# THE BUSHES

# THE BUSHES

## PORTRAIT OF A DYNASTY

PETER SCHWEIZER AND
ROCHELLE SCHWEIZER

DOUBLEDAY
New York London Toronto Sydney Auckland

PUBLISHED BY DOUBLEDAY
a division of Random House, Inc.

DOUBLEDAY and the portrayal of an anchor with a dolphin are registered
trademarks of Random House, Inc.
1745 Broadway, New York, NY 10019

*Book design by Elizabeth Rendfleisch*

The Cataloging-in-Publication Data is on file with the Library of Congress

ISBN 0-385-49863-2

First Edition
1   3   5   7   9   10   8   6   4   2

*To our mothers, Evelyn Rueb and Kerstin Schweizer, who have taught us much;
and to our children, Jack and Hannah, from whom we continue to learn*

# CONTENTS

# THE BUSHES

On election night, November 1994, governor-elect George W. was beaming in his hotel suite in Houston. Fourteen hundred miles to the east, younger brother Jeb was sitting dejectedly in his hotel suite in Miami.

Both men had decided to run for governor of their respective states of Texas and Florida in January 1993. They had not really consulted each other or coordinated their plans. "Maybe the Kennedys handle this part of the job better than we do," Jeb Bush noted, "but it's just too complicated."

Conventional wisdom in the family had it that Jebbie would win and W. would go down in defeat. Jebbie was, after all, the serious one, the one who had been meticulously planning to run for office for more than a decade, the one who really knew his stuff, and the one who would drop everything whenever his father needed him. He actually read those briefing papers put out by the think tanks in Washington and had headed up the local Republican Committee in Miami. And, if he won the governorship, he would probably run for president in 2000.

And his older brother? Well, W. was smart and shrewd. But he was also the rebel, edgy and unpredictable. His mother, Barbara, thought that his running for governor was a big mistake and had told her eldest son precisely that. Governor Ann Richards would likely come up with something during the campaign to set him off, and he would probably lose and lose big. Only a few years earlier, when a family history was being written, Marvin Bush, a younger brother, had described his oldest sibling as "the family clown."

But on that election night, when the tallies came in, the results were stunning to most in the family. Jeb was going down to defeat in Florida and W. was beating Ann Richards big. When W. was finally over the top and Richards had conceded, he got a phone call in his hotel suite; it was his father.

Aunt Nancy Ellis was standing nearby as W. chatted with his dad. When he hung up the phone, a disappointed W. simply shook his head. Almost the entire conversation had apparently been about Jeb's loss, with barely a mention of his win. His aunt listened as he said, "Why do you feel bad about Jeb? Why don't you feel good about me?"

A little more than six years later, 274 members of the extended Bush family converged on the nation's capital. Washington, D.C., was cold and dreary. But that didn't matter to the group of Bushes, Walkers, Clements, Houses, and Ellises that had arrived from eighteen different states. They were there, after all, to help coronate the second member of the Bush clan to be elected president ("Two and counting . . ." cracked one of the young cousins).

The backgrounds of those family members covered a broad spectrum—young and old, Easterner and Midwesterner, partisan and apolitical, conservative and liberal. Some were staying in a large bloc of rooms at the elegant Jefferson Hotel while others were in the Marriott downtown, and buses had been hired to take them from venue to venue. This event was part inauguration, part family reunion. Former president George Herbert Walker Bush ("41" in the lexicon of the family) was making the rounds as he always did, graciously trying to greet everyone. On Thursday evening he met with his sister, Nancy Bush Ellis, and his brothers Bucky, Pres, Jr., and Johnny, to reminisce. They talked about the pending tenure of George W. Bush and swapped family gossip. But as they always do, they also talked about the past. They laughed quite a bit, but they all kept tearing up.

Two days later, many of them stood on the podium of the West Lawn of the Capitol Building as George W. Bush took the oath of office. The remarkable rise of the eldest son, the rebel, was now complete. The family's political fortunes, expected to be carried by Jeb, were instead now on his older brother's shoulders. "As in all things, it's always good to be the winner," said cousin John Ellis. "So they saddled up with ol' George W."

Tears welled up in the eyes of both George Bushes. On his wrists, the new president wore the cufflinks that his grandfather had worn in the Senate and that his father had worn in the White House. It is remarkable to think that had the electoral fortunes been in Jeb's favor in 1994, a Bush still might have been sworn in as president, only the first name would be different.

When the Bushes gathered in Kennebunkport, Maine, a few months later, the elder George Bush relinquished his seat at the head of the family table; that spot would now go to his eldest son. During the next several years, some of the most eventful in American history, W. would consult with his father regularly. Sometimes they would agree; at other times, over issues such as the war in Iraq, they would express differences. And as President George W. Bush conducted the affairs of the country, he would find himself at times dealing with foreign heads of state or international players in the Middle East and Asia who had business dealings with his family.

For more than a century the Bushes have been at or near the center of America's public life—as friends of presidents, captains of industry, capitalists, senators, congressmen, ambassadors, governors, federal judges, and two American presidents. While the Bushes lack the flamboyance of the Roosevelts or the enormous wealth of the Kennedys, they have surpassed those two great dynasties. There can be little question that the Bushes are now the most successful political family in American history. Yet precious little has been written about the Bushes in contrast to the hundreds of books about the Roosevelts and Kennedys.

Biographies have been written about both former president Bush and President George W. Bush, but details about the larger family are scant. To the extent that the family has been studied at all, it has emerged as a caricature. *New York Times* columnist Maureen Dowd has compared the Bushes with a sinister Mafia clan while at the same time declaring that they are a boring group of cutouts from a Brooks Brothers catalog. Michael Kinsley claims that he can find nothing serious about them. They are motivated, he claims, by a "preppy ethic that one should be serious about games and casual about life." Journalist Evan Thomas of *Newsweek* is equally unimpressed. "The Kennedys flew too close to the sun. The Bushes just ask for more pork rinds."

Why the caricature? Mystery often invites these kinds of labels. Unlike the Kennedys and even to some extent the Roosevelts, the Bushes have been famously disinterested over the years in speaking to the media about their family and the dynamics within the greater Bush clan. *Time* magazine has accurately dubbed them "the Quiet Dynasty" because they have quietly gone about their business, flying below much of the media radar.

Inside the family there is an unwritten code about dealing with the media, a code that is firmly enforced. "There is an inner circle in the family," Bush cousin John Ellis explained. "If you haven't said anything bad to the press, you're in pretty good shape. But if you said anything bad, Barbara [Bush] kind of puts you in the deep freeze for a while. And then you have to work your way out. I think you could burn down the house in Kennebunkport and you'd be in less trouble than if you gave a bad quote to the *New York Times*."

The family's distrust and at times disdain for the media has deep roots, running back some fifty years to when Prescott Bush was making his first bid for the U.S. Senate. That distrust runs particularly strong when it comes to writing about family matters.

"The public glare can be distorted, it can be mean," Jeb Bush said. "You have the political press writing about nonpolitical issues. Most of these people are not the most brilliant people in the world, and when you get them out of their area, writing about the family, it can be a little bit scary."

Even on the few occasions when these family walls were penetrated by journalists, they often came up dry. The simple fact is, members of the Bush family don't like to talk about themselves. The Bushes consider self-focus and self-analysis to be dangerously close to self-centeredness. In an era of media saturation and confessional politics, the Bushes have little interest in playing the game. Too much self-reflection, Jeb Bush says, "is self-absorption and it's part of our problem in this country. There needs to be a limit to constantly reflecting on yourself. You should keep your head up, help others, and be well versed in the world around you. My dad is not going to write a memoir; it would make him feel really uncomfortable. That is an odd thing in America today. Bill Clinton just signed up for $10 million for the book rights, and he'll *love* writing about himself. His editors will probably say, 'You'll have to cut it in half.' "

The Bushes also have a disinterest in publicity because they consider themselves to be the "un-Kennedys." When they talk about themselves both in public and private, they often use the Kennedys for comparative purposes.

Senator Prescott Bush maintained a cordial relationship with JFK during his political career. But he was quietly dismayed about their focus on publicity. "He thought that old Joe Kennedy was unseemly in the way he courted the media," says Nancy Ellis. "The sort of imagery around Camelot, he just thought it was ridiculous." So while the Kennedys often tried to Waspify themselves and play the aristocrats, the Bushes migrated in the opposite direction. While the socially ambitious Kennedys were giving white-glove teas, the aristocratic Bushes were barbecuing in Texas.

Prescott Bush was also proud of the fact that the Bush boys, unlike the Kennedys, were expected to go out and earn a living in the marketplace. Work was the great democratizer, an experience unfamiliar to the Kennedys.

But the Bushes also differ from other prominent families in their intense sense of loyalty. Their keen sense of self-identity runs deeper than in just about any other American dynasty. The Kennedys, for example, cultivated close relationships with a host of advisers and friends and made them, as Garry Wills has put it, "honorary Kennedys." The Bushes have no such appendages. Marlin Fitzwater, who served as White House spokesman for President George H. W. Bush and remains a close family friend, noticed pretty quickly that even the closest of friends and advisers could not penetrate the family's inner circle. "The Bushes will never have their Ted Sorensen," he told us. "They are just too close-knit for that."

Bush cousin John Ellis saw this unique difference between the Bushes and a dynasty like the Kennedys close up as a young man. His summers were spent with the extended family, and he keeps close contact to this day. He also happened to forge a close relationship with Joe Kennedy, Jr., when the two roomed together at Milton Academy.

One Thanksgiving, the two boys headed to the Ellis home in Lincoln, Massachusetts. Sandy Ellis, John's father, came and greeted young Joe.

"What are you doing for Thanksgiving?"

"I'm going back home," young Joe told him.

"That'll be great."

"Well, I'll have to leave early from here to get home."

"Why do you need to leave early?"

"To get a bed."

"Excuse me. What?" asked the elder Ellis, raising his eyebrows.

"Yeah, when we have Thanksgiving at home," Joe explained, "we have all these people come—Arthur Schlesinger, all these people—and if I don't get there in time to claim my room, mother just gives it away."

Ellis concluded with a serious tone: "And that would never happen *in a million years* in our family."

For the Bushes, blood runs thicker than politics or patronage. John Adams called it "family spirit," a desire to promote the essence of our families. For the Bushes it is an idea deeply ingrained from their earliest youth. Longtime family friends note that they possess a strong tribal sense, a dynastic instinct, that drives them.

"They are a clan, pure and simple," says Fitzgerald Bemiss, a family friend of more than sixty years who has known four generations of Bushes. "They think like a clan and act like a clan. Loyalty is very important and so is their sense of heritage. Everyone is independent but also part of the whole."

Children are brought up with stories about past generations and taught to respect their elders and their contributions to both family and country. When Prescott Bush served in the United States Senate, he insisted that his grandsons call him not grandpa but "Senator." They were also strongly encouraged to come to the Senate Gallery to watch the action, to listen, and to learn.

The family makes a conscious effort to pass along its heritage. Just as the young John Quincy Adams would listen in on his father's conversations with Thomas Jefferson, the Bushes make a conscious effort to train future generations as history is being made. When George H. W. Bush was president, he saw to it that not only his children but also his grandchildren became familiar with the White House and saw the pageantry of the presidency.

Bush kids are also encouraged to experience the same rites of passage that their ancestors did. When George H. W. Bush was a young man on vacation in Kennebunkport, he would be awakened in the early morning and encouraged to jump off the dock and swim in the cold waters off Walker Point. Several generations of Bush toddlers have skinny-dipped in the "Boony Wild Pool," a small pool of water collected in the rugged rocks by the Atlantic. Even today these practices are encouraged among the Bush children, although today's generation is decidedly less interested in complying.

With the Bushes it really is true, as Oliver Wendell Holmes said, that a child's education begins 250 years before it is born. In the case of the Bushes, genes play a remarkable role in their success. According to genealogist Gary Boyd Roberts, the Bushes are related to fifteen former presidents including George Washington, Millard Fillmore, Franklin Pierce, Abraham Lincoln, Ulysses Grant, Rutherford B. Hayes, James Garfield, Grover Cleveland, Teddy Roosevelt, William Howard Taft, Calvin Coolidge, Herbert Hoover, Franklin D. Roosevelt, Richard Nixon, and Gerald Ford. The Bushes are also related to the Indian princess Pocahontas, who married colonist John Rolfe. (A Bush relative married the couple's only American great-grandchild.) A Bush ancestor completed Paul Revere's Midnight Ride in 1775. A passenger on the *Mayflower*, Thomas Mitchell, had two children, and through them the Bushes are related to the late Princess Diana. Indeed, according to Roberts, George W. Bush is distantly related to roughly half of the entire American population.

Over the course of their history the Bushes have forged thousands of friendships and alliances with both individuals and families. The Bushes try as best they can to see that these relationships are passed from one generation to another. Sometimes they fail. But during the past century the Bush family has proven remarkably adept at handing down relationships. It is not unusual for a young Bush to visit a close friend of his grandfather to ask for help or a favor.

This has translated into an enormous universe of friends, allies, and supporters. More than any other single factor, this informal network has allowed the family to develop and construct the largest network of supporters inside the Republican Party. They form what could be called a Bush caucus, individuals of diverse backgrounds and differing political views who are united by their respect and affection for the Bush family. George H. W. Bush used it when he ran for president. George W. accessed it in 2000. Should Gov. Jeb Bush choose to run in 2008, he will hope to tap into it as well.

"There are some thirty thousand people across the country who will raise money and work on campaigns," says John Ellis. "That's the only real political network that exists in the Republican Party."

IN EARLY 1999, WE BEGAN INTERVIEWING FAMILY MEMBERS FOR THIS BOOK. We spoke with three generations of the family. Some are at the center of the family's rise to power, including former president George H. W. Bush and Florida governor Jeb Bush. Others are part of the family's inner circle; still others are members of the extended family and longtime friends who have been deeply involved in the family's activities. In the course of these conversations we found the family members to be remarkably candid and observant about how the family works and what makes it tick as they provided stories and details about the family's past and present.

What follows is the untold story of the remarkable rise of America's most powerful family.

## PART ONE

# RISE

### 1880·1972

#### CHAPTER 1

# IRON

F OR AN AMBITIOUS AND INDUSTRIOUS YOUNG MAN JUST BEFORE THE turn of the twentieth century, there were few better places to be than Columbus, Ohio. Next to the large coal-producing areas of Ohio, Columbus was not Cincinnati or Cleveland with their tall buildings and keen sense of culture. But, situated at the center of the great highways of commerce, it was well poised to explode into prominence.

Arriving by train from New Jersey, a tall, slender man named Samuel P. Bush saw the opportunity to be had in the great American Midwest. Not wanting to become an Episcopalian minister like his father, S. P. (as he was known) had balked at attending prestigious Yale University, the college of both his father and grandfather. Instead, he had enrolled at the less regal Stevens Institute of Technology on Long Island. While Stevens lacked the history and spires of Yale, it offered something S. P. was more interested in, namely, the new field of scientific management and engineering.

It was a novel concept in late-nineteenth-century America, applying the principles of science and mathematics to managing a business. One of his classmates was Frederick Taylor, who would later be considered the acknowledged father of scientific management. S. P. would apply many of those principles in his work, and great-grandson George W. Bush would study Taylor's organizational theories and use his case study approach in his business and political life.

While at Stevens, S. P. excelled not only in his studies but also in baseball and tennis. During the evenings he sang baritone in the glee club.

Shortly after leaving Stevens, S. P. joined the Pennsylvania Railroad and headed for the great railroad operations of the Midwest. Decades later he would regale his grandchildren with stories about his life on the railroad. "The work was hard," his grandson Prescott Bush, Jr. recalls, "but he told stories about adventure and being free with a sparkle in his eye; so you knew he must have enjoyed it."

In 1894, S. P. fell in love and married a local Columbus woman, Flora

Sheldon, the daughter of a dry goods merchant and bank officer. Her family was not particularly wealthy, but her pedigree was pure: one ancestor was Robert Livingston, the Puritan dissenter who had left Scotland after the Stuart restoration and arrived in America in 1673. The Livingstons were deeply interwined with American history. Philip Livingston signed the Declaration of Independence, Robert R. Livingston, Jr. gave the oath of office to George Washington, and Edward Livingston negotiated the Louisiana Purchase while serving as minister to France.

Flora was slender, elegant, and loving, a woman of grace and beauty who was profoundly attached to her husband. As he traveled on business, she wrote to him constantly. "Let me know dear, what you are doing," she would write, "the little details of your days and nights—for they are my greatest interest in life."

Flora saw the marriage as a providential act. As she later wrote to her husband, "I went to church and sat where we usually sit together and read the words under which we were united—for as I sat in Emmanuel Church my thoughts were always of you and our life and love—our children and the beautiful blessings that we have known."

S. P. applied himself diligently at the railroad, keeping accurate financial records and supplying plenty of suggestions to cut costs and boost profits. His work in middle management did not go unnoticed. But the Pennsylvania Railroad was a massive company with more than 110,000 employees. Rising through the ranks would be a long, arduous process. So when he was offered a job at Buckeye Malleable Iron and Coupler Company (later renamed Buckeye Steel) in Columbus, Ohio, he seized the opportunity.

Buckeye was far from a profitable venture when S. P. joined the company. Founded in 1894 by Col. W. F. Goodspeed, the company produced automatic couplers that joined railroad cars together. Instrumental in raising capital for Buckeye Steel was Cleveland-based financier Franklin Rockefeller, younger brother of John D. The two brothers had made a fortune together with Standard Oil, but later experienced a nasty falling out. Franklin Rockefeller was considered "genial, adventurous, quick to love and hate." S. P. would grow to have a complex and at times awkward relationship with him, but it would serve the family well over the next century. When a young politician named George H. W. Bush met Nelson Rockefeller more than fifty years later, their families were already very familiar with each other.

Stockholders of the company agreed to give Rockefeller fifteen thousand dollars worth of stock and a share in any future increase in proportion to these holdings. In return, Rockefeller promised to use his influence to persuade the railroads to buy Buckeye couplers. Meanwhile, almost immediately after his arrival at Buckeye, S. P. began working feverishly to turn the firm around. Using some of the new, groundbreaking techniques he had learned at Stevens, S. P. figured in both indirect and overhead costs when calculating the cost of production. Most companies at the time ignored such expenses; but by meticulously watching them, S. P. was able to cut costs. For S. P. it was an extremely important responsibility. His ledger features broad cursive letters and finely crafted numbers tabulated down to the penny.

Producing couplers was dirty and dangerous work. But S. P. was often on the plant floor, keeping things moving and giving orders. Worker Albert Stock remembers S. P. as "a snorter . . . Everyone knew when he was around; when he issued orders, boy it went!"

Accidents were a common occurrence. Stock later recalled that one worker died after being caught in the ropes of the machinery; another was decapitated when an emery wheel flew off. But Buckeye paid a good living wage, considering the alternatives. Laborers at Buckeye put in twelve-hour days, and many worked seven days a week, just as workers did elsewhere.

S. P.'s passions went beyond home and work. During his time at Stevens he had been introduced to a strange new game. And when he arrived in Columbus, it was just catching on in Ohio. On the campus of Ohio State University, young men were gathering on a dusty field to play football. Unlike the more pastoral and skill-based game of baseball or the aristocratic pastime of tennis, football appealed to S. P. because of its raw energy. It was a game of strength, speed, and will.

S. P. had not only seen the game back east, he had participated in scrimmages. So when the first OSU team was assembled, S. P. signed on as an assistant coach.

The Buckeyes did not prove to be much of a team. In their first meeting with Michigan, the team was shellacked 34–0. Playing before a wooden grandstand that could seat seventeen thousand, OSU lost regularly to smaller Ohio schools. But S. P. and the other coaches were determined to win. Unable to recruit solid players like the surrounding schools, OSU became one of the first to integrate the football team. A speedy Ohio State flanker named Julius B. Tyler made the first touchdown by a black player in the history of college football.

S. P. coached with the team for five years, during which time it never had a winning season. But for S. P., that mattered little.

For S. P., sports was the great equalizer, offering universal rules, fair play, and measurable performance. Athletics also appealed to his idealized sense of honor and was a critical ingredient in the development of the complete man, which his Episcopalian faith led him to believe every man should strive to be. At Buckeye Steel he encouraged the workers to participate in sports because it was good for both body and soul. Later, when S. P. ran Buckeye, the company would boast eight bowling teams in the local YMCA and one of the first basketball teams in Ohio. The Buckeye track team and other sporting groups were racially integrated, a radical idea in turn-of-the-century America.

S. P. AND FLORA HAD FOUR CHILDREN. PRESCOTT, AS THE OLDEST, WAS EX-pected to keep his siblings in line. S. P., busy as he was with his work and travel, nevertheless undertook to train his sons. There were Bible readings at home and lessons on etiquette. Recollections about the home, however, were not particularly warm. "He was a stern man, that's what my father always said," says Teensie Bush Cole, daughter of James Bush. "It was that era of seen and not heard. He kept that attitude throughout his life."

The one reprieve was sports. On Saturday afternoons in the late spring and summer, S. P. would bring his sons to the South Side Industrial Athletic Field directly east of the plant to see the Buckeye Steel team take the field against a rival squad from a nearby town or another plant in Columbus.

S. P. insisted that the boys attend public school rather than one of the elite private schools in and around Columbus. The Douglas School, in one of Columbus's middle-class neighborhoods, was an amalgamation of students from all sorts of backgrounds. S. P. wanted his sons to learn the rigors of life and not be isolated from its difficulties. For young Pres Bush, it opened up a new world. "We had a very large negro population," Prescott recalled years later. "We had a very large German population. In fact, we had representatives of most every ethnic group in this public school."

The Bush children got good marks at the Douglas School, but the real interest of the boys came after school. When the school bell tolled, they would rush off to Franklin Park, a stretch of green grass between East Broad Street and Franklin Avenue on Columbus's east side. Once the grounds of the state fair, the park by then was mostly made up of makeshift baseball diamonds. Boys from every neighborhood, rich and poor, black and white, would choose up sides for games. It didn't matter who your father was or what he did; it only mattered if you could hit and field. Young Pres was particularly adept at both.

In 1905, Frank Rockefeller was elected president of Buckeye. A man who certainly knew his way around investments, Rockefeller was nonetheless a bad manager. The company soon began to face more financial difficulties. At times bank loans became necessary to make payroll and retire other loans. But how do you tell a man like Frank Rockefeller that he's not up to the job?

Fortunately, that task fell to no one. In 1907, Rockefeller himself saw that Buckeye was in trouble, so he turned the company over to young S. P. Bush. He would run it for the next twenty years.

Rockefeller was critical to the success of the company. He had good contacts in the railroad industry and could help Buckeye win much-needed and coveted contracts. But Rockefeller's contentious family life was often a source of discomfort for S. P. At times Bush found himself in the awkward position of fending off Rockefeller family requests for company stock and cash that had not been authorized by Frank.

With his new role as company president, S. P. could now join the elite club of manufacturing industrialists dotting the American Midwest. He was well compensated for his efforts. His annual pay was $25,000 per year. (A survey by Harvard University at the time showed that CEOs of companies with similar capital and size received average salaries of $9,958 per year.) S. P. also began traveling more, negotiating deals from St. Paul, Minnesota, to Birmingham, Alabama. He was also responsible for dealing with Buckeye's investments, which meant making frequent trips to New York City. It was a place he didn't care for very much. New Yorkers, he wrote to his wife, "are not quick in their methods and we all have to wait on them."

All his time away from home made it difficult for Flora to manage the teenage boys. She would ask for help in her letters, but there was little S. P. could do from a distance. After receiving one letter, he wrote back explaining that she needed to assert herself. Thus began a practice that would be carried out over four generations of the family: while the man was off making his way in the world, a strong and loving mother would raise the children and hold the family in place. As Jeb Bush has described it, the family has a strong "matriarchal" quality.

S. P. worked constantly and Flora worried openly. What he needed to do was to "find the courage to say no" to some of his responsibilities. But that was too much to ask of S. P. When his nonstop schedule continued and his health weakened, she expressed her concerns with gentle words. "I now want to send you my heart full of tender love . . . all the tenderness in my being goes out to you—without whom I could not live."

The one reprieve for the family came when the hot winds of summer rolled across the Midwest. Like so many who were financially comfortable, the Bushes took refuge from the heat by heading for the rocky coasts of New England. They often went to Cape Cod and stayed at the East Bay Lodge near Osterville, Massachusetts.

S. P. would continue to keep up with business and often made trips to New York City. So during the day, Flora would visit with friends and play bridge while the children delighted in swimming, crabbing, rowing, and tennis.

As Pres reached adolescence, he became a particular frustration for the family. Perhaps it was because of the promise that his father saw in him. The boy was attractive, charming, and intelligent. But he seemed to lack the seriousness that S. P. expected from him. So the decision was made to send him away to school. Flora had misgivings but agreed that it was necessary.

The choice was St. George's, an Episcopal Church school in Newport, Rhode Island, that had a solid reputation for academics and a stern atmosphere. After his struggles in Columbus, young Prescott seemed to take to St. George's instantly.

But St. George's was a church school, and in addition to his regular course work, Pres read church doctrine and learned about Christian service. His grandfather was a member of the clergy, and young Pres began to think seriously about pursuing the same career.

Prescott participated in athletics, especially football, baseball, and basketball. He also joined the civics club. "We debated the issues of the moment on the national level," he recalled. "Are we for or against the popular election of United States senators? How do we feel about a protective tariff versus a tariff for revenue only, and that type of question."

He also worked as a caddy on the nearby golf course at Watch Hill. The experience not only put cash in his pocket and allowed him to play the course for free; it also brought him in contact with wealthy and glamorous people. At one point he caddied for Douglas Fairbanks, Hollywood's leading man, stimulating a brief interest in the theater.

Pres had to work for spending money because, despite his father's growing wealth, the old man was as frugal as could be. S. P. expected an accurate accounting of household expenses from Flora, much as was done at Buckeye. She would often catalog expenses in letters that he could read while traveling.

S. P.'s tastes, like his general demeanor, were anything but ostentatious. He was tight without being miserly, occasionally offering to buy something for Flora when he visited New York City. "Which would you rather have," he wrote her, "a fur coat, a collar, a party wrap, a string of pearls or a pair of shoes?"

As for himself, however, S. P. remained a practical man. During one out-of-town trip he considered purchasing a billiards table. But after deliberating for a while, he decided against the extravagance. "I was afraid it would be throwing away money," he later wrote to his wife.

Deeply influenced by his parents' brand of Episcopalianism, which bordered on Puritanism, S. P. saw thrift as a virtue unto itself. As president of Buckeye, he even created a Thrift Committee to instruct employees in the virtues of frugality. "Only fifteen percent of the American people are in the habit of saving, whereas from forty to sixty percent of foreigners living in our midst habitually save a considerable portion of their income," read one company flyer. "Thrift is not meanness or stinginess, or the mere hoarding of money, but the intelligent conservation of our financial, physical and mental resources for development of fuller, broader, happier, and more efficient lives."

During these prosperous years for S. P., Columbus was growing as well. In 1902, Columbus had a population of 136,000. Just four years later it was 160,000 and continuing at a rapid pace. The city that once possessed what one observer called "a nice balance between urbanity and solid farm philosophy" was becoming both more urban and diverse. And with its rapid expansion and growing industrialization, new problems emerged.

In 1910, Columbus was rocked by a bitter streetcar strike, the sort of violent labor confrontation that the city had never seen before. Men who worked on the Columbus municipal streetcars were organizing a union, and by the end of March, labor leaders were demanding increased pay and the right to organize. They also wanted a shorter workday and overtime pay. The workers went on strike, and the company tried to run the cars with nonunion workers under armed protection.

The next several weeks saw a series of clashes as strikers threw rocks and shots were fired. The rioters obtained dynamite, which they used to blow up some railway cars. Several business leaders, including S. P. Bush, offered rewards for the capture of the dynamiters. Blowing up the railway cars seemed to alienate many workers who had initially sympathized with the strikers. Four rioters were arrested and sent to the penitentiary. The strike ended with little gained by the workers.

As a result of the streetcar strike, fear of labor agitation grew. A socialist party was organized and garnered ten thousand votes in the 1912 mayoral election. Some in the business community advocated a firm response to stem the rising strength of "anarchists." S. P. undoubtedly had mixed emotions. Violence was unacceptable in his mind, but he recognized the need for reforms. He had a paternalistic view toward labor based both on his view of the need for capital and labor to cooperate and his Episcopalian sense of the natural order of things. S. P. wrote to Buckeye board members that labor unrest was a serious problem requiring both firmness and a recognition that "industry in this country" needed to understand that a happy labor force was a critical ingredient in both social stability and profitability. "Labor will never be reasonably contented without a living wage that is economic . . . Everyone in a community must have decent living conditions as well as facilities and advantages for bringing up families, facilities for education and recreation, and these the average industrial community has not supplied and does not supply at the present time."

The key was managing and directing such a balance. For S. P., it was the duty of the enlightened in the community to lead.

But leadership required guiding without reverting to paternalism. "Paternalism must be avoided but there is no reason why those responsible for the operation of industry should not educate and show the way, and assist its employees to help themselves." This hierarchical view of society was not unusual at the time. S. P. was particularly outspoken regarding the duties and responsibilities of those in leadership positions. A close friend and business associate later wrote to him, summing up S. P.'s views of public service in classical terms, "I have always thought of you as a Spartan citizen, what may be termed a Roman senator of the finest type."

But S. P. also believed in charity. Shortly after he became president of the company, he impressed on the board the need for "appropriations for charitable purposes." It was the company's first commitment to philanthropy, and soon after, regular donations were being made to the South Side Settlement House, the Children's Hospital, the Knights of Columbus, and the Salvation Army. By far S. P.'s favorite charity appeared to be the YMCA, with its commitment to Christianity, education, and self-help.

Many of these efforts were aimed not simply at meeting the immediate needs of the poor, but toward their self-improvement. One charitable enterprise S. P. was a heavy supporter of was the "potato patch" initiative sponsored by Associated Charities of Columbus. Seventy-two acres were brought under cultivation, and more than twelve hundred families received food from the patches. The arrangement was simple. Associated Charities would pay for supervision of the plots, the seeds, and the plowing. But the families were expected to pick the potatoes themselves. This was the sort of endeavor that his great-grandson, President George W. Bush, might call a "faith-based initiative."

Some people lived in squalor near the Buckeye plant, and S. P. took notice. Blacks were living in shacks near the facility, so in 1925 he directed the company to retain land along the Groveport Pike. He made this purchase to improve the land, he told the board, because "quite a number of our colored employees and those of other plants had located near the property," and "it was desirable to provide suitable quarters for community gatherings, religious services and other public events." A year later, concerned that "the plight among the colored people of Columbus is in many cases deplorable," he pestered fellow directors into contributing money to fund a camp for blacks. Later he urged the company to fund construction of the Mount Carmel Baptist Church and Community Center to boost "the morale and efficiency of our colored employees."

S. P. took his faith seriously, particularly the reading of Scripture and the teachings of the Episcopalian High Church. His upbringing had taught him that faith was a matter of introspection, a private covenant between the Lord and the Christian. Those views were challenged in December 1912 when it was announced that William A. "Billy" Sunday and a group of evangelists would be visiting Columbus at the request of local clergy. Soon a tabernacle was constructed at Goodale and Park Streets, with a seating capacity for 12,000. A choir of 1,200 was organized.

While many of the Baptists, Methodists, and other Protestant churches were enthused about the visit, the Lutherans were rather aloof. So, too, were Episcopalians like S. P., who disapproved of both Sunday's doctrines and methods. As anticipation built up for the visit, religion became the first topic of conversation all around Columbus. Business and social engagements were deferred, and everyone seemed intent on hearing and discussing the evangelist. It is unlikely that S. P. attended the event, but he did allow employees at Buckeye to attend. When Sunday left town, there were 18,333 conversions.

These were times of contentment for S. P., who took pride in his growing family and the growth of Buckeye Steel. The years from 1906 to 1914 were prosperous. Several companies, including the Pennsylvania Railroad, tried to lure him away with offers of better pay and less work, but to no avail.

#### CHAPTER 2

# BONES

I N THE FALL OF 1913, PRESCOTT, FOLLOWING IN THE STEPS OF HIS grandfather and great-grandfather, enrolled at Yale University. Tall, handsome, and athletic, he found a campus both steeped in tradition and on the cusp of change. If in the nineteenth century Yale had been the preserve of an American aristocracy, students now included the sons of merchants and industrialists.

Yale's rejection of modernism, the very thing that had led S. P. Bush to go elsewhere for his education, was also beginning to change. If before Yalies had moved into the law, academe, or church service, now a future in business and industry inspired many of the students. It was much as Van Wyck Brooks characterized the era in *America's Coming-of-Age*: "The highest ambition of young America is to be—do I exaggerate?—the owner of a shoe factory."

Pres Bush fell between two distinct groups that tended to dominate campus life. The wealthy Northeasterners from prominent bloodlines lived at a leisurely pace. They did not yearn to win at anything because they had, by definition, won already. At the same time, campus life included upper-middle-class sons who had made it into the university by virtue of their academic skills and intellectual gifts. Young Pres was awkwardly in the middle. He had more drive than the rich, but more wealth and style than the sons of the middle class; both accordingly viewed him with some level of suspicion. Later in life, Pres would try to align himself with the middle-class sons who attended Yale, misleadingly telling one interviewer that his father had "a modest income" and lacked the funds to send him to law school.

Pres studied history, literature, and politics. But he considered wearing Yale blue and white on the baseball diamond his most important accomplishment. With a powerful swing, he could muscle an inside pitch deep into the opposite field. He batted fourth on the 1917 Yale baseball team, and his exploits would be long remembered among the Eli coaches. Teammates found him affable and friendly. His greatest joy, based on his letters to his parents, was apparently his selection as team captain. When his son George played for Yale three decades later, coaches and trainers were still talking about his father.

It was Pres more than anyone who would make baseball and golf the games of choice for generations of Bushes. If life was prose, golf and baseball were poetry. Both games, he insisted, had an innate purity, and he spoke of them with reverence. "The appeal to him was the pace of the game and the skills involved," says William Bush, his youngest son. "Neither game depended on your size or strength. And neither game ends at some predetermined time. It's over when the pitcher or the batter triumphs and the last out is made, or in golf when the last shot has gone in the hole."

---

ON A GENTLE EARLY EVENING IN THE SPRING SEMESTER OF HIS JUNIOR YEAR, a Yale senior approached him from behind and tapped him on the shoulder. "Go to your room!"

Pres Bush complied. Even the young student from Ohio knew what this meant. Some young men at Yale hinged their success at the school entirely based on this night.

When Pres arrived at his small apartment, two other students were waiting for him.

"Skull and Bones—accept or reject?"

Pres nodded. "Yes." He was then handed a message wrapped in a black ribbon sealed with black wax that had a skull and bones emblem and the mystical number 322 embossed on it. The message revealed the time and place to appear on initiation night.

None of Yale's secret societies were more legendary than this one. Bones had been memorialized in the classic 1902 American novel *Dink Stover at Yale*. F. Scott Fitzgerald would write about the society's mystique in *The Beautiful and the Damned* and *This Side of Paradise*.

Skull and Bones was an elite within an elite, an incubator for members of future generations who would rise to power in their respective areas of professional life. Where else could college students sit informally with former president Taft, a member and frequent attendee of Bones events? Where else might an ambitious young man suddenly find himself in a small, closed universe populated with planets that had names like Rockefeller, Pillsbury, Whitney, Wadsworth, and Adams?

Founded in 1833 by William Huntington Russell, the Skull and Bones

Society is legally known as the Russell Trust Association. Each year, since its inception, fifteen Yale students are "tapped" for the society, which still owns an Egyptian-style crypt at the center of the college. Unlike other societies such as Scroll and Key, which chooses its members based on family background and prestige, Bones is a meritocracy; name helps, but members are chosen overwhelmingly because they are smart, ambitious, and bound for success.

Prescott attended at a time when Yale was the college of bankers, industrialists, intellectuals, and lawyers, professions in the vanguard of a burgeoning American society. That evening, when he attended the initiation rite, he would join a class of 1917 that included Roland Harriman, son of financier E. H. Harriman, and Percy Rockefeller, son of William, the treasurer of Standard Oil. He would soon meet other recent Bonesmen including Henry Stimson, Averell Harriman, and Henry Luce.

Why he was tapped is difficult to say. It might have been his father's connection with the Rockefellers; Percy Rockefeller was active in Bones. But more likely, he was simply selected on his own merits. The society drew its members from a combination of legacy candidates: those whose fathers were members, the intellectual leaders on campus, often including the editor of the school newspaper, and those with athletic prowess. Given Prescott's role as captain of the baseball team, it is probable that this was the reason for his choosing.

Despite the wealth and position evident among Skull and Bones members, the society prided itself on an irreverence toward both. Above the entrance to the crypt, a German inscription reads, "Who was a fool, who was the wise man, beggar or king? Whether poor or rich, all's the same in death." The society alleges a mythical bond with the past, claiming that it possesses an ancient mission dating from 322 B.C., when, legend holds, the society was founded by Demosthenes in Athens.

At a ceremony held every April, as many alumni as possible attend to watch the young charges go through a ritualistic initiation. A Yale junior such as Pres is assigned a mentor, known as Uncle Toby. Members then dress in a costume and the pledges enter one by one into a room decorated with coffins and skeletons. As members chant mystical oaths, someone yells, "Who is it?" Then alumni and current members bellow the pledge's name. The aspiring member is then pushed toward the table where the secrecy oath has been placed. The alumni chant "Read! Read! Read!"

The pledge is then picked up and carried to a picture of Eulogia, the goddess of eloquence, and all assembled yell, "Eulogia! Eulogia! Eulogia!" After repeating the oath of secrecy once more, he is put in front of a portrait of a woman that the Bonesmen call Connubial Bliss. When they are finished, the newly minted member is declared a Knight of Eulogia and is now and forever a member of the secret society.

Every Thursday and Sunday evening of his senior year, Pres and the other Bonesmen would disappear into the windowless "tomb" on High Street. Each member was assigned a secret name. Long Devil went to the tallest member, Boz to the varsity football captain. Many names were drawn from myth, religion, and Shakespeare.

Bonesmen were infused with a strong sense that they had a unique obligation and duty to lead. Within the tomb, clocks were set at Skull and Bones time, which is five minutes ahead of the rest of the world; Bonesmen were ahead of the world, out front, in the name of the greater social good.

The group had plenty of social functions, but they included no outsiders. Pres might sit in the Firefly Room for dinner, its darkened atmosphere touched off with light fixtures shaped like skulls. Or he might gather with Bonesmen in another room to drink out of skull-shaped cups. Alcohol was never served; Skull and Bones was and is strictly dry.

Behind the crypt's padlocked iron doors, members could speak with complete candidness about everything. They were encouraged to strip bare any secrets so that their bonds might be strengthened. Frankness and secrecy bred trust, which encouraged greater secrecy and frankness. In this atmosphere, Pres forged a close bond with men who would remain his friends and allies for the rest of his life. Closest among them was Roland "Bunny" Harriman, younger brother of Averell Harriman and joint heir to the Harriman fortune.

Once the Bonesmen left Yale, they were expected to continue their active membership and show allegiance to their fellow Bonesmen. The society also owned Deer Island on the St. Lawrence River, in Alexandria Bay, a forty-acre retreat for alumni and current members. There, tennis courts and softball fields were surrounded by rhubarb plants and gooseberry bushes; stewards brought catered meals.

Pres was the first in what would become a long line of Bonesmen in the family. His future brothers-in-law George Herbert Walker, Jr. and Lou Walker would join, as would his own sons George and Jonathan. Following them was a third generation, including George W. Bush, George Herbert Walker III, and Ray Walker. No family could claim to have a longer and stronger bond with Bones than the Bushes.

IN MARCH OF THE YEAR BEFORE, FIFTEEN HUNDRED MEXICANS HAD INVADED American soil and attacked several villages in New Mexico, killing nineteen civilians. President Wilson ordered Gen. John J. Pershing to launch a military expedition deep into the Mexican countryside. Pershing pushed south of the Rio Grande but was hampered by logistical problems and the poor training of his men. Bloodied and defeated, he was forced to retreat. It was an embarrassment to many Americans, and in New Haven the young men of Yale were watching.

Former (and future) secretary of war Henry Stimson (Skull and Bones, class of 1888) called for America's best and finest to take up arms. He pushed for special training camps for Ivy Leaguers and appealed to his fellow Yalies to join the glorious crusade and win the war.

Young Pres enlisted in the Connecticut National Guard as a private. For three months that summer, he and fellow classmates received military training at U.S. Army facilities in Tobyhanna, Pennsylvania. When they had finished, they returned to campus and formed the Yale Battalion, hoping to head south for Texas and quite possibly action in Mexico. But the call never came; Yale University's President Hadley wrote to the War Department and encouraged them not to use the Yale Battalion.

One year later, when the United States entered the First World War, Pres and fellow members of the Yale Battalion got their chance. They were called up and soon on their way to Fort Sill, Oklahoma, the U.S. Army's artillery school. The unit was divided into four batteries of field artillery, with one hundred young men in each battery. Pres excelled during training, was given command of a battery, and commissioned as a captain in the field artillery.

During his brief stay at Fort Sill, Pres and a few coconspirators were said to have performed a deed that would go down in the annals of Skull and Bones. According to a private document published by Bones on June 17, 1933, Pres and fellow Bonesmen Ellery James and Neil Mallon sneaked off under cover of darkness and went to the grave site of the famed Apache chief Geronimo.

"An axe pried open the iron door of the tomb, and Pat[riarch] Bush entered and started to dig. We dug in turn, each on relief taking a turn on the road as guards . . . Finally Pat[riarch] Ellery James turned up a bridle, soon a saddle horn and rotten leathers followed, then wood and then, at the exact bottom of the small round hole, Pat[riarch] James dug deep and pried out the trophy itself . . . We quickly closed the grave, shut the door and sped home to Pat[riarch] Mallon's room, where we cleaned the bones."

"The bones" were said to be the skull of Geronimo. Neil Mallon reportedly applied carbolic acid to the skull to clean it up. Later it was supposedly taken back to the society's tomb on campus, where it was displayed. Whether true or pure legend, the story soon spread and would echo seven decades later in the lives of Pres's children.

When Pres's son George was running for president in 1988, members of the Apache tribe tried to arrange a meeting with him to discuss the matter, hoping that the skull might be returned. Tribal leader Ned Anderson engaged in private discussions with Pres's son (and Bonesman) Jonathan Bush to determine whether the skull was indeed in the crypt. Later he raised the issue with his congressman, John McCain, who promised to approach Vice President Bush about the matter.

———

ALTHOUGH COLUMBUS WAS A CITY THAT PRIDED ITSELF ON ITS PATRIOTISM, IT was also home to a large German population. With more than seven thousand German-born citizens living in Columbus at the time and an even larger group of first-generation German-Americans, the outbreak of World War I divided the city in a mood of suspicion and fear. A fire at the American Chain Company plant was "officially believed to have been the result of a pro-German plot," reported the local paper. Two employees of the Ralston Steel Car Company were indicted for allegedly attempting to destroy machinery in an effort to help the German cause. And several men were arrested for making derogatory remarks against Liberty Bonds.

The city's response was to make both literal and symbolic changes in the community. The study of German in the public schools was first restricted and later banished entirely. Unpatriotic actions by teachers were reported to the Board of Education, which adopted a resolution warning that anyone engaged in "disloyal acts and utterances" would be promptly investigated. Woodpiles were made at street corners, and German-language books were burned while members of the Columbus Reserve Guards stood by to see that no one interfered. The city council voted to change the names of Schiller Park to Washington Park and Germania Park to Mohawk Park. They also changed the names of some streets, such as Bismarck Avenue to Lansing Avenue. After sixty years of using German in its ritualistic work, the local branch of the Order of Druids substituted English. The First and Second

German M.E. Churches dropped the word "German" from their names and substituted the word "Zion."

While there is no record of where S. P. stood on these questions, he was plainly concerned about the divisions that the war was creating at Buckeye Steel, which employed a large proportion of German-American workers as well as other Europeans who were not pro-German. So he launched an ambitious "Americanization" effort to ensure greater unity.

"In the past many men of foreign birth have been employed at the plant," read a Buckeye publication. "A systemic effort has been made to encourage them to attend night school, to take out naturalization papers, and to adopt American ideals and customs." An Americanization Committee was formed to work with the foreign-born employees.

Like so many companies, Buckeye switched to war production. By the end of 1917 the Buckeye plant was producing thirty-four hundred tons of steel castings per month, which were used to forge 75mm guns. Buckeye also signed a lucrative contract with the Railroad Administration, the federal agency running the railroads during the war, to produce couplers and other railroad parts.

The First World War was not only a conflict on the battlefield but also a race in industrial mobilization, and it was widely assumed that whichever power could best harness its industrial might would be the victor. People like S. P. Bush, who spent their lives applying scientific management to industry, were no longer simply businessmen; they could be potent weapons in an industrial war.

Leading the effort to organize American industry was Wall Street financier Bernard Baruch. Gruff, opinionated, and demanding, Baruch had been asked to head the War Industries Board (WIB) and serve as a liaison between government and industry. Captains of industry were brought to Washington to oversee planning and production of war matériel. In the spring of 1918 a telegram arrived at Buckeye from Baruch; he wanted S. P. to become chief of the WIB's Ordnance, Small Arms and Ammunition Section. S. P. accepted the offer, and by June 1 he was in Washington.

Prior to the war the production of munitions was restricted to a small number of plants situated on the eastern seaboard—in Connecticut, Rhode Island, Massachusetts, and New York. By the spring of 1918 congestion and bottlenecks were a serious concern. Plants were behind schedule, and there was a shortage of power, fuel, and transportation; the most pressing concern was ammunition.

Much of S. P.'s time was spent haggling with Remington Arms, which supplied machine guns, Colt automatic pistols, and millions of rifles to the United States and the Allies. Samuel Pryor, head of the company, was a bombastic and aggressive negotiator.

S. P. effectively negotiated several large deals with Remington and tried to help harmonize the production and distribution of munitions.

The merging of business and war stirred controversy. With business executives and captains of industry serving in important board posts while they held large contracts with the government, there was a blurring of private and public purposes. Senator James A. Reed of Missouri assailed companies like the Aluminum Company of America. "Practically all the big trusts and monopolies" were benefiting from the collaborative efforts, he complained, "making contracts for their own use, enrichment and benefit." In 1918, Mississippi senator James Vardaman urged that the WIB be disbanded because it "lends itself to favoritism, overcharge and graft."

Buckeye prospered enormously during the war years. Company sales increased to $10 million per year and assets rose to $9.1 million. But much of it was the result of increased work. The contracts themselves were not particularly lucrative. While large companies such as U.S. Steel and Bethlehem Steel signed open-ended government contracts that could easily be abused, Buckeye placed caps on profit. Net earnings rose only slightly faster than sales.

S. P. spent the war years working at a frenetic pace; it was as if he were fighting the war himself. Dividing his time between Washington, D.C., and Columbus, he was rarely home. When he saw his family, he simply reminded them that this was about responsibility and duty. S. P.'s eldest daughter wrote some verses, expressing her supreme confidence in him. He was a distant giant in the eyes of his children.

> Now I have figured out a way
> That's clever and quite clear
> To rid the world of its dismay
> And do away with fear.
> There is a man who's qualified
> To rule all lands on earth
> His training in all fields is wide,
> He's worked quite hard since birth.
> His father was a minister,
> His mother was a Fay,
> So there is nothing sinister

At home to spoil his play.
He worked and schooled and schooled and worked
At least he tells us so,
And he was never known to shirk
Good deeds for friend or foe.
An athlete of great renown
He proved that he could be
And there is not a man in town
So good to charity.
Among the men most everywhere
He has a lot of pals
The statement certainly is fair
He's first with all the gals.
An answer to the world's great need
My candidate would be,
So very fine in word and deed,
I'm sure you will agree.
Get all the nations' flags unfurled,
A plebiscite please push,
Elect the Moses of this world,
Whose name is S. P. Bush.

With S. P. engrossed in his work, it fell to Flora to hold the family to-gether. She devoted her time and energies to the war effort, working on be-half of relief organizations and promoting campaigns that encouraged housewives to can fruits and vegetables. As chairwoman of the Women's Auxiliary, she instituted a drive to raise money to support young soldiers training near Columbus. The auxiliary held religious services, opened read-ing rooms, and provided entertainment for soldiers who were coming and going by the thousands. "At the end of the luncheon many played ald lang syne," she wrote her husband about one event. "And then the Star Spangled Banner. What could be better than that?"

FOR PRES THE WAR BEGAN IN EARNEST IN JUNE 1918 WHEN HE SHIPPED OUT with the 158th Field Artillery Brigade bound for France. The so-called Yale Battalion was expected to see action soon as artillery was the great workhorse and destroyer of the war.

The trip to Europe was long and arduous. Quarters were cramped, with the threat of lurking German U-boats. Once on the Continent, Pres and his comrades found the days difficult and long. First they made the trek to the front. Drivers and horses would wait until dusk to begin moving since all vehicles were prohibited in forward areas during daylight. Once they reached the front near the French town of Meuse, a vigorous routine became their daily life. During the day, supplies were drawn from the depot and ammunition from the dump. Then at nightfall the caissons were loaded with shells, and they and other wagons filled with rations and supplies were moved forward. When night reached its darkest, the real action would begin.

Flares and rockets gleamed and faded in the darkness, and the sound of machine guns chattering nearby was common. Blasts from the big guns to the right and left could blow out an eardrum, and the flashes threw the column into sudden silhouette. Occasional bursts of enemy shells nearby had the men ducking for cover. But the explosions might lead the restive horses to bolt, which meant hunting them down all night.

When the orders came to fire, the cannoneers would unload the shells and carry them to the guns, stacking them in orderly rows. Forward spotters identified the targets and relayed the coordinates back to the crews. The full-throated booming of the guns would go on literally for hours.

IN EARLY SEPTEMBER 1918, GENERAL PERSHING, DETERMINED TO BREAK THE stalemate on the Western Front, moved more than 1 million American soldiers into action, including the Yale Battalion. Fighting was particularly fierce east of the River Meuse, which flowed between a dominating range of hills. Pershing's goal was simple, "to draw the best German divisions to our front and to consume them." It was to be an inglorious battle of attrition.

Using seven double-size divisions against eight battle-weary German divisions, Pershing reduced the German position in four days. Then he quickly shifted his forces for a giant Allied thrust all along the Western Front. For the next five weeks the Americans slugged it out with the Germans. By late October, one-fourth of the German forces on the Western Front were crowded into one-tenth of the entire front to face the American army. Casualties on both sides were mounting at an alarming rate.

Captain Pres Bush and his men spent most of the time under enemy fire, which tried to knock out the American guns before they could wreak havoc on the German trenches. The guns of the 158th returned volleys onto the

German positions. The actual weight of the ammunition fired by American forces during the battle was greater than that used by the Union Army during the entire American Civil War. More than 4.2 million artillery shells were fired before it was all over.

American casualties were high, more than 256,000.

When the German guns finally fell silent, Pres was jubilant with victory. Suddenly the mischievous and humorous side of the young man returned in a letter he wrote his parents. Describing what he claimed were his exploits during the battle, he wrote that as the Germans launched a great offensive on July 15, three Allied leaders—General Foch, Sir Douglas Haig, and General Pershing—were making an inspection of the American positions. Pres told his parents that he was guiding the three generals when a German 77mm artillery shell suddenly descended from the sky. As he described it, he drew his bolo knife, stuck it up as he would a baseball bat, and parried the blow, sending the shell off harmlessly to the right. He had saved the lives of the three great Allied generals and was to be rewarded with a chestful of medals and ribbons!

The letter was utterly fantastic. And yet he never indicated that it was a joke. When his proud mother finished reading it, she shared it with the local newspaper, the *Ohio State Journal*. "The three generals marveled at the exploit," the *Journal* reported on its front page. "Apparently, they couldn't believe their eyes . . . Within 24 hours young Bush was notified of the signal recognition that was to be accorded him." Captain Bush was to receive the Cross of the Legion of Honor from the French government, the Victoria Cross from the English, and the Distinguished Service Cross from the United States.

"Possession of either one of the three is in itself considered a notable distinction," the paper wrote. "Conferring of the three decorations upon one man at one time implies recognition of a deed of rare valor and probably of great military importance as well."

News of Prescott's exploits created a sensation in Columbus, where much of the reporting in the paper had been the endless casualty lists issued by the War Department. When Prescott received a clipping of the *Journal* article in France, he was sickened and devastated to see that his obvious joke had been mistaken for the truth. He immediately cabled his mother explaining that the letter had been written in humor. A brief notice of correction was published on the front page of the September 6, 1918, edition of the *Journal*.

For Flora and S. P., the sense of embarrassment must have been great. As prominent citizens of Columbus and possessing a strong sense of social honor, they were particularly troubled by the fact that the erroneous news report appeared in the *Journal* near long lists of dead and wounded.

After the war, when Pres returned from Europe, he would find that his relationship with his father was strained. In a way, it would never recover. He would never ask his father for help, and the two men would see each other only occasionally. As for the war years, Pres would leave them behind. According to his son Bucky, he never spoke about them later in life.

#### CHAPTER 3

# WHISKEY

JAB TO THE HEAD, JAB TO THE HEAD, BODY BLOW, BODY BLOW.
While Samuel P. Bush was studying statistics and mathematics at the
Stevens Institute on Long Island as a young man, a strong, solidly built
Bert Walker was pummeling his opponents as a heavyweight boxing champion in the state of Missouri. Large and powerful with a thick mop of sandy
hair, Walker could deliver jabs with unbelievable speed. Yet his most devastating punches were the powerful body blows thrown at the abdomen. The
sport was brutal as fighters squared off without gloves, often striking each
other until only one was left standing. This was a test of stamina, cunning,
and raw strength, and Walker rarely lost.

In a sport dominated by frontiersmen, the sons of poor immigrants,
and young men from hard-soil farms seeking a better life, Bert Walker was
an unlikely figure. A young man born to privilege, who had the attentions
of both his own personal valet and a nurse, he reveled in the pure glory
of besting his opponents. If the Bushes were self-contained, duty-bound, and
steady, the Walkers were aggressive risk-takers who wanted to win at all
costs. The fusion of these two families would make for a potent genetic cocktail.

Bert was the son of a prominent St. Louis family that owned a large stake
in Ely and Walker, one of the biggest and most successful dry goods wholesalers in the Midwest. Unlike the restrained Presbyterian and Episcopalian
Bushes, the Walkers were staunch Catholics, and his devout mother had
named him after George Herbert, the great English poet. ("Help thyself, and
God will help thee," Herbert wrote.)

His father, David Davis Walker, was a remote and distant figure who had
come to St. Louis from Maryland. His own father had wanted young David
to become a lawyer, but he refused and ran away from home. In St. Louis he
started Walker Dry Goods store, which merged with another to produce Ely
Walker. Thanks to the Missouri Pacific Railroad, which was pushing into the
American hinterland from Mississippi to the New Mexico Territory and

south from Colorado to the Rio Grande, it was an enormously profitable enterprise. Construction of the railroads helped propel a new wave of immigrants to the American Midwest and Southwest. Small settlements were burgeoning into medium-size towns and small cities, and in places like Little Rock, Wichita, Pueblo, Denver, Dallas, Houston, Fort Worth, and San Antonio, retailers and small general stores looked to St. Louis wholesalers for their supplies.

Ely and Walker became one of the most successful companies at meeting this new demand. Using full-time buyers in New York, London, Paris, and Brussels, the firm struck alliances with merchants like Sears, Roebuck and J. C. Penney. But it was a competitive business. Price was everything for the middleman. David Walker was often on the road, trying to cut expenses and reduce transportation costs.

St. Louis of the mid-nineteenth century was a city of marked contrasts—sophistication and Western ruggedness. A major manufacturer of beer and cigarettes, it also boasted the largest drug company in the United States. These industries generated immense wealth and brought both elegance and extravagance to the city. Homes like the one the Walkers owned were "veritable palaces in every particular of richness, appointment and setting—even in size," recalls one contemporary account.

Yet St. Louis was also a frontier city. Along with its elegance, St. Louis had the largest cattle market in the world and was home for tens of thousands of immigrants from Germany and Ireland. For the elite of St. Louis, culture and high society were just small islands in a sea of commonality.

The Walkers spent their summers in Kennebunkport, Maine, at an old hotel. Traveling to the Maine coast was an adventure in itself. Servants would pack up large crates, and they would dine in a private car en route. Once they arrived, the Walkers and their brood would spend warm summer afternoons at the home of novelist Booth Tarkington, playing bridge or mahjongg and eating baked beans and blueberry pie. In the afternoon they would head to the coastal home of author Kenneth Lewis Roberts.

Bert's mother, fearing that the Catholic education in St. Louis was "too raw and too German," sent her young son off to boarding school in England. When Bert left, his valet went with him.

Stonyhurst was an all-boy school housed in an imposing sixteenth-century estate surrounded by ornate gardens. It was a Jesuit institution guided by the *ratio studiorum* of St. Ignatius where students received rigorous instruction in the classics and were required to engage in daily worship in the chapel. Most students were sons of prominent English Catholics, who would later enter the Church, go into politics, or receive a special commission to the military academy at Sandhurst.

Bert excelled in his studies, including heavy doses of history, mathematics, and Latin. But his greatest passion was sports. In addition to boxing, he developed into an exceptional polo player. Bert also discovered a new game, still little known back in the States. Although golf lacked the physical contact of his other two choice sports, the game required a mental toughness that he grew to appreciate. He was soon on the links every day, rain or shine.

After four years at Stonyhurst, Bert headed north to Scotland to begin studies in premedicine at the University of Edinburgh. But he found the courses boring and the tempo of his life slow going. So after just one year, he abandoned his studies and returned to St. Louis.

Unlike so many young men his age, Bert did not need to make a place for himself. A spot had been reserved for him at Ely and Walker. It was an enormously successful enterprise, and his brother was also expected to join the business. But Bert was an aggressive free spirit who had little interest in the nuisances of running a dry goods distribution business. He was determined to make his own path, much as his own father had done, and as S. P. Bush was doing in Columbus. Accordingly, Bert sold his stake in Ely and Walker and formed G. H. Walker and Company, one of the first investment banking firms in the American Midwest.

If S. P. Bush was like the trains he made his couplers for—steady, sure, and direct—Bert Walker was altogether different. Like the stallions he rode on the polo grounds, Bert was fiery and unpredictable.

"The old man was a dealmaker," says his son Lou Walker. "Nothing more, nothing less. He wanted a piece of the action, and took a lot of risks. He *liked* taking risks."

Risk-taking fueled Bert like a shot of adrenaline. He would invest in mining, railways, banks, and cattle breeding operations, leveraging his position as best he could. He never expected them all to work out, and over the course of his lifetime he would lose and double his money many times over. Samuel P. Bush saw his wealth rise steadily, accumulated over the course of several decades of loyal service to Buckeye Steel.

One deal that worked out magnificently for Bert was his investment in the Missouri, Kansas, and Texas Railroad. The young businessman landed a spot on the corporate board and, along with the dividends that rolled in, he enjoyed a special pass that allowed him to travel the rails free of charge. Bert visited distant locales from Santa Barbara, California, to the rugged coast of

Maine. Later, when he could afford it, Bert built vacation homes at both lo-
cations. In Maine he bought an outcropping of rocks near the small village
of Kennebunkport that would later be known as Walker Point.

Making money was for Bert, in some respects, like boxing. It was more
than a competition. It was the measure of a man.

Soon after G. H. Walker and Company was off the ground, Bert met a
beautiful young girl and fell in love. Lucretia ("Luli") Wear was blonde, gentle, and affectionate. Her family had social prominence, with ancestors who
had fought in the Revolutionary War and under General Jackson at the Battle of New Orleans in 1812. Her four brothers all attended Yale University
and were superb athletes. But unlike the Catholic Walkers, the Wears were
staunch Presbyterians.

Luli's older brother Holliday played baseball for the Cincinnati Reds. He
barnstormed the Midwest as a star outfielder in a sport that was still in its infancy. When the Reds came to town to play the St. Louis Cardinals on a
Sunday afternoon, Holliday and his teammates strutted down the street to
the sounds of a marching band. It was the sort of spectacle that the boister
ous Walkers could appreciate; but for the Wears it was too much. Mrs. Wear
rang for the maid to come in and close the windows and draw the curtains.
Son or no son, it was a Sunday. Games of any kind were generally forbidden
in the Wear home, and there were no playing cards or games with dice.

"Chess was acceptable, though, because it was not a game of chance,"
says Nancy Bush Ellis.

Bert spent considerable time at the Wear house as he courted young Luli.
To see her, he would need to come to the front door; telephones, just coming into use, were unacceptable to Luli's father. "Any young man who wants
to see my daughter *should* come around and ask properly," he insisted.

As Bert and Luli's relationship blossomed, the courtship ran into an un-
avoidable problem. When Bert proposed and Luli accepted, it came to the
fore. Bert went to his parish priest to discuss the wedding ceremony; he
didn't get the reception he expected.

"I'm going to marry Miss Luli Wear," he told the parish priest.

"You'll go to hell if you marry Luli Wear," the priest apparently responded.

"I'll go to hell if I *don't* marry her," Bert snapped before storming out of
the church. In the end the couple decided to hold two weddings. But Bert's
parents, devastated that he had not married a Catholic, refused to attend.
The chill lasted for several decades until Bert's mother grew to accept her
Protestant daughter-in-law.

"Luli is a Catholic at heart," she would tell her son. For the Walkers, there could be no higher compliment.

With his growing personal wealth and a beautiful young bride, Bert Walker took his place in St. Louis society. Anyone seeking membership in the city's elite needed either ancient lineage (at least three generations of relative affluence) or current wealth and power. Bert qualified on both counts.

Local civic affairs were run by a small group of power brokers known as the Big Cinch. Politics in turn-of-the-century St. Louis was largely a struggle between competing ethnic groups searching for power in city hall. The Democrats were dominated by Irish pols. The growing Republican Party was largely run by ethnic Germans. Like many prominent families, the Walkers were Democrats, and Bert became a friend of up-and-coming pols like David R. Francis, who later went on to be governor. It was a mutually bene-ficial relationship. For Francis, Walker was a source of campaign funds. For Walker, Francis was a way to protect his growing business and financial em-pire, a friendly face in local government. While they were not particularly close, Francis trusted Bert's judgment. When Francis was appointed U.S. ambassador to Russia by Woodrow Wilson in 1916, he hired several people for the embassy staff in Petrograd at Bert's suggestion.

But despite his increasing involvement in dignified St. Louis society, Bert Walker retained his rough edge. One winter night at the exclusive St. Louis Club, Bert and friends were celebrating the birthday of Blakesley Collins. In a private room elaborately decorated for thirteen, they listened to a six-piece string-and-brass band. After several rounds of drinks, Bert and the others be-gan singing with the orchestra and finally were bellowing. The noise became so loud that other patrons in the club began to complain. A white-gloved waiter arrived and delivered the news: Please quiet down. When Bert read the note, he and his friends only intensified their singing. When another re-quest arrived, Bert stood up and snatched the bass drum from the drummer. Taking the cue, his friends grabbed the other instruments and tried to strike up a tune. Minutes later they threw open the doors and began a drunken pa-rade through the entire club.

The next morning Bert was told to go before the board of the St. Louis Club and explain his loutish behavior. Bert went to the meeting, where he promptly announced that he was going to form his own club. He hired the manager from the St. Louis Club and formed the Racquet Club of St. Louis. Proclaiming an end to stuffiness, the club motto was "Youth Will Be Served."

Bert was equally boisterous as captain of the St. Louis polo team. When the club headed to Chicago for the regional championships, Luli and the Wears went to watch and cheer him on. St. Louis was not expected to do much at the event, but the team eventually found itself in the finals.

The night before the big match, Bert gave a rousing speech, shot glass in hand, and offered numerous toasts. The next morning when he arrived at the polo grounds, word had spread about his raucous behavior at the previous night's festivities. Bert ignored the whispers and climbed atop his stallion. He rode hard and yelled in his booming voice, "Get me Whiskey! Get me Whiskey!" The crowd murmured that the hard-drinking captain of the St. Louis squad required more liquor to finish the match. But actually he wanted to switch ponies. His other horse was named Whiskey.

Bert would tell his children and grandchildren that physical contests forged spiritual qualities and encouraged certain virtues that made one a better person. He certainly seemed to stake a lot on athletic ability. His children were all expected to compete fiercely and win. Years later, when he went to New York to run the Harriman Brothers investment banking firm, he often hired tennis champions and baseball players, convinced that their competitive spirit was more important than their academic accomplishments. You can always teach someone the finance business, he would tell his sons; you can't teach them how to compete and win.

"He was a superb athlete and brought up all of his kids as athletes," recalled his son Lou. "Sometimes he seemed more like a coach than a father. Either he had his business or he had his own game of golf with friends. We didn't see much of him."

The physical aggressiveness that served him so well on the polo pitch, the adrenaline that drove him in business, seemed to fail him when it came to being a father and husband. What was creative energy in his outside pursuits seemed to transform itself into destructive energy at home.

Bert and Luli Walker had four sons—Herby, Johnny, Jimmy, and Lou. When the boys had a disagreement, Bert had little patience for determining who was in the right. Instead, he would grab two sets of boxing gloves, give them to the feuding boys, and let them go at it with no rules or time limit.

"The old man figured that whoever was left standing was right," says Lou Walker, "and whoever was laying on his ass was wrong."

As the boys got older and entered their early teens, matters got worse as Bert himself would enter the ring.

"We had to box with him, you know," says Lou. "He fixed this room up like a boxing ring and he would take us in there and knock the hell out of us. We got used to it, of course. My brother Johnny was the boxing champion at the Hill School and if he had wanted to he could have let him have one. But he was a little afraid to do that."

The boys often found the relationship with Bert adversarial rather than paternal. When he wasn't boxing with his sons, he was criticizing. "He'd catch you up on details and keep you off balance," says Lou. "I was always scared as hell of him."

Bert had high hopes that his sons might become professional athletes. He financed a small baseball league in Kennebunkport during the summers to help them hone their skills. He hired Jack Coombs, the coach at Duke University, and recruited nine college captains to play ball with his sons. Even semipro teams were brought in to play them.

While none of the Walker boys made it in the pros, the youngest, Louis, got a shot at it. A lumbering pitcher for Yale, Lou received an offer for a tryout with the New York Giants. Bert was ecstatic and saw his son off.

Lou spent three days in training camp in Florida waiting for a chance to show manager Bill Terry what he could do. Finally his opportunity came.

"Walker, go in and throw some batting practice," Terry barked, cigar clenched in his teeth.

Lou grabbed his glove and ran onto the mound. Much to his chagrin, the first man at the plate was the legendary Mel Ott.

"The first pitch I threw hit him in the back of the neck," recalls Lou.

Grimacing with pain, Ott turned to Bill Terry and bellowed, "Get that college jerk out of there before I get killed!" Thus ended the Walker sons' chance for baseball stardom.

———

IF THE BOYS WERE FRIGHTENED OF BERT, THINGS WERE SCARCELY BETTER for Luli. Lou Walker never remembers seeing his father strike his mother, but Bert could be harsh in his criticism. Often after leaving the offices of Walker and Company for the day, Bert would go to the St. Louis Racquet Club and play bridge. Luli and the children would wait patiently at home with dinner warming on the stove. After he failed to show an hour later, Luli would call the club and inquire, "Is Mr. Walker there?"

When she discovered that he was, she would gather the children. "All right, children, we'll start dinner," she would tell them, and the children would eat and then complete their homework before going to bed. Hours later, after nightfall, Bert would stroll in and blow up at Luli, angry that the family had not waited for him.

"Do I count for nothing in this household?" he would yell.

"No, no, darling, the children had homework," she would respond quietly.

Every morning the toast would arrive on the table in a little silver holder with small slats. Bert would usually pick it up and examine it. "Luli!" he would bellow. "Do you call this toast?!"

"Bert, darling," she would say ever so graciously, "there's nothing wrong with the toast."

"It's a sponge!" he would snap, complaining that the bread had not been crisped to perfection. "*This* is not *toast!*"

Like a coiled spring he would snap at the most inopportune moments. "He just jumped all over her when things were wrong," says granddaughter Nancy Bush Ellis.

Although Luli appeared to maintain her poise throughout, the criticism had a withering effect. Once Bert took her out on the golf course to play a game of alternate shots with her brother Joe Wear and his wife. Joe teed off and fired a shot straight down the fairway. Bert shot next and did the same. Next came Mrs. Wear's turn to play the ball her husband had shot. Walking over to the ball, she measured the club and swung, missing it completely. Embarrassed, she stepped away. Luli then approached Bert's ball and took her turn. She took a hard swing and connected with the ball, shanking it at a right angle into a sand trap. Bert was furious.

"Well, Bert, darling, at least I didn't whiff the way Irene did," she said, trying to appease him.

"Luli," he snapped back angrily, "I wish to God you had!"

So hurt by the incident, Luli reportedly never played golf again.

Despite it all, Luli worked to maintain her graceful disposition. She read her Bible daily and spoke gently to her husband, even when he was full of froth and fury. "My mother was an unbelievable woman," says Lou Walker. "We often wondered how she stayed married to my father."

While life at home was difficult and even brutal for the boys, Bert was extravagant when it came to his girls. If S. P. Bush believed in the virtue of frugality, Bert Walker spent his way to a luxuriant lifestyle. A French governess cared for young Dorothy and Nancy, and they were outfitted with the latest silk fashions from Paris, which would arrive several times a year in pretty boxes. They attended the St. Louis Country Day School. They also traveled overseas regularly, unusual for young girls from the Midwest. One year they headed off to Paris for the entire summer with their eccentric Aunt Min. For Dorothy and Nancy it was an entire summer of daydreams. They attended extravagant weddings and other social events, rode through the city by horse and buggy at night, and even frequented the gaming tables of Paris salons where Aunt Min could play cards. The girls watched as she racked up large sums of money at the poker table.

If Samuel P. Bush in Columbus believed in the virtues of eating basic foods on reused tablecloths, the Walkers enjoyed rich foods, expensive silver, cakes, and pastries. Bert imported the finest wines, dined on rich European cuisine, and enjoyed drinking the finest bourbon, which he pronounced "bubbin."

The children grew up strong and spirited. The boys were particularly keen on terrorizing any French governess that came along. When Mme. Gramillot insisted that they stop playing on the rocks in Kennebunkport, they set fire to the tortoiseshell mirror of her prized dresser.

Second-oldest Dorothy (Dottie as she was called) had a way of taking charge and rejecting pretension. In St. Louis, when a neighborhood girl would parade around in her fine clothing, Dottie would line up the neighborhood kids to see if she should be allowed to play with her white gloves on. Dottie carried the day; the vote was no.

When competing in sports, she fought valiantly to keep up with her brothers. She spent most of her time playing tennis, particularly when they went to Kennebunkport. She won tournaments by playing with abandon, and her brothers preferred not to play her—for fear of losing to a girl. In spite of their competitive nature, the boys were intimidated by their sister. And for good reason. One summer in Kennebunkport, Dottie returned to the house and discovered that her favorite tennis racket had been damaged by her brother. Furious, she grabbed young Herby, Jr. and tied him to the front gate to teach him a lesson. When Bert returned home a few hours later to discover the family heir affixed to the gate, he was horrified.

But it was the sort of competitiveness and spirit that Bert could understand. One summer in Maine, Dottie and her brother Louis were engaged in a game of doubles against another team. When they took a break from the afternoon heat, Lou headed for the clubhouse, where a wedding reception was being organized. Discovering an unattended champagne foundation, he drank ten glasses before returning to the court—too drunk to play the next set; the match ended then and there.

Later that evening, when Bert found out about it, he called Lou into his study. "You won't be going to school next year," he informed his son without discussion. "You'll be working in a Pennsylvania steel mill. The train leaves tomorrow morning at 8 A.M. Be on it." Lou was on the train the next morning.

By the early 1900s, Bert Walker's world began to expand as head of the G. H. Walker and Company. What started as a successful Midwestern investment firm was now a major force in American finance. By forging strong working alliances with the Guaranty Trust Company in New York and J. P. Morgan and Company, Bert was becoming a player in the consolidation of major corporations.

He was a premier deal-maker in the Midwest, well known in corporate offices from Minnesota to Mexico for his ability to find lucrative deals. Larger investment firms in New York City often looked to him for advice as they considered investment opportunities in the region.

Bert's success attracted the interest of the Harriman family, which possessed one of the largest fortunes in America. Edward Henry Harriman had created the Union Pacific and was known as the Napoleon of American railroads. A stern man with grandiose visions of a global transportation network linking railroads with vast shipping empires, E. H. Harriman instructed his sons Averell and Roland in true aristocratic fashion. They played croquet and polo with the Morgans, Vanderbilts, Whitneys, and Rockefellers. When E. H. died in 1904, his sons were still in their youth.

By 1919, when Averell and Roland had graduated from Yale, they were looking for a new man to manage and direct their investment banking efforts. Their father had dealt with Bert when he was amassing his railroad empire; they contacted Bert to see if he might be interested.

Roland and Averell Harriman were establishing a new investment bank, W. A. (William Averell) Harriman and Company, to be active in the securities and underwriting business. The young men saw the company as an organization that would have branch offices around the world. Young Averell Harriman made two trips to St. Louis in an effort to recruit Bert Walker. If Bert seemed difficult to convince, it was probably a front. He was eager to move on to bigger and better things.

Bert began spending months at a time in New York, assisting with the organization of the new private bank. In November 1919 the firm opened for business. A few months later Bert was made president and chief executive. He moved the family to New York City.

As Bert was making a new home on Wall Street, young Pres Bush had arrived in St. Louis in 1919 to make a place for himself. He was a Yale graduate and decorated veteran, but his relations with his father were still strained. He had gone to Yale for a Skull and Bones reunion in the spring and met Wallace Simmons, founder of the Simmons Hardware Company. Simmons (Bones, 1890) offered Pres a job as a salesman. Pres took the train to St. Louis and began pushing the company's Keen Kutter tools, Karpet King sweepers, Klipper Kut ice skates, and Krystal Klear lanterns

While visiting a St. Louis social club, Pres met Nancy Walker, Bert's oldest daughter. Pres asked if he could call on her at home a few days later. She agreed, and when young Pres came calling, she took him to the parlor where they chatted for almost an hour. Then suddenly Dottie came bursting through the front door, sweating and rosy-cheeked after a game of tennis, adorable blonde curls dancing on her shoulders. Pres was immediately smitten. The next time he came to the Walker home, it was to see Dottie.

An intense courtship began, followed by a long engagement. Nancy Walker would never marry.

Dottie was just eighteen when they met, carefree, strong, and vibrant. She had spent time at Miss Porter's School in Rhode Island and traveled to Europe. But she was in some ways still only a girl, under the protective wing of her father. Pres on the other hand was twenty-five and a Yale man. He had been to war and was working hard at his job. He had plans for the future.

Pres and Dottie courted for quite some time, regularly attending social functions together when Pres was in town. It was unclear to many whether the courtship would lead to marriage. But then, as is so often the case, tragedy struck, and the yearnings of both came to the fore.

Pres received word from his father that his mother, Flora, had been killed in a freak automobile accident. Struck by a car while standing on the street, she died instantly. Pres was devastated and returned to Columbus immediately. It was one of the few times he ventured back home.

Dottie met him before he left and saw the pain in his eyes. She yearned to go to Columbus to be with him.

"I have to go, I have to go to Columbus, to be with Pres," she told her mother.

But Luli explained that it just wouldn't be acceptable. "A young lady can't just hop up and go to Columbus."

Dottie was forced to stay in St. Louis and wait. The difficulty in having to wait for him, to know that he was suffering alone, revealed to her for the first time how deep her love was for him. "She knew then that she was going to marry him," says her daughter Nancy.

The marriage was not socially advantageous to Dottie. As they would say at the time, it was Pres who would be moving up. But convincing Bert and

Luli was not a difficult thing. Bert, while enjoying a luxuriant lifestyle, was himself a rebel against the social classes in St. Louis. And perhaps even more important, he could see that the young man from Yale wanted to take care of his daughter. What carried currency with Bert was a young man's *drive*. He had seen Pres on the golf course several times—his natural swing, his intense concentration, and his gentle putts on the green. This was how Bert measured a man.

Pres and Dorothy were engaged the following year. Kennebunkport, Maine, and not St. Louis, was selected as the site for the wedding. All the Walkers and some of the Bushes were there. S. P., by most family accounts, did not attend.

On the night before the wedding, August 5, 1921, Dottie Walker spent the evening with her mother, sorting through her life in an upstairs room of the family's grand seaside home. Dorothy had just turned twenty, and the independent and spirited young woman wondered out loud whether she should go through with the wedding. A phenomenal tennis player by this time, who had aspirations of joining the tennis circuit, she openly wondered what the future might hold.

"Oh, mother, I don't want to leave," she told her, showing a hint of concern and fear. "I don't want to get married. I don't want to leave you all, my sister and my four brothers and you. I can't bear to leave you."

Luli listened and gently consoled her. "Now Dorothy, darling, you're going to have a most wonderful life."

The next morning, men dressed in high starched collars and charcoal gray suits and women in ankle-length dresses and sunhats began arriving at the Walker house by boat. When they were all seated, the minister took his place in front and a small orchestra began to play. Pres Bush walked forward with his groomsmen, which included six of his friends from Skull and Bones. When Dottie came forward, dressed in white, tears came down Pres's face. The two exchanged vows and afterward, the celebration began.

#### CHAPTER 4

# DEALS

FTER THE WEDDING, PRES AND DOTTIE RETURNED TO ST. LOUIS.
For Dottie the marriage was a sobering adjustment. Pres was
working for Simmons Hardware and spent much of his time
traveling to cities such as Wichita, Kansas City, and Minneapolis. Gone
were the French governesses, the endless selections of silk dresses from Paris,
and the dreamy trips to Europe. A young hardware salesman could not hope
to offer that kind of lifestyle. And Pres Bush lived by an important principle:
You don't take money from your family. After leaving Yale, he never took a
penny from his father. (When S. P. passed away years later, Pres gave his portion of the estate to his sisters.) Now that he was married, he was no less determined to keep up the practice with his wealthy in-laws.

Seven months after their wedding, Pres was sent to Kingsport, Tennessee, to
arrange for the sale of a factory. The plant made horse saddles in what was now
clearly the automobile age, and their large orders from the army during the
war had dramatically declined. Pres and Dottie moved to the small town in the
foothills of the Smoky Mountains while Pres worked to reorganize the factory.

That spring of 1922, Dottie discovered she was pregnant. As summer approached, she asked to go to Kennebunkport to visit her family. With his
work done, Pres agreed and the young couple headed for the Maine coast.
When they arrived, it was as it had always been for the Walker brood—
lobster, tennis, and baseball. According to family lore, Dottie was standing at
the plate ready to bat when she went into labor. She hit the ball deep and
rounded the bases before asking to be taken to the doctor. Their oldest son,
Pres, Jr., was born hours later.

The joy of the birth was quickly overshadowed by a cloud of uncertainty.
When the young couple returned to St. Louis, Wallace Simmons announced that he was selling his hardware business to the Winchester Repeating Arms Company. The new management asked Pres to stay on, but
there seemed little future in the company. Suddenly Pres Bush was twenty-
seven, married, a new father, and looking for a job.

Back in Columbus, his father, S. P., was also struggling. He was still stunned by the death of his beloved Flora, and life was painful and difficult. Other than Buckeye Steel, he had little else in his life.

"My father was very lonely," Pres would later recall.

Hearing of his son's situation, S. P. asked him to return to Columbus to help turn around a business that Buckeye Steel had just acquired. Hupp Products produced floor coverings and had been run by corrupt management. S. P. was hoping that Pres might be able to save it, and that the time together would heal their relationship.

Without an immediate job prospect, Pres reluctantly took his father's offer and decided to return home. Their relationship warmed but remained distant. Relatives remember that S. P. Bush was not a demonstrative man. "He was very stern, always, that's how I remember him," recalls Teensie Bush Cole, his granddaughter. "And Pres was always so kind and gentle. They were different people—really different people."

As it turned out, the arrangement lasted only a year. "The thing had failed completely," Pres later recalled, "and we had to sell out for what we could get for it." The company was sold to Stedman Products, a manufacturer of rubber flooring based in South Braintree, Massachusetts. The company offered Pres a job, which he accepted. Again the young family was on the move. Pres and Dottie had been married for a little over two years, and they were now heading off to establish a new home in their fourth city. What's more, Dottie was pregnant again.

They settled into a Victorian house at 173 Adams Street in Milton, a town just south of Boston. It was there that Dottie gave birth to her second son, named after Bert: George Herbert Walker Bush. Pres liked the name okay, but became slightly irritated when Dottie's brothers started calling him Poppy. Since they called their father Pop, little George became Poppy. The name stuck with him throughout his life.

With two young boys at home, Pres hired a nurse to help Dottie. Money was tight.

When Pres wasn't putting in long days at Stedman or singing in the church choir, he was attending local town meetings. The process of New England meetings was rather quirky to this son of the Midwest. Elders of the town would gather with the members of the community to discuss their concerns over various issues, and a wide-open debate would follow. At first Pres was amused by it all, but he soon became fascinated by this demonstration of local democracy in action.

The young family spent two years in Milton until Pres got a better offer from U.S. Rubber, the largest rubber manufacturer in the United States, based in New York City. Pres was intrigued by the opportunity to advance his career, and Dottie was enormously pleased by the chance to be closer to her family. When they got the news of the transfer, Dottie wrote a friend from school, Helen "Didi" Gratz. Didi had married Godfrey Rockefeller, and the two had settled comfortably in Greenwich, Connecticut.

Greenwich was still mainly a resort town dotted with large homes, and it catered to wealthy New Yorkers who wanted to escape the summer heat. In many respects it was a divided community. Bisected by the Boston Post Road, the northern edge and outlying countryside had large estates, where Didi Gratz and her wealthy husband lived. To the south were comfortable but simpler homes; it was here that the Bushes would settle.

For Pres, the move to New York represented more than a new job. It was in a sense a return from the wilderness. After graduating from Yale, many of his closest friends had gone to work in the city. This was particularly true of his friends from Skull and Bones, who were now firmly ensconced on Wall Street. Knight Woolley, characteristically snappy in a double-breasted suit and fedora hat, pipe firmly clenched between his teeth, was working for the American Exchange National Bank. Bob Lovett, with his penetrating eyes and quiet demeanor, was also in the financial district, helping to secure major investment deals for his clients. And Pres's closest friend, Bunny Harriman, was deeply involved with W. A. Harriman and Company, now being run by Pres's father-in-law, Bert.

While Pres and Dottie had spent the past five years trying to make their way, Bert and Luli Walker were lapping up the life in New York. All the facets of the city that had bothered S. P. Bush—the speed, the innate tension of the place—attracted Bert. Like a moth dancing around a flame, Bert was captivated by the opportunities. After only a few weeks in the city, he felt right at home. "The old man considered himself a New Yorker after that point," recalled his son Lou, who made the move with his parents. "He never even thought of going back to St. Louis."

For the Bushes—S. P. with his strict mannerisms, Pres with his sense of guilt and duty—pleasures were sought and valued but could not be allowed to intrude upon the serious affairs of life. For the Walkers, pleasures *were* the serious things of life. Bert's New York was Gatsby's: high society, luxuriant galas, dinner parties that seemed never-ending, gambling, and high finance. "My grandfather was the worldliest man that ever lived, the very worldliest," says Nancy Bush Ellis. "Two Rolls-Royces, the place on Long Island, and two butlers—First Man and Second Man. One did the silver and one was his valet."

Thanks to the full coterie of business relationships that Bert had developed over the years, the Walkers entered New York society at a gallop. Bert quickly became the master of the deal, financing everything from the construction of Madison Square Garden to the Aviation Corporation of America, later Pan American Airways. He was one of the big wheels at the Belmont Race Track and had even been asked to sit down and chat with an ambitious young politician named Franklin D. Roosevelt.

When they first arrived, Bert and Luli had stayed at the home of Dwight Laurel Reid, owner of the *Herald Tribune*. The Madison Avenue townhouse proved to be a perfect location to explore the nightlife of the city. After a few months the Walkers settled into a beautiful home at 453 Madison Avenue, just behind St. Patrick's Cathedral. Times were good, so Bert also bought a place out on Long Island near Belmont. Bert would spend weekends there with two male servants who wore striped vests and beige linen jackets. For dinner, Bert dressed in a formal white tie.

What had brought him to New York was the opportunity to run W. A. Harriman and Company. Averell and Roland Harriman had seen their father build a financial empire in railroads. Now they wanted to use that capital to build an even larger empire of their own.

And in the years following the First World War, there were plenty of opportunities. International commerce was booming, and Wall Street was discovering a new world of wide open financial markets. Europe was recovering from the war, and both the victors and the vanquished were anxious for capital and goods.

Most of the financial houses were doing business with the European victors, France and Britain. These were places to make safe and sound investments for a comfortable return. But if you wanted to make a killing, you needed to venture further east into the heart of war-ravaged Europe. Germany was still reeling. Plagued by political instability and hyperinflation, weighed down by punitive war reparations, the German economy was a risky place to make an investment. But if you were successful, the rate of return could be enormous. The same was true if you looked even further east, to Russia. In that country the Bolsheviks were nationalizing industry and growing increasingly isolated, but they needed Western capital and technology.

W. A. Harriman and Company began by taking a stake in Hamburg-Amerika, a commercial steamship line the U.S. government had seized after the war. It had first-class vessels and well-trained crews, but was now largely idle. Bert looked over the assets and liked what he saw. So Averell Harriman went to Germany to negotiate a deal. In exchange for the capital needed to reopen the line, Harriman wanted a 50 percent stake in the business. The hope was to link the Hamburg line with the other steamship lines the Harrimans already owned.

In 1922, Averell made a visit to Berlin and opened a branch office. There he found it easy to meet and deal with German industrialists such as Fritz Thyssen (son of August Thyssen, the so-called "Rockefeller of the Ruhr"), who was running the family's iron, steel, and coal empire. Fritz Thyssen wanted alliances with American firms that could provide him shelter from Germany's hyperinflation. Harriman was a willing partner, and in 1924, Averell Harriman and Thyssen formed the Union Banking Corporation. Bert Walker structured a deal in which the company would put up about four hundred thousand dollars and become a full-fledged partner in Thyssen's overseas investments. At the same time the firm financed zinc mines in Polish Silesia in partnership with other German investors. Some of these deals made a substantial return; others failed miserably.

The other risky place to do business in the early 1920s was the Soviet Union. Vladimir Lenin had come to power loudly condemning the crimes of capitalism and unleashing a wave of terror in the country. But the Bolshevik leaders soon realized that they needed capital from the West to keep the communist state viable. Working from his offices in Berlin, Averell Harriman joined with a German firm and the Soviet government to form a short-lived joint trading corporation to ship raw materials out of the country. To arrange the tricky deal, Harriman negotiated directly with Lenin and Trotsky. Little trade resulted. But in 1924 the company learned that the Soviet Union was willing to grant mining concessions for the world's largest deposit of manganese ore, which was vital to the manufacture of steel. The massive field, located near Tiflis, Georgia, had supplied half of the world's output before the revolution.

Bert Walker dispatched company vice president J. Speed Elliott to Moscow to negotiate directly with the Kremlin. Elliott haggled with Soviet leaders for several months and sent updates to Bert in New York. Finally, after three solid months, a deal was struck. At a cost of just over $3 million, Harriman bought the rights to mine the field for twenty years and export the ore. W. A. Harriman and Company was required to loan the financially desperate Soviet State Bank $1 million as a "security deposit" and put down another million as advance royalties. Speed Elliott penned the contract in a Kremlin ceremony on June 12, 1924. Signing for the Bolsheviks was Felix Dzerzhinsky, the Soviet secret police chief. Decades later, Russian emigrants were still receiving royalties from the mine.

Harriman's growing business activity in Soviet Russia soon started to draw criticism. Western political leaders such as British MP Winston Churchill believed that commercial agreements with the Bolsheviks served only to strengthen the regime and thus were not only unwise, but immoral. But the Harrimans and Bert Walker didn't see it that way. Averell Harriman disagreed in principle: Commerce would mellow the Bolsheviks. Bert Walker really didn't care; he derisively called diplomats and politicians the "striped pants set." They had little business meddling in, well, business. In a private 1927 letter to Averell, he wrote, "It seems to me that the suggestion . . . that we withdraw from Russia smacks somewhat of the impertinent . . . I think that we have drawn our line and should hew to it." What both Averell Harriman and Bert Walker failed to understand was how entangling such business dealings would ultimately prove to be in a rapidly changing world.

IN EARLY 1926, BUNNY HARRIMAN WAS HAVING A DRINK WITH HIS GOOD friend Pres Bush and chatting about business. Pres was still working at U.S. Rubber and Bunny was cutting big deals on Wall Street. After reminiscing about Yale, Bunny explained that W. A. Harriman and Company was looking to bring some new talent into the firm. Pres had experience in manufacturing and possessed a list of contacts that ran through the Midwest and into New England. Would he be interested in joining the firm?

The obvious answer was yes. He was good friends with Bunny and the firm was on the rise. If he could make partner, the financial returns would be tremendous. But he also had concerns. At W. A. Harriman he would be working with Bert. He loved Dottie dearly, but being with Bert could be difficult at times. Compared to his own father, who was quiet and detached, Bert was often loud and overbearing.

Yet in the end, the opportunity proved too tempting. W. A. Harriman offered a better future than U.S. Rubber.

Joining the firm brought Pres back to the club atmosphere he had known at Yale. The men at Harriman were bonded together by a congenial familiarity and cooperative spirit they had learned on the playing fields at prep school and in the Ivy League. As at Yale, the firm wanted young men who had "sand"—perseverance, diligence, and grit. Pres was deemed to have all of these qualities and more.

Pres adapted quickly. Focusing less on the exotic deals that Averell and

Bert were cooking up, Pres concentrated instead on solid conservative investments in undervalued American firms that he could underwrite, reorganize, and then take public.

Dresser Industries of Bradford, Pennsylvania, was such an enterprise. A producer of steel railroad parts and machinery for the oil and gas industry, Dresser was a respectable company with a dominant position in a growing sector. It had five years of solid profits and no debt to speak of. Pres believed that if the company went public, it would have the capital to significantly expand its operations and produce even larger profits.

But the Dresser family was divided over the idea, so Pres went about planning a reorganization. Working with a few members of the board, Pres scripted a plan to take the company public. After months of extensive research and secret negotiations, the day of action finally arrived. On the afternoon of December 28, 1928, a series of meetings took place at the company's offices in Bradford. A group of directors led by Robert, Richard, and Carl Dresser voted to increase the number of shares available from 5,000 to some 300,000. That opened the door to a listing on the New York Stock Exchange. Next came the reorganization. A majority of the board voted that someone new needed to be brought in to run the company, and the current president was let go. Robert and Richard Dresser then appointed W. A. Harriman and Company to come up with a candidate.

As Pres sat in his office a few days later discussing the matter with Bunny Harriman, his secretary interrupted them to announce that Neil Mallon, a fellow Bonesman, was waiting to see him. The two had allegedly opened Geronimo's grave site, and had served in Europe together. Mallon was now working in Cincinnati for a canning company.

Pres was immediately seized by an idea: Why not make Mallon the new president of Dresser? Pres immediately contacted the company, and when Mallon left later in the day, he had been offered the job of president and general manager for twenty-five thousand dollars a year.

For Mallon it was the break of a lifetime, and the ambitious young man knew it. Over the next five decades he would eagerly repay Pres and his sons for help in getting the Dresser job. When Pres's son George ventured into the oil business after the Second World War, it would be with substantial assistance from Mallon. When Pres and later his son George ran for political office, Dresser would provide substantial financial contributions. The specter of Dresser Industries even lingered when Pres's grandson George W. ran for president seventy-two years later. Dresser was no longer an independent company, but part of an oil and gas conglomerate called Halliburton, headed by vice-president-to-be Dick Cheney.

WORKING AT HARRIMAN WAS NOT SIMPLY A JOB; IT WAS A WAY OF LIFE. UNLIKE U.S. Rubber, which had been strictly nine-to-five, Pres was now expected at social gatherings where business was often discussed.

If before Pres and Dottie had spent quiet weekends playing tennis in Greenwich, they were now spending weekends at house parties given by world-class financiers like James Brown, a senior partner in the venerable Brown Brothers banking firm. At his lavish home in Oyster Bay, Brown threw big bashes for men of finance from firms like Harriman, Dillon Reed, and Warburg. The Bushes also attended a swirl of Long Island and Westchester house parties frequented by the New York industrial, financial, and social elite.

The experiences of the war had dissolved many of the social barriers between the patricians of old society, new money, and the creative community of café artists and writers. So when Pres and Dottie joined fellow Bonesman Bob Lovett for dinner, Lovett would also invite Knight Woolley, the Harriman brothers, the poet Archibald MacLeish (whose older brother Kenneth had served with them as a member of the Yale Battalion), and playwright Philip Barry (another Yale man). Making occasional appearances were Lillian Hellman, Dorothy Parker, and Robert Sherwood.

While Pres, with his abundance of charm and wit, moved comfortably in these circles, he probably felt a bit out of place. His views on social mores were more conventional than some of the more Bohemian members of this set. Like the young Midwesterner in *The Great Gatsby*, Pres probably felt as if he were on the outside looking in at the odd excesses of 1920s Long Island society.

Pres and Bert spent considerable time together during these productive years. They shared a mutual respect, but they could also grate on one another. The way each man conducted business and dealt with family matters was radically different, and a subtle tension was often the result.

"Pres had terrific respect for the old man," recalled Lou Walker. "But it wasn't a 'hey, fella,' sort of relationship where they slapped each other on the back. It was more distant than that."

Bert Walker relished the trappings of high society. "He liked the style in which Averell Harriman lived his life," recalls Nancy Bush Ellis. He bought a yacht with Harriman, a large, white cruiser with detailed woodwork in mahogany inlaid with brass, named the *Pawnee*. The two men would cruise out on Long Island Sound with a set of society friends along for the ride. Bert went to the Links Club for lunch and would spend the afternoon at Belmont, watching the ponies with friends as they drank on the terrace. He won and lost large sums of money at the races and later shared a racing stable with Harriman called the Log Cabin Stud.

Bert also enjoyed his liquor. "During prohibition, he had his supplier," said Pres Bush, Jr. "Only the finest whiskey would do."

Pres Bush did none of this. At their home in Greenwich, the Bushes ate simple fare: roast beef, chicken, mixed vegetables. Pres liked it that way, neat and simple. He detested gambling and had mixed views about prohibition. His tastes were so different from his in-laws' that if he arrived home and saw pheasant or goose being prepared, he knew in an instant who was coming for dinner.

In part these differences were exacerbated by money. Pres was like his father, steady and conservative. Bert Walker would make or lose as much on one deal as Pres would make all year. Even years later, when he was doing well at the firm, Pres could not escape his Midwestern sense of frugality. When he took his children to the Algonquin Club in New York, he would complain about the cost. "$12.50 for eggs benedict! Ridiculous!"

Bert enjoyed needling his son-in-law for his lack of interest in the rich trappings of life. When filling out an order for imported French wine he would ask his son-in-law: "Would you like to lay down some money for twenty cases?"

"I'll take one case," Pres would say.

"A single solitary case?" Bert would respond with a condescending chuckle.

"I knew Prescott Bush well and he had a much softer side to him than Mr. Walker," said Gerry Bemiss, a family friend who has known four generations of Bushes. "The Walker boys grew up being tremendously aggressive, and competitors in sports, and Mr. Bush was a great competitor himself. But he kept it more fun than total warfare. If you got in front of Mr. Walker on the golf course and held him up for one minute, there was hell to pay. He didn't want anyone to stand in his way. Mr. Bush wasn't like that at all."

Despite their differences, Bert and Pres did share a few things in common. Along with their mutual devotion to Dottie, both men were crazy about golf. American golf in 1920 was still very much in its infancy. The nation's first crude golf course had sprung up in a pasture outside of Yonkers just forty years earlier. Only after wealthy New Yorkers William Vanderbilt, Duncan Cryder, and Edward Mead discovered the game in Biarritz, France, in the winter of 1890 did it catch on. The first incorporated golf club appeared at Shinnecock Hills in 1891, and the U.S. Golf Association was formed three years later.

When the Walkers moved to New York City in 1920, there were a variety of courses and clubs to choose from. But being a golf purist, Bert investigated the courses with great vigor before joining a club. When he learned that the national Golf Club Links course in Southampton was based on several classic Scottish holes, he joined immediately.

Bert also became increasingly involved in managing and organizing the United States Golf Association. He was on the USGA executive committee, and in late 1920 went with the committee to Scotland for a series of meetings with the Royal and Ancient Golf Club of St. Andrews Rules Committee to discuss the possibility of international play with the Scots. Bert believed that a dose of patriotism would help the game catch on more quickly in the United States, so he presented a plan to field international teams, including the United States and Great Britain, and offered to donate the trophy. The USGA loved the idea and when it was presented to the public, the press dubbed the trophy "the Walker Cup."

The next year the USGA invited all golfing nations to send teams to the United States to compete. No country other than Great Britain was able to send a team. So it was decided that the Yanks would square off against the Brits. Thus began the semiannual Walker Cup, an event that continues today.

LIKE BERT, PRES IMMERSED HIMSELF IN THE WORLD OF ORGANIZED GOLF. IN 1926 he was appointed chairman of the USGA's Championship Committee, with responsibility for establishing rules and identifying the courses that would host the championships. For Pres, the game had a grace that could be enjoyed with friends or alone. With his children he would play baseball and tennis. "But golf he reserved for himself," said Nancy Ellis. And while he never played for a championship, the game would serve him well as he later ventured into politics. Political leaders like President Eisenhower were always eager to play with "the senator with a smooth swing." But he would never compromise the game. "Regardless of whoever it was, he never let up on the course," recalled Pres Bush, Jr. "He played to win, whether he was playing a good friend or the president."

#### CHAPTER 5

# WORRY

I N THE SPRING OF 1930, ELLERY JAMES, KNIGHT WOOLLEY, AND PRES Bush were in the parlor car of a train headed for a Skull and Bones reunion. They were playing cards and discussing the panic on Wall Street. Vast fortunes had been lost in the months following the 1929 Crash.

Woolley was now working with Pres at W. A. Harriman and James was firmly ensconced at Brown Brothers, a white-shoe banking operation that had been on Wall Street since 1843. The markets were still shaky and only a few investment banks could hope to survive. Many were expected to do so only by merging with their competitors.

As he dealt the cards, James casually suggested that perhaps Brown Brothers and Harriman should consider a merger. People at both houses knew each other well and they could wait out the financial storm together. No one took the idea seriously, and they returned to their game. That weekend, they helped initiate the new class of Bonesmen in the secret crypt on the Yale campus. On Sunday, they returned home.

A few days later, James went to see Woolley at Harriman to discuss the matter further. The financial carnage was continuing, and more than a thousand banks around the country had already failed. Companies were laying off workers and industrial production was being dramatically reduced. No one seemed immune. The venerable Brown Brothers was in trouble, too. The firm needed new capital, caught with a mountain of what it politely called "undigested securities." "It became clear to us," said senior partner Thatcher Brown, "that we were doing too large a business for our capital."

Brown Brothers and W. A. Harriman were two very different houses. Brown was staid and solid, with a rich tradition of financial operations in both the United States and Great Britain. Harriman was a rich up-and-comer, willing to take risks. What bonded the two firms together were their mutual needs in the midst of the financial crisis. Brown Brothers needed capital. Harriman on the other hand was looking for the imprimatur of a first-class firm that Brown Brothers still enjoyed. More important, perhaps, were the deep social relationships between the managers at both houses. Pres Bush, Knight Woolley, and Bunny Harriman at W. A. Harriman and Company and Robert Lovett and Ellery James at Brown Brothers were all members of Yale's Skull and Bones.

On the evening of December 11, 1930, Thatcher Brown, a tall, rather scholarly-looking man with graying hair and a broad, comfortable mustache, walked into the crowded library in an opulent home at 775 Park Avenue. Peering through round, horn-rimmed glasses, he read a prepared statement. The fifth-generation banker announced that his revered family firm was merging with W. A. Harriman and Company.

In financial circles it was quite a story. Brown Brothers was, as one newspaper put it, "a venerable banking power, whose history is closely linked with American history." W. A. Harriman in contrast was the upstart, flush with money from lucrative overseas investment but lacking status and position in the banking world.

Overnight the newly minted Brown Brothers Harriman became one of the "big four" investment houses that would come to dominate Wall Street in Depression-era America.

For Bert Walker the merger provided an ideal time to cash out and leave the firm for an early retirement. He was past fifty-five years old and still enormously wealthy despite the Crash. His sons were running his old firm G. H. Walker and Company. Retirement would allow him to dabble in other investments and spend most of his time focusing on golf and the racetrack.

For Pres Bush the merger proved a booster rocket to his career. Partners at Brown Brothers Harriman selected him to serve, along with Knight Woolley, as managing partner. Days after the public announcement, Pres moved his office to 59 Wall Street, an imposing marble building where Brown Brothers had been since 1843. Pres took his place at a bulky rolltop desk as silent and properly attired British floor attendants served as clerks.

Every Thursday morning, precisely at a quarter to ten, the partners' meeting would take place in the venerable Partners' Room, the inner sanctum of the company. Pres and Woolley would run the meeting as stark and imposing portraits of the four original Brown Brothers scowled at them from the dark, wood-paneled wall. The meeting would last half an hour to forty-five minutes, in which they would analyze operations for the previous week and discuss pending policy matters. The partners worked on the basis of strict consensus—they never voted. If there was a disagreement, they discussed it like gentlemen.

Pres Bush would spend the next forty years at Brown Brothers Harriman except for a brief respite in the United States Senate. From time to time offers came to move to larger corporate banks, but Pres always turned them down. Consensus and camaraderie forged behind closed doors suited him perfectly. The American West was settled by wagon trains, he would tell his sons, not cowboys. Well-intentioned, upright, and intelligent men could always arrive at the right conclusion absent outside pressures. It would be that way at Brown Brothers, and later when Pres went to the Senate. His sons and grandsons would adopt a similar attitude.

---

THE DEPRESSION HAD TAKEN A BIG BITE OUT OF PRES BUSH'S INVESTMENT accounts, and for several years his reserve capital account was in the red. The Harrimans carried him for a bit, and he continued investing until he eventually put the account back in the black a few years later. It was an arduous task, investing in the market during the Great Depression. "It took courage," he later recalled, "because the market was going down, week by week, week by week, and so some of our younger partners got heavily in the red."

The merger led the firm to concentrate on three areas: commercial banking, investment advisory service, and brokerage. Pres was given responsibility for handling the investment advisory service and the task of attracting new clients. In 1931 he set up an advisory department and began charging a fee for investment advice. The client received a formal contract and agreed to pay half of 1 percent on the first million dollars. Pres relied on a large network of contacts at Yale reunions, golf outings, and social events to secure clients.

"When we'd talk to somebody who'd say, 'Look, I have half a million dollars. I don't know what to do about this market. What should I do?' We'd say, 'Well, why don't you let us do this for you? We're doing it for the Harrimans, our own partners, so and so's wife, and the children, and my own wife' and so on — 'We can do for you just what we're doing for ourselves, if you think that's good enough,' and we'd explain how it worked. In this way we built up a fine business."

In 1933, Pres wrote a small book describing the importance of making good investment decisions. Titled *Scattered Wealth: A Brief Discussion of Investment Management*, the book appealed to the virtues of steady and secure investing under the management of a professional. It reflected his conservative temperament. "There is nothing about bonds and stocks that looks particularly hard to manage. Superficially they seem like a very simple means of conserving wealth. Probably you have experienced that sense of security which accompanies leaving some of them in a safe deposit box. As the gate of the vault closes behind you, you leave with the comfortable feeling that your wealth is safely locked up and cannot get away. Of course this is an illusion." He went on to describe the various threats the investor might face — inflation, market fluctuations, or economic calamity. The solution: accounts professionally managed and broadly diversified.

Producing the book took considerable effort. When it was finally released, Pres sent a humorous memo to his partners entitled *Shattered Health*.

There is nothing about a book on investment management that looks particularly hard to write. Superficially it seems like a very simple thing. Probably you have experienced that sense of superiority which accompanies reading such a book written by some one else. As you yawn and close the book, you have a comfortable feeling that you could have done much better with one hand tied behind you.

Of course this is a joke. Maybe you have never tried to edit such a book, not to mention writing it; but I have. What you think is something pretty swell turns out to be merely pieces of paper on which 18 different people think it is their God-given duty to scribble criticisms and sarcastic comments. Somebody in Chicago thinks it's too elementary and what is really needed is a 400-page *Compendium of Universal Knowledge*. Somebody in Boston or Philadelphia says it's too long and nobody will read it and what you ought to have is a one-page letter. Three of the partners in New York think the whole idea is lousy and should be abandoned in favor of a Christmas card.

The salesmanship and hard work were paying off by 1934. Despite the Depression, the firm had some $22 million under management.

When Pres wasn't running the firm's advisory business, he was making corporate deals. In January 1932 opportunity walked through the door when two young men named Bill Paley and Herbert Swope entered the office to discuss a deal. Radio was still in its infancy at the time and it was unclear whether the new medium would really take off. But Paley believed it would, and he had heard that the Columbia Broadcasting System (CBS), a small radio company owned by Paramount, was for sale. He wanted to buy it. Paramount was willing to give up half an interest in CBS in exchange for $5 million. Paley could come up with only half of the money. Could Pres Bush and Brown Brothers Harriman come up with the rest?

Pres knew next to nothing about radio. But the idea was intriguing, so he fell back on his extensive network of social and business contacts. He chatted with his good friend Richard Dupree, then vice president of Procter & Gamble. The advice Dupree offered was direct and simple. "Pres, if you ever get a chance to get into radio, on the right basis, that's the coming advertising medium. Tremendous impact." The next call he placed was to Stanley Resor, head of J. Walter Thompson, the biggest advertising agency in the country. Pres handled his money at Brown Brothers, and the two men often commuted together from Greenwich. Resor echoed what Dupree had said: Radio advertising was going to be big in the years ahead.

Pres took the advice and rounded up the money. Some of it was his own, but most was from outside investors. Paley bought CBS and in return gave Pres a slot on the CBS board of directors, where he served for close to twenty years. Paley would also become a lifelong family friend. He would support Pres's political ambitions and help his son George when he became director of the CIA.

Despite his long involvement with CBS, Pres never pretended to be particularly interested in broadcasting. When television was in its infancy, Paley sent a TV to the Bush house in Greenwich. Family members recall that Pres plugged it in, turned it on, watched for a few minutes, then shrugged his shoulders and shut it off. He couldn't figure out what all the excitement was about.

Pres performed a similar service for other companies in need of capital. In exchange he became a board member at such firms as Simmons Company, Dresser Industries, Prudential Insurance, the International Shoe Company, and the Pennsylvania Water and Power Company.

Unlike Averell Harriman, Pres was not a Europhile. He was quite comfortable staying in the United States, thank you very much. "My father never thought it was important to go to Europe," recalled his daughter. "I said once, 'Why don't we go to Europe, the way my friends do?' And my dad would say, 'Nothing is more beautiful than the Connecticut River Valley. It's just as pretty as the Rhine River. We should take a trip to see the Connecticut River Valley and Vermont.'"

When Adolf Hitler seized power in 1933, the investment banks in the United States waited to see what would happen. All the major financial houses had large stakes in Germany—Dillon Reed and Company, Guaranty Company of New York, Equitable—everybody. American industry had large stakes there, too, including GE, Du Pont, Ford, and ITT. In the case of Brown

Brothers Harriman, the troubling link was Fritz Thyssen, with whom Averell Harriman had forged a partnership a decade earlier. Thyssen suddenly emerged as a major financial supporter of the Nazi Party.

Like the other major investment houses, Brown Brothers Harriman elected to stay in Germany, fearing that they would lose their investments there entirely if they left. In 1935 they sold their stake in two German mining operations that were directly linked to the Nazi Party. But other investments remained in play. The most troubling to Pres Bush was the Union Banking Corporation, a deal the Harriman brothers had secured before Pres joined the firm. After he joined Brown Brothers, Bunny Harriman gave him a single share (of the five thousand created) to ensure that he could participate in any banking board decisions that needed to be made. Pres, busy with his work on the domestic ledger, probably paid little attention. After war broke out in 1939, the United States was still officially neutral, and the Union Banking Corporation limited its operations to the Nazi-occupied Netherlands. But when America joined the war in December 1941, the federal government seized the assets of the bank on the grounds of "trading with the enemy." A banner headline was spread over the front page of the *New York Tribune*. Even though he had no direct responsibility for the international portfolio, Pres was listed as a shareholder (because of the one share he held) along with Roland Harriman and Knight Woolley.

During the decade of the Great Depression, life with the Bushes moved at a steady rhythm. Every morning their father would sit at one end of the dining table with the *New York Tribune* in hand and scour the headlines while Dottie sat at the other end looking through the *New York Times*. The children, Pressy, Poppy, and Nancy (and later Johnny and Bucky) were seated in between. Pres was consumed with the paper, and when it was time to go he would take the *Times* with him on the train.

At night, when Pres was expected home, the maid, Lucy Larkin, would come into the library and find the kids slouching on the chairs, arguing, or playing.

"All of you out of the room, right this minute!" she'd say in her thick Irish accent. "Your father's coming home and there's not a one of you that will be half the gentleman your father is. Get up and go to your own room."

She would fluff all the pillows, put fresh ice in the bucket, and turn on the radio. When Pres arrived, he'd nurse a drink while listening to Fred Waring and his orchestra, and the news.

He was often irritable and brooding, troubled by the financial situation and world events. He was also burdened by his involvement in local politics.

He ran and served as a selectman for the town of Greenwich. He also became an early leader in the Greenwich Taxpayer Association, which worked to limit local taxes. And if that were not enough, he worked to raise money and campaign for Republican candidates. He raised thousands for Alf Landon in his unsuccessful 1936 bid against Roosevelt and later for friends like Bob Taft of Ohio and New York governor Tom Dewey.

"There were a lot of phone calls about local issues and politics," recalled his daughter. "He seemed to enjoy it, but also got frustrated a lot. He'd slam down the phone and exclaim, 'That jackass!' Jackass was one of his favorite words."

Pressy and Poppy often spent their free time playing baseball in their room upstairs, running the bases on their knees. They used a stick for the bat and a pair of their father's socks as the ball. Pres would come home after a tough day of work and discover several pairs of socks missing. "Would you please put the socks back in the drawer," he would lecture his sons. "All I ask is that people put things back."

At times, when Pres was in a particularly foul mood, Dottie would sneak Pressy, Poppy, and Nancy up the back steps to have them avoid seeing their father. At other times she would gather the children and try to get them to cheer him up. "Now go and tell your father about the game today," she would tell them, "and speak up."

Pres was often detached. As the children played, he would be downstairs looking over financial reports or reading about market trends. "He was busy and troubled by the world," recalled his daughter.

"He didn't get down and play with you on the floor," said William "Bucky" Bush, his youngest son. "He wasn't big on vacations and going sightseeing. He was more formal than that. To a large extent it's a generational thing. Fathers simply didn't do that sort of thing back then. But dad was always there for your games. And you always knew that he loved you."

Jonathan Bush described his father's sense of decorum and formality more bluntly: "I never heard him fart."

In large part, his sour moods grew out of working in the difficult world of Depression-era finance and worrying about money. "Dad was a worrier," said his daughter Nancy. "And he worried about money *a lot.*"

The Bush home was not extravagant. But the family had three maids living on the third floor, to help Dottie. A nurse and laundress also came in. "There was a lot of help," says Nancy Ellis, "and not much work to be done."

Dottie looked for ways to save money and cut costs. She sewed her own curtains for the maids' room and shopped at Macy's. At one of their many house parties, her children even observed her recycling the ice. A departed guest hadn't touched his drink, so she removed the ice from the glass, rinsed it, and returned it to the bucket.

━━━━━━━

ONE THING THAT COULD ALWAYS PULL PRES OUT OF HIS FUNK WAS THE SWEET melody of a song. He listened to music incessantly. When *The Music Man* came to Madison Square Garden, he caught the show six times. In Greenwich he formed the Silver Dollar Quartet. The two Howard brothers from down the street would play piano as Pres and three other neighbors would sing in four-part harmony. During the summer months they would sing out on the front porch with the piano in the front hall. The music would float upstairs, where the children would listen intently to the songs interspersed with the sounds of laughter.

His love of music also led to a nocturnal life he tried to keep secret from his family. Pres would slip out at night and trek up to the Cotton Club in Harlem to catch a show by the Merrimac Quartet or the Ink Spots. The family learned about it only by chance when Dottie was driving the kids around in the car one night. Pres Jr. was fiddling with the radio and Poppy and Nancy were in the backseat. Suddenly a voice on the radio declared, "Live from the Cotton Club on 125th Street in Harlem, New York, the Ink Spots!"

After the quartet sang their first melody, a loud and enthusiastic "Attaway boys!" could be heard amidst the applause.

"That sounds like dad," said Pressy.

"Oh no," said Dottie, thinking that her husband was at the New York apartment they shared with her sister Nancy. "Dad's at the apartment, sleeping."

The next evening at the dinner table, Pressy said, "Dad, we were driving home and we heard the Ink Spots were at the Cotton Club. We heard someone say, 'Attaway boys, way to go boys.' And it sounded like you. Was it?"

Pres turned scarlet but never answered the question.

With Pres preoccupied at work, it was Dottie who put most of the time into raising the children. She had strong views on how children should be raised and the values that mattered most.

Dottie believed that the family was crucial in tempering self-love, which in her mind was one of the great evils in life. The individual ranked below the family—far below. To encourage this view, Pressy and Poppy shared a bedroom in their early years, even though there was plenty of space for each to have his own. The two boys became very close.

"Finally one year mother decided that we ought to each get our own separate bedrooms," Pres, Jr. recalls. "She gave us the two rooms in the back of the house. That lasted for a couple of months and then Christmas came along. When Mom asked us what we wanted for Christmas, we said to room together. So that was it."

The two boys played together constantly. The few times they fought, both would get disciplined regardless of who started it.

"We were taught that brotherhood was more important than winning an argument," says Bucky Bush.

This had the effect of infusing the children with a fierce sense of family loyalty. When Poppy was only a little more than two years old, his parents bought him a pedal car to climb into and push along with his feet. The toddler was thrilled with the toy, but soon after he went to Pressy and offered him half of the car.

"Have half," he said. "Have half, have half." The family was so amused by it, they started calling young George "have half."

Friends remember one summer when Pressy and Poppy were in their teens and both entered a weekend tennis tournament. Poppy was a far superior athlete because Pressy had poor eyesight. But this weekend both were playing exceptionally well. Pressy was showing real hopes of breaking through and finally winning his first tournament, something Poppy had already done several times. On late Saturday afternoon, as Dottie sat in the clubhouse, Pressy came running to her glowing with enthusiasm.

"Guess what! Guess what!" he was yelling.

Dottie lit up. "Yes?! Yes?!"

"*Poppy* won!"

This fierce sense of loyalty not only formed a tight cohesion in the family, it also served as a powerful means of disciplining the children. If you did something wrong, Dottie would remind the kids, "*We* don't do it that way." By *we*, she meant the Bushes. To be a Bush you had to uphold certain standards. When you disobeyed, you were not simply rebelling against authority, you were letting down the whole family.

The end result was that good behavior came out of shame, not fear. "The greatest punishment for us as children was not a spanking or getting grounded," says Bucky Bush. "Knowing that we disappointed our parents. That was the most painful punishment we could get."

For Dottie, the evil twin of self-love was self-importance, or what she called "the la-dee-das." When Poppy would come home from baseball and report that he had hit a home run, Dottie would retort, "That's fine dear. But how did the *team* do?" When he reported that he had lost a tennis match because "my game was slightly off," she dismissed him with, "You don't have a game."

Nancy once came to her mother in tears. She was supposed to be a bridesmaid at a wedding party and was upset because she felt her hair "looked so terrible." Dottie told her to stop crying immediately. "This is the bride's day, not yours. Nobody will be looking at you."

Even in later years, when her husband and son went into politics, Dottie kept reciting Emily Dickinson's poem "I am nobody, who are you?" to both of them as a reminder.

> I'm nobody, who are you?
> Are you nobody too?
> Then there's a pair of us.
> Don't tell—they'd banish us, you know.
> How dreary to be somebody,
> How public—like a frog—
> To tell your name the livelong June
> To an admiring bog.

She continued correcting her son George in this regard even when he became vice president fifty years later. She complained that he tended to "talk about himself too much" and once became angry when it appeared that he was reading while President Reagan was giving a speech. When he explained that he was only following the prepared text, she still admonished him for setting a poor example.

Dottie was the family's north star, the point that the boys navigated by to chart their progress when they became young men. George's speeches in Congress, and as vice president and president, were usually elliptical and had a choppy syntax. Often this was because he failed to use personal pronouns—words such as "I" and "me." Those sorts of words were not uttered with great frequency in the Bush home.

Dottie seemed unconcerned with pretension. "She never worried about how she looked, she never had any fashion sense," says Nancy Bush Ellis. "My grandmother Luli Walker was very fashionable, she had lovely suits made to order in New York, and beautiful shoes. Mom never went to New York to shop if she could possibly help it. She would order something from Macy's."

When formal socializing had to be done for Brown Brothers Harriman, Pres and Dottie would hold elaborate dinners. But when the party broke up, out would come a game of Tiddlywinks. An old, soft brown blanket was laid over the dining table and for the next several hours, in black tie and evening gowns, the Bushes and their guests would play a fierce game.

At other times the Bushes would be downright casual. One night Henry and Clare Boothe Luce arrived for dinner. It was a hot summer night, but Henry, an old Yale friend and fellow Bonesman, was dressed in a white dinner jacket. Clare was dressed in a beautiful summer organdy. Pres Bush greeted them in a Hawaiian shirt. According to family members, Clare was horrified. Pres Bush didn't miss a beat.

"Oh Henry, haven't you discovered these?" he asked. "They are so wonderful. Bing Crosby wears them and now I wear them and they are the most wonderful things in the world. I'll have to send you one."

But after the Luces left, Dottie prodded her husband. "C'mon Pres, you are not really going to send Mr. Luce one of those shirts, are you?"

"Sure I am," Pres said confidently. "They're very cool in the summer."

"Mr. Luce isn't going to wear it, darling. He has air-conditioning."

The relationship between the Luces and the Bushes would be cordial. But never far from the surface was the dislike and political rivalry between Clare and Pres, which would erupt publicly in the early 1950s.

———

BECAUSE OF DOTTIE'S DISDAIN FOR THE "LA-DEE-DAS," AND GIVEN THE FAMily's Midwestern roots, the Bushes didn't have the same class consciousness that many other residents of Greenwich possessed. The children were encouraged to play with good kids, and good didn't necessarily mean "good breeding."

"The Bush house was a revolving door, and kids from everywhere were welcome," recalls Fay Vincent, a childhood friend of the Bush children. "The parents might not have had anything in common or been particularly close. But there was always a sense that the kids could play with whoever, as long as they were good kids. Whatever your background, if you were a friend, that's all that mattered."

Big plastic bowls with spaghetti and salad were placed on the table for the children to eat as they played games and sports.

When Dottie wasn't purging her children of self-love and self-importance, she was encouraging them to be risk-takers, undoubtedly something she had learned from her father. For the boys, this risk-taking began with the dogwood trees in the yard. While other neighborhood mothers dissuaded their sons from climbing trees and risking a cracked skull or broken limb, Dottie encouraged Pressy and Poppy to climb as high as they could.

"She never said anything to make us worried or cautious," says Pres, Jr. "She never wanted us to say, 'I can't do that.' "

The boys were expected to make their own evaluations of what they could handle and then do it. Dottie would often call her sons "little man," a sign that they were expected to use their own judgment and live with the consequences, even if that included a broken limb. Failure was acceptable; timidity was not. When the boys hesitated or demonstrated doubt, Dottie would prod them forward, sometimes by example. One summer the boys expressed reluctance about swimming in the rough waters off Walker Point. Dottie slipped into her bathing suit and dived into the surf, swimming from the Point to the clubhouse and back—a distance of two miles. She then walked out of the water and asked the boys if they *really* had a concern about the surf.

The children were also expected to be fiercely competitive. Pres and Dottie were good athletes and competitive-minded, but Dottie was perhaps more so, having grown up in a family with an aggressive father and fiercely competitive brothers. Barbara Bush would later describe her mother-in-law as the "most fiercely competitive person I have ever known."

Along with the fierce competition came the Bush version of trash-talking: jabbering and needling each other in the midst of a contest. Even Dottie and Pres would engage in this sort of banter. While Pres excelled on the golf course, Dottie was better at tennis, a fact that she enjoyed reminding her husband of. Nancy Ellis recalled, "They would come home from a tennis match and she couldn't resist. 'Pres,' she'd say, 'if you had only lobbed more over Margaret's head, the match would have gone better.' And dad would get furious. And we all thought, 'C'mon Mom, lay off.' He'd get silent and say, 'Well, your mother knows so much more about tennis than the rest of us.' "

Family friends would marvel at the keen competitiveness and verbal banter that accompanied any Bush sporting event. On the tennis court a sprained shoulder, dislocated finger, or scraped knee was not uncommon. George once chased a shot at Kennebunkport and ran into the porch, separating his shoulder.

The family also developed its own code of words for shots. Some are obvious. A drop shot in tennis is "the falling leaf." A weak shot might elicit yells of "power outage!" But other references are downright bizarre and had embedded political significance. During a game of doubles tennis, George might look over to his partner who is serving and exclaim, "Unleash Chiang!" a reference to the call in government circles during the 1950s and 1960s to allow Chiang Kai-shek to invade the Chinese mainland from Taiwan. In Bush-speak, George was calling for a power shot. Later, after his loss in 1992, there would be much-more-colorful references to Bill Clinton.

The competition between the boys was keen, but Dottie channeled it. Rivalry was acceptable at designated times, when the boys could take no prisoners. But after the contest was over, so was the rivalry.

For many visitors, the first experience with the Bushes in athletic competition was surprising. "Unmerciful," says Richard Bond, who served as Republican National Committee chairman when George Bush was president. "They are all unmerciful. I've played horseshoes with President Bush and George W. and basketball with Jeb. They are unbelievably fierce in competition. Elbows flying in basketball, tennis balls fired right at you. But when it's over, it's over and all forgotten." Like other large dynastic families such as the Kennedys, the Bushes saw the value in harnessing competition and using it for constructive ends.

WHEN PRESSY AND POPPY WERE OLD ENOUGH FOR SCHOOL, THEY WERE dressed in black sweaters with orange stripes on the left sleeve and knickers before heading off for the Greenwich Country Day School. GCDS was founded in 1925 by a group of well-connected parents. Dottie was familiar with the school thanks to her friend Didi Gratz Rockefeller. Didi's sister-in-law Florence Rockefeller had been involved in setting up the school.

The curriculum centered on Latin, history, English, and mathematics. But the school also had strong programs in music and athletics. Most appealing to Pres and Dottie, however, was the teaching of values. The GCDS report card carried a line that read: "Claims no more than his fair share of attention." In the Bush home, high marks here were a must. "How'd we do in 'claims no more'?" Pres would ask when the report cards were due.

Sister Nancy was sent to Rosemary, an all-girls school. Having children attending both schools was expensive, and Pres often reminded them of that fact. "He made us know that we were very lucky to be going to the schools we were," recalled Nancy.

These were "prep-prep schools," often gateways to the great prep schools of New England. When Pressy and Poppy were at school, headmasters from Andover, Exeter, and Groton would visit to discuss the prospects of having the Bush siblings attend their institutions. Pres expected his children to make the ultimate decision themselves. "If it was my choice and not his, I couldn't come and complain to him afterward," Pres, Jr. recalled.

On Sundays the Bush family attended Christ Church, an Episcopal church in Greenwich that placed a heavy emphasis on piety and responsibility. In the Bush home, Sundays were a time for reflection, not a great deal of activity. After the Sunday sermon, Pres would sometimes supplement the teaching with Bible lessons or a reading. His favorite source was a slender book by John Bailey entitled *A Diary of Private Prayers*. The book emphasized the inner experience of God's direction. It was by your God-directed conscience that your inner life was regulated and your external life controlled. Conscience is the force that led people to avoid doing wrong—even if they could get away with it.

In the Bush home, religion and faith were profoundly personal matters, and not to be discussed openly unless you were prompted. Dottie often cited I Corinthians 4:2, a verse she had been taught by her mother. "Now it is required that those who have been given a trust must prove faithful." This sense of faithfulness was deeply felt by the family When Pres's brother James left his wife and children to take up with Philadelphia socialite Janet Rhinelander Stewart, he was incensed. He barred Mrs. Stewart from ever visiting his home. Instead, he flew off to visit his brother's ex-wife and his daughters. "You will always be a part of our family," he told them. When the marriage to Mrs. Stewart also ended in divorce, Pres decided that he would have nothing more to do with his brother.

After church and a lesson from their father, the family would sit together and read books aloud to each other. A particular favorite with Pressy and Poppy were adventure books. The heroes were often supreme individualists, acting alone to save lives in the face of enormous odds. On Sunday evenings the family would retire to Pres and Dottie's bedroom, pull their two beds together, and listen to the radio. Fred Allen or Edgar Bergen and Charlie McCarthy might be on and they would laugh together for hours. Pres Bush particularly liked "stingy Jack Benny," says his daughter Nancy.

During these years the Bushes saw very little of S. P. Bush. Instead, they spent the bulk of their time with the Walkers. Bert had free time now, and he led an active, playful life. It seemed that by sheer force of personality, the Walkers were crowding out the Bushes of Ohio.

During Christmas the Bushes would often journey south to join the Walkers at Duncannon, Bert's plantation and hunting lodge situated in the uplands of western South Carolina near Aiken. Bert played polo there with Averell Harriman and other wealthy aristocrats from the northeast.

Bert would often venture there in early December with several dozen business associates and other friends in tow. The family would arrive a few weeks later for Christmas.

Bert kept a kennel of twelve dogs, all beautifully trained setters and pointers that were good at finding quail. Every morning the plantation manager would determine where the party was going to shoot. Then he would load a small pack onto a wagon and head off.

The family would leave the plantation at twelve and, after a few hours of shooting quail, snipe, and dove, a large grill would be unfolded right at the shooting site. They would enjoy a full spread for lunch before doing more shooting in the afternoon. As Pres, Jr. recalled, "In later years, when we got older, my grandfather would let George and me take a dog or two in the morning and go out in the fields near the house to look for birds. Both of us loved to go down there."

At night the family would sleep in the bedrooms upstairs, and black servants in white gloves would appear in the early morning to light crackling pinewood fires to warm their rooms from the early morning frost.

For Christmas, as much of the country struggled through the Great Depression, Bert regularly gave his grandchildren five hundred dollars cash each. "We were getting an allowance of twenty-five or fifty cents a week from mom and dad," Nancy Ellis recalled. "So here was Gampy Walker giving us five hundred each to spend on ourselves. Mom and Dad would have to bring us down to earth after that." Young Pres and George were impressed with their grandfather's wealth, his style, and his battling spirit. If their father was detached, distant, and somewhat understated, Gampy Walker was larger than life.

"He was a man of such presence," Pres, Jr. recalled. "And he doted on us." The toughness and brutality that he spilled out on his sons was nowhere to be seen with his grandchildren. With them he was affectionate and doting. It was as if the anger was already out of him.

The arrival of hot, muggy summer weather saw the Bushes heading north from Connecticut to spend time with the Walkers in Kennebunkport. Gampy Walker owned a rugged sliver of land that jutted into the rich blue waters of the North Atlantic. He loved the place; it was here that he voted and would eventually be buried. For the Bush children, a youth spent at Walker Point meant times of fishing, racing on the rocky beaches, boating, and assorted mischief.

Family members were invited: Walkers, Bushes, Houses, and Clements were all encouraged to turn inward and toward one another. Spending time at Kennebunkport was an important family ritual that added to the Bushes' cohesiveness. You didn't go to Kennebunkport to spend time alone or curl up for hours with a book.

Gerry Bemiss, whose family owned a home nearby, remembers those carefree years with Pressy and Poppy. "We had a gang of five or six, including Pres and George. Every day it was something different. One day we were pirates and sailors chasing each other through the trees and bushes. The next day we went to the boat club and offered to clean boats for a small fee." The young boys might head for the golf course and shag errant golf balls, which they could trade for small change. When the boys got older they created a secret smoking club in the heavy shrubs near the beach, tasting cigarettes taken from the bureau or half-smoked butts they had found.

Kennebunkport at the time was a small village where wealthy industrialists spent summer afternoons boating or playing golf and tennis. "It was a pretty homogeneous place," Bemiss recalled, "like relaxing next to like. There was only one Jewish family, for instance, that had a place there that we knew of. They were welcomed and everyone was gracious, but they were considered somewhat exotic at the time."

For Gampy Walker, Kennebunkport was a playground where he could enjoy his favorite activities and toys. In addition to a sterling yacht at the boat club, he owned a thirty-eight-foot motorboat named *The Tomboy* that he would take out with the grandchildren, appointing Pres, Jr. the captain and George the first mate. With a good, broad beam on the stern, it could take the pounding of the surf, and Gampy Walker would attack the surf with abandon.

"We were allowed to take the boat out and ride it around, take our friends out, and would go out and ride it into the waves," recalled Prescott Bush, Jr. When the boys weren't on *The Tomboy*, they would accompany Gampy on his yacht or speedboat, which were both docked at the club. The speedboat was slender, stylish, and outfitted with a loud siren. Gampy Walker enjoyed blasting the siren as he approached the club, sending the attendants scurrying to greet him dockside.

#### CHAPTER 6

# CHAPTERS

W HEN PRESSY HAD FINISHED HIS TIME AT GREENWICH COUN-
try Day School, Pres and Dottie sat down to deliberate on
which prep school would serve him best. They were also
aware that wherever Pressy went, his young brother Poppy would follow him.

Bert Walker was pushing for the Hill School, where he had sent all four
of his sons. But the school was in Pennsylvania, and Dottie feared that was
too far away. Pres also wanted something different for his sons. For that same
reason he decided against his alma mater, St. George's. He had fond memories of going to school there, to be sure. But he thought it was "not democratic enough," recalled Nancy Bush Ellis, and was too dependent on
aristocratic East Coast families for its enrollment.

The Bushes had plenty of other schools to choose from. Groton, Choate,
the Deerfield Academy, Phillips Exeter, Andover, the Kent School, and Milton were all possibilities. They were all forthrightly Christian schools with
good academic traditions. Pres and Dottie could have made the decision
themselves, but instead they let Pressy decide.

The family toured several schools, walking the campuses, talking with students and faculty. In the end Pressy chose Phillips Andover Academy, largely
because he knew an older boy in Greenwich who was going there. Pressy enrolled in 1935 and for the next two years, Poppy was at home without his brother
and somewhat depressed. He followed Pressy to Andover two years later.

Andover, an old-line New England prep school dating from 1778, was being infused with new money from the rising industrial and commercial elites
of the Midwest. While its alumni included plenty of Rockefellers and Vanderbilts, it was apparently less elitist than some of the other New England
schools. Andover even had a few black students, which at the time was un-
heard of elsewhere. Dottie was undoubtedly encouraged when she read the
school's motto: *Non Sibi*, "Not for self."

In the early fall of 1937 the family drove up to Andover to drop Poppy off
for school.

"He looked so young when he went off," recalled his sister Nancy. "I can still remember him looking at us with those excited but nervous eyes, standing in front of Washington Hall."

Pres and Dottie intended to have his arrival at Andover signify a clean break from his childhood. The Bushes seemed to live their lives in chapters, and young George was turning a page. When Pressy and Poppy had attended GCDS, their parents had been a daily influence on their lives. They still lived at home, attended church together, and played together. But at Andover the boys would be on their own for considerable periods of time. Dottie and Pres wanted their "little men" home for holidays, summers, and special occasions. But weekend visits home were discouraged.

One thing that did go home weekly, however, was the laundry. Pressy and Poppy mailed home their dirty clothes, which were promptly returned by post, clean and folded.

Phillips Andover was patterned after a New England village, its centerpiece the chapel, its spire rising well above the abundant trees. The buildings were elegant as far as Puritan architecture went, with some of the originals designed by Charles Bulfinch, the nineteenth-century Boston architect. The school also had a world-class art gallery, including paintings by Eakins, Homer, and Whistler.

The campus had undergone a beautiful upgrading in recent years thanks to the kindness of Thomas Cochran, an alumnus and partner at J. P. Morgan. During the 1920s he had donated large sums of money that led to the construction of numerous new buildings on campus. A new library had also been built and named for Oliver Wendell Holmes, Andover class of 1825. But Poppy preferred to spend his time at the sanctuary, sixty-five beautiful acres that included a brook, two ponds, well-manicured lawns, and flower beds of rhododendrons and laurel.

The school was committed to developing the "whole man." Academics was certainly important. But discipline and character were more so, with strict rules on dress, table manners, and an academic code of conduct. Students were expected not to leave the campus without the approval of the headmaster. In one famous incident, a ninth-grader just barely crossed over the school boundary to retrieve his hat, which had been blown away by the wind. Headmaster Alfred Sterns saw it and immediately ordered the young man to pack his bags.

By the time Pressy and Poppy were at Andover, the headmaster was Claude Feuss, a history teacher at Andover since 1908 and a towering figure on campus. Feuss was in many respects a first-rate scholar, having written important biographies on, among others, Calvin Coolidge. He was as tough and strict as Sterns had ever been and was feared even by the faculty. He would walk the campus, his starched white collar like a tall, white picket fence around his neck, barking out orders to students and faculty alike.

Prominent on campus was the Latin phrase *Finis Origine Pendet*, "the end depends on the beginning." As far as the school was concerned, the young men in their charge were arrows, pulled from the quiver of America's leading families. The purpose of Andover was to load them into the bow and fire them on a straight trajectory that would allow them to go great distances and accomplish great things. But to hit the target, the aim needed to be near perfect. And aim had less to do with intellect than with discipline and focus.

"Other schools had boys, Andover had men," was a common campus refrain.

While the faculty and headmaster held a tight rein, they relied on student leaders to regulate student behavior. In his second year at the school, Poppy performed this task as a member of the student council, monitoring students during tests to deter cheating. He was also selected to keep order at social events such as movies and dances.

In part his selection resulted from his newfound physical strength. Poppy, rather slender as a boy, was now tall, strong, and athletic. He was captain of both the soccer and baseball teams, and his physical prowess was well known on campus.

One day a young student named Bruce Gelb was being harassed by a fellow student. Gelb was fourteen, in his second year, and fairly small. A bigger boy approached him in the lounge and began hassling him, insisting that he move an enormous couch situated in the corner. Gelb tried, but couldn't move it. The bully then put him in an armlock and began to squeeze. Suddenly a voice came from the corner. "Leave the kid alone." That was all it took.

"This guy dropped me like a hot potato," Gelb later explained.

Gelb didn't recognize the boy who had rescued him and then walked off. After asking around, the answer came back quickly. "That was Poppy Bush," he was told. "He's the greatest kid in the school."

Gelb never did speak to Bush on campus. But Poppy's small act of mercy eventually paid handsome dividends. Only many years later, in 1978, were the two men introduced. Gelb's father was the founder of the Clairol Company, and the younger Gelb never forgot what Bush had done. When Bush was planning to run for president, Bruce Gelb wanted to help. He went on to serve as Bush's finance cochairman in New York for the 1980 presidential run, collecting nearly $3 million.

Much as his father had at Yale, Poppy threw himself into activities at Andover—a swirl of sports, theatrics, music, and more sports. He was president of
the senior class, secretary of the student council, and a member of the editorial board of the student newspaper, *The Phillipian*. Poppy also helped collect
the tithes and offerings in the chapel, and in his senior year headed the annual
charity drive on campus. His greatest source of popularity seemed to be that
among the students, Poppy was a regular guy, unpretentious and natural.

In the spring of his junior year, Poppy was approached about joining
AUV, a secret society founded in 1877. AUV stood for *Auctoritas, Unitas,
Veritas* (Authority, Unity, Truth), which were considered cardinal virtues by
society members. Pledges were selected by faculty members and AUV
alumni. Poppy Bush might have been sponsored by Godfrey S. Rockefeller,
a family friend and former member, or possibly AUV faculty adviser Nor-
wood Penrose Hallowell. Hallowell was the son of the chairman of Lee Hig-
ginson and Company, a Boston banking firm, who did business with Pres
Bush at Brown Brothers Harriman.

AUV had an elaborate initiation rite. Once a pledge had been approved, he
was given a list of unusual commands to follow. The initiate might be told not
to wash his face or comb his hair for a week, or he might be forced to smoke a
clay pipe filled with Lucky Strike tobacco. The pledge was expected to perform these acts in public while never offering an explanation for his behavior.
At the final ceremony, held in the basement of the society's lodge, the pledges
were asked to strip down to their skivvies, blindfolded, and battered around by
current members and alumni. As the blindfold was removed, there would be
chants of "Let him have light . . ." and he became a member for life.

In the year Poppy joined, other initiates included Godfrey Anderson
Rockefeller. The society sponsored scholarships and supported fellow members, but little is known about how it functioned. Headmaster Feuss eventually banned all secret societies from Andover, declaring that they promoted
"social cleavage" and "exclusiveness" on campus. His decision set off a storm
of protest from AUV and other secret society alumni, but the decision stood.
Gone from campus by 1950, it is now largely forgotten.

---

ONE SUNDAY MORNING, AS HE WAS WALKING ACROSS THE CAMPUS WITH A
friend, Poppy got the word. It was December 7, 1941, and news had just arrived that the Japanese had bombed Pearl Harbor.

Dr. Feuss ordered the students to gather at George Washington Hall for a special assembly. The young men shuffled into the chapel. After an opening prayer, Dr. Feuss spoke about the importance of keeping the American fighting spirit. Americans needed to demonstrate courage. Courage prolonged becomes morale, and Andover men were expected to demonstrate courage. Poppy Bush and some of his friends all pledged their commitment to join the fight as soon as they could.

When classes ended for the Christmas break a few weeks later, Poppy went home to Greenwich. His older brother Pressy was now at Yale. He found his father consumed with his work, as war made the complexities of international finance even more difficult. With America at war with both Japan and Germany, the federal government moved to halt all business activity with both countries. Hundreds of joint ventures were shut down, and millions in assets were frozen. Pres Bush watched with other partners as the Union Bank was shut down and had its assets seized under the Trading with the Enemy Act.

The outbreak of war created fear and energy among the teenagers on the eastern seaboard. Fear because they knew that it would be a war they would fight; excitement because they knew that the world would never be the same again. They all seemed to feel this unbelievable energy.

That Christmas of 1941, Poppy Bush went with some friends to a dance in nearby Rye, New York. Dressed in white coats and black ties, they arrived at the country club and congregated along the far wall with the other boys. Poppy had always been a little awkward around girls, so he stood there looking at the cluster of young society girls across the room. The band suddenly struck up a Glenn Miller tune, and a girl across the dance floor caught his eye.

Dressed in a festive green-and-red holiday dress, she was blonde, slender, beautiful, and athletic. Poppy approached Jack Wozencraft to ask if he knew the girl.

"He said she was Barbara Pierce, that she lived in Rye, and went to school in South Carolina." Wozencraft took Poppy across the room and introduced them.

The Bushes by and large don't believe in love at first sight; but this was pretty close. For young Barbara Pierce, the attention of the slender and tall seventeen-year-old from Andover was overwhelming. "He was the handsomest-looking man you ever laid your eyes on, bar none," she said.

Poppy asked her to dance and she accepted. Much to his misfortune, the bandleader changed tempo from foxtrot to waltz. "I don't waltz," he later recalled. "So we sat the dance out."

Instead, the young couple sat at a nearby table and began talking under the watchful gaze of chaperons. They had a certain magical way of talking. They fed off each other, constructing a conversation together. Poppy was funny but direct; pretty young Barbara was charming.

Barbara Pierce was the daughter of Marvin and Pauline Pierce, originally from Ohio. They had settled in Rye, Westchester County. The Pierces were descendants of the fourteenth president of the United States, Franklin Pierce, but it was hardly something they advertised. Barbara's only exposure to the man was in school. "The only thing I remember about him was years ago as a child, reading that he was one of our weakest presidents," Barbara recalled. "I was humiliated."

Her father was vice president of the McCall Corporation, publisher of *Redbook*. The theme of the magazine was family and togetherness; warm family portraits graced the pages. But the Pierce home itself didn't entirely fit that image.

Marvin Pierce was a fun-loving man who enjoyed sports, particularly golf, but Pauline Pierce was distant and austere. Barbara recalled years later how her mother had handled her first day at school. "At age six, in 1931, my mother led me by the hand into the public school at Rye, New York. We met the teacher, then my mother was gone. She disappeared with no good-byes. I felt abandoned."

Her mother seemed to have difficulty getting close to people; she was constantly worried about reputation and status. "Barbara idolized her father," George H. W. Bush recalled, "but she was not particularly close to her mother."

Barbara also looked up to her older sister, Martha, a pretty young girl who went on to become a model. But with her older brother James, she often squabbled. Jimmy and Barbara would fight incessantly, oftentimes Barbara giving as much as she got. Once Jimmy accidentally shot Barbara in the leg with a BB gun and warned her that he would kill her if she told their mother. "For a week, I wore high woolen socks and feared death," Barbara said.

Her younger brother Scott was an object of doting at the time. He suffered from a cyst in the bone marrow of his shoulder, so she was constantly caring for him. Out of this experience, Barbara developed a remarkable capacity for kindness and a strength that would carry the Bush family through its most trying times.

Barbara was in many respects a mirror image of George's mother, Dottie. Pretty, funny, with a definite sense of direction, she was also very strong. And the Bush men were attracted to strong women. S. P. Bush had expected

Flora to be his equal partner. And Pres had seen the strength in Dottie early on. The first chance George got, he told his family about this "great gal from Rye" he had just met.

For Barbara, Poppy Bush was like her father, strong yet gentle. When she got home that night, she told her mother that she had met someone she really liked named Poppy Bush from Greenwich. She went to bed that night with a joy she had not felt in a long time. The next morning she woke up to find that her mother had been on the telephone trying to find out what she could about the Bushes of Greenwich. Would this be a good social match? she wondered. Barbara was furious.

The next evening Barbara went to another dinner dance, at the Apawamis Club in Rye. She was dancing with a nice young man when suddenly George tapped on his shoulder and cut in. This time he was determined to ask her out. But before he got the chance, Barbara's brother James cut in. He asked Poppy if he would join him in a game of basketball in a couple of days. Poppy agreed, but only if Barbara would come and he could drive her home.

The night of the game, George borrowed his father's Chevrolet and headed off to Rye. He was thankful the car had a radio, because of those long silences that often occurred on first dates. He arrived at the game and played his heart out as Barbara and the other Pierces watched. After the game, George and Barbara went out for ice cream sodas. He never did have to use the car radio.

When Christmas vacation was over, George returned to Andover. "George was smitten," recalled his brother Pres. "No doubt about it. He was always talking about Barbara from Rye."

Barbara returned to South Carolina where she was attending Ashley Hall, a small school in the heart of Old Charleston. About 150 girls were attending at the time, almost all from the South. Barbara's room, in one of the school's old houses, had a fireplace and large bay windows looking out over oak trees dripping with Spanish moss. The place had a formality that was like nothing Barbara had experienced in Rye. When young ladies left the campus, they were expected to be well dressed with a hat, gloves, and no lipstick.

Her classmates immediately noticed that Barbara seemed different. She was distracted and dreamy. And then the letters started to arrive. Every day she was getting a letter from that boy at Andover. Barbara dropped her other boyfriend and started to write Poppy back. Figuring that he must be cold in Massachusetts, she started to knit him a pair of argyle socks.

Poppy and Bar would not see each other again until spring break. Even then, they didn't have much time. Their vacations overlapped by one day and they went on a double date to see *Citizen Kane*. After the movie, George walked Barbara to the door and kissed her goodnight. Barbara was only sixteen and he was first boy she had ever kissed.

———

IN EARLY JUNE 1942, THE YOUNG MEN OF ANDOVER GATHERED IN THE COLLEGE chapel to receive their certificates of graduation. Secretary of War Henry Stimson stood to deliver the convocation address. Stimson, an Andover graduate and graying image of what all young Andover men were expected to be, had served five presidents in every capacity from secretary of state to secretary of war. Poppy Bush and the other young men sat with rapt attention and listened.

Stimson spoke of pride, character, honor, and the war. He told the graduates that the war would be long, and they, the leaders of tomorrow, should go on to college to gain more knowledge and wisdom. If they wanted to serve, they would get their chance. And when they went, they should be "brave without being brutal, self-confident without boasting, part of an irresistible might, but without losing faith in individual liberty." After the applause died down, Poppy went to meet his father in the hallway. Older brother Pressy was already at Yale and Poppy was expected to follow him.

Had Stimson's advice made his son change his mind? his father asked.

"No sir," Poppy said. "I'm going in."

Pres Bush only nodded. Poppy would be eighteen on June 12 and could do what he wanted. Instead of arguing, Pres extended a hand to his son. George was doing what his father had done twenty-four years earlier.

Pres seemed resigned to the decision, and everything seemed fine the rest of the afternoon as they spoke with teachers and alumni who had returned for the ceremony. When they finally headed to the car to return home, Pres Bush, so often distant and remote, broke down and cried. "It was the first time we had ever seen our father cry," Nancy recalled.

Poppy wanted to be a naval aviator and fly combat missions from an aircraft carrier. So on his birthday he drove to Boston and enlisted in the navy. Plenty of excitement was associated with aviators, who were the new mythical heroes in American culture. But by going on to become the youngest pilot in the U.S. Navy, George Bush was not taking an easy route. Landing on an aircraft carrier was difficult, as a carrier's landing area was only 70 feet wide by 350 feet. In order to stop, the plane's tailhook needed to catch one of nine cables extending across the deck. Casualty rates were higher percentage-wise for pilots than for infantrymen, artillerymen, or sailors serving aboard ship. It was more dangerous than almost any other field in the armed services.

On August 6, George reported for active duty at the navy's preflight training center in Chapel Hill, North Carolina. Assigned to the 6th Battalion, Company K, 2nd Platoon, he was housed in Lewis Hall where he shared a room with three other men. He was the youngest recruit on base, and the experience of those first few weeks was a shock. After growing up in Greenwich and attending elite schools, it was his first real exposure to the world outside the cloister of wealthy institutions. The men in his unit came from all sorts of backgrounds. "They are a darn good-hearted bunch," he wrote to his parents, and "so many different types of fellows."

It was an awakening in many respects. His father had never really spoken to him about sexual matters, and young George was shocked at the number of "rather attractive girls that after a couple of drinks would just as soon go to bed with some cadet. They are partly uniform conscious I suppose, but the thing is they, as well as the cadet, have been brought up differently. They believe in satisfying any sexual urge by contact with men."

"These girls are not prostitutes," he explained delicately to his mother, "but just girls without any morals at all." Most of the cadets "take sex as much they can get it," he wrote. While George admitted having the same feelings as these cadets, he was restrained, falling back on the Bush tenet of self-control. "The difference is entirely in what we have been taught; not only in 'what' but in 'how well' we have been taught it."

America had a great need for pilots. The war in the Pacific was turning out to be a series of naval battles in which aircraft were making a critical difference. Japan had used them to great effect in the attack on Pearl Harbor. The United States had returned the favor at Midway, when Adm. Chester Nimitz had used dive-bombers and torpedo planes to sink four Japanese carriers.

In October 1942, George and his unit were transferred to Wold-Chamberlain Naval Air Station near Minneapolis. With their basic training complete, it was time to fly. They started by flying P-18 training aircraft (the civilian Piper Cub). "I was so nervous," he wrote his mother, "that in the beginning my legs were shivering around. Once in the air, I was completely cool much to my surprise." The trainees practiced takeoffs and landings and emergency drops, in which the instructor cut the gas and forced the pilot to glide the plane in for a landing.

"I thought when I was away at school I understood it all," he wrote his mother from Wold-Chamberlain, "but being away in the Navy for this long and with so many different types of fellows has made me see more clearly still how much I do have to be thankful for . . ."

Despite the importance of naval aviation to the war, it was still in its infancy. George's training aircraft were plagued with problems. Engines would cut off on cold days, requiring the pilots to restart them quickly in the air. Mechanical failures were common, and the landing gear would malfunction regularly. Flying navy planes was downright dangerous.

Christmas of 1942 was the first one that George ever missed with his family, at home or at Duncannon. He spent it alone in Minnesota. But he did receive a bathrobe from his mother and some goggles for flying. Gampy Walker sent him twenty-five dollars and some socks. And Barbara sent him "a big box of food" and a photograph of herself that George had requested.

The sense of duty and responsibility impressed upon him at such a young age now weighed heavily on him, and he was eager to get into combat. "I will never feel right until I have actually fought," he wrote to his mother. "Being physically able and young enough I belong out at the front and the sooner there, the better."

But he also worried about holding on to Barbara. The Bushes were big on loyalty; it was one of their most important tests of character. As he courted Barbara, he wondered if she might "fluff him off" as so many of the other cadets had experienced with their girlfriends. He was writing her regularly, but the letters coming back were more sporadic. He wondered if she was keeping her options open. As he wrote to his mother, "Barb is really a smart girl in that she can be sweet and all that without committing herself to any great degree . . ."

In February 1943, George was transferred to the U.S. naval air station in Corpus Christi, Texas. Having passed flight training, he was chosen as a torpedo bomber pilot selectee. While fighter planes were the bad boys of the navy, the torpedo bombers did the heavy lifting. Fighter pilots could fire back at the enemy, but torpedo bomber pilots had to keep a steady hand while flying into the teeth of enemy fire.

The navy had young men from all over the United States, and George seemed determined to meet every one of them. One morning he spotted a lanky, sandy-haired pilot trainee chatting with some of the boys. He looked familiar, and George approached him and extended a hand. "I'm George Bush," he said.

"I'm Ted Williams." Like so many sports stars of the era, the Boston Red

Sox phenom had enlisted and was going through flight training. The two became fast friends, which began a relationship that would last sixty years.

On June 9, 1943, silver-haired Adm. Alfred Montgomery pinned wings on his young, newly minted pilots. It was three days before George's nineteenth birthday, making him the youngest pilot in the navy. He received five days' leave and returned home. After visiting briefly with his parents, he headed off to see Barbara.

When he left for training he had seemed very much the Andover boy. Now he was coming back a man. His sister and brothers remember him being taller and thinner than before. He was six feet, two inches tall now; not quite as tall as his father, but close. And he weighed 160 pounds, largely muscle. His fitness score for the navy was 103, up from the 77 he had received when first inducted.

The Bush home in Greenwich was frantic with activity. President Roosevelt had asked the American people to contribute generously to the National War Fund, and Pres had been asked to serve as chairman.

It was a massive undertaking. The National War Fund was a consortium of six hundred war relief groups from around the country. Pres's job was to bring them together and give the effort real firepower. John D. Rockefeller, Jr., John Foster Dulles, and Chester Barnard, president of Bell Telephone Company, were all recruited to join the board. Thomas D'Arcy Brophy, the advertising giant, agreed to handle public relations.

Using the client list at Brown Brothers Harriman and his extensive business contacts, Pres spent almost all of his time raising money for the cause. He tapped into his network of friends from Skull and Bones, Yale, and just about every association he had ever been a member of. He also asked his father S. P. to help in Ohio, along with Bert Walker, who was retired and enjoying the good life at his homes in Maine, New York City, and Long Island.

If the First World War had been the first truly industrial war that required people like S. P. Bush to organize the manufacturing of war matériel, the Second World War was the first great war of business finance. In all, the National War Fund raised an astonishing $321 million during the war. The vast majority of the money went to support American servicemen. Clubs were established to entertain troops through the United Service Organizations (USO), and personal items were bought for soldiers overseas and their families. But the National War Fund had a secret side that Pres could not tell his family about. His good friend from Wall Street, Allen Dulles, had been recruited to work for the Office of Strategic Services (OSS). Dulles had handled legal matters for Brown Brothers for many years, so when he went into the OSS as a gentleman spy, Pres was one of the few people who knew about it. Dulles was given the sensitive post of station head in Bern.

Switzerland was the crossroads of the war in Europe, filled with Allied and German spies, and anti- and pro-Nazi networks and groups. Dulles was deeply involved in the great game of espionage. At times he needed financial resources to help the underground resistance in Nazi-occupied Europe. On at least one known occasion he called on his friend Pres Bush. In early June 1944, Pres authorized the secret transfer of some fifty thousand dollars to the OSS, to be given to Christian trade unions working in occupied Europe.

George had come back to Greenwich with his navy wings. In a family that valued competition and accomplishment, it was a moment of notable pride for his parents. Things were more difficult for older brother Pres, Jr. Pres had also been eager to serve and went to a recruiting post to enlist in the army. But when he took the medical exam, he failed because of blindness in one eye. Pressy had been declared 4F and rejected for service; he was devastated.

Still wanting to do something, Pressy went to work for Pan American Airways, which was doing government contract work. Pan American, launched with money from Grandfather Walker, was building airfields in the remote South American jungle to help airmen grapple with German submarines in the Atlantic. Pres moved to Brazil and spent the first eight months in the small city of Recife.

His work in Recife was mostly warehousing, which, as he told a friend in a letter, kept him "busy as a beaver." After eight months he was transferred to Rio, where he was supposed to do "confidential radio work," he wrote to a family friend. But he didn't have much work to do, and "as a result I am nearly stark, raving mad." He applied to the company for more work, but they failed to transfer him until months later. So he spent much of his time at the tennis club near Copacabana Beach. For the namesake and eldest son in a competitive family, it was a difficult blow.

———

THAT AUGUST THE BUSHES GATHERED IN KENNEBUNKPORT. GEORGE HAD some leave before he reported for duty in Norfolk, Virginia. Barbara came up to spend some time with the family. She was only eighteen, but the young couple was very serious and deeply devoted to each other. For Barbara, the time in Kennebunkport was her first introduction to the competitive world of the Bushes. The clan played tennis, golf, cards, and softball, and cycled.

At night the family would gather to listen to the CBS radio broadcasts of Edward R. Murrow and William Shirer. Pres and Dottie loved Bar. But Dottie had doubts that they would wed. When the two played tennis together, Dottie would switch the racket to her left hand to make it easier for Bar. But the young lady seemed to lack the killer instinct, the fierce competitive spirit so important to the Bush clan. Bar wasn't that tough. "She won't play net," Dottie told family members after she left the court.

As the brief vacation ended, George prepared to leave for Norfolk. The two pledged their love and became secretly engaged. For both George and Bar, so used to convention, it was a silent form of rebellion. Both families believed that emotions were running so strong between the two that taking it slow was in order.

As George headed to Norfolk, Barbara headed to Smith College in Northampton, Massachusetts. To take her mind off George, she joined both the soccer and swim teams and also played lacrosse. But despite making a great many good friends, her time at Smith was accentuated by a curious clash of cultures. Her father would send her copies of *McCall's* magazine each month in order to keep her abreast of what he was doing. Smith administrators were not pleased.

"One day they came up to me and they said, 'We notice you're getting pulp magazines in the mail. We don't allow pulp magazines,'" Barbara recalls. "I phoned my dad and said, 'Dad, I can't get those magazines. They're pulp magazines.' He said, 'You tell that lady you're getting those magazines, and you wouldn't be there if it weren't for pulp magazines.'"

George arrived at the Chincoteague Naval Air Station, a base still under construction, in early September. Beyond the half-finished buildings and loose construction material, out on the newly built runway, he saw the TBFs with their folded wings standing in a row in the golden Virginia sun.

George was training to fly the "pregnant turkey," the name given to the TBF Avenger. It was the largest single-engine plane in the navy. Designed to carry and drop bombs and torpedoes, the Avenger was slow and difficult to maneuver. TBF pilots were expected to have steady nerves; unlike fighter pilots who could maneuver and evade the enemy, TBF pilots were expected to fly straight into enemy fire.

Except for occasional weekend visits from his parents, most of George's time was spent in the air. In his plane, which he christened *Barbara*, he practiced takeoffs, landings, flying in formation, and bombing runs. But the training for his Torpedo Squadron 51 (VT-51) was often rushed as the navy pushed desperately to put together as many flight groups as possible to meet the threat in the Pacific.

In late October, George was bringing his plane down after practicing carrier-landings on a makeshift carrier platform at the base. As he approached the runway, he gingerly moved the stick forward and then back as the ground rose to meet his aircraft. But instead of the familiar bump of tires hitting the tarmac, George felt a huge bang and his head slammed forward in the cockpit. His Avenger slid along the runway until it finally ground to a stop. The landing gear had failed and the plane was a total loss. Fortunately, he was not hurt.

One morning George was summoned into Squadron Commander Douglas Melvin's office. The navy was launching an intense intelligence operation and he wanted George involved. George then received training in aerial photography, including film processing and chemistry. However, he could share very little with family and friends about what he was doing.

In December word came that George would be in Philadelphia for the commissioning ceremony of the USS San Jacinto, a new aircraft carrier. The San Jac, as they had come to call it, was not a pure carrier. In early 1942, President Roosevelt had scrapped plans to build light cruisers and instead converted them to carriers. The San Jac, named after a Texas battlefield, was one of these.

George wrote to his parents and Barbara, inviting them to the festivities in Philadelphia. George was getting ready to go off to war, and everyone knew that he was going to ask Barbara to marry him.

Dottie called Barbara and suggested that they travel together; it would give them a chance to talk. Sitting in the first-class car, the women chatted about everything. But Dottie was also quietly probing. She asked Barbara what kind of ring she wanted from George when they became engaged. Barbara said she didn't care.

"Does it *have to be* a diamond?" Dottie asked, obviously checking to see if her prospective daughter-in-law might succumb to the "la-dee-das." Again Barbara said she didn't care.

When they arrived at the commissioning ceremony, they stepped out to meet George, who was dressed in a heavy overcoat and navy dress uniform. When he had the chance, he took a ring out of his pocket and gave it to Barbara. It wasn't a diamond, but a star sapphire that had belonged to his aunt.

"I was thrilled," recalled Barbara. "I don't know to this day whether it's real and I don't care. It's my engagement ring and it hasn't been off my finger since the day George gave it to me." Their engagement garnered mention on the society page of the *New York Herald Tribune*: "Barbara Pierce and Ensign Bush, Navy Flyer, to Wed."

The *San Jac* steamed out of Philadelphia and for the next several months the pilots practiced landing on the carrier. Over the next three months, as the carrier went from Chesapeake Bay through the Panama Canal en route to Pearl Harbor, more than half of the air group's planes were involved in crashes. They would overshoot the flight deck and end up in the sea. Or they would approach too quickly and send the plane into the tower. Two pilots were killed and nine injured. Captain Harold "Beauty" Martin, the ship's commander, considered the pilots to be "below average in fundamental carrier operations." George kept his nerve up and continued flying. He would land 116 times without a mishap.

When the *San Jac* arrived in Pearl Harbor that spring, the war in the Pacific was reaching its peak of intensity. Admiral Chester Nimitz was glad to have the *San Jac* at his disposal, and he immediately assigned it to Adm. Marc Mitscher's Task Force 58, which was expected to strike the Japanese fleet as soon as possible.

In Pearl Harbor the *San Jac* took on new supplies, and George met with military intelligence officers assigned to the Joint Intelligence Center for the Pacific Ocean Areas (JICPOA). The intelligence photos he was expected to take in combat would be brought here and evaluated by analysts. Two weeks later the task force headed west to help take back the chains of Pacific islands that led to the main island of Japan.

As the armada proceeded west, George and the other pilots continued practicing landings. Given the sometimes rough seas and the narrow flight deck, accidents continued. In one instance George saw a plane lose too much airspeed, hit a gun mount, and smash into the gun's crew, "wiping them out." Before him was a man with a severed leg, quivering. George had never seen death "that close, that suddenly," he wrote his mother. "Four seamen who also had been with us seconds before were dead because of a random accident."

On a cool morning, as the ship cut its way through the choppy waters of the Pacific, the crew of twelve hundred gathered on the flight deck for a brief service. George probably thought he was lucky not to be among those being memorialized. For unlike almost every other pilot on the *San Jac*, George was left-handed, and that made flying his Avenger particularly difficult. The controls were designed for a right-hander. The propeller, throttle, and fuel mixture knobs were on the left side of the cockpit. So George had to shift the flight stick back and forth between his left and right hands in order to use the controls.

As part of the Pacific command's island-hopping strategy, now in full force, the carrier's first mission was to strike Japanese fortifications on Marcus and Wake Islands. The fighters and torpedo bombers of the *San Jac* were expected to help take out enemy strong points so the Marines could clean them up. The pilots gathered in the ready room, waiting for their orders. Some played cards or maybe a game of chess, and others sat in the overstuffed black leather lounge chairs. When the call came early on May 19, George and the other pilots flew their planes into the sunny morning sky. The three-man crew of *Barbara* flew several reconnaissance missions in search of enemy trawlers, but returned empty-handed.

On the morning of May 24, George and his crew received their first bombing orders. The target was Wake Island, which had been invaded by the Japanese early in the war and was still under occupation. A strange coincidence tied George to Wake Island. Wake had been a stopover and refueling post for Pan American Airways before the war, when the airline made regular flights from California to Hong Kong. Pan Am's startup had been financed by his grandfather Bert Walker in the 1920s.

With an eight-by-eight-inch map of Wake Island strapped to his leg, George and his squadron mates were expected to locate the island and hit two particularly important targets: the radio-direction-finding unit and the headquarters of Admiral Sakaibara, commander of Japanese forces on Wake Island. The admiral was particularly despised by the American navy because in 1943 he had massacred ninety-eight American prisoners of war he was holding on the island.

These were not easy targets. The headquarters was heavily fortified and protected by a picket fence of 5-inch antiaircraft guns. About sixty guns were concentrated in a four-square-mile area.

George and his crew went to the ready room and checked the chalkboard for their assignment. To their distress they would not be flying *Barbara* today, as it was undergoing maintenance. Instead they would fly a substitute plane. As they walked onto the carrier deck at 0715, skies were clear and visibility good. Reports indicated cumulus clouds rising to nine thousand feet. George and the others checked the bomb bay. Four 500-pound bombs were mounted inside.

As they climbed into the plane, George and his crewmen were reminded that a rescue sub code-named "Lovely Louise" was available in case of an emergency.

The *San Jac's* catapult drove the Avenger off the flight deck just after 0730, and George pulled up into the clear morning sky. Their formation was shadowed by a group of fighters, which would escort them to the island. They rose to nine thousand feet, and as the island came into view they moved into attack formation. George put his Avenger into a steep dive. Plunging toward the earth at a 50-degree angle, the plane picked up speed. Some antiaircraft fire was sent up, but less than expected. George steadied the plane and kept a firm fix on the target. As the plane approached three hundred knots, they reached a thousand feet and the bombs were released. George pulled out over the water and then banked slowly to the west, back toward the *San Jac*. The air strikes lasted most of the day as torpedo-bombers from other carriers—the *Essex* and the *Wasp*—joined in the attack.

The entire dive had taken maybe thirty seconds, but it was an intense adrenaline rush. George had flown his first mission against an active target and returned safely. But when the sun began to set, he became concerned that his roommate, Jim Wykes, was not back. It wasn't until hours later that he got the word: Wykes would not be returning.

George was upset but he didn't show it to the crew. Instead he retreated to his bunk and cried in private. He wrote to his parents. He then, with difficulty, penned a note to Wykes's mother. "I know your son well and have long considered myself fortunate to be one of his intimate friends. His kindly nature and all around goodness have won for him the friendship and respect of every officer and enlisted man in the squadron . . . You have lost a loving son, we have lost a beloved friend; so let us be brave—let us keep faith and hope in our hearts and may our prayers be answered."

In the days following the air strikes, navy intelligence assessed the effectiveness of the attack. Admiral Alfred Montgomery, the gruff pipe-smoking commander, was disappointed in the results. The pilots of the *San Jac*, *Essex*, and *Wasp* had missed 95 percent of their targets. Also, in the excitement of battle, the pilots had broken radio silence on several occasions, possibly endangering themselves and "Lovely Louise," the nearby rescue sub.

After the air strikes, the crews of the *San Jac* had a layover on the island of Majuro. Having seen death for the first time, George's crew tried to relax by playing baseball, drinking beer, and listening to music. George went out of his way to bolster morale and encourage confidence in his men despite the pain he was still feeling over his friend's death. After a few days the task force was ordered to move west to the Marianas, where the Japanese had built immense fortifications. Admiral Nimitz wanted to smash the Japanese positions with Operation Forager, which would become one of the great naval air battles in history.

George's VT-51 squadron was assigned antisubmarine patrols in the waters off the Marianas (Saipan, Tinian, and Guam). Using handheld K-2 cameras, they were also asked to take surveillance photos of Japanese positions on the islands. Marines and U.S. Army troops were soon going to hit those beaches. Commanders needed to know what kind of resistance they might face, and whether they could establish a beachhead at all.

Snapping photos was a tricky business. Pictures taken from a distance were not particularly useful. To see how the enemy had his forces dug in and where they were located, you needed to get in close, and you needed to do it alone. If you went in with other aircraft, you would attract too much attention. Because of its risky nature, aerial photography duty was voluntary. George took the assignment, and in early June 1944 began making reconnaissance flights over Japanese positions. Command was particularly concerned about the Charan Kanoa invasion beach on the west coast of Saipan, where Marines were expected to push in quickly and root out the Japanese forces.

On an early June morning, George and his crew were flying alone toward the islands at a thousand feet. Through smoke and the real possibility of enemy fire, George brought his Avenger in over the white sandy beaches of Charan Kanoa. Behind him, crewmate John Delaney snapped away. When he was finished, George banked the plane out to sea and returned to the *San Jac*. The photos were immediately processed and then sent back to Pearl Harbor for evaluation by navy intelligence. What they discovered was important: The Japanese had taken over a nearby sugar mill, which they were using as an observation post. Unless that position was taken out, the Japanese could use it to report on U.S. troop movements when Marines did hit the beaches. The photos also let Marine Corps general H. M. "Howlin' Mad" Smith see that there were extensive fortifications and bunkers in the area.

Days later, on June 12, his twentieth birthday, George and the other torpedo-bomber pilots were summoned to the ready room. Lieutenant Martin E. Kilpatrick, a baby-faced intelligence officer, was writing a note on the chalkboard. As the pilots and crewmen sat back in their comfortable leather chairs, Kilpatrick explained the situation. Intelligence reports indicated that Japan was using the Aslito air base in southern Saipan to protect the islands from American airpower. Until it was hit—and hit hard—American planes would be vulnerable. George and seven other Avenger pilots were expected to take it out.

As they suited up and prepared for the mission, word came that *Barbara* was grounded with mechanical problems. Instead they would take a substitute. Twelve F6F Hellcats went up first. They would provide the escort. The eight Avengers, including George's, took off next. They flew seventy-five miles toward the air base on Saipan, climbing slowly to ten thousand feet. When George reached his target and put the plane into a steep dive, he could see antiaircraft batteries and machine guns firing at them. He tried to avoid looking at them, focusing instead on the target. Then suddenly he saw that one of the escorting Hellcats was hit. The plane disintegrated and fell to the ground, burning. He knew by the plane's markings that his friend Ens. Robert McIlwaine was on board.

George quickly shifted his attention back to the attack. When they reached the target, all four bombs were released. George pulled out quickly to avoid being hit by the heavy ground fire, then returned to base safely with the other pilots. Later he learned that the mission had been a relative, but not a complete, success. The bombs had failed to hit the Japanese radio command post directly, but did sever the radio control lines, which knocked out radio communication at least for a time.

Over the next several days George was constantly flying missions. He was given difficult and sensitive reconnaissance tasks as well as bombing missions. He watched as the casualties continued to mount. Every night when the pilots retired to their rooms, another bed would be empty.

On the morning of June 19, the tired flight crews gathered for another briefing. The planes were being prepared to support the pending ground attack by U.S. Marines. Then suddenly an alarm sounded; radar indicated enemy aircraft approaching. Four great waves of Japanese planes—some four hundred in all—were on the way.

"Scramble all fighters!" came the order over the intercom.

The deck of the *San Jacinto* became a frenzy of panicked activity. Crews dashed about madly to get the fighters off first. The Hellcats had orders to climb to twenty-four thousand feet and meet the Japanese head-on. George watched from the deck and saw wisps of white vapor and smoke in the sky as the dogfights ensued above him.

Minutes later, Japanese aircraft began making runs at the American fleet while the carrier's antiaircraft guns blasted away. Suddenly George and his crew were ordered into the Avenger. At 1155, with the airwar exploding around him, he was catapulted into the sky. The air was thick with smoke and he could feel the rumble of the navy's antiaircraft guns. As he climbed to fifteen hundred feet, he suddenly saw a Japanese dive bomber falling down from above, blasted by one of the carrier's guns.

George fixed his attention on the horizon in front of him. Suddenly black smoke covered everything. He checked the gauges and noticed that the engine was gone.

"We're losing oil pressure," he told his navigator and gunner. "I think the oil lines have sucked up shrapnel."

He thought about returning to the San Jac, but the carrier was still launching aircraft. Trying to land would only mean disaster.

"Prepare for a water landing," he calmly told his crew.

He had been flying at only fifteen hundred feet and was beginning to drop rapidly. There was no time to ditch the four 500-pound bombs. The waves were high and there was a crosswind. Recalling the training he had received time and time again in Virginia, he landed by lowering the tail into the water first, to slow the plane, before setting its belly down in the water.

"We skidded along until the nose dropped," recalled Leo Nadeau, his gunner. "Then it was like hitting a stone wall. The water cascaded over the entire aircraft."

George popped out of the cockpit and quickly inflated the raft. As the air battle continued to rage overhead, he rowed away from the sinking plane as fast as possible. He was soon joined by his crew and they waited only minutes before being picked up by a passing destroyer.

When they were pulled from the water, they were taken to the ship's doctor, who checked them out before giving them a tumbler of "medicinal" brandy. For the next two days they stayed on the Bronson. It was a welcome respite from the normal rhythm of combat. As he wrote to his parents, the destroyer's crew "treated me and my crewmen like kings." Later, George was summoned for a meeting with Adm. James Kauffman, the commander of the Pacific Fleet's destroyers. George thanked him for the rescue, but the meeting had another purpose. George's brother Pressy was engaged to Kauffman's daughter.

During his time waiting to be returned to the San Jac, George saw himself change. The young warrior had tasted battle, seen people die around him, and heard the howls of men in pain. He wrote to his parents: "I hope John and Buck and my own children never have to fight a war. Friends disappearing, lives being extinguished. It's just not right. The glory of being a carrier pilot has certainly worn off."

He found himself thinking about his youngest brother, Bucky, who reminded him of the innocence that was so lacking around him. "I get such a kick out of Buck—I picture him so clearly at all times—He is sort of a symbol to me in a way. I remember how Bar and I used to play with him. We'd pretend he was our little boy, I don't know why, but little old Buck so often is brought to my mind—even when I'm up flying I'll burst out laughing at times . . . Perhaps it's because he's so young and innocent . . ."

It wasn't until June 24 that George was transferred back to the *San Jac*. By then the carrier group was preparing for the invasion of Guam. George literally dropped his bags in his room, returned to the briefing room, and began flying missions again later that day. Over the next ten days he would spend forty-six hours in the air, making thirteen strikes against the enemy in all. When they were finished, Guam had been conquered, and the Pacific commanders were already looking at the Philippines.

North of that important outpost was the island of Chichi Jima, part of what the Japanese regarded as the Chichi Jima barrier in the Bonin Islands: literally the last line of defense for the main island of Japan. If the navy could take out the facility, it would clear the way for the invasion of Iwo Jima.

One key objective was knocking out a military listening post in the center of the island. Seven massive radio towers, each two hundred feet tall, served to relay Japanese military communications and intercept U.S. transmissions. They were protected by an array of antiaircraft guns and an extensive radar system that allowed the fifteen thousand soldiers on the island to be well prepared for any attack by American aircraft.

American navy planes had repeatedly hit the listening post and failed to take it out. Most of the pilots who tried had returned. But those who did not faced a grim future. Eight American fliers were captured by Japanese forces and taken prisoner, and some were killed and actually eaten. Colonel Kato, a senior officer on the island, enjoyed dining on the flesh of American pilots, which he washed down with sugarcane rum.

George and his crew gathered with dozens of other men on the flight deck of the *San Jac*. They had just completed the 6 A.M. briefing and nerves were tense. No one said much. They just watched as the ordnance men wheeled the 500-pound bombs across the deck.

The orders had come for an assault on Chichi Jima, which had a formidable arsenal of weaponry. The island was a maze of bunkers, so it was hard to find your target. A heavy complement of antiaircraft batteries and machine guns had brought down eight pilots so far. On top of it all, it was assumed that the Japanese would be well versed on the combat formations and flight patterns the Avengers would use in the strike. Japanese AA gunners could be expected to know their angle of attack, relative altitude, and exit speed.

Standing next to George on the flight deck was a new face. His normal gunner, Leo Nadeau, had been asked to step aside so a young lieutenant named Ted White could come along for the ride. White wanted to go on a mission, and the change had been okayed by the commanding officer.

White was a squadron ordnance officer and a good friend to George and the family. He was a Yale man and a member of Skull and Bones, and his father had been a good friend to Pres at Yale. The two men had met on the *San Jac* by coincidence. He was eager to fly with George, who was in turn glad to have him along.

At 7:15 A.M. the order was given, and the Avengers lined up to be pushed into the morning sky. As *Barbara* was moved into line, George checked to make sure that his crewmates were secure as the plane was attached to the catapult. He then ran the throttle up, made sure the flaps were on full, and signaled the catapult officer. In one quick motion the Avenger was thrust into the air.

After the Avengers were airbone, they were joined by a cluster of Hellcat escorts. Together they climbed to twelve thousand feet, flying in a V-formation and maintaining radio silence. After about an hour the rugged geography of the island came into view. The orders came to assume attack formation and they fell into line.

The Japanese were ready and waiting. Douglas Melvin, the squadron commander, dived toward the target in a rapid descent. As his Avenger reached the radio station, he unloaded his bombs, scoring a direct hit. Next in line was *Barbara*. George came in at a 35-degree angle, closing fast. His vision was obscured by smoke from the antiaircraft guns and tracer fire streaming up into the sky, but he kept his eyes fixed on his target, one of the large radio towers. As Lieutenant White prepared to drop the ordnance, they suddenly felt a jolt, "as if a massive fist had crunched into the belly of the plane," Bush recalled later. Smoke poured into the cockpit and all he could see were flames ripping across the crease of the wing, edging toward the fuel tanks.

The smoke became so thick, he couldn't read the instrument panel. But he continued to dive, and once over the target, White released the 500-pound bombs.

George couldn't look back at the target. The Avenger was losing speed and he was losing control. He guided the plane back out to sea.

"Hit the silk!" he yelled through the intercom at White and Delaney.

But George didn't hear anything in reply and couldn't see them, as a thick armor plate behind him divided the cockpit from the crew.

He checked his altitude, now only twenty-five hundred feet and dropping rapidly. Removing his headset, safety belt, and harness, he pushed himself out into the stiff wind. He jumped and pulled the ripcord to the parachute prematurely. His head hit the horizontal stabilizer at the rear of the plane, and his parachute snagged on the tail of the aircraft and was ripped.

When it was finally free, he and the damaged chute plunged to the sea quickly. After he hit the water, he swam desperately up so he could breathe. Bleeding from a heavy gash on his head, he spied the small life raft nearby that automatically inflated when he pulled his parachute. He swam toward it quickly, feeling the stings of several large jellyfish before climbing inside. Above him he could see the other planes from his squadron circling in support. On the horizon, he could see Japanese boats approaching. No doubt they were hoping to reach him first so they could claim their ninth pilot as a trophy.

The water tossed his tiny raft around for half an hour as he watched the Japanese boats getting closer. Fortunately, he spotted an American submarine farther out at sea that was closing more quickly. The USS *Finback* was on "lifeguard" duty and picked him up. Crew members pulled him onto the deck and immediately took him below. The sub submerged moments later.

After he got cleaned up and was checked out by the doctor, George had time to rest in a narrow bed. As he lay there, he was haunted by what had happened. He had made it out of the Avenger, but what about his crew? He had not heard from them and never saw another parachute exit the plane. A few planes had circled after his rescue to see if there were any other survivors, but none were ever found.

To his family he wrote about his pain in not knowing what happened. "The fact that our planes didn't seem to be searching anymore showed me pretty clearly that they had not gotten out. I'm afraid I was pretty much of a sissy about it cause I sat in my raft and sobbed for awhile. It bothers me so very much . . . I feel so terribly responsible for their fate. Oh so much right now."

That night, George tossed and turned, unable to sleep, reliving the whole experience. He gained a little peace of mind when it was later reported that witnesses had seen a second man jumping from the plane. Unfortunately his chute hadn't opened. As he wrote to his parents, "I am sorry over that, but am glad that someone at least got out of the plane besides myself." But the memory of that day would haunt him for years. "I cannot get the thought of those two boys out of my mind," he would say.

George spent thirty days on the submarine as it attempted to evade the Japanese fleet. Consequently, no mail got out. George had been a regular and frequent writer of letters. But now, for several weeks, his parents and Bar heard nothing. Pres Bush contacted a friend at the War Department and found out that his boy was missing. He shared the information with Dottie, but they elected to keep it from Barbara and the children.

But with no letters, Barbara worried anyway. George had been writing several times a week, describing in vivid detail the sort of missions he was undertaking. But now, nothing. Finally one morning a telegram arrived at the Bush home in Greenwich. George was safe and being returned to the *San Jac*. Dottie and Pres immediately called Barbara.

George returned to the *San Jac*, and because he had been shot down he was eligible for rotation back to the States. But he was determined to fly again. He flew eight more missions near the Philippines, striking enemy shipping in Manila Bay.

When he wasn't flying, George thought about his plans for the future. By late 1944 there were clear signs that the war might soon be coming to an end. He wondered what the future might hold. Before the war he had expected to follow in the tracks that his father had laid before him. But now he was thinking differently, unconventionally.

First and foremost was Barbara, and wedding plans. He also thought about skipping college and going to work instead. He was particularly struck with the life that his brother Pres had described in South America, and he wrote to his parents, suggesting that he might take such a route. But even from the Pacific he could hear his father's heart breaking at the thought that his son would not follow him to his beloved Yale.

On November 9 he wrote his kid brother Johnny with the news. "Whip out your top hat and tails, 'cause I want you to be one of the featured ushers at my wedding—when it will be I do not know, but get hot on shining your shoes, cause the day is not far off. Also get pants that are plenty big, because we're going to fill you so full of champagne it'll be coming out of your ears . . ." They settled on the date of December 17.

Barbara had the invitations printed and the plans were set. But then they heard no word from George, who was expected back stateside. When news finally came, it was on December 22, when his squadron finally reached San Diego. George phoned her before catching a commercial flight to Pittsburgh, followed by a sleeper train to New York. He arrived at the Rye railroad station on Christmas Eve, 1944.

On the sixth of January, a cold day marked by blowing snow, George Bush was dressed in navy blues and standing at the altar of the First Presbyterian Church in Rye. The entire Bush family was in the pews, awaiting the arrival of the bride. His brother Pressy, recently married to Admiral Kauffman's daughter, was standing next to him as best man. Bert Walker and the whole Walker clan were also there.

The music started playing and down the aisle came a young, slender beauty dressed in white. It was Bar, wearing Dottie's wedding dress.

#### CHAPTER 7

# LIFTOFF

URING THE SUMMER OF 1945, SHOUTS OF JOY WERE HEARD IN THE Bush home just as they were around the country. Japan had surrendered; the war was over. For the first time in years young Americans began thinking again about getting back to a normal life.

Because George was a combat veteran, he was discharged just months after the war ended. His parents, brothers, and sister could all see that the war had changed him.

But while those events left a lasting impression, he was determined to leave the war behind him. He never showed his Air Medal, two Gold Stars, or Distinguished Flying Cross to anyone unless repeatedly prompted, and he rarely spoke about his wartime experiences.

"George lives his life in chapters, like a lot of the Bushes do," said his sister Nancy. "The war was over and he left it behind. Some people had trouble doing that. George didn't."

Two months after he returned home, George was enrolled at Yale University. Although he had talked loosely about getting a job, there was never really any doubt that he would attend Yale. Not going would have hurt his father too much. Pres was on Yale's board of trustees and had worked doggedly for the university ever since he graduated. The young Bush men were expected to follow suit (and they all did). "Going to Yale was like going to Kennebunkport in the summer," William "Bucky" Bush told us. "It was just part of what you were expected to do."

Yale in the fall of 1945 was full of servicemen. Of the 8,000 freshmen who entered that year, fully 5,000 had been to war. Yale seemed every bit the same as it was when Pres Bush had been there twenty-five years earlier, with its graceful Dutch elms, trolley cars, and tradition. But that first semester, it took a while for khaki to give way to gray flannels.

The bond among students had less to do with family and pedigree than a generation earlier. "We came out of the war like a band of brothers," recalls Lud Ashley, a friend of George's at Yale. "All of the people we knew on campus had been in Europe and the Pacific. We had a shared experience. We didn't talk about it much. We wanted to put the war behind us. It was time to get on with our lives. But we all knew the bond was there and we felt it."

With housing in short supply, George and Bar took a small apartment on Chapel Street near campus. George put his medals and ribbons in a small box and packed them away. Living conditions were cramped, and certainly George's parents could have provided some money for a larger place. But in keeping with the tradition he had learned from his father, George was not about to ask for money. Instead, they lived on the money that he had saved during the war. And while George was at class, Barbara worked at the Yale co-op. She discovered, too, that she was pregnant.

George quickly immersed himself in Yale—the classes, the social life, and the athletics. He reveled in the opportunity to meet people and connect. Met someone whose old man went to school with dad? Gotta invite them over. Saw a fella who went to Andover? Drop by for a bit. George had a lot of identifiable qualities in his youth—charm, athleticism, and a sense of duty. But he had something even more advantageous and useful—the gift of friendship. Strangers weren't strangers for long; they were only possible friends. Before long he began simply inviting people over for dinner without consulting Barbara. As Barbara cooked in a cramped kitchen with an old stove and orange crates on the wall for a pantry, George would show up ten minutes before dinner with three unexpected friends in tow. Barbara would be sent scrambling. Finally she called her mother-in-law in Greenwich to find out what to do. "Set the table for eight every night," Dottie counseled. "Then subtract from there depending on who shows up."

George got straight A's in economics and made Phi Beta Kappa. But like his father, he was a decidedly practical man. He concentrated on business courses and took little interest in the impassioned ideas of guest lecturers Jean-Paul Sartre, Arnold Toynbee, or T. S. Eliot. He also had little interest in politics. "When it came to the hot political issues on campus," recalls classmate William F. Buckley, Jr., "he was never in the thick of it." Indeed, while Buckley and his brother-in-law Brent Bozell worked tenaciously to build a conservative movement on campus, George never attended any of the events.

Instead he concentrated on making friends and forging relationships. He was active in the DKE or "Dekes" fraternity, where he was well known and liked. Fellow Deke John H. Chafee, later the U.S. senator from Rhode Island, recalled, "We didn't see much of him because he was married, but I guess my first impression was that he was—and I don't mean this in a derogatory fashion—in the inner set, the movers and shakers, the establishment. I don't mean he put on airs or anything, but . . . just everybody knew him."

On a hot July 6, 1946, Barbara gave birth to a small, boisterous baby boy. Dottie and Pres were there to see little George Walker Bush come into the world. The choice of name said something about the Bushes and the family itself. As it had been for two generations, as the eldest born son he was given his father's first name. But George and Bar also gave him the middle name Walker. It was a tilt to the Walker clan, which had injected so much energy into the Bush family blood. Little George, as he quickly became known, was not just a Bush; he was a Walker, too.

Little George was born in the busiest year of the baby boom. Young newly married couples were having children at an astonishing rate. Expectant mothers were thumbing through the pages of Dr. Benjamin Spock's best-seller *The Common Sense Book of Baby and Child Care*, which advised parents to adopt a more relaxed form of parenting. Parents should avoid schedules and other structural impediments to being a parent, Spock advised. Let the infant decide when he is hungry, and sleep in a communal bed together as a family. Bar thought it was all utter nonsense; that was no way to parent. "Barbara was a lot like my mother when it came to child-rearing," Nancy Ellis recalled. "The child could rightfully expect a lot from their parents. But the parents had a right to expect certain things from their children." Bar quit working and stayed home with little George. When she went out to run errands she would have him in tow. But George and Bar also believed that they had a life of their own. Only weeks after giving birth, the couple was plugged back into campus life. And Barbara was rarely left behind.

George was on the baseball team, and Bar would often travel with the team to keep score. As they warmed up for the game, Bar would sit in the bleachers with a bundled Little George at her side, drawing up the scoring sheets. Bar had that ability to latch onto what George was doing and lay claim to some of it herself. "You had a sense even then that George and Barbara were a team," Jim Duffus, a teammate, told us. "Baseball was important to George so—wham—it was equally important to Barbara."

When the team played at home, the games became a family activity. Pres would break away from Brown Brothers and come to watch his son play. George was now a young man and in some respects that made it easier for Pres to connect with him. Sitting near the first-base line, Pres would watch his son with an intensity that had frankly been lacking when George was younger. Pres would often cast off other responsibilities, even skipping a board meeting at CBS or forfeiting a six-hundred-dollar fee, to catch a game against Princeton. Family members were surprised because Pres would never have dreamed of doing that when George was younger.

Unlike his playing days at Andover, where George was a star athlete, things were more competitive at Yale. When Pres played first base at Yale, he'd had the sheer physical strength and size to muscle the ball into the outfield even if the pitch was tight and inside. George lacked that strength but was still capable of moments of brilliance, as when he went 3-for-5 with a double and a triple during a game in Raleigh, North Carolina. His performance brought half a dozen scouts to Coach Ethan Allen with queries about the "new pro prospect." But the interest didn't last long. "They thought he did that every game," recalls Jim Duffus.

Overall he was average at the plate, hitting .239 in 1947 and .264 in 1948 while batting seventh in the rotation, with two career home runs in fifty-one games. But what he lacked at the plate he seemed to make up for in the field, where he played with surprising confidence, even cockiness. "You could see him at first base, just glaring at the batter with this stern look on his face," recalls his brother Bucky Bush. "He was almost daring them to hit it down the right baseline."

Selection as team captain was George's crowning moment at Yale. He had achieved what his father had done three decades earlier. He also managed to do it in the same way his father had. Success wasn't necessarily about being the smartest or the best player on the team. (The man he beat out for team captain ended up playing for the Detroit Tigers.) It was instead the innate quality that he carried with him. "When he came into the clubhouse the first day, everyone just knew he was going to be team captain," Duffus says. "He had an air about him. But it was the sort of thing he could turn on and off—like a light switch."

George was affable and friendly in the clubhouse. But on the field he was all business. "He didn't mind telling you whether you weren't playing the way you should or you weren't trying hard enough," Duffus recalled. "If you ran the lines too slow or didn't work hard enough on your base-running, Poppy would let you hear it."

For George, like other members of his family, there was a mythology about sports, and near the top of the pantheon was baseball. Later in life he would actively encourage his sons and grandsons to play the game. Long after he had entered the world of politics, family members can remember few moments when George lit up any brighter than in 1981 when, as vice president, he was in Denver giving a speech. When he learned that a group of former pro players was in town for an old-timers game, and thrilled at the chance of meeting them, he invited the group to visit. They swapped stories at his hotel room and then one of them asked: Do you want to give it another try?

The vice president of the United States suited up and arrived at the ballpark in an unmarked car. (The Secret Service went crazy; this was unplanned and unsafe!) Sitting in the dugout, he chatted with the players until he was called out to the field to pinch-hit. Against Warren Spahn, the Hall of Fame left-hander, he popped up. Later he faced Milt Pappas. With a fluid swing of the bat he managed to squib the ball over second base for a single. It was, he would later recall, one of the happiest moments of his life.

Less than a decade later, when he became president, George kept his old Yale first baseman's glove in a drawer in his Oval Office desk. He oiled it regularly, as if to make sure it would be ready for use at a moment's notice.

***

IN THE SPRING OF 1947, GEORGE WAS TAPPED FOR SKULL AND BONES. IT WAS not really much of a surprise. The Bushes were now replete with Bonesmen: His father had been the first family member to join in 1917, followed by his brother James and brothers-in-law Herby and Lou Walker.

But unlike the other Bonesmen in his family, George received the honor of being "last man tapped," a distinction that went to the top prospect. His father attended George's initiation rite.

George became a fixture in Bones. Every Thursday and Sunday night during the academic year, he would gather with fellow members behind the triple-padlocked door of the windowless crypt to discuss what was happening in his life.

For Barbara, George's membership in Skull and Bones was a source of minor irritation and amusement. Now growing used to being in a marriage in which the two shared everything, she was suddenly told that her husband could not share the details of his conversations with fellow members.

Skull and Bones was every bit the secret society it had been in Pres Bush's days. If anything, the legend had grown as the group's practices and rituals became part of the lexicon of the American establishment. Ernest Hemingway had written about Bones in *To Have and Have Not*. F. Scott Fitzgerald rhapsodized about it in "A Woman with a Past" and *This Side of Paradise*. During the war, Bonesman and FDR confidant Averell Harriman had used the Skull and Bones numerical code 322 as the combination for the lock on his briefcase. Other Bonesmen had served in the Office of Strategic Services (OSS). Even nonmembers were caught up in the group's legendary secrecy. John Mc-

Cloy, adviser to President Truman, had informed the commander in chief about the importance of keeping the atomic bomb secrets hidden. Failing to do so would be "like mentioning Skull and Bones to good Yale society," he told Truman in the Oval Office. Truman didn't have to ask what McCloy meant.

But while the ritual and tradition of Bones remained, the group was beginning to evolve because Yale itself was changing. The society's penchant for recruiting the lily white sons of old-line bankers and blue-blood lawyers was changing as the GI Bill brought thousands of veterans to the Yale campus. The group's insistence on the absolute secrecy of its members, which had once evoked suspicion, was now the subject of Ivy League humor. When it was learned that the Harvard Hasty Pudding Show would include a joke about Skull and Bones, the Harvard Lampoon hired a group of blacks to sit in prominent positions all over the orchestra. The moment Skull and Bones was mentioned, they all got up and left the theater.

George was uncomfortable with the makeup of Bones. Like his father, George believed that race relations needed to be repaired and discrimination was a problem. He was active in the United Negro College Fund along with his father.

In the spring of 1949, two years after George's selection, Bones took a historic step when Levi Jackson, a black football player, was tapped for membership. One of the alumni most supportive of Jackson's membership was George Bush. But as Jackson himself wryly noted, more changes needed to be made. "If my name had been Jackson Levi," he joked, "I'd never have made it."

While both George and his father favored changes in Skull and Bones, not everyone in the family shared their views on race. In 1948, when George went to Harlem to meet with a group of black leaders to discuss racial discrimination, Gampy Walker became furious. "You're wasting your time!" he bellowed. Others were incensed about the changes taking place in Bones. Louis Walker, George's uncle, feared that it was becoming less masculine, less establishment. "God damn," he told George and Lud Ashley. "When I was in Bones club, everyone played football. Real men. Look at them now. They're all so soft!"

After George left Yale, he would remain active in Bones just as his father and uncles had. He would attend reunions, give money to secret fundraising drives, and help fellow Bonesmen as best he could. When he became vice president and president, some of his first celebratory events were small, secret meetings of fellow Bonesmen in Washington.

FOR THE EXTENDED BUSH-WALKER CLAN, THE POSTWAR YEARS WERE GOOD. Pres Bush was prospering at Brown Brothers and serving on seven corporate boards. G. H. Walker and Company was doing a booming business, too. Herby Walker, the eldest son, was now running the place, and his brothers Louis and Johnny were there, too. When the clans would gather at Kennebunkport in the summers, you could see the seismic shift taking place in the family. The currency, particularly for the Walkers, was success. "There was this Walker ethos about having to be big shots," Elsie Walker Kilbourne said. "It dominated everything."

Herby's sons were going to Yale and on the rise. The Bush boys were rising fast, too. Pressy worked for G. H. Walker and then founded his own firm on Wall Street. Johnny and Bucky were off to school at Hotchkiss, to be followed by Yale and successful careers in finance. But the one rising fastest was George, who was becoming the North Star of the family's new generation. And in this competitive clan, it was causing problems.

When George got his military decorations and went to the College World Series, Uncle Herby made sure his boys knew how proud he was of his nephew. He was always talking up George, how sharp that boy was and what a future he was going to have. It was Uncle Herby who first posited the idea that he would be president one day. "In many ways, Herby was better to George than to his own sons," Shellie Bush Jansing, James's daughter and George's cousin, said. During the next three decades, Herb Walker, Jr. would play a central role in George Bush's rise to power. George was everything that he wanted in a son—attractive, athletic, charming, and successful. His sons, by comparison, simply didn't measure up. Unable to compete, Herby's son Ray basically dropped out of the game. He became a Jungian therapist and moved to rural Vermont. George Herbert Walker III struggled throughout his adult life with the knowledge that his own father thought less of him than of his cousin George.

As graduation approached, the subject of George's future arose. Thanks to his status as a GI, George made his way through the Yale course work in two and a half years. With one son already, he struggled quietly over what to do next. "My mind is in turmoil," he wrote his good friend Gerry Bemiss. "I want to do something of value and yet I have to and want to make money."

Uncle Herby came up to him at his parents' house and slapped him on the back. (Uncle Herby was always slapping someone on the back.) Herby wanted to make George a star by hiring him to work for G. H. Walker and

Company. For George it would be an easy move, one that would bring him into the world of investment banking at a high level. But he wanted something more. "I am not sure I want to capitalize completely on the benefits at birth—that is on the benefits of my social position," he wrote Bemiss. "Such qualities as industriousness, integrity, etc. which I have or at least hope I have had inculcated into me by my parents, at least to some degree, (I hope) I do want to use, but doing well merely because I have had the opportunity to attend the same debut parties as some of my customers, does not appeal to me."

Besides, for the Bush men, success was always best achieved far from home. George's grandfather S. P. had left a comfortable life on Long Island to venture to Ohio. His father had turned down a chance to work for Buckeye Steel and join Columbus society based on his family's name, and migrated to St. Louis.

So with the offer from Uncle Herby dangling in front of them, George and Barbara considered just about everything—teaching, attending Oxford University, even farming. Both Barbara and George had read Louis Bromfield's *The Farm* and found the idea of living off the land appealing. George investigated and was immediately deterred by the economics of farm life.

George was in conflict as the battle raged inside him. It was as if the two strands of the family were struggling to gain mastery. "The Walkers were Get goin' kind of guys, whereas the Bushes were more steady as she goes," Lud Ashley said. "George has a little bit of both in him. Part of George just wanted the steadiness of a regular job and a paycheck. But there was also a risk-taking element in him that he inherited from the Walkers."

In the late 1940s there were few better places to strike out and make your fortune than the American Southwest. Young George had read about the great oilmen in *Life* magazine and *Fortune*. Gampy Walker had also told him stories of his dealings with bigger-than-life oil mavens like H. L. Hunt, Clint Murchison, and Sid Richardson that seemed like tales of fiction. His favorable impressions of Texas grew during his time in the navy. The *San Jac* had been named after a famous battlefield in Texas, and at the insistence of Admiral Halsey it flew not only the Stars and Stripes but the Lone Star flag of Texas. The Texans he served with told him about the boom that was rising from the prairie ground itself. "They filled George's head with stories about all the money that could be made in oil," Pres Bush, Jr. said.

In April 1948 the phone call came that S. P. Bush had died in Ohio. Days later, George was on a chartered plane to Columbus with his father and other family members, including some of the Walkers. Seated next to his father on the plane was the charming Neil Mallon, the longtime family friend and head of Dresser Industries.

Mallon was one of his father's best friends. They had been through Yale, Bones, the Great War, and business dealings together; Pres Bush had arranged for his appointment at the helm of Dresser more than twenty years earlier. On top of that, Neil Mallon was the kind of man who, in the words of Bucky Bush, could "charm the fangs off a cobra." Like everyone in the Bush-Walker universe, Mallon saw George's drive, intelligence, and discipline. So as they sat on the plane together, he pitched young George on how he could make it big in the oil business. George's cousin Stu Clement was on the plane, and he recalled how Mallon worked George over. Smooth and direct, he told George that he could be like the men of action who were making a fortune in the oil business. If he came to Dresser and worked hard, "You'll have a chance to run it someday," Mallon told him.

The group stayed in Columbus a day or two as S. P. was laid to rest near his beloved Flora. He left behind a sizable fortune, which Pres Bush ensured all went to his sisters. He could always say, for the rest of his life, he never took a penny from his old man.

When they all returned to Connecticut, George seemed convinced of what he should do next. He talked to Bar about it and then announced it to his parents: They were going to move to Texas.

Although Bar didn't object to his plans, she certainly wasn't thrilled about them. She had expected that they would settle in the New York City area or perhaps in New England. The idea of bare and hardscrabble Texas held no allure for her. But what did entice her was the chance for adventure, and if things didn't work out, they could always return east and start anew.

In June 1948, shortly after the College World Series, George graduated from Yale University. His father gave him a shiny, new red Studebaker—the first car George ever owned. He took Barbara and little George for a drive around New Haven. Then his parents were off to Kennebunkport to escape the coming heat, and George and Bar joined them there for a while.

Compared to the job Uncle Herby had offered him, the work at the International Derrick and Equipment Company, a Dresser subsidiary, was not much to get excited about. George would be clerk in their Odessa, Texas, office, as he needed to learn the business from the ground up.

While Bar and Little George stayed with his parents, George drove the red Studebaker south, off to a new land, just as his father and grandfather had done before him. Cutting a path through the American South, he arrived days later in Odessa on a hot afternoon. What he saw was barely worth looking at. Flat land covered with sagebrush surrounded a town that had no parks, few trees, and a skyline of equipment yards and oil derricks. When the wind blew, sand and dust got in your eyes. When the air was still, the pervasive stench of natural gas from the nearby oil wells burned your nostrils and made you wish the wind would rise again.

George found a house for his family, showed up at his new office, then sent for his wife and son. When Bar arrived, she discovered that her husband had utilitarian standards.

Their half of a duplex on East Seventh Street had one bedroom, a living room, and a kitchen. The paint was barely clinging to the old walls and there was no air-conditioning, only a rattling window fan. The cramped space meant that Little George slept in the bedroom with his parents. When the couple wanted privacy, Georgie was relegated to the living room.

Most disconcerting to Barbara were the neighbors, with whom they shared a bathroom. The single mother and her teenage daughter seemed nice enough, even downright friendly. But then they heard the sounds and saw strange men coming and going all afternoon and into the evening. Bar was the first to realize that their first Texas neighbors were in fact a mother-daughter prostitution team, who not only entertained guests in their bedroom, but also used the bathroom when space became a problem.

With George trying to get accustomed to his job, Barbara was left to fend for herself and Little George through the long, lonely days. Barbara had been accustomed to living in large spacious homes with lush gardens and nearby clubs. Odessa offered none of that. George was bringing home $375 a month and they had no friends. When the mail arrived there might very well be a package from her mother with a discouraging note. Why they were in West Texas, God only knew, Pauline Pierce would write. She began sending provisions of Ivory Soap through the mail, convinced that Texas lacked hygiene products.

Although Barbara was outgoing and friendly, making friends was still not easy as she had so little in common with her neighbors. And George had managed to move to one of the few places in the United States where a Yale background and New England pedigree worked heavily against you. "We find some west Texans are . . . Eastern-prejudiced," Barbara wrote her family.

As with all the Bush men, who were always in a hurry, George threw himself into his work, and it was left to Barbara to deal with most of the harsh realities in Odessa. The Bushes always tried to marry strong women because they expected them to carry most of the family's emotional and organizational burdens. It was here, in the harsh physical and emotional climate of West Texas, that the family pattern emerged that would last their whole lives.

Teensie Bush Cole, George's cousin, saw how Barbara was stretching herself for her husband. "You've got to understand your husband if you are going to be happy," she said. "You've got to understand what he wants and go with it. Barbara did."

"He could go and do anything he wanted, anything he needed to do; he had an anchor," John Ellis explained. "I don't know how many people are lucky enough to have Barbara Bush as their wife. Everything gets done."

George saw it, too. "Anyone would like to be around her own friends, be able to take at least a passing interest in clothes, parties, etc.," George wrote his mother at the time. "She gets absolutely none of this. It is different for me, I have my job all day long with new things happening, but she is here in this small apt. with people whose interests cannot be at all similar to Bar's because they have never had any similar experiences."

But for all the burdens, Bar also found West Texas a strangely liberating place. Away from the cloistered world of her youth, thousands of miles from a difficult mother, out of the shadow of her older sister who was modeling, she was no longer measured by her name or family, closely examined by her mother, or compared to her beautiful sister. "It was the first time in our lives that we had lived in a place where nobody said, 'You're Marvin Pierce's daughter or Pres Bush's son,' " she recalled. "It's pretty nice to be judged on your own."

George embraced that freedom and quickly worked to blend into what was still an alien place. Just as he had learned to do in the navy, he began chatting with the locals and eating the standard diet of chili with crackers and ice-cold beer for lunch and chicken-fried steak for dinner. Once George was asked if he had attended college. George replied, "Yale."

The man shrugged his shoulders. "Never heard of it."

So the college tie and class ring were put away, and he disguised the fact that he was a college man from back East, concentrating instead on talking about his job, his family, and church. But it was hard to escape the cultural contradictions. Months after they arrived, George ran into a black worker for the NAACP on the street and invited him home for a drink. For George it was the natural thing to do. His dad had entertained black musicians and civil rights workers at home for almost twenty years. But this time the man politely declined. George was puzzled but soon found out why. When word got around about what he had done, neighbors informed him that they were not pleased.

And there were other lessons to be learned. On Christmas Eve, 1948, just months after he and Barbara arrived, George was given the responsibility of cohosting the office Christmas party, held in the company's supply store. George was put in charge of mixing drinks. As Barbara and Little George waited back home to decorate the tree, George kept mixing, filling an occasional glass for himself. When the party was over, a colleague had to put him in the back of his pickup truck and drive him home, depositing him gently on the front lawn. Barbara, needless to say, was not amused.

Still, George was able to do something the Bushes had now done for at least two generations—adapt, fit in, reinvent not your values but your mannerisms and your way of talking. S. P. had worked the railroads with hardened men. Pres Bush had gone from Skull and Bones to selling Keen Kutter tools in St. Louis in a matter of months.

To prove himself, George always showed up early and stayed late. He also made frequent trips out of town. He learned how to change the clutches and brakes on oil rigs by accompanying IDECO servicemen to oil fields throughout Texas and New Mexico. He frequently worked Saturdays. But despite these harsh realities, George saw Texas as a place of his dreams. He was hearing reports every day of young men making their fortunes. Why couldn't he? "If a man could go in and get just a few acres of land which later turned out to be good," he wrote his friend Gerry Bemiss, "he would be fixed for life."

On the weekends when George wasn't working, the family attended church and tried to come up with ways to amuse themselves. Golf, such a genteel affair in Greenwich and Rye, was decidedly different in hardscrabble West Texas. Courses were not carpets of lush green, but flat and brown. To avoid sunstroke, players would drive jeeps on the fairways to get to their balls.

As the months passed, Little George began sprouting up. A rambunctious and at times demanding two-year-old, he was more Texas than anything. "Whenever I come home he greets me and talks a blue streak, sentences disjointed of course but enthusiasm and spirit boundless," George wrote a friend. "He is a real blond and pot-bellied. He tries to say everything and the results are often hilarious."

But the demands of George's work meant that he had little time to spend with his son. "I was gone all the time," former president Bush said, "busy with my job. It was Barbara who really raised him."

The Bushes lived in Odessa less than a year. Neil Mallon had big plans for George, and he was transferred to another subsidiary, this time in California. Having learned a thing or two about oil rigs, he was moved into sales, which meant the family was on the go, moving five times in a single year: Huntington Park, Bakersfield, Whittier, Ventura, and Compton.

George's travel schedule was grueling. He might travel a thousand miles in a week trying to sell company products around the state. While on one of those trips, Barbara received terrible news from home. She was forced to face it alone. On a November morning, while her father and mother were in their car, a freak accident had occurred. Pauline had set a hot cup of coffee on the car seat next to her. Marvin saw the cup starting to slide toward her, so he reached over to grab it but lost control of the car. The automobile crashed into a stone wall on one of Westchester County's narrow country lanes. Pauline was killed instantly; Marvin was in the hospital with broken ribs. He spoke with his daughter by telephone.

A funeral was being planned for Pauline back in Rye. But Bar was seven months pregnant. She anguished about whether to head back east or stay at home for the baby. Given that George was traveling all the time, she decided that she couldn't make the trip. The guilt would always haunt her.

Two months later Barbara gave birth to a beautiful thin sliver of a girl. They named her Robin. The birth was relatively easy, which was fortunate. The family had been on the move so much, traveling from town to town, that she first met her doctor the day Robin was delivered.

Shortly afterward the Bushes were transferred back to Texas by Dresser Industries, this time to Midland. If Odessa was a town where men drank their liquor straight from the bottle and chewed tobacco instead of smoking it, Midland at least included a small enclave of young, smart, and ambitious couples who had been educated back east.

George and Barbara were newcomers in town, but so was just about everybody else in Midland's burgeoning oil business. The average age in town was twenty-eight, and many of the young couples there were Easterners who had moved to the area after the war in the hope of finding their fortune in oil. And fortunes were being made and lost in town on a weekly basis. Independent producers poured money into prospective oil fields that either made them a fortune or went bust. Some three thousand wells were being drilled in the Permian Basin every couple of months. Competition was intense.

The sons of America's aristocracy were also in Midland trying to make the next big strike. The Gettys, the Mellons, and the Rockefellers all had young men in town doing their bidding. So while Midland was pure West Texas, it also boasted a Harvard Club, a Yale Club, and a Princeton Club.

The Bushes settled first into a small, wood-paneled motel on Main Street called George's Court. Each morning George would rise with the sun and head off for a long day at work trying to sell Dresser Products to oil drilling companies. Barbara would stay behind with Little George and Robin. When they heard about a new housing development going up, George and Barbara bought a home there, on East Maple Street. It was a small place, only 847 square feet, including a carport and a small paved-over slab of concrete that passed for a patio. The house was painted bright blue in keeping with the vivid colors of the neighborhood. George financed the seventy-five-hundred-dollar purchase with a Federal Housing Administration mortgage.

Early in June 1950, George faced another difficult decision. Weeks earlier he had received a letter that he couldn't get off his mind. Tom McCance, a partner at his father's investment firm, had written to offer George the opportunity to work for Brown Brothers Harriman in New York City. "This suggestion," McCance assured him, "did not originate with your father and, in fact, he has nothing to do with it . . . others of us here [feel] this would be an excellent move for us and are most hopeful that you will react favorably to the suggestion."

The offer was tempting. His path would certainly be easier, and George could trade his soiled workingman's clothes for a wool suit, his small metal desk for a mahogany rolltop. For Barbara it would mean returning from an exile of sorts.

For more than a month, George and Barbara wrestled with the offer. They talked with friends, drew up a checklist, and prayed about the decision. (Curiously, George did not call his father for advice.) In the end, Barbara left it to George.

On June 25, George wrote McCance a note. "Many personal factors tended to make us lean toward moving back," he wrote. "The decision has been a most difficult one to make for the choice was between two wonderful jobs." But he informed McCance that he was going to stay with Dresser. Like his father some thirty years earlier, he was determined to chart his own course and write his own chapter in the annals of the family's history.

George was convinced that he had a future in the oil business. Unlike the oil fields in East Texas, run by big landowners and big oil, in Midland there were still opportunities for smaller independents. It was just a question of taking a chance.

Still, there wasn't a lot to do in Midland, Texas. Outside of high school football, there wasn't a lot of entertainment available. Young couples needed to make their own fun, which usually meant backyard barbecues and casual socials. George and Barbara, always voracious about meeting new people, made a seamless transition from the cotillions and socials in the East to the down-home socializing in Midland. They met one neighbor who became a lifelong friend when they walked across the street barefoot and joined him in the backyard for a beer.

Another neighbor was an independent oil operator named John Overbey. Twenty-six-year-old George listened intently as his neighbor described trading oil leases and mineral rights. The secret to the oil business, Overbey told him, was not in drilling for oil. That was expensive and risky. You could hit oil and make it rich, but it was much more likely that you would come up dry and lose a lot of money. You were better off selling and trading the rights to drill on land to the oil companies. You assumed none of the risk but could make a tidy profit.

As he peddled Dresser equipment in towns with names like Muleshoe, Wink, and Pecos during the day, George found himself increasingly eager to return home for his evening chats with Overbey. The conversations soon turned from the theoretical to the practical as the two men decided to form a partnership and go into the business of selling and trading drilling rights. They would call it the Bush-Overbey Oil Development Company.

What Overbey brought to the partnership was expertise in acquiring the mineral rights from owners. He had been doing this for a while now. What George brought was an overwhelming drive to succeed and access to capital. Buying and trading oil leases required money if you were going to do it right. So George boarded a plane and headed east to raise some capital.

George went home to spend some time with his parents. But most of his time was spent with Uncle Herby, who was running G. H. Walker and Company. He was always happy to see his favorite nephew.

Herby was much like his father had been: hard, gruff, and demanding. George was none of those things. "George was always so funny with the Walker uncles," says Lud Ashley. "His uncles were aggressive and hard-charging. George was so calm and polite. He was amused by them and their ways."

George laid out his plans to his uncle, who was making huge money on Wall Street and in New York City real estate. The gambler in Herby liked the idea of going into the oil business. But more important, he loved George like his own son—only more. Herby offered to open some doors for his nephew.

Over the next several weeks, George traveled the eastern corridor of the United States to raise some $350,000 for the venture. His father invested and so did Uncle Herby. So, too, did Eugene Meyer, publisher of the *Washington Post*. Meyer coughed up $50,000 and then invested some for his daughter, Katharine Graham. It was an initial investment that planted the seed for what would become a several-decades-long friendship between George Bush and Katharine Graham, who eventually took over as publisher of the *Washington Post*. The relationship suffered, however, in 1987, when *Newsweek* magazine (which was owned by the *Post*) published a hard-hitting cover story calling George Bush a "wimp." "They blamed Katharine Graham for that," Harry Catto, George's longtime friend told us.

With the capital lined up, George had one more visit to make. He flew to Dresser's corporate headquarters in Dallas and laid out his plans. Neil Mallon listened intently and then pulled out a legal notepad and began to write. "I really hate to see you go, George," he told him, "but if I were your age, I'd be doing the same thing—and here's how I'd go about it."

So over the next half hour, Neil Mallon, the man who had become president of Dresser Industries with the help of Pres Bush, explained to George exactly how to structure the business. It was in George's words "a crash course not only in how to structure but how to finance an independent oil company." When George left, he did so with Mallon's blessing and their friendship intact.

In a matter of weeks, Bush-Overbey Oil Development Company, Inc., opened up offices in the Midland Petroleum Building across the street from the county courthouse. To save money, George insisted that they rent only one room of a two-room office. (The other went to an insurance company.) They bought two desks, two chairs, a couple of typewriters, a file cabinet, and a map rack.

Buying and trading mineral rights was a business that rested almost entirely on personal relationships, something George excelled at. Once some prospective land was identified, George and Overbey needed to negotiate for the rights with the owner. It often meant being charming and shrewd at the same time. George wrote personal notes to everyone he met: people he met at the courthouse, someone who dropped by for a casual chat, even a chance encounter with someone at the coffee shop might prove to be a lead on some property. "We spent our time in the county courthouses, checking land records," Overbey recalled. "Then you'd go talk to a farmer who usually thought you looked suspicious and was busy with his cattle anyway. Just when you'd get him convinced to sell his rights, somebody else would show up. Pretty soon, you were bargaining among six guys and the price kept going up."

Once you secured the rights, you needed to offer them to oil drilling companies. This was a fast-moving business, and deals were often consummated with a simple handshake. "It wasn't like you had a thick contract for them to sign," said Jerry Finger, a longtime Bush friend from Texas. "You had to get a measure of a man quickly to know whether you could trust him. If you lied or didn't hold up your end of the bargain, no one would do business with you."

In those first years the company experienced moderate success. As John Overbey put it later, the company "rocked along and made a few good deals and a few bad ones." Like his father, George began to worry about money, eventually developing bleeding ulcers. "I would worry a lot," he recalled. "I'd keep a lot inside me."

In August 1951, George, Barbara, Little George, and Robin headed north to Kennebunkport to escape the heat of West Texas. For George it was the first opportunity in several years to spend some time with his extended family. Johnny and Bucky were at the Hotchkiss School in Connecticut. Johnny was interested in singing and proving to be quite the wit. Bucky, like his big brother George, was a good athlete. Nancy was getting ready to finish at Vassar.

Bert Walker, the aging lion and patriarch of the Walker clan, would hold court in the big house on Walker Point. All the Walker boys would be there. Dottie Bush, by virtue of being the only daughter, got the bungalow on the property. Over the next several weeks the families engaged in a constant bedlam of tennis, golf, fishing, boating, cards—anything and everything was a competition. But with the young members of the family rising in their careers, the atmosphere was beginning to change. Elsie Walker Kilbourne explained how it was no longer the generally safe family place that was all about unity. "This game started, with everyone trying to prove who knew more impressive people. Competition as a child is fun and doesn't need to be unattractive. But among adults, as name-dropping, it can be ugly."

The Walker boys would show up with brand-spanking-new powerboats and line them up at the marina. Who had the larger engine, the most impressive paint job, the most impressive horn became subjects of keen argument. When they finally went out on the water, the spontaneous fun of years earlier evaporated. Instead, they were competing, driving their boats fast and hard. "There was a lot of anger out on the water," Elsie told us.

Bravado, so disdained in the Bush home, became a regular houseguest at the Point. Herby Walker, who was married but also "friendly with the ladies" in Elsie Walker Kilbourne's words, might offer a veiled comment about one of his conquests. The situation became so difficult and ugly to Pres Bush that he found himself increasingly retreating from his time with family. Eventually Pres would insist that they stop coming to Kennebunkport for a while. Instead, they would buy a place on Jupiter Island, Florida.

During these visits to Kennebunkport, George spent considerable time with his Uncle Herby, and they talked often about the oil business. Not that Herby knew that much about it. But as an investor and a man with a good financial mind, he wanted to know about George's plans. He also had a zillion ideas about how the business might be better run. George took his advice in stride.

"There wasn't a damn thing to do out there in Midland except make friends," recalled Hugh Liedtke. Across the street from Bush-Overbey was a small law office run by two fresh-faced boys from Tulsa, Oklahoma, Hugh and Bill Liedtke. Sons of the chief counsel of Gulf Oil, they had headed east to Amherst College before entering the University of Texas Law School. It was only a matter of time before the Liedtkes and George Bush met.

Trading land leases was fine, they told George. But drilling for oil was the way to make big money. Just like the California gold rush, when the suppliers selling all those prospectors supplies had made a killing, a good drilling company could be busy for a long time.

By early 1953, discussions with the Liedtkes led to a new partnership. Bush and Overbey raised half the capital for the new company, which they named Zapata Petroleum, after the Brando film *Viva Zapata* playing in downtown Midland. They were now bona fide oilmen.

They began in early March, drilling a patch of sandy prairie land in nearby Coke County that was too inhospitable for just about any other use. Hugh Liedtke was convinced he could find oil deep below the crusted surface of the earth there. Liedtke, later called the "boy genius of West Texas oil," proved to be right. They drilled six wells there and found a rich deposit in each case. A year and a half later they had drilled seventy-one wells, producing an average of 1,250 total barrels of oil per day. They never struck a dry hole. In all, this first field eventually sprouted 130 wells that produced handsomely for the company.

As always, these were busy times for George, and it was Barbara who maintained the home, keeping the family happy as her husband threw everything into his work. On weekends, when George had the time, they often spent it at the First Presbyterian Church. The church taught a brand of Christian piety that must have reminded them of New England. "Presbyterians are determined people," reads the church's official history. "Hardships and discouragements do not stop them. Because of their nature, they often turn stumbling blocks into stepping stones. The history of the Midland Presbyterian Church is splendid evidence of that traditional spirit and experience." George and Barbara taught a Sunday school class, leading discussions about Proverbs and the Gospel of John. After services, they would gather in a nearby field to play a game of touch football. George was quarterback.

In early 1953, Barbara gave birth to their third child, a large boy they named John Ellis Bush, or Jeb. (George's sister Nancy had married Boston businessman "Sandy" Ellis, hence the name Ellis.) Jeb joined a precocious brother, Little George, who was already at age seven growing comfortable in the ways of West Texas. Little George was enrolled at Sam Houston Elementary School and he simply lived in the cowboy clothes that his mother had bought for him in a shop downtown. Little George was picking up the local language, too, but to Bar's disdain. One day he stood in the house and blurted out something about a "nigger." Bar grabbed him and washed his mouth out with soap.

Little Robin with her graceful curls and sunny smile seemed to be thriving, too. That is until one morning in early 1953, when she woke up listless and pale. Barbara looked her over and noticed that she had some bruises on her body that didn't seem to go away. George had already left for work. Zapata was just being formed and he was putting in long hours as they attempted to drill the first wells in the Jameson Field.

Barbara loaded up her daughter's frail body and took her to the pediatrician. The doctor ran a few blood tests and then asked Barbara to return that afternoon with George. When they arrived late that afternoon, the doctor sat the two down and made a stunning announcement. Little Robin had advanced leukemia; she had only a few weeks to live.

Bar sat silently and George announced his refusal to believe that the case was terminal. He went home and immediately called his uncle, Dr. John Walker, back east. Gampy Walker's second son was a brilliant surgeon whose career had been cut short by polio. But his immense knowledge and gift for medicine had led to his appointment as president of Sloan-Kettering Memorial Hospital in New York. In a long conversation, Uncle John urged George and Barbara to let the Kettering specialists examine little Robin immediately.

George dropped everything and the family flew her to New York. After extensive testing, John advised that they use new cancer drugs to treat little Robin.

The treatment would be painful. Robin underwent difficult bone marrow tests and blood transfusions. At times the little girl would cry out, tired of the prodding and testing. For George, who had seen the horrors of war and the face of death up close in the Pacific, nothing could compare to this. He simply couldn't watch. As George later wrote to a friend, "Someone had to look into Robin's eyes and give her comfort and love and somehow I didn't have the guts."

As such things so often did, the difficult task fell to Barbara. They moved into Aunt Nancy's apartment on Sutton Place in New York so Barbara could be near the hospital. And she laid down a stern rule with iron steadiness: There would be absolutely, positively no crying in front of Robin.

It was for Bar the most painful thing imaginable. She stayed with her daughter constantly, playing games with her, reading to her, laughing, tickling, and combing her blond hair. When Robin was tired and wanted to sleep, Barbara would lie down next to her. When she was in pain, she held her, knowing there wasn't a thing she could do about it. But Barbara never wavered. During the entire seven-month ordeal, no one in the family ever saw her cry.

While Barbara was caring for Robin in New York, George was back in Midland looking after Little George and Jebbie. Little Georgie, always so curious, was popping off questions: Where's mom? Where is Robin? Early on, George and Barbara had made a critical decision about how to handle the news with Little George. He was seven years old. Feeling that he was incapable of handling the news and hoping for a recovery, they shielded him from the realities of what Robin was going through. Robin was sick, they told him, but it was really nothing to worry about.

At first the treatments seemed to stabilize the situation, and Bar returned to Midland with her little daughter. But as the weeks passed by and Robin became increasingly frail, the family braced itself for the worst. Bar and Robin returned to New York, and George would join her every weekend, leaving the boys with the Liedtkes. Dottie and Pres watched from Greenwich. Dottie, worried about Little George and Jebbie, dispatched a nurse to Texas to care for them. Pres, stoic and reserved, tried as best he could to share his affections. As death approached, he called on Barbara and asked her to come to Greenwich. He took her to a cemetery to pick out a grave site where all the family would be buried. Together, they identified a spot for Robin, under a shady tree, and he planted a small bush there as a marker.

"We saw a lot of her the last months of her life because she was staying at mother and dad's house and we were living in Greenwich," Pres, Jr. said. "It was so painful, a terrible blow. You could see her getting weaker and weaker—literally dying in front of you. And there was not a thing anyone could do."

George, for the first time, was feeling completely powerless.

By early October even Dr. John Walker was losing hope. Robin was very weak, everyone could see that. X rays were showing that the cancer drugs were eating holes in Robin's stomach, causing internal bleeding. The doctors wanted to operate, convinced they might stop the bleeding, but the prospects were not very good. Her tiny, delicate frame could take only so much. It was a Friday and George was on his way by airplane from Texas to New York; Bar had to make the decision by herself.

"You don't have to do it," John Walker told her. But they had gone this far and everyone was trying so hard to save Robin's life. She gave them the go-ahead.

They went into surgery and George arrived at the hospital. Robin never came out. She died on the operating table, two months short of her fourth birthday.

Throughout the ordeal it was Barbara who had been the emotionally strong one as George struggled to come to grips with the tragedy. He avoided seeing Robin in pain; Bar stayed and suppressed her own emotions. She pushed them so deep inside that her hair literally began turning gray. She was only twenty-eight.

When Robin was gone, Barbara fell to pieces. It had been half a year of pain and struggle. She could now let it go.

She collapsed with exhaustion and fell into a deep depression. George was by her side, attending to all of the grim details. They elected not to bury Robin in the spot under the shady tree where Pres had planted a small bush. Instead they donated Robin's body to the hospital, so that the doctors could perhaps discover more about the grisly disease that had taken their daughter. The next morning, George went to the hospital and personally thanked everyone who had cared for Robin—the doctors, nurses, even the orderlies.

To help Barbara, George put her on the same plan that he was on—keep busy and hope the grief drifts away. They held a large memorial service with dozens of family members and friends. And when they arrived back in Midland, George took Bar directly from the airport to see friends rather than going straight home. Too many memories remained there.

Robin's death marked the most painful experience in the family's life. And it revealed that the emotional currents of the family ran strongest not with George, but with Bar. They would keep a portrait of little Robin in their living room. But while Barbara might have wanted to talk about it with her husband, for forty years he couldn't. "For forty years I wasn't able to [talk about it]," George H. W. Bush said. "I was too weak to, I guess. Barbara could."

The most difficult task awaiting them in Midland was explaining to Little George why his sister wasn't coming home. The fact was, Little George didn't have a clue about what was going on. When they arrived that afternoon to pick him up from Sam Houston Elementary, he was carrying a phonograph back to the principal's office. When he saw his parents, Little George set the record player down and ran toward them. Eager to welcome everyone home, he noticed that Robin was missing. Bar broke the news to him; Little George was shattered.

While it was difficult for Bar and nearly impossible for George to talk about Robin, Little George had a thousand questions. Was she in heaven? Will she be the same size in heaven? Was she buried standing up or in a prone position? Because the earth rotates, they said so at school, and . . . does that mean that Robin is standing on her head? Bar did her best to answer. But the news still hadn't sunk in. Months after her death, while the family was at a football game, Little George said he wished he were Robin. Bar looked over at him, stunned. "Why?"

"Because she can probably see better from up there than we can from down here," he replied.

As he stopped asking his parents clumsy seven-year-old questions, the news slowly sunk in. His Uncle Bucky recalls taking his young nephew to a baseball game at Yankee Stadium in New York after she died. "You could tell it was taking a toll on him," Bucky said. "He wasn't weepy or anything like that, but you could see the pain in him. I guess we didn't appreciate at that time that he was having an adult reaction to her death, even though he was so young."

Barbara responded to the tragedy and Little George's questions by trying to desperately overcompensate with her sons. She had been gone so much over the past half year that she had seen very little of them. She began spending most of the time with Little George and became known as Little League Mom, attending every game that he played in. "Mother's reaction was to envelop herself totally around me," George W. Bush later recalled. "She kind of smothered me and then recognized that it was the wrong thing to do."

Like his mother, Little George kept up a strong front when he was melting inside. Seeing that his mother was suffering, he tried as best he could to carry the burden for her. Once, when a friend came to the door, Little George told him he couldn't play. He needed to stay home and play with his mother, who was lonely. Barbara recalled, "I was thinking, 'Well, I'm being there for him.' But the truth was, he was being there for me."

Little George, who had always been rambunctious, now suddenly became the family cutup, trying to bring his parents back to that happy place they had been in before Robin died. Elsie Walker, who had earlier lost a sister to polio, had the same sort of response to her family's suffering. "He and I both saw our parents suffer enormously when we were very vulnerable," she recalled. "We both became clowns trying to lift them out of their depression." (Elsie once told Bar that this common experience explained why she was so close to George W. "Don't be so psycho-analytical," Bar responded.)

But clowning was more than an attempt to distract. It was the only response possible in a family that prided itself on strength and shunned any expression of vulnerability or weakness. "There is a real emphasis on being and staying positive—almost to a fault, you are not to complain," Elsie said. "And you are not to draw attention to yourself. These are very strict rules. It's all fine when life is good and well but when things go wrong and you are full of complaints, you don't feel you can say anything. It's a bit of the 'stiff upper lip,' a little bit of Midwestern stoicism, and a little bit of machoism thrown together. It's a lethal combination."

The grief that George and Barbara felt about Robin never really went away. In 1957, his brother Bucky Bush and friend Fay Vincent drove the new car that George had ordered from New York down to Midland. By now George was a rich man, one of the first independents in Midland worth more than a million dollars. They were living in a new house that had a swimming pool and twice as much room as before. Little George was playing Little League and Jebbie had been joined by younger brothers Neil and Marvin. The house was a frenzy of activity, and George was busy with work. But Vincent recalls that the loss of Robin still hung over the house like a heavy rain cloud. "You could tell they were struggling with it," he recalled. "They talked about it just a little bit—like they didn't want to burden anyone with it. But you could just tell they were still in pain."

#### CHAPTER 8

# POLITICS

WHEN GEORGE LEFT YALE IN 1948, HE LEFT BEHIND A FATHER who seemed every bit as restless as his son. Pres Bush had enjoyed a bounty of financial success on Wall Street. Brown Brothers Harriman was expanding and profit margins were at record levels. The dog days of the Depression and war years were gone. If he had been comfortable before, he was now, at age fifty-three, becoming comfortably rich. That might have been enough for most men; but Pres Bush never saw money as an end in itself.

Many of Pres's friends and colleagues had already made the jump from Wall Street into public service. James Forrestal, who had been president of Dillon Reed, became the first secretary of defense. Averell Harriman had served in the Roosevelt administration and was now advising Truman. Bob Lovett, another Brown Brothers partner, was helping to forge American defense policy. John Foster Dulles and his brother Allen, friends and lawyers who did work for BBH, were spending considerable time in Washington. Allen was the first head of the CIA; Foster would soon become Eisenhower's first secretary of state. To the wise men of Wall Street, the new badge of merit was public service.

Pres had served on the Greenwich Representative Town Association and on the board of his beloved Yale. He had been active in the Republican Party for more than a decade now, serving as finance chairman for the state party in 1948 and as a delegate to the 1948 Republican National Convention. But clearly this was not enough.

Moreover, unlike so many of his Wall Street friends, he was less interested in an appointed position than in an electoral office.

The idea had first been raised in 1946 when Bill Brennan of the Fairfield County Republican Party approached him to run for Congress in the state's Fourth District. The seat was being vacated by Clare Boothe Luce—the correspondent turned politician—who was leaving for California and a new career in the entertainment business.

When Brennan suggested that he run for her seat, Pres was instantly intrigued.

"Let me talk to my partners about it," he told Brennan. Pres took the idea into the Partners' Room and talked it over with his close friend Roland Harriman. Bunny was less than enthusiastic.

"Look, if this was the Senate we'd back you for it and we'd like to see you do it, but for the House, don't do it," he advised Pres. "We need you more here than the House needs you."

When he mentioned the idea to Dottie, he got the same response. She was clearly enjoying her life in Greenwich. She had helped form a children's shelter and was active in the Greenwich chapter of the American Red Cross. She had joined the Garden Club and played on the Greenwich Field Club tennis team, which played weekend matches against teams from Connecticut, New York, and New Jersey. At the Greenwich Country Day School she was captain of the "mothers' team," a group of ladies who played against their sons in a sunken field behind the school.

Pres was also worried about finances. A man should run for public office only if his family is financially secure, he had repeated over the years. He still had Bucky and Johnny in school and was paying tuition for Nancy at Vassar. There was also the added burden of his two young nieces. During the war, his brother James had fought bravely in Burma and China. But he had come back a changed man. By 1946 he had left his wife and children. For Pres it was the ultimate betrayal. Family was not so much about blood; it was about commitment. "The instant it happened," recalls Shellie Bush Jansing, James's daughter, "Pres and Dottie were on a plane to St. Louis. He told us, 'You are still family. Let me know whatever you need.' Both he and Dottie basically adopted us."

So he decided to balk at running. As he later recalled, "At that time I was not financially independent enough to be comfortable about my family's future . . . I just didn't feel I could afford it, without very considerable sacrifice by others."

Three years later, in the summer of 1949, the subject came up again when Pres sat down with Harold Mitchell of the Connecticut Republican Central Committee to discuss a run for the U.S. Senate, where the incumbent was retiring. Mitchell was an old friend, a former member of the State House and state chairman in 1945. The two had spent time in the political trenches, raising money, screening local candidates, pushing the Republican agenda in Greenwich. They had also attended the Republican National Convention the previous summer. In the 1948 presidential race, Pres had been an early supporter of Sen. Robert Taft of Ohio. The Tafts and the Bushes were longtime family friends from Ohio. Bob Taft was also a member of Bones. But Pres was a reluctant supporter of the senator. Taft's brand of Midwest conservatism was not the future of the party, in Pres's mind. Mitchell shared his view. Did Pres want to give a run for the Senate a shot?

At first Pres didn't take the idea very seriously. Running for Congress in Greenwich was one thing; statewide office was another. Greenwich, a commuter town, wasn't considered a real Connecticut town by many state residents. On top of that, Pres was an international banker. Local politicians such as Jasper McLevy, the openly socialist mayor of Bridgeport, would have a field day with that one.

But as he mulled the idea over, it began to intrigue him. The race was for an open seat, which would give him a fighting chance. And with all that he had done for the GOP, he could count on a good base of support and plenty of money.

He took the idea to Dottie to see what she thought of it. Her short answer was, "Not much." But Pres and Dottie's marriage had been well oiled by plenty of deference and love that helped the machinery run smoothly. Pres would ask Dottie what she thought because he generally wanted and needed her input. And Dottie would respond in a way that always seemed to leave little doubt that she was putting his needs first. "Mom was definitely not enthusiastic about getting into politics," Pres Bush, Jr. recalls. "She didn't like politics per se. But she knew it was important for dad."

In the weeks following his meeting with Mitchell, Pres began crisscrossing the state by car with his son Pressy behind the wheel. He met with local party committees, social clubs, and business groups. When he wasn't on the road, he was at home in planning sessions. "A bunch of guys would show up in Chevys and Cadillacs and they would all go into dad's library and talk politics," Bucky Bush recalled for us. "Mom was a patient woman. There was *always* someone there."

As things started to fall into place, Pres suddenly heard that his friend and fellow Bonesman from Yale, Henry Luce, was thinking about running for the same seat. Clare was now out of Congress, and the publishing magnate was living in Litchfield.

Henry Luce had been intrigued with the idea of going into politics for quite some time. Pres had known him for decades and they were friendly, but not particularly close. A large divide separated them, as they were very different men with distinct temperaments.

As he had learned in Bones, matters between gentlemen were best resolved in private. So Pres called him up and the two men sat down with state party chairman Cappy Baldwin to discuss the matter. Cappy laid out to Luce what the Senate race would entail: traveling to small towns, dropping in at schools, kissing babies, shaking a lot of hands, and smiling all the time. He would have to stop spending so much time in New York City and more time in Connecticut, boning up on issues that mattered to ordinary voters. As Baldwin continued, Luce raised his hand. Maybe running wouldn't be such a good idea after all. He decided to write a check to Pres's campaign instead.

In April 1950, Pres made a public announcement that he would seek the nomination for the U.S. Senate. The only real opposition came from Vivian Kellems. A petite woman with delicate features, Kellems was a fiery business leader and tax protester who had a small but enthusiastic base. In 1948 she had refused to collect income taxes from her one hundred employees. Withholding estimated taxes from their paychecks was not her job, she said; it was the government's. The federal government disagreed and seized eight thousand dollars from her bank account, which further secured her populist reputation as an enemy of the IRS. Pres Bush, she told her supporters, was part of the elite that was betraying the country's ideals. He was an international banker and a Yale guy, making him even more suspect.

Back in the days when he had served in local government, he had railed to his children about "those jackasses" who couldn't have a civil argument about anything. Now his discomfort was compounded by the fact that he was being attacked by a woman. Pres had grown up in a man's world—a gentleman's world. You didn't publicly criticize a woman the way you would a man. (Privately he was less restrained, however, calling Kellems "a wicked little woman.") Instead of verbal fisticuffs, Pres and Pressy figured the best way to deal with her was to ignore her. So they began the Bush Campaign Train to attract voters.

When his campaign pulled into a small Connecticut town, a campaign truck would pull off the side of the road and unload some bicycles. Pres would stand in the bed of the truck and "a bunch of beautiful ladies would ride those bicycles into town," he recalled. "With the music blaring and campaign signs on the truck, we attracted a lot of attention." And they would strike up the recorded music—maybe a quartet of former Yale Whiffenpoofs, or the Brooklyn Dodgers symphony band. The shortest part of the event was his speech.

The rest of the family threw their hearts into the race. Dottie and daughter Nancy held teas with Republican ladies from across the state. Bert and Herby Walker helped raise money from friends on Wall Street and their

Connecticut neighbors. Pressy, Johnny, and Bucky worked the polls and passed out campaign material. The only member of the family who did not work for the campaign was George, who was still trying to run his new business in Texas.

Campaign contributions were not a problem. Pres tapped rich veins of money from his BBH partners and friends in finance. He also contacted friends he had met while serving on corporate boards. Neil Mallon cut him a check and so did William Paley. Cornelius Vanderbilt Whitney, chairman of the board at Pan American Airways, even held a fund-raiser.

With little effort he managed to dispatch Vivian Kellems at the state party convention. That fall he faced the Democratic nominee, William Benton, an advertising executive who had served as assistant secretary of state from 1945 to 1947. Benton tried to mold himself as the Connecticut incarnation of President Harry Truman—tough, honest, and down-to-earth.

It was a tight race as the two candidates debated the merits of Harry Truman and how to end the war in Korea. Pres ran as a strict conservative, opposing "socialized medicine" while favoring cuts in domestic spending. He also railed against "confiscatory taxes" and favored limiting the power of trade unions. Labor laws should "protect the rights of union members and the public," he said, not "labor bosses." In short, the issues of the campaign were in his words, "Korea, communism, confusion, and corruption." As election day approached, the Bush-Benton race was running close with most observers giving Pres a slight edge. It all seemed to be working out until two days before election day. Then a bombshell exploded.

That Sunday morning, thousands of cryptic flyers appeared in Catholic church pews of Waterbury, Torrington, and Bridgeport. "Listen to Walter Winchell's radio broadcast tonight at six," they read. Winchell was a famous New York columnist; his column was published in newspapers all over the United States. He also had a weekly radio program that was popular in Connecticut, and a reputation for being aggressive.

That night, thousands in Connecticut tuned in when Winchell came on the air. In a monotone voice, the columnist announced his prediction that Benton would win the Connecticut Senate race "because it has just been made known that Prescott Bush, his opponent, is president of the Birth Control League in this country, and of course with Connecticut's heavy Catholic population and its laws against birth control, this is going to be too much for Bush to rise above." Moments after he uttered those words, the phone began to ring at the Bush home. Dottie would pick it up a dozen times that night.

"Mrs. Bush, have you heard the broadcast? Is it true?"

"No," Dottie responded again and again. "It is not true. He's never been on the Birth Control League at all."

With only forty-eight hours until the polls closed, Pres scrambled and tried to set the record straight. But the damage was done. Two days later he lost the election by a mere 1,000 votes out of 862,000 cast.

The fact that Winchell had so recklessly intervened in the race without even contacting Pres's campaign to see whether his report was accurate infuriated Bush and darkened the family's views about the media. They can attack and we can't respond, said Pres. It created a sense of helplessness. "No doubt about it," Pres Bush, Jr. said. "It left a bitter taste in all our mouths."

In the months following his narrow loss, Pres returned as an active partner with Brown Brothers Harriman. But he was not about to swear off politics entirely. In 1950 the Republican Party had fared poorly across the country, and Pres was convinced that the GOP needed to change. Word was out that in 1952, Pres's good friend and fellow Yale trustee Sen. Robert Taft of Ohio was going to make yet another run for president. Pres believed that if he won the nomination, the results would be disastrous for Republicans in 1952. "Dad admired Bob Taft to the day he died," Bucky Bush told us. "But he felt he didn't have the personality to win."

So in November 1951, while on business in London, Pres called his friend Charles Spofford, who was chairman of the NATO Council of Deputies. Spofford was serving on the Council on Foreign Relations staff when he had met Pres Bush years earlier, and the two had become friends. Now Pres wanted a favor.

Concerned about the fate of the GOP, Pres wanted a meeting with Gen. Dwight David Eisenhower. Pres had joined the clamor of Republicans who believed that the war hero, then based in London and commander of NATO forces in Europe, could be the savior of the GOP. Ike agreed to the meeting, and the two sat down in his London office for a lengthy conversation. They chatted first about golf, a love they shared. Then Pres asked him about his future. Did he want to run for president? Ike didn't answer directly and wouldn't commit.

"General, there's been some question as to whether your sympathies really are with the Republicans or the Democrats," he asked him pointedly.

"Well," Ike told him, "there shouldn't be any question. I've always been a Republican and I am a Republican."

As the conversation came to a close, Pres offered to be helpful. If he ever did decide to run and needed help raising money, Pres would be glad to help. Eisenhower politely thanked him but said no more.

A few months after Pres returned home, Bob Taft came by to pay him a visit. The two had a long association together—Yale, Bones, the Yale board—and Pres's father had known the Tafts for who knows how long. Taft explained that he was going to make one last bid for the White House in '52 and wanted his help. Pres listened politely as Taft laid out his plans. When he was finished, Pres told him about his conversation with Ike. The future of the Republican Party was in London, not Ohio, Pres told him. Taft said he understood and the two departed friends.

In the spring of 1952, Pres was looking for a chance at redemption. Ike had decided to join the presidential derby, and Pres was excited about his chances. In Connecticut, Senator Benton was up for reelection after only two years because he was completing Raymond Baldwin's unexpired term. Pres wanted another crack at Benton. He campaigned hard that spring for the Republican nomination, mimicking the strategy he had used in 1950. This time, however, he faced a strong challenge from William Purtell, a West Hartford businessman and former president of the Connecticut Manufacturers Association. Purtell was no Vivian Kellems. In many respects he had better ties to the Connecticut business community than Pres did. At the Republican nominating convention that summer, Purtell won relatively easily. Pres figured his life in elective politics was over.

But one month later the situation had changed. In mid-July, the state's senior senator, Democrat Brien McMahon, died suddenly. A special election was called. Now there would be two U.S. Senate races in Connecticut.

Pres had an inherent advantage given that the machinery from his nomination push only one month earlier was still in place. But before his second campaign began, Gov. John Lodge, a Republican, would have to appoint an interim senator to fill the remaining few months of McMahon's term. Governor Lodge was the grandson of Henry Cabot Lodge. Like the Tafts, the Lodges were longtime family friends of the Bushes. But before the governor could even seriously consider the matter, Clare Boothe Luce suddenly reemerged. Having left Connecticut for California a few years earlier to write movie scripts, Clare had heard of McMahon's death and called Lodge herself. She wanted the interim appointment and, as a former congresswoman from Connecticut, could make a strong claim to it.

Lodge was stuck in the middle. To avoid offending anyone, he chose William Purtell, who had just won the Republican nomination for Senate seat #1, to serve as interim holder of seat #2. If Pres and Clare Luce both wanted a seat in the Senate, they would have to fight it out in a special primary.

While Pres had always been relatively close to Henry Luce, his relations with Clare were somewhat strained. The divisions had been apparent in the early dinners the Bushes and the Luces had together in Connecticut. Clare lived her life with flair and verve. Pres saw some of that as pretense. Then there was her blunt manner. "Clare—I've always been a little frightened of her," he would admit later, "because I don't deal easily with women who are severe or terribly determined. I've always been afraid of women who are pithy and sharp and sarcastic."

In the run-up to the State Republican Party Convention on September 5, Clare Luce began running newspaper ads and radio and television broadcasts to push her candidacy. She also declared that "the fix is in" for Pres Bush, that the party establishment was secretly backing his candidacy despite its promises of an "open and free process." Pres responded with broadcasts of his own, buying time on Channel 8 television. Unlike in 1950, he spoke little about the issues. Instead, he listed his qualifications while his grown children Johnny, Bucky, and Nancy sang in the background.

In Hartford, Clare set up a lavish hospitality suite at a nearby hotel and entertained hundreds of delegates. They feasted on prime rib and lobster and sipped champagne. In the end, though, she could muster only 50 delegates while Pres piled up 412. Clare Luce was extremely disappointed but gracious. Perhaps she felt that a divisive fight would doom her political future.

"I stand before you as a defeated candidate," she told the convention from the podium. "But no battle is worth fighting that is not worth losing. Defeat is the mother of victory." She then came over to Pres and shook his hand and whispered some advice in his ear. Based on her years in Congress, she had learned that "there are three things to remember. Claim everything. Explain nothing. Deny everything."

The day following the Republican convention, Democrats gathered to pick their nominee: Abraham Ribicoff, a plain-talking congressman and former assistant secretary of state to Harry Truman. The choice of Ribicoff was no great surprise, but what stunned Pres were the people on the podium with him. Smiling and waving to the crowd were none other than Pres's business partners, Averell Harriman and Bob Lovett.

Harriman and Lovett had always been active and loyal Democrats, just as Bunny Harriman and Pres had been GOP. But the club atmosphere at the firm had always prevented personal attacks; it was just not done. Pres had always been quiet in public about Harriman's service to FDR and Truman and had applauded Lovett's service to Truman. But now Averell stepped to the podium and threw down the gauntlet.

While Bob Lovett had kept his remarks focused on Ribicoff's merits, Averell gave a ringing speech decrying the need to defeat Pres Bush. Friendship apparently had its limits; politics ranked higher for Harriman. It was a supreme act of betrayal, and few things mattered more to Pres than loyalty.

A few days later, Pres returned fire in a speech at a Republican Party dinner. It was an angry Pres Bush, something no one had seen publicly before.

"At the Democrat state convention which nominated Ribicoff, Harriman made a speech calling for my defeat. Why did he do that? The answer, of course, is that he has become a captive of the extreme left wing of the Democrat Party, which I have constantly attacked. Harriman, of course, applauded Ribicoff's nomination, which is all the evidence needed to show that they both represent the extreme left-wingers who have taken control of the Democrat Party away from the true old-line Democrats. So it is Abraham Ribicoff and Averell Harriman who are partners—in politics, that is. When did either of them speak out against the corruption of the Truman administration? When did either of them protest against its soft attitude toward Communism? When did either raise his voice against the reckless policy that landed us in the Soviet trap in Korea?"

Averell Harriman's opening salvo and the war of words that followed soured relations between the two men. It would be a long time before their friendship would recover.

The campaign began in earnest, and Pres staked out positions on the war in Korea and the international situation. He also linked himself with Ike, who was running well ahead in the polls. But as the election date approached, he worried about a replay of 1950. Sensitive to the fact that he was a Protestant in a mostly Catholic state, he sat down with his Irish Catholic campaign manager, Elmer Ryan, to discuss the matter.

"Elmer, do you think that my being a Protestant and not a Catholic is apt to affect me in this 1952 election?"

"Oh no, Pres, don't worry about that," Ryan told him. "We just look upon a Protestant as a Catholic who flunked his Latin."

Religion did not play a direct role in the campaign, but it was a factor, particularly as it related to passions about Sen. Joe McCarthy. An October 1952 Gallup Poll showed that fully 52 percent of the American public approved of McCarthy while only about 38 percent disapproved. The numbers in Connecticut were probably even more favorable to McCarthy. The Wisconsin senator was extremely popular in Connecticut and made regular trips to the state throughout the fall, giving speeches and raising money for his anticommunist campaign.

In early October, McCarthy came to Bridgeport to speak before several thousand political activists. While not a Republican Party event per se, most party leaders were going to be there, and Pres was encouraged to show up and at least welcome the senator to the state.

Pres was uncomfortable with McCarthy and his tactics, but he heeded the advice of party leaders and put in an appearance. As he later recalled, "I went out on the stage with my knees shaking considerably to this podium, and I said that I was very glad to welcome a Republican senator to our state, and that we had many reasons to admire Joe McCarthy. 'In some ways he was a very unusual man' [I said]. At least he had done one very unusual thing—he had created a new word in the English language, which is 'McCarthyism.' With that everybody screamed with delight. I said, 'But I must in all candor say that some of us, while we admire his objectives in his fight against Communism, we have very considerable reservations sometimes concerning the methods which he employs.' "

The roof went off of the place with boos, hisses, and screams of "Throw him out!" Pres said a few more inaudible sentences and then, sensing that the crowd wouldn't settle down, returned to his chair on the stage. The catcalls continued, and then Joe McCarthy stood up. Dressed in a dark tie and gray suit, his hair gently brushed across his head, he walked over to Pres before he went to the podium.

"Pres, I want you to have dinner with me after this show's over," he said, offering his hand. "I want you to have dinner with me, I want to talk with you."

After the rally, the two men went to a local restaurant and sat in a corner booth with Cappy Baldwin, the state party chairman, and Elmer Ryan. They chatted mostly about politics and the upcoming election. When they talked about communism, they found common ground: The threat was real. But they parted ways in how to root it out. The dinner was cordial and they agreed to disagree. Before it ended, McCarthy offered to help Pres's campaign.

"Do you need any money?" Joe asked.

"Well, a candidate usually needs money, but we're in pretty good shape up here."

"Would you like me to send you five thousand dollars?"

"Well, Senator, let me think about that," Pres responded, dodging the offer. "I think perhaps there are other candidates that need it more than I do. We're really in pretty good shape, as far as our campaign finances are concerned."

McCarthy grinned, understanding Pres's discomfort. "Pres, you're a real gentleman and I'd like to help you. I can either come into the state and speak for you or speak against you . . . Which would help you the most?"

Everyone at the table laughed. "Well, thanks Joe," Pres told him. "But maybe it would be best just not to come, and we'll see each other down in Washington."

In the final weeks of the campaign, Pres hammered away on defense and national security issues. With a stalemate on the Korean Peninsula and American losses mounting, he proposed winning the war by "unleashing" Taiwan's army. He also declared that only by electing Ike and other Republicans would America's security needs be met.

On November 4, Pres and the family gathered at the Bush house as voting began. That evening they went to an election party to await the results. Ribicoff won big in Hartford, which was to be expected. But Pres carried the traditionally Republican small towns in an election that became a near clean sweep for Republicans across the state. Pres won by more than 37,000 votes, and the GOP captured control of the state legislature and the governor's mansion while winning every congressional seat except one. Eisenhower, who won the state by nearly 130,000 votes, proved to have very long coattails.

After all the struggle and intrigue, all the internal party machinations, Pres Bush was finally going to the Senate. Nancy Bush Ellis remembers seeing her father all "aglow" that night. This was certainly his greatest triumph, and it mattered more to him than any business deal he had ever put together.

William Purtell had won the other Connecticut Senate seat that same night. But since Pres had won a seat left vacant by the death of Senator McMahon, he would go to Washington immediately. Purtell would not be sworn in until January. Thus in an instant, Pres Bush became the senior senator from Connecticut.

CHAPTER 9

# CAPITAL CITY

AYS AFTER THE ELECTION, PRES AND DOTTIE ARRIVED IN WASH-
ington and checked into a hotel. Then Pres headed for Capitol
Hill. Dottie began the search for a new home, and settled on an
elegant brick townhouse on Volta Street in Georgetown.

Small, but big enough for entertaining, the house had enough help to
make sure that everything was just so, with one lady cooking in the kitchen
and another passing the food. It wasn't long before the gregarious Dottie had
the place filled up all the time. She invited senators and their wives for
drinks on first sight or had neighbors over for games of tiddlywinks, and
within weeks she was firmly embedded in the social life of Washington. The
Bushes would dine with the Fulbrights, the Dulleses, and even the
Kennedys. Perle Mesta, the legendary Washington socialite, would have
them over sometimes for one of her extravaganzas.

Even though Pres Bush was new to the Senate, he was a well-connected
freshman as his friends and business associates took up senior positions in the
new Eisenhower administration. His old friend Allen Dulles was the new CIA
director, and John Foster Dulles was to become secretary of state. Despite his
support for Ike, Pres was still close to Senate majority leader Robert Taft. So
when committee appointments came, Pres not only got a powerful assignment—the Public Works Committee—but another that was even more interesting: the secretive Joint Congressional Committee on Atomic Energy
(JCCAE). The Atomic Energy Committee, a powerful voice in drawing up
America's nuclear policy, dealt with everything from nuclear reactors to hy-
drogen bombs. But most of their work on military matters was classified. No
numbers were published on precisely how much money we were spending on
the nuclear weapons program. In fact, few people in Washington knew precisely what sorts of nuclear weapons were being developed. The committee
was also a hotbed of political tension. William L. Borden, the departing executive secretary of the committee, was absolutely convinced that Robert Op-
penheimer, head of the U.S. Atomic Energy Commission, was a Soviet agent.

Pres quickly assembled a staff. On advice from friends and colleagues, he selected Margaret Hampton, who had worked for Bob Taft, to serve as his chief of staff. She was responsible for hiring and firing subordinate staff, handling press relations, and being the liaison with organizations back in Connecticut. They worked hard together and she quickly became his most trusted adviser, laboring alongside him on Saturday mornings when most other Senate offices were closed. He would later call her "the most remarkable woman that I have ever come in contact with in business or professional life."

When Pres came into the Senate, the shadow of his dinner partner in Connecticut, Joe McCarthy, was hanging over the chamber. McCarthy, who had begun his campaign to root out communists by asking tough questions, had quickly descended into making wild accusations. He was attacking fellow senators, Gen. George Marshall, even Ike.

Pres had denounced McCarthy's tactics during the 1952 election and held firm to that position during his first year in the Senate. As McCarthy's attacks on Eisenhower, Marshall, and other senior government officials mounted, he became frustrated by the sideshow it was becoming. "He gloried in the press that he created," Pres said.

McCarthy was a demagogue, Pres had no doubt about that. But it was the media that gave demagogues fuel, supplied an audience, and fanned the flames. One night in late 1953, Jim Linen, president of *Time* magazine, came over to the Bush house in Georgetown for dinner. "Why don't you fellows do something about this Joe McCarthy down there?" Linen asked.

"Well, it's pretty hard, Jim, when *Time* magazine puts his picture on the cover, and gives four pages of the paper of such and such an issue, to tell everybody about Joe McCarthy. Why don't YOU do something about it?"

On the Senate floor, efforts were building to do something about McCarthy. A censure motion was pending; debate was intense, and the Connecticut delegation divided. Senator William Purtell, the other senator from Connecticut, rose from his chair and gave a ringing defense of McCarthy. With Dottie and Nancy watching from the gallery, Pres Bush rose moments later to become one of the first Republicans to denounce him.

Joe McCarthy had "caused dangerous divisions among the American people because of his attitude and the attitude he has encouraged among his followers: that there can be no honest differences of opinion with him. Either you must follow Senator McCarthy blindly, not daring to express any doubts or disagreements about any of his actions, or, in his eyes, you must be a communist, a communist sympathizer, or a fool who has been duped by the communist line." Bush then turned to face Sen. Arthur Watkins, chairman of the censure committee, who had been repeatedly savaged by McCarthy. "Mr. President, if I have ever met a brave and noble senator, Arthur Watkins is that man. And, Mr. President, I for one will not walk off and leave him standing in this chamber with a coward tag on him—not without protest."

It was a bristling speech, the first of several from other senators who had simply had enough of McCarthy. He was censured by a vote of 67–29. And while McCarthy continued his attacks against Eisenhower following the vote, for all intents and purposes he was a spent force politically.

The last time Pres Bush saw McCarthy was in the summer of 1957. McCarthy by then was isolated from official Washington and persona non grata among many in the power elite. He had fallen about as far as he could fall. Pres had gone to the Bethesda Naval Hospital for a physical exam and learned that McCarthy was on the same floor, on his deathbed. Pres went down the corridor to McCarthy's room, where a nurse was standing out front. "I'm Senator Bush of Connecticut. I wonder if I could see Senator McCarthy for a moment, just to wish him well?"

"Oh, no, Senator, he's much too ill for that," she told him. "He's much too ill to see anybody."

"Well, would you take a little note to him?"

The nurse agreed, and Pres scribbled him a note telling him he hoped he would recover soon. When Pres returned to his office, he found a telephone message dictated by McCarthy to his office. He thanked Bush "very warmly for coming to see me. I can't tell you how much I appreciate that." The next day McCarthy died.

AS A NEW MEMBER OF THE SENATE, PRES APPLIED THE LESSONS HE HAD learned as a young man at Yale and Brown Brothers Harriman: Forge relationships to succeed. In the spring of 1953, Pres helped organize what he called "a little club within a club" that included the sixteen new Republican senators. Every Wednesday, in the office of the secretary of the Senate, the club would lunch with some veteran member of the Senate or a cabinet officer. Sometimes his good friend Bob Taft, the Senate majority leader, would join them. Other times Secretary of State John Foster Dulles or Vice President Richard Nixon stopped in for a talk. These were closed-door meetings, strictly-off-the-record sessions, which created a certain intimacy among the club's members. Pres seemed to fit right in, maintaining friendships with everyone from Bob Taft to William Fulbright, Wilbur Mills, and John F. Kennedy. The notable exception was Margaret Chase Smith, the fiercely independent and sometimes acerbic Republican senator from Maine.

In the early months of his Senate career, Pres was asked by several Republican senators to organize a dinner in honor of President Eisenhower. Knowing that Ike liked to play golf, Pres made arrangements for a quiet dinner at the Burning Tree Country Club. The invitations went out, including one to the good senator from Maine. It seemed to be the perfect plan except for one small fact: No women were allowed at Burning Tree. When Pres realized his mistake, he tried to convince the board at Burning Tree to make an exception for Margaret Chase Smith; they steadfastly refused. Pres then went to the Senator and explained his predicament. She was furious.

Pres promptly changed the location and sent her a dozen roses, including a hand-scribbled note, "For the rest of my life I will apologize."

The senator was unmoved. "I'm not about to forgive you," she wrote back.

Outside the Senate chambers Pres enjoyed an active social life as a member of the capital's most exclusive private clubs. He joined the Alfalfa Club, which counted among its members the most prominent politicians in the country, and was immensely popular because of his quick wit. In 1959 he was selected to be the club's joke nominee for president, which required him to give a ribald acceptance speech. A recording of that speech reveals that his presentation was punctuated with howls of laughter. But the jokes are certainly off-limits by today's standards. "I hasten to mention an issue that I do not intend to overlook, namely, integration," he remarked in his baritone voice. "This issue we must face squarely. I frankly admit, friends, that my sympathies are with the Southerners. And the Northerners. Now, I propose that we settle the matter this way. Select a group of leaders from the NAACP, and another group selected by say Governor Faubus of Arkansas, and we shall lock them in their conference suite, and let nature take its course. For the convenience of the conferees and their families, I suggest a private suite at a funeral parlor."

Even more exclusive was the Alibi Club. Founded in 1884 and limited to only fifty members, Alibi was housed in a three-story, brick row house at 1806 I Street N.W.

During the Second World War, Gen. George C. Marshall would secretly meet with world leaders at the club to avoid any attention. Through the decades at least four CIA directors, four Supreme Court justices, three secretaries of state, three secretaries of war, and numerous military commanders have been members. One of the friends Pres made at Alibi was Gordon

Gray, the tall, young, dark-haired heir to the R. J. Reynolds tobacco fortune who was an adviser to President Eisenhower. Gray's son, C. Boyden Gray, would later serve as counselor to the president for George Bush.

The Alibi Club proved useful for conducting Senate business, particularly when it was sensitive. When Pres's good friend Eugene Black, president of the World Bank, wanted to set up a quiet meeting to discuss plans for expanding the bank's mission, Pres organized a dinner at the club. A dozen senators were quietly invited, including Fulbright, Bricker, Capehart, and Monroney. Thus began the Bush manner of conducting political business: quiet consultation with an emphasis on secrecy. Pres Bush's son and grandson would also handle their presidencies with a keen commitment to secrecy, more to ensure honesty than to conceal what was being done. Secrecy breeds candor and candor breeds wisdom; at least that is how the Bush family sees it.

If relationships were established and built in intimate clubs and private groups, they were solidified with a good game of golf. Pres Bush loved golf, and in Washington the fact that he was a scratch golfer had great currency with plenty of weekend duffers. The opportunity to play with a former president of the United States Golf Association was a real treat for President Eisenhower, who was a passionate if inconsistent player. Over the course of Ike's tenure in the White House, the two men would play dozens of rounds of golf together. Sherman Adams, the president's chief of staff, would call in the morning, Pres would meet Ike at Burning Tree around noon for lunch, and then they would play a round or two in the afternoon. Sometimes a foreign dignitary like Japanese prime minister Nobosuke Kishi would join them. But often they played alone.

Pres was shrewd enough to know that this was no time to discuss politics. "This was Ike's chance to get away from it all," he would later say. So instead they would chat about the game, the course, or some other unrelated subject. One thing Pres would not do, however, was compromise his game. After the first few games they played together in the winter and spring of 1953, Sherman Adams openly asked Pres whether he might go easy on the president. Pres just shook his head. "That would never do."

While he never extracted a hard favor from Ike on the golf course, he certainly gained plenty of soft favor that brought great admiration from Ike. By 1956, when Ike put together a list of possible successors, among those he put on the list were Pres Bush, to whom he gave an "A."

Vice President Richard Nixon also enjoyed the chance to hit a few balls with a bona fide pro. "I remember driving out to the club with him in his great big Cadillac," Pres Bush later recalled, "and we would talk, going out and coming in, and he was always very interesting." But for all the time they spent together, Pres never really felt close to Nixon. Mainly, he was troubled by what he saw as Nixon's lack of loyalty to Ike. During the height of McCarthy's attacks on the president, Pres had asked Nixon whether he would join in denouncing McCarthy. "He refused to do that," Pres later recalled.

He was also somewhat put off by Nixon's demeanor. "He's not much fun," he'd tell his children. "You wouldn't want to have him around in Kennebunkport sitting out in the sun laughing."

For the Bushes, a moment of personal triumph is also a family victory. And for Pres Bush, election to the United States Senate was not simply a career move; it was a stark shift in the journey of the entire family. His children remember how he changed while serving in Washington. "Dad just blossomed in Washington," recalls his daughter Nancy. "He loved the life. He loved being away from the financial pressures he had been under his whole professional life."

But Pres was also starting to think about his legacy. Having reached the pinnacle of power, getting the chance to serve in what he considered "the best job in the world," he was thinking not simply about the shadow he would cast but about the entire Bush clan. The changes happened suddenly. Bush had never been big on titles. Even the youngest workers at Brown Brothers had been able to call him "Pres." Now he asked his grandchildren and others in the family to start calling him "Senator." When members of the clan would arrive for a visit, Pres would try as best he could to relay to Little George, Jebbie, and the others the business of the Senate. Lud Ashley, George's good friend from Yale, had been elected to Congress from Ohio. "It's like a tree against a wall, where you know you can control where the limbs are going to go. He was consciously trying to transmit what you could do in public service to these little tiny kids."

The formality and serious demeanor of Pres Bush had a powerful effect on his grandchildren. Ashley remembers the "silent fear" that was evident on the face of Little George. But it was a fear of the awesomeness of this distant grandfather. "You can't underestimate the influence Senator Bush had on his grandchildren," Ashley told us. "To have a grandfather who is a U.S. senator is an impressive thing. And he was a tall man—six foot four—which added to his sense of grandeur. The boys had real reverence for the man. It was not the sort of warm grandfatherly type of relationship."

For other members of the family, visits to Washington were remembered as times of excitement. Bucky Bush remembers seeing his father talking and chatting with people he had read about in school or seen in the newspaper. Pressy recalls the sense of awe as he accompanied his father to the Capitol Building and realized that this was now where the old man was working. For daughter Nancy, attractive, charming and just out of Vassar, it was pure adventure. But Dottie was always there to make sure the brood was protected.

One morning she took her young daughter to the Senate balcony, which was reserved for wives, to watch a debate on the floor. Someone was giving a monotonous speech when suddenly a young senator named John F. Kennedy came bounding up the stairs to the balcony. Pres and Kennedy had worked together on several issues, and Pres had given a speech at Teddy Kennedy's University of Virginia Law School class at John's request.

"How are you, Nancy?" Kennedy asked with a warm smile, extending a hand.

"Fine, Senator," she responded.

Dottie smiled politely but was glad when the senator left. "Why did he come up and say hello?"

"Because he's polite, mother," Nancy said with a grin.

"Well, he doesn't come up and say hello like that to every woman in the world."

The rise to the Senate had other repercussions for the family. For the first time they were confronted with the competing claims of money and power. As a United States senator, Pres could do quite a bit to affect the fortunes of the family and all of those in it. Herby Walker recognized this early on, in a not-so-subtle way. Just months after Pres was appointed to the Joint Congressional Committee on Atomic Energy, he formed a partnership with several other investors to get into the commercial nuclear energy business. The enterprise received early encouragement from federal authorities but never turned into a viable company.

For son George, having a father in the Senate was both a blessing and a curse.

In early 1956 a bill was introduced to deregulate the natural gas industry. It was a revolutionary piece of legislation and Pres favored the bill's objectives, but he had reservations about its implementation, as did several other senators. Passage of the bill was not certain, and lots of money was at stake. Francis Case, a Republican from South Dakota, was even offered a direct bribe to support the bill.

With Pres Bush they tried a different tactic. As President Eisenhower recorded in his private diary, the president of one oil company had lunch with "two or three Republicans, among them Len Hall and Cliff Folger. At that luncheon, he announced in unequivocal terms that he had supported Senator Bush of Connecticut with funds for his first election, but because Senator Bush was trying to get the bill reasonably amended, the oilman announced that never again would he support such a fellow and referred to him in indecent language. He further stated that he had helped to see that the senator's son [George] had been deprived of a large volume of business. In what business the senator's son is, I don't know, but the blackmailing intent of the oilman was clearly evident."

George was indeed being pressured just as he was charging ahead with Zapata. He went to Washington to visit his father and described the threats that were being made against him. Some oil companies were threatening to run him out of business. "I think you ought to know these things," he told his father.

Pres listened to his son but was unyielding. "Don't you believe them," he told him. "They'll never put you out of business. They wouldn't dare, because this would be the worst possible mistake they could make. This will not affect you at all. I'm going to vote against the bill because on the whole I think that's in the best interest of my state, as well as the United States, to vote against this bill. But don't you worry about it, and if there's any after-effects from it, just tell me about them, and we'll take care of that."

George left for Texas understanding, but nonetheless disappointed. "What I did was the last thing my son wanted me to do," Pres would later say.

Pres worked with a broad range of senators during his tenure. Part of it was his affable personality. But it was also a testament to his political philosophy. Pres was a proud Republican, but he was what many at the time were calling a Modern Republican. Behind Modern Republicanism was a simple premise: After twenty years of Democratic control in Washington, the party of FDR and Harry Truman was the majority party. The only hope Republicans had of changing that was by promoting a mix of fiscal conservatism and social liberalism. As Eisenhower explained: "It is a type of political philosophy that recognizes clearly the responsibility of the federal government to take the lead in making certain that the productivity of our great economic machine is distributed so that no one will suffer disaster or privation through no fault of his own."

It proved to be a formula for political success in '52. Pres Bush had joined other GOP candidates such as Clifford Case of New Jersey and John Sherman Cooper of Kentucky to serve as standard-bearers for this new approach to Republican politics. As he explained in one speech, Modern Republicanism could be traced to the principles of Abraham Lincoln and Theodore

Roosevelt. Notably absent from the list were Republican presidents Harding and Coolidge. This was not an oversight on Bush's part. "Our philosophy recognizes that in this complex industrial civilization of modern times, the problems of government are more complicated and more comprehensive than they have ever been before." In short, Pres Bush was pragmatic, not ideological.

Pres's pragmatism was a reflection of both the political realities of the 1950s and his own temperament. In his twenty-five years at Brown Brothers Harriman, Pres had learned that forging a consensus required flexibility and an affable touch. The same had been true on the Greenwich town council, where things could quickly get out of hand without calm deliberation and some give-and-take.

Pres sought out opportunities to work with both Republicans and Democrats. As he bluntly put in on the CBS News program *Face the Nation*, his approach was to take "the best out of the traditional positions of the Democrat and Republican party, and put them together in what the president calls the moderate progressivism of our new Republican party . . ." He sponsored legislation in favor of desegregating schools, protecting voter rights, abolishing the poll tax, and establishing an equal employment commission. When it came to budgetary matters, however, Pres was a strict conservative. He opposed Medicare when it was first proposed, fearing that it could bust the budget, and sponsored legislation for a government-funded insurance program that could "pay its own way." He was firmly opposed to high taxes, arguing from common sense that when taxes went up there was less money for people to invest and save. When government services failed to perform, he favored encouraging private efforts to fill the gap.

In 1954, Catholic leaders from Connecticut came to see him concerning parochial schools. They argued that parochial schools, which were privately funded, were taking a burden off public schools because students were taken out of the system. Parochial schools were meeting student needs and therefore should have access to public funds in proportion to their enrollment. It was a fractious issue in Connecticut and other states, but Pres Bush introduced legislation calling for local funds to be used for private as well as public schools. It was the Bush family's first foray into what would later be called school vouchers and faith-based initiatives sponsored by the federal government.

Pres opposed government regulation of business and finance, resisting efforts to raise the minimum wage because it would throw people out of work. But he was also generally supportive of labor unions, provided they worked with business and not against it.

Pres's ability to swim in the sea of politics with several different schools of fish was attractive to President Eisenhower. And when that ability was wedded to the personal trust he had in him, it made Pres the natural candidate to help chart the new direction of the GOP. So at the president's suggestion, Pres was tapped to serve as the chairman of the Republican Party Platform Committee for the 1956 convention.

This campaign was largely going to be about Ike, whose personal popularity was immense. But this was also the party of conservative Barry Goldwater and Liberal Nelson Rockefeller, of Everett Dirksen and Jacob Javits. The party was split by deep divisions over many issues, including the size and role of government in the lives of people, and national defense. Only four years before, at the 1952 national convention, Sen. Everett Dirksen had instigated a major floor fight by attacking Eisenhower floor managers from the podium. No one wanted a replay of that event.

Pres Bush was given the responsibility of unifying Republicans around a platform that would outline several key principles. The goal was to hammer together guidelines that would offend few in the party while keeping all of its factions energized. Differences would be blurred, the language fuzzy.

One issue that Pres did not want to be lukewarm on, however, was civil rights. The example of his father, and his own involvement with organizations such as the United Negro College Fund, made him a strong advocate of federally supported civil rights legislation. After more than twenty years' commitment to the cause, he was not about to avoid the issue now. He called on Americans to elect "Eisenhower Republicans like myself who have been working for civil rights legislation and the removal of harsh and discriminatory provisions" of the immigration laws. He was particularly interested in having the party endorse the recent U.S. Supreme Court ruling against racial segregation.

In early August, Pres huddled with top Republicans in San Francisco's St. Francis Hotel to draft the platform. Working with him were Sherman Adams; William P. Rogers, the deputy attorney general; and Max Rabb, special White House assistant on minority problems. For the civil rights committee, Pres approved a list of witnesses that included A. Philip Randolph, president of the Brotherhood of Sleeping Car Porters. Randolph told the committee, "We believe in this and recommend the earliest possible implementation of the Supreme Court rulings and the prompt and forthright elimination of all forms of state-imposed segregation."

The platform committee endorsed the controversial civil rights plank and a platform that managed to keep the peace among the various party factions.

As he recalled years later, "I have always been a little bit pleased with the fact that we produced a plank in that platform dealing with labor which was immediately praised by Barry Goldwater, who sent a telegram congratulating our subcommittee on the draft of this language. And the next day we got a very nice letter from Nelson Rockefeller in which he fully endorsed the language we had put together."

With the convention behind him, Pres returned to Connecticut. Since he had won a seat in a special election filling out Brien McMahon's term, he was up for reelection in 1956. In one sense it was good news. He would be running the same year as Ike.

His challenger was Congressman Thomas J. Dodd, a two-term representative from Connecticut's First District. Dodd was dynamic and a good speaker who had championed Joe McCarthy. The race was receiving national attention because Bush was deemed to be vulnerable. At the Democratic Party State Convention the keynote speaker was Sen. Albert Gore from Tennessee, who advised voters to "turn Pres Bush out" and put Dodd in office.

The race was a tight one. As some in the party began to wonder whether Pres could win, they began to abandon ship. A few local party bosses stopped sending volunteers; others stopped sending money. "I was amazed . . . that they would take as small a view as that of a man who is trying to do his damnedest for the Republican Party," Pres later recalled. "It was almost inconceivable to me that they wouldn't go all out. It hurt like mad."

Carried by Ike's coattails and buoyed by the long hours he had put in answering correspondence to constituents, Bush did win the election, by almost 130,000 votes. But the election experience deeply shaped both Pres and his family. Local party officials had failed to go all out, to be there for him when he needed their help. His family, on the other hand, had worked tirelessly in doing everything asked of them. When his son and grandson ran for the presidency decades later, they would heed these lessons and rely on a network of family and friends to guide their campaigns, not the Republican Party machinery.

#### CHAPTER 10

# ONE-ON-ONE

NYTIME THE RAINS CAME TO MIDLAND, REJOICING COULD BE heard in the Bush home. Little George would anxiously pace around the living room in a soiled T-shirt and jeans waiting for it to let up. When it did, he would burst out the front door and join his friends at a nearby pond.

Thousands of frogs would be there, croaking and hopping about. "Everybody would get BB guns and shoot them," recalls Terry Throckmorton, a childhood friend. "Or we'd put firecrackers in the frogs and throw them and blow them up."

For the Bush children, Midland was an idyllic place of adventuresome days and placid, star-filled nights. Little George, Jebbie, Marvin, and Neil had the run of the house. Each had his own place in the family, and each tried to define himself within it.

Little George, the eldest by more than six years and also his father's namesake, spent his free time riding around on his bicycle looking for adventure. It could be something very simple like throwing dirt clods, or catching the matinee at the theater in town. "On Saturdays we'd meet at the ball field and put together a ball game," recalled Robert McCleskey. "In the afternoons we would ride our bikes down to the Ritz and watch the serials, mostly Buck Rogers and cowboy movies."

Little George was, like his father, a great collector of friends. They came from school, the neighborhood, or the baseball diamond. To those he was particularly close to, he would assign nicknames. It was his mark of friendship.

Most of his time was spent dreaming about baseball. He had heard from family and friends about the great triumphs of his grandfather, father, and uncles on the baseball diamond. Little George played catcher on the Midland little league team and was a member of the Midland All-Stars. While not the most gifted athlete, he more than made up for it with an innate aggressiveness. He swung the bat so fiercely, coaches would have to urge him to loosen his grip. "He tries so very hard," his father wrote to his friends.

George often arrived early at Sam Houston Elementary School to play baseball with his friends. The school principal, John Bizilo, would come out on the field, take off his jacket, loosen his tie, and hit a few balls for the boys. Some neighborhood girls would come and watch. One who didn't was a small, pretty girl named Laura Welch, who lived only a few blocks away. Laura and her friends were interested in more refined matters, at least as defined by a young girl. They spent their Saturdays at the Rexall Drug Store sipping Cokes and passed their free time reading or listening to 45s—mostly Buddy Holly, the Drifters, and Roy Orbison—and dancing in their socks.

Little George didn't have much interest in that sort of thing. If his father was a gentle and obedient child, this son was different. George Walker Bush was, many in the family said, more Walker than Bush. He did little reading except for the occasional Hardy Boys story or a series of mystery books about baseball. He did make one early run at electoral politics, however. In the seventh grade he ran for class president against Jack Hanks, a popular kid. Few expected him to win, but with heavy campaigning and a smile he managed to do so narrowly. (Hanks went on to a political triumph of his own. Four years later he went to Boys Nation and was elected vice president, defeating a young candidate from Arkansas named Bill Clinton.)

Perhaps baseball more than anything gave George something to share with his father. Big George coached his son's team, which usually played its games on Saturday mornings. Then in the afternoon the fathers would play a pickup game. Word got out—not from George himself—that the coach had been a star player at Yale. And his skills were on display for all to see during the afternoon dads' game.

"If he was standing in the outfield when someone hit a fly ball, he could put his glove behind him at belt level, drop his head forward, and catch the ball behind his back," recalls Joe O'Neill, a childhood friend. "We'd try to do it too, but the ball would always hit us on the back of the head. We all had scabs on our heads from trying to catch the fly balls like Mr. Bush did."

For Little George, life would be defined by the need to live up to his name. He had seen his father's photos of the Yale team and heard stories from his uncles and great-uncles about Poppy's playing days. Little George would have trouble matching those accomplishments. Fay Vincent, a family friend who later went on to be baseball commissioner, remembers visiting Texas in the 1950s and watching Little George play. "I remember him striking out a lot. Wild swings with lots of muscle; but he was swinging so hard, trying so hard, he didn't take the chance to watch the ball."

Little George loved the game and became fixated on becoming a star.

"All George ever wanted to be was a major league baseball player," recalls Terry Throckmorton. "That's all he ever talked about." In an instant he could recall the batting averages and slugging percentages of his favorite players. He swapped baseball cards with a passion and proved to be so shrewd at it that his friends had to carefully think through any deal or they might be taken.

"He would sit there on the floor with his brothers and they would argue for hours about the value of a Pee Wee Reese card," recalls Elsie Walker. "He was so tenacious about it, it was ridiculous. He either convinced them to make a bad trade, or he just waited them out." Soon he was writing notes to famous players, offering words of encouragement and enclosing a baseball card with return postage. His diligence paid off as he got signed cards returned from Mickey Mantle, Willie Mays, and some of his other favorite players.

At school Little George was not exactly a serious student. He would get into trouble because of that Walker swagger. In the fourth grade he was clowning around in class and used an ink pen to draw a mustache, beard, and long sideburns on his face. When he shared his artistic work with his classmates, they erupted in laughter. The teacher, Frances Childress, promptly grabbed him by the arm and took him down the corridor to see the principal.

"Just look at him," she said. "He's been making a disturbance in class."

The principal took George by the hand and told him to bend over and reach for the ground. He then promptly administered three licks with a paddle.

"When I hit him, he cried," John Bizilo recalls. "Oh, did he cry! He yelled as if he'd been shot."

When Bar found out, she was furious. With the death of Robin, she had become fiercely protective of her oldest son. She called Bizilo immediately. "My husband's going to kill you," she said with slight exaggeration. "He's out of town, but he's coming home to kill you immediately."

Bizilo calmly explained what Little George had done: When sent to the principal's office to explain his actions, he had been far from contrite. Instead, George had "swaggered in as though he had done the most wonderful thing in the world." When Bar heard the full story, she ended up supporting Bizilo.

When George Sr. was at home, he sometimes clashed with his oldest son. "Georgie aggravates the hell out of me at times (I am sure I do the same to him)," he wrote his father-in-law, "but then at times I am so proud of him I could die."

Little George was strong-willed and stubborn. Even as a young boy, Little George constantly butted heads with his father, recalls Gerry Bemiss, who saw them frequently in Kennebunkport. Otha Taylor, who helped out in the Bush home, recalls the two Georges "were always tussing about something."

His younger brothers each seemed to move in a different path to make room for themselves in this busy and active family. Marvin grew up with a wicked sense of humor, trying to communicate and establish himself by making fun. He would pee in the housecleaner's iron or switch the liquids in the kitchen. When you reached for the apple juice, you'd find vegetable oil instead. Neil was the attractive little kid. Pleasant and well-mannered with shining white blond hair, his father would call him Whitey. He became the good kid, the one who got attention and identity by being the most obedient son.

For Jebbie, being the middle child proved to be the most difficult. Too young to compete with his older brother as a boy, he had also spent scarce time as the family baby, with Neil being born just two years after him. He quickly emerged as the most serious of the Bush children, but also the one that family members saw go through the most changes. "Jeb I thought of as somebody who as a kid was experimenting and trying to figure out his role," recalls cousin John Ellis.

Despite their age differences, the boys were expected to compete on an equal footing. It was the family's currency of communication, a way of showing that you were a Bush. Competition was also a way to channel their natural rivalries. "The boys absorbed the family's competitive nature at an early age," says Bucky Bush, their uncle. "I remember watching them playing baseball, basketball, board games, just about everything, and just going nuts, playing over and over again, each one trying to win one over on the other."

Robert Mosbacher, a longtime family friend, remembers that when the Bushes would visit in Houston, the Bush boys were always eager for a game. "We played touch football in the backyard and a game called wonder tennis, a game of table tennis with a larger table," he told us. "What was so interesting was that the sense of competitiveness was much greater at wonder tennis than touch football. Touch football is a team sport and they weren't as fiercely competitive at that. But wonder tennis—it's one-on-one, that really brought it out in them." One-on-one sports—not team sports—really brought out the competition among them, particularly as the boys became older. "We played basketball," recalls Neil Bush, "and we'd throw elbows at each other and duke it out."

"I remember one afternoon up in Maine," Marvin Bush recalls. "My brother George and I were playing tennis when things got a little tight on the tennis court. I was about ten years younger than he and it got to an especially tense point in the match. I think I was fairly brash and was making sure he knew exactly what the score was. The next I knew he was chasing me up a fence."

In those early years, Little George was the lead boy. It was a function of both his age and personality, which could come on strong at times. But as they grew older, Jeb began to assert himself. "At first George was in charge and Jeb always seemed to be finding the place where he fit in," recalls John Ellis. "But as they got older, Jeb started to chart his own path and at one point had surpassed his brother in terms of success."

In Midland the boys would fight over toys, the rules of the game, or the proverbial pecking order. When a fight did break out, it was Barbara who usually got in the middle to break it up. "Sometimes they'd come up the driveway yelling dirty words at each other and Barbara would send them to their rooms and that kind of discipline," George Bush, Sr. said. "She would say, 'Your dad will be disappointed in you.' "

That was the family's most powerful tool for imposing discipline: instilling a profound sense of disappointment that you had let the family down and hurt everyone. George Bush says he considers it the most effective parenting tool they had; he rarely spanked his boys.

George and Barbara still reserved a special place for Robin. They placed a portrait of their late daughter in the living room for everyone to see. Barbara worried at the time whether it was fair to "our boys and to our friends" to give her such a prominent place in the home. George never thought so.

Barbara and George were desperate to have another girl. "What I'm going to do," Barbara told everyone, "I'm going to keep trying until I get another girl." In August 1959, Barbara gave birth to Dorothy Walker Bush, whom they called Doro. Big George in particular was beaming. Robin was still very much on his mind, and Doro added a touch of softness in a home with four rowdy boys. She instantly received special attention from her father. It was as if he had a special place in his heart reserved for a little girl.

"My dad would just spoil me with love," Doro Bush recalls. When she was a small girl and George was in town, he would tuck her into bed at night, telling her about Robin. "We would both cry," she says. The whole family saw Doro as a living reminder of Robin. "Dorothy is enchanting," George wrote his friend Lud Ashley. "She is a wild dark version of Robin. They look so much alike that Mom and Dad [Pres and Dottie] both called Dorothy 'Robin' all last week when Bar went to visit at Hobe Sound."

———

DESPITE THE TIME HE TRIED TO RESERVE FOR HIS CHILDREN, GEORGE SPENT most of his time traveling on business. Zapata was now heavily involved in offshore drilling. That meant, instead of trips to West Texas or Houston, George was increasingly venturing to Europe, Latin America, and the Persian Gulf. He was in many respects a distant figure for his sons, much as his father had been to him.

His heavy travel schedule also caused tension at home. "I had moments where I was jealous of attractive young women out in a man's world," Bar later recalled. "I would think, well, George is off on a trip doing all these exciting things and I'm sitting home with these absolutely brilliant children, who say one thing a week of interest."

Compounding the problem was the fact that Barbara was often left to handle problems on her own. When Jebbie was diagnosed with what was thought to be a rare bone disease, Barbara had to handle it by herself. "George was away, so my friends held my hand," she recalled later. "But it turned out to be only an infection in his heel. Neil had an eye emergency and I had to rush him from Midland to Houston, but it turned out to be nothing."

George and Bar would argue. She would complain about the burdens on her, and George would counter with how hard he was working for the family. Bar finally figured that the arguing did little to improve anything. "What's the point?" she recalls. "He would just let you flail and flounder . . . I mean, it's no fun to argue in a one-sided argument. He knows what he thinks and he's perfectly willing to let you scream and yell, but I gave that up. That was a waste of our energy."

———

AFTER THE EARLY YEARS OF EUPHORIA IN THE MARRIAGE, THEIR RELATIONSHIP was changing. Teensie Bush Cole recalls seeing how the two, who were very much in love, started relating to each other differently. "Love matures and becomes more understanding," she told us. "You become friends and if you're not friends, you don't have a good marriage. Somehow when he was away it didn't matter, they stayed close. She understood George. You've got to understand your husband if you are going to be happy. If Barbara had said, 'I can't take another house, I can't take the politics,' he might not have done it and really been damaged, because he loved her that much."

George could sometimes be less than sensitive. One day George and his friend C. Fred Chambers were sitting and drinking beers when Bar called them in for dinner. They sat down at the table. George took one bite and grimaced. "You expect me to eat this shit?" Bar ran away in tears as George and Fred laughed.

This sort of bantering went on until Barbara developed her own defenses. Shellie Bush Jansing recalls having dinner with George and Bar one night. When Bar reached to take another helping, George said, "Don't you think you've had enough?" It was a particularly insensitive comment because Barbara was always concerned about her weight. This time, rather than get upset, Bar simply smiled and began humming the tune "Old Gray Mare." "And he shut up," says Jansing. "That was her way of saying absolutely cut this out or you've had it."

The offshore side of the oil business was still in its infancy, and George was determined to see it through because he believed it had so much promise. Several offshore ventures had already failed: The rigs tipped over or never found any oil; others had been destroyed by tropical storms.

Zapata was using new rigs designed by L. G. LeTourneau of Vicksburg, Mississippi. LeTourneau had designed a self-elevating platform on three legs that he thought would be stable enough to withstand major storms. George was intrigued enough by the idea that he struck a bargain with him. In exchange for a $400,000 advance, LeTourneau would build a rig at his own expense. If the thing actually worked, LeTourneau would receive some Zapata stock and $550,000 more.

LeTourneau tested the rig in the Mississippi River, where it worked fine. But when it began operations in the Gulf of Mexico, saltwater destroyed the gearboxes. George spent considerable time with him, watching over his investment. It was a slapdash operation most of the time. "His design was questionable," George Bush later recalled, "but if something didn't work—if one of the legs squeaked when the barge was jammed up—he'd climb up there with a piece of chalk and just start marking up the steel. He'd tell his workers to cut this out here and cut that off there, and they'd get a welding torch out to do it. That inspired confidence in us because he could fix something and get it going. He was a creative genius. But more conservative engineers would have been horrified by the way he did things . . ."

The first rig was the *Scorpion*, a $3.5 million project financed by a bond offering in 1956. The next year Zapata financed construction of another rig, the *Vinegaroon*, named for a West Texas insect. The *Vinegaroon* began drilling in Block 86 off Vermilion Parish, Louisiana, and it was the first offshore rig to make a major find. Soon it was producing 113 barrels of oil and 3.6 million cubic feet of natural gas per day. Zapata received a half interest in all the royalties that came from the field.

The international offshore oil business was a high stakes game influenced by a variety of political factors. In 1956, while George was meeting in London with Zapata investors and other oil company executives, the Suez Crisis erupted. He watched anxiously as the Suez Canal was closed, threatening the northward flow of Persian Gulf oil. In 1958, Zapata's *Scorpion* rig was moved from the Gulf of Mexico to a location in the Cay Sal Bank, just fifty-four miles north of Isabela, Cuba. Tensions were high because of a festering revolution being led by Fidel Castro.

During the latter half of the 1950s, George Bush turned Zapata into a global company, with operations in the Gulf of Mexico, the Persian Gulf, Trinidad, and the north coast of Borneo. Negotiations for these contracts were tough and George was often directly involved, meaning he oftentimes was not home.

In his foreign travels George would sometimes bring Little George along. They traveled together to Latin America and went to Scotland several times, where they stayed with Jimmy Gammell, a Scottish investor who had a major stake in Zapata and sat on the board. They spent time at the Gammells' family farm in Perthshire, going over finances and discussing their contract with the Kuwait Shell Petroleum Development Company. Over the course of those visits, Little George became friends with Gammell's son, Bill. It would prove to be an enormously helpful relationship later in life. Gammell's son went off to boarding school and became good friends with a classmate named Tony Blair. At a critical juncture in the days after September 11, Gammell would solidify the relationship between the two men and convince Blair that Bush was someone to take seriously.

Little George would also travel with his father to Medellín, Colombia, where Zapata had an office headed by Judge Manuel B. Bravo, a Texan. While George Bush would visit, Little George would go to the Bravos' house for homemade meals. "My mother fed him tortillas and arroz and frijoles," recalls Manuel B. Bravo, Jr. "He didn't want to go back home . . . He would say that this is the best food I ever had."

Like his father, George Sr. was focused on his work. In Midland he helped start two banks and soon was involved in several other ventures, including serving on the board of an oil field equipment company named Camoc, Inc. He joined the boards of the American Association of Oilwell

Drilling Contractors, the Independent Petroleum Association, and the Texas Mid-Continental Oil and Gas Association.

By the late 1950s, Zapata was going in two different directions. The firm was not really making much money. George saw the firm's future in offshore drilling. His partners Hugh and Bill Liedtke wanted instead to concentrate on building a larger presence on land in Texas.

The two visions might have been reconciled, but there was also friction concerning the interference of George's uncle, Herby Walker. A major investor in the firm who had helped round up other investors, Herby wanted his voice heard on just about every matter. Forceful and tough, Herby irritated Hugh Liedtke to no end. Finally it was decided that the business should be split. George would take Zapata Offshore and the Liedtkes would take Zapata Petroleum. Herby and his fellow investors bought out the Liedtkes' 40-percent stake in Zapata Offshore while the Liedtkes bought out the Bush-Walker interest in Zapata Petroleum. At the time, George owned about 15 percent of the company, a stake worth about six hundred thousand dollars.

Despite the split, however, the friendship between George Bush and Hugh Liedtke would last, as they so often do with George Bush, for a lifetime. Liedtke would go on to run the oil giant Pennzoil, and by 1973, fifteen years after their split, Liedtke wanted drilling rights in China. George Bush, who had just ended his term as the U.S. representative there, accompanied him to Beijing to meet with Chinese officials. Shortly afterward, Liedtke was granted the first drilling rights in China.

By splitting Zapata, George was now a self-made man. He was running his own operation, and the gamble on offshore oil was paying off. "He was the first in our group, along with Hugh Liedtke, to make a million, and in that day a million was a bundle," recalls Earle Craig, Jr., a Midland friend. "I was pea green with envy."

George would no longer need to spend his days driving through the bone-dry fields of West Texas. He was working with larger companies now, renting out his rigs to the world. That meant a change in his work and a change for his family. Tiny, comfortable Midland, which seemed so very much to be home, was no longer big enough for George or Zapata. To be a player with the big companies would mean moving east, to the booming city of Houston.

Midland had been comfortably middle-class, a community too small and tight-knit to allow for the formation of wealthy enclaves. Little George and Jebbie had gone to public schools there and played with the children of laborers, lawyers, and teachers. In Midland the family had attended First Presbyterian Church, a congregation made up of a cross-section of people from the community. Houston was very different. Settling into Oak Haven, with its large homes, graceful oaks, and expansive green lawns, their world changed overnight. They joined St. Martin Episcopal Church, a formal and wealthy congregation made up of people from Houston's nicest suburbs. George joined the Houston Country Club, the Ramada Club, and the Bayou Club.

For Little George the change was most dramatic. Gone was San Jacinto Junior High School, where he knew just about every kid. Now he was attending the Kinkaid School, a prestigious prep school for the children of wealthy Houstonians. It was competitive, and prestige suddenly mattered. Little George quickly realized how different things were going to be.

"One day at Kinkaid a guy walks up to me after practice and says, 'Hey, you want a ride home, Bush?' " he recalled years later. "I was waiting for the bus. This was an eighth-grader, who might have been fourteen at the time, and he was driving a GTO—in the eighth grade! I remember saying, 'No thanks, man.' It was just a different world."

In Houston, George Bush set about making friends and social contacts as his business operations expanded, just as his father had done in New York City some forty years earlier. In Washington, Prescott had joined every social club that he could. George did the same in Houston. At parties and socials, he developed friendships and alliances with families that would make critical contributions to his family's success for the next two generations.

While playing tennis at the Houston Country Club, he met a young lawyer named James A. Baker, scion of a family of Texas lawyers going back three generations. Baker had gone to the Hill School in Pennsylvania (where three of George's Walker uncles had also gone), then on to Princeton University and the University of Texas Law School. His grandfather had founded Baker and Botts, the second oldest law firm in the state.

Though George and Jimmy had never met, their families were not exactly strangers. Robert S. Lovett, Pres's friend and partner at Brown Brothers, had been a partner at Baker and Botts and was counsel to the Harriman family's Union Pacific Railroad. "My father had done some work with Brown Brothers Harriman before I met George," James Baker said. "And Baker Botts had contributed to Prescott Bush's Senate campaign."

On the day Bush and Baker first met, they played a match of doubles tennis. They complemented each other on the court in a way that would serve as a metaphor for their entire relationship. "George was good at the net, and I was good on the baseline," Baker said. Each, it seemed, had different strengths.

Another one of the young bucks that George met was Robert Mosbacher, a charismatic independent oilman who had set up his own oil company in Houston. Like George, Mosbacher had been born back East, in Mount Vernon, New York. His father, Emil, was a wealthy stockbroker who had managed to sell his holdings before Wall Street crashed, and like George, Mosbacher had gone through the Depression largely untouched by the tumult around him. Educated at Choate and Washington and Lee University, he headed west after college in September 1948, only a few months after Bush had done the same. Mosbacher settled in Houston and became a wildcatter, poring over county real estate records searching for possible oil leases. After a few failed attempts, in 1954 he found a million-dollar natural gas field in South Texas at just about the same time George and Zapata Petroleum made their first major find.

Like George, Mosbacher was interested in expanding his operations overseas, and the two talked about offshore drilling together. In the end the business plan fell through, but the two later invested in Hollywood Marine of Houston, a limited partnership that operated barges moving petroleum supplies along the Gulf Coast.

George also became friends with a Houston attorney named Leon Jaworski. Founder of Fulbright and Jaworski, a law firm, he had served as chief of the War Crimes Trials Section during the Nuremberg tribunals after World War II. A conservative Democrat like Baker, Jaworski ran in George's social circles. In 1974, Jaworski would be appointed special prosecutor in the Watergate investigation, which would lead to Nixon's resignation. In 1980 he would run an organization called Democrats for Reagan and Bush.

Another Houston lawyer he became close to in these years was Robert Strauss. A lawyer with great influence and many friends, Strauss would later serve as head of the Democratic National Committee during Watergate, at the same time that George was head of the GOP.

As the universe of Bush family friends continued to expand, Barbara took to writing out note cards to keep track of them all. The list included Poppy's friends from Andover, his war buddies, his teammates and classmates at Yale, friends and neighbors from Midland, investors and partners in Zapata, and new acquaintances in Houston. She even had the names and addresses of the men who had rescued George in WWII. Friendships were becoming institutionalized, so they could be tracked and nurtured. Barbara would take meticulous care of the card file, noting birthdays, funerals, hobbies, and interests. At first the cards were kept in a small recipe box. By the time George was president, they would number in the *tens of thousands*.

Samuel P. Bush (back row, third from right) as a member of the Stevens Institute of Technology football team. The paternal grandfather of George H. W. Bush, he would make a fortune at Buckeye Steel with the financial backing of the Rockefellers. *(George Bush Presidential Library)*

Above (left), Prescott Bush as a member of the Yale baseball team. For the Bushes, sports were an obsession, but athletic prowess mattered less than the sheer will to win. *(Prescott S. Bush family scrapbook)* At right, Dorothy Walker, matriarch of the dynasty, circa 1915. Fiercely competitive in her own right, she once tied her brother to the front gate of the family home after an argument over a tennis racket. *(George Bush Presidential Library)* Below (at far right), Pres Bush with fellow members of Skull and Bones. Few families have deeper roots or stronger ties to Yale's secret society than do the Bushes. *(Prescott S. Bush family scrapbook)*

Above (left), George Herbert Walker, the current president's great-grandfather, was a hard-charging dealmaker who lost and made huge fortunes in his lifetime. Hard on his wife and children, the Missouri boxing champ would pummel his sons in the ring as a form of discipline. *(Prescott S. Bush family scrapbook)* At right, Luli Walker in Palm Beach at the turn of the century. The long-suffering wife of Bert Walker instilled a sense of grace and strength in her daughters. *(Prescott S. Bush family scrapbook)* Below, the family home at Walker Point (1902). Purchased by Bert Walker with money from a railroad deal, it would serve as the family's compound for more than a century. *(George Bush Presidential Library)*

Above (left), the Walker brothers in Kennebunkport. Dorothy's brothers were aggressive and rambunctious and would loom large in future President George H. W. Bush's life. *(Prescott S. Bush family scrapbook)* At right, Nancy and Dorothy Walker in a tidal pool at Walker Point. Four generations have gone skinny-dipping in the "Booney Wild pool" in the rocks off Walker Point, an important family ritual. *(Prescott S. Bush family scrapbook)* Below, G. H. Walker and his daughters at Walker Point. Few families have a greater sense of identity than the Walkers do. *(Prescott S. Bush family scrapbook)*

Above, Dorothy Walker playing tennis at a club tournament. Despite their love of baseball, the Bushes encouraged their children to play individual rather than team sports, believing they were better for one's character. *(Prescott S. Bush family scrapbook)*

Left, Prescott Bush on the golf links. Bush served as secretary of the U.S. Golf Association, and his father-in-law, Bert Walker, bankrolled the Walker Cup.

*(Prescott S. Bush family scrapbook)*

Above, Pres and Dorothy with their children in Greenwich in the 1930s. Pres was often concerned about money and detached from his children. *(Prescott S. Bush family scrapbook)* Below, the Bush home on Grove Lane in Greenwich. There was a constant swirl of entertaining; everyone from jazz musicians to Henry and Clare Booth Luce would dine here. *(Prescott S. Bush family scrapbook)*

Above (left), George H. W. Bush with his sister, Nancy. Their mother discouraged self-importance, which she called the "la-dee-das." *(George Bush Presidential Library)* At right, George H. W. Bush at age twelve. Encouraged to be independent, he went to Andover at a young age but sent the laundry home. *(Prescott S. Bush family scrapbook)* Below, George and his brother Pres Jr. in Duncannon, South Carolina, with their grandmother. If the Bushes were austere, the Walkers were extravagant. For the young Bushes, visiting their grandfather's plantation in South Carolina was like a journey back in time. *(Prescott S. Bush family scrapbook)*

George H. W. Bush circa 1942 as a member of the Andover baseball team. He went on to star at Yale as a player and team captain. Years later, as president, he kept a well-oiled glove in a drawer of his Oval Office desk. *(Prescott S. Bush family scrapbook)*

THE MOVE TO HOUSTON HAD BEEN ABOUT MORE THAN BUSINESS. GEORGE was also thinking seriously about politics. Certainly he had taken an interest in his father's career and had participated at the local level in politics. In 1952, while living in Midland, he had arranged an airport reception at the request of his father for a young vice presidential candidate named Richard Nixon. Nixon arrived and started to speak when a couple of protesters began to disrupt the event. "Bush took one look at them and tore over there," recalls John Overbey. "He ripped up their signs and told them to get the hell out of there."

George could think about getting involved in politics because he was financially secure for the first time in his life. His father had established the threshold: Take care of the family first. But the road would not be easy. In the early 1960s, Texas was largely a one-party state controlled by Democrats. They held every major statewide office but one. In 1961 a Republican college professor named John Tower had managed to win the Senate seat vacated by LBJ when he became vice president. But the GOP was a minor factor in the state. Even George's friends like Jimmy Baker wouldn't consider leaving the Democratic Party. Another challenge for George: Larger-than-life Democratic personalities, true-blue Texans like LBJ and John Connally dominated the process.

Compounding the problem was the disarray of Texas Republicans. At the local level in Houston, Jimmy Bertron, the Harris County GOP chairman, had been besieged by squabbles over how to define the party while mainline conservatives battled more extreme elements, including members of the John Birch Society. Robert Welch, head of the Birch Society, declared in 1961 that Los Angeles and Houston were the organization's two strongest cities. Bertron was trying to broaden the base of the party by promoting conservative economic issues and appealing to the business community. But the Birchers were making it difficult, with talk of blowing up the United Nations, violently resisting the income tax, and claims of a global conspiracy.

The Birchers in Houston were far from a group of ragtag protesters; they were a formidable force. Some of the most powerful and influential Texans at the time supported the organization. H. L. Hunt, the legendary oilman and patriarch of the powerful Dallas family, was sending large contributions to the organization, and his son Nelson Bunker Hunt was friends with Robert Welch. The local leader of the Birch Society was a state senator named Walter Mengdon, and a charismatic former general named Edwin

Walker was very active in the Houston chapter. Bertron had battled them for several years, but by 1963 had had enough. He was moving to Florida and wanted to turn the Harris County GOP chairmanship over to someone else.

Bertron had tried for quite some time to get George Bush involved in the party, but with little success. Now, with Bertron retiring, the GOP needed a new man to serve as county chairman. And they wanted George Bush.

Party leaders came to the Bush house for lunch, and Bar served up a meal and drinks while they explained the situation. Would George consider running for county chairman?

It was not an easy decision. Zapata Offshore now had four rigs in operation. They had contracts with Gulf Oil and Standard Oil of California and Royal Dutch Shell to drill oil in the Persian Gulf, Latin America, and the Far East. Zapata also had two hundred people on the payroll. The company made great demands on his time.

Yet the desire to get involved in politics was great. It was what had animated his father more than anything. And the idea of service, hammered into his head by his mother, seemed to have no greater expression than in public life.

The next year, at the February 1963 Harris County GOP Committee meeting, George appeared as a candidate for county chairman. He was the unanimous choice. In his acceptance speech George promised to end the factionalism, bring all elements of the party together, and work with both moderates and Birchers.

George's selection as county chair was widely touted around Houston as evidence that the GOP was heading in a new, youthful, and vibrant direction. But it failed to get off to a good start. The *Houston Chronicle* ran a short article on his election, declaring that George Bush wanted to "hone the party to a fine edge for the important job ahead in 1964." Unfortunately, the photo that appeared above the caption was not George Bush at all, but somebody else.

In the weeks that followed he had various faction leaders over to his house, hoping to forge a conservative coalition. Friendship was his great gift, and he considered it one of the most powerful tools in his arsenal. But it would not be easy. George, like his father, was a conservative by temperament, not ideology. The Birchers, with their strong views on every single issue, were an alien force to him. George had underestimated the extent of the divide.

Instead of getting bogged down in ideological disputes, George took the reins of the party and immediately began working on organization, assembling a group of friends to help him remake the party. William B. Cassin, a lawyer with Baker and Botts, was appointed party counsel. A group of business friends became committeemen. William R. Simmons, a young Houstonian, was appointed executive director.

George started a research library to help the party keep up on the issues and launched a county newspaper that could be sent to party activists. Then he made a point of visiting each of the county's 202 precincts. "My job is primarily an organizational job since the Republican Party has quite a few unorganized precincts," he wrote to his friend (now congressman) Lud Ashley. "So far I like it a lot and although it takes a tremendous amount of time I think it is worthwhile."

Using his contacts and a large base of friends, George set about to raise $90,000 for the party, an unheard-of amount in local Texas politics. He moved the headquarters out of the old digs on Audley Street and into a spacious house on more desirable Waugh Drive. George took an office upstairs in the front bedroom. Increasingly he spent his time at party headquarters rather than at Zapata. Barbara began spending more of her time there, too, stuffing envelopes or knitting while George met with party officials. The hard work quickly paid off. In a matter of six months he had raised his $90,000.

Yet despite his success in energizing the Harris County GOP, it didn't take George long to get entangled in the web of political disputes. After one of his first speeches in a small town south of Houston, George was asked by one activist about his position on the Liberty Amendments. The Birch Society had proposed a series of constitutional amendments designed to get the U.S. out of the United Nations, abolish the Federal Reserve, and get rid of the income tax. George was dumbfounded by the question and didn't know anything about the so-called "Liberty Amendments." All he could tell the man was that he would study the issue in depth. Days later, George went public with his views of what the party should stand for. As he told the *Houston Chronicle*, he wanted to focus on convincing the public that the GOP was not "extremist" but "conservative."

"The Republican Party in the past," he said, "and sometimes with justification, has been connected in the mind of the public with extremism. We're not, or at least most of us are not, extremists. We're just responsible people."

What George was facing with the Birchers was similar to what his father had faced with McCarthy in the 1950s. Determined to chart a course as what he called a mainstream conservative, he was loath to offend hard-liners. George no doubt drew from his father's experience in Connecticut, and his choice of words was remarkably similar. The Birchers engaged in what he called "smear and slander and guilt by association," the exact phrase his father had used against McCarthy supporters.

Even so, George was no Republican moderate. In 1963 he supported Sen. Barry Goldwater for president. This was more than a question of party loyalty. George believed that Goldwater was a good man, based on what his father had told him. As George's brother Bucky recalls, "Dad liked Barry a lot. They had their differences, in part because Arizona and Connecticut are very different states. But dad thought Barry was a good and decent man." George also embraced quite a bit of the Goldwater message. He read Goldwater's seminal *Conscience of a Conservative* and gave a copy to Little George. People who considered Goldwater an extremist didn't understand him, George told his friends.

The mood in the Houston office was enthusiastic the first year of Bush's tenure. GOP activists at headquarters tossed darts at balloons that covered a photograph of Lyndon Johnson. The number of volunteers was rising along with campaign contributions. But the fissures continued as George was attacked by both sides. The Birchers called him a "Rockefeller Republican," even though he was supporting Goldwater and not Rockefeller for the nomination. Liberal Republicans were upset because of his early and active support for Goldwater. George tried to ignore his critics and stuck closely to the Goldwater message.

In public speeches he was aggressive when he discussed issues ranging from Vietnam to race relations. Like his father, he was convinced that black voters were a natural for the GOP. They simply had never received accurate information about what the party stood for. "First they [the Democrats] attempt to present us as racist," he told one newspaper. "The Republican Party of Harris County is not a racist party. We have not presented our story to the Negroes in the county. Our failure to attract the Negro voter has not been because of a racist philosophy; rather, it has been a product of our not having the organization to tackle all parts of the county." He went on to blast Democrats, who were the biggest segregationists in Texas and still managed to attract a large black vote because of their stance on poverty programs. "We believe in the basic premise that the individual Negro surrenders the very dignity and freedom he is struggling for when he accepts money for his vote or when he goes along with the block vote dictates of some Democratic boss who couldn't care less about the quality of the candidates he is pushing."

———

IN LATE 1961, SEN. PRESCOTT BUSH WENT TO SEE HIS DOCTOR IN GREENWICH. He had served ten years in the Senate and was sixty-eight years old. His spirit was still strong and he was making plans to run for reelection the next year. But his body seemed to be failing him. His six-and-a-half-foot frame was slightly stooped now and plagued with arthritis. The doctor checked him over, and as Pres was getting dressed he asked about his condition in light of the coming reelection campaign. The words from the doctor were direct: "You would be crazy to run for reelection," he was told. If he did, he might not live to see election day.

Pres went home and discussed the matter with Dottie and his sons. It didn't take Dottie long to make her feelings clear: No campaign was worth dying for. The boys, particularly Pressy, shared their mother's concern. But as they talked the matter over, they could see in their father's eyes that he was being asked to give up a job that meant almost everything to him.

A few weeks later, his office in Washington issued a press release. The senior senator from Connecticut would not seek reelection. "Fortunately, we have able younger men available," it declared. After the news went public, Pres sat in the study of his Georgetown home and quietly wept.

One month after the announcement, Pres traveled to New Haven and his beloved Yale University. Pres sat on the stage in front of the graduating students as the university president read a citation for his honorary doctorate. Seated next to Pres was his friend and fellow senator (now president) John F. Kennedy. "You have served your country well," read his citation, "and personified the best in both political parties." Pres Bush received his award graciously, but family members left the ceremony feeling they had attended not an awards ceremony but a funeral.

The decision to retire would haunt Pres Bush the rest of his life. He would live another ten years in generally good health. After the Senate, he returned to Brown Brothers as a senior advisory partner. He was by now a relic of an earlier era of the firm. New partners never consulted him on serious business. He was bored and frustrated and deeply bitter about having given up his seat.

"He was always bitter about that decision," recalls Pres Bush, Jr. "He was simply miserable after he left the Senate. He was bored and felt that he had made the biggest mistake of his life in leaving."

#### CHAPTER 11

# TWEED

As George Bush embarked on the beginning of his political career, his son George W. Bush was on his way to Massachusetts. Like his father, he was to attend Phillips Andover. It was a tremendous transformation. In a matter of fourteen months the young man had gone from the relative security of life in Midland to the competitive world of a cold and distant place. It would represent an enormous turning point in his life.

Getting into Andover was not easy; 80 percent of applicants were being turned down. Each prospective student was given a score ranging from four to twenty based on grades, test scores, and references. If, like George W., you were the son of an Andover graduate, you were given a three-point "legacy" bonus. But even this was no guarantee of getting in. The acceptance rate for the sons of Andover graduates was still below 50 percent.

When George Walker Bush arrived on the Phillips Andover campus in the fall of 1961, it looked every bit the school that his father had attended almost thirty years earlier. The straight and proud spire of the chapel was still visible through the trees on the main quad. Students still wore the same blue jackets, white shirts, and ties. But appearances were deceiving.

When Poppy had attended with his brother Pressy, the school had been all about raising young men who were committed to service and merit. Poppy had been appointed the enforcer of school rules and decorum and was lauded by his classmates. But times were different now. A pervasive sense of sarcasm had descended on the campus and seemed to pollute everything. "The Andover atmosphere of sarcasm was sort of the language we spoke," recalls George W.'s dorm-mate James Lockhart III. "When anybody did something good, the first comment was always something bad. Just to sort of even everything out."

Headmaster John Kemper worried openly about students who were more interested in a "credential" than character development. A "lucky-me attitude . . . affects many Andover boys," he told one magazine. He wanted to teach his young charges "a sense of humanity and public service," but they seemed largely uninterested. Emory Basford, chairman of the English Department, who had taught at the school since 1929, lamented how the atmosphere on campus had changed. "The spirit of man is neglected in his school," he said. "This has become a strange, bewildering, killing place."

Unlike the lazy pace of life in Texas, with its informality and laid-back style, Andover was regimented. Students were allowed seven minutes between classes and every aspect of life was scheduled: a mandatory chapel service every morning but Wednesday and Saturday; a mandatory lights out at 10 P.M.; the strict dress code and the lack of girls on campus didn't help. Nor was it a place to find a warm sense of community or acceptance, particularly for a young man with a thick Texas accent. Here George found that friends and classmates were competitors. Everyone was expected to attend an Ivy League school and accomplish great things in their youth. This was an environment that he felt unprepared for. "We went from being at the top of our classes academically to struggling to catch up," recalled Clay Johnson, a friend from Houston who also attended Andover. "We were so much less prepared than kids coming from Massachusetts or New York."

When George was assigned his first essay in English class, he was told to write about an emotional experience in his life. There was little doubt what subject he would write about: the death of his sister Robin. But as he looked at his first draft, his sense of inferiority overwhelmed him. So he began looking for big, impressive sounding words in the *Roget's Thesaurus* his mother had given him. Trying to describe the tears he had shed at Robin's death, he wrote that "lacerates" were falling from his eyes.

When the essay was returned to him, he received a zero. The teacher wrote the word "disgraceful" on his notebook so firmly that "it stuck out of the back side of the blue book," George later recalled. He spent his first year on campus staying up late at night, placing his book on the floor of his room so he could read by the light from the hall.

W.'s shock was compounded by the fact that he was not only competing against bright young men from around the country, but also one bright young man who had been on campus decades ago but was still legendary. Although he was a thousand miles from home, he kept running into his father's legacy everywhere. In Benner House he saw the large photograph of his father looking strong and confident in his baseball uniform. When he saw teachers and coaches, they would often talk about his father's exploits.

Poppy had been one of the finest athletes ever produced by Andover. Little George on the other hand was second-string on the basketball team, a marginal player on the baseball team, and a role player on the junior varsity football team. His most remarkable quality was not his athletic skill but the sense of fierce competitiveness he had been raised with and continued to carry with him. Once during a basketball game, when he was angry about a referee's call, George W. threw the ball at an opposing player. Coach Frank Di Clemente (who had also been his father's coach) had to pull him out of the game.

In the fall of 1963 one of the team's guards was injured, and Di Clemente went to young Bush before the game against Exeter. "George, looks like you're going to start today."

George was excited and played a decent enough game that night. When the team stepped off the bus back at Andover, George and Barbara were waiting for him.

"Well," Coach Di Clemente told Barbara, "your kid did a helluva job today."

Barbara just smiled. "Well, what did you expect?"

But the expectations that seemed to weigh mostly heavily on George W. were not those of his immediate family, but those around the family. Poppy's boy, his namesake, surely would be the athlete and man on campus his old man had been.

It didn't take George W. long to realize that he would not be able to measure up to the man whose name he carried. So it was on the snowy campus at Andover that W. developed his first mechanism to blunt the pressures and divert them in a different direction.

"George really saw the value of lowering expectations," said Elsie Walker Kilbourne. "He became a master at it. The whole family clown thing was as much about lowering expectations so he wouldn't disappoint than anything."

Cousin John Ellis saw the shadow that he was living under. "For George, everywhere he went his father was there: Andover, Yale, Texas. In the circles he ran in, George Bush the father was like Tiger Woods in a golfing community. He was just really high up there on a pedestal. And of course every year the pedestal seemed to get bigger and bigger because he continued to achieve and achieve. As a young man, how do you compete with that?"

W. found he could lower expectations by quietly mocking the system. Andover seemed to prize two qualities in its young charges: brain and brawn. W. realized that he was not the smartest of the students there, nor was he the most athletic. But what he did possess was a remarkable ability to make friends and keep them. Within the first few months the gregarious teenager was spending his time playing table tennis, throwing the Frisbee on the front lawn, playing touch football, and shooting pool. He set out to become every bit as popular as his father had been, but to do it in arenas where he could succeed.

He gained friends by, in his words, "instilling a sense of frivolity on campus." At uptight and strict Andover, it was just the sort of thing that most of his classmates wanted. While his father had excelled under a system that placed an emphasis on conformity, punctuality, athletic prowess, and acceptance of authority, W. grew in stature because of his easygoing demeanor and minor rebellions against the finer points of discipline at Andover.

Students were required to wear a mandatory jacket and tie for meals, but George would wear sneakers without socks, wrinkled shirts, and ties that were purposely contorted around his neck. Instead of a winter coat, he strolled around campus in a beat-up army jacket. Poppy never would have considered such a thing.

Most of George's classmates became aware that his grandfather was a senator only when Pres visited campus in his Chevy with his "Connecticut 2" senatorial license plates. It wasn't that W. was turning his back on his heritage. He was proud of his father and respected his grandfather, but by drawing attention to their accomplishments, it was as if he were setting himself up to meet a standard he was not certain he could meet.

Although not a premier athlete himself, W. managed to befriend the campus jocks. "He was less a jock; he was more of a jock hanger-on-er," says Peter Schandorff, a classmate. "He was a member of our teams, but he never really distinguished himself in sports."

But because W.'s position came from whom he spent time with on campus, he seemed to be much less secure as a student than his father had been. He felt uncomfortable stepping out from the confines of the social groups he ran with. "When I was at Andover, I was not part of the cool crowd, and George was," recalled Matthew J. McClure. "If you were not cool, then George ignored you. When you're that age and the people who are cool ignore you, it's unpleasant, and that was my experience."

One group on the outside socially that W. did connect with were the two African-American students in his class. Race was a complex issue at Andover at the time, and many of the students had experienced precious little contact with ethnic minorities. W. had no hesitations.

"Much to my astonishment, the fellows from the South, especially the guys from George's little Texas group, were more friendly than their Northern counterparts," recalled Conway Downing, a classmate from Virginia. "At least with respect to the African-American guys in the class, he got along very well with them."

His ability to put people at ease and humor them was apparent his senior year. After he figured out that his football career would go nowhere, he elected to become a cheerleader rather than try out for the team. (Ironically, George W. Bush is not the first Republican president to have been a cheerleader. Dwight Eisenhower was a cheerleader at West Point as was Ronald Reagan at Eureka College.) Every week Andover held a school assembly to build school spirit. As head cheerleader, W. began initiating unique pep talks and skits to energize the crowd. These antics proved so successful that G. Grenville Benedict, dean of students, worried that they were drawing too much attention to the cheerleaders and not enough to the teams. He pointedly asked W. to tone down his capers or call them off completely. But the pep talks and skits proved so popular that the school newspaper. *The Phillipian*, felt compelled to run an editorial entitled "Bush's Antics" in defense of him. "George's gang has done a commendable job, and now is not the time to throw a wet blanket over cheerleading." Benedict promptly reversed course, and when the next head cheerleader, Michael M. Wood, took his post the following year, Benedict explained that George W. Bush had raised school spirit to the highest level he had seen since 1930 when he first came to Andover.

An ability to ad-lib and make people laugh was evident in 1963 when, as head cheerleader, W. delivered a speech at the traditional bonfire celebration the night before the annual football game against Exeter. He stood before the students and spoke through a megaphone for more than an hour without any notes. "He talked about each player, telling little stories about us," recalled John Kidde. "He called me 'Surfer,' because I was from California, and said I should be at the beach. He made a real production of it, making everyone laugh." (George never mentioned his exploits as a cheerleader to his friends back in Texas. "Texans have a hard time relating to male cheerleaders," he would later explain.) As classmate Jim Nelson recalled, "George was really learning how to work a crowd, how to exploit a captive audience, how to come off wholesome and energetic and winning."

Elsie Walker Kilbourne saw W. developing as a young man in a most unusual way. He had great interpersonal intelligence; he could understand other people, what motivated them, what they wanted, and how to persuade them. But he lacked self-understanding. He didn't really understand himself because, as with all of the Bushes, introspection was not encouraged.

Perhaps the pinnacle of his crowd skills emerged in the spring of his senior year when he organized an informal stickball game on campus. W. was the commissioner and he appointed his cousin, Kevin Rafferty, his deputy. In keeping with his sense of frivolity, he named the teams the Crotch Rots and the Stimson Steamers, the latter derived by combining Henry Stimson (whom his father and grandfather revered) with "what a turd did" in the winter snow. He named another team the Nads, so the Andover boys could cheer "Go, Nads!" to the utter confusion of faculty and visitors. He also created rules about everything: what the spectators could do and what players could wear. And as he had done with his friends back in Midland, each player was given a nickname. Students returned the honor by calling him Lip because of his speaking ability, or Tweed, in honor of Boss Tweed.

The whole effort was immensely popular in part because it represented a stark break with the competitive spirit of the school. Stickball was about fun, not excellence. W. peppered the students with funny irreverent talks about the rules and mocked the "seriousness" of the competition. It was a spoof of Andover, and the boys loved it. "Stickball was a way to send up Andover and let off some of the inevitable senior year springtime steam," says David T. Mason, a classmate. "To George's eternal credit, it did this without getting anyone expelled."

On a campus where athletic ability was so highly prized, W. made a point of drawing attention to those who were not very gifted but played stickball nonetheless. Alan Wofsey recalls the time that he caught a fly ball—to everyone's surprise. W. stopped the game and insisted that everyone applaud. But beyond his antics, teachers saw that in a strange sort of way, W. had an influence over his peers that even those who were in real positions of leadership—class president, football captain—simply didn't. His desire not to compete and to lower expectations had found deep resonance with the other boys.

In his senior year, W. was appointed proctor of a tenth-grade dorm, an appointment that spoke of trust and honor by the powers-that-be on campus. Proctors had the responsibility of enforcing dorm rules against drinking, girls, cheating, or excessive roughhousing. The college administration recognized that it was best to appoint popular students to the post, because they were much better than others at persuading other students to follow the rules.

Despite his grandfather's position and his father's growing interest in elective office, George W. had little interest in campus politics. When speakers came on campus, he was rarely one to attend unless it was mandatory. When he returned to Andover after a visit to Texas in his senior year, he brought back a copy of Goldwater's *Conscience of a Conservative*, which his father suggested he read.

"I said, 'What the hell is this?' " recalls John Kidde, his roommate. "We didn't have any time to read anything extracurricular. If we did, you would read a novel. But W. seemed honestly interested in the book. He said his father had asked him to read it. I remember him telling me what Goldwater stood for."

When graduation finally rolled around, W. was not a finalist in the voting for "most respected" or "most likely to succeed" or any of the main awards that his father had managed to win. But his ability to create his own form of success by connecting with people and making them laugh helped him cultivate a second-place vote as "big man on campus." It was an astonishing feat, given that the other finalists were all top athletes at the school. What his father had accomplished by performance on the playing field, W. had nearly matched by the sheer force of his personality.

As graduation approached, W. turned his attention to thoughts of college. He saw few other choices than trying to gain acceptance to Yale University. It was after all the school of his great-great grandfather, his grandfather, his dad, and seven of his uncles.

But unlike his father and uncles, who had made it into Yale through academic excellence or athletic ability, George seemingly had neither. He had never made the honor roll at Andover, and his College Board scores of 566 for verbal and 640 for math were far below the average for Yale freshmen. He was also not the athlete that his father or uncles had been. So when he met with the counselor at Andover and announced his desire to go to his father's alma mater, the counselor kindly advised him to consider an alternative. George W. picked the University of Texas as his "safe school." He was so anxious about getting into Yale that he again tried to lower expectations. Yale was not really where he wanted to go, he said; the University of Texas was his preferred choice.

When he learned two months later of his acceptance by Yale, he felt a mix of both excitement and relief. He was in. But he also knew that having his grandfather and great uncle Herby on the board of trustees undoubtedly helped.

#### CHAPTER 12

# BID

O N September 11, 1963, George H. W. Bush stood in front of the podium of the Capitol Press Room in Austin to announce his plans to run for the U.S. Senate. A few months earlier GOP state chairman Peter O'Donnell had dropped by to tell George that he was doing a magnificent job in Harris County. He also came in hopes of persuading George to challenge Democratic Senate incumbent Ralph Yarborough in the 1964 election. It didn't take too much arm-twisting, as George had been thinking the same thing himself.

In a simple and straightforward speech, George outlined what he was for and what he was against. He was opposed to Kennedy's civil rights bill because he believed that it threatened the Constitution, much as Barry Goldwater was arguing. America did have a race problem, he declared, but it would best be solved by education and persuasion, not laws. He was also opposed to any federal government effort that would curtail state power. In foreign affairs he was opposed to Kennedy's arms control proposals and argued instead for a more firm American policy of fighting communism.

At age forty, George had already accomplished much in life. He was a war hero with a good education and, thanks to his oil business, a sizable personal fortune. But he also had some serious hurdles to overcome. He was a Republican running in a very Democratic state. George Brown, a confidant of LBJ's, had suggested to George that he run for office, but as a Democrat. George had politely declined. His pedigree was also a problem. He was not a native Texan and didn't talk like a Texan or carry himself like most Texas politicians.

His performance at the announcement speech was typical of the problems he would encounter. He waved his arms and spoke in a high-pitched voice. He talked about the issues in sentences that sometimes ran together. George never seemed to want to talk about himself, carefully avoiding those la-dee-dahs his mother had warned him about, and often avoided eye contact with reporters and the camera.

But not all hope was lost. Republicans were making strides in Texas for the first time since 1890. During the 1960 presidential election, John F. Kennedy and favorite son LBJ had carried that state. But Nixon had made it a much tighter race than expected. Indeed, he had carried high-growth areas like Harris County and Houston by a comfortable margin. And in the 1961 special election to fill LBJ's Senate seat, John Tower had won on a platform very similar to George's.

George wanted to run the sort of intensive campaign that Pres had: plenty of television and radio commercials; billboards, campaign speeches; music and entertainment at the campaign stops. In a small state like Connecticut that was not so difficult. But doing the same thing in Texas would take a massive fund-raising effort: on the order of $2 million, a daunting sum for a candidate in 1964. C. Fred Chambers, his good friend from Midland, agreed to serve as finance chairman for the campaign.

Shortly after he decided to run, George began working to solidify his position in the Republican Party. He was the only announced candidate, and he took the opportunity to visit potential supporters and adversaries. Among those he visited was H. L. Hunt, the Dallas-based oilman and backer of the John Birch Society. The two men discussed the political situation in the state. Both wanted to see Ralph Yarborough defeated. But Hunt's ideological convictions were much further to the right than George's. The Senate candidate had gone to Dallas hoping to leave with a pledge of support and perhaps a campaign contribution. Instead, Hunt gave him a large brown envelope stuffed with material from *Lifeline*, a newsletter produced to advance the Bircher cause.

The man Hunt would support was Dallas oilman Jack Cox. Like George, Cox had made good money in Texas oil and had the political bug. In 1962 he had run as a Republican for governor against John Connally. The race was never really close. Connally was a centrist Democrat and popular in the state, but Cox did manage to collect 710,000 votes, an impressive enough showing. Cox therefore came into the primary contest with statewide name recognition and a good financial base. The Hunt family immediately began making large contributions, and Cox reactivated the campaign network that he had used for the 1962 governor's race.

George Bush had positioned himself as a Goldwater conservative, so Cox moved further to the right. He was boosted by the early endorsement of Gen. Edwin Walker, a former army divisional commander in Germany who had been relieved of his command a few years earlier after ordering his troops to read John Birch Society materials. Walker had come to Texas, where he enjoyed a considerable following.

George Bush was concerned by what he saw as an extremist strain in some Republican circles. He had experienced firsthand the verbal banter at the Harris County GOP between the Birchers and the party regulars. He quietly wondered whether it might go further than that.

The day of the JFK assassination in Dallas, his fears seemed to be realized. Shocked and saddened by the killing, he placed a phone call to the FBI to offer a tip on a possible suspect.

"On November 22, 1963," reads the FBI file, "Mr. George H. W. Bush, 5525 Briar, Houston, Texas, telephonically advised that he wanted to relate some hearsay that he had heard in recent weeks, date and source unknown. He advised that one JAMES PARROT has been talking of killing the president when he comes to Houston. PARROT is possibly a student at the University of Houston and is active in politics in the Houston area." The FBI eventually sent two agents to Parrot's home, and he was cleared the next day. But the event indicated just how disturbed George was about the swirl of conspiratorial politics enveloping the Republican Party.

Both Cox and Dr. Milton Morris, a Dallas surgeon who had also entered the race, tried to paint Bush as a liberal. George mostly ignored what they said and focused on spreading the Goldwater message and trying to generate excitement and attention. Compared to Cox and Davis, Bush was clearly the most telegenic of the group. The media reported that George's campaign was a mix of "Goldwater's policies, Kennedy's style . . . he is the sort of fellow the ladies turn their heads to see at the country club charity ball."

Money poured into George's campaign coffers. Uncle Herby Walker sent a large check and got several of his partners in New York to do the same. In Midland and Houston a large network of friends and business colleagues lined up to support his candidacy. One man who was surprisingly disengaged from the race was George's father. Out of the Senate for two years and in retirement in Connecticut, he didn't seem to be watching the race much.

Bob Mosbacher recalls visiting with Pres Bush in New York City during the height of the campaign. "I suppose I expected him to know a lot about George's race and the politics in Texas," he said. "But the fact is he was asking all the questions, and they were very basic questions. He didn't know about anything that was really going on."

As it had been with both S. P. Bush and Pres, George seemed determined to go it alone as far as his father was concerned. But George had learned a few tricks by watching his father's campaigns in Connecticut. The Bush Belles, the group of attractive young ladies that Pres, Jr. had organized for the 1952 race in Connecticut, were re-created in Texas as Bush's Bluebonnet

Belles. The Belles were made up of friends and Republican Party volunteers (Jim Baker's wife was a Belle).

Dressed in red, white, and blue with white skimmer hats, they wore sashes emblazoned "Bluebonnet Belles for Bush" and sang "The sun's going to shine in the Senate some day/George Bush is going to chase them liberals away." The young ladies attracted attention in towns such as Tyler and Midland, and emotions picked up even further when they were joined by the Black Mountain Boys, a country music band that the campaign had hired. It was a replay of what Pres had done with former members of the Whiffenpoofs during his campaign.

The campaign schedule was intense. George was up every morning and ready to go by 6 A.M., awaiting the arrival of campaign workers at headquarters. When he was on the road, he was going all day, shaking hands and meeting people.

During this first campaign, Barbara demonstrated a shrewd political acumen that few had seen in her earlier. While George campaigned, Barbara would walk door-to-door, talking to people about her husband. But she purposely wore a name tag that had only her first name. She was interested in knowing what people really thought about her husband, in what were perhaps the first focus groups in American politics.

"Barbara, really very early on, understood the intricacies of politics," Pres, Jr. said. "It was instinctive. And she complemented George in a very good way." She managed the card file of family friends, writing letters and mailing out flyers. The network became an enormous source of funds. She was also very sensitive to imagery. George was forty years old and running as a young, dynamic candidate. But Barbara's beautiful auburn hair had turned silver during Robin's slow death. Now, with the television cameras looking on, she was self-conscious about it.

As the campaign kicked off, she went to a beauty parlor. The beautician told her, "Let's try this rinse called Fabulous Fawn." "So we rinsed with Fabulous Fawn and off I flew to East Texas to campaign . . . It was a hundred and five degrees in that plane. I asked the pilot to turn up the air-conditioning, but he told me it had just gone out. And my Fabulous Fawn began to run. It ran down my neck, my ears, my cheeks, and my forehead. I began to blot myself with Kleenex, used all that up, then started on toilet paper. I spent the whole flight mopping myself up."

In the end she elected to keep her hair silver and continued working hard for her husband. The children were involved at various levels, too. George W. helped in the summer during his vacation from Andover. Jeb worked in the precincts and helped stuff envelopes at campaign headquarters.

On foreign policy George staked out a strong position, influenced by his experiences in the oil business. His work drilling for oil south of Florida had put him in contact with Cuban-Americans, and George became an advocate of a strong anti-Castro policy. "I advocate the recognition of a Cuban government-in-exile and would encourage this government every way to reclaim its country," he said on the campaign stump. "This means financial and military assistance." He declared that if the U.S. failed to do so, it would be a sign of weakness. "I think we should not be found wanting in courage to help them liberate their country." He also criticized U.S. foreign aid to Indonesia, where hundreds of millions in aid was being given to President Sukarno even as the dictator was taking a strongly anti-American position in Asia.

On domestic issues George was very much in the Goldwater mold. "Only unbridled free enterprise can cure unemployment," he said. "But, I don't believe the federal government has given the private sector of our economy a genuine opportunity to relieve this unemployment. For example, the [war on poverty] contains a new version of the CCC, a Domestic Peace Corps, and various sundry half-baked pies in the sky." He also opposed affirmative action and other programs designed to help certain groups in the United States. "I don't think we can afford to have veteran-Americans, Negro-Americans, Latin-Americans and labor-Americans." It was an echo of his grandfather's "Americanization" efforts in Columbus forty years earlier.

On civil rights, however, George found himself in a position distinctly different from his father's. No doubt this was in part a reflection of the political distance between Connecticut and Texas. While Pres had been a strong supporter of federal civil rights legislation, George echoed the view of many Texans that this was a state matter, not a federal one. Yet this was apparently a pragmatic concession to local sentiment rather than a principled position. George (like his father) had been a longtime proponent of civil rights and a supporter of the United Negro College Fund, even going against the wishes of Gampy Walker. He had encouraged the GOP to reach out to black voters, and as county GOP chairman he put the party's account in one of Houston's few black-owned banks.

But there was more to the differences between George and his father than a pragmatic sense of politics. Pres Bush had spent his business life working in the corridors of finance capital, where the relationship between the banking world and the federal government was at least in part cooperative.

George's experience in the world of oil had been completely different. For the oilman, federal power was intrusive and a barrier to successful operations. When Barry Goldwater talked about the dangers of federal power, it was something that George Bush believed in 1963. As he told one audience, "The most dangerous portions of the [civil rights] bill are those which make the Department of Justice the most powerful police force in the nation and the attorney general the nation's most powerful police chief."

Privately, however, he anguished about the whole issue. He did not question the correctness of Goldwater's position, but in letters to friends he worried about the atmospherics of the debate. "We must develop this position reasonably, prudently, sensitively—we must be sure we don't inflame the passions of unthinking men to garner a vote; yet it is essential that the position I believe in be explained." The reality was much more complicated. George's opposition to the civil rights bill was being cheered in part by segregationists and racists. He wrestled with the fact that he was getting support from such quarters. "What shall I do?" he asked a good friend in a letter. "How will I do it? I want to win but not at the expense of hurting a friend nor teaching my children a prejudice which I do not feel . . ."

The debate over civil rights took an unexpected turn in April 1964 when Sen. Edward Kennedy rose to deliver his first speech in the Senate. Kennedy invoked his dead brother's belief that "we should not hate, but love one another." Kennedy went on to attack not only the critics of the Civil Rights Act, but their integrity. His clear implication was that those who opposed the bill were hatemongers. Back in Texas, George was furious. "Kennedy's dramatic, almost tearful plea for passage of the bill presented all those who disagree with it as hatemongers," he said on the stump. "In other words, Ted Kennedy was saying that anyone who opposes the present civil rights bill does so because there is hate in his heart. Nothing could be further from the truth. This is not a question of hate or love, but of constitutionality."

George spent his time giving speeches, talking to the press, and writing a flurry of letters to just about all of the people he met. After he returned home late at night, Barbara would often find him typing letters on a typewriter, with a note in the corner "self-typed by GB" just to excuse the errors. It was a hectic pace and it began to take its toll. He had been plagued with ulcers once before and was on his way to another. To counteract the pain in his abdomen, he would take a swig of Pepto-Bismol and move on.

George ended up winning the Republican primary, carrying 44 percent of the electorate with 62,579 votes. Jack Cox was second with just over 44,000, and Dr. Morris came in third. But because George had failed to win an absolute majority, a runoff was required.

Dr. Morris threw his support to Cox and formed an organization called Coalition of Conservatives to Beat the Bushes. Declaring that George was too liberal for the state, he circulated a newsletter attacking George's father and his work on behalf of Brown Brothers Harriman. George Bush was not an independent man, the organization claimed, but a tool of "Liberal Eastern Kingmakers." Zapata Offshore did a lot of business with the Rockefellers' Standard Oil of New Jersey, Morris declared. Jack Cox picked up on the same theme, attacking the Bush family and its connections: "Conservatives of Texas will serve notice on June 6 that just as surely as Rockefeller's millions can't buy a presidential nomination, the millions at George Bush's disposal can't buy him a Senate nomination."

While Cox aggressively went after him, George enjoyed the support of the Republican Party leadership, and the day of the runoff he won 62 percent of the votes cast. Now he could set his sights on the Democratic incumbent.

Ralph Yarborough was the quintessential Texas populist. He exuded confidence in himself and his cause, and his words were often demagogic and sharp. If you didn't agree with him, there was something wrong with you. When LBJ, who agreed with him on quite a bit, took a different view on a particular piece of legislation, Yarborough called him "power-hungry."

Still, Yarborough had courage. He was one of only five Southern senators to vote for the Civil Rights Act of 1957 and one of four to vote for the Civil Rights Act of 1960. His commitment to civil rights legislation led the short, solidly built Texan to become involved in one of the most riotous events in the history of the Senate. Before a vote on one of the civil rights bills, Sen. Strom Thurmond tackled Yarborough in the Senate cloakroom and pinned him to the ground. The senator from South Carolina was trying to prevent him from reaching the floor so they could call a quorum.

For all his rhetorical flourishes and attacks on those who disagreed with him, Yarborough was a seasoned and effective politician. He eventually rose to become chairman of the Senate's Committee on Labor and Public Welfare, which gave him enormous power in funding infrastructure and education in Texas.

When the dust settled from the GOP primary runoff, Yarborough took up where Cox and Morris had left off, attacking George's work, family, and connections. Zapata Offshore, which was drilling for oil companies in Kuwait, Borneo, Trinidad, and the Persian Gulf, was a frequent target. "Every producing oil well drilled in foreign countries by American companies means more cheap foreign oil in American ports, fewer acres of Texas land under oil and gas lease, less income to Texas farmers and ranchers,"

Yarborough told voters. "This issue is clear-cut in this campaign—a Democratic senator who is fighting for the life of the free enterprise system as exemplified by the independent oil and gas producers in Texas, and a Republican candidate who is the contractual driller for the international oil cartel." Yarborough also zeroed in on George's relationship with the "sheikh of Kuwait and his four wives and 100 concubines." He was a "carpetbagger from Connecticut who is drilling oil for the sheikh of Kuwait to help keep that harem going."

But the Bush campaign was facing a more serious problem than Yarborough's withering attacks: a real lack of party organization in most parts of the state. Close to two hundred counties had no real GOP organization, making it virtually impossible to organize campaign events.

George tried to peel off some of Yarborough's support by appealing to Democrats who didn't care for his antics. George's friends developed an organization called Conservative Democrats for Bush, which was chaired by Ed Drake and included former Texas governor Allan Shivers. Another ad hoc group was East Texas Democrats for George Bush, headed by E. B. Germany, a former state Democratic Party leader and chairman of the board of Lone Star Steel. George also made a pitch to bring Lloyd Bentsen, a rising young star in the Democratic Party, on board. Bentsen did declare on April 24 that George was a "good conservative" but did not endorse his candidacy.

Former vice president Richard Nixon, his father's acquaintance from Washington, paid a visit to Houston to campaign for George and delivered a withering blast against Yarborough. GOP presidential nominee Barry Goldwater also made an appearance with George, urging Texans to vote for him. But neither gave him much of a boost.

As election day approached, George and his campaign aides began searching for solutions. C. Fred Chambers wanted George to talk more about himself. Yarborough was talking about his war record. "Why don't you mention your own service?" Chambers asked.

George shook the suggestion off. "I'd just feel funny doing that." The box with his service medals remained firmly closed in his closet.

One step George did take was to begin distancing himself from Goldwater, who was not doing well in Texas. Bush campaign material began focusing less on the GOP ticket and more on George Bush the person. As Yarborough put it, "You can find everything on those [Bush] billboards except the word Republican . . . He's got it so small you have to . . . get out of your car and look for it with a magnifying glass."

But Yarborough responded to the challenge by making some changes of his own. His very public dispute with LBJ ended. He apologized for calling him a "power-mad Texas politician." For his part LBJ, who didn't like Yarborough, recognized the political realities he confronted. He didn't want two Republican senators from his home state of Texas. So he flew back from Washington and the two men held a press conference. When they greeted each other, LBJ not only shook his hand, he gave Yarborough a bear hug.

"You have heard and you have read that Senator Yarborough and I have had differences at times," the president said. "I have read a good deal more about them than I was ever aware of. But I do want to say this, that I don't think that Texas has had a senator during my lifetime whose record I am more familiar with than Senator Yarborough's. And I don't think Texas has had a senator that voted for the people more than Senator Yarborough has voted for them. And no member of the U.S. Senate has stood up and fought for me or fought for the people more since I became president than Ralph Yarborough." The meeting made the front page of just about every newspaper in Texas.

On election day 1964, George Bush was still optimistic, telling friends and supporters that he could win. He was hoping to accomplish what his father had not—victory in his first campaign. But as the early returns came in, it quickly became clear that Yarborough had won. George kept up his hopes and waited with his family and parents until all hope was lost. Then at 11:30 he issued a statement that was characteristically modest. The defeat weighed heavily on him. Someone was to blame, and it had to be him. "I have been trying to think whom we could blame for this and regretfully conclude that the only one I can blame is myself," the *Houston Post* quoted him as saying. "I extend to Senator Ralph Yarborough, who I believe beat me fair and square, my best wishes."

Despite the defeat, the news was not all bad. George had managed to get more votes than any other Republican in Texas state history, and he did much better than Goldwater, who lost in Texas by more than six hundred thousand votes. Still, for someone who had been competitive about everything in his life, defeat was difficult to take. It was perhaps even more difficult for George W., who had come from school to be with his father on election night. While the father was certainly teary-eyed, it was his sons, particularly George W. and Jeb, who cried the most.

In December 1964, George was asked to give his assessment of the campaign for William F. Buckley's *National Review*. In his article George argued that his loss—and Goldwater's for that matter—was largely a result of how conservatism was being presented. A "nut fringe" had succeeded in being fanatical in its criticism of the welfare state, he argued. "We should repackage our philosophy. Emphasize the positive, eliminate the negative . . . Conservatism can and will survive—it needs to be practical and positive." In a way, George was walking in the same steps that his father had in 1950 during his first run for the Senate. Although his father had lost by one thousand votes, largely because of a biased news broadcast, Pres Bush had concluded that his campaign had been too shrill and his focus too much on the negative. George was now coming to the same conclusion about his own campaign.

In a letter to Richard Nixon, his father's friend who had been passed down to him, George expounded in much the same vein. The party needed to strike a balance between ideology and inclusiveness. If the party stood for nothing, it would fail to motivate voters. On the other hand, those who insisted on ideological purity would keep the party from winning. In 1964, he wrote Nixon, victory had been lost by those "who through their overly dedicated conservatism are going to always keep the Party small." It was the sort of tightrope that the next generation, George W. and Jeb, would have to walk three decades later.

#### CHAPTER 13

# YALIE

THE YALE CAMPUS THAT GEORGE W. BUSH ARRIVED AT IN 1964 WAS radically different from the one his father had walked less than twenty years earlier. During his father's time the campus had been coat-and-tie. The young men who had served in the war were eager for learning and quick to adopt the cultural traditions of the university. But in the 1960s that veneer was beginning to change. The new generation of Yalies was less interested in the traditions of the school as the growing turbulence of the era began to take root. In 1964, Yale was still a conservative place. But the time George W. spent there heralded the cusp of change. By the time he graduated in 1968 the transformation was in full swing. When Tom Wolfe visited the Yale campus in the late 1960s, he compared the place to a 1930s mining camp with its overalls and worn blue jeans instead of coats and ties.

W. half considered going to the University of Texas instead of enrolling at Yale. After all, at Andover he had already experienced life in a new world where the spirit of his father seemed ever-present. At Yale it would be no different. Only this time he would be joined by the specter of his grandfather, who had not only graduated from Yale and been a baseball star but had gone on to serve on the Yale board of trustees. Also, as a senator, he had pushed through legislation to use urban renewal funds to clean up parts of New Haven that bordered the Yale campus.

Yale was George's first opportunity to completely break away. If at Andover he had been constrained by the rules and restrictions of the headmaster, at Yale he could be a free agent. Drinking was not only a possibility; it was a social lubricant, something you were expected to do. George happily joined in and began smoking cigarettes, too. His mother, Bar, had smoked for years (never in public), but not as much as George, who was putting away a pack a day.

When he arrived at Yale, W. brought with him a list of people his father and grandfather had known from the old days at Yale—college teachers, friends, and fellow classmates. The Yale family, as Pres Bush would call it, was a group that W. needed to get plugged into. In the early winter of 1964, shortly after his father's defeat in the Senate race, W. went to the Yale chapel to meet with Rev. William Sloane Coffin, the chaplain of Yale. Coffin had been at Yale with his father and was a member of Bones. W. went in and introduced himself. After only minutes of talking, Coffin said, "I knew your father, and your father lost to a better man."

W. was stunned. In the Yale family, these sorts of things were not supposed to happen. It was a rude awakening for a young student who had expected to find the same Yale his father and grandfather had rhapsodized about; he found nothing of the sort.

Like his father and grandfather, W. came to Yale believing that while academics mattered, they were clearly of secondary importance. Both his father and grandfather had found Yale to be a place to make friends and forge the kind of relationships that can last a lifetime. That seems to be the Bushes' unofficial college motto: Grades are important but soon forgotten; good friends made in your youth can last a lifetime. It was a conscious approach, one that was apparent to fellow classmates.

Robert McCallum picked up on it pretty quickly. As a fellow student and member of Bones, he saw W. regularly.

"More than anything, George was a student of people, not subjects. He knew everything about everyone and you could see him making a conscious effort to learn about others. He decided pretty early on to be people smart, not book smart."

He happily coasted along as a solid C student in the era before grade inflation hit Yale, but his course load was not particularly demanding. Unlike his father, who had taken courses in economics and business, George W. concentrated on softer courses in philosophy and anthropology. One semester he studied under Margaret Mead. Later he would tell family members that he didn't really learn "a damn thing at Yale."

One class that did seem to interest and stimulate him was offered by Professor H. Bradford Westerfield. Westerfield taught political science, and in particular was an expert in the field of intelligence and covert operations. Three years before George W. took the class, another student who never graduated from Yale did: Dick Cheney.

Westerfield saw covert operations as the great game, a tool that great powers could legitimately use to advance their interests, prevent war, or evaluate threats.

George W. displayed a level of emotional empathy with people that his fellow students found surprising. "He was third-generation Yale," recalls Calvin Hill, the football great who was a fellow student. "I was first-generation Yale—first generation college, for that matter. Yet nothing about him suggested he thought he was better than other people. I guess you'd say his mother and father raised him right." The expanse of his friendships was impressive even to his most outgoing friends. "George probably knew 1,000 of the 4,000 undergraduates at Yale," estimates Roland Betts, his friend. "There probably was no one else who knew 200."

Fellow student Lanny Davis, who would later serve in the Clinton administration, recalls sitting around the college common room late at night discussing fellow classmates. Someone made a nasty comment about a student who was regarded as one of the biggest nerds on campus. At Andover, George might have been tempted to take part or at least laugh along. But this time when everyone laughed, George demurred. "Hey, it's not so easy for him," he said calmly. "He's a good guy—leave him alone."

Early in his freshman year, George W. made a vow to his friends that he was going to assume a leadership position at Yale. His father had been team captain in baseball and lettered in soccer. W. didn't have those athletic skills, but he did play sparingly as a member of the Yale freshman baseball team. So he continued along the path he had followed at Andover.

In his sophomore year he pledged to join the DKE fraternity, his father's frat. It was a highly coveted group. Deke held the best parties, attracted the most campus stars, and enjoyed a reputation for raucous fun. When girls from surrounding colleges came to a Yale party, it was often a Deke party.

George took to the Deke house instantly and began for the first time in his life to drink seriously.

"George was a fraternity guy, but he wasn't Belushi in *Animal House*," recalls fellow DKE member Calvin Hill. "He went through that stage in his life with a lot of joy, but I don't remember George as a chronic drunk. He was a good-time guy. But he wasn't the guy hugging the commode at the end of the day."

He did have his moments, however. One time George drank so much that, while walking home, he fell in the street and started rolling around. Unable to get back up, "he literally rolled back to the dorm," recalls his classmate Russ Walker.

But George could be rowdy whether he had been drinking or not. When his roommate Fred Livingston got married, George was asked to serve as an usher. At the wedding reception that followed, it was George who tossed both the groom and the father of the groom into the swimming pool. Years later, Livingston's dad met Vice President George Bush in a receiving line in Washington.

"Your son once threw me into a swimming pool," he told him.

George Bush just nodded. "That sounds like George," he said without skipping a beat.

During the spring semester of his junior year, George W. was tapped to join Skull and Bones, the secret society of his grandfather, father, and four uncles. As it had been for Pres Bush in 1917, the door to George W.'s dorm room swung open and a Bonesman touched him on the shoulder and asked: "Skull and Bones. Do you accept?"

For his father the decision had been an easy one. But George W. hesitated. He knew about Bones; his father had told him about it and he had expected to be tapped. But with all of its ritual and secrecy, it held little attraction. Skull and Bones by the 1960s was still tied up with the traditions established generations earlier. He had told friends and family members that instead of Bones, he was thinking of joining Scroll and Key, a rival society better known for its parties that shied away from the rituals that were so much a part of Bones. But family tradition probably weighed on him too heavily, and he accepted.

Despite the prestige still associated with membership, George W. seemed to be more of a Deke than a Bonesman. In his senior year, George attended the regular meetings in the society's crypt, just as his father and other ancestors had done. He would hear the stories about how his grandfather had helped secure the bones of Geronimo for display in the crypt. And he undoubtedly knew that his father was making contributions to the RTA, the legal entity that funded Skull and Bones. But George W. never seemed to really jump into the group the way his other relatives had.

When he was initiated into the group in the elaborate ritual that all Bonesmen are given, he was asked what his Bones "name" should be. Both his father and grandfather had taken this responsibility seriously. W. didn't seem to give it much thought. When he couldn't think of one, he was given the name "Temporary." Bonesmen would call him that for the next thirty years.

When it came to Bones, George W. was the outsider in the Bush family. His father and grandfather gave regularly to the RTA fund-raising drives organized by Nicholas Brady to upgrade the tomb. His uncle Johnny Bush handled some of the group's administrative duties. But George W. never did immerse himself in the group and rarely if ever attended reunions. And while his friendships with certain members remained intact, W. was far less committed to Bones than any other member in the family.

During his junior year George W. announced that he was engaged to be married. His friends were stunned. They all knew that he had been seeing Cathy Wolfman, a pretty coed from Smith College who had recently transferred to Rice University. But they had not really expected this.

What emotions lay behind the decision are impossible to decipher. But the arrangements did appear to be an eerie replay of his father's relationship with his mother. Cathy Wolfman, like his mother, had attended Smith College; the young couple made their decision to marry over the Christmas holiday, just as George and Barbara had; George W. was twenty years old, the same age his father had been; and the couple planned to live in married housing on the Yale campus during George's senior year, just as his parents had done.

George and Cathy eventually drifted apart and never married. Perhaps it was due to the geographical space separating them· George stayed at New Haven and Cathy remained in Houston.

It was a meandering time for George. He was actively dating and bringing girls to Kennebunkport all the time, but they never quite fit in and none of them seemed to impress. One girl who came to Kennebunkport made the mistake of explaining quite confidently that she was a very good tennis player. Grandma Dottie Bush, never much for people who talked about how good they were at sports, quickly arranged a game of doubles. She placed the young girl at the net and promptly fired several shots straight at her.

"George I think was really struggling with which direction to go with his life," says Elsie Walker Kilbourne. "He was battling in a way between imitating his father and going in a different direction. I think he almost felt he was being disloyal if he went on a different path from his dad. That's not because of anything George or Bar said. It was just the strong example that he saw in front of him."

Yale in the early 1960s was not exactly a hotbed of political action. But it was an incubator for a surprising number of people who would rise to political prominence. George Pataki, future governor of New York, was head of the Political Union's Conservative Party, a campus group. John Kerry, future senator from Massachusetts, was leader of the liberals. Future senator and presidential candidate Joe Lieberman was head of the *Yale Daily News*. Others, including Russia expert Strobe Talbott and filmmaker Oliver Stone, might not have had leadership positions on campus, but they were nonetheless embroiled in the political issues of the day.

As divisions over the Vietnam War deepened, teach-ins and demonstrations featured speeches by author John Hersey and playwright Arthur Miller. But George W. didn't participate in any of this. While a growing number of Yale undergraduates listened to the protest songs of the 1960s, George listened to soul music. When the Beatles entered their psychedelic period, George stopped listening to them.

While for many students the debate over politics was abstract, or centered at best on their prospects of going to Vietnam, for George W. it was highly personal. His grandfather had seen how political differences could damage professional relationships. The Bushes never operated that way; they carefully divided the world of politics from their world of personal friendships. They saw nothing wrong with being friends with those on the other side of volatile political debates. But the mounting activism of the sixties was changing all of that. The political was becoming personal.

"One time he came back to the room, and it was the only time I ever saw him perturbed," recalls roommate Robert J. Dieter. "Somebody had attacked his dad over the Vietnam War. George had a hard time with what is now known as the politics of personal destruction, where you don't debate the merits of an issue but instead you attack the person. Apparently people had disparaged his father as a person, and that upset George a lot."

While he avoided campus protests and other events, he increasingly debated the issue with his friends.

"I can remember him telling me why I was chicken for not just going into the air force or the army and doing my job like I'm supposed to. Just letting me have it," recalls Robert Birge, a classmate. "He was never shy about telling people where he stood and where they should stand."

During his senior year, a young fraternity brother named Glenn Dechaubert founded an organization called the Black Student Alliance, which was dedicated to convincing the university to offer courses in Afro-American studies. George encouraged Dechaubert even though he didn't fully agree with everything he was saying.

But George was frustrated by what he saw going on around him on campus. William Sloane Coffin was encouraging students to defy Selective Service laws. Strobe Talbott circulated a petition in which Yalies declared their unwillingness to serve in Vietnam. Yale was quickly becoming ground zero in the antiwar debate. In October 1967, when draft cards were turned in to the Justice Department in protest, the largest number from any college came from Yale.

What bothered George was not so much the issue of Vietnam but the tenor of the discussion. As he later recalled, he was put off by the sanctimonious and condescending attitude of Vietnam War critics who "think they're all of a sudden smarter than the average person because they happen to have an Ivy League degree." Moreover, while the protesters claimed to be motivated by a strong commitment to morals, George saw it as a lack of courage. He noted to family members that Vietnam had not been much of an issue on campus until 1967, when LBJ got rid of graduate school deferments. He was also struck by the sense of guilt and even self-loathing he saw on campus, emotions he didn't share.

"I always felt that people on the East Coast tended to feel guilty about what they were given," he said later. "Like, 'I'm rich; they're poor.' Or, 'I went to Andover and got a great education, and they didn't.' I was never one to feel guilty. I feel lucky. People who feel guilty react like guilty people: 'I will solve this problem for you.' It's being motivated toward largesse for the wrong reasons. Everybody has been given free will, and everybody has a chance to succeed. If someone has failed economically, that does not mean that the rest of us should be judged differently."

Perhaps nothing personified this divide more than the feud that would develop between cartoonist Garry Trudeau and the Bush family.

In 1968 a young student named Garry Trudeau began drawing a comic strip in the *Yale Daily News* called "Bull Tales." (He would later rename it "Doonesbury.") Trudeau took regular swipes at the traditions of the university and at some of George's friends, including Brian Dowling, Yale's star quarterback, who Trudeau turned into B.D., the helmet-wearing athlete who is just slightly out of touch. Trudeau was also a member of Scroll and Key, the rival secret society to Skull and Bones. Rumor had it that Trudeau had wanted admission to Bones but was never tapped.

The differences between Trudeau and George W. Bush might have come to nothing except for the fact that the Bush family would go on to political prominence and Trudeau's cartoon strip would eventually gain a national following. Along the way, Trudeau had fun taking potshots at the family, making wry social commentaries about Barbara Bush, Jeb, Neil, and George W. In 1984, Trudeau provoked the family's fury when he drew a cartoon declaring that then–vice president George Bush had placed his manhood in a blind trust.

"I wanted to go up and kick the hell out of him, frankly," George H. W. Bush later recalled.

George W. did take the matter directly to Trudeau, confronting the cartoonist. (No one will say exactly what transpired.) All Bush will say is: "I didn't like it. I didn't like it at all. And I made it absolutely clear to Mr. Trudeau. And if he didn't like me telling him that, I don't care."

The feud grew more intense during the 1988 presidential campaign when Trudeau's wife, Jane Pauley, sat down to interview Barbara Bush. During the live interview, she looked at her guest and asked pointedly: "Your husband is a man of the *eighties*, and you're a woman of the *forties*. What do you say to that?"

Barbara kept her composure but later admitted that she was angered and hurt by the rudeness of the question. When asked later about Trudeau and Pauley, all she would volunteer was, "They're a *perfect* pair."

The attacks continued when Neil Bush faced allegations over his involvement with Silverado Savings and Loan. In 1994 they seemed to reach their peak when Jeb Bush was running for governor of Florida. In some of his "Doonesbury" strips, Trudeau accused Jeb of trying to block the fraud investigation of a former business associate. Trudeau timed the strip to appear just days before the election, but it proved to be so pointed that some Florida newspapers refused to run it. Later, the distributor of "Doonesbury" admitted that the strips had been "misleading."

When George W. Bush ran for president in 1999, Trudeau devoted a comic strip to the controversy over branding at the Deke house. The strip claimed Bush "once presided over savage initiation rites that included beatings and the searing of flesh." Later, when W. was president, Trudeau would run a strip that claimed Bush had been found to have the lowest IQ of any president in American history. (The cartoonist was later forced to admit that no such study existed.)

In the spring of 1968, George W. and his fellow graduates gathered on the lush green lawns on campus to receive their diplomas. For George W. it was a bittersweet moment. While he could feel good about his accomplishments at Yale, he was feeling very much alone. While his grandparents were in the audience, the person he wanted there most was not. So he had sheepishly asked his friend Roland Betts's father to serve as his "father-in-absentia."

"Nobody's closer to their father than George," says Betts, "but his father was down in Texas. Busy."

After George left Yale, the family's break with the school seemed complete. Yale was no longer an institution they could trust. George H. W. Bush attributed much of that distrust to what President Kingman Brewster had done to the university. As George wrote a few years later to his children, "My hang-up with Brewster was not his own honestly held views on the war but his unwillingness to insist that other views could be expressed. He did not lead—he followed the mob. In fairness so did many, many others. Thank God, George, you got the best from Yale but you retained a fundamental conviction that a lot of good happens for America south and west of Woolsey Hall."

#### CHAPTER 14

# MAINSTREAM

F OR MONTHS AFTER HIS ELECTORAL DEFEAT IN NOVEMBER 1964, George H. W. Bush was in a funk. He resumed his work for Zapata, which continued to be successful. His biggest challenge came on September 9, 1965, when Hurricane Betsy struck the Gulf Coast of Louisiana. Zapata had an oil rig, the *Maverick*, working in 220 feet of water twenty miles off the Louisiana coast. When Betsy struck, it spawned several dozen small tornadoes that spun off randomly in several directions. One of those twisters struck the *Maverick* with full force. When the skies cleared, the *Maverick* had disappeared completely.

The crew had been evacuated, so no lives were lost. But what was potentially at stake was the future of Zapata. Some $8 million worth of company assets was sitting on the bottom of the Gulf of Mexico. George could never hope to get the *Maverick* working again. But what he did need was proof of what had actually happened. George immediately headed off to Louisiana and boarded a search helicopter. For the next several days he flew with a pilot over a vast expanse of the Gulf, searching for clues and evidence of the *Maverick*'s demise. Eventually remnants of the *Maverick* were found and evidence was provided to Lloyd's of London. The firm paid Zapata's claim.

Along with his work for Zapata, George continued his political activities. He had no formal position with the Harris County GOP, but that didn't stop him from voicing his views on a variety of issues. Bush called on local Republicans to take an "anti-extremist and anti-intolerance pledge." Too many in the local GOP were driven by a "far-out fear psychology," and he called for a mainstream conservatism that would unite a large proportion of the American people.

On July 1, 1965, he participated in a public debate with Texas writer Ronnie Dugger that ranks as one of the most fascinating of Bush's career. The exchange, which took place in front of the Junior Bar of Texas, covered a vast expanse of issues from Vietnam to civil rights. The debate offered insights into Bush's thinking about the world and the direction of the country.

Most interesting was George's growing dismay at the radicalization of the civil rights movement. As a regular and active supporter of the United Negro College Fund since 1947, George knew several civil rights leaders quite well. But he was concerned about the broader civil rights movement, which he believed was "being made over into a massive vehicle with which to attack the President's foreign policy in Vietnam." To prove his point, he quoted from Conrad Lynn, the black civil rights attorney who had declared, "The United States white supremacists' army has been sent to suppress the nonwhite people of the world." During a speech at George's beloved Yale University, Lynn had spoken approvingly of the fact that several blacks had gone to Asia to enlist in the North Vietnamese Army. (The students, he noted with apparent disappointment, had applauded this.) He also quoted Coretta Scott King, who was linking "global peace and civil rights." She had "somehow managed to tie these two things together philosophically," Bush said. George also quoted Ossie Davis as saying, "If we can be nonviolent in Selma, why can't we be nonviolent in Vietnam?" Bush proposed giving Davis an award for "what's got to be the fuzziest thinking of the year."

In George's mind, the problem with the civil rights movement was that it was becoming increasingly anti-American, and that anti-Americanism was clouding the activists' view on a variety of issues. As he put it, "They talk about civil rights in this country, but they are willing to sacrifice individual rights in the communist countries." He also declared that critics of Vietnam, who he conceded had some points, were becoming increasingly extremist. "I am sure you know what an extremist is," he told the crowd. "That's a guy who takes a good idea and carries it to simply preposterous ends. And that's what's happened. Of course, the re-emergence of the political beatnik is causing me personally a good deal of pleasure."

The debate signified that for Bush, politics was less about winning a seat than debating the issues at hand. In his debate with Dugger, Bush was passionate and direct but with his customary good-natured demeanor.

George was increasingly divided between the demands of Zapata and his hopes for a political career. Yarborough had turned Zapata into a liability in the domestic oil industry. If he wanted to seek office again, he knew that he would have to sell the company.

Meanwhile, a lawsuit that Bush had filed as chairman of the Harris County GOP challenging the recent redistricting in Texas was bearing fruit. A Houston federal district court had declared that the suit had merit. A three-judge panel of the federal circuit court of appeals had ruled likewise, and in March 1965 the suit received favorable action by the U.S. Supreme Court.

The end result was that the congressional districts in and around Houston would be substantially redrawn.

The new Seventh Congressional District was made up of affluent areas such as River Oaks and some surrounding upper-middle-class precincts as well as some working-class neighborhoods and small black and Hispanic enclaves. The result was enormously beneficial to George. During the 1964 Senate race he had beaten Yarborough in these precincts by an eight-to-five margin.

But George still had important decisions to make. As he later told his Episcopalian pastor, John Stevens, in the campaign against Yarborough, "I took some of the far right positions to get elected. I hope I never do it again. I regret it." George was particularly troubled by his failure to take a clearer stand on civil rights and by what some saw as his condemnation of civil rights protesters.

In late 1965, George began assembling a campaign team for his run at the Seventh Congressional District seat, and in early 1966 sold his stake in Zapata. "I feel like I am selling a baby," he wrote to a friend and Zapata investor. In part this was because so many Zapata investors were family and friends. Investors included his childhood friend Gerry Bemiss, Lud Ashley, his friend from Yale, and of course several Walkers and Bushes.

George owned 15 percent of Zapata Offshore, a rather sizable stake. He made it known through friends at the Petroleum Club in Houston that he wanted to sell his interest, and soon a buyer in Fort Worth was offering a good price.

As Jim Allison, who was involved in the congressional campaign, later recalled, "One Saturday morning I was sitting in George's office, discussing his campaign, when a telephone call came from the foreman of one of his off-shore drilling rigs. The foreman told George that the prospective buyers had come to the rig and had been shown around, and then had been quite vocal about how, when they took over the company, they would get rid of some of the old employees and reorganize things."

The foreman, of course, was quite upset. He had been a longtime Zapata employee and was worried about his future. George was so disturbed that he called the prospective purchasers right on the spot. He told them he would not sell them his company, and that part of the deal was to keep his old employees and to honor their longevity and service. Less than a week later George sold the company to another firm that agreed with his principles. He took a personal loss on the sale of about $400,000.

The sale did net George some $1.1 million, but it could have been even more. Later in the year, a large strike was made in the North Sea that would have ballooned George's stake to some $4.5 million. His response to the news was nonchalant, much as his father's would have been. "I didn't have as a goal a stacking-up of money," he said later. "If you're going to build something like that, I could make a very stimulating case that would be worth doing. But the idea of just going out and making money for the sake of it doesn't interest me."

What the money did offer was a chance to meet the main requirement that his father had laid down for public office: The family must be provided for. With the sale of Zapata, the Bushes' financial future was secure. And now, for the first time since 1953, he was free from the demands and pressures of running Zapata; he could campaign full-time.

George asked Jim Allison, a friend from Midland, to serve as his campaign manager. But more than anything, family members see the 1966 congressional campaign as the first time that Bar emerged as a political partner and in many respects a key political adviser. "Barbara's political instincts have always been underestimated," says nephew John Ellis. "She is very shrewd politically, in some respects more so than George Bush." The failure in 1964 had many causes, Barbara thought, chief among them the fact that George Bush the man was never known to the voters. When she had wisely gone around meeting with voters incognito, she had gained a valuable perspective that no one else possessed. George needed to let the voters get to know him; issues were of less importance. It was a view shared by George's father, who for the first time began playing an active role in his son's campaign.

In keeping with the changing face of politics, George tapped advertising executive Harry Treleaven in New York to help define his message. Treleaven had been working at the J. Walter Thompson Agency for close to twenty years, developing ad campaigns for Pan Am, RCA, Ford, and Lark cigarettes. He had learned the advertising business under the legendary Stanley Resor. Pres Bush had first met Resor in the 1920s, when they commuted from Connecticut into Manhattan in the club car. By the 1930s, Resor was one of Pres's clients and an occasional sounding board for investment ideas and advice.

Treleaven took a leave of absence from J. Walter Thompson and headed for Houston. Almost immediately he did some quick polling of the district to find out what the voters thought of his candidate. According to a memo he sent to Bush, most people he spoke with thought George was "an extremely likable person," but they had "a haziness about exactly where he stood politically." This was not necessarily a problem, Treleaven noted. As he wrote in a memo, "Most national issues today are so complicated, so difficult to understand, and have opinions on that they either intimidate or, more often, bore the average voter . . . Few politicians recognize that fact." With his professional expertise and advice, Treleaven was telling George what Bar had been telling him.

The important thing was that George was likable—and that was key. As Treleaven put it, "There'll be few opportunities for logical persuasion, which is all right—because probably more people vote for irrational, emotional reasons than professional politicians suspect." In the age of media—newspapers, radio, and most important, television—politicians were not simply leaders. They were, according to Treleaven, "celebrities." The most successful campaign concentrated on generating a sense of celebrity for the candidate. The end result was that the 1966 election would be radically different. If against Yarborough, George had been firmly focused on the issues at hand, staking out his position on every one—including foreign aid to Indonesia!—this race would instead be about George Bush the man.

George's father had been one of the first to use the medium of television to convey the sense of the man to the voters. Treleaven did the same with George in 1966, producing casual spots focused on the man and not his message. There was George walking in the sunshine with a coat slung over his shoulder; another with his sleeves rolled up, clearly a hard worker; still another as he walked the streets, grinning and shaking hands. Nary a word was said about any of the issues.

To add to his sense of celebrity, George brought in Republican Party luminaries to hold campaign rallies. Richard Nixon, who was beginning to make plans for his run for president two years later, urged the people of Houston to vote for his "good friend" George Bush. Congressman Gerald Ford also made an appearance at a Houston fund-raiser. Dwight Eisenhower, still in contact with Pres Bush, wrote a letter of endorsement for the Bush campaign. So did Sen. Everett Dirksen, who had served with Pres.

George easily won the primary and faced Democrat Frank Briscoe, a former district attorney, in the general election. Briscoe was an old-line Democrat who was running to George's right politically. As district attorney, Briscoe had gained a certain notoriety by maintaining a "ten most wanted convictions list" on his office wall to keep the public advised on how he was doing. The liberal *Texas Observer* declared that "Frank Briscoe was one of the most vicious prosecutors in Houston's history."

While George had renounced the John Birch Society, Briscoe embraced the organization. He called George Bush "the darling of the Lindsey-Javits crowd." Briscoe was opposed to civil rights legislation, LBJ's war on poverty, and foreign aid of any kind. What he favored was getting rid of "extravagant domestic spending" and forcing France and the Soviet Union to pay debts accumulated during the Second World War.

George campaigned as a "mainstream conservative." When he talked about the issues, he proclaimed his support for LBJ on Vietnam, the necessity of keeping taxes down, support for right-to-work laws, and opposition to gun control. But discussions about the issues were an afterthought. Campaign flyers and billboards proclaimed him as a "successful businessman . . . civic leader . . . world traveler . . . war hero." Unlike the Senate race, which had been statewide, the race for a seat in the House of Representatives allowed George to spend more time simply talking with people. The Bluebonnet Belles were revived and they passed out literature on their candidate.

One of the most effective campaign tools proved to be a letter from Barbara, which was sent out to the district's seventy-three thousand women voters. "George has a marvelous sense of humor, a great sense of being open-minded and fair," she wrote in a mimeographed, handwritten note. "He is kind and a very hard worker, eager to learn more. All these qualities he uses to help bring up our five children. George leans heavily on his church and, in turn, serves his church. What I am trying to say is that George loves his God, his family, his friends and his fellow man. Please . . . vote with me for George!"

On election night the family gathered at the Richmond Street headquarters. George W., visiting from Yale, posted the returns on a large board as family, friends, and volunteers watched. George H.W.'s brother Johnny had flown in from New York and his brothers Bucky and Pres and his parents were all checking in by telephone. The other Bush kids sat near their mother as the returns came in.

As the evening went on, George W. proudly added new numbers to the board that showed his father's lead increasing. By 10:30 victory was assured; Frank Briscoe was on television announcing his concession. The family cheered and George quickly called to let his parents know that he had won. George carried the Seventh District with 57.6% of the vote. Now, just as his father had done fourteen years earlier, another Bush was headed to Washington.

#### CHAPTER 15

# WAYS AND MEANS

T HE MOVE TO WASHINGTON WAS NOT EASY, PARTICULARLY FOR THE children. George W. was away at Yale, but the rest of the children were forced to leave behind a passel of friends and a way of life they had come to enjoy. Jeb, now twelve, found it so difficult that his parents, after much discussion and debate, allowed him to stay behind. He finished out his year at school in Houston, living with the family's good friends Baine and Mildred Kerr. The following year he headed off reluctantly to Phillips Andover.

George went to Washington ahead of the family to set up his office and find a place to live. He actually purchased a house sight-unseen from retiring Sen. Milward Simpson. When Barbara arrived with the kids soon after, she discovered that the place was too cramped for entertaining and set about finding a new home, closer to Washington's National Cathedral, where the children would be attending school. But the house was situated in a cul-de-sac, with plenty of room for the children and a nice backyard.

Introducing themselves did not prove particularly difficult. Living nearby was Supreme Court Justice Potter Stewart and his wife Mary Ann. Stewart was a Yale graduate and member of Skull and Bones who had developed a reputation as a superb jurist. Eisenhower had nominated him to the Court in 1958, and he had received strong support from Sen. Pres Bush. Stewart became good friends with Pres and joined the Alibi Club at his suggestion. Years later, when George became vice president, he asked Justice Stewart to administer the oath of office.

George threw himself immediately into his work, leaving it to Barbara to bring order out of the chaotic move. Barbara saw to it that the boxes were properly coded and made snap decisions about furniture and other decor with amazing efficiency. "She could walk into a furniture store," marvels Nancy Bush Ellis, "and know what she wants and needs *in an instant*. There would be no doddling around." Among the items that made the journey was Barbara's growing card file with the names of thousands of family friends.

One of her first tasks was sending out Christmas cards by the hundreds, providing the new family address and news of George's victory to those who didn't already know.

In January 1967, little Doro was enrolled in the Cathedral School, an independent Episcopal day school for girls. For her, the transition was difficult. Shy, a little insecure, and sensitive, Doro was concerned that she wouldn't fit in right and that her clothes were not in fashion. So her father took her across the street to ask a neighborhood girl what the current fashion was. Doro quickly realized that the short socks she had worn in Texas were nothing like the kneesocks the girls in Washington were wearing.

Neil, now twelve, and Marvin, ten, were enrolled at St. Albans, which was the boys' school connected with the National Cathedral. St. Albans was an incubator for political families and counted on its rolls the sons of Kennedys, Gores, Jacksons, Buckleys, and Mondales. There were so many that the master of the school was known to quip: "Your father may be making history, but you still have to pass it."

Neil had immensely enjoyed the excitement during his father's election campaign. But once in Washington, his sensitivity and innocence stood out. As John Davis, the St. Albans headmaster recalls, "So many of these kids were political products. They were very careful about how and when to use their names—they were brought up that way, dealt with life that way. But Neil seemed oblivious to that. He was very much like his mother, very open, warm, never on his guard. I think he assumed that people are all basically decent." This naive presumption would cause trouble for Neil later in life.

St. Albans was a difficult place for him. "I had a terrible first half year," Neil recalls. His frustrations increased as his English teacher began sending back his papers with a flurry of red marks. He made so many grammatical errors and misspellings that he was forced to come to school on weekends to write the words over and over again. When his work did not improve, the school counselor called Bar into the office. It was doubtful that Neil was going to make it at Albans, the counselor told her. He should consider going elsewhere.

Neil's problem was dyslexia, a minor disorder that impairs the brain's ability to interpret printed symbols. His mind transposed letters and words so that they seemed out of order—jumbled. It was not an unusual malady in the Bush-Walker clan.

Instead of moving Neil out of St. Albans, Bar did what she always did—took control of matters herself. Even with everything else she had to do, Bar spent hours pushing him through exercises, asking him to read flash cards and stories. She also enrolled him in remedial courses. It was a long process, but his grades did improve.

During the day, Barbara began gardening, planting, and weeding in the yard. She also became active in the 90th Club, an organization made up of freshman Republican congressmen and their wives. Many became instant friends like Janet Steiger, wife of Congressman Bill Steiger of Wisconsin. Bar also joined the International Club II, a group of congressional wives who made it their goal to help foreign dignitaries "feel at home in America." Dottie Bush had founded the group ten years earlier.

But most of Barbara's time was devoted to maintaining some semblance of order amidst the swirl of social and political activity. George, who had established the habit at Yale of inviting people over without telling Bar, perfected the art in Washington.

"I remember there was always a chaotic environment in our house," recalls Marvin Bush about those years. "Happy, but chaotic in the sense that Sunday morning my dad might bump into somebody at the grocery store and have them come on home for lunch. And he'd just show up, with three or four people, then two others would hear about it. The next thing you know, they've got a cookout with twenty-two people eating lunch there."

Uncle Herby might be visiting Washington on business and stop by to see his favorite nephew. Or George W. might come from Yale, borrow dad's car with the congressional plates, and take it for a spin. Pres Bush, who had trouble staying away from Washington, also liked to visit for the weekend. Congressman Lud Ashley, still a bachelor, would spend the afternoon. And of course neighbors like the Stewarts and Franklin Roosevelt, Jr. made regular appearances.

George had an office in the house, something he considered essential in any home. His door was always open, but the children rarely interrupted him, sensing that dad was doing something important and shouldn't be disturbed.

George Bush was one of forty-three Republicans elected in 1966 in the wake of mounting problems in Vietnam and economic concerns raised by LBJ's war on poverty. As a freshman, George could expect to have very little influence in the legislative process. The congressional hierarchy was largely governed by seniority, which determined leadership posts and committee assignments. But George Bush was not a typical freshman. His father was well regarded in Washington and the family had made many important friendships over the years. And the old man was quite willing to help his son advance. Pres believed that his son was an extension of himself; how George fared in Washington would be a reflection on him.

In Congress, committee assignments were everything. They determined which issues you worked on, your ability to bring federal dollars back to your district, and your leverage with other House members. George recalled how his father's membership on the Senate Armed Services Committee had strongly influenced his ability to help the Connecticut shipbuilding industry.

Back in December 1966, Pres Bush was a senior adviser to Brown Brothers Harriman—a largely ceremonial post—and bored out of his mind. He did not have any formal power in Washington. But he was a master at the art of exercising influence. Pres had a vast network of former colleagues and friends on both sides of the aisle with whom he maintained contact with great attention. In the years following his retirement, Pres had established a winter home in Hobe Sound, Florida, a small community that included the elite of American society. Hobe Sound and next-door Jupiter Island became the winter refuge for Bob Lovett, who was now advising LBJ. The Harrimans had a home there as well, as did the Paysons, banker Paul Mellon, and Douglas Dillon. As a former senator, Pres retained his privilege to attend the Monday Morning Club, the weekly gathering of GOP senators. He also kept up his membership in the Alibi Club (George would later become a member) and played golf at Burning Tree. Pres's trips to D.C. were more than casual social visits. Pres wanted very much to be on the inside.

So when George contacted him about advice on committee assignments, Pres went to work immediately. George had set his sights on membership in the House Ways and Means Committee. Any major piece of legislation was influenced by this powerhouse committee and membership was highly coveted, even by long-serving congressmen. No freshman had served on the committee since 1900.

Pres phoned his old friend and golfing partner Gerald Ford, the Republican leader in the house, and asked him to support his son's bid. Next he contacted former vice president Richard Nixon. Although out of office since 1960, Nixon was still a major player in Republican politics. Nixon already knew George from his visits to Texas and was immediately on board. Pres then began working the other side of the aisle. As a moderate Republican, affable and reasonable, he had many friends in Democratic circles. He remained good friends with Sen. William Fulbright of Arkansas, although increasingly they were of different minds about the war in Vietnam. Fulbright called his fellow Arkansan Wilbur Mills, chairman of the House Ways and

Means Committee, and told him to expect a call from his good friend Pres Bush.

Mills had chaired Ways and Means since 1958 and ruled the committee with a firm hand. Because so much important legislation went through his committee, even Republicans were deferential to Mills. What Mills wanted he usually got. As he later recalled, "I got a phone call from [George's] father telling how much it mattered to him. I told him I was a Democrat and the Republicans had to decide; and he said the Republicans would do it if I just asked Jerry Ford."

Mills did talk to Jerry Ford and by early January, George had a slot on Ways and Means. News of the assignment instantly brought national attention. The *Christian Science Monitor*, in a series on the new Congress, pronounced that "Rep. George Bush of Texas" was now part of a "new power elite" in Washington. "That assignment," Lud Ashley said, "was seen as evidence that George was a real comer."

Mills took an instant liking to George, who was deferential to the committee chairman and humored him with stories and jokes. Mills in return helped the young congressman along. One day United Auto Workers leader Walter Reuther appeared before the committee to answer questions. At around five o'clock, Reuther informed Mills that he had a plane to catch and would have to leave shortly. Mills told the labor leader to stay put until the young congressman from Texas could have a crack at him.

Later, in 1974, Mills faced embarrassment and ridicule over public disclosure of his drunken escapades with a Washington stripper named Fanne Foxe. The powerful congressman fell quickly, left Congress, and sought to get control of his drinking problem. In retirement and out of power, he would get occasional letters and phone calls from George Bush, who encouraged him in his battle against liquor.

In 1967 the GOP was in search of a new champion and believed they had found him in Richard Nixon. The Democrats had been in the White House for nearly eight years and controlled both houses of Congress. Nixon, a former senator and vice president, was preparing to make another run for the presidency (he had lost narrowly in 1960). In the spring of 1967 he gathered a small group of Republicans in Mission Bay, California, to make plans for the campaign. One of his priorities was to put together a short list of surrogates who could make campaign appearances for him when he was not able to personally attend. He wanted young and exciting speakers who knew the issues and whom above all Nixon could trust. It didn't take long to get to the name George Bush. It was an odd fit.

"Richard Nixon hated the whole Ivy League persona," says Robert Mosbacher, a good friend to both men. "You would expect that George, with his family history and Ivy League pedigree, would be anathema to Nixon. But the fact is that George had made his own money in Texas, and that mattered enormously to Nixon. He respected self-made men. He also appreciated George's toughness. Nixon associated Ivy League types with weakness, but he didn't see that in George."

George agreed to serve as a surrogate, and throughout 1967 and early 1968 he traveled around the country speaking on Nixon's behalf. Meanwhile, a quiet campaign was being launched to get George on the national ticket.

Pres Bush spoke with President Eisenhower at his farm in Gettysburg in 1967. He also spoke with George Champion, chairman of Chase Manhattan, a strong Nixon supporter whom Pres knew from his days at Brown Brothers. Pres even extended his efforts to Tom Dewey, the former New York governor and GOP nominee in 1948. Pres knew Dewey well and considered him one of the brightest political leaders in the GOP. He also talked with Bill Middendorf and Jeremiah Milbank, two of Nixon's chief fund-raisers. Middendorf was not only a Bush friend; he was a neighbor. "I remember sitting out in my backyard and you could hear Pres Bush and his boys singing harmony out back," he recalled. "It was just beautiful."

It was an astonishing idea: Nixon should choose George Bush, a first-term congressman, as his running mate. Still, it made sense in a lot of ways, Middendorf said. "Nixon was embracing a Southern strategy and so he needed someone from the South. And he also needed someone young and dynamic." Middendorf, Milbank, and Champion all concurred and joined the bandwagon. "The idea made sense," says Middendorf. "But we also did it because of our immense respect for Pres Bush."

Ike wrote to Nixon and told him to give consideration to George, and so did Dewey. Champion told him that he thought the young Texas congressman "had what it takes" to be vice president. At the convention, Middendorf and Milbank went to see Nixon to make a hard push. "When we raised the idea he told us that he had already made up his mind," Middendorf recalls. "He had picked Governor Spiro Agnew of Maryland instead."

It was a bitter disappointment to Pres Bush. But as Tom Dewey wrote to him, "I think there was simply a feeling that he had not been in public office long enough. Everything else was favorable."

George Bush came to Washington able to stand on the shoulders of what his father had learned in the Senate. Consciously or not, he imitated his father's manner in office. Like Pres, George spent Saturday mornings on Capitol Hill, writing correspondence to his constituents. George also hired a woman for a senior post in his office. In 1960s Washington, politics was still largely a man's game. But George hired Mrs. Rosemary Zamaria as his administrative assistant, and she became a fiercely loyal aide. Women, the Bushes would say in private, are often more loyal than men.

Pres's regular golf outings gave him an intimacy with Ike and Nixon and others that simply would not have developed in the Senate cloakroom or at Georgetown parties. George started playing paddleball regularly with fellow congressmen like Thomas Railsback and golf with Republican senators. Like his father, George was fiercely competitive even when it might not have been politically prudent. At times his athletic competitiveness even fueled political rivalries within Republican ranks. This was nowhere more true than on the House Republican baseball team. Every year congressional Democrats and Republicans gathered on a grass field to play a series of baseball games. The Republican team was led for years by Gerald Ford, who had played football at the University of Michigan and was a fine all-around athlete. His baseball exploits in Washington included a famed inside-the-park grand slam against the Democrats in 1957.

George Bush and Gerald Ford were friends, but on the baseball diamond they also proved to be competitors despite the fact that they were on the same team. George was a better player than Ford and took his position at first base. The Republicans continued their dominance on the baseball diamond, but George and Illinois congressman Bob Michel increasingly challenged Ford as the best player on the Republican squad.

George Bush came to Washington as a Texas conservative, committed to maintaining low taxes and reducing government spending. He made LBJ's "guns and butter" spending on both Vietnam and the Great Society a target of criticism. "The nation faces this year just as it did the last a tremendous deficit in the federal budget," he warned after LBJ's State of the Union Address. "But in the president's message there was no sense of sacrifice on the part of the government, no assignment of priorities, no hint of the need to put first things first. And this reckless policy has imposed the cruel tax of rising prices on the people, pushed interest rates to their highest levels in one hundred years, sharply reduced the rate of real economic growth and saddled every man and woman and child in America with the largest tax burden in our history. And what does the president say? He says we must pay still more taxes and he proposes drastic restrictions on the rights of Americans to invest and travel abroad. If the president wants to control inflation, he's got to cut back on federal spending and the best way, the best way to stop the gold drain is to live within our means in this country."

In May 1968, as a member of the Ways and Means Committee, he backed a successful proposal to cut spending and raise taxes in an effort to reduce the deficit. He also favored reducing regulations on business and putting limits on social spending. When he did support social programs, it was usually with a proviso that they encourage "responsible behavior." He supported the Family Assistance Program (FAP) because it provided an income floor for the poorest Americans but also required that able-bodied recipients take a job. "The present federal-state welfare system encourages idleness by making it more profitable to be on welfare than to work, and provides no method by which the state may limit the number of individuals added to the rolls," he said. Likewise, he favored federal programs that encouraged birth control and family planning for poor Americans. The poor, he said on the floor of the House, "cannot hope to acquire a larger share of American prosperity without cutting down on births."

In elective office for the first time, George was forced to make difficult decisions about his political philosophy and values. The result was a belief system that was instinctively—but not ideologically—conservative. "Do I remember him sitting down and reading political books?" says Pete Roussel, who served as his press secretary. "The answer is no. I remember him reading a biography, not necessarily of a politician. Usually not. He also liked to read a lot of fiction—historical fiction, thrillers, stories about people. George Bush has always been more about people than abstract political ideas."

George had been raised and schooled in an America that he saw as decidedly nonideological. When he had encountered debates over core ideas on the Yale campus, he avoided them. To the extent that he espoused any philosophy, it was that of Edmund Burke, who intensely disliked ideology. Burke's prescription that conservatives should stand above all for slow and gradual change fit the young congressman comfortably. George voted instinctively, relying on the lessons of his youth, advice from friends, and his own personal experiences. Those experiences would sometimes lead him to reverse course completely.

In both of his races, George had been resolutely against sweeping federal civil rights legislation. His opposition was similar to Barry Goldwater's: concerns about creeping federal power. But his view changed dramatically based on a deeply personal experience.

On December 26, 1967, George Bush paid his own way on a sixteen-day trip throughout Southeast Asia. He stopped in Honolulu to meet with U.S.

military officers and then went on to Tokyo, where he met with Ambassador Donald P. Gregg. He proceeded to Saigon, where he held discussions with Ambassador Ellsworth Bunker. Bush found the meetings informative, but his views about both Vietnam and civil rights crystallized when he went into the field and met with American soldiers. Flying in a Huey helicopter courtesy of the U.S. Army, he traveled to military outposts from the Mekong Delta up to Da Nang. As he later wrote, "We went out on a new patrol boat and headed up a little inlet to a village and we talked to the people. Six months ago we'd have been zapped by the V.C.—there are still V.C. there, but the area is much more peaceful." He also spent time on an American aircraft carrier, talking with pilots about their bombing runs over North Vietnam. The morning he arrived in Da Nang, mortar shells landed at the base. During one trip to the field his chopper had to be diverted to avoid heavy ground fire.

He came away enormously impressed with the fighting spirit and commitment of the American soldiers he met and returned convinced that the war in Vietnam was just and could be won if the U.S. simply remained committed. But he also realized that he had been wrong about civil rights legislation. It was a question of basic fairness, in his mind. How could America send young black men off to fight a war but deny those same young men a chance to buy a house wherever they wanted?

Three months after his return from Vietnam, George Bush voted for passage of the Civil Rights Act of 1968. The most controversial provision guaranteed "open housing." As he told the press after the vote: "I could not have it on my conscience that I had voted for legislation that would have prevented a Negro serviceman, who has the funds, and who upon returning from Vietnam where he had been fighting for the ideals of this country, would know that he could not buy or rent a decent home."

The vote was a total reversal of his position and very unpopular in Texas. Thirteen of his fellow Texans in the House had voted against the bill. The only other two who voted in favor were Jim Wright of Fort Worth and Kika De La Garza of Mission, who were in safer districts. Days after the vote, nasty telephone calls and hate mail started finding their way to George's office. Former political allies were suddenly talking about finding another Republican candidate to run against him. Politically, George Bush was in trouble. "I voted for the bill and the roof is falling in—boy does the hatred surface," he wrote to a friend. "I have had more mail on this subject than on Vietnam and taxes and sex all put together."

A few weeks after the vote, Houston's Memorial High School hosted a public forum with several candidates on hand who were running for everything from the local school board to governor. The place was packed, and when George Bush showed up to make his statement he was greeted by a chorus of boos and nasty signs.

Bush stood at the podium with only a few notes in hand and began to speak to the crowd in a steady, confident tone. He quoted from Edmund Burke: "Your representative owes you not only his industry; but his judgment, and he betrays instead of serves you if he sacrifices it to your opinion." It was a bold statement, which told the audience that he was more concerned with his conscience than about public opinion.

Pete Roussel, standing near the podium, remembers how amazed he was that Bush spoke with so few notes. Instead of talking about the bill itself, he spoke instead about what he had seen in Vietnam, about the bravery of America's black soldiers and basic questions of justice. In the end, according to newspaper accounts, Bush succeeded in turning at least some in the crowd around. He left the podium to a partial standing ovation.

George had reversed course on civil rights, but when it came to Vietnam he remained a steadfast supporter of the war. The growing protests were both bewildering and difficult to grasp. He had been all too eager to sign up after Pearl Harbor, not simply to fight Japs but to serve his country. The Gulf of Tonkin was not Pearl Harbor, but in George's mind the issues seemed very much the same. A country that provided so much to its people was now asking those very same people to serve in time of need. Service and duty were not conditional.

Despite the fact that an overwhelming majority in his district shared his views, George became an evangelist in trying to explain the merits of the American cause in Southeast Asia. It was as if he and his generation were on trial, and he was determined to make a ready defense. While many in Congress were avoiding the issue, George seemed to go out of his way to discuss it with his opponents. On May 11, 1970—exactly a week after the Kent State shootings—students and faculty members from Yale came to Washington to lobby Congress to end the war. Their position was clear: Vote to end the war or we will work to unseat you. Among those leading the charge was Kingman Brewster, the Yale University president whom Pres Bush blamed for ruining Yale. Rather than avoid the group, George met with them eagerly, patiently listening to their arguments while making several of his own.

There was no similar dialogue within the immediate Bush family, but, as in the country at large, the war was dividing the Bush clan. Nephew George Walker was in the Airborne and fought in Vietnam. Barbara would write him religiously every week. But nephew John Ellis was working to end the war and campaigned for George McGovern in 1972. As the clan gathered in Kennebunkport, a new emotion not seen before became apparent—political tension.

"You could sense the divisiveness in the air," Elsie Walker Kilbourne recalled. Some of the Bush kids (particularly Jeb) started to wear their hair longer. One time Elsie Walker had a boyfriend visit who was from a good family, played great tennis—and wore an earring. "That set off a firestorm. The Walker men in particular were *outraged*. But the women kind of liked him. They showed up to watch him play tennis as an act of solidarity."

But despite the fact that this was a political family, they spent little time actually discussing the issues. The last thing George wanted to do on his vacation was debate Vietnam with his relatives. Bar, on the other hand, made an effort to be available, particularly to the teenagers in the clan. "She was so ingenious about it," recalls Elsie Walker Kilbourne. "She would have a jigsaw puzzle out on the table, and you would just start looking for pieces. Before you knew it, you were talking about all sorts of things: boys, school, you name it. Most of the people in the family were just inaccessible when it came to talking about what you faced in the sixties. Bar was always open."

George W. remained the dutiful son, completely supportive of Vietnam and standing firm against the radicalism of the day. But for Jeb it was more difficult. "When I was at Andover," he told us, "I had fellow students who were chaining themselves to the federal building in Boston. It was not a great time to be at that school. It was not a happy place." The general mood on campus seemed to rub off on Jeb.

"He wasn't disrespectful," recalls family friend Gerry Bemiss. "But he had some rough edges in a way the other boys didn't."

He was troubled by the war in a way that his older brother and father were not. "In Vietnam, people didn't have a sense of what the plan was, what the exit strategy, what guiding principle there was," he recalled. "It seemed that it just crept up."

Jeb became active in politics, joining the socialist club and engaging in campus debates. When it came time to register for the draft, Jeb gave serious thought to filing for conscientious objector status. He spoke to his father about it.

"Whatever you decide," he told his son, "I will be with you 100 percent."

Jeb eventually did register for the draft and in late 1971 he received lottery number 26. "I went and took the physical in Houston, and I was prepared to serve if called," he said. Given his low number, the prospects were good that he would receive "Greetings" from Uncle Sam. But by then the war was winding down and he was never called up.

#### CHAPTER 16

# AIR GUARD

Military service in 1968 most often meant service in Vietnam. For George W. Bush, there was never any question about the military occupation he wanted. "Being a pilot," Robert McCallum, his friend at Yale, recalls. "That was all he ever talked about. He mentioned it his freshman year."

George had been raised on a strong diet of stories about his father's exploits during the war. He had seen the photo albums, and once went into his father's bedroom to sneak a peek at his medals. He asked about the war from time to time, but his father was reluctant to talk about it. Mostly W. learned about it from his mother and uncles, who knew the stories well.

But the lingering question of Vietnam raised many doubts. George W. was supportive of the cause but troubled by the execution of the war. After his father had returned from a fact-finding mission to Southeast Asia, he came to a greater understanding that the war was being poorly executed. Likewise, he heard secondhand through his mother about how his second cousin, George Walker, who was fighting with the Airborne in Vietnam, was discouraged by events there. Had he been called to fight, there can be little doubt that George W. would have done so. But there can also be little doubt that he had reservations about how the war was being fought.

To be a pilot required eighteen months of basic training, course work in officer candidate school, and flight training to earn his wings. As graduation from Yale loomed, George discovered that the only real route open to him was the Texas National Guard. Back home in Houston on a break, he went to visit with Col. Walter "Buck" Staundt, a cigar-chomping air force veteran who commanded the 147th Fighter Wing of the Texas Air National Guard. Staundt was typically blunt. "Why do you want to join the Texas Air National Guard? What's the real reason?"

"I want to be a fighter pilot because my father was," he told him.

Getting a slot in the Air National Guard was not easy. There was a waiting list, and Bush was not a military veteran, which could move him to the top of the list. He scored in the 95th percentile on tests regarding "officer quality," but only in the 25th percentile on the pilot aptitude section of the air force recruiting test.

Ben Barnes, former speaker of the Texas House of Representatives, placed a call in late 1967 or early 1968 and asked a friend at the Texas Air National Guard to help George W. get into its pilot program. Barnes says he placed the call at the request of Sidney Adger, a Houston businessman and friend of the Bushes. Former President Bush insists that he never tried to help his son move to the front of the line. And Col. Walter Staundt, who headed the Air Guard unit, insists: "There was no special treatment."

Fortunately for Barnes, it was not a hard sell. Staundt and other senior Air Guard officials were suitably impressed with the young Yale graduate and undoubtedly knew the influence of his father. "Applicant is a quiet, intelligent young man who has the interest, motivation and knowledge necessary to become a commissioned officer," Staundt wrote in his report.

On May 28, 1968, George enlisted as an Air Basic in the 147th Fighter Interceptor Group stationed at Ellington Air Force Base in Houston. He was selected for pilot training and a direct commission as a second lieutenant. He then went off for six weeks of basic training at Lackland Air Force Base in Texas. After the training finished on August 25, he went to Houston to visit his parents and then headed off on September 5, 1968, to take an eight-week leave of absence to work on a Senate campaign in Florida. Taking a leave of absence would become a regular occurrence during his military service.

In the fall of 1968, George packed up his blue Triumph convertible and drove east to Moody Air Force Base in Valdosta, Georgia, where seventy other airmen were training in a Consolidated Pilot Training Program that brought together prospective pilots from all of the services. The other men were air force and navy pilots. George, as the only National Guardsman, was almost immediately cast as the outsider. The others were suspicious of Bush. While they were all active-duty pilots who were expecting to see service in Vietnam, it was not likely that George as an Air Guard pilot would.

"We made fun of him for being in the Guard," recalls Bruce Henry. "I'd tell him, 'Hey, George, you've got a real tough job defending Texas.' "

But much as he had done at Andover and Yale, George made friends and seemed to win people over. He gave the trainees nicknames—Fly, Road, Chubby. When they weren't taking mind-numbing courses on instrumentation or the basics of flying, they hung around at the officers club. "He was a fixture in the officers club," recalls Roger Dahlberg, "always having a beer and a good time."

George began training in the T-41A Cessna, a four-seat, single-engine, prop-driven aircraft (known to civilians as the Cessna 172). George and the other pilots received about thirty hours of flight training before moving to the T-37, a jet training aircraft. George was assigned to learn to fly the F-102 Delta Dagger, a single-engine Convair jet with a cruising speed of six hundred miles per hour.

The training was difficult, and the most challenging aspect was flying in tight formation. Pilots were instructed to fly within three to five feet of each other while traveling at more than four hundred miles per hour.

In December 1969, while his father was back from Washington and in Houston for Christmas, the elder Bush pinned his second lieutenant wings on after fifty-five weeks of active duty.

The Texas Guards 147th was no slouch unit. In 1966 it earned the Air Force Outstanding Unit Award when it was proclaimed "the most combat ready of all Air Guard units." After successful completion of F-102 tactical combat training at Ellington AFB on June 23, 1970, W. was required to take the Delta out only a few times each month.

While he completed the training and became a solid pilot, it was clear that George W. had other priorities during his tenure in the Guard. In addition to his leave of absence in the summer of 1968, he also transferred to the Alabama National Guard in 1972 so he could work on a Senate campaign in that state. Alabama Guard records are unclear whether Bush actually reported for duty, and then–Lt. Col. William Turnipseed of the Alabama Guard doesn't remember seeing him. But Emily Martin, a former Alabama resident who dated George W. during that time, recalls him spending a week or ten days after the campaign on Guard duty in Montgomery. National Guard records also indicate that he reported for duty nine times between November 1972 and May 1973, giving him a total of 56 duty points, more than the 50 needed to maintain his standing in the Guard.

His jumping around at this time was no doubt a reflection of his general attitude toward life. George W. would spend those five years after Yale drifting. He had seven apartments in three different states, held three different jobs, and had many girlfriends. If his father had come out of Yale on a straight-line trajectory, the same could not be said for George.

"There are some people who, the minute they get out of college, know exactly what they want to do," he said later. "I did not. And it didn't bother me. That's just the way it was."

WHEN GEORGE W. RETURNED TO HOUSTON IN JUNE 1970, HE JOINED WHAT came to be dubbed the "Campaign Unit" of the Texas Air National Guard, where he saw plenty of familiar faces. Among them were John Daughtery, whose father was in the oil business and knew Congressman George Bush, and John Adger, whose father was also a prominent oilman. Ironically, Congressman Lloyd Bentsen's son was there, too.

With his training complete, George rented an apartment at the Chateaux Dijon, a singles place in Houston. It was on the southwestern edge of town, just far enough away from his parents' home in the north. The complex included a mock French chateau and three hundred semitropical garden apartments that overlooked a courtyard and pool area. It was the place to live for upwardly mobile, young, and ambitious Texans, where friends held banana daiquiri parties. He worked on his dad's Senate campaign and in his time off drank beer, dated girls, and played volleyball in the pool. Dan Gillcrist, who was the scheduler for his father's 1970 Senate race, remembers those years as a time of hearty socializing. "He had fun and partied and raised a little hell like the rest of us."

He seemed most directed when it came to dating. With the Bush men, many times it seemed to be their women who gave them direction. As Nancy Bush Ellis said, "Dad taught that you pick a wife and remain loyal and move forward together. George, Pres, Bucky, and Johnny all learned that lesson. I think the younger boys—George W. and Jeb—saw all that."

By his own admission, George W. spent "enormous amounts of time and energy courting women." It wasn't a heavily romantic thing with George. "I spent a good deal of time with him," recalls Nee Bear, who dated George for some time. "Mr. Lothario I never got the idea that he was. Do you get the impression he's a big romantic? I don't. He never was wolfish. He was a decent guy. He would never be a kiss-and-tell guy. Never."

In early 1971, George took his first year-round job in the private sector. Robert Gow was a Yale man, friend of the Walkers, and former vice president of his father's old firm, Zapata Offshore. In 1969 he had left the company and started Stratford, an agricultural company, and had managed to build it into a major enterprise, with chicken processing plants in Texas, Louisiana, and Mexico, major hog operations near Houston, and nursery greenhouses in central Florida, Jamaica, and Costa Rica.

George was looking for a job, so his great uncle Herby Walker placed a call. Gow plugged him in as an assistant trainee for the executives, working mostly in negotiating the purchase of horticultural operations in the U.S. and Central America.

George W. moved from Chateaux Dijon to a garage apartment off North Boulevard in Houston that was close to downtown. His roommate was Don Ensenat, and they rented the place together from Georgia Corbett, a widow who lived with her daughter. George would banter with Mrs. Corbett and seemed to be coming and going all the time. But as Mrs. Corbett told her daughter, "He doesn't seem lonesome, but you never see him with groups of other people. He's always alone."

GEORGE TOOK TRIPS TO FLORIDA AND CENTRAL AMERICA TO LOOK AT BUSI-nesses that Stratford might purchase. He mulled over reports and attended meetings where detailed discussions took place about egg production, horticultural yields, and new seeds for houseplants. It didn't take long for George W. to discover that he was just plain bored by the whole thing. Up to that point his life had been plenty exciting: Andover, Yale, Washington, political campaigns, flying jets. Now he was trudging off to a corporate job that he didn't much care for. He stayed there less than a year.

In 1972, Jimmy Allison, who had known his father since the Midland days and run his father's campaigns in 1966 and 1970, was working for Winton Blount in his Senate race in Alabama. Blount had been postmaster general under Nixon and was running as a Republican against the George Wallace political machine. George W.'s father had played tennis with Blount when he was in Congress.

Blount was facing John Sparkman, the Democratic incumbent. Allison knew that George W. was interested in politics and had worked on the 1968 Senate campaign in Florida. So he called him up in May and offered him a job on the Blount campaign. George jumped at the opportunity and immediately made plans to move. He also asked for and received a transfer to the Alabama National Guard for the duration of the campaign, but never reported for service.

George enjoyed his work, which was primarily organizing on the local level: putting bumper stickers on cars in parking lots, handing out leaflets, and working the telephones to encourage people to vote. It was an exercise in retail politics. Unlike his father's race in 1970, when he had been a surrogate candidate and been given managerial responsibility, here George W. was not the candidate's son but just another campaign worker.

He kept a close watch on the polls and realized that Blount was not going to win. Still he continued to labor throughout the summer in the heat. In the end Red Blount captured only 36 percent of the vote.

#### CHAPTER 17

# WING TIPS

C ONGRESSMAN GEORGE BUSH WAS IN HIS OFFICE IN MAY 1969 when the phone rang: President Nixon wanted to see him immediately. George was surprised and grabbed his press secretary Pete Roussel to come along.

The two men left the office, jumped in George's car, and started down Constitution Avenue. George turned to Roussel. "Hey, I gotta go by my house first."

"He said it like it was some kind of emergency," Roussel recalls.

They nevertheless headed for George's house on Palisades Lane in northwest D.C. When they pulled up to the driveway, George got out and walked quickly to the house. A few moments later he reappeared and jumped in, and they proceeded to the White House. Roussel wondered what the visit was about: Why had George gone home before meeting the president?

When they arrived at the Old Executive Office Building, George went up to meet with the president. Forty-five minutes later, he returned.

"The president wants me to run for the Senate in Texas, against Yarborough," George told his aide enthusiastically.

For the next several minutes they discussed the pluses and minuses of giving up a safe congressional seat to run against a three-term incumbent who had already beaten Bush once. As they approached the congressional parking lot, Roussel had a nagging question in his mind. "Hey, by the way, I know we made that unexpected stop along the way. What was that all about?"

George glanced down at the floor. "Remember those shoes I had on earlier today? I had on a pair of loafers. You don't go to see the president of the United States in a pair of loafers." Roussel looked down and, sure enough, Bush had changed into a pair of dark wing tip shoes.

Ever since leaving Yale, George Bush had enjoyed a series of mentors who had guided his career and offered fatherly advice. The first of these had been Neil Mallon. His father's friend from Yale had given him his first job and advised him on how to structure his oil business. When George decided to leave Dresser and strike out on his own, his uncle Herby Walker had advised him in his career as an independent oilman. It was Herby who had helped him raise money and meet the right people. With both men George had enjoyed an intensely personal friendship. Mallon, with his charming, wily ways and relaxed manner, had rubbed off on George in a way even the family could see. Uncle Herby, though he could be aggressive, rude, and meddling, never left a doubt in George's mind that he cared for him deeply.

As George's trajectory in politics began to rise, Richard Nixon became a new mentor of sorts. He had met Nixon, like his other two mentors, through his father. Indeed, it was his immense respect for the father that led Nixon to embrace the son. "President Nixon always seemed to bring up Pres Bush when he talked about George," Al Haig told us. "He clearly considered him a very good friend."

But unlike with Mallon and Uncle Herby, the relationship with Nixon was a frustrating one for a man who offered and expected a level of trust and even intimacy with his friends. Nixon could offer neither, much to George's disappointment. "He [Nixon] is unable to get close to people," George wrote to his sons at one point. "It's almost like he's afraid he'll be reamed in some way. People who respect him and want to be friends get only so close—and then it is clear—no more!"

Despite these limitations, George was attracted to Nixon. Even if Nixon was inaccessible at a certain level, the Bushes came to know the larger Nixon family. Bar and Pat hit it off well, and the kids spent time together now and again. George W. even flew to Washington to go on a date with President Nixon's daughter Tricia. The Nixons were thoroughly charming and kind. How a family behaves and acts is an important measure for the Bushes, who often pepper correspondence with the approving phrase "and I like their family" as a seal of approval. "We were all taught you measure a man by how his family conducts itself," said Bucky Bush.

George was attracted to Nixon because he was hardworking, tenacious, and loyal, attributes that ranked high in the pantheon of Bush family values. For his part, Nixon took a keen interest in the young two-term congressman from Houston. George had demonstrated intense loyalty to Nixon and the president thought he had a big future in politics. The relationship seemed based less on the strong bond of friendship that George Bush had developed with so many others than on the attractiveness of the presidency. For George there was a mythical quality about the office, and no matter how well or how long you had known the president, you wore formal shoes in his presence. As

George told one reporter in 1970, he experienced a "tingly feeling when the president is near."

Richard Nixon called George Bush into the Oval Office in 1969 because he was eager to gain a Republican majority in the United States Senate. Not since Zachary Taylor in 1848 had a sitting president confronted a Congress so completely in the hands of the opposition. Nixon was facing a House dominated 242 to 190 by the Democrats and a Senate the Democrats controlled 57 to 43. He had written off the House; but the Senate seemed to be within reach.

Retaking the Senate would be no easy task. But Nixon believed that with the right candidates—young, dynamic, exciting—it could be done. So he was recruiting bright young sparks in states that had vulnerable Democrats. Texas was such a state and George Bush was one of his first recruits.

Never had a president been so involved in candidate recruitment. He met with George Bush, William Brock of Tennessee, Lowell Weicker of Connecticut, Glenn Beall of Maryland, Thomas Kleppe of North Dakota, William Roth of Delaware, Robert Taft of Ohio, Laurence Burton of Utah, and Gov. Paul Laxalt of Nevada. When George left the Oval Office he was intoxicated. Nixon was committing himself personally to help George's campaign. He would make appearances, raise money, do whatever he could to help him beat Yarborough. And if for some reason he failed, Nixon had promised George a "soft landing."

George called his father to ask what he thought. Pres Bush's career had been all about patience. He had worked his way up through the ranks at Brown Brothers Harriman and run for the Senate when he was in his fifties. It was best for George to keep his safe congressional seat and work his way up the chain of the powerful Ways and Means Committee, the father said. He had a good thing going, and he could have a long and prosperous career in the House.

George also went to see the old warhorse, former president Lyndon Johnson. George had first met LBJ when his father had been in the Senate. ("Dad considered LBJ a master manipulator," says Pres Bush, Jr. "But he liked him personally.") George and LBJ developed something of a friendship after Johnson left the White House. As Nixon was being sworn in on January 20, 1969, George was skipping the ceremony and going instead to Andrews Air Force Base to see LBJ off. George was the only Republican there, a gesture that LBJ did not forget. "Thanks for coming," he told George before boarding Air Force One. Weeks later he asked George and Bar to come and visit him at his ranch.

George and Bar went to see him in May. They arrived on a warm, sunny day and LBJ gave them his typical treatment. He gave them a tour of the place, driving 80 mph on the dirt roads of his ranch in his open Lincoln Continental. Then they had lunch on the veranda. After the last bite was gone, they talked politics.

Johnson had served in both the House and the Senate, so he could offer a unique perspective. George asked him: Was it worth leaving a safe House seat for a crack at the Senate? Both bodies of Congress were honorable, Johnson told George. But there was a difference between the two, and it was huge. In the House you were one of the masses. In the Senate you could be much more your own man; have real influence. "It's the difference," he said, slapping his thigh, "between chickenshit and chicken salad."

Not that it would be an easy race, Johnson advised. Democrats had a four-to-one registration advantage in Texas and it would be an uphill battle for any Republican. But Johnson encouraged George to make the run nonetheless and offered to help. While he couldn't endorse George, he said he wouldn't do anything this time to help Yarborough. In the 1964 race, LBJ's last-minute support had made all the difference in Yarborough's victory.

George left the ranch believing that the path to a serious run seemed to be clearing. He commissioned a poll to see what the Texas political landscape looked like statewide. He also began mentioning the idea to friends, a term that comprised a large universe of people across the country. Bar's card file had been growing by leaps and bounds over the previous couple of years. Aleene Smith, who worked on Capitol Hill for George, says that he managed to keep in touch with about four thousand people through phone calls and personal letters. Now, many of these friends offered immediate help with the proposed campaign.

In the late spring of 1969, friends who were members of the prestigious Republican Boosters Club, a group of wealthy GOP donors, invited him to speak. After being introduced by Robert Finch, the secretary of health, education, and welfare, he made some remarks on the issues of the day. The Boosters Club would raise more than one hundred thousand dollars for the campaign. Bob Mosbacher, Jim Baker, and others from the oil business all agreed to hold fund-raising events and line up supporters.

In January 1970, with his campaign team in place, George announced his plans at a Houston press conference. Ralph Yarborough was too liberal for Texas, he told the assembled press. He was out of touch with most Texans, not pro-business enough, and too interested in using the powers of the federal government. The speech was effective, but the tectonic plates of Texas politics were shifting and George did not realize it. George was not the only one who knew that Senator Yarborough was out of touch. Democratic Party leaders had come to the same conclusion.

Yarborough was a fiery populist whose base of rank-and-file Democrats, minorities, and union members was beginning to erode. In part it was because Yarborough had continued to move to the left, becoming more outspoken on environmental issues and disassociating himself from the LBJ wing of the party.

"We all saw it—Yarborough was going to lose," recalls Bob Strauss, a Dallas attorney who later became head of the DNC. "Particularly when you saw the kind of race George was planning to run. He was young, attractive, and running as a mainstream conservative. Yarborough wouldn't have LBJ to pull his chestnuts out of the fire."

Strauss and Texas governor John Connally, a conservative Democrat, moved quickly to find a centrist to run against Yarborough in the primary. It didn't take them long to find a suitable challenger.

Lloyd Bentsen was a lot like George Bush, a young and attractive congressman from Houston who had a good reputation and a patrician demeanor. He also had a lot of friends in the oil business who were Democrats and didn't like Yarborough. With their support, and help from Strauss and Connally, Bentsen decided to plunge into the race.

At first Yarborough didn't take the challenge too seriously. Rumblings from conservative Democrats had been heard before, and he had always beaten back any challengers. Yarborough was chairman of the powerful Senate Labor Committee, and he spent the first four months of 1970 back in Washington, D.C., pushing projects for the state of Texas. When he finally did return to campaign in earnest, it was too late. Bentsen had successfully painted him as too liberal for Texas in what was by all accounts a dirty fight. The *Houston Chronicle* called the primary "memorable for its meanness."

Meanwhile, George was winning the Republican primary by more than a ten-to-one margin. But it was hardly a day for celebrating. The race the Bush family had been expecting—liberal against conservative, older pol against the young dynamic upstart—was replaced by a tough fight against a conservative Democrat who reminded a lot of people of George Bush. Both men had been decorated pilots in World War II (although Bentsen was a bomber pilot), both had served in the House, and both had worked in the oil business. To most Texas voters, there were more similarities than differences. And in that case, a voter registration that cut four-to-one for the Democrats would prove decisive.

Almost immediately, important defections began to affect the Bush campaign. Conservative Democrats such as Texas oilman Clint Murchison and industrialist George Brown, who had wanted to replace Yarborough, suddenly no longer expressed interest in supporting George's campaign. But despite these defections, the money kept flowing in. George had a national financial network now, whose inner circle was made up of family members and close Texas friends.

His father was slowing down because of declining health and was not very much involved in the campaign. Robert Mosbacher was struck by George's energy but also by how passive his father was. "I remember meeting [Pres] in New York at a club," Robert Mosbacher recalled. "I expected him to be up on the campaign but he really wasn't. He was asking me all sorts of very basic questions."

Still, Pres managed to contact some friends in New York banking circles. Tim Ireland, a partner at Brown Brothers, remembers Pres Bush encouraging the partners to make donations. Uncle Herby did the same with the partners at G. H. Walker and even passed the hat to some of his clients.

Senator John Tower was eager to help. As chairman of the Republican Senate Campaign Committee, he earmarked more than $72,000 for the race, nearly twice what other Senate candidates were getting. Nixon also kept his promise and tapped into his so-called Townhouse Fund, a secret slush fund he maintained to support friendly candidates. Run from the basement of a Washington apartment near Dupont Circle, it was managed by a group of Nixon loyalists and Bush friends, including Bob Mosbacher and William Liedtke, George's old business partner. The Townhouse Fund sent more than $106,000 to the Bush campaign.

But the embrace of Nixon complicated matters in Texas. Nixon was in some respects liberal by Texas standards. So when Bentsen denounced Nixon's welfare reform package as a "giveaway program," George was forced to defend it. When Bentsen attacked Nixon for too much government spending, George said programs were necessary to help poor Americans.

George moved to the political center, trying to attract Democrats and independents. Through his sister Nancy, he sought out and received the endorsement of her friend, the liberal economist John Kenneth Galbraith. The Harvard professor signed a letter of support that appeared in the *Texas Observer*. George also tried to lure young voters by arguing that the penalty for marijuana possession should be reduced from a felony to a misdemeanor. Lots of kids in Texas (including his son Jeb) were smoking pot. He also supported calls to end the draft and move to an all-volunteer army. Above all, he tried to stay positive. "I say in 1970 you've got to be positive, to be for something," he explained on the campaign trail. "And I'm for block grants, decentralization, revenue sharing, greater protection for society as a whole, and a return to fiscal sanity." This was far different from the right-wing Goldwater campaign he had run six years earlier.

Given that Bentsen would run on the same mainstream conservative message, George needed something to give him traction. Harry Treleaven, the New York City ad man, came back to Texas to put together his media package. He would spend more than half a million dollars on television and print advertising, adopting the campaign slogan "He can do more." George positioned himself as an outsider. "Sure, it's tough to stand up against the machine, the big boys," he said in his television ads.

For the first time George also found himself having to define his views on "women's issues." "The concept of a women's movement is unreal," he said much to Bar's chagrin. "You can't get two women to agree on anything." But it did play well in Texas.

Yet when pressed on the issue of abortion, he committed himself for the first time to the pro-choice position. This was also Barbara's view, and she helped convince him to adopt a more liberal stance. "I realize this is a politically sensitive area," he told one reporter. "But I believe in a woman's right to choose. It should be an individual matter. I think ultimately it will be a constitutional question. I don't favor a federal abortion law as such."

As in every previous campaign, the election was a family project. Bar walked precincts in Houston and traveled with George around the state. She also reviewed his television and print ads, often giving astute political advice. George W. would help with the primary campaign and again during the summer. He had matured to the point where his father felt comfortable for the first time making him a surrogate, the same role George himself had played for Nixon in 1968. George W. spent most of his time, however, working at the Houston campaign headquarters, where he recruited student interns. He had a knack for hyping the campaign and getting students excited.

During the summer of 1970, Jeb returned from Andover and walked with his father in campaign parades and helped distribute literature. For Jeb it was an act of familial loyalty rather than politics, and he was glad to be away from school. He had a distinct dislike for Andover. "The signals that they sent were not subtle to people from outside the region," Jeb told us. "Everybody thought they were a lot smarter than everybody else. It was not a very nurturing environment. It was very competitive intellectually. The culture at the times was very cynical and [it was] not a happy time to be sixteen, seventeen, or eighteen. I don't look back with fond memories."

Jeb worked long hours in the campaign office, dressed in torn jeans with a Marlboro hanging from his mouth.

The race remained surprisingly close as summer turned to fall. Suddenly a bump in the road appeared when word leaked from the Nixon White House that George might not stay in the Senate long if he managed to defeat Yarborough. David Broder of the *Washington Post* ran a piece quoting unnamed White House sources saying that if George won, he might replace Spiro Agnew as Nixon's running mate in 1972. No doubt this was encouraging news to George, but it could not have come at a worse time. Texas voters did not want a candidate who had his sights set on something else. George issued a quick denial, but the news no doubt hurt him with some voters.

By early October the polls continued to indicate a close race. In the White House, Nixon aides were looking for chinks in Lloyd Bentsen's armor, something that could derail his campaign. Chuck Colson in particular had people digging for dirt on Bentsen. Finally, when he thought he had something, White House aides contacted Bush. George wasn't interested.

"He refused to allow us to use some very derogatory information about Bentsen," Colson recalled later.

"Don't ever send anything of that nature up here again," George allegedly told Colson's assistant. "Tell Mr. Colson I called and to be sure he understands."

Tensions with the White House grew more pronounced as Nixon began flirting with Gov. John Connally. Connally was Bentsen's chief backer and a conservative Democrat. Nixon saw him as someone who could serve in his cabinet and give it a solid bipartisan hue. George was furious when he heard the news.

"Nixon had immense respect for Connally," said Robert Mosbacher. "He was a self-made man and had charisma, just like George. But he was one of those larger-than-life Texas politicians in a way that George was not. Nixon was attracted to that, and he was hopeful that Connally could be an ally with Southern Democrats. That was something George could not offer him."

When Peter O'Donnell, head of the Texas GOP, heard about Nixon's interest in Connally joining his cabinet, he contacted the White House immediately and told them that Bush and his supporters felt betrayed by the news. George had campaigned for Nixon twice while Connally had campaigned against him twice. George considered Nixon a friend.

The White House failed to respond to O'Donnell's concerns. George, who like all the Bushes placed a high value on loyalty, was enormously saddened.

In the waning days of the campaign, Nixon made two stops in Texas to bolster George's run. The crowds were large and excited on October 28 as he gave a rousing speech. He defended his Vietnam policy ("What we have done is after five years of men going into Vietnam, we have been bringing them home") and talked tough about crime and inflation. Nixon also hammered away on welfare reform, an issue that George was closely identified with. "If a man is able to work, if a man is trained for a job, and then if he refused to work, that man should not be paid to loaf by a hardworking taxpayer in the United States of America."

In the days before the election, Nixon spoke with William F. Buckley about the Senate race in New York, where Buckley's brother James was running for the seat on the Conservative Party ticket. "The only other race he mentioned was Bush's race in Texas," Buckley told us. "It was clear he believed Bush would win."

But as election day neared, George seemed to run out of partisan steam. As the *Washington Post* reported about a campaign appearance at Southern Methodist University, George lectured "with a great feeling on the problems of pollution and population control. The speech seemed nonpolitical, without a single jab at his Democratic opponent." His demeanor, reported the *Post*, was that of "the youthful modesty of a high school quarterback who had just been kissed by the prettiest cheerleader." Partisanship came hard to George, even in the waning days of a tough campaign.

The day before the election, Pres and Dottie flew down from Connecticut. George was cautiously optimistic. The poll numbers indicated that the race would be close. Given that this was an off-year election, turnout would be everything.

On election morning a tide of voters, unprecedented in Texas for an off-year election, turned out to vote. In heavily Democratic San Antonio voters stood in long lines, but Republican Houston also had a higher turnout than expected. Most surprising to the Bush campaign, however, was the rural vote. In small West Texas towns and East Texas ranching counties, voters were flocking to the polls. As the Bush campaign quickly discovered, the turnout was less driven by the Senate race than by two proposed constitutional amendments. One would allow saloons to operate on extended hours; the other would allow all undeveloped land to be taxed as farmland. Both proposals were highly unpopular in rural Texas, which also tended to vote Democrat.

As the numbers rolled in, the result was clear by early evening. Bentsen would carry the day, beating George by 150,000 votes out of more than 2 million cast.

George took the loss hard; he had failed both himself and the family. "I can't find anything to blame—not the president, not my campaign workers, not finances," he told the dejected crowd that night. "I'm looking introvertedly and I don't like what I see. I must've done something wrong."

George characteristically showed little emotion. But the loss weighed heavily on Bar. It not only meant that George would not serve in the Senate, but that their pleasant life in Washington would change. "When I called her up after the loss of the Senate election," says Nancy Bush Ellis, "she couldn't stop crying."

George W. cried openly, just as he had done in 1964. Little Doro, who was now eleven, was also in tears. Her father tried to console her, explaining that everything would be all right. "Oh no it won't," she retorted. "I'll be the only girl in the fifth grade whose daddy doesn't have a job."

The Republicans lost nine seats in the House and eleven governorships in 1970. In the hotly contested Senate races they did manage to pick up two seats. Nixon's most gratifying win was James Buckley's in New York, he would later say. His greatest disappointment: George's loss in Texas.

The loss was a deeply personal one for George, but he tried to remain optimistic. "I've got a house, a wife, some kids, a dog here in Houston. A man doesn't need much else." But deep down he couldn't help feeling that he was losing out on something grand. A person was defined by what he did, and he had missed out on an opportunity to prove himself in his father's arena. "It was not just ambition," he explained. "It was the feeling that the Senate is the zenith of politics, or public service, *the best a person can be.*"

———

HOURS AFTER HIS DEFEAT, GEORGE RECEIVED A TELEPHONE CALL FROM Washington columnist Charles Bartlett. Bartlett lived in Georgetown near Pres and Dottie and had won a Pulitzer Prize in 1956 for a series of articles on corruption at the Department of Defense. Pres, who was on the Senate Armed Services Committee at the time, had been a source, and the two had been friends ever since.

Bartlett had received a tip that Treasury Secretary David Kennedy was leaving the Nixon administration and suggested that if George was interested in the job, he should move quickly. George, clearly recalling Nixon's offer of a soft landing should he lose the Senate race, contacted the White House. Nixon aides were noncommittal. Days later it became apparent why: Nixon's flirtation with Gov. John Connally of Texas was quickly advancing toward some kind of nuptial. On November 30 the president appointed Connally to his Foreign Intelligence Advisory Board, and by the first week of December, Connally was offered the Treasury job, which he accepted. Barbara in particular saw this as a supreme act of disloyalty. Nixon was clearly aware of how it would look to the Bushes. As H. R. Haldeman put it in a memo to the president: "Connally set. Have to do something for Bush *right away*."

Having given up his congressional seat and with the Treasury job now filled, George fell into a funk. Finances were not an immediate concern. His net worth was a comfortable $1.3 million. But for the first time since Yale, it was unclear what his future might be. After the loss in 1964 he had Zapata to keep him busy. Now he had lost two statewide races and his political future in the state was more than a bit shaky. Rumors in Washington had it that he might be appointed head of the Small Business Administration, undersecretary of commerce, or perhaps even head of NASA. But none of these jobs held much interest for him. Then he received an unexpected summons from the White House.

H. R. Haldeman, Nixon's chief of staff, wanted to meet with him immediately. George went to the West Wing and Haldeman made a proposal. The job of ambassador to the United Nations would be open soon, but it was hardly a plum assignment. Nixon's first appointee to that post was Charles Yost, a career diplomat and a Democrat. But Nixon was clearly not pleased with Yost and had offered the job to Daniel Patrick Moynihan, another Democrat, in an effort to maintain a "bipartisan foreign policy." Moynihan's selection was savaged in the press, which questioned his foreign policy credentials. Moynihan (who had not yet embarked on his political career) quickly announced that he was not interested in the job, preferring to stay at Harvard. So the White House was turning to Bush.

"I was in a discussion with the former president Nixon and Henry Kissinger when he was making some observations about young George, as he called him, and the fact that he had lost the Senate race in Texas to Lloyd Bentsen," Al Haig recalled. "He wanted to make sure that he was offered a high-level position in his administration because he had such high regard for his father. And that's how he was appointed to the U.N."

———

GEORGE WAS ENTHUSIASTIC ABOUT THE IDEA. THE JOB SOUNDED IMPORTANT and interesting. It might also fit in nicely with his long-term plans to run for president. What he lacked, of course, was background for the job.

He asked his friend Congressman Lud Ashley for advice.

"That's great, George. But what do you know about foreign policy?"

"Ask me that in four weeks," George snapped, determined to secure the job.

Ashley's concerns were echoed in the *Washington Star* and the *New York Times*. George had "nothing in his record that qualifies him for this highly important position," wrote the *Times* in an editorial. Senator Adlai Stevenson, who had held the job under Kennedy, declared that his selection was "an insult."

But while George had no formal foreign policy background, most of his critics were not privy to the extensive private diplomacy he had engaged in during his Zapata days. Under George's ownership the firm had drilled for oil in highly sensitive areas that required an acute understanding of local and regional politics. Zapata had operated rigs near the coast of Cuba around the time of the revolution; in the Persian Gulf in the aftermath of the Suez Crisis; and in the Far East in the midst of the Malaysian civil war. In none of these instances was George a diplomat, but he had frequently met with foreign officials from time to time to protect his company's interests.

When George appeared before the Senate Foreign Relations Committee on February 8, 1971, he was fortunate to be among friends. Several key members of the committee knew his father well, and it quickly became apparent as the hearings began. Senator Stuart Symington, one of Pres Bush's closest friends in the Senate, encouraged George to work with both the National Security Council and the State Department in his capacity as ambassador. Senator Claiborne Pell, who also had a cordial relationship with Pres, declared that George would help the U.N. immensely given his contacts and access to the Oval Office. With the seal of approval from these two key Democrats, it never became necessary for the Republican members of the committee to make the case for Bush. He won easy confirmation from both the committee and the full Senate.

At George's swearing-in ceremony in February, George and Bar gathered with family and friends. President Nixon made an appearance and encouraged George in his new position. In a hint that he still had great expectations for his protégé, Nixon noted that William McKinley lost an election in Ohio but went on to be president. "But I'm not suggesting what office you should seek and at what time," he said warmly.

For Bar the move to New York represented another dramatic change. She had spent her entire adult life as the wife of an oil supply salesman, independent oilman, and congressman. Now she would be the wife of an ambassador whose work would be heavily oriented toward social functions. Bar threw herself into the task with typical abandon. All the boys were now off at school, so only little Doro would be living with them in New York. Family members remember her seeming particularly liberated as they headed off to the United Nations.

The Bushes took up residence in a forty-second-floor apartment at the elegant Waldorf Towers in the Waldorf-Astoria Hotel. It was a sprawling place, nine rooms in all with a forty-eight-foot-long living room and five bedrooms. It had once been the quarters for Gen. Douglas MacArthur and still looked it. The place was staid, drab, and musty. Using a little known State Department program, Bar arranged to borrow paintings by Mary Cassatt, John Singer Sargent, and Gilbert Stuart from the Metropolitan Museum of Art and had them hung in the entryway. She also had some antique Steuben glass placed in the reception area. Always sensitive to politics, she returned two Monets that the Met had also offered. She wanted their art to be strictly American. She also had the place repainted and installed new carpets.

The daily routine in New York remained pretty much what it had been since their days at Yale, with George up every morning like he was shot out of a cannon and Bar trying to keep up. George would rise early and ride the exercise bike for twelve minutes while he watched the morning news. Then he would eat a quick breakfast and meet his driver in the lobby for the short trip over to the mission. He looked at the overnight cable traffic from U.S. embassies around the world and went into a meeting with his assistants, Tom Lais and Aleene Smith. If any policy discussions needed to be held, he met with the delegation's professional diplomats, Ambassadors Christopher Phillips and W. Tapley Bennett.

Most of George's time was spent on the diplomatic social circuit, an endless stream of luncheons, receptions, formal dinners, funerals, and other ceremonies. For George it was the perfect assignment. If the Moroccan ambassador was hosting a dinner, George and Bar were expected to attend. If the Egyptian ambassador's son was in town, George and Bar might drop by for a drink. It was a dizzying blur of chitchat interspersed with the important business of forging social relationships with his counterparts.

When George wasn't involved in official business, he was giving political speeches for Republican candidates around the country, appearing at luncheons, or meeting with party supporters. His quest for the presidency was not dormant. As a case officer at the National Security Council at the time, Al Haig spoke regularly with George about foreign affairs and noticed that even then he seemed keenly aware of the political situation. "George was very ambitious and he saw this as an important stepping-stone," he said. "I could sense that very early in my association with him that he wanted to be president. He was consciously aware of a larger goal."

George set a frantic pace. "I try to get to bed by 11:30 if possible," he told a reporter in 1971, "but often my calendar is so filled that I fall behind in my work and have to take it home with me."

Despite the diplomatic niceties, George retained the casual style he had adopted in Texas. His mannerisms might have been appropriately patrician, but he was, as one newspaper put it, "breezily casual—an impression reinforced as he stood talking, wearing a wrinkled suit, hands stuffed in his pockets." George would, with Bar in tow, breeze into receptions, call on foreign dignitaries, and end with a dinner at a swank New York restaurant. But sometimes his sense of ease and the frantic pace presented problems for Bar. One night they were hopping from reception to reception as part of the New York social set. Bar was dressed in a short, bright red cocktail dress with gold threads. George was in a conservative blue suit.

After three receptions, it was getting late.

"Where to now?" Bar asked him.

"Come on, I'll tell you about it later," he said as they headed up some stairs at a diplomatic mission. Next thing Bar knew, she was in a memorial service for the ambassador of a Central American country who had passed away. George in his dark suit fit in fine with the men and women who were appropriately dressed in black. Bar, however, in her bright red cocktail dress, was forced to hide just as a television announcer declared, "And here comes the United States ambassador and Mrs. Bush."

"To this day he doesn't realize how sore I was at him," recalled Barbara. "It was *really horrible*."

But Bar was a quick student, and shortly after arriving in New York she asked someone for a copy of the Diplomatic Blue Book. It was a boring tome that provided personal information on the U.N. representatives: where they went to school, place of birth, spousal names, children. Bar studied it vigorously, memorizing names, faces, and any other information that might be of use. When she did find some free time, she volunteered at the Sloan-Kettering Cancer Institute, where George's uncle John Walker was president.

For little Doro, life in New York was an embarrassment of riches. She was driven by a chauffeur to the U.N. School, but she asked the driver to drop her off a block away so no one would see the car. She would spend time with her mother or her caregiver in museums or shopping on Madison Avenue or visiting nearby family. The one thing she seemed to lack was time with her father, who was always busy. The moments he did have with her, he was often tired. "I thought I was really hot stuff going there to meet him," she recalled of one dinner with dad. "We were going to spend the night at the Waldorf, and after the speech he took me to the 21 Club for dinner. I thought that was the neatest thing in the world. We were sitting there at dinner and all of a sudden dad started to fall asleep because he was so tired."

The most divisive issue then facing the U.N. was China. The People's Republic was seeking admission and calling for the expulsion of Taiwan, and the move had growing support in the international community. The State Department was taking the position that the United States should support the admission of Beijing but oppose the expulsion of Taiwan. Henry Kissinger, the national security adviser, and Secretary of State William P. Rogers called this the "two Chinas" policy.

Shortly after George's arrival it became clear that the entry of Red China into the U.N. was a given. The only real question was whether Taiwan would retain its seat.

China had been a subject of political passion for the Bushes going back to 1950, when Pres Bush had raised the issue in his Senate race. He had accused the Truman administration of being soft on communism and failing to support the Nationalist government. Ever since then the family had been firmly pro–Chiang Kai-shek. George had even declared when he ran for the Senate in 1964 that if Taiwan were expelled from the U.N., the U.S. should leave the international organization entirely. So George threw himself into the task with real zeal. Within the first six months of his tenure in New York, George had lobbied sixty-six countries on behalf of Taipei, meeting with their representatives and discussing possible deals. By late September he had personally spoken with ninety-four delegates about the Taiwan question.

Based on what the delegates had told him, George believed he had a better than 50 percent chance of winning the vote in the U.N. When the General Assembly finally convened on September 21, George was working frantically on the vote count. The State Department was checking in twice a day to get the best estimate.

George sat and watched when the vote tally finally came on October 25. The final tabulation was a shock. Taiwan was out on a 76 to 35 vote. It was a stunning defeat.

George left the hall visibly angry. Only days earlier he had been told by delegates to his face that they would vote with the U.S. Some had even received trade-offs from the United States in exchange for their vote. It was a long way from Midland, where all it had taken to seal a deal was a handshake.

As a show of solidarity, George escorted Liu Chieh, the Taiwan delegate, out of the hall. Third World delegates were dancing and cheering the American defeat. George brushed tears from his eyes and looked straight ahead. He later conveyed to his sons that the situation was "something ugly, something harsh that transcended normal disappointment or elation."

George's defeat at the U.N. was caused by delegates who had betrayed him despite their assurances. But he had also been undermined by Henry Kissinger, who had been on his secret mission to Beijing and made it clear to a number of Allied countries that regardless of what Bush was telling them at the U.N., a vote for Red China was fine with the United States.

George had now faced several instances where the loyalty that he so valued was not returned, but it never seemed to change his attitudes toward Nixon or Kissinger.

Relations with the Soviet Union were also a complicated matter. Ambassador Jacov Malik decided to test George early by organizing a small meeting days after he arrived. Malik, a hard-nosed diplomat of the old school, was everything that George was not: gruff, aggressive, and rude. It was Malik who in 1950 had walked out of a U.N. Security Council meeting in the middle of a discussion about the North Korean invasion of the South. He had done it as a sign of protest, but by leaving he allowed the United Nations to approve a U.S.-backed effort to support the South. Since then, Malik had demonstrated great skill at offending Western diplomats with his withering attacks on the West and boisterous verbal blasts at U.N. social functions.

Shortly after George arrived in New York, Malik called a private meeting with Britain, France, and the United States. He billed it as a get-acquainted session, but soon after George arrived Malik launched into a blistering attack on Israel, calling for its withdrawal from the Gaza Strip. (Israeli forces had occupied the territory during the 1967 Six-Day War.) Malik turned to George and proclaimed that the United States was a puppet of Israel. George responded calmly, telling Malik that his statements were so absurd that they did not even justify a response. Throughout his tenure at the U.N., George bantered with Malik on a host of issues. But at the heart of his relationship with Malik were Soviet concerns about the Jewish Defense League. George, for whom civility was a requirement, found himself in agreement with his nemesis on this issue.

The JDL was conducting angry and sometimes violent protests against Soviet delegations, including a harassment campaign under the slogan "Never Again." Automatic weapons were fired at the Soviet mission and protesters tried to storm a Soviet delegation meeting at Glen Cove on Long Island. One night, while George was dining with the Belgian delegation, he received an angry call from the Soviets. A refrigerator in the apartment of the

Soviet mission had been pierced by a bullet fired through the window. George instantly appeared at the Soviet mission to assure them that he would try to prevent a reoccurrence. He also made an immediate call to New York mayor John V. Lindsay, a family friend, requesting that security be increased.

George became outspoken in his views about the JDL, which in turn made him a target. In one instance Rabbi Meir Kahane, founder of the JDL, showed up at the U.S. mission and tried to prevent George from walking in through the front door.

"Why won't you talk to me?" Kahane shouted as he blocked the entrance. "All I want is a dialogue."

"I've seen your idea of a dialogue," George snapped back as he walked by him.

When talk show host Dick Cavett tried to arrange a program with Bush and Kahane to discuss Jewish immigration from the Soviet Union, George refused, saying that he would appear with someone else, but not Kahane.

George practiced a highly personalized form of diplomacy with friends and enemies alike. That gave the Bush clan an important role to play. U.N. diplomats regularly dined with him at his parents' home in Greenwich. Uncle Herby gave George the use of his box at Shea Stadium so a dozen or so members of the U.N. Economic and Social Council could take in a Mets game. Herby had purchased the team more than ten years earlier with a group of fellow investors, including the Whitney family of New York.

George also took delegates to the Lynx Club and the Palm. *The Nation* magazine called Bush "a mixture of Gary Cooper and John Lindsay—with money." And money it did take. While the State Department provided some funds for entertaining, it never went far enough and George was constantly tapping into his own funds to maintain what Brian Urquhart called his "aristocratic embrace."

What George was in fact doing was something that his father had learned at Brown Brothers and from his tenure in the Senate. Forge relationships; make friends. But while that approach worked well among those with common interests, it went only so far at the U.N. As Seymour Finger, who worked with him at the U.N., put it, George was amazingly popular among delegates at a time when "U.S. policy was so defensive and generally unsupportive."

Still George's sense of friendship and loyalty led him to trust in these relationships even when interests were opposite. It was a mistake he would make again when he returned to Washington.

George W. would sometimes fly to New York with some of his Texas friends and stay a few days. Often it was left to Bar to remind Lone Star visitors of the need to maintain a certain decorum. One night while W. and his friend Doug Hannah were dining with a small group in the Waldorf apartment, Hannah reached for a piece of Steuben glass and joked that he might stuff it in his pocket as a souvenir. He glanced over and noticed that Bar was staring at him.

"Neither you nor I can afford to get caught," she told him sternly.

---

THROUGHOUT THE SUMMER OF 1972, PRES BUSH HAD NOT SEEMED HIMSELF. Normally energetic and active, he was lethargic and labored to do the most basic tasks. He was losing interest in just about everything, including his family, his son's career, and politics.

"All that summer dad was ill," recalls Nancy Bush Ellis. "Mom would wrap him up in a blanket and say, 'He's just got a cold.' But you could sense dad was not doing well."

In September, Pres went to Sloan-Kettering in New York at the suggestion of Dottie's brother Dr. John Walker. Pres was now seventy-seven years old; the diagnosis that came back was bleak. Pres had lung cancer and didn't have much time. He was admitted to the hospital.

Dottie moved into the Waldorf apartment so she could be closer to Pres, who was medicated to ease the pain. All John Walker could do was try to keep him comfortable. They all came by to see him, Pressy, Johnny, Nancy, Bucky, and the Walkers.

George, who had characteristically thrown himself into the 1972 campaign by helping Republican candidates around the country, sharply cut back on his schedule. He tried to buck up the old boy by sharing news about his work. "Well, Dad, I had dinner with Andrei Gromyko." He described what they discussed, how he was getting to know the foreign minister, and the intricacies of superpower relations. "I had a wonderful dinner," he concluded. At which point Pres perked up enough to ask, "Who picked up the check?"

Pres Bush died a few days later, on October 8, 1972.

Christ Episcopal Church in Greenwich, where Pres and Dottie had attended for more than forty years, was selected for the funeral. Dottie, fighting back the grief, made all the plans. But she was no longer herself. "It was so atypical of her, but I remember her saying she wished that she had gone with him," Elsie Walker Kilbourne told us.

Dottie sat alone and quietly composed a eulogy, which was read by Rev. Bradford Hastings. Pres, she wrote, was a father who "believed in the necessary discipline when the occasion demanded, but was always loving and understanding. As the children grew older he respected each as an individual, ready to back any decision thoughtfully reached, and giving advice only when sought." For her part, Dottie was thankful that he was a man who had a "lack of pride in material possessions." In short, she said, he had given her "the most joyous life that any woman could experience."

The ceremony signified the passing of Pres Bush, who had led the family for several decades. But the funeral also signified the rise of a new generation of Bushes. At Dottie's suggestion, the pallbearers were not her sons but rather her grandchildren, including George W., Jeb, Marvin, and Neil.

More than a thousand turned out for a memorial service that spilled into the streets. Johnny Bush, the son who most inherited his father's gift for music, sang a solemn song. Community leaders from around the state turned out in force, as did the Walkers and the Bushes. One who didn't turn out was Pres's only brother, Jim, who had never reconciled with him over the issue of his divorces.

In Washington, senators on both sides of the aisle paid homage to the loss of one of their own. It was a moving service, recalled Nancy Ellis, marred by only one irritating act. "As we left the church, Lowell Weicker was standing on the steps talking to the cameras and holding court, telling them how close he was to dad. It wasn't true and it wasn't appropriate." Weicker was a newly elected senator from Connecticut. Ten years later Pres Bush, Jr. would run against him (and lose) in the Connecticut Republican primary.

Weeks after the funeral, George got word that President Nixon wanted to make some changes following his reelection. Nixon had told John Ehrlichman that he wanted to do a little housecleaning. What his administration needed, he said privately, was "not brains but loyalty." Nixon wanted to reshuffle his cabinet and revamp the GOP party organization. "Eliminate the politicians," he told his aides. "Except George Bush. He'd do anything for the cause."

One of the people whom Nixon wanted to replace was Sen. Robert Dole of Kansas, head of the Republican National Committee. The man had an "attitude," Nixon complained. He was a "poor-mouther" and "sour." Dole had a Senate career that was keeping him busy, and party fund-raising was way down.

"Dole—he must go," Nixon wrote in one memo. "In self interest. Need a full-time man. RNC chairman must be 1. Youth. 2. Image. 3. Builds new majority. 4. Center. 5. South or Midwest. 6. Bush?"

On November 20, 1972, George was flown by military helicopter to Camp David, where the Nixons were spending the weekend. Before he was ushered into Aspen Lodge to see the president, George met with George Shultz, the treasury secretary. Shultz offered him the job of undersecretary of Treasury, which essentially meant he would be responsible for the management of the entire department. Shultz would handle the major policy issues.

The offer had a certain appeal for George, who was comfortable in the world of finance. But when he was ushered into the Presidential Lodge to meet with Nixon, it soon became clear that the president had his own plans.

"George, I know that Shultz has talked to you about the Treasury job. And if that's what you'd like, that's fine with me. However, the job I really want you to do, the place I really need you, is over at the national committee running things. This is an important time for the Republican Party, George. We have a chance to build a new coalition in the next four years, and you're the one who can do it."

Nixon's choice of Bush for the RNC post was based on the enormous energy George had put into campaigning, not only in his own run for office but also for Nixon's campaigns. Perhaps even more important, George was a fantastic fund-raiser. George had helped to recruit his former business partner Bill Liedtke to serve as a regional finance chairman for the Nixon campaign in both 1968 and 1972, and he had raised an astonishing seven hundred thousand dollars for the 1972 campaign. George's good friend Robert Mosbacher was also an enthusiastic Nixon supporter and donor. The two had been centerpieces of the secret Townhouse Fund.

Truth be told, however, George had little interest in the job. Being RNC chairman was all about raising money, pressing the flesh, and giving speeches. He had done it all before with some reluctance. Now he was more interested in public service and policy than the mechanics of party politics.

George tried to sidestep the offer by asking whether he might instead take the number two job at the State Department, where he could serve as Kissinger's deputy. The experience at the U.N. had given him a taste for foreign policy. But Nixon was cool to the suggestion and pressed ahead with the RNC idea.

When the meeting broke up, George asked Nixon for a little time to think about it. But according to Nixon's own notes of the meeting, George also promised to dutifully do what Nixon asked. 'I'll do what you tell me. Not all that enthralled with RNC but I'll do it."

George took the offer home and talked with Bar about it. If George was "not that enthralled" with the idea, Bar was strongly set against it. She had already spent enough time in politics and knew what the job would mean. It would be tough on her and bad for his political career. His presidential ambitions were now a franchise for the both of them. She was investing as much time and effort as he was. For the first time in their marriage, she specifically asked him not to take a job he was considering.

George didn't respond directly, probably because he knew that she was correct.

"You can't turn a president down," was all he could muster.

"It was really about loyalty," aide Pete Roussel told us. "He didn't want the job. But few things matter more to George Bush than loyalty. He expects it from others and demands it from himself."

George did consult with other members of the family and a few friends. But in the end there was little anyone could say to dissuade him. The one bit of valuable advice he did get was from Sen. Hugh Scott of Pennsylvania, who had served in the Senate with his father. Scott told him to take the job only on the condition that George remain in the president's cabinet. It was good advice; Nixon was all too glad to agree.

Before the official announcement could be made, however, there was still something left undone. Although Nixon had offered the job to Bush, he hadn't told Bob Dole that he was being replaced. Instead of telling him straight out, Nixon concocted a ruse, telling Dole that he wanted his help to find his own replacement. He suggested that the senator fly to New York and talk with George about it. Dole did go to New York, only to discover later that the trip was pointless. Dole was furious and blamed George in part for his unceremonious dumping. As he later told his aides, he had been "bushwacked." A simmering feud between the two men was born.

PART TWO

# CONSOLIDATION

1972 · 1992

#### CHAPTER 18

# WATERGATE

C HRISTMAS 1972 WAS A TIME OF CHANGE FOR THE BUSH FAMILY. It was the first Christmas without Pres, and Dottie was missing him terribly. The family gathered in Washington, coming from different corners of the country. Jeb was eighteen and attending the University of Texas. He had said good riddance to Andover and never gave an instant's thought to going to Yale.

The one highlight from Andover was a trip he had taken to Mexico. While there, he had met a young Mexican girl. He was quite serious about her, but didn't introduce her to the family. He was quiet about his plans, reserved, and not sharing much of anything with anyone.

George W. flew in from Houston. He was now twenty-six years old and still searching for his way. He had graduated from Yale four years before and since that time had hardly moved out of the gate. He was finishing his stint in the National Guard and had taken a few jobs. To his father it was a complete mystery. When George had been that age he was married, with kids, trying to build a successful business. He didn't see much of a spark in his son and it was beginning to bother him.

"You have to understand," Elsie Walker Kilbourne told us, "big George is so direction-driven. Little George was not. He was enjoying himself, not doing much of anything in particular. His father didn't relate to that sort of existence."

Carrying around his father's name as he lived and worked in Houston was not an easy thing for George W., and rather than live up to the expectations that he would be his father's son, he seemed intent upon reducing those high hopes. He also had his quiet and not-so-quiet rebellions.

The family spent Christmas together as they always did, but there was a simmering conflict between big George and his eldest son. Matters seemed to come to a head one day when George W. asked his brother Marvin, then fifteen, to go with him to visit a friend. Marvin, who was attending Andover just as his father and oldest brother had, was struggling at school. He was clashing with school authorities and his marks were not particularly good. Finally he was asked to transfer. Marvin's godfather, Gerry Bemiss, arranged for his acceptance at a school in Richmond, Virginia.

"Marvin was having some difficulty," Bemiss remembers. "He was, as they say, acting a little too big for his britches. George and Barbara wanted him to transfer. We arranged to have him come to Woodbury Forest in Richmond."

That night George and Marvin spent several hours at the friend's house, drinking quite heavily. When they finally headed back late at night, George W. was driving erratically. As they approached his parents' house in Washington, he barreled the car into a neighbor's trash can. The can was jammed under the front fender, so when George W. started driving again, he created a tremendous racket that promised to wake everyone in the neighborhood.

When George W. finally pulled into the driveway, his father was waiting for him. Seeing that Marvin was clearly inebriated, he told Jeb to ask W. to come see him in his study. When the eldest son arrived, he was keyed up. And the emotions came pouring out.

"I hear you're looking for me," W. told his father. "You wanna go *mano a mano* right here?"

The family watched as the astonishing confrontation unfolded. Jeb apparently sensed that it was as much about his older brother's lack of clear direction as it was about the incident that had just occurred. Now over six feet tall, he stepped between the two and made a surprising announcement: W. had been accepted to Harvard Business School.

It was a secret that W. had been keeping from his parents, who didn't even know he had applied. And it was the sort of news that seemed to allay some of the father's concerns.

"You should think about that, son," George told him.

"Oh, I'm not going," W. retorted, with alcohol doing what it always did, making him arrogant. "I just wanted to let you know I could get into it."

The rest of the Christmas holiday, father and son didn't discuss Harvard much, but W. clearly knew that attending would be beneficial. What his father did do, however, was instruct his son in the best way he knew: He let him find his own way.

Harvard classes didn't start until September, so George suggested that his son might want to take an interim job in Houston with an organization called PULL. As he described what would be a very hands-on working experience, W. saw the instant appeal.

Professionals United for Leadership (PULL) was a charity run by two former professional football players, John L. White and Ernie Ladd. The two had come to Congressman George Bush in the late 1960s to discuss their plans to start a mentoring program for underprivileged kids in the poorest neighborhoods of Houston. George embraced the idea; he knew what a difference mentors had made in his own life and agreed to become honorary chairman and help raise money for the organization.

Shortly after the holidays, W. moved to an apartment at 2910 Westheimer in Houston, a world away from Chateaux Dijon. The place was a dump. Because a neighbor had a dog and refused to let the landlord spray for bugs, roaches were everywhere. There was little furniture and W. had little money. He lived cheap and drove his white Cutlass around with dirty laundry, tennis shoes, and papers stacked in the backseat.

Most of PULL's programs were centered in the Fifth Ward, the scene of serious racial tensions. A few years before, at nearby Texas Southern University, black students had barricaded themselves and lit a bonfire to protest police brutality. When George W. showed up with Marvin, they were quite a sight. "They stood out like a sore thumb," recalled Muriel Simmons Henderson, one of the organization's counselors. "John White was a good friend of their father's. He told us that the father wanted George W. to see the other side of life. He asked John if he would put him in there."

Despite the fact that W. was a white guy from an affluent family, the employees at PULL quickly found that he did not have any pretense in his attitude. "He never put himself in the position of looking down his nose at someone, like, 'I've got all this money, my father is George Bush.' He never talked about his father." W. worked with the others in an old warehouse building, playing and teaching the kids.

One day he was playing basketball with Zeke Moore, a defensive back for the Houston Oilers, and some of the kids. This was the sort of tussling on the court that W. had been accustomed to growing up. But as one of the twelve-year-olds went up for a shot, a pistol fell out of his pocket. W. was stunned, and the PULL staff had to ask the boy to leave for violating the group's strict antiweapons policy.

To the surprise of many, W. was a natural with the kids, playing basketball, checkers, and helping them in art classes. He also escorted them on prison trips to teach them about the dangers of a criminal life. He even took some of them up in an airplane. For many of the kids it was their first exposure to a white person who wanted to be their friend.

"He was the first real white boy that all of the kids really loved," recalled Ernie Ladd.

One boy in particular formed a close bond. Jimmy Dean was a scrawny kid who would show up at PULL without shoes and hungry. W. would get him a snack, take him to the store to buy some shoes, and help him in art class. One night he took Jimmy home. The house had a ripped door and a front porch that was sagging. A woman answered the door as loud music was blaring inside. W. could tell she was stoned out of her mind. "Jimmy was happy to be home," he recalled later. "But I was incredibly sad to leave him there."

Several years later W. learned that Jimmy had been shot and killed as a teenager.

GEORGE, SR. TOOK THE HELM OF THE REPUBLICAN NATIONAL COMMITTEE in January 1973 and found the party's affairs in disarray. Much of the money raised for the 1972 election had been siphoned off by the Committee to Re-elect the President (CREEP). As a result, the RNC was short of cash and in heavy debt. George's first task was an unpleasant one: firing a sizable portion of the staff.

As he had before at Zapata, he handled the matter personally. "He called them in and told them himself," recalled Nancy Thawley, who worked at the RNC. "He was very up front and honest about it and talked to them, and told them why it had to be done." The axe fell on more than one hundred, and when he was finished he was left with a staff of eighty-five.

He also cut back on spending. For out-of-town speeches or meetings, he flew coach, not first-class. And when in Washington he drove a small American Motors car. Bob Strauss, then head of the DNC, had a limousine and driver.

George also made changes to office policy that reflected a new tenor for the party. During his first week on the job he discovered that plenty of booze was being passed around during the day. George ended the practice immediately, telling the staff that if they wanted to drink, they would have to do so on their own time.

As party chairman and a member of the cabinet, George had unusual access to the president. While the RNC office was in the new Eisenhower Building, he spent much of his time in a government office next to the White House. His was the world where party politics and government met.

For the Nixon administration, that intersection had brought forth allegations of "dirty politics" in the fall of 1972. Some of the charges were major, as the Watergate scandal would prove. Others were relatively minor, even sophomoric. Such was the case involving one of the first allegations that George promised to investigate.

Karl Rove—later to mastermind W.'s ascent to Texas governor and then president—was then a student leader in the College Republicans, and had been accused of teaching "dirty tricks" to students around the country. He had instructed them on how to "dumpster dive," i.e., purloin the enemy's political secrets by digging through their trash; infiltrate Democratic political events to obtain information; and pass out faux invitations for hippies and pot smokers to attend DNC events. The allegations surfaced just as George was taking the job, and, as he told the *Washington Post*, he would "get to the bottom of the accusations." After a monthlong investigation, he determined that the charges had been exaggerated by a rival group of College Republicans.

Still, in the midst of the investigation George took a liking to Rove and no doubt saw some of himself in the young man. Rove was extremely high energy, fascinated by the mechanics of politics, and intensely loyal. He could also be tough as nails, something George himself found difficult at times. So after Rove was cleared, George hired him as an assistant. Over the next thirty years, Karl Rove would come as close as anyone to entering the inner sanctum of the Bush family.

But something much larger was already beginning to loom: the trial of the Watergate burglars. Charged with breaking into DNC headquarters at the Watergate Hotel, the burglars were assumed to have been hired by a group of overzealous partisans. Senior White House advisers were assuring George that the president and the people around him were completely clean of the scandal.

George immediately began a counteroffensive, defending the president and declaring that the break-in was not evidence of anything deeper. Over the next year and a half George would travel 124,000 miles and give 118 speeches and 84 press conferences echoing that theme. When party activists needed someone to come to town to rally the troops and fend off criticisms about Watergate, George was a willing soldier. Even when the evidence began to mount and others hesitated, George defended Nixon. When asked about dirty tricks in politics he would say, "I don't think it is good for politics in this country and I am sure I am reflecting the president's views on that as head of the party." Throughout it he seemed decidedly upbeat, even in the face of mounting criticism.

Meanwhile, he continued to expand his list of friends and allies around the country. Rich Bond was a young political operative in New York when he met Bush at the airport to take him to an event on Long Island. "I picked him up in the car and took him to the event," he recalled for us. "I was amazed when he got up and spoke. He stood there confidently and defended the president in front of the audience and then in front of the press. There were very few Republican leaders who were willing to go out and mix it up like that at the time. I was deeply impressed with his willingness to even show up." Bond would later serve Bush as a campaign aide and then serve as chairman of the RNC.

Andy Card, then head of the Massachusetts Republican Party, had a similar experience. Card had scheduled George to deliver a talk for local party officials, and six hundred chairs were set up. Only sixty people showed up, but George went gracefully through the speech. Card was particularly impressed with George's willingness to take the stinging criticism of some in the audience. Card would later serve as George's transportation secretary and as his son's chief of staff.

While in Washington, Barbara kept up a heavy schedule of entertaining. She was a full partner now in his ambitions, and worked every bit as hard as he did. Bar would go to social meetings and then return, writing down notes in the card file about whom she had met, details about their families, and common friends and interests they might have.

George was convinced that Nixon was not involved in Watergate and that the Democrats were trying to make hay for political gain. Their zeal to investigate Nixon was an expression of partisanship. So George was determined to investigate the investigators and give them a taste of what they were dishing out. On July 24, 1973, George released affidavits signed by several men who claimed that the chief investigator of Sen. Sam Ervin's Watergate Committee, Carmine Bellino, had recruited spies to defeat Nixon back in 1960. At a press conference George declared, "This matter is serious enough to concern the Senate Watergate Committee, and particularly since its chief investigator is the subject of the charges contained in the affidavits. If these charges are true, a taint would most certainly be attached to some of the committee's work."

The charges were quite specific: that Bellino and other Democrats "had bugged the Nixon space or tapped his phones prior to the television debate [in 1960]." While admitting that some in the Nixon White House might have gone too far in their political activities—there was "corruption," George said—he also pointedly claimed that Democrats had done the same.

Bellino was furious with the allegations and declared that they were "absolutely false." "I categorically and unequivocally deny that I have ever ordered, requested, directed, or participated in any electronic surveillance whatsoever in connection with any political campaign. By attacking me on the basis of such false and malicious lies, Mr. Bush has attempted to distract me from carrying out what I consider one of the most important assignments of my life."

George was getting down in the trenches for the first time in his political life. The capital was awash with charges and countercharges, and George was in the middle of it. George also blasted away at Democratic senators Talmadge and Inouye, declaring that they had tried to prevent a full probe of LBJ intimate Bobby Baker back in 1963. All of this, which was so out of character for George, was a reflection of the personal loyalty that he felt for Nixon.

While George was willing to pursue what he saw as legitimate counterattacks on Nixon's opponents, in Nixon's inner circle they knew there were limits. In an Oval Office meeting in January 1973, Nixon met with Chuck Colson to discuss some possible dirty tricks that could be used to undermine the Watergate investigation. Nixon was all for the idea, but according to the White House tapes, a long discussion went on about who exactly might be willing to carry them out. When George's name came up, the president proclaimed, "Bush will never do it. He'll do position things [to help], but that's all."

As the investigations progressed, George was unwilling to follow the harder line demanded by the White House. John Ehrlichman had hired retired cops to probe the personal habits and drinking patterns of Nixon's political opponents. When George found out, he was outraged. "Crawling around the gutter to find some weakness of a man, I don't think we need that," he snapped. "I think opposition research is valid. I think if an opponent is thought to have done something horrendous or thought to be unfit to serve, research is valid. But the idea of just kind of digging up dirt with the purpose of blackmail or embarrassing somebody so he'd lose, I don't think that is a legitimate purpose." Little surprise that as the crisis reached critical mass, Nixon told Haldeman that George was just a "worrywart."

As the Senate and House Watergate investigations continued, the trail appeared to lead to someone in the White House. As a result, Nixon and his closest aides became increasingly insular and secretive, even with George. The head of the RNC found himself defending the administration when he had little idea of what exactly was going on.

"You can't image the tension," said Eddie Mahe, Jr., who was RNC political director at the time. "There was never any good news. Bush was the epitome of the good trooper. At staff meetings, he'd tell everyone to hang in there. Then, privately, he'd be very distressed. He would just moan: 'What is going on?' "

What seemed to sustain George were the personal assurances from Nixon that he was clean. The word of a man is of great value to the Bushes. So

George continued to preach the gospel that Nixon was not involved. "Watergate was the product of the actions of a few misguided, very irresponsible individuals who violated a high trust and who served neither the president nor their country very well," he told one audience. He made a point of telling the crowd that Nixon "wasn't involved in the sordid Watergate affairs. I believe him."

But despite his public face, privately George was troubled. He was growing tired of Watergate and the persistent questions and, along with Bar, he was feeling isolated in Washington. For the gregarious Bushes it was the first time they did not have a busy social life. Those at the RNC and in the White House were seen increasingly as pariahs, even among Republicans on Capitol Hill. The only tennis partner Bar could find to play with her was childhood friend Milly Dent, whose husband, Frederick, was secretary of commerce.

George continued to seek consolation through his friendships, which at times spanned the political divide. One of his most unusual at the height of Watergate was with DNC chairman Robert Strauss. While in Congress, George had befriended many Democrats, such as Congressman Dan Rostenkowski. But Strauss was the man who ran the political shop that was targeting Nixon and the GOP.

Strauss was a Dallas lawyer who had known Bush slightly during the Texas days. (He was also a business partner of George's friend Jim Baker.) But the friendship took on a deeper form during the adversity of Watergate.

"It was a sort of oddball pairing," Strauss said. "We were both going through a difficult time. George was dealing with Watergate, and we had problems of our own. It was a friendship made during adversity, and that is what I think makes it so strong and special to me."

George and Strauss would meet for lunch or drinks, certainly an unusual sight when Watergate was at its height. George would pour out his frustrations, and Strauss would encourage him to hang in there: Things would get better. At one point George asked him what he would do to end the mayhem. "When a gorilla wants to make love to you," he told George, "you don't stop when *you* want to. You stop when *the gorilla* wants to."

Strauss could offer very little advice on how to get through the Watergate mess. But their bond of friendship helped George when things finally imploded. While many Democrats on Capitol Hill were lambasting Nixon and members of his team, including George, Strauss was remarkably restrained. "I pledged to myself that I would not attack George personally," Strauss remembers. "He was a friend, but more important, he didn't have any part in Watergate."

As the tidewaters continued to rise, George and Bar were rocked by a phone call from Jeb. He was attending the University of Texas and getting terrific grades. But he had news: He was going to marry Colu, the Mexican girl he had met, and it was going to happen fast. The news was like a bolt of lightning from a West Texas thunderstorm. Jeb was only twenty years old and Colu was nineteen. George and Bar had never even met the girl. Colu was the only girl Jeb had ever seriously dated and by his account ever really *been with*.

They had first met three years earlier when Jeb was an exchange student from Andover teaching English in Mexico. Colu was from a middle-class family and had never really known her father, who had walked out on the family when she was three. When she first met the tall, gangly student, she wrote him off as a playboy, not being interested in serious matters. Jeb, who was smitten, vowed to prove to her that he was serious. His grades improved substantially, and he was on schedule to graduate from the University of Texas Phi Beta Kappa in just two and a half years.

When George and Bar had married thirty years earlier it was after a long courtship, and both families had been involved. This situation was a lot different, and Bar in particular worried about whether they would make it. "How I worry about Jeb and Columba," she wrote in her diary. "Does she love him? I know when I meet her, I'll stop worrying . . . I am praying to be like Dottie Bush but it will be hard."

"I didn't make it easy for them in retrospect," Jeb Bush admitted. "I hope that my kids don't do to me what I did to my parents. I told them that I was going to get married and they had not met her. My mom came early, but my dad did not meet her until the small dinner before the wedding, which wasn't very nice of me."

Bar flew down to Texas and went with her son to pick out his wedding band at Boone and Sons. She also pulled out Grandmother Pierce's wedding ring and had it fitted for Colu's hand. The rest of the family arrived days later for the ceremony. On February 23, 1974, a small party gathered at the University of Texas chapel. Colu's mother and sister made the journey, and for the first time they met the Bushes. It was a simple, joyous ceremony, but because Colu spoke no English, portions of the service were conducted in Spanish.

Colu's entry into the Bush family would prove difficult, a process that even after thirty years is still a work in progress. At family gatherings the family would laugh, play, and tell stories. Colu would just sit, smile, and wonder.

Colu learned the language quickly, but more difficult were the behavioral barriers between the quiet, shy young lady who had grown up without a father and the active, boisterous, robust Bushes.

"The family was going a mile a minute and involved in national politics at the highest level," says Gerry Bemiss. "And then here comes this kind, shy young girl thrust into the middle of it. She naturally retreated in the face of it."

She started by withdrawing from family activities. Family members saw it as a rejection, particularly of Barbara, who worked hard to reach out to her first daughter-in-law. "It was a huge strain for Jeb, and taken in the context of that family, which was that she never fit in," Shellie Bush Jansing said. "One of the things that I think we all resented is that Bar tried so hard for her. She has broken her back and Colu has never reciprocated. A lot of situations like that have made us all resentful."

The family rallied around Barbara, which led to Colu's further isolation. Then she became resistant to anything political. It caused tension for Jeb and within the family and complicated his later ambitions to go into politics.

"Jeb carried a huge chip on his shoulder for a long time," says Jansing. "Everybody in the family knew that, because of Columba. Jeb was always the one who had the brains. But in the real bosom of the family we never thought Jeb would go national because of Colu."

In the spring of 1974 a series of dramatic political explosions reverberated through the nation's capital. Perhaps none was as loud or rocked the Bushes' world more than the news that President Nixon had a taping system in the White House. For George it was a shocking breach of confidentiality, which he believed was the twin brother of trust. Everything his father had taught him about the importance of discretion, about how things worked in Bones, at Brown Brothers, and in the Senate, had been predicated on confidentiality.

Immediately there were demands that Nixon release the tapes to reveal what if anything he knew about the Watergate break-in. George sent a "confidential and eyes only" letter to this effect to Al Haig, Nixon's chief of staff. After all, wouldn't the tapes prove his innocence? In George's mind there seemed little doubt that Nixon had nothing to fear. If he didn't release them, George warned, "Each congressman and senator will have a justifiable reason to try to put distance between himself and the White House. There will be a major outcry. The press will play this Republican outcry for all it is worth."

The second explosion was Nixon's firing of Archibald Cox, who was handling the Watergate investigation at the Justice Department. The so-called Saturday Night Massacre was cited as proof that Nixon was covering something up.

Nixon replaced Cox with Leon Jaworski, a Democrat and an attorney from Houston who happened to be a longtime friend of George's. Jaworski was a partner in one of Houston's largest law firms and heavily involved in Texas business circles. George had first met him in the 1960s during his days with Zapata. When he was in Congress, Jaworski lived in his district.

Nixon had hired Jaworski because he thought that he might be a more compliant investigator. But Nixon proved sorely mistaken when Jaworski pushed aggressively for release of the tapes.

The third and final explosion came when the U.S. Supreme Court ruled 9–0 that Nixon could not prevent release of the tapes under the guise of "executive privilege." Weeks later the so-called "smoking gun" tape was released.

A tape recording of a June 23, 1972, conversation, about one week after the break-in, revealed that Nixon did have knowledge of the burglary and had a role in organizing a cover-up. The mask came off of Richard Nixon. George suddenly realized that Nixon had lied to just about everyone, including him.

As calls for Nixon's resignation mounted, Chuck Colson sent George memos urging him to mount a more vigorous defense. George refused, arguing that the party and the White House were separate entities. If the president wants to talk about it, George told Colson, have him call me direct. Nixon never did.

Ehrlichman pleaded with him to circle the wagons and fight to the bitter end. Father John McLaughlin, who was also working on the White House staff (and who later went on to become a television personality), asked George to provide the RNC fund-raising lists so he could ask for letters and statements in favor of Nixon. George refused. The party was bigger than one man, even the president. He was not going to destroy the party base for the sake of a White House that was spinning out of control.

The most difficult appeal came from Julie Nixon, who visited George to talk about her father. In tears, she begged George "to do more to help my dad." The emotion brought tears to George's eyes.

But George could mount no defense of Nixon—what sort of defense was possible? Instead he steadfastly avoided criticizing the president in public. In part it was his sense of loyalty. But he was also no doubt thinking about his own father, who had always spoken highly of Nixon's commitment to the country.

For the next several weeks the Nixon administration lumbered along on the edge of crisis. Moves were made on Capitol Hill to bring charges against Nixon. Defections in the Republican ranks indicated that a vote of impeachment just might succeed. Still, Nixon was determined to hang tough, seemingly unaware that many of his allies in Congress had abandoned him.

On August 6 the matter came to a head at a cabinet meeting in the White House. Nixon began by saying that he wanted to "discuss the most important issue confronting the nation." Cabinet members, including George, undoubtedly assumed that he was going to finally address the Watergate issue and settle the matter. But instead Nixon began talking about inflation. He went on for several minutes, dissecting the subject, acting as if the Watergate mess did not even exist. George later remembered the discourse as giving the cabinet meeting "an unreal feeling."

As Nixon went on to propose a national summit on the economy, his attorney general, Bill Saxbe, suddenly interrupted him.

"Mr. President, I don't think we ought to have a summit conference," he told him bluntly. "We ought to make sure you have the ability to govern."

The president tried to deflect Saxbe's concerns, but then George suddenly asked for a chance to speak. Nixon refused to give him the floor but George spoke anyway.

Saxbe was right, George said. Watergate had sapped public confidence. Then he flat-out asked Nixon to resign. He wasn't expecting Nixon to comply on the spot, so he was also carrying a letter in his jacket pocket requesting that Nixon resign.

It was a bold move on George's part and certainly not his usual style. He had in the past handled sensitive matters privately. As Al Haig recalls, "Remembering the blizzard of historic precedents produced by Watergate, this particular snowflake, in which the chairman of the Republican National Committee called on a Republican president to resign in the presence of his cabinet, stands out in my memory."

A silence came over the room. Then, as Haig recalls, someone said, "Shut up, George, we're trying to do business here."

Yet Haig and the others saw George as merely stating the obvious. "It was like bringing snow to an Eskimo," he told us. "He did it for effect rather than substance. That was how we viewed it at the time." But it was the first request uttered by a member of his cabinet that the president should step down. After the meeting, Henry Kissinger followed Nixon back to the Oval Office and told him that resigning was indeed the best thing he could do for the country.

George went ahead and submitted the letter he had written asking the president to step down. The letter, although direct, indicates how conflicted

George felt between the twin imperatives of doing what was right and maintaining personal loyalty.

> Dear Mr. President,
> It is my considered judgment that you should now resign. I expect in your lonely embattled position this would seem to you as an act of disloyalty from one you have supported and helped in so many ways. My own view is that I would now ill serve a President whose massive accomplishments I have always respected and whose family I love, if I did not now give you my own judgment. Until this moment resignation has been no answer at all, but given the impact of the latest development, and it will be a lasting one, I now firmly feel resignation is best for the country, best for this President. I believe this view is held by most Republican leaders across the country. This letter is much more difficult because of the gratitude I will always have for you. If you do leave office history will properly record your achievements with a lasting respect.

The letter sat on Nixon's desk. The next day, prompted by more than this, the president delivered his resignation.

All George could say was, "I'm really glad Dad's not alive, it would have killed him to see this happen. He thought we were the party of virtue and all the bosses were Democrats."

---

To say that Watergate was a failure of American institutions would have been too antiseptic for George. Institutions are only as good as the men who populate them, in the Bushes' worldview. Failure is a profoundly human matter. This sense of the meaning of Watergate came through in a private letter he wrote to his sons.

Watergate represented the profound failure in judgment and action of everyone involved. H. R. Haldeman was "unable to exercise political judgment—condoning things he should have condemned—arrogant to a fault." Ehrlichman was a man who appealed "to the dark side of the Nixon moon." Colson had "no judgment, a mean and vicious streak—so insidious and ugly." John Dean was "a small slimy guy—unprincipled—groveling for power."

In the face of all this, George told his sons that he found himself wondering "for heaven sakes where was what Dad always called conscience." Conscience was the great restrainer in the Bushes' world. Pres and Dottie had always been very big on conscience. George and Bar had often appealed to it, rather than a paddle, when disciplining their sons.

"Listen to your conscience," he advised them. "Don't be afraid not to join the mob—if you feel inside it's wrong. Don't confuse being 'soft' with seeing the other guy's point of view." Above all, understand that "power accompanied by arrogance is very dangerous. It's particularly dangerous when men with no real experience have it—for they can abuse our great institutions. Avoid self-righteously turning on a friend, but have your friendship mean enough that you would be willing to share with your friend your judgment. Don't assign away your judgment to achieve power."

George already had a jaded view of the media, dating back to his father's defeat in 1950. The media in his view picked favorites and went after those they didn't like. In Watergate, the press had been on a search-and-destroy mission from the beginning. "Long before any evidence was on the table many in the press had concluded that RN was evil and no good," he wrote.

George was also sensitive to the fact that for the first time in his public life, his associations and affiliations might be a source of potential embarrassment for his sons. For a family that embedded in its young the importance of carrying the name, it was a difficult admission to make. "I expect it has not been easy for you to have your Dad be head of the RNC at this time," he wrote. "I know your peers must put you in funny positions at times by little words in jest that don't seem funny or by saying things that hurt you because of your family loyalty."

For a man with an acute sense of ancestry and family mission, these were difficult words to write. But the letter was not an effort to convince them that he had followed the course his conscience dictated. "It's important [to write] not from the sense of my interpretation of the fact; but it's important because as Dad helped inculcate into us a sense of public service I'd like you boys to save some time in your lives for cranking something back in. It occurred to me your own idealism might be diminished if you felt your Dad condoned the excesses of men you knew to have been his friends or associates."

Despite his pain and anger, George remained optimistic that American institutions would survive the human failings exposed by Watergate.

"Civility will return to Washington eventually. The excesses condoned by the press will give way to reason and fair play. Personalities will change and our system will have proved that it works—more slowly than some would want—less efficiently than some would decree—but it works and gives us— even in adversity—great stability."

#### CHAPTER 19

# BOOZE

IN THE FALL OF 1973, GEORGE W. DROVE HIS SPRAY-PAINTED CUTLASS north out of Houston and headed for Cambridge, Massachusetts. Whether consciously or not, he retraced some of the same roads that his father had taken in 1947 when he had left Yale bound for Texas.

Everyone in the Bush family was enthusiastic about W. going to business school. None more so than uncle Johnny Bush, who was now ensconced in the world of finance after a brief fling with theater and music. Johnny thought the experience would be like boot camp and instill a sense of discipline. Johnny and W. got along well. They both had that sassy sense of humor and high spirits that put them in the center of the family's activities. Now that George W. was back in the Northeast, he would see his uncle more regularly, and Johnny would begin to assume the role of mentor/adviser that uncle Herby Walker had played for his father.

Cambridge in the mid-1970s was everything you might expect it to be: liberal, liberated, and very self-confident.

George W. took an apartment off Central Square and began his course work. The classes at HBS were intensive, with plenty of emphasis on quantitative management techniques and case studies. It was very different from what W. had been used to at Yale.

From the earliest days he was determined to be the ultimate iconoclast in a community that championed diversity. Among the long-haired students and preppy establishment kids, George W. would strut into class wearing a Texas National Guard flight jacket with a tin of Copenhagen chewing tobacco in his pocket. He would sit in the back, spitting into a cup that he kept on the floor next to his desk.

From the earliest days he made a point of being different. "While they were drinking Chivas Regal," recalls April Foley, a girl he dated in Cambridge, "he was drinking Wild Turkey. They were smoking Benson & Hedges and he's dipping Copenhagen, and while they were going to the opera he was listening to Johnny Rodriguez over and over and over and over."

W. spent his free time hanging out at the Hillbilly Ranch—one of the few places in Boston that would play country music—drinking beers and chatting with whoever might show up. He studiously avoided talking politics, usually not volunteering even to friends who his father was. W. had not had an anonymous childhood. He had always been George Bush's boy, carrying his name and walking in his shadow. At Harvard he wanted it to be different.

Being in the Northeast again gave W. the opportunity for the first time in several years to spend time with family and friends from his Yale days. Roland Betts, one of his best Yale friends, was living in New York City. The two men were opposites in just about every way. Betts was a liberal Democrat, and his social background was not like anything George had experienced. Still, the two had a strong bond and enormous respect for each other.

Shortly after W. arrived in Boston, Betts called to say he was coming to introduce him to his new wife. Betts was excited for W. and Lois to meet and curious as to how Bush might react. Lois was black. "It was very important to me that George meet Lois," Betts recalls. "Although there's a lot of interracial stuff now, at that time it was pretty controversial. So we went up to Boston. They were best friends that night and forever."

W. felt comfortable with his friend and would escape Boston and head to New York for a chance to visit and maybe play a pickup game of basketball. On a court near Riverside Drive and 100th Street they would join with some younger kids in the neighborhood and play a no-holds-barred game. It was the sort of relaxed and informal atmosphere in which he felt at home.

Another important outlet was his friendship with Karl Rove, who was working for his father. The two stayed in touch, talking on the telephone about politics and the intellectual snobs that W. was encountering on a daily basis.

W. also had the opportunity to see more of his family. His Aunt Nancy was nearby, Uncle Johnny was in New York, and Uncle Pres was in Greenwich. He would come over on a weekend for a home-cooked meal or someone would take pity on him and offer to help with the laundry. Through it all W. seemed to be his same irascible self. Sassy humor, sarcastic wit, and a glimmer in his eye. The same cockiness was there, too, but family members also noticed for the first time that his drinking was becoming a problem.

The Bushes had always been casual drinkers. Gampy Walker enjoyed his bourbon, Pres and Dottie offered a full-service bar in their home, and George and Bar enjoyed the cocktail hour with friends. But George W. was spending a lot of time socializing around alcohol and it was affecting his behavior.

His aunt Nancy recalls how he was hung over from the night before with some frequency. She would phone him at his apartment, sometimes late in the morning. W. would answer with the groggy voice of a man barely awake. "Sorry, Aunt Nan," he would apologize. "The Black-jack got me last night."

His uncle Pres also noticed that his nephew was drinking more. "George was becoming a real boozer," he recalled.

At Yale he had seemed on top of the world. After Yale he seemed to be looking around with no idea of what to do next. Alcohol gave him a sort of escape; a replay of his identity from college days. "He was always the big man on campus," Shellie Bush Jansing said. "Now he would come to family parties with three or four friends dragging in behind him and they had been out drinking, full of bravado."

---

Nixon's resignation elevated Gerald Ford to the presidency, and speculation began almost immediately as to who he would pick as vice president. The Twenty fifth Amendment would require confirmation by a majority of both houses of Congress, so Ford wanted to select someone he believed could sail through without a fight. Dean Burch, a White House aide, told Ford in a memo that it was essential to pick a candidate who would not only serve him well, but also be able to carry the torch for the party into the next decade. Of those being given serious consideration, wrote Burch, "My personal choice is George Bush."

George was clearly interested in the job, and hours after Nixon resigned, his friends began organizing a draft effort on his behalf. While George was not directly involved in this work, he certainly didn't discourage it. Jim Baker, who would later run Ford's reelection campaign, helped start a whispering campaign, as did other friends like Robert Mosbacher. A few zealous party activists even set up a "campaign" office in Washington.

Could George rise Phoenixlike out of the ashes of Watergate? Clearly he was a long shot. Much of the talk centered on Nelson Rockefeller, the former governor of New York. Rockefeller was the ultimate establishment choice, a safe and steady partner for Ford who enjoyed strong support in the cabinet. Caspar Weinberger, the secretary of health, education, and welfare, James Lynn of Housing and Urban Development, Attorney General Saxbe, and Frederick Dent of Commerce were all for Rocky. On the White House staff, Pat Buchanan and John McLaughlin were also for Rockefeller.

But Ford was not so sure. He announced that he would poll Republicans across the country to determine who might be the most popular choice. The jockeying soon began, and while Rockefeller enjoyed a large built-in advantage, the Bush forces quickly mobilized.

Richard A. Moore, a member of the White House staff, wrote to the president declaring that George would be a great help in the area of economics. After all, wrote Moore in a memo, "His father and grandfather were both highly respected investment bankers in New York."

In the Congress, George's friends from his years in the House rallied to his support. Bill Archer, who had taken George's seat in Houston, led the campaign, but plenty of support came from his broad cluster of friends on both sides of the aisle. Republicans Barber Conable of New York, Pete du Pont of Delaware, Glenn Davis of Wisconsin, and Ed Derwinski of Illinois all came out for Bush. Trent Lott, then a young congressman from Mississippi, declared his support for Bush because Ford needed someone "young and clean." Jack Kemp, an up-and-coming congressman from New York, also made Bush his first choice.

Lud Ashley of Ohio, George's friend from Yale days, and Dan Rostenkowski indicated to Ford that Bush was someone that Democrats could work with.

When the White House staff tabulated the results from the House, George was the first choice of 101 congressmen as opposed to 68 for Rockefeller.

Rockefeller supporters protested the efforts being made on George's behalf. Tom Evans, a former RNC cochair, wrote to the president that "no one should campaign for the position and I offer these thoughts only because of an active campaign that is being conducted on George Bush's behalf which I do not believe properly reflects Republican opinion." He then slammed George as unqualified for the job.

"Certainly one of the major issues confronting our country at this time is the economy and the related problems of inflation, unemployment, and high interest rates. I respectfully suggest that you need someone who can help substantively in these areas. George is great at PR but he is not as good in substantive matters. This opinion can be confirmed by individuals who held key positions at the National Committee."

Then another whispering campaign began. If George Bush was the choice, it would mean trouble for Republicans. There was a skeleton in George Bush's closet, notably his ties to Nixon's slush fund during the 1970 campaign. The two men who had run the so-called Townhouse Fund, Jack Gleason and Herbert W. Kalmbach, had pled guilty to running an illegal operation. Although there was no evidence that George knew about the irregularities, the large contributions that went to his Texas Senate campaign could prove embarrassing, the *Washington Post* reported. If George were selected as vice president there would be hearings, and questions raised about the Townhouse Fund. Some eighteen Republican senators who had received money from the fund but had never been named publicly might be exposed.

By the middle of August the intensity of speculation about Ford's choice was matched by the late summer heat that had hit Washington. George, recognizing that he could do nothing more to tip the odds in his favor, suggested to his aide Pete Roussel that they escape to Kennebunkport.

The two men spent a few days playing golf and riding the choppy waters of the Atlantic in George's boat. They awaited the president's decision eagerly, says Roussel, but didn't talk much about it. On August 20 they finally got word that the president was close to making a choice, so they brought a television out on the porch and watched for the news intently. Moments before the announcement, the phone rang; it was the president. George spoke with him for a few minutes before hanging up. Ford had made his choice. It was Rockefeller.

As the two men sat on the front porch, watching Ford announce his selection on television, Roussel couldn't help but notice the emotion on George's face. Roussel had worked for Bush now for five years and had never seen his emotions so strong. It was as if he believed he had failed. When a local television crew approached the house to ask for a comment from George, all he could say at first was, "It hurts so much."

---

George's loss in the vice presidential sweepstakes stung him deeply. In a note he sent to his good friend Jim Baker the day after Ford's announcement, he wrote, "Yesterday was an enormous personal disappointment." But there was anger, too. He alone had been on the firing line around the country, delivering speeches, giving press conferences, when so many Republicans like Rockefeller had stayed quietly on the sidelines. After all of that, the idea of returning to his post as head of the RNC had little appeal. "He thought he had it [the vice presidential slot]," recalls Eddie Mahe, a Republican consultant. "He said they could shove the RNC job."

President Ford certainly knew of George's disappointment. The two had been friends, and Ford was indebted to George for his service to the party.

He invited George to the Oval Office in late August to discuss his future. But Ford was not offering anything particularly substantive. No seats on the cabinet were available. Instead, the choice he offered was a plum ambassadorship in either London or Paris. A European capital might be a welcome change from the rough-and-tumble of post-Watergate Washington.

On the other hand, George had some economic realities to confront. The American ambassador was expected to provide lavish entertainment regularly, well beyond what the State Department budget would allow. While in New York, George had dipped into his own funds to entertain foreign dignitaries. But he was not in any sense a rich man. Since he had left Zapata and sold his stake in the company, his personal net worth had actually declined.

As Ford and Bush discussed his options, the president mentioned another opening, as U.S. representative in China. Mainland China was just beginning to open up. Kissinger's secret breakthrough meetings had occurred a few years earlier, and a lot of diplomatic work still needed to be done. This sounded much more intriguing to George.

It would also be more helpful in attaining his goals. Despite the setbacks of Watergate and his disappointment with Nixon, his eyes were still fixed on the presidency. As he wrote in his diary, "I told him [Ford] that I was very interested in foreign affairs . . . I indicated that way down the line, maybe 1980, if I stayed involved in foreign affairs, I conceivably could qualify for Secretary of State. The President seemed to agree."

George spoke to Bar about the decision at length. Bar was attracted to the idea, but for her own reasons. The children were all in their teens now, or older. W. was at Harvard, Jeb was married and employed by Texas Commerce Bank, Marvin would soon be attending the University of Virginia, and Neil was off to Tulane. Little Doro was enjoying herself at Miss Porter's School, where her grandmother Dottie had gone.

Over the previous twenty-plus years, Bar had devoted herself to raising the kids and backing George in whatever he undertook. She had dutifully supported him without much complaint and with very little opportunity to share fully in the fruits of his work. And while George had traveled to dozens of foreign countries in his work as a businessman, congressman, and U.N. ambassador, Bar had never once been overseas.

They had also felt the sting of Watergate. Although George had not been involved in the cover-up, he was still one of the scandal's casualties. Bar sensed the growing isolation as social acquaintances drifted away while the scandal grew deeper.

George decided to call his old mentor, Richard Nixon, to discuss the matter. He was hopeful that their relationship might be able to pick up where it had been before Watergate, when George was the bright young congressman and U.N. ambassador for whom Nixon had generously served as patron.

Was the position worth taking? George asked. Nixon said yes, but as George recorded in his diary, the ex-president was "very formal, very perfunctory" as he spoke to his friend. Perhaps he was depressed or still feeling the sting of what George had said at the August 6 cabinet meeting. At any rate, Nixon "was less than warm personally" on the phone.

George accepted the assignment and officially resigned as head of the RNC. Before he headed off for Beijing, however, he went to New York for the annual meeting of the United Nations General Assembly. China's vice minister of foreign affairs, Qiao Guanhua, was in New York, and Kissinger arranged for them to meet at his Waldorf Tower suite.

The two exchanged pleasantries and Qiao offered to be of help to George in any way he could. According to secret State Department notes of the meeting, Kissinger made sure to emphasize to Qiao that George was a man of ambition, "one of our best men—a good friend—also a presidential candidate."

—————

BY EARLY OCTOBER, GEORGE AND BAR WERE OFF TO BEIJING. THEY PLANNED to return to Washington soon and kept their house on Palisades Lane for good measure.

Beijing was an impressive city but hardly elegant. The old city walls had been removed and high-rise buildings were being built out of large concrete blocks. The city had few parks and very little greenery, and occasionally high winds blew in from the Gobi Desert bringing in a thick brown dust that covered the city like dark snow. China was a developing country and the capital city showed it.

The liaison office and residence where they would live and work was also austere. With two connected two-story buildings surrounded by a wall, it was unlike anyplace they had lived in since the early days in Odessa, Texas. The gates were guarded by People's Liberation Army soldiers, and the house staff was furnished by the Chinese government's Domestic Service Bureau. They were dutifully friendly but presumed to be informants. Chinese employees were constantly trying to collect information on the American delegation. The United States on the other hand was using the delegation as an outpost for its own intelligence operations. James Lilly, who worked on the staff ostensibly as a diplomat, was actually a CIA officer.

All foreigners were restricted in their travel, and access to information was limited. The Bushes were free to take the main roads with their Chinese driver, but side roads were strictly off-limits. Unplanned stops were also disallowed. With so few sources of news or information, they were largely isolated from the outside world. So George and Bar took to listening through the shortwave crackle to Voice of America broadcasts at the residence. George also wrote CBS in New York, where William Paley was still president, asking for programs on videotape to be sent so the delegates could keep up with the news.

To reduce their sense of isolation, George and Bar abandoned their car and driver and began traveling by bicycle. Other diplomats were shocked at the informality. But if diplomats were taken aback, ordinary Chinese on the street were more than a bit amused at the sight of two Americans pedaling around town. As George took the time to meet with people, he found himself surprised by what they thought of America.

"The American people do not have any concept of how others around the world view America," he wrote in his diary. "We think we are good, honorable, decent, freedom loving. Others are firmly convinced that though they like the people themselves in our country, that we are embarking on policies that are anathema to them. We have a mammoth public relations job to do on this."

The Bushes quickly established their routine. George arrived at his office at 8:30 for the daily staff meeting. Then he would read the mountains of cables and mail that had been sent overnight before meeting with the other diplomats or attending to visiting congressmen or businessmen. Just before lunch he would take a Chinese language lesson. After eating lunch with Bar, he would return to the office and stay until 5:30.

This was hardly the frantic pace that George had maintained for so long. The lunches with Bar were also something new. That had not happened since their days together at Yale. So the assignment in China was both a job and a sabbatical. Henry Kissinger had warned George before he left that he would be bored with the job in Beijing. But even for hyperkinetic George and Bar, the time of solitude was welcome. For Bar it proved to be a time for "delving deep" into the private pool of emotions that had been so long neglected.

"I don't mean to say that I didn't do a lot of things before," she recalls. "But I was always a nice little follower."

For George the time in Beijing had a similar effect. "Here one sorts out his values," he wrote his friend Gerry Bemiss. "Freedoms we take for granted come to the fore here as treasures but for us it's family and close friends— ever thus in our lives, but here it's vivid and in perspective."

The sojourn in China was also a time in which their personal faith was reinvigorated. While they had always been the regular churchgoing sort, in China the practice took on a special significance. In Greenwich, Midland, Houston, and Washington—every place they had ever lived—church was something you were expected to do, especially in their social circles. But here in China, Christianity was an oddity, an alien faith, and a perceived threat to the regime.

Shortly after they arrived, George and Bar began regularly attending a Protestant service which was held in the reading room of a bible study organization. A simple service conducted by an older clergyman speaking in Chinese, clearly it was unlike anything they had seen at the National Cathedral in Washington or their Episcopal church in Houston. This small church in Beijing had a simple altar, a lectern, an old piano, and about thirty chairs. As the worshipers entered, they would pick up a worn copy of the Bible and a mimeographed copy of the service. George and Bar were the only Americans who attended these services, along with the Austrian ambassador and Christians from Africa and other countries in Europe.

When it came time for the hymns, congregation members would sing in whatever language they happened to speak. The result was "ecumenical bedlam," recalls Gerry Bemiss, who attended one of these services when he visited the Bushes.

But the spirit of the place was overwhelming. As George admitted in a letter to his children, during the service they would often get "choked up— here we were worshiping in a land where this kind of worship is all but forbidden."

Shortly after their arrival, Henry Kissinger swept into Beijing with a large entourage. Kissinger was hoping for a breakthrough in relations, but matters were in a state of flux. Mao Zedong, the Communist leader, was ill, and everyone was waiting to see who might emerge as the new power in the leadership.

George had had only limited dealings with Kissinger. As ambassador to the U.N. he had worked with Al Haig, Kissinger's deputy on the National Security Council. George's tenure in Beijing gave him his first real opportunity to work directly with a man he had grown to admire. But admiration from a distance soon became irritation and frustration up close.

It started with the meeting at the airport. George was waiting with several Chinese VIPs as Kissinger and his following disembarked. Kissinger greeted them and then drove away, leaving them all (including George) standing on the tarmac.

During the meeting that followed, George found himself put off by Kissinger's rude manner and gruff style. "Kissinger is brilliant in these talks," George wrote in his diary. "Tremendous sweep of history and a tremendous sweep of the world situation. He is at his best. It is a great contrast to the irritating manner he has of handling people. His staff are scared to death of him. The procession is almost 'regal.' People quake, 'He's coming. He's coming.' And don't dare tell him when he's keeping them waiting. In a Wednesday morning meeting [he said], 'I want my staff. I want them all in this room. I want them right here now. Where are they?' All kinds of yelling of that nature goes on."

Kissinger also proved to be a control freak, in contrast to George's more free-flowing style. Later, after returning to Washington, Kissinger expressed concern that George was inviting too many members of Congress to come to China. So he ordered that all such requests needed State Department approval. George was dumbfounded by Kissinger's ambition to dominate every aspect of American foreign policy: "I am wondering if it is good for our country to have as much individual diplomacy. Isn't the president best served if the important matters are handled by more than one person?"

Despite these frictions, Kissinger and Bush did have a chance to talk privately. Kissinger pressed George about his plans for the future. Did he still expect to be on the ticket in 1976? Would he run for president in 1980? George was noncommittal. Rockefeller was the vice president, he told Kissinger. As to 1980, he "couldn't see that far ahead."

During Christmas of 1974, Bar flew back to the United States to be with the children. George remained in Beijing and awaited the arrival of his mother and aunt, who were spending the holidays with him.

During this time, rumors first began to circulate about George's relationship with Jennifer Fitzgerald, a personal assistant in the RNC he had brought to work on his staff in Beijing. Fitzgerald was an efficient and effective aide who would later move with him to a variety of other assignments. During these early months in Beijing, with Bar out of town, George and Jennifer would spend time shopping and dining out together. At one point she accompanied him alone on an official trip to Hawaii.

Family members say that they do not believe the rumors are true. But they also note that the relationship bothered Barbara. Physical relationship or not, George and Jennifer had developed a close emotional bond that Bar found hurtful and troubling. It would only be later in Washington, when Fitzgerald left George's staff, that Barbara's anxiety would go away.

While George and Bar welcomed the time in Beijing as a reprieve, they were still firmly fixed in the world of politics and eyeing his political future. With news and information difficult to obtain, George wrote to his friend Congressman William Steiger of Wisconsin for political news about Washington. He also made a point of inviting friends and supporters to visit China. Some that did included Neil Mallon, still head of Dresser Industries, who was now eighty years old.

During the day, while George was engaged at his office, Bar made a point of keeping in touch with their thousands of friends and family halfway around the world. Her card file now included more than ten thousand entries, with vital information on just about anybody they had come in contact with over the past thirty years. It was something Bar attended to constantly.

Speculation in the American press continued as to how long George would remain in China before returning to the political stage in Washington. If he had a clear-cut plan, he wasn't talking. "Sure, the place is very different but I wanted a change of pace," he told the *Washington Post* from Beijing. "What the hell, I'm fifty. It won't hurt anything."

What George did worry about was his children. Being at this distant outpost, thousands of miles from home, he hoped the family wouldn't fragment and the children go their distant ways and lose contact with each other. He was pleasantly surprised when he discovered several months after arriving that the children were all calling or writing each other with some frequency. In a sense his absence had created a breathing space into which the children had moved on their own. As he wrote in his diary, "It is as if each one of these five kids, recognizing that the family was undergoing a different experience, are pulling together much more." Still, he worried about the lack of time in Kennebunkport. It was now George, more than anyone in the Bush-Walker clan, who looked forward to spending time there. As he wrote Pete Roussel, "They [the kids] are all doing good but Maine for us is like a magnet—we are drawn to it, and I want it to be that way for all our kids, forever."

During the summer of 1975, the family gathered not in Kennebunkport but in Beijing as the children flew in for an extended visit. It was the first time so many had been together in more than a year. George W. made the trip, as did Marvin, who was interning for George's old colleague, Representative Steiger. Doro also came, as did Neil. The only no-show was Jeb.

The newlywed, now working at Texas Commerce Bank, seemed to be charting an increasingly independent course.

For the next couple of months the residence in Beijing came to resemble Walker Point as the Bush clan took to a vigorous regimen of sports, games, and day trips. The competition was as fierce as ever, only this time ordinary displays of competitiveness risked turning into diplomatic incidents. When during one tennis match Marvin threw his racket in anger, his father set him straight immediately.

On June 29 the Bushes gathered at the church for a simple ceremony. Little Doro, now sixteen, had asked to be baptized. The ceremony was simple and moving as the baptismal waters graced Doro's head. As her brother Marvin recalls, "It was so humble and yet so powerful to see this happening in the middle of the largest Marxist nation in the world."

When the family wasn't competing, they were entertaining, much as they had done their whole lives. On July 4, George and Bar hosted an all-American Independence Day celebration with hot dogs, Miller beer, Coca-Cola, and American cigarettes.

---

BACK IN WASHINGTON IT WAS BECOMING INCREASINGLY CLEAR THAT NELSON Rockefeller was not working out as vice president. His poll numbers were down, and he was unpopular with the rank and file of the Republican Party. Speculation began about who might replace him. It didn't take long for some to suggest that George should come back to Washington to serve in the cabinet and then join the ticket for the 1976 election.

Russ Rourke of the White House staff wrote to presidential counselor Jack Marsh: "It's my impression and partial understanding that George Bush probably had enough of egg rolls and Peking by now (and has probably gotten over his lost V.P. opportunity). He's one hell of a Presidential surrogate, and would be an outstanding spokesman for the White House between now and November 1976. Don't you think he would make an outstanding candidate for Secretary of Commerce or a similar post sometime during the next six months?"

Ford was well aware of the concerns being raised about Rockefeller. He also believed that his cabinet was in need of reshuffling. Secretary of Defense James Schlesinger was unpopular with many of his colleagues, and CIA director William Colby was under siege by congressional critics. Don Rumsfeld, his chief of staff, was interested in moving to a more policy oriented post.

The jockeying for positions soon began. George, halfway around the world, could do little to enhance his position except to stay in touch with friends and allies.

The most difficult post to fill would be CIA director. The agency was reeling as as reports began to trickle out about domestic spying, psychedelic drug experiments on unwitting people, and efforts to stymie the press. William Colby, the embattled director, was on his way out. Ford had already quietly offered the job to Washington lawyer Edward Bennett Williams, but he turned it down.

Dick Cheney, an assistant to Ford who would shortly become chief of staff, put together a short list of suggested candidates that included lawyer Robert Bork, businessman Lee Iacocca, and George Bush. Jack Marsh also suggested Bush as a possible candidate, as did Chief of Staff Donald Rumsfeld. But Rumsfeld worried whether Bush was right for the post. He had the right experience and was "generally familiar with components of the intelligence community and their missions," but he was primarily a politician, and his appointment might lend an "undesirable political cast" to the job.

George was privy to very little of what was going on in Washington. He had never expressed the remotest interest in being director of Central Intelligence. It was not the sort of position that would help his chances of getting on the ticket in 1976. Some even believed that certain people were forwarding his name for DCI to take him off the vice presidential short list.

So George waited, unaware that his political fate hung in the balance. Jack Marsh drafted a "Suggested cable to George Bush" for President Ford's approval once the decision was made. The original telegram read: "Congratulations on your selection by the President as Secretary of Commerce." That memo was never sent. Instead, Ford had Marsh cross out Secretary of Commerce and insert "Director of Central Intelligence" by hand in its place.

One morning in mid-October 1975, George and Bar were out riding their bikes in Beijing when a messenger tracked them down with an urgent cable from the State Department. They eagerly cycled back to the residence before opening it. The letter was from Kissinger, outlining the president's plans to reorganize the administration. When George read the cable aloud to Bar, tears of sorrow came to her eyes.

President Ford was not, of course, ordering George to take the post. But Bar knew that a request from the Oval Office was all it would take. "Remember Camp David?" she said to him, referring to his comment in 1970 about not being able to refuse the president's offer. "I think I know your answer."

The news was especially devastating for Bar. China had been an island refuge for her. For the first time in a long time she'd had George all to herself. There were no long business trips, few distractions from his job, and the nest at home was empty. The feverish pace he had maintained for so many years had been replaced by a steady, if still quick-stepping, stroll.

If he got the DCI job, George would be stepping into a maelstrom. In December a story broke that the CIA had been investigating the antiwar movement in the United States. According to the reports, the agency had been monitoring antiwar activists by tapping their telephones, tampering with their mail, and putting them under surveillance. Weeks later word leaked that the CIA might have been involved in foreign assassination plots. The floodgates were open, and in the wake of the American defeat in Vietnam, cynicism was running high.

In 1975 a Senate select committee under Sen. Frank Church, a CIA critic, was established to investigate CIA abuses. The next month the House of Representatives would do the same, making Congressman Otis Pike its chairman. The storm was just beginning.

George knew that the job would be thankless and was sensitive to the fact that it might cause complications for his family. As he wrote his brothers and sister: "It occurs to me that my controversial new job may cause concern—if not to you, to some of your kids . . . It's a graveyard for politics, and it is perhaps the toughest job in government right now due to abuses of the past on the one hand, and an effort to weaken our capability on the other. Besides, it's not always a clean and lovely business . . . When the cable came in I thought of 'Big Dad'—what would he do, what would he tell his kids—I think he would have said, 'It's your duty.' It is my duty and I'll do it. I love you all."

His bid for the DCI post also brought back a strange echo from the past. Pres Bush, as a member of the Senate Armed Services Committee and the Joint Committee on Atomic Energy, had been involved in secretive matters that he could not discuss with his family. But now, as George prepared for the DCI confirmation hearings, some of that activity began to spill out.

Back in the 1950s, when Pres had been in the Senate, there was no intelligence committee. Intelligence and espionage matters then were handled instead by the Senate Armed Services Committee. So Pres had been deeply immersed in the early establishment of American intelligence. In the early 1950s some in Congress had argued for greater congressional oversight. Pres, whose friend Allen Dulles was then serving as DCI, was strongly opposed. "I consider it to be absolutely impossible for the Agency to function in that manner," he told his colleagues. "If it tried to do so, it would endanger the lives of Americans who may be in the service of this Government behind the Iron Curtain, and of persons who may be prisoners of war or who may be, indeed, nationals of some of the countries which are behind the Iron Curtain."

The family also came to realize that Pres had been heavily involved in developing and structuring the American spy satellite program, which was still highly classified. Pres had strongly favored making use of Dr. Werner von Braun and other German rocket scientists, who came to the United States after the war, to enhance America's ballistic missile program. And he had been a supporter of the aborted Bay of Pigs attack in 1961. (The failure, he said in his oral history, was due to Kennedy's unwillingness to back the insurgents fully.)

The administration's choice of George Bush was unpopular in many circles. The *Washington Post* editorialized that the CIA had become "a political parking spot" and that public confidence in the agency would decline. Senator Church declared that Bush's appointment was merely an exercise in "concealment," aimed at halting the congressional investigations.

As the confirmation hearings loomed, rumors again began to circulate about the heavy baggage he was carrying. The Nixon Townhouse Fund and Watergate were both mentioned, and the rumors became so loud that there were concerns they might derail his appointment. Leon Jaworski, the Watergate prosecutor and friend of the Bushes, even took the unusual step of publicly speaking out on the matter. In a speech before former FBI agents in Houston he declared, "This was investigated by me when I served as Watergate special prosecutor. I found no involvement of George Bush and gave him full clearance. I hope that in the interest of fairness, the matter will not be bandied about unless something new has appeared on the horizon."

DNC head Bob Strauss also let it be known that while raising questions about George's professional qualifications was legitimate, questions about Watergate were not.

In keeping with the confirmation process, George was required for the first time to fully disclose his financial assets and holdings. He listed his memberships, including being a trustee of Phillips Andover Academy and a board member of the Episcopal Church Foundation in New York City. In terms of his financial holdings, he mentioned publicly for the first (and only) time the Bush Children Trust, which he had established for his five children. It was made up of a "diversified portfolio," mostly stocks and bonds, to fund his children's education and provide an inheritance. In a letter to Sen.

John Stennis, who was chairing the hearings, George declared that he would be willing to resign as a trustee of the Bush Children Trust if needed to avoid any conflicts of interest.

When the hearings got under way on December 15, 1975, George saw several friendly faces in front of him in the committee room. Senators Harry Byrd, Barry Goldwater, and Stuart Symington had all been good friends with his father, and they declared their respect for the family as the hearings began. But the encouraging words did not last long. Several members began immediately questioning his ability and his political plans in 1976. Senator Mike Mansfield, the Democratic majority leader, had already told President Ford that Democrats needed assurances that George would not be the vice presidential candidate if he wanted to be confirmed.

Senator William Roth, Republican of Delaware, expressed the same view in a letter to George. "It is my deep conviction that the security of this nation depends upon an effective viable Central Intelligence Agency. This depends in part upon the intelligence agency being involved in no way in domestic politics, especially in the aftermath of Watergate. For that reason, I believe you have no choice but to withdraw your name unequivocally from consideration for the Vice Presidency, if you desire to become Director of CIA."

Senators Gary Hart and Patrick Leahy began pressing George on the issue. If confirmed, would he stay out of the 1976 race?

George tried to sidestep the question. "I can tell you that I will not seek any office while I hold the job of CIA director. I will put politics wholly out of my sphere of activities." That of course left the door open for him to resign and then run. As Hart and Leahy pressed him harder, Stennis intervened. "If I thought that you were seeking the vice presidential nomination or presidential nomination by way of the route of being director of the CIA, I would question your judgment most severely." The line got a good laugh, but it didn't soften the senators' concerns.

When White House aides met later that afternoon, they tallied up the votes and determined that, as it now stood, George had at best a bare majority. In addition to the Republicans on the committee, George could count on votes from Senator Stennis and his late father's friends, Byrd and Symington. That gave him only nine of sixteen votes.

On the second day, Sen. Frank Church made an appearance before the committee to argue strenuously against what he saw as the politicization of the CIA. "We stand in this position in the close wake of Watergate, and this committee has before it a candidate for director of the CIA, a man of strong

partisan political background and beckoning political future . . . At the very
least this committee, I believe, should insist that the nominee disavow any
place on the 1976 ticket . . . Otherwise his position as CIA director would be
hopelessly compromised."

It was a passionate appeal by a senator who had presidential ambitions of
his own. As he left the room, a newspaper reporter asked him bluntly: If
Bush was too partisan, should "the investigation of the CIA and other intelligence agencies be headed by a man who aides say is 80 percent certain to
enter politics and run for the presidency?" Church was visibly angered by
the question and never answered it. But the damage was done. Church had
made his point quite effectively.

Later that day President Ford reluctantly concluded that to ensure
George's confirmation, he would have to exclude him from his list of possible vice presidential running mates. On December 18 he called George to
the White House and informed him of his decision.

For George it was a painful blow. His ambitions would have to be held
in check yet again, in order to obtain a job he really didn't want. George
was approved by a 12–4 vote in the committee and by 64–27 in the full
Senate.

George Bush came to the job of DCI with little formal training in intelligence. While serving in Congress he had done little work in the area of national security policy, and at the U.N. and in China he had been a diplomat,
not a spy. And yet he was not unfamiliar with the ways of the Central Intelligence Agency. His father's good friend Allen Dulles had headed the agency
in the 1950s, and George knew plenty of people who had worked there as
well.

George had come of age at Yale at a time when that university was intimately connected with the CIA. "There was an easy flow between Yale and
the CIA," says history professor Robin Winks. CIA heavyweights such as
James Jesus Angleton, Cord Meyer, and Richard Bissell were all Yale men.
Yale professor Sherman Kent established the CIA's Board of Estimates in
1950. While George had been on the Yale campus during the mid-to-late
1940s, a number of professors and coaches had doubled as CIA recruiting officers. The crew coach, Skip Walz, received ten thousand dollars per year to
identify and recruit young Yalies. George knew Walz as a member of Yale's
Undergraduate Athletic Association and the Undergraduate Board of Dea-
cons. Elliott Dunlap Smith, master of Yale's Saybrook College, and Thomas
Mendenhall, master of Berkeley College, were also agency recruiters.

Members of Skull and Bones were particularly well represented. Lud

Ashley had worked for the CIA's Radio Liberty before running for Congress. The CIA's ill-fated Bay of Pigs operation in 1961 had been organized by no fewer than three Bonesmen.

George's swearing-in ceremony was attended by President Ford and out-going director William Colby. The oath was administered by his friend and fellow Bonesman, Justice Potter Stewart.

In the days following his appointment, George went to New York to at-tend a banquet in honor of William Paley. While there, George took the op-portunity to meet with a few people at CBS to talk about what he was planning to do at CIA. But if George was expecting a friendly reception, he was soon disabused. Walter Cronkite started railing against the CIA and complaining that it was destroying the credibility of newscasters. Others joined in the chorus. George was defensive; it was not what he had expected.

Paranoia about the CIA was running high at CBS, especially over disclo-sures that Paley had been cozy with the agency and that he had asked re-porters in the 1950s to sit down with agency personnel to discuss overseas stories they were working on. Rumors also surfaced that broadcasters like Cronkite had been working for the agency. Paranoia seemed to reach a fever pitch months later. CBS reporter Daniel Schorr, after working on several stories critical of the CIA, was a target of scorn for agency employees. One day as he was driving on the Washington Beltway, he was suddenly rear-ended. When he stepped out of the car, he discovered that the car that hit him contained none other than CIA director George Bush.

But the attacks on the agency were just beginning. The Senate Select Committee began its investigations in earnest, and Chairman Frank Church made it clear where he stood: He was planning an extensive investigation into all sorts of agency excesses. "We must focus on abuses," he told one of his staffers during the committee hearings. "That's what this committee is for: to investigate wrongdoing. We need to begin hearings with something dramatic."

---

AFTER HIS CONFIRMATION, GEORGE AND BAR MOVED BACK INTO THEIR house on Palisades Lane. Bar was eager to pick up where they had left off from his days in Congress. But this time it was different. Due to security con-cerns, George's work was secret, and his schedule was brutal.

Early in the morning a driver would show up with a security person and a folder containing an intelligence briefing. George would read the report before heading to the office to read the overseas cable traffic. At nine he had a half hour staff meeting before turning to the work for the day. Often that meant going to Capitol Hill to attend another hearing or meeting with members of the press. In 1976 he would make fifty-one appearances before Congress. Extensive overseas travel was also part of the job, to visit CIA posts and hold private meetings with his counterparts in Britain's MI5 and MI6 and France's SDECE.

It was a frantic pace, busier than he had ever experienced. Not only did he have the normal duties of the DCI; he was also in crisis-control mode, answering questions being posed by two congressional committees and the press.

Bar had always been strong and supportive, but that was because she had been deeply involved in his work. Now it was different. George couldn't share what he was doing. When he returned from an overseas visit, sometimes he couldn't even tell her where he had been. It was enough to throw her into a terrible depression.

"She was really, really, deeply depressed," Shellie Bush Jansing recalls. "Part of it was George's schedule and his job as CIA director. But she was also at the age when she went through a 'change of life.' We feared for her, really feared for her."

The depression was so profound that Bar started considering drastic measures. Life seemed to have lost much of its meaning, and she thought about driving her car into a tree or an oncoming car. At least that way, the pain would come to an end.

Compounding the problem was Bar's difficulty in opening up to friends, fearing that she might not be able to trust them. It was what Elsie Walker Kilbourne called the "curse of the family," the ethos of never showing your weakness. Bushes and Walkers were strong; to be otherwise was somehow disloyal.

One person she did confide in was Mary Ann Stewart. Bar told her that for the first time in her life she felt left out of George's career. Mary Ann told her that she knew all about that. Being the wife of a Supreme Court justice, she wasn't privy to most of what went on in chambers. Stewart advised Bar to just accept the reality of his job and move on.

Eventually she did turn to George. Twenty years earlier, when Robin was dying, Bar had been the strong one, staying with their little girl as he left the room to deal with his pain. It had been Bar who dealt with the illnesses of their children when he was gone on the road. "People don't realize how much of George Bush's success was because of Bar," says nephew John Ellis. "She took care of *everything*. He simply didn't have to worry about the details of life that most men do."

Now suddenly he did. The kids were all gone and, like a dam that had been holding back pent-up emotions for years, Bar finally burst. "She would just sob and George would just hold her," said Shellie Jansing. "It was hard on George, no question about it. But I think it was all very, very good in the end for their marriage."

While George was spending the evenings he had at home emotionally nursing Bar back to health, during the day he was on the verge of war with congressional investigators. He was in a very real sense struggling to keep secrets secret and agents alive.

Two days before Christmas in 1975, the CIA station chief in Athens, Richard Welch, was gunned down in front of his home by masked members of a terrorist organization called "November 17." Welch's name had been made public by an anti-CIA group in the United States, and George feared that further disclosures would put other agents at risk. He fiercely resisted efforts by the congressional committees and Justice Department to depose CIA officials as witnesses or disclose their names.

Fiercely fighting for his employees was an important factor in boosting agency morale. But he also tried to encourage CIA personnel by inviting outsiders to come and visit. He brought in Averell Harriman, his father's old partner, to give a speech on the value of intelligence. For the agency's Christmas party he asked musician Lionel Hampton to perform.

He also worked to maintain enough wiggle room to allow the agency to continue its activities. In February 1976 the Church committee expressed its concern "that the use of American journalists and media organizations for clandestine operations [was] a threat to the integrity of the press." It was the very issue that had prompted the confrontation at CBS. At the time it was estimated that the agency had some fifty people working for U.S. media organizations on the payroll.

George agreed to end the practice, but with a few loopholes. "Effective immediately, the CIA will not enter into any paid or contractual relationship with any full-time or part-time news correspondent accredited by any U.S. news service, newspaper, periodical, radio, or television network or station," he told the committee. But the declaration was less straightforward than it seemed. "Accredited by any U.S." news outlet meant the agency was still free to use journalists who were not accredited or were accredited by a non-U.S. news outlet.

He was also a strong advocate of using intelligence to help U.S. allies.

When terrorists hijacked a plane full of Israeli citizens and flew it to the Entebbe Airport in Uganda, George counseled President Ford to provide aerial and satellite reconnaissance photographs to the Israelis. They were able to use the information to plan and execute a successful raid to free the hostages.

As DCI, George brought his informal manner to the job. Once in a while he ate lunch in the staff cafeteria, and he put in regular appearances at the agency's basement jogging track, running with CIA staffers. Shortly after he became DCI, George was invited to join the Alibi Club, where his father had spent so much time during his Senate career. He invited the Joint Chiefs of Staff to join him for lunch there and would chat casually with members of Congress or senators. Without any aides or staff members present, they were able to enjoy a cordial if frank discussion out of earshot of just about anyone.

With the election of Jimmy Carter in November 1976, George made it known that he was interested in staying on at Langley. Up to this point, many CIA directors had been retained by the incoming administration. George mentioned the thought to Carter during a briefing session following the election and asked his friend Bob Strauss to put in a good word for him. "But Jimmy had made up his mind," Strauss recalled.

Carter wanted his own people at the agency and he openly questioned Bush's abilities, declaring that he was a "failed politician" who had been "dumped" on the CIA. Not everyone saw it that way, however. Senator Daniel Inouye, Democrat of Hawaii, admitted that he had had his doubts about Bush at first, but they were dispelled by his service at the agency. "You might say Bush was one of the best [directors] we had," he told the *New York Times*.

#### CHAPTER 20

# OIL AGAIN

I N THE SPRING OF 1975, GEORGE W. WAS THINKING ABOUT LIFE AFTER Harvard. Most of his classmates were looking for a slot in a major corporation or a position with a major Wall Street firm, the sort of work Pres Bush and the Walkers had done for most of their lives. A place for him was open at G. H. Walker if he wanted it. Pres Bush's brother had worked there, as had Uncle Johnny Bush.

But the prospect of working business deals from an office didn't have much appeal for George W. His real interest was in his father's world of the entrepreneur, and oil. Like his father, W. was determined to hit it big, and oil seemed to be an inviting prospect. Harvard Business School had released a survey in the spring of 1975 indicating that the oil patch was where the action would be. OPEC's efforts in 1973 to create a shortage in the West had led to a boom in domestic oil production. The highest paying jobs for recent HBS graduates were not in finance or corporate America, but in the petroleum industry.

In early March, George W. went back to Midland to see his father's friend Jimmy Allison, who had given George Sr. both of his political jobs. Allison told him that there was real money to be made in oil again. Given the Bushes' good name in West Texas and the deep reservoir of capital that could be made available from family and friends, W. had a good chance of making it big.

According to George W., this conversation crystallized everything for him. "All of a sudden it dawned on me that this is entrepreneurial heaven. This is one of the few places in the country where you can go without portfolio and train yourself and become competitive. The barriers to entry were very low in the oil sector. I can't tell you how obvious it was."

So after graduation from Harvard, George W. loaded his few belongings into his old Cutlass and drove to Midland. Word spread quickly that the Bushes were back in the oil business. Martin Allday, an attorney who had run George Sr.'s 1964 Senate campaign, offered to do whatever he could. So did Walter Holton, a local businessman whose uncle had played golf with W.'s grandfather. Holton took W. to the Petroleum Club and introduced him around. Many of the old-timers had known his father and offered a few choice stories about his rise. But there were also plenty of new faces, and the fact that a young, newly minted Harvard MBA was trying to make it in the business made them defensive.

"Harvard, at first, was a hindrance" for him, says Ed Thompson, former director of the Permian Basin Petroleum Association. As a result, he remembers George W. as mostly being quiet and listening his first year in Midland. "He did a lot more listening than talking. He was pretty cagey. He didn't force himself. He played his hand close to the vest. He got involved in civic things. He began to fit into the group. Eventually he was invited to sit in."

George W. was close to broke when he arrived in Midland. He had fifteen thousand dollars left over from the trust fund his parents had established for his education, but that was supposed to be seed money for the company he planned to start. So he needed to watch every dime. Never that comfortable in a suit and tie, he nevertheless understood that it was the uniform you needed to wear in order to be taken seriously. Mostly he wore a couple of ill-fitting, Chinese-made suits he had picked up when he visited his parents in Beijing. For good luck he also sported a pair of sharkskin shoes he had inherited from his uncle Johnny. Joe O'Neill, an old Midland friend from grade school, gave him some old dress shirts that he would wear for the next several years. Keeping his meager clothes in presentable condition presented another challenge, and wives of his friends often took pity on him and did his laundry.

That first year in Midland, George W. spent his time learning the business and, more important, studying people. He was, as his Yale friend Rob McCallum had said, foremost a student of people. And in the oil business, whom you chose to partner with was of critical importance. Drilling for oil could end in a bonanza or, more likely, complete and utter failure. Those alternate outcomes could strain any business relationship.

While his father was in China and then at the CIA, George W. kept a low profile in the world of politics. But in 1976, at his father's suggestion, he became the Nineteenth District coordinator for Jerry Ford's presidential bid. Along with his responsibilities as a local surrogate, he also introduced vice presidential nominee Bob Dole, his father's old rival, at a speaking event in Lubbock. But he did little else in politics, aware that he would be constantly compared to his father in whatever he did.

"Being the son of George Herbert Walker Bush in Texas is like being the son of Tiger Woods in a golf community," says his cousin John Ellis. "I mean he's not just admired and respected, at some level he's adored in Texas. Particularly in the circles George W. was likely to travel in."

After W. got familiar with the business, he set up an office in the old Midland National Bank Building. (His father had helped found the bank in the 1950s.) "Office" is a generous term to describe the small room with no furniture that he used for the company he named Arbusto. He used soda-bottle crates for chairs but managed to avoid paying rent. Two oilmen gave him the space for free in exchange for getting first crack at any promising deals he developed.

The next thing he needed was cash, so he could buy oil and gas leases to begin drilling. Although his father had the contacts and resources, George W. did not turn to him. Instead, much like his father twenty years earlier, he turned to an uncle for help in raising the money. Just as his father had relied on Uncle Herby, W. relied on Johnny Bush, who had given up a career in theater for a job at G. H. Walker. He was now branching out and running his own investment firm.

Johnny managed to raise several million dollars for his nephew over the next five years. He invested twenty-five thousand dollars of Dottie's money in the company, but most of it came from outside the family. He tapped fellow Yalie Russell Reynolds, who Johnny had selected to join the elite Whiffenpoofs. He also tapped John Macomber, CEO of Celanese Corporation, another old friend from Yale. Venture capitalist William H. Draper III put money into the venture, too. It became a true family effort when Barbara's brother Scott Pierce tapped George Ball, CEO of Prudential-Bache Securities, and George Ohrstrom, head of an investment management company in New York who had gone to school with George and Pressy at Greenwich Country Day School. Lewis Lehrman, founder of the Rite-Aid drugstore chain, took a stake in the company, as did Gerry Bemiss, who put in eighty thousand dollars.

By early 1977, Arbusto was drilling its first holes. Two local oilmen named Mills and Sutton were drilling in Sutton County, and they gave George a "participatory interest" for a few thousand dollars. George waited eagerly for news as the crews drove the drill into the hard, crusted earth of a desolate ranch. After a few days he received the first report: The well was completely dry.

"I'll never forget the feeling, kind of, 'Oops, this is not quite as easy as we all thought it was going to be," he later recalled.

George W. was not the risk-taker that his father had been. He began to get nervous, wondering if he would run through all of the money quickly. But Mills and Sutton were old hands and encouraged him to stick with it. They gave him a stake in two more deals and these met with some success. By the middle of the year he had recouped his losses and made a meager profit.

"Let me tell you, Bobby, how you do quantitative analysis," he told Yale buddy Bob Reisner. "You do all your analysis, you do all your statistics, and then you punch a hole in the ground. And if there's no oil there, you just lost five million bucks."

George W.'s career path took a radical detour in the hot summer of 1977 when seismic political news hit Midland. Congressman George Mahon, a Democrat who had held the seat since 1934, announced that he was going to retire. The chairman of the House Appropriations Committee, the longest-serving member of Congress at the time, had finally had enough. For the first time in a long time, his West Texas congressional district was in play.

Mahon made his big announcement on July 6, which happened to be George W.'s birthday. He took it as something of an omen and impulsively began thinking about running for the seat. He called his father, now back in private life in Houston, for advice.

The demographics of the district looked good. The two main centers of population, Midland and Odessa, were places where George W. and his father both had plenty of friends. And the district was conservative. A Republican could win now that Mahon was retiring.

George W. made his decision quickly, telling friends days later that he was entering the race. They all supported him instantly. Don Evans became his campaign chairman; Robert McCleskey, a high school chum, agreed to handle the money and the campaign's books. Bob Blake, his father's friend twenty years earlier, took him to Mahlouf's Fine Apparel to buy him a suit. On July 19, sporting that new outfit, George W. made his announcement at the Midland Regional Air Terminal.

Every Bush campaign had been a family affair; this one would be no different. George W.'s brother Neil, who had just graduated from Tulane University, moved to Lubbock to serve as a county campaign chairman. Neil would try very hard in the campaign, sometimes too hard. He wanted to fit in and be everyone's friend, eager to do every task. He was growing up as the younger brother of two young men who were trying to fly very high. Jeb was working in international banking for Texas Commerce Bank and George W. was running for Congress. This, he believed, would be a chance to prove himself.

W.'s father played an enormously important role in the campaign, but it was often hidden lest voters confuse the two Georges or suspect that W. wasn't his own man. Karl Rove, who had worked for George at the RNC, was now in Houston heading George H. W.'s political action committee. Rove did considerable work for W.'s campaign over the next fifteen months.

George also placed an early call to Republican National Committee headquarters in Washington to protect his son's interests. Charlie Black was the political director at the time.

"You know George is getting in this race down here in Texas," the former chairman told Black. "I hope you all will stay neutral through the primary."

"Absolutely," Black told him. "By all means."

The main concern was Jim Reese, a former television sportscaster and ex-mayor of Odessa who was jumping into the Republican primary. Reese was a longtime Republican activist, having campaigned for George during his 1970 Senate run. In the 1976 presidential race, Reese had backed Ronald Reagan in the primary against Gerald Ford. As a result, Reagan was strongly backing him now with contributions from Citizens for the Republic, the former California governor's political action committee. He also agreed to appear in television commercials endorsing Reese.

When George Bush got wind of what Reagan was doing, he telephoned to say how upset he was. Other than Reagan and Bush, no one knows exactly what was said, but it did not go well. George saw it in the larger context of his own national aspirations. "I'm not interested in getting into an argument with Reagan," he told the *Washington Post*. "But I am surprised about what he is doing here, in my state . . . They are making a real effort to defeat George."

Relations remained frosty between the two for quite some time thereafter. William F. Buckley recalls an encounter between the two in 1979 at the Bohemian Grove, a gathering place for the American corporate elite in northern California. Bush and Buckley were members of the same camp and they were sitting around a fire talking about the election in Texas. "I was really pissed off about Reagan," Bush told Buckley. An hour and a half later they went to Reagan's camp and everyone filed by Reagan to shake hands. "It was very funny because I've known Reagan awfully well and I know when a look comes over his eyes when he is simply not concentrating. And by the time George came by he just sort of shook his hand as though he were an utter stranger."

"Ron, it's me, George," he told him.

Reagan, startled, apologized. "I was really sorry about that Texas thing," he said.

"There was a little heaving there," Buckley recalls, "but big George was very upset about that."

George also took W. to Dallas for a meeting with Bob Strauss to get an accurate assessment of what the Democrats were planning in the district. "I told him that the Democrat he would be facing if he won [the primary] was Kent Hance," Strauss recalls. "Hance was smart as a whip and mean as a snake. I told him it was the wrong race at the wrong time." George W. thanked him and left. Then Strauss and George discussed George's plans for a possible presidential run in 1980. Strauss encouraged him. "After all," Strauss said. "Reagan sure as hell won't be the nominee."

George also saw to it that a national network of contributions was made available to his son. While 63 percent of W.'s campaign war chest came from friends and supporters in the district, his father shook the money trees far from West Texas. Bar pulled out the thick card file of family friends. Letters went out. Weeks later contributions rolled in. Former President Gerald Ford sent a check, as did baseball commissioner Bowie Kuhn, a friend of Uncle Herby's. Film producer Jerry Weintraub, husband of a longtime family friend, also ponied up some money, as did Gen. Douglas MacArthur's widow, who had lived in the Waldorf-Astoria when the Bushes were at the U.N. In all, the George W. Bush campaign raised over four hundred thousand dollars.

Just weeks after George made his announcement, the O'Neills, old friends from Midland, invited him over for a backyard barbecue. Joining them that evening was a quiet young woman named Laura Welch.

Laura was the only daughter of Harold B. Welch, a successful builder, and Jenna Welch, who kept the company's books. Laura, who had grown up in Midland and was now living in Austin, had been raised only blocks from George W. but the two had never met. While George W. was blowing up frogs with firecrackers, Laura was lining up her dolls and pretending to be their teacher. While the Bushes were Presbyterians, the Welches were decidedly Methodist, at a time when such distinctions mattered.

They attended the same junior high school together. With W.'s outgoing personality and his sometimes bombastic demeanor, Laura certainly knew who he was. But W. never recalled meeting the quiet and serious young girl.

Laura went to Southern Methodist University to study education. After graduating, she worked in a racially mixed elementary school in Dallas, then taught at John F. Kennedy Elementary in Houston. The school was in a predominantly black neighborhood, and she grew so attached to the children that when they moved on to the third grade, she asked to teach that grade instead.

Laura had even lived at Chateaux Dijon when W. was there. But again, they never seem to have met, with Laura staying in the quiet wing and W. enjoying the parties at the pool. As W. continued to fly his jets and try his hand in the business world, Laura moved to Austin and got a master's degree in library science from the University of Texas.

That night at the O'Neills', W. and Laura talked and talked. Most of the words came from W., describing his plans and his family. But Laura talked in her way, too, with her quiet concern and interest in what he had to say. A strange confluence began to emerge that few would have expected.

"I would never have matched them together," said Charlie Younger, who knew them both in childhood. "Laura is more ladylike. She was a teacher-librarian-type lady and George was more the rambunctious reveler and rambler." Members of the Bush family noticed the contrast, too. Brother Marvin likened Laura's entry into the Bush family to Katharine Hepburn starring in *Animal House*.

For Laura the initial attraction was W.'s energy. While she was intense, it was in a quiet intellectual way. "She keeps things more inside," says Elsie Walker Kilbourne. "George tends to carry things on his sleeve. But it's a mistake to think that she is just very laid back. She just doesn't show it."

For W., who seemed to have trouble finding exactly his place, Laura was someone who seemed to know exactly who she was and where she wanted to be. "George saw that Laura's feet were firmly planted on the ground," says Nancy Bush Ellis. "I think after all the transitions in his life, he wasn't interested in marrying someone like himself. He wanted someone steady and calm."

Laura was also, interestingly enough, quite different from Bar. While Bar was a woman very much like George's mother, Dottie, the same could not be said of Bar and Laura.

W. and Laura had many differences, but they did share one thing in common, the experience of a sudden, unsettling death. W. still thought about Robin, who had died over twenty years earlier of leukemia. He didn't talk about it much, but it had left a permanent mark on his psyche. The death in Laura's youth occurred when she was seventeen years old. On November 5, 1963, while driving her friend Judy Dykes to a party in Midland, Laura hit a Corvair at an intersection, throwing the driver from the car. Laura had failed to see the car and broadsided it. Laura and Judy were taken to the hospital and treated for minor injuries. But the driver of the Corvair died at the scene. Laura discovered later that the victim was Mike Douglas, a friend of hers. She was devastated and is still uncomfortable talking about the event some four decades later.

The next evening W. took Laura out on a date that included a game of miniature golf. Five weeks later they announced their engagement. The family was stunned.

"I was truly amazed," says Elsie Walker Kilbourne. "Amazed not only that George moved so fast, but that his parents were in favor of it. They must have seen instantly how good Laura would be for him."

There was that sense in the family that a good woman could round out a man's life, improve him, make him better, give him strengths where before he had weaknesses. Bar, who was rarely impressed with the girls W. brought home, liked what she saw in Laura. Where there had been language and cultural barriers with Jeb's wife, Colu, Bar felt an instant synergy with Laura.

For Bar, Laura was a bit of a mystery. On Laura's first visit to the family home in Kennebunkport, Bar walked over to her and asked, "And what do you do?" "I read, I smoke, and I admire," she said matter-of-factly. And while she would mostly give up her Winston cigarettes, the other two pastimes would remain an essential part of the woman.

News of the engagement was welcomed by the Bushes, who were pleased that their son was finally settling down. The nuptial plans were viewed with more skepticism by Laura's father, Harold, who feared that the aspiring young politician might be interested in a quick marriage for the sake of improving his image. Laura tried to convince him that W.'s intentions were honorable, but he believed it only after they were married and had children.

On November 6 the two families gathered at the United Methodist Church in Midland. George and Bar were there, as were W.'s brothers, who served as ushers. Dottie also came and met the young bride. Following the exchange of vows, a luncheon reception was held at the Racquet Club. As George's father sat quietly, emotions clearly stirring deeply, it was Bar who finally rose to give the customary toast.

Because of the pending election, the young couple delayed their honeymoon and returned to the campaign trail. It was a difficult time for Laura. "I worried about the stress of the political campaign combined with the stress of being newlyweds."

W. threw himself into the campaign. As it had been for both his father and grandfather, a political contest was for W. as much a test of endurance as anything. Consequently, he was gone most of the first several months of their marriage. Laura, who had quit her job, took to organizing the Bush home. The bachelor messiness W. was so accustomed to was soon gone as she organized everything, including their library of books, which she placed according to the Dewey decimal system. She arranged her shoes according to hue while W.'s loafers were organized by most worn to least damaged. While W. ate with a speed and fury that he was used to in a family that had little time to waste, Laura was barely into her meal when he announced he was done.

Yet despite their differences, W. seemed to appreciate the change. He saw in Laura the sort of steely discipline that he had been lacking in his life and that his parents epitomized. Family members also noticed that Laura had that ability to influence her husband, and to regulate or restrain his behavior.

"Laura and Bar have that same quality, in that the two Georges can get a little bit full of themselves," Shellie Bush Jansing told us. "And those two women in a sentence or even with a wink or a look can get them right back down to where they belong. It's the most loving possible way you can do it. I've seen a lot of people do it the wrong way, and there goes the marriage. But they are great in how they do it. A lot of humor. The most important thing in the world."

Still, there were tensions. W. was stressed out because of the race, and Laura was just learning to navigate as a political wife. One night after a long day of campaigning, the young couple was driving home from Lubbock to Midland. W. had just given a speech that he seemed particularly proud of.

"Tell me the truth," he asked her. "How was my speech?"

"Well, your speech wasn't very good," Laura said as their house came into view.

W. said nothing but promptly pulled the car into the driveway and drove into the side of the garage.

Each week W. would drive the 20 miles from Midland to Odessa and then move along the 115-mile stretch north to the farms of Lubbock, stopping at every gas station, farm co-op, and strip mall along the way. His campaign staff scheduled his appearances for all hours of the day.

"You could schedule him for a 6 A.M. breakfast and an 8 P.M. coffee," recalls Mike Weiss, chairman of his campaign in Lubbock. W. would always be there with a smile, shaking hands, chatting about the weather, talking about his plans. His focus was on the positive. "People are tired of negative politicians . . ." he would say.

With a tight race for the Republican nomination and the candidates all running as mainstream conservatives, it didn't take long for the Bush family itself to become an issue. First there was the charge that W. was an outsider, a carpetbagger, who didn't deserve to represent West Texas. "He's a personable young man from back east who apparently has been misleading the people about his West Texas background," Jim Reese declared on television, producing a copy of W.'s birth certificate. The Bushes were "Rockefeller-type Republicans," he said, noting the family's connection with the Rockefeller clan.

Despite these attacks, W. won the tough primary. But Reese refused to endorse his candidacy. George H. W. and Reagan were already starting to position themselves for the 1980 campaign, and that competition was playing a role in the tensions over this race. W. faced Kent Hance in the general election with a divided Republican Party.

Hance was a local boy, the son of farmers, who had graduated from Dimmitt (Texas) High School, Texas Tech, and the University of Texas Law School before being elected to the state senate. He talked the language of the district's farmers and ranchers, and knew hundreds of people by name. "My daddy and granddaddy were farmers," he would tell people on the stump. "They didn't have anything to do with the mess we're in right now, and Bush's father has been in politics all his life . . . George Bush hasn't earned the living he enjoys. I'm on my own two feet and I can make my own living." He ran radio spots contrasting Dimmitt High School with Andover.

Hance could be, as Strauss had put it, "mean as a snake." But he was not without his charm. To make his point, he enjoyed telling stories contrasting the Bush clan with his own.

"There was a farmer sittin' on his fence one day when this big, fancy limousine comes rolling up the dirt road and stops right in front of him. The windows roll down and the fella inside says, 'You know the way to get to Lubbock?'

"The farmer, he chews on the straw for a couple of seconds and points up the dirt road and he says to the chauffeur, 'Go on up the road a couple of miles till ya' see the cattle guard, then go left and pretty soon you'll be in town.'

"Well, a while goes by and the farmer sees the big fancy limousine coming back down the dirt road. The window rolls down and the chauffeur says, 'Forgot to ask. What color uniform is that cattle guard wearing?'"

It was the sort of joke that went down well in West Texas. Hance would turn and look at W. on stage with him. "You see, that limousine wasn't from around these parts. I think it had one of them Connecticut licenses. That where you from, George?"

Reports were circulated that George Bush was a member of the Trilateral Commission, an organization that conspiracy theorists believed was trying to bring about a world government. Late in the campaign, at a luncheon in Odessa, a local radio host named Mel Turner asked whether he or any member of the family was involved in an effort to bring about a one-world government. W. was so angry that he turned red and ignored the question.

Afterward, when he was leaving the room, Turner met him at the door and extended his hand.

W. refused to shake it.

The attacks on his family angered him most, more than questions about his ability or qualifications. He often lashed back at the critics, speaking in rapid bursts that revealed his anger. "[My father] has the highest security clearance, and ran the CIA during its most troubled times. Against tough congressional inquiries, he stood firm so as not to weaken the CIA . . . When it comes to the integrity of my father, I will fight back. They are trying to slam me by slamming my father."

W. had spent half his life in Midland and had come back to live there by choice. But the family legacy, the name, the background, those very things that had brought him to the point where he could seek a congressional seat with so little experience, proved also to be his biggest hurdle.

"The problem is," he said at one point of frustration, "I can't abandon my background."

Despite Hance's aggressive campaign, the race remained tight going into the final weeks. W. tried to show people that he was not the uptight preppy his opponent was making him out to be. He and Laura even rented an apartment in Lubbock so he could get to know people there personally. But in the final week, his fate was sealed by a Bush campaign staffer who placed an ad in the Texas Tech University student newspaper advertising a "Bush Bash" for students with "free beer" for all. One of Hance's people saw the ad and decided to exploit it.

A letter was sent to more than four thousand members of the decidedly dry Church of Christ who lived in the district. "Mr. Bush used some of his vast sums of money in an attempt, evidently, to persuade young college students to vote for and support him by offering free alcohol to them," the letter read. Kent Hance also issued a statement declaring that while it "may be a cool thing to do at Harvard or Yale," people in Texas didn't take kindly to liquoring up college students.

It was a heavy blow. The Bush campaign was reeling.

Then suddenly information emerged that could be used to counterattack.

Kent Hance was leasing some property he owned near the Texas Tech campus to a bar called Fall Dogs, a well-known college drinking hole. If Hance was going to slam W. about the Bush Bash, why not call Hance a hypocrite?

Bush campaign employees leaked the information to the local press, but they would print the information only if candidate Bush made the charge with his own lips. When asked by his staff to do so, W. refused. He told one campaign worker: "Ruthie, Kent Hance is not a bad person and I'm not going to destroy him in his hometown. This is not an issue. If I try to destroy him to win, I don't win."

On November 7 turnout was heavy. W. and Laura spent the day meeting people at polling places around Midland. At five o'clock they went back to campaign headquarters and awaited the news.

The early returns looked promising, but his lead began to fade as the rural vote and the tallies from Hance's base in Lubbock came in. By eleven o'clock, W. was conceding the race.

"I have to congratulate you," he told Hance by phone.

Hance had captured barely 53 percent of the vote. Yet W. was devastated by his defeat, not so much for himself, but because he felt he had let his family down.

#### CHAPTER 21

# EXILE

AFTER BEING DISMISSED AS DCI BY JIMMY CARTER, GEORGE Bush left Washington in early 1977, driving Bar's Volvo back to Houston. He was out of politics for the first time in more than a decade.

Since 1965, George had either been running for office or between presidential appointments. He counted these times as some of the best in his life, but they had drained the family's financial resources. He told family members shortly after he left Washington that he was planning on running for the presidency in three years. But before then he needed to repair the family's sagging finances. It didn't take long for this perpetual motion machine to burrow deep into the corporate world.

Houston was booming, the fastest growing city in America. It was the new oil capital of the world, the second largest port in the country, and it boasted four of the top ten law firms in the United States. Land development was hot, and millions were being made every day as the city spread south toward the Gulf of Mexico and north toward Dallas. On top of all this, George had a zillion friends there.

Bob Stewart, the enthusiastic chairman of First International Bankshares of Dallas, asked George to come on board as chairman of the bank's executive committee. He offered the former congressman, U.N. ambassador, and CIA director an annual fee of $75,000. Invitations to join other corporate boards quickly followed. He also hit the lecture circuit, speaking before corporate and political audiences for $5,000 a pop.

In the late spring, George and Bar made a quick trip to Kennebunkport. While there, a diminutive but aggressive Texan came calling with a proposal. Ross Perot had made a fortune with a thriving database and computer company called Electronic Data Systems. Based in Dallas, he had been an active Nixon supporter and a donor to George's campaigns. George knew the man fairly well.

Perot, branching out from EDS, was eager to move heavily into the oil business. And he was coming to ask George to run the company.

The two spent time together out on George's boat and Perot pitched him the idea. George said he appreciated the thought, but would have to consider it. George and Bar admired Perot. He had all the qualities that Bush men aspire to: hardworking, driven, a self-made man. But George was no longer interested in the grinding work of running and managing a company. The Zapata days were behind him. He had been bit by the political bug and the fever just wouldn't abate.

He turned Perot down gently in a letter. "You called when I was kind of down," he wrote. "Though things didn't work out, I will always be grateful for your interest."

It was a soft "no thanks," but Perot was not used to being turned down and took the news badly, seeing it as a personal rebuke. Bush would hear from him again.

Despite his uncertainties about what direction to take, twelve years of public service, especially the pioneering work he had done in China, afforded George plenty of business opportunities. His knack for making and keeping friends meant that he knew people at the top in Beijing. And in China, contacts were everything. The friend who had been Chinese ambassador to the U.N. was the new vice foreign minister. Any company that wanted to do business in the Middle Kingdom needed those sorts of connections. The Chinese leadership was like an Asian version of Skull and Bones, secretive and select. While George was not exactly in the club, he was generally trusted by its members.

When the Chinese government celebrated its National Day in September 1977, it also invited a small group of Americans, including George, to come and observe the festivities. This was an opportunity for George to operate in the world of soft power his father had thrived in. George assembled a twenty-three-person delegation to accompany him. Along for the trip was Dean Burch, his friend from the Ford White House, who had so often pushed his name as a possible VP or cabinet officer. So was Jimmy Baker, who had served in the Ford apparatus and was practicing law in Houston. David Broder of the *Washington Post* got an invitation, as did international broadcaster and explorer Lowell Thomas, then eighty-five. Most important, perhaps, George invited his old partner Hugh Liedtke, who was now chairman of Pennzoil. Liedtke was interested in drilling for oil in China.

The group arrived to watch a ceremony in Tiananmen Square, where thousand of marchers paraded in precise formation carrying red banners. The real work began in the following days when they held a series of closed-door meetings with Chinese officials, including a ninety-minute session with

Deng Xiaoping. The meetings went well. Deng made a point of telling George that he was welcome in China anytime.

The next day George took Hugh Liedtke to a private meeting with the foreign trade minister. Pennzoil wanted a crack at drilling for oil offshore in the East China and South China Seas.

Four months later a senior delegation of Chinese officials traveled to the United States. They spent a few days speaking with State Department and White House officials, then they made an unprecedented trip to Houston and checked into the Galleria Plaza Hotel. George and Bar had the delegation over for dinner with a few select friends.

In August the Chinese government invited four big American companies to China to discuss the exploration and development of offshore oil reserves. One of the four was Pennzoil. A year later, Pennzoil became the first oil company to drill in China.

George's relationship with Beijing also reaped enormous rewards for the Bush family, which has served for many years as a bridge between China and corporate America. George's older brother Pres would later go on to serve as the longtime head of the China-America Chamber of Commerce.

———

IN EARLY SEPTEMBER 1977, GEORGE RECEIVED WORD THAT UNCLE HERBY Walker was seriously ill. For George it was a crushing blow. While George had loved his father, Pres Bush could be remote and formal with his children. If he had deep passions—and he did—Pres would conceal them. Uncle Herby was a Walker to the core.

George wrote him a grief-stricken letter on September 17. It was apparent that George was losing more than a doting uncle. "You have shown me how to be a man," he wrote. "You have taught me what loyalty is all about. You have made me understand what it is to make a commitment, 'bet on a guy,' as you'd say, and then stick with it through thick and thin. Without your friendship and support, I'd never have had the confidence to dream big dreams . . . I'm with ya, Herby, not just cause you handed me the future and made my life sing; but selfishly, because I need you as my father, my brother, and my best friend. You see, I love you very deeply." There is no record of George Bush ever writing a similar letter to his father.

Herby died a few weeks later, leaving a hole at the center of the Bush-Walker clan. For more than three decades he had fueled George's ambitions, hired Bushes and Walkers to work at the family firm, and kept the keys to the family's summer retreat in Kennebunkport. Now he was gone.

For George and his mother, Dottie, one of the immediate concerns was Walker Point. Herby's widow, Mary, was tired and didn't think she could keep the place. She sent out feelers to real estate brokers to see what she could get. It was a prime spot and offers quickly rolled in. One particularly lucrative offer came from Arab investors, who were interested in buying the land and splitting it up to build condos. The very thought was horrifying to a family that had seen four generations grow up at Walker Point, swimming in the Boony Wild pool and jumping off the dock into the cold waters of the Atlantic. Giving up Walker Point would be like shredding the family history.

Herby's brother, Dr. John Walker, got in touch with Mary and pleaded with her to keep the property in the family. George did the same. He was keenly interested in taking over the place, but he couldn't afford to match the offer on the table. Mary agreed to put off the sale for a couple of years until George could cobble together enough money.

Back in Houston, George and Bar moved seamlessly back into the city's social life. They had plenty of friends in the area—they seemed to have friends everywhere—but many of their closest lived in Houston: the Bakers, the Mosbachers, the Kerns. Life soon became a swirl of parties, socials, luncheons, and cocktails in the backyard. But George often found himself bored by it, numbed by the frivolity of so much of the conversation, particularly of those outside his inner circle.

"There is a missing of stimulating talk," he wrote his friend Gerry Bemiss. "I just get bored silly about whose daughter is a Pi Phi or even bored about who's banging old Joe's wife. I don't want to slip into that 3 or 4 martini late dinner rich social thing. There is too much to learn still."

Things perked up when someone from his past life in politics came to town. Houston was the central nervous system of the world oil market—most of the international oil giants were based there—so there was a steady flow of interesting guests. In 1977, King Hussein of Jordan and Prince Saud of Saudi Arabia came to the Oil Capital, and after their meetings with the titans of the oil business they both made special plans to see George. He was well known to both men, who were familiar with the role he had played in the Persian Gulf oil business back in his Zapata days. The relationship with Prince Saud had been further solidified when George was DCI. He had traveled secretly to the kingdom and met with Saud's brother, Prince (later King) Fahd, the Saudi intelligence chief. George Bush was a friend and ally as far as the Saudis were concerned.

George and Bar sent out invitations to a select two dozen guests to meet both King Hussein and Prince Saud. One of these was former vice president Nelson Rockefeller, a good friend and sometimes political rival. Rocky was the great-nephew of Franklin Rockefeller, who had invested in Samuel P. Bush's Buckeye Steel seventy years earlier.

In the summer of 1977, George helped set up two political action committees (PACs), the first embryonic organizations for his presidential run. Karl Rove was given the job of running them. Contributions rolled in from members of the Bush Christmas list, including Bob Mosbacher and his grateful friends at Pennzoil. A sizable check also came from Bruce S. Gelb, whom George had rescued from a harassing bully at Andover so many years ago. Gelb was now the head of Clairol.

PAC dollars went to friendly Republican candidates running for office in 1978, but George also used them to keep his toe in the pool of politics. He traveled around the country—96,000 miles to some 42 states—speaking for Republican candidates. George enjoyed doing it and was thinking about making a run for president—he'd been thinking about it for close to ten years now—but he wasn't certain. George had always been big on getting advice on major decisions, family advice, from someone you could trust. But his father had been gone for five years, and with Uncle Herby's passing, another light in his life had been dimmed.

So he dawdled back and forth on what to do. When he did finally commit, the moment of decision didn't come from on high. He was riding in a pickup with his friend Don Rhodes. It was the spring of 1978 and he'd been batting the question around forever.

"Don, I've really gotta decide if I want to run for president."

Rhodes kept driving.

"Run," he finally said, shrugging his shoulders. "Y'don't have anything better to do."

George got on the phone and called the family. Bucky in St. Louis, Johnny in New York City, Pres in Connecticut, Nancy in Boston, cousin Shellie, cousin Elsie. They all pledged their immediate support. The only negative came from Dottie. Politics had changed since her husband had served in the Senate. In the post-Watergate world, it was a particularly nasty business. "Mom didn't want George to run," recalls Nancy Bush Ellis. "She knew politics was a lot about self-promotion and that it could be very destructive. She was afraid of what it might do to George."

George then telephoned his children. W. was supportive, but distracted. He was newly married and in the midst of his own congressional race in West Texas. Marvin, Doro, and Neil were still in school, but eager to help. Jeb was then living in Venezuela as a vice president of Texas Commerce Bank. After some small talk, the father told his son that he was going to run for president.

"President of what?" Jeb asked.

But it was Jeb who would jump highest to support his father's campaign. He quit his job in Venezuela and moved his wife and two young children, George P. and Noelle, back to Houston. Over the next two years he would pour his heart and soul into his father's campaign. George W. would have a much smaller involvement.

In the weeks before his announcement, George held a series of private fund-raising dinners. Harry Catto, his longtime friend, held a $250-a-head dinner at his McLean, Virginia, home. It was a reunion of personal and family friends. Representatives Pete McCloskey, Joel Pritchard, John Hammer-schmidt, and Barber Conable were there, as well as his dad's old Senate colleagues Hugh Scott and Glenn Beall.

After the food and drinks, George said a few words but avoided talking about the issues. His message was upbeat and decidedly noncommittal.

"Wherever I go, people ask, 'What are you? A moderate, a conservative, a liberal? How do you fit in?' The people here tonight transcend these labels. And I think that's good. I want to be a national candidate."

Senator Hugh Scott held a fund-raiser days later at his suburban Virginia home. George spoke a little about Jimmy Carter but mostly about his kids, letting everyone know that W., Jeb, Marvin, Neil, and Doro were all doing fine. (He did admit to being a bit concerned about Marvin, who had taken up driving in demolition derbies as a hobby.) It was more like a family get-together. The guests all made their donations, but they were for the man, not necessarily his politics.

Plans were made for an official announcement at the National Press Club. Everyone in the family had an opinion. Dottie insisted that he get a new suit and asked Johnny to help him pick it out. They settled on a nice-fitting, conservative dark blue suit. "It's the only decent one he's got," Johnny informed campaign workers. "He's got these baggy gray things. They cost $80 and he thinks they're terrific. I've seen him with two different colored socks. We've got to give this boy some counsel."

Bar convinced him that those half glasses he wore—they looked like reading glasses—had to go. But efforts by his media adviser Robert Goodman to move to contact lenses were resisted to the bitter end. He took to wearing full lenses instead.

Johnny took him to a speech coach named Lilyan Wilder to improve the rhythm and intonation of his speeches. He needed to stress key words. She also got him to stop pointing in the air with his index finger every time he wanted to make an important point. But he replaced it with a karate chop that irritated Bar no end.

At his announcement, George talked about the ills of the Carter administration, the foreign policy failures of recent years, inflation, taxes, excessive regulation, and high energy prices. But he also directed his fire—without mentioning any names—at Reagan. Unlike the front-runner, he was promising to wage a campaign "of substance, not symbols; of reason, not bombast; of frankness, not false promise." With that his campaign was launched. In no time he had thirty-five people on the payroll in Houston and fifteen in Alexandria, Virginia.

In the days following, Bar turned over her massive card file to members of the campaign staff. David Sparks, the campaign field director, was amazed at how deep and long the ligaments of friendship extended in the Bushes' life. Friends from U.N. days. The CIA. Congress. The RNC. Yale. Andover. Texas. The oil business. "I guess it's a fact of life that graduates of Andover and Yale hang together further in life than graduates from the 1969 Neoshoba Regional High School," Sparks said.

"You have to remember," George's classmate William Clark told a reporter, "that there hasn't been a Yalie in the White House since William Howard Taft and we've had all those Harvard guys in the interim."

George headed north to New England for an eight-city campaign swing. The media immediately put him to the test, asking him questions about complex foreign policy problems. George stumbled and the press smelled blood. "If we're going to maul him," the *Washington Post* reported one journalist telling another, "let's set up in the [TV] lights."

Next George headed off for a fund-raising breakfast in Miami. He gave a speech to 425 Republicans and raised fifteen thousand dollars. But his speech was awkward. After reeling off a long list of America's troubles he angrily blurted out: "What the ffffff . . . in heaven's name is going to happen to our country?"

Days later the same thing happened, explaining to an audience that he wasn't offering a new deal, a new frontier, or a great society, but a "new condo" for government.

He was struggling on the stump, especially compared to his rivals. John Connally—always brash and filled with Texas flamboyance—was waxing eloquent about what he was going to do to solve America's ills. Ronald Reagan was his naturally smooth and solid self. Connally and Reagan were like luxury sedans at the podium—powerful, steady, with a low and confident rumble. George was pure economy car, slow starts and sudden stops. Friends fretted that this was not the same man who had been so effective on the stump in Texas.

"George was more hesitant than he had once been," Bob Mosbacher told us. "Everything he had done over the past decade—U.N. diplomat, RNC chairman, China ambassador, CIA director—forced him to be diplomatic and very careful with his words. It seemed to suck the life out of him. He never seemed to get that out of his system."

Still George pressed on, always the happy warrior. From Florida he flew to Alabama, where he met with George Wallace. The next evening he was in Clanton, Alabama, speaking at a six-dollar-a-plate dinner organized by the Possum Growers and Breeders of America. They gave him a membership card, a certificate of appreciation, and a license plate that read EAT MORE POSSUM. (Somehow, it did not find its way onto Bar's Volvo.) For good measure, George held up a baby possum with the mayor of Clanton for the traveling media to see. "He did it with a certain horrified grace," noted one reporter.

A few weeks later Dottie put together an event in Connecticut. In Hartford, four men in bow ties and vests played oompah music as George spoke before three hundred who had gathered under a large banner that read CONNECTICUT IS BUSH COUNTRY. When the media asked for her thoughts about the campaign, Dottie said, "It was always Senator Bush's policy and my own to let them do whatever they strongly wished. I was apprehensive at first, because George can get tired. Actually, I think he'll win the whole thing."

From Connecticut, George went to Boston, where Sen. Bill Saltonstall helped arrange a press conference at Logan Airport. On the flight up, George was encouraged when four people leaned over and shook his hand after recognizing him. "Two of them were from Maine," he recalled, "a third was a prof from Harvard who reminded me we'd met in China, and some other guy."

Saltonstall had been a classmate at Andover, and his father had served with Pres in the U.S. Senate. When George arrived, Saltonstall went up to the mike. "Ladies and gentlemen, you've come to hear George Bush, and here he is."

George awkwardly approached the mike. "Uh, my cochairman believes in a crisp introduction," he said, looking at Saltonstall with a bit of irritation.

George went on to talk about the Carter administration and his ability to lead the country. He took some questions and then walked around Logan Airport shaking hands. "Say, which one is George Bush?" asked an elderly lady in a raincoat. "He's in films, isn't he?"

As the campaign officially began, the Bush-Walker clan was loyal and energetic. When the campaign opened an office on Lexington Avenue in New

York, the place was crawling with family members. Shellie Bush Jansing remembers it being a bit like a family reunion, "sometimes with members of
the Walker clan that I had never met before." They worked the phones,
licked stamps, and served as an insulation of sorts for Barbara, who was dis-
trustful of advisers and politicos. She preferred to have members of "the
tribe" around.

Each member of the family had a critical role to play. The Bushes were
fiercely competitive and, by harnessing that spirit, believed there was little
they couldn't accomplish.

Johnny Bush, now forty-seven and doing well with his own investment
firm, cochaired the campaign's finance committee. Big brother Pres chaired
the finance committee in Connecticut, where he was able to tap longtime
family friends from Greenwich. Before the campaign was done, Pres had
raised more than $1 million for his brother.

Doro was eager to help, but unsure how best to do it. "George told her
nobody wanted her if she didn't have a talent," Barbara Bush recalls. "So she
went nine straight months to Katharine Gibbs [secretarial school] and put
herself in his office." Doro hated secretarial school but she stuck to it, wanting to serve her father as best she could. She typed memos and took short-
hand at the campaign's Boston office.

Marvin took the semester off from the University of Virginia and caught
a flight to Iowa, where he rumbled around the state in a banged-up Chevy
Blazer that sported GEORGE BUSH license plates. He knocked on doors,
passed out literature, and called talk radio programs telling people to vote for
his dad. For Marvin, his work was an act of love, not political expression.

"Look, I don't always agree with the guy," he told one reporter about his
dad. "I don't like his stand on abortion. But he works his tail off. He deserves
to be president."

Neil did the same in New Hampshire, helping to rally the volunteer
troops in another critically important state.

But the biggest sacrifice came from Jeb, who had moved back stateside
with Colu and the kids to work on his father's campaign full-time. He received no salary, and when the campaign was over he was largely broke. Flu-
ent in Spanish, Jeb would spend most of his time in Florida, signing up two
dozen delegates from Miami's Little Havana for the Florida straw poll.

Jeb was focused and determined, throwing himself into the Florida campaign like no one else. One of the first to arrive in the morning, he frequently
worked late into the night. He also scolded his brothers when he felt they
were not sacrificing enough for their father. When Marvin expressed a desire

to return to the University of Virginia to finish classes, "Jebby bawls him out," George Bush recorded in his diary. Clearly the father saw a spark in his second-oldest son. "God, Jeb is doing fantastic though. Has such good judgment, good with people, great grasp of the issues."

If Jeb was living and breathing the campaign, George W. in contrast was only dabbling. He made brief forays into Iowa and placed phone calls to raise money. But his mind was elsewhere. Having lost his congressional race, he was facing an uncertain future. It was a curious repeat of what his father had done in 1950 when Pres Bush launched his first Senate campaign. George had remained in Texas trying to build his own company and left the campaign to his brothers.

The heaviest burden would fall, as usual, on Bar. Lacking the resources and name recognition of front-runner Ronald Reagan, it was critical for the Bush campaign to reach as many people as possible. So George asked Bar to spread the word by traveling extensively around the country on her own. George had his way of convincing her. "He uses psychology on me," she recalled later. "He always has. Some way or another, he makes me *feel wanted.*"

Traveling with just one aide, Bar pulled out the card file of eight thousand friends and starting speaking to small groups around the country. For close to a year Bar rarely saw George and the kids. She would fly into a city and make contact with a local Republican activist or a family friend. She traveled to Michigan where she spoke to a group put together by Patsy Caulkins, who had lived next door during their Yale days. Then she flew off to Grand Rapids, where Patsy's sister-in-law brought together a few friends. Then it was off to Muskegon, where another friend had put together a wine-and-cheese party. Then to Midland, Michigan, where a former neighbor from Washington, D.C., held a coffee.

The pace was often so frantic that Bar at times didn't even know where George was. One time, while changing planes in Chicago, Bar and her assistant Becky Beach ran into George and his assistant David Bates. "We were literally carrying all our bags, a lot of them, and we looked up and here come Mr. Bush and David," recalls Beach. "It was the first time they had seen each other in a week."

Any politician who aspired to the White House was judged, along with his wife, by the youthfulness factor. Jackie Kennedy had made it so back in the early 1960s. Bar, with her silver hair, was seen as a liability by some in the campaign.

During a fund-raiser in her hometown of Rye, New York, Bar and Dottie met with a group of Republican women to talk about George's campaign. One lady approached Bar on the mistaken impression that she was the candidate's mother. Bar was devastated but recovered gracefully. "I'd like you to come over and meet George's mother," she told the woman.

As her profile rose, her white mane became a source of regular discussion among supporters and contributors. The campaign was even forced to produce a form letter to respond to the myriad of comments about it. "I was very much interested in your views of my hair," it would say over Bar's signature. Some on the campaign staff insisted that she dye her hair to look more youthful, but Bar stubbornly refused and George backed her up. It was George's unconditional support for Bar that propelled her to work so hard for him.

The family and the forest of friends that George had carefully tended over the years provided the foundation for his presidential run. His strategy was in fact more about relationships than ideas, but he needed to broaden his base of supporters to have a chance of claiming the nomination.

That summer George traveled to San Francisco to a secluded camp deep in the Redwoods north of the Golden Gate Bridge. Sixteen hundred other men were there, too, gathering for the annual retreat held at the Bohemian Grove.

The Grove was in many respects similar to the other private clubs the Bush family had been associated with over the past fifty years. Skull and Bones. Alibi. Links. Gampy Walker had even started his own club in turn-of-the-century St. Louis when his revelry got out of hand.

The Grove's blue-chip membership rolls over the years included Richard Nixon, Ronald Reagan, Herbert Hoover, David Eisenhower, Earl Warren, and Robert Taft. Titans of industry like Stephen Bechtel of the Bechtel Group and Leonard Firestone of Firestone Tire also belonged, as well as an officer or board member from forty of the largest companies in America.

But it was also decidedly different. In keeping with its name, the Bohemian Grove encouraged free-spirited behavior. Where else could you spot former California governor Pat Brown parading around in the nude or a former president urinating on a tree?

The political significance of the Grove was unmistakable, particularly for Republicans. Ike, Goldwater, and Nixon had all made visits there the year before they ran for president. At the Grove you had the chance to mix with hundreds of major figures in a secluded environment for two weeks in the summer. Where else could you do that?

A sign over the club's entrance proclaimed SPIDERS WEAVE NOT HERE. It was a line from Shakespeare's A *Midsummer Night's Dream*, a warning to members not to discuss business, politics, or other worldly concerns. The Grove was supposed to be about fun, not networking. But everyone knew that within the portals of Bohemia the rule was often broken, at least in spirit. The Grove was a place to forge relationships with hundreds of men who could help you in the outside world.

The men participated in skits, frolicked in the woods, and ended with an operetta-like extravaganza called "High Jinks." There were elaborate rituals with men dressed in pointed red hoods and flowing robes. But the best time at the Grove was spent in the various camps, lounging about, drink in hand, talking about the world.

The Grove was divided into smaller fireside camps that carried endearing names like Cliff Dwellers, Woof, Toyland, Moonshiners, and Land of Happiness. Each camp had about fifty to one hundred members. Some camps became famous for their food and drink. Jungle Camp made a keen mint julep. Owl's Rest (where Ronald Reagan was a member) produced a famous gin-fizz breakfast. Less popular was the culinary delight at Poison Oak, which featured a Bulls' Balls Lunch: testicles from a castrated herd cooked to perfection. (George carefully avoided that one.)

In 1978, George was initiated as a new member and assigned to the Hill-billies Camp, whose members included Donald Rumsfeld, Walter Cronkite, and William F. Buckley, Jr. By joining the Grove, George was consciously planting his foot on Ronald Reagan's turf. Reagan was a longtime member and the place was filled with his supporters.

The experience was not lost on George. Over the next several years he would be a regular attendee. And more than twenty years later, when George W. was preparing to make a run for the White House, his father would bring him out for a visit.

From the time George Bush left the Bohemian Grove until election day 1980, he was hardly ever home. He traveled across the country making speeches to Republican clubs, civic groups, and business associations. David Bates, a friend of Jeb's from college who was a young lawyer in Houston, would swing by the house at 6 A.M. Don Rhodes would arrive a few minutes later in his pickup. They would throw their bags in the back and then head for the airport to wing it somewhere and make an appearance. George would stump for Robert Livingston, who was running for Congress in Louisiana. (Livingston was a distant relative, but George didn't know it at the time.) He'd raise money for a young freshman congressman named Dan Quayle, who was up for reelection in Indiana. Any Republican anywhere who had a decent shot at winning a local race could call on George Bush and he'd be there.

In the first four months of 1979 he made eleven trips to New Hampshire and nearly that many to Iowa. The strategy was straight out of Jimmy Carter's playbook from four years earlier. Jack Germond and Jules Whitcover had laid it all out in their book *Marathon*: concentrate on winning Iowa and New Hampshire to gain momentum. Jim Baker had read the book during his trip to China in September 1977. Then he read it again and again. "We read that book," he would say on the campaign trail. "Damn carefully."

The strategy required full immersion in the early states, going county by county, precinct by precinct in Iowa and New Hampshire. At the time, George was an asterisk candidate, hovering in the low single digits in national polls. If he were going to win, this would be the only way he could do it. The strategy was not glamorous and it required patience; you had to be the tortoise, not the hare. "Yeah, the turtle's kind of an ugly reptile," he said on the campaign trail. "But he's got persistence. Not too charismatic, but persistent. Determined. Successful."

The campaign was a test of Bush stamina, an athletic competition par excellence. George maintained an astonishing pace that impressed even seasoned campaign watchers. The Walkers and the Bushes believed in physical contests, whether on the athletic field or in business. Politics too was a contest of will, stamina, and determination. Pres Bush had thought that very thing when he ran in Connecticut. George had run his campaigns that way in Houston, and George W. did the same when he ran for Congress in West Texas. You out-hustle the other guy and prove to the voters that you want it more. "I have covered a lot of political candidates during the last twenty-five years but I have never known one—not even Hubert Humphrey—who ran with more zeal and determination," wrote Roy Reed of the *New York Times* about George's presidential campaign.

It was also a test of sheer toughness. While on the campaign plane, a television producer was joking around with him, mocking him, almost taunting him. When the man stood in the aisle of the airplane with a foot on each seat, blocking his progress, George walked up to him calmly, grabbed him by the private parts, and directed him out of the way.

George had inherited from his father the view that the race was less about the issues than it was about the character of the candidates. Ronald Reagan, Howard Baker, Phil Crane, John Connally: No one else had his breadth of national experience. "George Bush," ran the campaign slogan. "A President we won't have to train."

George wanted it to be a war of attrition. The front-runner, Ronald Reagan, was sixty-seven years old. "The age thing is going to get him," George quietly told his aide, Karl Rove.

George wanted to make an issue of it, remind the world that the front-runner was just not fit to be president. But he wasn't going to come out directly and say so. Instead, George started jogging in every city he visited. Give a speech, put on the shoes and running gear, and hit the streets. Soon his image, in full stride, was in campaign commercials, posters, even the nightly news. "I don't think we're running for athlete of the year," he quipped to one reporter. "But if we were, I'd win."

George was playing it cautious, always cautious. But while caution might have kept him out of trouble, it had less effect in firing up voters. After four years of Carter, people were looking for decisiveness. George was out to convince people he was qualified for the job, but without talking much about the issues. George had principles by which he lived his life and certain instincts about the way the world worked. But like his father, he was not committed to a particular political philosophy. Like Edmund Burke, the one political thinker he read and embraced, he was skeptical of political ideologies. "George Bush has no political ideology," said his nephew John Ellis. "His ideology is friendship."

One of the most sensitive elements of his support came from CIA agents who had served under him and now wanted him to be president. They formed a group loosely called Agents for Bush (quickly nicknamed Spooks for Bush). Ray Cline, the CIA chief of station in Taiwan, was an avid backer, as was Gen. Sam Wilson, a former director of the DIA (Defense Intelligence Agency). Harold Aaron, former DIA deputy director, was on his national steering committee, as was Henry Knoche, who had served with George at the CIA. Robert Gambino, CIA director of security, was so excited that he left his job at Langley to work full-time for Bush. The move caused concerns in the Carter camp that "dirty tricks" might be in the offing.

Bruce Rounds, director of operations for the campaign in New Hampshire, was a former CIA officer as was Tennessee finance chairman John Thomas. The Virginia coordinator was the former director of the Association of Former Intelligence Officers, and Harry Webster, who worked in clandestine operations for more than twenty-five years, became field coordinator in northern Florida. Active volunteers also included Gen. Richard Stilwell, who had served as the CIA's chief of covert operations for the Far East. In all, some twenty-five retired directors, deputy directors, and/or agents were working in the campaign.

The Bush team was an amalgam that reflected George's ideology of friendship. Jim Baker called the shots, and a network of New Englanders who had been displaced by the rise of the Goldwater-Reagan faction in the GOP helped staff key slots. Politicos like Paul Celluci, Andy Card, and Ron Kaufman, all from Massachusetts, eagerly joined the campaign. It was a coalition so broad that the only common factor was that they all knew George Bush.

Henry Cabot Lodge, Jr., the sartorial aristocrat of New England and heir to his family's political tradition, announced his support for George. Lodge was decidedly Eastern establishment liberal. "I'm for Bush, and I think he is a decent, generous, open-minded guy." On the other hand, the Bush campaign was also being supported by George Wallace's brother-in-law and former campaign manager. Wallace and Lodge: Never before had the two names backed the same political cause.

The first major hurdle came in November 1979 when Maine held an informal straw poll. Senator Howard Baker was presumed to have it locked up because of an endorsement from Sen. William Cohen (R-ME). But George worked Maine hard, relying on friends and family to get out the vote. He had lots of acquaintances there, having spent every summer but three there since he was a small boy.

The night of the straw poll, Senator Baker arrived in Portland on a jetliner with fifty reporters ready to cover his victory. George drove up from Massachusetts by car, with Doro and one aide along for the ride. Each candidate was given ten minutes to explain why he should be president. When the speakers were done, George left early, figuring that at best he could expect second or third. When the tallies came in, it was a stunning upset: George came in first with 35 percent of the vote.

It was a little win, insignificant in terms of the larger campaign, but it gave George a much-needed boost. In December, Robert Mosbacher had expected to raise perhaps $185,000 for the campaign. Instead, $850,000 rolled in.

Next came the straw poll in Florida, where Jeb was working the Cuban-American community hard. Relying on his father's contacts from CIA days, Jeb put together an impressive list of delegates. Reagan won the poll and John Connally came in second. But George was third, only seventy-four votes behind his fellow Texan. While Connally had spent $300,000 in the state, George had used only $40,000. Jeb had passed his first political test.

It was a long race, a marathon, like nothing George had experienced before. As he continued to crisscross the country, talking with voters, meeting with donors, doubt crept in as he wondered whether it was really worth it.

He was neglecting his kids, he lamented in his diary. "We haven't given proper attention to Neil. He's engaged, and we've really said nothing about that, done nothing about that. The girl must wonder, what kind of family we are . . . Doro has a boyfriend, the first time. Yet, we haven't taken them out to dinner together—and any of the things that normally we do." But he plodded on, hopeful that he might break out of the single digits in nationwide polls. Iowa was his chance to do just that.

George had been working Iowa hard. Governor Robert Ray was on his team, as were Iowa's Republican National Committeemen Mary Louise Smith and John McDonald. Still, Reagan was expected to win the state easily. The Gipper had been well known there since his days as a sports announcer in 1930s Des Moines, and his conservative philosophy seemed to resonate in the Hawkeye State. In 1976, Reagan had upset Jerry Ford—a sitting president—in the caucuses by a two-to-one margin. John Sears, Reagan's campaign chairman at the time, was so confident that he decided to keep Reagan out of the *Des Moines Register* debate days before the voting.

That proved to be a mistake. George stunningly won the caucuses. Once the so-called asterisk candidate because his poll numbers were so low, George was now the front-runner. Lou Harris found that while Reagan had led Bush nationwide before Iowa 32 to 6 percent, Bush was even at 27 percent within twenty-four hours of his victory. George claimed "the big mo," and Walter Cronkite, his fellow camper at the Bohemian Grove, seemed to agree. "George Bush has apparently done what he hoped to do, coming out of the pack as the principal challenger to front-runner Ronald Reagan," he declared on the evening news.

The campaign moved next to New Hampshire, where George already had an extensive operation. Hugh Gregg, a former governor who had supported Reagan in 1976, was the state chairman for the Bush campaign. Neil was working there night and day. But Reagan seemed energized by the Bush challenge and began maintaining a dawn-to-midnight campaign schedule. He focused on the issues and called for a tax cut, which George opposed.

Then the long knives came out.

William Loeb, publisher of the *Manchester Union Leader*, the most influential paper in the state, was a Reagan supporter. The curmudgeonly Loeb had assailed Gerald Ford in 1976 as "Jerry the Jerk." Now he started blasting away at George with the sort of rhetoric that had worked against George W. in Texas two years earlier. Bush campaigns always seem at some point to return to the issue of the family—its connections, its social position, and its money.

The paper declared that George was "a spoiled little rich kid who has been wet-nursed to succeed and now, packaged by David Rockefeller's Trilateral Commission, thinks he is entitled to the White House as his latest toy." The only question remaining was, "Will the elite nominate their man, or will we nominate Reagan?" George's win in Iowa was dismissed as a possible dirty trick. "The Bush operation has all the smell of a CIA covert operation . . . Strange aspects of the Iowa operation [include] a long, slow count and then the computers broke down at a very convenient point, with Bush having a six percent bulge over Reagan."

George bristled at the idea that he was an "elitist."

"It's undeniable that by God's will I was born to a family of comfortable means and given many opportunities," he wrote to a friend. "I suppose this makes me one of the elite. But an 'elitist' is a person who wants to associate only with other elites; in other words, a snob. I assure you I would never have moved to the oil fields of West Texas if I were an 'elitist.' "

Events in New Hampshire came to a head when plans were made for a candidate debate the Friday before the primary, sponsored by the *Nashua Telegraph*. The Reagan campaign had proposed to Jim Baker that the debate include only the two front-runners, namely Reagan and Bush. The newspaper agreed, and Baker saw it as proof that this was now a two-way race. They jumped at the chance to make it Reagan vs. Bush, confident that they could win.

On the night of February 23 the high school gym in downtown Nashua was packed with more than two thousand animated voters. The other candidates still in the race, Bob Dole, Howard Baker, Phil Crane, and John Anderson, were all furious at being excluded and showed up to demonstrate their displeasure. As the time for the scheduled debate approached, feverish negotiations were still taking place behind the scenes. George, oblivious to most of it, went out and took his place onstage.

The audience was now cheering for the four excluded candidates to be offered a chance to speak. J. Herman Pouliot, owner of the *Telegraph*, tried to calm the crowd. "This is getting to sound more like a boxing match," he said from the podium. "In the rear are four other candidates who have not been invited by the *Nashua Telegraph*." A chorus of boos erupted, and members of the crowd started to yell. Then suddenly Ronald Reagan appeared, declaring that his campaign now wanted to include the other candidates.

"Turn Mr. Reagan's microphone off," snapped John Breen, editor of the paper.

The crowd erupted and so did Reagan.

"I'm paying for the microphone, Mr. Green," he said, getting the last name wrong.

The crowd loved it. It was the sort of decisiveness that the public seemed to desire in the wake of the Carter administration. They cheered Reagan some more. George sat quietly at the podium and said nothing, sticking to the original rules and waiting for Breen to sort it out. To some in the audience he looked weak and aloof.

"You have to understand," said Johnny Bush, "George had given Breen his word. With George, manners are his compass, his unfailing guidance system."

The taunts now began. George Bush "wants to be king," snapped Bob Dole from the floor. "I have never been treated this way in my life. Where do we live? Is this America? So far as George Bush is concerned he'd better find another Republican Party if he can't talk to those of us who come up here." John Anderson and Phil Crane took their shots, too. When the night of chaos was finally over, George was the clear loser. He was furious with Reagan, believing that he had been set up.

George wrote to the four excluded candidates explaining his anger. "You should know that Governor Reagan never contacted me on any of this even though he had been in contact with most of the other campaigns. The first we heard that Governor Reagan might not debate as planned was when the newspaper contacted our New Hampshire manager. Confusion reigned until debate time . . . Unlike Governor Reagan, I have not ducked joint debates, having joined you on many occasions in joint events in many states . . . I felt that Governor Reagan has definitely not played fair with me."

Fair or not, the damage was done. Film footage of the encounter played throughout the country over the next two days. When voters in New Hampshire went to the polls a few days later, Reagan won 50 percent of the vote in the state. George came in second with 23 percent, a considerable drop-off.

His poll numbers were slipping. Characteristically, he became even more cautious, concerned about making a mistake or an error in judgment. The trouble was, in 1980, Republicans were looking for someone who did more than avoid making mistakes. While Reagan was talking about his "vision of America," George was sticking with his theme of competence. He was almost running the campaign as if he were ahead and not behind. George and Jim Baker placed their hope in the belief that Reagan would eventually screw up.

"George Bush, Jim Baker, and the people around them were all men who had specific, technical skills," says nephew John Ellis. "They were lawyers, bankers, businessmen who had run companies and executed major business deals. And here was Reagan, coming out of Hollywood. He had never run a company, never started a bank, nor had he been involved in finance or served in government at the national level. They considered him a light-weight."

Six days after New Hampshire, Massachusetts held its primary. Aided by his strong Massachusetts team, George managed to pull off a razor-thin win. Team Bush went on to win in Connecticut on March 25, Pennsylvania on April 22, and Michigan on May 20. But while they were racking up some victories, Reagan was winning big in the South and Midwest. The "big mo" was now with Reagan.

On May 3, Texas held a critical primary. By now Gov. John Connally was out of the race, and George was hopeful that he might be able to carry his home state as a "favorite son." He poured half a million dollars into televi-sion while Reagan could do very little to match him. But Reagan won Texas anyway, 53 to 47 percent, carried by his strong support in rural areas of the state. George carried only Houston and northwest Dallas.

George now faced a critical decision. Ohio was coming up in days. He could drop out of the race and hope that he might be picked as Reagan's run-ning mate, or he could stay in and hope that his opponent might screw up, sending uneasy Reagan delegates his way.

Fiercely competitive, the Bushes wanted him to stay in. George figured he ought to stay in, at least until California. Jim Baker had seen that look on George's face before, usually on the tennis court: unflinching, win at all costs, never give in. But while that might be a virtue in tennis, in politics it could be disastrous. Knowing how competitive the Bush clan was, he wanted to protect George from himself. So Baker quietly began negotiating with the Reagan camp—without George's knowledge—to assure that the Bush dele-gates would have a role to play at the convention. "I also knew," Jim Baker said, "that if there was any chance of George being on the ticket, he had to get out before the California primary."

After Reagan's win in Nebraska, Bush campaign officials met in Houston to discuss what to do. George clung to the fading hope that he could still win, and his family was telling him to fight on. Jim Baker told him he was licked; it was time to give in. The conversation was heated and no decision was made. It was only a week later that George finally dropped out of the race; losing was difficult to take.

In a monotone, almost sullen voice, George stepped up to the microphone and, with his family nearby, announced that he was withdrawing from the race. Bar was next to him, crying. George W., Marvin, Neil, and Doro were there, too. But none was more disappointed than Jeb, who was so upset he could hardly handle it. Jebbie had wanted his father to fight all the way to the convention; he had poured his life into the campaign. His son, four-year-old George P., was next to him, blinking back tears, aware at even such a young age that he should be disappointed.

#### CHAPTER 22

# VEEP

I N THE SPRING OF 1980, WITH THE NOMINATION ALL BUT ASSURED, members of Reagan's inner circle began exploring voters' attitudes toward possible running mates. Throughout May and June they conducted extensive in-home surveys on each of twenty possible candidates. The results were forwarded to Reagan, his campaign chairman Bill Casey, and Ed Meese. Based on the polling, three names emerged—Sen. Howard Baker, Gerald Ford, and George Bush. Reagan pollster Richard Wirthlin found that former president Gerald Ford was the most popular choice, with George coming in a distant second. For the first time in his political career, his father and his network of friends were not able to intervene. In both 1968 and 1976, George had been able to count on a small army of family and friends who could influence the process. This time there would be none of that. The Reaganites were a new factor in the Republican Party.

Instantly there was talk about a possible "dream ticket": Reagan and former president Ford. As the Republican National Convention approached, talks began between the two camps. Casey, Meese, and Wirthlin haggled with Henry Kissinger, Alan Greenspan, and Jack Marsh. Kissinger and Greenspan were particularly keen on the idea that Reagan could handle domestic matters and Ford could be in charge of foreign policy. But other former Ford administration officials had serious doubts.

"I don't know what Greenspan and Kissinger were thinking," recalls Donald Rumsfeld. "Picking a former president as vice president had to be the dumbest idea I've ever heard. Personally, I think they were well meaning, but wrong—flat wrong. You don't want four hands on the steering wheel. It would have weakened Reagan and made him look like he was not a full president. People don't want a president who isn't president."

The Republican National Convention in 1980 was held in Detroit. At his suite in the Pontchartrain Hotel, George was sitting around with family and friends, resigned to the fact that Ford was the choice for VP. "That's the way it goes," he told his friend Leonard Garment. "Give it your best shot. On to the next damn thing, whatever."

Meanwhile, as rumors spread about a pending deal between Reagan and Ford, Gerald Ford went on CBS for an interview with Walter Cronkite. The broadcaster began probing him about the exact nature of the possible arrangement. "It's got to be something like a copresidency?" asked Cronkite.

"That's something Governor Reagan really ought to consider," Ford replied confidently.

When word reached the Reagan team about what Ford had said, there was a complete meltdown. Negotiations stopped. Reagan sat in his hotel room frustrated and furious. He was expected to make an announcement about his running mate shortly, and now Ford had implied to a national audience that he would really be calling the shots.

Wiping his brow he turned to an aide. "Now where the hell's George Bush?"

Back at the Bush suite, the family had gathered to hear the pending news. Jeb was dejected, nursing a beer as he rumbled over rumors of the apparent Reagan-Ford marriage. "It's not fair, it's not fair," he kept repeating. His father told him to buck up, and Jeb headed back to the convention. George retreated to the television with a beer and some popcorn. Bar was sitting next to him at 11:37 P.M. when the phone rang. Jim Baker picked up. It was Reagan.

Baker quickly hustled everyone out of the room except George, Bar, and Marvin. Then he handed the phone to George.

"Hello, George, this is Ronald Reagan. I'd like to go over to the convention and announce that you're my choice for vice president . . . if that's all right with you."

George grinned. "I'd be honored, Governor."

But before he made the announcement, Reagan needed some assurances. He needed George to fall in line on the issues, particularly on his plans for a tax cut and on abortion. George quickly agreed. As he headed down to the convention floor for the announcement, he ran into Len Garment again and simply shrugged his shoulders in a gesture that said, "Go figure."

When Reagan stepped to the podium to announce that his choice was George Bush, many were stunned. After a few moments of silence the Bush delegates erupted in cheers, but Reagan's selection met with resistance among some of his own supporters.

Howard Phillips of the American Conservative Union declared it a sell-out of conservative principles. "Governor Reagan sounded like Winston Churchill but behaved like Neville Chamberlain," he said. Some announced their intention to draft Jesse Helms as the vice presidential choice. But that died down when word spread that George had agreed to support the party's platform—federal law against abortion, everything.

Still, most conservatives were far from thrilled. "Certainly, I'm disappointed," said conservative congressman John Rousselot from California. "But I can live with it."

Reagan and Bush left the convention enthused and energized. The economy was a major focus of their campaign, with emphasis on reducing government spending, slashing regulations, and cutting taxes. But also looming large was the holding of fifty-two American hostages in Iran.

Polls indicated that it would be a close race. They also showed that if the hostages were released before election day, Carter might very well win. Reagan-Bush staffers began to worry that Carter might be working on a secret deal with the Iranians to free the hostages. Rumors were circulating that Carter might cede to Iranian demands for money and arms in order to get them out before November.

To prepare for a possible October surprise, the informal Agents for Bush network went to work monitoring American military and political activities. Experienced ex-CIA and military intelligence officers watched U.S. air bases to see if we might be flying military spare parts to Iran. George's older brother, Pres, had a friend working in the Carter administration who offered to pass along any unusual information coming from the National Security Council. They had the situation wired—just in case.

The fall campaign kept George on the road, and he and Bar had little direct contact with the Reagans. The ticket was a marriage of convenience, and the two couples were still getting acquainted. Reagan and his top aides were hearing good things about his running mate. George was a good soldier on the campaign trail, both in front of the cameras and in private meetings with Republicans. "All the reports were positive," recalled Ed Meese. "He was being completely loyal to Reagan."

But the Bushes were slowly learning about the Reagans, particularly the power that Nancy Reagan wielded.

Two weeks before election day, Nancy sat down with campaign aides Michael Deaver and Stuart Spencer in a Dallas hotel room to discuss who would play what role in any future Reagan administration. Nancy had strong opinions on the matter and was supportive of placing Jim Baker in the position of White House chief of staff. It was a curious idea at first glance. Baker was hardly part of her husband's loyal inner circle, but she liked him. He was wealthy in his own right, possessed social graces learned in his youth, and had an air of great ambition. Nancy would become a big supporter of Jim Baker. She would also make life difficult at times for the Bushes.

On election day Reagan-Bush defeated Carter-Mondale in a resounding victory. For George it was the culmination of a nearly two-decades-old dream. But for the family, it would change the world almost completely.

———

SHORTLY AFTER THE VOTES WERE COUNTED IT BECAME CLEAR THAT A powerful and vibrant new force had entered the world of electoral politics. Evangelical Christians had helped propel Jimmy Carter to the White House in 1976. Now they had switched sides and gone heavily for Reagan. The American political and cultural map was changing as "born-again" Christians became part of mainstream society.

For the Bushes, evangelicals were a somewhat exotic bunch. Their faith was open, their emotions apparent, their commitment to the Bible uncompromising. Certainly the Bushes shared some of these traits. But they were most comfortable in the world of "high church" Episcopalians, who were reserved and not demonstrative. To both the evangelicals and the Bushes, faith was precious. For evangelicals, that required sharing it with others. For the Bushes, however, you didn't flaunt your faith; instead you demonstrated it by quiet action.

George and Bar were distinctly "high church." But in early December, George heard about a private service being organized at the Georgetown Baptist Church in Washington. Billy Graham was going to be preaching from the pulpit. George had first met Graham years ago, when his father had been in the Senate, and the two became friends during the Nixon administration when Graham was a frequent First Family guest.

The service was being organized by Sen. Mark Hatfield (R-OR), an evangelical and another family friend. George asked him if he could come by. Hatfield agreed. "President Carter and all of us would like to make a Baptist out of you."

George arrived with, of all people, Henry Kissinger, not someone you would expect to show up at a Baptist service. But Kissinger was also intrigued by Billy Graham. "I went to see one of his crusades twenty years ago because I wanted to see what it was like, and I was very condescending about it," Kissinger later said. "But at Madison Square Garden I was so moved that I thought I ought to meet him. I think he's a man of great substance, a man of great value."

Senator Hatfield declared that the "spirit of the Lord" had brought everyone together for the service. People in the pews raised their hands in praise during the singing of hymns. The event was an indication that faith would play a greater role in America's public life in the years ahead.

George was uncomfortable with some elements of the evangelical community. But he defended the so-called religious right in private conversations and in correspondence with his more mainline friends.

Bart Giamatti, president of Yale University, was one of these. The two men shared a common Yale history and a passion for baseball, but were often at odds politically. Giamatti in particular was troubled by the rise of evangelical churches and their involvement with politics, and wrote the new vice president on the subject. George wrote him back. "Why do you feel a threat from the Religious Right and not the Left? I'm not sure what God wants of us; but that others think they know what God wants is okay with me. Why is it all right for [Rev. William Sloan] Coffin to urge defiance on Vietnam, tolerance on Khomeini, or advocate 'gay marriages' but it's not okay for the Right to get together to work against abortion or for prayer in school?" Evangelicals were getting involved in politics because of the traumatic changes in America over the previous twenty years. "We must understand," Bush wrote, "that in our post-Vietnam post-Watergate guilt, we have condoned things we should have condemned."

George admitted that he was uncomfortable with some who were "totally intolerant, but in my view most are not . . . I love Billy Graham, I really do: some of the flamboyant money-mad teary temple builders worry me."

He struggled with issues of morality and politics, particularly abortion. He had been, prior to joining the Reagan administration, "personally opposed to abortion" but not in favor of legally restricting it. But his attitude had changed somewhat as his religious convictions evolved. The most profound change came when his son Marvin adopted his first child. The child could have been aborted rather than adopted. "When I have real doubts, and I do, I look at Marshall," he wrote his brother Buck.

Being elected vice president had brought George to the pinnacle of public life. For more than a decade his name had been bandied about as a possible vice president. Now he could only be saddened that the two men who had been so central to the ambitions in his life, his father and his uncle Herby, were not there at the summit to enjoy the view with him. Still, it was a family victory, and before the seriousness of doing the job they had time to celebrate.

In mid-January, just under five thousand Texans gathered in Washington for the Texas Ball. Ladies in mink coats drank from cans labeled J.R. BEER, in honor of fictitious oil baron J. R. Ewing. The men wore black-tie-and-boots, some arriving with a gowned date on one arm and a stuffed armadillo in the other. After a few hours of drinking the crowd loosened up and began dancing the "One-Eyed Joe." George W. made sure he enjoyed himself, and George and Bar made an appearance onstage.

Many of the couples had limousines to carry them from party to party. But so many members of the extended Bush family were in town that they had rented a fleet of four buses. All 130 family members wore large, bright BUSH FAMILY name tags because many of them had never met. George and Bar knew all of them, and they were hopeful of fusing the many branches of the family—Bushes, Pierces, Coles, Clements, Houses, Walkers, and Ellises—together for the first time.

The Bushes worked with typical efficiency. They transported people from event to event, serving lunch on board so no time was wasted. There were also delectables, including chocolate-dipped strawberries soaked in liquor.

The day before the swearing-in, the family gathered for a reception at the Museum of American History and took turns greeting the eighteen thousand people who passed through. For three and a half hours, each guest shook hands with someone from the family; Jeb and George W. would step in when their father needed a break.

That night former senator John Sherman Cooper, Pres Bush's good friend from the Senate, held a reception for one hundred family members at his Georgetown house. Longtime family friends who had been dormant in public life suddenly reemerged. It was a testament to the family's unique ability to pass friendships from generation to generation.

The next morning, as George was getting dressed, his telephone rang. It was Vice President Walter Mondale with good news: The American hostages in Iran were being released after 444 days in captivity. In exchange, the Carter administration was releasing Iranian assets, which had been frozen in the United States. It was for George a tremendous relief: That nightmare would not hang over the new administration. George finished dressing, and he and Bar went to the Capitol Building to receive the oath.

George had taken the unusual step of asking that the oath be administered by an associate justice of the Supreme Court; it was only the second time in American history. George tapped his old friend and fellow Skull and Bones man Potter Stewart to do the honors. The ceremony lasted a mere fifty-five seconds. Stewart said, "God bless you, George," when it was done. Then Bar kissed him.

After the ceremony the family went inside the Capitol Rotunda for the traditional lunch with the Reagans and members of Congress. It was the first real chance the Bush clan had to spend time with the Reagans. They didn't exactly hit it off.

George's sister Nancy Ellis sat next to Sen. Howard Baker and Reagan's daughter, Patti Davis. The genial Baker watched as Nancy tried to make polite conversation, but Davis said nothing. "She sat there pouting," Ellis recalls. "She was upset about something and refused to talk to anyone."

Watching George W. greet Ron Reagan, Jr. was another source of family amusement. W., wearing cowboy boots, looked at the aspiring ballet dancer suspiciously. It was not the sort of thing he saw very often in West Texas. They spoke awkwardly for a few moments before young Reagan slinked off to look for a friend. W. just shrugged his shoulders, laughed, and went back to his table.

After the luncheon, George and Bar drove to the vice presidential mansion. This was their thirtieth move in thirty-six years, and Bar wanted to enjoy it. The clothes were hung upstairs, and a large collection of orchids that Bar had bought days earlier was lined up for immediate planting in the garden. Stewards lit the fires and put out food as the family arrived.

That evening there were nine balls. George W. and Laura spent time with fellow Texans while Jeb and Colu stayed with the Florida delegation. George spent most of the night jumping from party to party with little time to do anything but shake hands.

The next morning the furniture arrived from Texas. It was classic Chinese, a collection they had assembled during their time in Beijing. The dark, wood pieces were blended with a menagerie of Chinese porcelain miniatures. Some of Bar's most prized possessions were beautiful antique Mandarin robes, which she had had framed. One hung in the reception hall, the other over the buffet in the dining room. When an inquiring Bush relative reached out to touch one of them, Bar snapped, "If you do, I'll cut your finger off."

Their most cherished piece, however, was not an item they had purchased, but the elaborate needlepoint rug Bar had been working on for several years. It was in many respects the family's scroll or parchment, eight by twelve feet in size and green, with flowers, a water garden, frogs, rabbits, and birds. Bar had carefully packed it up and taken it to thirty-six states and seventeen countries. She could look at that rug and tell you which stitch she had been working on when George W. got married, when her first grandson was born, when her husband had announced for president. The rug, still being worked on, was placed in the dining room, but family members were careful not to step on it.

Days after the move was complete, George and Bar characteristically invited Ron and Nancy Reagan over for dinner. The foursome had drinks upstairs in the private residence before heading downstairs for dinner. George and Bar had reached out to the Reagans repeatedly. Days after the election, George had written them a private note.

"This is just a quick thank you—thanks for making us feel so welcome, thanks for the joy of working with you, thanks for those little touches of grace and humor and affection that make life sing. Please know that we both want to help in every way possible. I will never do anything to embarrass you politically. I have strong views on issues and people, but once you decide a matter that's it for me, and you'll see no leaks in Evans and Novak bitching about life—at least you'll see none out of me . . . Call me if I can lighten the burden. If you need someone to meet people on your behalf, or to turn off overly-eager office seekers, or simply someone to bounce ideas off of—please holler." He signed it, "Respectfully and with friendship."

But the gestures were not reciprocated. In part, it was a case of the gregarious Bushes bumping into the more reserved Reagans. George and Ronald Reagan were very different men. Reagan was the son of a small-town shoe salesman, in a faceless Illinois town, who had graduated from tiny Eureka College. George of course grew up in Fairfield County, Connecticut, a universe of stone mansions, tennis clubs, and country day schools. If Eureka was Middle America, Andover and Yale were the ramparts of the WASP elite.

Still, despite these differences, the two men would grow close over the next decade. George committed himself to being supremely loyal, and Reagan appreciated Bush's abilities. The relationship they forged was reminiscent of the sort of clubby partnerships that Pres Bush had mastered first at Brown Brothers and then in the Senate: no public discord; disagreements handled in private.

One sign of compatibility came early when a particularly difficult budget battle erupted on Capitol Hill. Reagan was reportedly proposing cuts in social programs and an increase in defense spending. The new administration was getting hammered in the media, and moderate Republicans were abandoning the president. One moderate Republican senator wrote to George and advised him, for the sake of his own political future, to distance himself from Reagan or at least not lead the charge.

George rejected the advice in the strongest words possible. As he wrote to

Richard Nixon, "I don't believe a President should have to be looking over his shoulder wondering if the Vice President was out there carving him up to undermine his programs in one way or another." At a meeting with GOP party leaders, a Republican senator lectured everyone in the room about how his supporters were not being taken care of by the Reagan administration. "Aside from being elected president yourself," George snapped sarcastically, "just how damn much do you think you ought to have to say about who is working there?"

George's sense of loyalty extended to cabinet meetings, where he was unwilling to join the fray. "It's more than [reluctance]," he said. "It is an absolute determination not to express myself. Suppose several Cabinet members, or even one Cabinet member, expresses a view, and I express a contrary view. I don't think the president should ever have to choose between me and a Cabinet member. That's not the way to have a relationship of confidence."

If George did voice disagreements with Reagan, he did it during the weekly luncheons they held together. No one else attended the luncheons, and that led, in George's words, to "the development of a good confidential relationship with the president . . . in an environment where I feel perfectly free to discuss controversial things with him and give him my honest opinion and best judgment."

To Reagan's utter amazement, there was not one leak from the luncheon meetings over the course of eight years. George Bush never talked to the press about them, nor did he ever talk with aides about their private discussions.

Rivals for the presidency and very different in temperament and style, the two men nonetheless came to rely on each other. As George wrote in his diary, "I do feel close, and he makes you feel totally relaxed. He's hard to read; he doesn't ask for advice; he doesn't say, 'what do you think about this,' very much—but the other side of that is, I feel uninhibited in bringing things up to him. When I do bring up something controversial, he might not comment; he might not say anything right there; and he might not look particularly enthralled about it or say, 'tell me more'; but I never get the feeling that he doesn't want me to tell him, so I do and try not to overdo it . . ."

George made clear to his aides early on that his goal was not to make policy. "Don't expect me to make policy," he told Rich Bond. "I'll take some hits on this, but my job is to cement my relationship with Ronald Reagan and articulate his policies." This was the way it had been throughout George's life. Relationships reigned supreme. Relationships had always been key to his ambitions, but nowhere was that more true than in Washington. "If I don't have his confidence," he quipped to aides, "I'll be going to funerals in Ecuador."

But Reagan found George to be exactly what he needed. His cautiousness, the fact that he was a team player, meant that he could give George assignments and know he would assiduously avoid taking any of the limelight. One of George's first assignments was to go to Atlanta to meet with local and state officials about providing federal assistance to help solve a series of high-profile child murders in the city. George went to extraordinary lengths to avoid media attention. He discouraged senators and congressmen from accompanying him and banned direct photos or press coverage of the meetings.

In return for his loyalty, George found Reagan to be a genuinely kind individual. At Reagan's seventieth birthday party, the president leaned over and asked Bar, "I want to ask you a very personal question. Is George happy with his job? Does he feel what he's doing is worthwhile? I just want to be sure he's doing enough. If the awful-awful should happen, George should know everything."

The two men forged a bond. "Reagan is a guy's guy, a man's man," says John Ellis. "They male bonded. But I don't think [George] ever felt that he got close to him."

But while the Bushes' relationship with Ronald Reagan blossomed, the same could not be said for their ties with Nancy. Following the election, relations went from ice-cold to nonexistent.

Problems began from the start. "When the Cabinet and Barbara would meet with a high-level state delegation, they were all shoved over to one side of the room and never even saw the visitor," said Al Haig, who was secretary of state. "Barbara was treated like dirt. And Barbara cried. Believe me, it's hard to do that to Barbara."

"It was hurtful to Barbara," says Shellie Jansing. "But she never complained, never once during the White House years said anything about it. It was only after [the Reagans] left that she told us how difficult it really was."

The most painful snub for Barbara and George was the fact that their children were never invited to the White House. "They did resent that," Harry Catto explained.

Even more troublesome, however, was Nancy's penchant for spreading gossip about George. In the spring of 1981, rumors surfaced that George was having an affair with the widow of an ex-congressman. George was not particularly bothered by the rumors. This was, after all, Washington. But what concerned him was their source: He learned from several people that the flames were being fanned by none other than Nancy. George and Bar were furious about it but said nothing, never raising the matter with her or the president. But George lamented in his private diary: "I always knew that Nancy didn't like me very much, but there is nothing we can do about all of that. I feel sorry for her, but the main thing is, I feel sorry for President Reagan."

Complicating matters was the fact that Jim Baker was one of Nancy Reagan's favorites. She liked his customary elegance and Southern Comfort voice; the silky confidence and cowboy business image he put forth. Baker could put in a good word for George and try to temper Nancy's anti-Bush tendencies. But it also complicated the longtime Bush-Baker relationship, because Baker was beholden to Nancy. As he told friends, "She is responsible in part for my being here."

There had always been a mysterious cocktail of friendship and competition between Baker and George Bush. In their early years it seemed as if their professional relationship mirrored their partnership on the tennis court: George was up front, playing the net, swatting at close shots; Baker backed him up, playing the baseline and chasing down ground strokes. But in the Reagan White House the game was different.

As vice president, George had the position. But as White House chief of staff, Baker had the real power. He managed the president's schedule, attended cabinet meetings, and participated in all National Security Council discussions. In addition, he helped forge the legislative strategy and had responsibility for all press relations. Particularly for a president like Reagan, with a laid-back administrative style, Jimmy Baker was the gatekeeper.

Baker kept his head down in Washington, maintaining a low profile. "The higher the monkey climbs," he was fond of telling friends, "the more you see of his behind." But he was quietly forging relationships in the GOP and the administration. And by the summer of 1982, Lou Cannon of the *Washington Post* was reporting that Baker might very well have presidential ambitions of his own.

Baker was also fond of making statements in the press that seemed to bolster his position at George's expense. He made sure the public knew that it was he who had largely engineered the choice of Bush for VP. "Everyone knows the president didn't want to pick Bush," he told one reporter. "He was not particularly popular with Governor Reagan. If George had further alienated him back then by entering a primary in Governor Reagan's home state as a pure spoiler, there is no way he'd be where he is." Baker further claimed that George had rejected his advice to drop out of the race in 1980 and that he had saved George's career by holding a news conference to announce the end of the campaign without George's knowledge.

———

LIFE AS VICE PRESIDENT WAS LIVED UNDER THE GLARE OF CONSTANT PUBLIC attention. For Bar, who had grown comfortable with a casual style, it was clear that some changes were in order. She started wearing Bill Blass rather than clothing right off the rack. "I realized I never had a suit that fit before!" she told her family. George, on the other hand, kept to his preppy Brooks Brothers look. When the clothier had its semiannual sale, George roared to the downtown D.C. store in the vice presidential limo and picked up some new clothes. Characteristically, they were plain gray flannel slacks, no cuffs or pleats.

National politics in the media age meant that the image of a man mattered even more than his substance. Your ability to project a certain image was critical to creating a national persona. To the Reagans, who had both been in Hollywood, this was something that came easily. The way they carried themselves, the way they interacted with each other captured part of the national imagination. Media advisers and photographers suggested that George and Bar try to do the same thing. After all, Ron and Nancy Reagan's love affair was very public; their talk, the looks, the hugs and kisses. But for the Bushes it was very different. Like their faith, their love was very private, and Bar in particular did not want that to change. When asked by a White House photographer to kiss her husband for a shot, Bar refused. "We don't do that in public. There are some things you just don't spell out."

George spent much of the first several months doing the sorts of politicking that Reagan didn't particularly want to do: a heavy schedule of foreign travel, public appearances, and campaigning for Republicans around the country. As VP he would travel more than a million miles and visit seventy-four foreign countries.

In late March 1981 he was traveling through Texas. The schedule called for stops in Fort Worth, Austin, and Dallas. On the morning of March 30, George was in his limousine on the way to Carswell Air Force Base near Fort Worth with several members of the Texas congressional delegation, including Jim Wright and his friend Bill Archer. Air Force Two was being prepped for a trip to Austin, when shocking news arrived. Ed Pollar, head of his Secret Service detail, told George that there had been a shooting in Washington. Two Secret Service men were down; President Reagan was apparently not hit.

"Where did it happen?" George asked.

"Outside of the Washington Hilton. I'll let you know when we get more information."

Reports trickled in, but they were confusing. A troubled twenty-six-year-old named John Hinckley, Jr., had fired five shots at the president, who had been pushed into his limousine. The car had raced off for the George Washington University Medical Center. Reagan had not been directly hit, they knew that. But for some reason he was getting medical treatment. George turned on the black-and-white television set in the staff cabin of Air Force Two and waited for a news update. The telephone lines to Air Force Two were not considered secure, so it took several minutes for a telex communication from Secretary of State Alexander Haig to arrive. He was advising George to return to Washington as soon as possible.

Then came phone calls from Don Regan, the treasury secretary, who had oversight of the Secret Service, and Ed Meese. The reports were now alarming. While Hinckley had failed to hit Reagan directly, one bullet had ricocheted off the bulletproof limo and lodged under the president's left arm. It was resting only an inch from his heart.

The flight plan for Air Force Two was immediately changed; planned events in Austin were canceled. But the return flight to Washington would take time. Air Force Two needed refueling, and it would have to stop in Austin as planned.

George was outwardly calm, recalls Jim Wright, demonstrating "a complete command of his emotions." But inside he was a tempest, and he released his feelings through the tip of his pen as he scribbled notes on his Air Force Two flight information card.

"Pray—literally—that RR recovers." Reagan, he jotted, "was a friend not just C. in C. [commander in chief]. President, decent, warm, kind." He made a note to ask Bar to call Nancy Reagan. As if to mark his own dread and uncertainty about the situation, he wrote "unknown" in the center of the card and underlined it twice.

Back in the White House there was mass confusion. Larry Speakes, the deputy White House press officer, was standing before the assembled television cameras trying to explain the situation.

"Who's running the government right now?" asked one reporter.

"If the president goes into surgery and goes under anesthesia, would Vice President Bush become the acting president at the moment?"

"I cannot answer that question at this time."

In the nearby White House situation room, cabinet members sat in horror as they watched Speakes on TV. Al Haig and National Security Adviser Richard Allen feared that such an unclear answer could spawn national uncertainty and doubt, even tempt enemies into taking advantage of the situation. They both ran to the press room and Haig stepped up to the podium. The rest of the cabinet was back in the situation room and unaware of what Haig was doing.

"We were sitting there discussing the situation and Al showed up on television," recalls Caspar Weinberger, the secretary of defense. "At first we thought it was an old videotape of a press conference, but then we realized it was live."

Haig explained that he was "in charge" and that his authority came from the Constitution. That wasn't quite true, and later there were chuckles about the choice of words by what seemed to be an ex-general overeager to take command. As Haig later put it, he made a "poor choice of words."

As these events unfolded in the White House, Air Force Two was en route to Washington. George's military aide, Colonel Matheny, explained that once the plane touched down at Andrews Air Force Base, George could immediately board a helicopter and land directly on the South Lawn of the White House. That would create a clear picture that someone was indeed in charge, and that it was the vice president.

But George didn't see it that way. As long as Ronald Reagan was still alive, healthy or otherwise, he was still the president. George ordered the helicopter trip to the White House canceled: "John, only the president lands on the South Lawn." It was as if the instruction at the Greenwich Country Day School that mattered most to his parents—"never claims more than his fair share"—was returning in the crisis.

When Air Force Two finally landed, George instead took a helicopter to the vice presidential residence and rode by limousine to the White House. When he finally arrived at the situation room around 6 P.M., he was equally deferential. Leaving the executive chair at the head of the table empty, he instead calmly sat in his own. "The President is still President . . . I'm here to sit in for him while he recuperates. But he's going to call the shots."

———

THE FIRST SIX MONTHS OF 1981 HAD BEEN FILLED WITH PLENTY OF HEAVY lifting. With the arrival of summer the Bushes were able for the first time to think about family pursuits. In early June the family gathered in Richmond, Virginia, for Marvin's wedding to Margaret Conway Molster, the daughter of a department store executive he had met at the University of Virginia. Like his older brothers Neil and Jeb, Marvin was getting married at a relatively young age. After the honeymoon, the couple moved to Boston, where Marvin was training with an investment firm. Unlike his three brothers, he had absolutely no interest in politics.

Summer meant spending time at the beloved Walker Point. Now that he was vice president, George relished the chance to escape to Kennebunkport even more than before. He was so eager to smell the salt air and hear the water crashing on the rocks that when guests arrived late at the Portland airport, he fished quietly for an hour from the pier on the city's waterfront with the Secret Service in tow.

Only two weeks on the job and George had already written to Uncle Herby's widow, Mary, describing his plans to renovate the place. He was putting the money together to finalize the sale to the Bushes.

"We want the Point to be as Herby would want it to be—open to all family to come and go and love it as we all always have. I am grateful to you for your patience and understanding on all the details of transfer . . . I hope we can give the place the same love Herby did. We want it to keep its character. He wanted it to be the anchor for all the family."

Bar spent lots of time that first summer supervising changes to the house. A local man named Longley Philbrick and his son Danny were restoring the place and making structural modifications. Longley had done the work at Walker Point since 1925. As usual, the deal was handled without a contract; a handshake would do.

Only three of the rooms at the Point were heated, and George wanted to winterize the place. Bar also wanted to create order out of the chaos that characterized most Bush family vacations. She posted rules on the door: "Picnics should be planned early for the beach. Please pick up wet towels and use them twice. Please be down for breakfast between seven and nine or no breakfast."

More than anything, Bar wanted the place to be comfortable. No antiques were on the property, and she used fifteen-year-old slipcovers to make sure the grandchildren could do what they wanted. She reserved an end room for herself, painted in aqua with a large fireplace, latticework on the walls, and water on three sides. She planted both perennials and annuals outside to bring the place to bloom.

The job of vice president was constraining, unlike anything George had experienced. Even as director of Central Intelligence, he could walk around with anonymity. But the vice president could not go anywhere alone, and he was constantly traveling. Quick trips to Walker Point seemed to sustain him.

When he finally had a chance for an extended stay later that summer, he wrote about it in his diary. "It's a great joy being there with the sea pounding into the rocks, the boat, the new tennis court, being with Mother, seeing the Walkers and the kids, and our own grandchildren running around the place. It was supreme joy, a physical lift. I ran comfortable and fast, played reasonable tennis, took up golf again, learned to putt, and had two birdies on the front nine against Ed Muskie."

Walker Point was a place where a man could be steadied by the voice of his ancestors. George had even put his feelings about the place into verse.

Now it's Sunday at St. Ann's
The kids are passing the collection plate
Ganny's here—Great Ganny, too
My Dad and Herby there next to Lou.
The Powers and the Woodhulls all are blessed
Though long ago laid to their rest
I see the brides and the christened face
Soul strength from this sacred place . . .
They're all in bed now in the dorm
The pulse of generations firmly born
The sea's the same—the rocks stay fast
The new ones' strength—generations past
My God, the blanky's lost again
Fred's bit Sam—what should we do?
Just relax and watch the sea
Treasure the strength God's given you.

Walker Point was more than a physical place; it was a place in time. George would invite guests to come and then walk the grounds with them, pointing out the exact eddy where he took his first swim in the surf; where W. and his cousins would go skinny-dipping; where his father would sit to watch the sea.

"You had the clear sense," Marlin Fitzwater told us, "when he was there he wasn't just visiting. He was *reliving history.*"

George often used Walker Point as an informal place to politick. He had seen his father and the Walkers conduct business every summer in the sunshine and brisk winds of Maine. If the president had Camp David to entertain guests in a relaxed and private setting, George wanted to do the same in Kennebunkport.

One summer he and Bar hosted governors from across the country for a clambake. The meeting was ostensibly about pushing forward the administration's agenda to return some federal programs to the control of the states. But as always for George Bush, the meeting was also about forging relationships.

The guest list included young Arkansas governor Bill Clinton and his wife Hillary, and members of the Bush family, who mingled and discussed a host of issues in the late-summer breeze. When George Wallace arrived, he was in a wheelchair with his most recent wife, a buxom young woman wearing a rather tight-fitting dress. Dottie Bush tried to engage her in conversation but to no avail. Afterward she told her son, "George, I just can't see what that nice man sees in that woman."

But despite the intrusion of national politics, Walker Point remained preeminently a place for the Bushes. The family would gather and play tennis. The children would stage a "mini-Olympics." There would be lunch on the terrace—usually a cookout. Adults would have afternoon cocktails and dinner.

Marvin, Neil, and George W. would make their appearances during the summers, but Jeb and Colu didn't come as much. It was still difficult for Colu, who had trouble fitting in. She didn't play golf or tennis, and shopping for knickknacks or lobster pots in Kennebunkport was not exactly her thing.

But throughout, people would talk as much about the past as the present. And Harry Catto, a longtime family friend whom George would later appoint ambassador to Great Britain, remembers experiencing how the past and the present in the Bush clan seemed to merge. "They were recultivating the past and using it in part to encourage greater closeness of the family," he recalls. "It was quite remarkable."

Elsie Walker Kilbourne had seen plenty of "anger" during the gatherings at Kennebunkport as the men of the family competed against one another to prove their manhood. The anger may have gone, but George continued the family tradition of guiding his boat directly into the violent surf. In one instance NBC newsman Tom Pettit asked to come along for the ride. George granted him his wish and then, while out on the water, Pettit crashed to the deck after *Fidelity* smacked a wave particularly hard. The newsman lost ten days of work due to his injuries.

#### CHAPTER 23

# STRUGGLE

P EOPLE COULD SEE HOW MUCH STRESS GEORGE W. WAS UNDER. AT his oil company's small three-room office in Midland, you would find stacks of geological maps lying around and W. smoking cigarettes at a fast and furious pace. His language was explosive—cursing in a way that some in the family had not seen before. Plenty of investment money was being tossed into his struggling oil enterprise, but he really wasn't seeing much of it. Instead, he kept putting it back into the business, gambling that it would pay off. One of those who invested in the business was Stephen Kass, a classmate from Harvard Business School. "There are people who live in $4 million homes, and have a yacht and then drill dry wells. That wasn't the case with George. If you saw how George lived in Midland, no one could think he was living off their money."

Having a father who was vice president was proving to be both a blessing and a curse. It did offer him new opportunities, there was no doubt about that. The family was now at the center of national power, and people would return your phone calls pretty quickly. More people than ever would be interested in doing business with members of the Bush family. But it also posed a vexing challenge: His father was raising the bar of achievement yet again. It would be a more arduous climb than ever to live up to the expectations of his name.

"I think all the boys felt the pressure," said Elsie Walker Kilbourne, "but Little George in particular. He was the oldest, and the Bushes and the Walkers place a big emphasis on the oldest-son bit. The fact that he was also carrying his father's name added enormous built-in pressure. The other boys didn't face that; they could be anonymous if they wanted to."

W. was now in his mid-thirties. By this age his father was already worth close to a million dollars. W. was hopeful that he could strike it rich with one big strike. He called this mythical well "the Liberator." It would be the one that would not only free him from financial worry but release him from the high expectations that were squeezing the life out of him.

In his quest for "the Liberator," W. tried everything. He tried to convince the owners of the famous half-million-acre Waggoner Ranch near Wichita Falls to let him drill on the property. But he couldn't afford the huge lease fees. He tried joint ventures with other oil companies. He even ventured overseas with the help of a family friend.

General Vernon Walters had served as deputy director of the CIA under George Bush in the mid-1970s. Now retired from the military and temporarily out of government service, he was trying his hand at business consulting. Walters was a longtime friend of King Hassan II of Morocco: The two had first met during World War II when Walters as a young army lieutenant landed in North Africa to push back the Germans. Hassan was thirteen at the time and wanted to see the tanks from the U.S. Army 2nd Armored Division. Because Walters spoke French, he was selected to give the young man a tour. They had remained fast friends ever since. According to Walters, George W. approached him because he was interested in trying to drill in North Africa, which still offered tremendous opportunities. Libya and Algeria were already major producers. The same might be true for Morocco.

Walters says he took George W. to Morocco and introduced him to Hassan. They had a royal meal in the palace and then were asked to spend the night. "Everything went smoothly until King Hassan inquired as to whether George wanted a woman for the night," Walters told us. "He just froze." Sensing his discomfort, but also not wanting to destroy the prospects of a deal, Walters kindly explained to Hassan that the young American was not interested. An awkward moment was averted. But like so many others, the deal in Morocco never panned out.

W. was feeling pressure not only because of the heavy expectations he was laboring under, but because of the investors who were banking on him. Uncle Johnny Bush was helping to raise capital, and the money did roll in. In 1980, as W.'s father sought the presidency, $1.7 million came in from thirty-four investors. But much of it came from longtime family friends and even members of the family. Some of these investors had put up money in his dad's firm, Zapata, more than twenty years earlier, and with tax write-offs and a modest return on their investment had done quite well. The old man had done it. Why couldn't the son?

W. dealt with the pressure by continuing to drink, much to the chagrin of his wife. "He would go out with a group of friends and come back inebriated," Shellie Bush Jansing told us. "It was embarrassing to the family and Laura certainly didn't like it. But at that point he wasn't particularly listening to Laura."

Gerry Bemiss recalls sitting with his wife and some of the Bushes at a fish shack up in Kennebunkport one summer. George, Bar, and W. where all there enjoying some beer and chowder. Suddenly W. leaned over to Mrs. Bemiss. "So, what is sex like after fifty?" It was one of those embarrassing moments that Big George and Bar faced with some frequency. (But Bemiss reports that his wife exacted her revenge years later when W. hit the big five-oh. "So, George, how is it after fifty?" W. grinned and retorted, "Quite good, thank you.")

W. took to drinking, says Elsie Walker Kilbourne, because he had to bear the pressure largely alone. "Our family is not terribly good at allowing people to open up and ask for help. We all know help is there if we need it—no questions asked. But asking for help is interpreted as a sign of weakness. So we tend to keep it to ourselves and suffer alone."

In December 1981, W. was given an opportunity to buy a stake in a property owned by Pennzoil, which was run by the Liedtkes, his father's old partners. W. jumped at the chance and changed the name of his company from Arbusto to Bush Exploration. He also welcomed a major new investor named Phil Uzielli, who was a friend of Jim Baker's. Uzielli put $1 million into the company in exchange for a 10 percent stake. W. tried to leverage the company and go public to raise even more capital, offering chunks of stock worth $16 million. But his efforts failed miserably. "Going public was a mistake," he said later. "We weren't prepared for it. We didn't raise any money, we weren't able to get enough exposure for our partners as a result . . . I made a big mistake."

The underlying problem was not W.'s business plan, but the tumultuous oil market. Even when he was able to find oil, prices were so low it often didn't pay to bring it up to the surface. In 1984 he drilled ninety-five holes in four Texas counties. Forty-seven were actually spitting up crude and three were producing natural gas. But the days of high-rolling Texas oil producers were over.

It didn't take long for Bush Exploration to find itself in financial trouble. Salvation came, as it so often did for W., through his ability to acquire and keep friends.

Paul Rea, a Midland geologist, had been a friend for quite some time. Rea was now working for the DeWitt family of Cincinnati, who had owned the Cincinnati Reds, two Coca-Cola distributorships, several radio stations, and a chain of restaurants. They even ran their own mutual funds. In the great rush to the oil patch in the late 1970s, they had branched out and created an energy investment firm named Spectrum 7. Paul Rea was the exploration manager for Spectrum 7, and like everyone else in the energy business, the company was struggling.

The DeWitts wanted to turn the operation over to an experienced manager who knew the business. When they asked Rea, he thought immediately of George W. The DeWitts had met W. before and were familiar with the family. Bill DeWitt, Jr., living in St. Louis, knew about the Walkers and had spent time with W.'s uncle Bucky.

Bill DeWitt, Jr., went to Midland and had lunch with Rea and W. They quickly discovered that they shared a common pedigree—both were Yalies who had gone on to Harvard Business School. More important, perhaps, they shared a passion for baseball. Within minutes the two were chatting about the game like old friends. When DeWitt left that afternoon, it was clear he wanted W. on board. George W. became chairman and would earn seventy-five thousand dollars a year. He was also given 1.1 million shares of Spectrum 7, or about 15 percent of the company.

Family members could see the relief on W.'s face. He had never quite taken to the maverick world of the independent oilman. Now he had some stability. The company's worth would be determined by forces beyond his control. He tried to eke out a profit by investing in stripper wells—rigs that would draw oil from previously drilled wells. But the market continued to soften, and soon the company was $3 million in debt. He had to lay off employees; he had to put off his plans; he had to face those expectations again.

"I'm all name and no money," he lamented.

#### CHAPTER 24

# LIFTOFF II

W. HAD GONE BACK TO WORK IN THE OIL PATCH AFTER THE 1980 campaign. His younger brother Jebbie had packed up his bags and left Texas as quickly as possible. "I left Houston to get out from my father's shadow," he explained. "It took me about a week to figure out that the shadow a vice president casts is very large."

Jeb had always been the honest one, the serious one. He was the child who would tell Bar, "Mom, you look like you've put on some weight." He was also the fighter, the one who always believed in the underdog. It was that seriousness and drive that had brought Jeb into his father's campaign in 1979. No one worked harder than Jeb. And when defeat came, no one took it harder.

Now, Jeb was determined to avoid the pitfalls of living near his father's home base. Much as his own father had done, and his grandfather Pres before him, Jebbie was determined to make it somewhere else, alone. He turned down a chance to return to Texas Commerce Bank, where he had been working since college. Despite a successful career there—he was vice president of Venezuela operations in his twenties—he had never taken to the banking business.

"I wasn't very good at collecting on bad loans," he told us.

Family members remember little Jebbie talking about running for president when he was just eight years old. While he didn't talk about it openly anymore, no one doubted that he was still thinking about politics. But if he wanted to run for office, Texas clearly wouldn't do. There was not enough room for two Bushes.

It didn't take long for an interesting prospect to develop in Miami with Armando Codina, a Republican Party activist who had met George Bush during the 1980 campaign.

Codina was a true American success story. A Cuban immigrant with just a high school education, Codina had developed an automated billing system for doctors. Over the course of a decade he built a 220-employee firm with offices in Miami, Jacksonville, Orlando, and Tampa. He sold the company in 1978 and turned his energies to the less taxable domain of real estate. Jeb hooked up with him as he worked the Cuban-American community and called him after the election to see if he had any ideas.

Codina offered Jeb a job as vice president at his real estate investment firm, IntrAmerican. Success or failure would rest on the business Jeb generated; his compensation was almost entirely tied to commissions. Not only was this an opportunity to build something—and the Bushes are big on building things—Miami was the perfect place for Colu. The vibrant Latin culture would help her feel more at home than she had been in Houston.

In the early 1980s, Miami was booming with an influx of Latinos. In twenty years the city's Hispanic population had jumped from about 5 percent to roughly 60 percent. Jeb and Colu spoke Spanish at home, and Colu proudly maintained her Mexican citizenship. "*Beso, Jebbie, rápido,*" Jeb would blurt out to his young son as he ran around the house. It wasn't surprising that the first words the little boy uttered were *agua, jugo,* and *aquí.*

Many American companies saw the city as a window to the large Central and South American markets. Likewise, Latin firms were moving to the city in hopes of tapping into North America. Miami was in many respects the gateway city.

But while the city presented opportunities, it was not without risks. Miami was going through a deep recession; there were riots, and the Mariel boat lift had brought in thousands of criminals and mental patients from Cuba, which added to the skyrocketing crime rate. The place was also a favorite American outpost for drug gangs and petty criminals.

The work was hardly stimulating. IntrAmerican was channeling money from throughout Latin America into land speculation in downtown Miami. Jeb was spending most of his days—and plenty of evenings—hustling to lease office space owned by the firm's investors. If he lacked the overt charm of his older brother's backslapping ways, he made up for it with hard work, focus, and persistence. His first year on the job he earned a relatively modest $44,000. By 1990 he was pulling in $1.2 million.

While his older brother struggled in the oil patch, Jeb's star began to rise. The pecking order for this generation of the family was suddenly beginning to change. "When they were young, Jeb was somebody for George to torture," explained cousin John Ellis. "Then he grew up to be six foot four, and that got complicated. As a kid, George viewed him as a completely unnecessary addition to the family. It was just for the first part of it there was nothing; Jebbie was just a pain in the ass. I think that carried on for a long time.

Jebbie went off and did what he did and he rose more successful at certain points. Throughout George W.'s life people were measuring his progress versus what his father had accomplished. George has never said this directly to me. But he wasn't measuring up. And he was drunk on too many occasions, and he embarrassed the family on too many occasions and now all of a sudden his brother Jeb is married, has kids, is making a good living in the real estate business in Florida and George was floundering around. It had to be at some level annoying that his younger brother was doing better than he was."

As the pieces of his life fell into place, Jeb also started thinking about politics. If before he had been cynical about politics, the 1980 campaign had changed him. He had traveled with his father, worked the grass roots in Florida, and served as a surrogate speaker. "That experience shifted my thinking about politics," he told us. "I had thought it was kind of lacking in moral value. Once you get to do it the way that I got to do it, I was hooked."

Now when the family gathered, it was Jeb who was talking about politics, about the crisis in Central America, the demographics of south Florida, and the need to reduce regulations on business. The vague left-wing politics of his youth had melted quickly under the heat lamp of reality.

"All that left me when I had to start worrying about paying my bills," he said.

In early 1984, Jeb learned about an opening on the Dade County Republican Committee. The GOP was a rising force in south Florida, once a Democratic stronghold. But after 1980, Republicans gained 36,000 new registered voters while the Democrats lost 33,000. Much of it was fueled by the Cuban-American community, which identified with the Reagan-Bush administration's strong anticommunist politics.

The race for the county committee would be complicated—just like everything to do with politics in Miami. The GOP was beset with factions. There were the Republican liberals, mostly well-off retirees from the Northeast who thought of the GOP in terms of a social club. Then there were the fire-breathing Cuban-Americans, who saw everything in the context of Fidel Castro. Throw in the occasional John Birch supporter and the middle-class professionals who were new to party politics, and you had a potent and at times unappetizing cocktail.

Jeb called his dad for advice. George told him the situation reminded him of his first run for Harris County GOP leader in Houston. Stick to your guns and be firm, he advised.

The other candidates were Laura Hunt and Carlos Dominguez. Hunt was the wife of Watergate conspirator E. Howard Hunt and the widow of the Bay of Pigs hero Mañuel Artime. But more difficult to deal with was real estate investor Dominguez, who gave Jeb his first taste of Cuban-American politics.

Dominguez, a successful businessman who was used to getting what he wanted, had been laboring on behalf of the party for several years. He was furious that such a young upstart would challenge him and decided that it must be a conspiracy. He wrote to President Reagan insisting that he investigate Jeb's campaign. He was convinced, he wrote, that "Fidel Castro is behind all this."

Jeb managed to get the endorsement of several key Cuban-American leaders and, like his father some twenty years earlier, was elected county GOP chairman. It was the first political success for this new generation of Bushes, and George was so pleased that he sent his son the gavel he had once used as county chairman in Houston.

Many hoped that Jeb would be an ideal candidate to bring the party factions together. He was young and energetic and preppy, which would appeal to the party's middle-class base and the liberal country club set. But he also spoke perfect Spanish and was even developing a Cuban accent. He was the perfect fusion candidate. Still, there was tumult in the beginning. During one of his first meetings as chairman, local councilman Julio Martinez and newspaper columnist Eladio Armesto got in a fistfight. Martinez had Armesto pinned to the carpet before a security guard broke it up. Martinez then claimed that nothing had happened.

"I tripped," he said, dusting off his jacket.

Jeb gaveled the meeting to order and went back to business without skipping a beat.

Jeb quickly became an important voice in Miami. As son of the VP, he was considered an easy conduit for getting things done in Washington. On local radio stations he would be besieged by callers criticizing the Reagan administration or asking for help. "Does your father or President Reagan know about the social problems in Haiti? Do they know where U.S. money is going?" Any detailed foreign policy question or complex issue related to the tax code he was expected to know the answer to, or have the means to change. He labored hard, reading as much as he could about every imaginable issue he might be asked about.

Soon it all became a blur. He was attending dinners, appearing at social functions, and holding fund-raisers. "I'm on four or five tracks at once," he complained. On top of the long day in the real estate business, he had countless political meetings. Colu, although she knew politics was the Bush family business, was a private woman who didn't share his enthusiasm. While she supported him "because it makes him happy," it was not, she explained, because she shared his passion for politics. Above all, Colu worried about her children. George P. was on the cusp of his teen years and little Noelle, with her raven hair and beautiful smile, was a sight to behold. Little Jebbie had joined the family and was getting into everything. Sure, there were advantages for the children in being members of the Bush clan. George P. would attend the Army-Navy game with his grandfather, sit on the fifty-yard line, go out for the opening coin toss, and lift up his hands like Rocky Balboa to the thrill of the crowd. But George P. also had challenges. At summer camp he would get into fights with boys who criticized his grandfather.

The family settled in a 1970s rambler in Pinewood Estates, near Miami, deep in the heart of suburbia. George P., Noelle, and Little Jebbie lived a generally middle-class existence. But dad was gone most of the time. It bothered Colu, who had been abandoned by her own father when she was young. But it didn't faze Jeb, who had grown up with a busy father himself. "When I was growing up," he said at the time, "I hardly saw my dad either, but when I did see him it was really enjoyable."

---

MORE THAN TWO THOUSAND MILES AWAY, IN COLORADO, NEIL BUSH WAS EAger to make his own mark. The third son in the family had graduated from business school and during the campaign in New Hampshire had met a schoolteacher named Sharon. Wedding plans were announced quickly for what Shellie Bush Jansing described as a "need-to-marry situation."

Neil had always been the odd man out among his brothers. While they were all fiercely competitive, Neil was polite and less interested in winning. The most fiercely fought games of tennis or basketball never included Neil, who lacked his brothers' killer instinct.

In part it was a confidence problem. Plagued with dyslexia, he couldn't compete academically with his brothers. While George, Jeb, and Marvin had all gone to their father's alma mater, Andover, Neil struggled at St. Albans even when helped along by a tutor. George W. had set off for Yale and Harvard Business School, Jeb graduated Phi Beta Kappa from the University of Texas in two and a half years, and Marvin from the University of Virginia. Neil went to Tulane, where he graduated with a 3.2 GPA.

Growing up in a competitive family, Neil found other means to gain approval. "I always found ways to compensate," he told one reporter. "I was nicer. I volunteered to rake the yard when the others were bailing out." Family friends remember little Neil as a delight. "He was the most polite, the most compliant of the boys," Gerry Bemiss recalled. "His father called him Whitey not just because of Whitey Ford, but because he was the pure, clean kid." But Neil's way of compensating and gaining approval from his parents frustrated his brothers. "He drove us all crazy growing up," recalls Marvin Bush, "because he made us look just horrible." The boys all started calling him "Mr. Perfect."

In the early 1980s all the Bush boys were ambitiously pushing into the future. George W. was struggling but still the head of his own oil firm. Jeb was breaking into Miami real estate. Marvin was beginning to launch what would be a very successful career in the investment business. Neil, on the other hand, was still trying to find his way. So he sought to imitate what his father had done. "I didn't have a red Studebaker," he recalled. "But I wanted to be in the oil business."

In the 1940s, Texas had been the hinterland for the American oil business; still plenty of oil in the ground and not too many players crowding you out. But now his brother George was facing too many players in Texas. By 1981 the new frontier was in the central plains states. Denver, not Dallas, was the place to be for young upstarts hoping to break into the oil business. It had the additional virtue of being a place where Neil wouldn't be in the shadow of his brothers.

Neil interviewed with Amoco and was offered a position as a trainee landman at a starting salary of thirty thousand dollars per year. But it would give him the chance to learn how to secure leases for mineral rights, something his father had learned thirty years earlier.

Neil and Sharon moved into a Denver apartment. Neil proceeded slowly, waiting before he got to know people before telling them who his father was. But that quickly ended in late March when John Hinckley, Jr., fired five bullets at President Reagan.

By a strange coincidence, Neil was friends with Hinckley's family, who lived in the Denver area. Just days before the shooting, Neil had dined with John Hinckley's older brother. The ironic twist brought media attention and a few wacko claims that the Bush family had engineered the assassination of Reagan so George could take power. While no one bought the conspiracy theories, the entire Denver community now knew that a member of the Second Family was living in their midst.

Neil would spend three years learning the oil business at Amoco. During that time, he and Sharon joined the go-go social scene in Denver. They were frequent guests at the city's most selective galas, and blue-chip friendships quickly formed. Sharon helped organize charity balls and befriended Nancy Davis Zarif, the daughter of oil billionaire Marvin Davis. The two formed a small company called Cookie Express.

Neil was always looking for opportunities to branch out on his own and, in 1983, he took the plunge and formed his own oil company, JNB Exploration, just as his father and brother had done. Neil was hoping to make money quickly—perhaps a million by the time he was thirty—then get out and go into politics. More than anyone else in the family, Neil started pushing the idea of a Bush dynasty.

"At the time the talk in the family was W. in Texas, Jeb in Florida, and Neil in Colorado," John Ellis recalled. "All three were going to make a run for political office."

But the very audacity of his plans revealed his naivete about the ways of business. He was planning to make a killing in a deeply troubled industry. George W. was finding it tough going in Texas. But Neil remained absolutely convinced that it was just a matter of doing things right. "He was a classic babe in the woods," said Gerry Bemiss, who has invested in Bush family oil ventures. "Neil was very trusting, too trusting, of just about anyone who wanted to do business with him."

George W. had tapped out most of the investors his Uncle Johnny knew. So Neil started hustling around Denver, shaking hands, passing around his business plan, and meeting with prospective investors. Neil was charming, likable, and hardworking; the reports from Amoco were that this guy wanted to work very hard to succeed. Of course, the fact that his father was vice president didn't hurt.

Before long he was having lunch with Bill Walters, a prominent Denver developer. Walters was an architect who had started a real estate business from his basement. By the time he was forty he had amassed a fortune worth more than $200 million. He owned something like 24 million square feet of undeveloped land in the Denver metro area, about the size of the downtown area itself. Walters had the kind of established credentials Neil needed in a partner. For his part, Walters was intrigued by the chance to do business with America's Second Family. He quickly invested $150,000 in JNB in return for a 6 percent interest.

Neil then hooked up with Kenneth Good. Like Walters, Good was a self-made man who had earned his fortune in real estate. But if Walters was rock-solid, steady, and conservative, Good was flamboyant, a speculator. And like

Gampy Walker, he enjoyed showing off his wealth. He flew around the world in a six-seat private jet, sometimes winging to Monaco for a weekend of gambling. He closed high-powered real estate transactions in a jogging suit. He drove a Maserati and lived in a custom-built 33,000-square-foot home worth $10 million.

Good saw the value in hooking up with a member of the Bush clan—the kid's father might be president someday. He jumped at Neil's idea without even paying it much attention. "He was kind of free with his money," Neil later recalled. "He went for high-risk ventures, which is probably why he was interested in my oil business." Good slapped Neil on the back and got him a line of credit worth $1.7 million at a bank in exchange for a 25-percent stake in the company. JNB was now in business.

Neil had raised the capital he needed in a matter of weeks. But the timing couldn't have been worse. Like his big brother W., Neil was getting ready to drill for oil as the market continued to fall. As prices hovered below twenty dollars a barrel, the economics of the business became clear. Even if Neil hit a gusher, he still might end up broke. The cost of production was higher in the Rockies than just about anywhere else. By 1985, members of the Denver Petroleum Club were adopting the unofficial motto: "Stay Alive in '85."

The realities weighed heavily on Neil. Jeb was doing well in Florida, closing in on several million-dollar deals. W. was facing the same challenges in the oil business, but he had at least found a wealthy partner and merged with Spectrum 7. JNB was simply losing money, and Neil figured he was unlikely to find a partner to bail him out. Success was elusive and his ambitious plans had to be delayed.

"I keep moving the deadline back," he was forced to admit to friends. "By the time I'm *forty* I'll be able to do anything I want to."

As Neil searched for answers to his financial dilemma, a banker named Michael Wise called one day and asked to meet him at a Denver pancake restaurant. Neil had met Wise only once before, at a dinner party. But the guy sure seemed sharp. A former suit salesman from Kansas, he was now a player in the exploding savings and loan business as head of Silverado Savings and Loan. Popular in the Denver business community, he was also a board member of the U.S. League of Savings Institutions.

As the two men ate their syrup-laden pancakes, Wise made Neil an offer out of the blue: Would he consider joining the board of his financial institution? For eight thousand dollars per year in compensation, he would simply attend regular board meetings and try to drum up loan opportunities. Wise assured him that his firm was not the broken-down savings and loan of

George Bailey in *It's a Wonderful Life*; Wise was doing more than financing mortgages on single-family homes and automobiles. His institution was turbocharged, investing in commercial real estate, luxury hotels, condos, and shopping centers. Speculation was sending the price of commercial real estate higher just about everywhere, and Wise was along for the ride.

Neil knew next to nothing about financial institutions, other than what he had picked up on a summer job shuffling papers at a bank in Texas. The world of finance was otherwise unknown to him. But Wise was offering him a spot as an outside director, which was common with savings and loans. Doctors, businessmen, builders, retired military officers, ex-politicians—all showed up as directors at these places. The job didn't require much heavy lifting; an outside director was simply supposed to let people know about the company and try to steer business its way. The S&L's inside directors—lawyers and bankers employed by the thrift—handled the financial details.

Neil no doubt replayed in his mind the fact that his father had served on several bank boards over the years and had found them quite useful. And Wise had good credentials, so how risky could it be?

Before he took the job, Neil went to Silverado and met with the firm's senior officials. They pulled out a series of charts that demonstrated how successful it was. The financials were in order. An audit issued by an accounting firm indicated that the S&L was expected to make a profit that year. Everything seemed in order. Weeks later he was in the airy sky deck of a white building on the edge of Denver, attending his first monthly meeting at Silverado Savings and Loan. He took the opportunity because it was a chance to "pump iron with the big boys a bit," said Elsie Walker Kilbourne. "But he didn't have the wherewithal to do the pumping."

#### CHAPTER 25

# THE CALL

F OR CLOSE TO TWENTY YEARS, PRES BUSH, JR., HAD BEEN CONTENT
to watch his younger brother George carry the family's mantle into
the world of politics, standing patiently in the background while
his younger brother followed in their father's footsteps. When his father ran
for the Senate in 1950, it had been Pressy who drove him around the state
and served as his campaign manager. When George had run in Texas, it was
Pres, Jr., who had raised money for him on Wall Street. He did the same in
the campaigns of '66, '68, '70, and '80. For the presidential race alone he
had collected more than $1 million for his brother. It had been that way
most of their lives.

Over the years, Pres, Jr., had made a comfortable living in the world of finance and insurance. Living in Greenwich, he had remained deeply involved in Connecticut Republican Party politics—trying to make it more
conservative, recruiting candidates, and raising money. But deep inside he
had always possessed the desire to run for office.

In 1982, Republican senator Lowell Weicker of Connecticut was up for
reelection. For a long time Weicker had been a nemesis to the Bushes. Pres
Bush, Sr., had never cared much for his grandstanding, self-promoting ways.
In the Bush family there is still resentment over the way Weicker held court
at the old man's funeral in 1972.

When George was up for Senate confirmation as CIA director, Weicker
was one of only three Republican senators who voted against him. During
the 1980 presidential primary, after Weicker abandoned his own quixotic
campaign, he claimed that George had covered up illegal donations while
RNC chairman. (Weicker said George had told him about it in a secret conversation, something hard to believe given their adversarial history.) George
called the charge "an absolute lie." When in 1980 George was selected as
Ronald Reagan's vice presidential running mate, Weicker announced boldly
that he was supporting Reagan . . . but not Bush.

So there was plenty to raise the family's ire at Weicker. And Pres, Jr., now had his chance not only to win a seat in the Senate, but to serve as the family vanquisher.

A self-proclaimed moderate, Pressy began circulating word that he had some interest in seeking the seat. He garnered almost immediate support from conservatives and GOP stalwarts who were fed up with Weicker's maverick ways. In the Senate he was voting more with Ted Kennedy than he was for Reagan's agenda.

William F. Buckley, Jr.—another Greenwich resident—had organized a political action committee to oust Weicker, and the National Conservative Political Action Committee began running anti-Weicker television ads. Pres, Jr., worked to join forces to defeat Weicker in the primary, and then face a Democrat in the general election.

When family members got the word, many were surprised. But when the call came, they all joined in the crusade. Pres, Jr., began raising money, using the network of donors he had established for George's run for the White House. The family held a kickoff fund-raiser honoring "Prescott and George Bush." Almost everyone was there—brothers Johnny and Bucky, sister Nancy, and Dottie. But the George Bush being advertised at the reception was not the vice president, but his son George W. Pres's brother was conspicuous by his absence.

Big George was troubled by the campaign. He confided in Buckley that he thought it was a mistake. "He didn't think his brother would make a good candidate," Buckley related. Pres, Jr.'s, campaign also hurt George's political standing in Washington. Weicker was a worm, to be sure, but the Republican majority in the Senate was precarious, and if Pres, Jr., beat Weicker and then lost in the general election, it might help the Democrats retake the Senate, which would complicate things for the Reagan administration.

When Pressy first announced his campaign, George tried to ignore it. He was a sitting vice president, he explained, and couldn't become involved in a Republican primary. But by January 1982, polls in Connecticut indicated that Pressy was actually ahead of Weicker among likely Republican voters. They also showed that he would run far behind the expected Democratic nominee, Toby Moffett, a young, attractive candidate well known in the state, in a general election.

"George was in a fix," says Gerry Bemiss. "Friends were calling him because Pres had contacted them for support. The Senate was just barely in Republican hands and Weicker was the best chance to hold the seat for the GOP."

George started receiving pressure in Washington. Senator Howard Baker, the majority leader, and Sen. Paul Laxalt not only endorsed Weicker; they asked George to get his brother to back off. Connecticut GOP party officials made the same request. But George simply couldn't bring himself to ask his brother to exit. At the same time, George's lack of private support was deafening. For Pres, Jr., who for decades had supported his brother fully, it was a painful disappointment.

As spring turned to summer in 1982, party leaders in Connecticut began to panic. The state's unusual primary system called an endorsing convention in July. If Pres, Jr., managed to get more than 20 percent of the delegate votes, there would be a primary in September. Pres, Jr., did manage to stay in, and he vowed to hang tough when polls indicated he might win the primary.

Fearing that whoever won a divisive primary would lose in the general election, George felt the pressure from national party officials even more. Finally the call was made: Younger brother told older brother to get out of the race.

"Losing Weicker would have caused him a lot of grief in the Senate," Pres Bush, Jr., recalled regarding the conversation with his brother. "The message was, 'You need to get out for me and the party.' "

The other person who placed a call to Pressy was his mother. It was one of those rare instances in which Dottie injected herself into questions of politics. She, too, advised her son that it would be best for everyone if he dropped out of the race. In a simple statement to the media, Pressy did just that the next day.

Barbara Pierce as a young girl. The Pierces, like the Bushes, came from a lineage steeped in American history, including a former president. While Barbara was close to her father, her mother was a remote social climber. *(Prescott S. Bush family scrapbook)*

Above (left), Barbara Pierce in 1943. The young woman was smart, strong, and opinion-ated. For George Bush, she was a persona very similar to his own mother. *(George Bush Presidential Library)* At right, George H. W. Bush in his Navy pilot's uniform. He went into the war an isolated boy and came out a mature and purposeful man. *(George Bush Presidential Library)* Below, George H. W. Bush, Bar, and George's youngest brother, Bucky. Bar was completely absorbed into the Bush family. Members would later joke about the long-forgotten Pierces. *(George Bush Presidential Library)*

George H. W. Bush being rescued by a submarine after he was shot down over the Pacific. *(George Bush Presidential Library)*

Above, George and Bar's wedding, December 1944. *(George Bush Presidential Library)*

Left, George and Bar in 1945. Like several generations of Bushes before him, George was eager to step out on his own and get out from under the shadow of his father. *(Prescott S. Bush family scrapbook)*

Above (left), Big George and Little George, 1946. "Expectations are always high for the firstborn in our family," says one family member. The two Georges would spend a lifetime trying to understand each other. *(Prescott S. Bush family scrapbook)* At right, Bar with Little George. No one would loom larger in his life than his mother. *(Prescott S. Bush family scrapbook)* Below, Pres and Dottie celebrate their silver anniversary in 1947. To understand the success of the dynasty, say family members, you need to appreciate the strength of the Bush women. *(Prescott S. Bush family scrapbook)*

Above, Prescott Bush Sr. running for the U.S. Senate. Money for money's sake never interested the investment banker. Running for the Senate in the 1950s would mean navigating the minefields of McCarthyism and betrayed friendships. *(Prescott S. Bush family scrapbook)* Below, the Bush grandchildren eagerly working to send Pres to Washington. When a Bush runs for office, it's always a family affair. Money, friendships, alliances, and time are all put at the disposal of the candidate. *(Prescott S. Bush family scrapbook)*

Pres and Dorothy celebrate the victory of 1952. Long active in Republican politics, Pres now had his chance to shine. *(George Bush Presidential Library)*

Dorothy Bush and son George with her grandchildren George W. and Robin in 1953. Little Robin was suffering from cancer and would die a painful death. George would retreat, focusing instead on his burgeoning career in business and politics, and leave Bar to hold things together. *(Prescott S. Bush family scrapbook)*

# TRANSFORMATIONS

E VER SINCE MIGRATING TO MIAMI, JEBBIE HAD BEEN WORKING HARD in the real estate business and with the Dade County GOP. With the help of friends and his own innate drive, he quickly became a player in the byzantine ways of Miami. Alec Courtelis, a shrewd Cuban-American businessman who had helped finance his father's presidential bid, was serving as Jeb's mentor. Courtelis would let Jeb know about potential lucrative deals, chat with him over Cuban coffee about politics, and make sizable donations to the Dade GOP.

Jeb absorbed it all and was spinning in several different worlds at once— business, real estate, and party organizing. But running for office was never far from his mind. When he was eight and his older brother, George, talked about being Willie Mays when he grew up, it was Jeb who told the family that he was going to be president.

W. had run for office in 1978 and failed. Jeb was eager to be the first of his generation of Bushes to serve. Cousin Elsie Walker Kilbourne saw that, in contrast to George W., who was drifting, Jebbie was very much focused on one thing. "Politics didn't seem to be his [George W.'s] chosen career," she said. "With Jebbie you always had this sense that methodical planning was going on and that he was going into politics."

South Florida was becoming increasingly hospitable to Republicans, and several inviting congressional seats held by vulnerable Democrats caught Jeb's interest. He bandied the idea about with a few friends, who encouraged him to take the plunge. Raising money wouldn't be a problem. He was well known now and the family had a national fund-raising network in place. He recounted how he called his father in Washington and laid out the whole idea.

George listened patiently, and when Jeb was finished he asked a simple question: "What if you win?"

Jeb was taken aback. Wasn't that the whole idea?

But then his father started going over the financial realities of serving in

Congress. It meant having two residences, one in Washington and the other in Miami. It meant a cut in salary while paying for family trips back and forth. George had been a millionaire when he served and even so, money got tight.

Jeb was learning the family dictum that had first been established by his grandfather: Run for office only when you've made enough for the family to be comfortable. Pres Bush had waited until he was fifty and his kids were almost out of college before he first ran for the Senate. George and Bar had waited until they made their first million. George W. had made a run back in 1978, but he was single at the time.

So Jeb put his political plans on hold and began looking for opportunities to make more money. Becoming rich in real estate could be a slow and plodding process. So when a Cuban-American named Mike Recarey introduced himself to Jeb, he was intrigued. A refugee from Cuba, the young man had started a company called IMC that provided medical services to Cuban refugees. A fast-talker with a glowing charm, Recarey was an entrepreneur of the type that the Bushes could appreciate. Now he was pulling in about $12 million per year, with ambitions to make even more.

Recarey also had plenty of friends in high places. He was on a first-name basis with Congressman Claude Pepper, and a son of Pepper's chief aide was on his payroll. Former Jimmy Carter aide Maria Elena Torano was his lobbyist, and former Reagan campaign aides John Sears and Lyn Nofziger had lucrative consulting contracts.

Now Recarey wanted Jeb on board. So he started making contributions to the Dade County GOP to get his attention. "When he wrote a check," says Jeb, "it wasn't for fifteen dollars." Recarey also tried to cultivate a business relationship by telling Jeb that he wanted his help to develop a new headquarters for IMC. He offered a flat seventy-five-thousand-dollar fee for his efforts. Jeb quickly agreed.

Recarey was a subcontractor health management organization (HMO) to the U.S. Department of Health and Human Services. Each month the HHS would pay him 95 percent of the average Medicare payment for each patient Recarey handled, regardless of their health. If they didn't need any treatment, Recarey got paid anyway; he could pocket the difference. It was a good way to generate cash flow, but by 1985 he was running into trouble. An arcane HHS rule required that the number of Medicare patients that any HMO handled not go over 50 percent. Recarey was well above that number and in jeopardy of losing the contract. If that happened, his entire business empire might collapse. So he called in his chips.

He phoned Jeb and asked for a favor: Could you call the HHS and vouch for my character? Recarey said that all he wanted from the agency was a fair hearing. Jeb liked the guy and he had a good reputation in the community, so he placed a call to the HHS chief of staff, Kevin Moley, a political appointee. Jeb explained the situation and told him about Recarey.

"All I'm asking," he said over the phone, "is that you give him a fair hearing."

"Have no fear," said Moley. "I'm the chief regulator."

They both chuckled, and according to Moley the conversation ended there.

What difference the call made is difficult to say, as Recarey used his other contacts to send the same message to regulators. As a result, HHS decided to stay with Recarey. And although IMC never did go through with its real estate plans, Recarey paid Jeb a fee of twenty-five thousand dollars anyway.

What Jeb didn't know was that IMC was a house of cards. The HMO was insolvent and collapsed a year later. A grand jury indicted Recarey on fraud charges. Recarey promptly fled the country to avoid prosecution. Suddenly Jeb was learning what it means to be used.

But if being the son of the vice president attracted some unsavory types, it also yielded handsome rewards. When the secretive Bank Openheim Pierson of Switzerland opened a private financial institution on Brickell Avenue in Miami, it asked Jeb to serve on the board. The bank, which was aptly named Private Bank and Trust N.A., had no billboards and no advertising. Out front there was no sign, only the numbers "1438"–the bank's address. If you called the place, a polite receptionist would answer with "4643" — the last four digits of the bank's telephone number. It refused to accept deposits and never made loans.

Designed to cater to wealthy Latino investors who were interested in both security and discretion, the bank made money by handling the investments of its customers for a fee. Jeb sat on the board with only four other directors. It was one of those perks that came with being the son of the vice president and a man with connections.

IF BEING VICE PRESIDENT WAS CHANGING THE LIVES OF GEORGE'S CHILDREN, it was positively transforming Bar's. When they had first entered the national stage, Bar was the anonymous one, largely unknown and seemingly out of place. On the campaign trail, Bar was at times unsure of herself. Even after

George was elected vice president, she still had not defined herself. When George made a stop in San Antonio in 1982, a local news photographer was working feverishly to get a clean shot of him. But there was someone standing in front of him.

"Will the woman in the red dress please get out of the picture?" he shouted with real annoyance. When Bar turned around, she suddenly realized that the man was talking to her.

Even in official Washington she was an unknown entity. George and Bar attended a reception at the Swedish embassy and were placed in the receiving line to meet the guests. One woman asked her, "Who are you?" Another confused her with George Shultz's wife. One kindly American gentleman greeted her warmly with, "Welcome to our country."

Throughout George's career, Bar had been content to sit in the background. But now she seemed determined to find a place and a voice of her own.

Ever since the children were little, it was Bar who had been the enforcer. When it came to family matters, she retained a tight control that had been ceded to her by George. It was Bar who made the decisions about schooling, friends, and activities for the kids. She picked their houses and decided what should go where. And when George ran for office, it was Bar who was the epicenter of contact with family members.

But that tight control of family matters increasingly extended into the realm of politics, in part because the personal and the political were becoming increasingly blurred as the family entered the national stage. Politics was tough, and whether members of the family wanted to be in that world or not, they had no choice. To protect her family, Bar was becoming even tougher than before. "For some people Bar is not the sweet homemaker, she's some kind of dragon lady," Elsie Walker Kilbourne related. "I guess that's partly true. She is very strong and you don't want to cross her. But at the same time, she does have a huge heart. And she is very maternal."

But that instinct to protect was wedded with a shrewd sense of politics. While George was deliberative and would consult with others when making political decisions, Bar was instinctive, and those instincts were often correct. She saw increasingly that what her family did and said was open to national scrutiny, and she expected her children to fall into line.

Clashes were most frequent with George W., and they continued well into his thirties. Shellie Bush Jansing recalls a time when a few family members and friends were talking about politics and the media in the driveway at Kennebunkport. Someone mentioned the name Maureen Dowd of the *New*

*York Times*, and George W. suddenly went on one of his riffs, attacking and criticizing her in the strongest possible terms. "Well, George, that was certainly brilliant of you in front of all these people standing around," she snapped at her son. She want on to harange him for three or four minutes. "She just absolutely reduced him to ashes," said Jansing. "'If you want to think things like that, go ahead. But frankly we don't want to hear about it.' In other words, shut up."

In the Bush family, many opinions over the years were communicated through humor. "It's the coin of the realm for family communication," says Elsie Walker Kilbourne. "Messages are passed through humor, a lot of friends are judged by whether they are funny, and there is a lot of joking at the dinner table. Big George is always funny, young George's humor is more outrageous. Bar's is self-deprecating."

Now in the public light, Bar turned to the humor that she had used to communicate within the family to convey her thoughts and views to the public at large. In stunning contrast to the glamorous way Nancy Reagan presented herself, she started to make cracks about her hair, her weight, and her pearls. When Prince Charles arrived for dinner at the vice presidential mansion, Bar quipped that it was "like sitting next to one of my four sons, only he's better dressed and more polite." She was frank and open, speaking her mind when she considered it necessary. All of this had the effect of putting Bar in the limelight for the first time in their marriage.

George and Bar always had a competitive element in their relationship. It was part of the Bush family essence—competition without really appearing to compete. When it came to family gatherings, Elsie Walker Kilbourne remembers George and Bar bantering back and forth, "trying to one-up each other." Now the same thing was happening on the public stage. White House spokesman Marlin Fitzwater noted the transformation of Barbara Bush. Always fiercely loyal and supportive in private, Bar was now getting public attention and enjoying it.

"It was fascinating really," he told us. "They both enjoyed the attention and quite literally they were competing with each other for the public eye."

During a trip to Pintlala, Alabama, to fish on a friend's fifty-five-acre lake, they went out in a boat to spend the morning catching bass. When they returned, it was Bar who had landed the biggest catch—a six-pound-twelve-ounce bigmouth bass. Friends and photographers had gathered at the shore, and Bar, with a devilish grin, leaned over to her husband and said sweetly, "George, darling, would you like to have your photograph taken with *my* fish?"

Soon she was holding court on Air Force Two, chatting it up with reporters. Then suddenly aware that her husband was coming up behind her, she'd tell the press, "I better get back to my seat. The poet laureate has returned."

Those years brought Bar front and center in the family's political ambitions. "I think earlier on she was a bit more of an outsider on political matters," says Shellie Bush Jansing. "She was always there and supportive but maybe didn't have a place at the table, or at least she didn't have much of a place. Now she not only had a place at the table, she was making the seating arrangements. George saw what an asset she was."

She also became the one in the family with the keenest instincts. Gerry Bemiss recalled that when it came to George's presidential ambitions, family and friends were loath to make suggestions that Barbara didn't agree with. "She could be controlling in that way," he said, "not accepting any differing view from her own."

#### CHAPTER 27

# ULTIMATUM

A S THE 1984 ELECTION ROLLED AROUND, GEORGE'S OLD MENTOR Richard Nixon was quietly making waves. Nixon had always been big on George—smart, talented, and likable. But he had come to believe in the wake of Watergate that George wasn't tough enough, was unwilling to engage in the sort of political combat that Nixon considered essential in dealing with opponents. He quietly suggested to friends that Reagan put George on notice that he might be replaced on the ticket. Only when George was cornered and threatened, Nixon said, was he energized and tough.

Reagan failed to take his advice, and the Bushes were revved up for the campaign. The 1984 convention in Dallas was a coronation, and the whole family was there to enjoy it. George stayed on message during his convention speech and pledged his commitment to four more years of the Reagan agenda. As he stood with Reagan on the podium to accept the nomination, George whispered in Reagan's ear and pointed up to his sons, who were sitting in a luxury box in the back. "Hello, Bush kids," Reagan said into the microphone.

Afterward, Jeb went on national television and suggested that Mr. Zacarro, the husband of Democratic vice presidential candidate Geraldine Ferraro, debate his mother on national television. No chance he would win that one, family members agreed. Then all the Bush boys went to Dallas Cowboys quarterback Roger Staubach's house to play basketball. Staubach had a court in his backyard, including glass backboards, that was the envy of all the boys. Fellow Cowboy Cliff Harris was there along with two former college basketball players. As they stood around shooting baskets, one of the Bush boys proposed a friendly game. As it always seemed to be in these situations, it was the Bushes against everyone else. And while the boys lost the game, they fought together valiantly.

---

BEING ON THE TICKET WITH REAGAN SEEMED TO BE A SLAM DUNK FOR George's political career. Whoever was on the ticket in 1984 was the presumed front-runner for 1988. Still, he faced complications. The charge that he was soft, that his good manners and kindness made him a wimp, became tricky to handle as he went into the general election against Mondale-Ferraro. George wanted to show his toughness and stay loyal to Reagan. But how could he do that without sounding patronizing to Ferraro?

It was the same problem his father had faced when he ran for the nomination in 1952 against Vivian Kellems. George was fearful that if he made a misstep, the media would be out to get him. The seeds planted in the 1950 Senate race—that the media could not be trusted—had grown into a mighty oak. As George wrote to his sister Nancy during the 1984 campaign, "We are up against many in the press who hate to see the demise of Ferraro and the defeat of [Mondale]."

George kept quiet at first, sticking to his scripted talking points about the growing economy and the revival of America. But Ferraro and her campaign advisers soon started picking at those old scabs—money, class, elitism—that so irritated the Bushes. The same things had been said about Pres, George, and George W. in every campaign over the past thirty years. Issues became less important than the mystery surrounding the family, their money, and their connections to the inner circles of power. The irony was that, in this instance, the Ferraros were worth more than the Bushes. George and Bar had scrambled to buy Walker Point in Kennebunkport from Uncle Herby's widow, and they couldn't afford to keep two houses. So they lived in the vice presidential mansion and rented an apartment in Houston.

George, who never particularly cared for these kinds of tussles, tried to ignore the taunts. Characteristically, it was Bar who was the first to lose her cool. In early October, as Air Force Two flew to New York for the Columbus Day parade, Bar casually walked to the back of the plane to chat with reporters, as she was growing accustomed to. A few of them mentioned Ferraro's charges, particularly that the Bushes were out of touch with everyday Americans. Bar responded by noting that Ferraro and her husband, developer John Zacarro, were actually worth several million more than the Bushes. As the reporters elaborated further, Bar finally let loose: Gerry Ferraro was a "four million dollar—I can't say it but it rhymes with rich."

Bar knew instantly that she had made a mistake, but the damage was done. Later she apologized, and then tried to minimize the damage by saying that she really didn't think Gerry was a "witch."

"Witch is not exactly the word she was thinking of," Shellie Bush Jansing told us. "Barbara was just angry, angry, angry about what was being said about the family. That's what you get from Barbara, complete candor. And she's ready to go to war for the family if she needs to." Political disputes were fine and good, but for the Bushes, attacks on the family were verboten.

When the vice presidential debate began, George struggled to stay on script, sounding firm and tough. He managed to come out of the debate with a solid victory and was relieved when it was finally over. The next day he visited with some longshoremen in New Jersey, who congratulated him on the debate. One worker followed him with a sign that read GEORGE, YOU KICKED A LITTLE ASS LAST NIGHT. As he was getting into his limousine to leave, he leaned forward and said, "Yeah, I think I kicked a little ass last night." A TV boom mike picked up the comment.

Of all the Bush boys, it was Jeb who worked the hardest on the 1984 campaign. He set out on one of the most intensive recruiting campaigns in local history, and by June he was showing up at the Dade County Elections Department with stacks of voter registration cards from Democrats who were switching to the GOP, some four thousand in all. He also helped raise money for the campaign. In contrast, W. was conspicuous by his absence. While he did make a few phone calls and attended some functions in Texas, he did little work on the campaign.

Reagan and Bush won convincingly that fall. For the inauguration the whole Bush-Walker clan came to Washington. Bar ordered a $6,000 white wool coat with jeweled buttons and a $10,000 white mink blouson jacket for the events. It was the sort of extravagance that Bar had never enjoyed before. The family held its own private inaugural party one night before the main event. Merv Griffin handled emcee duties.

The morning of the swearing-in ceremony, family members went to St. John's Church with their children and left a passel of grandchildren back at the vice presidential mansion. It all went smoothly except when Jeb's daughter Noelle locked herself in the bathroom. She didn't want to go to her grandfather's swearing-in ceremony; she wanted to watch the movie *Annie* on the VCR. Members of the staff had to take the door off its hinges.

The family would remain at the center of national power. But for George there was uneasiness. On the brink of becoming president himself, he was torn between his sense of loyalty to Reagan and his desire to be his own man. "He was going to be loyal to Reagan come hell or high water," recalled his close friend Harry Catto. "He would never talk to anybody or discuss or criticize anything about Reagan. But he did express frustration at being vice president."

Days after the inaugural, George went to his friend Lud Ashley's house in northwest Washington for a quiet Skull and Bones reunion. Ashley noticed that despite the recent win, George was tense. After some drinks and casual chatter, Thomas Wilder Mosely suggested, "Let's repair to the inner sanctum."

For the Bonesmen, this was an orb of complete secrecy. Entering the inner sanctum was an invitation to unload your burdens, and George was eager to do it. As the men slowly went around the room sharing their secrets, George seemed particularly burdened by what was going on in his life. He was shocked at "the tone and substance of the attacks on him" by the press, Lud Ashley reported. He was being called a lap dog, a yes man, someone lacking his own identity. George couldn't respond to these attacks without drawing attention to himself and in effect undermining Reagan. He felt trapped by his office, unable to be his own man. He respected Reagan but didn't agree with him on everything. His iron grip of loyalty was clashing with his own political ambitions. These problems would not be easily solved.

———

In April 1985, Ronald Reagan offered George the use of Camp David to hold a private meeting about the coming presidential campaign. George's brothers Pres, Jr., Bucky, and Johnny were all there, as were his sons. Also attending was a small group of fund-raising consultants, media advisers, and campaign consultants who wanted to jump on board the Bush-for-president bandwagon.

One of these was Marlin Fitzwater, the presidential press spokesman, who recalls being struck by the way the meeting was organized.

"We sat at a long table," Fitzwater recalls. "Bush family members on one side of the table, all lined up in a row, and the rest of us on the other side of the table. They were firing off questions about everything: how we would run the campaign, our loyalty to George Bush, just everything. It struck me then and there that the Bushes were very different from the Kennedys in that they would never have their Ted Sorensen. No one outside the family would enter the inner circle."

That reality was underlined by the conversation George had with his eldest son. George W. was tougher than the other boys, and George had came to rely on his eldest son for strength. "George would call young George for advice," recalls Shellie Bush Jansing. "He always appreciated George because he knows George's strength. He has a steel ramrod in his back. He would call him when he had to make a tough decision. It's interesting because Reagan made George do some hatchet jobs that George didn't want to do. He didn't like to do them, so he used to call young George for bolstering up. They've always had that kind of relationship."

George wanted W. to be his enforcer on the campaign. He wanted him to be on-site at campaign headquarters, shadowing the major campaign leaders, participating in the key meetings, briefing him on the dynamics at work in the campaign office.

"What would my title be?" W. asked his father.

"You don't need a title," he responded. "Everyone will know who you are."

With his oil career on hiatus and the energy business in the toilet, W. had the time to devote to the job. Even more important, he had the sort of temperament that would allow him to do the work that his father didn't have the stomach to do.

"In the family we all know the temperament," cousin John Ellis told us. "George Herbert Walker Bush when confronting an enemy is strictly forgive and forget. Bar is never forgive and never forget. W. is forgive but never forget."

But while Laura Bush supported her father-in-law's political ambitions, she was nervous about her husband's diving into the campaign. She knew that he was doing it as both an act of devotion and because he was feeling the political bug. But things were unsettled financially. "For them there was no money," explained John Ellis. "Most of the wealth of the Walker-Bush clan was spread out. The larger concern for Laura was, 'How are we going to pay for all of this—retirement, the girls' schooling, weddings—given what happened in Texas oil? Now we're forty and we're still not financially secure on our own.' " But despite her conerns, Laura agreed that it was best for W. to work for his father's campaign.

Of particular concern to the family was political consultant Lee Atwater, whom they were considering for campaign manager. Atwater came highly recommended by Karl Rove, who had worked for George in the 1970s. He was sharp, aggressive, and blunt in his approach to politics, and was highly successful in helping candidates get elected in the South.

Still, there was plenty to separate him from the candidate. George was the child of privilege who had fought in World War II, joined the United Negro College Fund at a young age, and seemed most comfortable chatting with liberal Republicans from the Rust Belt. Atwater was a baby boomer from the South who relished the politics of the region, including explosive issues about race. He had worked for South Carolina senator Strom Thurmond and loved it.

W. had Atwater's aggressive personality and considered himself a son of Texas. His only hang-up about Atwater was the loyalty question. Atwater was a partner in the top political consulting firm in town—Black, Manafort, and Stone—and two of his partners were working for Bush competitors, Congressman Jack Kemp and Sen. Bob Dole. For Atwater, politics was both a passion and a business. The family was concerned about how committed he was to their man and the campaign.

As the family met that April weekend at Camp David, W. was blunt with Atwater.

"If there's a hand grenade rolling around George Bush, we want you diving on it first."

Atwater looked around at the assembled family members.

"Are you guys really worried about my loyalty?"

They nodded.

Atwater looked over at W. "If you're so worried about my loyalties, then why don't one of you come in the office and watch me, and the first time I'm disloyal, see to it that I get run off?"

It seemed like a reasonable suggestion and W. took the challenge. He would become Atwater's shadow.

In some ways for W., it was an opportune time. Jeb, who had quit his job for the 1980 campaign, was really building something in Florida. The real estate business was flourishing and he was becoming a player in the Florida GOP. For W. the collapse of world oil markets had brought about the buyout of Spectrum 7 by Harken Energy, an energy investment business run by New York investor Alan Quasha. W. joined a board that included investor George Soros. He also met Saudi sheikh Abdullah Bakhsh, a real estate investor. It was his first entry into the complex world of Middle Eastern oil politics, a world that his father had first been acquainted with back in the 1950s.

Harken was assuming the company's debt, taking over its operations, and planning to access the untapped oil reserves that it had not exploited. In the fall of 1985, W. stayed in Midland and tried to find jobs for all of his employees. Then he began commuting to Dallas, where Harken was headquartered, but he had few hands-on responsibilities.

The Harken deal would pay off handsomely. Harken was given the exclusive right to drill oil in Bahrain shortly after George W. joined the board. In 1990, W. would sell his stake in Harken, taking a $835,000 profit. He sold it two months before Harken announced big losses and the stock plunged. The timing of the sale set off a Securities and Exchange Commission (SEC) investigation, but no action was taken. Later in the year, the price was double what George W. sold it for.

"George was very useful to Harken," Stuart Watson, a former Harken director, recalled. "He could have been more so if he had had funds, but as far as contacts were concerned, he was terrific . . . it seemed like George, he knew everybody in the U.S. who was worth knowing."

W. did consulting work for Harken and flew to Washington regularly to meet with Atwater. But 1986 proved a difficult year. While his father had entrusted W. with his fate at campaign headquarters, W. continued with those fits of drinking that were so embarrassing to the family. In April, W. spotted Al Hunt, the Washington bureau chief for the *Wall Street Journal*, lunching at a Mexican restaurant in Dallas. Hunt was sitting with his wife Judy Woodruff and their four-year-old son. The *Washingtonian* magazine had just published the predictions of several pundits about the 1988 presidential election, and Hunt was predicting that Jack Kemp and Indiana senator Richard Lugar would be on the GOP ticket. In short, he was betting against George Bush.

W. had been drinking, and when he spotted Hunt, he stormed over to his table. "You no good f—— sonofabitch, I will never f—— forget what you wrote!"

At first Hunt didn't recognize him. Who was this raving lunatic? Only after the verbal attacks continued did he recognize who it was. He smelled the alcohol on W.'s breath and casually brushed aside what he said.

The incident was the latest in what had been a long chain, and the family was growing weary of it. W. had his four Bs—beer, bourbon, and B&B. It had been funny enough when he was in college, but now he was becoming an embarrassment, and the family let him know that things needed to change.

"There was a strong feeling that he had become an embarrassment to the family, there had simply been too many incidents," cousin John Ellis related. "I think several people, including George and Barbara, were just fed up."

Laura was also tired of it all, her titanic patience sinking fast. The roguish charm that she had been so attracted to had become something less appealing: obnoxiousness soaked in liquor. She had twin daughters, Jenna and Barbara, who were four years old, and they were starting to understand what their father was doing. W. and Laura were also not as close and intimate as before. They were spending less time together.

"He needed to have that braggadocio toned down," says Shellie Bush Jansing. "George had a lot of bravado. He used to get a lot of criticism for it. A lot of that had to do with the drinking. And Laura simply wanted it to stop."

Finally Laura delivered an ultimatum. The two were attending a Methodist church at the time, and Laura handed him a flyer about an alcohol abuse program. Contrary to published reports in which she is quoted as having said, "Pick Jim Beam or me," the appeal was more subtle, and it pointedly included mention of his daughters.

"Laura basically went to him and told him he had to make a choice," Doug Wead, a longtime friend, said. " 'You've got these two beautiful girls and you've got me. You don't want to lose us over a bottle do you?' "

While he wouldn't say it directly, family members also had the clear sense that W. was not where he wanted to be. He had mastered the art of minimizing expectations early in life so he could avoid direct comparison with his father. But now the minimizing became a self-fulfilling cycle as the drinking impeded his success. Elsie Walker Kilbourne saw the drinking as W.'s form of "self-medication," a way to deal with the stresses of his name and the expectations that went with it. "His father quite literally said and believed, 'We'll support you in whatever you want to do,' " says Elsie Walker Kilbourne, but deep down W. really didn't believe it. "He masked his disappointments by drinking."

That summer W. and Laura were in Colorado Springs with friends, celebrating his birthday. It was a landmark year for W. as he was forty, a time when men chart their life's progress in midcourse. Jebbie, his younger brother by eight years, had now surpassed him. He was building a solid real estate business in south Florida and was a player in the GOP. By any measure, little Jebbie, whom W. had enjoyed teasing as a kid, was now casting a larger shadow than W. was. Meanwhile, in Tennessee, a young politician named Al Gore was already making plans for his first run at the White House.

That night at the Broadmoor, W. and Laura were joined by their old Midland friends the Evanses and the O'Neills. Brother Neil was also there. They drank sixty-dollar bottles of Silver Oak cabernet and enjoyed themselves thoroughly.

The next morning W. woke up and saw the imprint that mask was leaving on his life. And he didn't like what he saw.

W. had always been a conventional Christian: christened as a small boy, attending Sunday school in Midland, sitting patiently through the Sunday sermon. But over the previous year his faith had been changing, becoming more than an act of routine obedience. His faith was alive.

A year earlier he had begun a series of conversations with Billy Graham, a family friend since Prescott's days in the Senate. Graham was definitely not one of those "temple builders" his father had been so leery of. At the Bush home there was a deep reverence and respect for Graham, not only because of what they believed to be his sincerity but because of his profound sense of humility. Graham talked to all the Bushes about faith, son Franklin Graham recalled. But he connected with W. because the young man was so candid and transparent with him.

The conversations between W. and Graham had begun in the summer of 1985 at Kennebunkport. After Graham gave a sermon at a church near the family's home, George asked him back to Walker Point. With the family gathered around, George asked Graham if he would answer some questions about faith.

Graham sat down by the fireplace and the family crowded around and began probing. The questions were basic and direct, about faith, belief, and the nature of God. For some it was an interesting intellectual exchange. But for W., it seemed to touch something deeper.

The next morning George W. joined Graham for a walk along the rocky shore. They went by the Boony Wild Pool, the spot where W. used to skinny-dip as a kid, and passed the pool of water where his father had first felt the icy waters of the Atlantic more than sixty years earlier. They discussed things as a grandson might with his grandfather. If Pres Bush had evoked fear and awe in young W., Graham seemed accessible and assuring. Finally Graham asked him directly, "Are you right with God?"

W. shook his head. "No, but I'd like to be."

Over the next year, W. and Graham spoke at regular intervals. They chatted at family get-togethers when Graham would drop by for a visit and they talked on the phone. The conversations intensified as W. struggled with both his drinking and his professional career. The hard-drinking, swearing first son forged a personal friendship with the preacher. When the prospects of a big oil strike faded, W. found himself searching for another sort of liberation. In their conversations, says George W. Bush, Graham "planted a seed in my heart."

For his part, Graham was not completely aware of the process. "Daddy had a number of conversations with George W.," Franklin Graham related. "I don't think he was certain which one made a difference."

If before he had been serious about games and casual about life, now W. was beginning to think about deeper matters. If before he looked into the mirror and saw the son of a superstar who couldn't measure up, now the reflection was of someone more comfortable with himself. He was now able to accept himself because of Graham's teaching that he was created by God for a reason.

Faith in the form of a personal relationship with the Creator, Graham's message, was transforming him. What had been a psychological dependence on alcohol quickly faded. Drinking, which had been a key pillar of his social life for twenty years, was now something he was willing to give up completely.

"It was not an overnight transformation," recalls his sister, Doro, "but when . . . he found happiness in his life and himself—we knew it right away. You could see a new confidence. He's always had the bravado, but [this was] real confidence."

Those who worked with him on George's presidential campaign saw several forces converging in his life at the same time. Doug Wead was a family friend and an ordained Assemblies of God pastor who worked directly for George W. in the campaign. "I was ignorant of what G. W. had been through when I first met him," he told us. "And I think his experience with evangelicals had not been so good. He had had the evangelical card played against him in the 1978 congressional race. But now he saw faith in God as the salvation of his marriage, a chance to keep his daughters. This was the solution to everything."

As the campaign began to gather steam, increasing attention was being paid to the question of evangelical voters. They made up a large voting bloc, and George W. took an interest not only in how they voted but in what they believed. Wead presented him with Gallup surveys showing how high the numbers were for born-again Christians. "These numbers can't be right," George W. told him. "They're too high. How do they define born-again Christian?"

"Personal faith in Christ, Bible as the word of God, accepting Christ as savior being a turning point in their life," responded Wead.

George W. chuckled. "Well, then by that definition I'm born again."

Some would question whether George W. simply adopted the pose of evangelical Christian because it was politically expedient. Later, when he ran for president himself, some would question the sincerity of his faith. "I'm always amazed when I read that George Bush is moving this way or that way for the religious right," says cousin John Ellis. "George W. Bush *is* the religious right."

George and Bar welcomed his newfound faith, but it was also a stretching experience. Some of that same brashness in his personality came out when he talked about faith. And unlike his parents, who were quiet when they talked about it, George W. was wide open. In part this was because his father "came of age in a different period of time than I did," W. explained. "He was not quite as forthright in being able to describe his faith in personal terms." But it also reflected a different sort of religious teaching, one that still divides the family.

W.'s understanding of "faith alone" contrasted a bit with his father's faith in the old-line Episcopalian view that he had been raised with. At one point Vice President Bush invited over some evangelical leaders to learn more about them and their beliefs. The evening went well, but he did get into a disagreement with Pastor Charles Stanley on the question of "faith versus works."

To better understand evangelicals, the vice president sat down and read C. S. Lewis's *Mere Christianity*. "I expected the apologetics to be the powerful thing," recalls Wead. But when he saw the book at Bush's bedside in Kennebunkport, it was dog-eared on the section about marriage.

As W. began speaking more openly about his faith, it sparked disagreements within the family. When he discussed the subject of salvation with his mother, they found themselves in disagreement about the path to eternal life. Bar took issue with the exclusive aims of evangelism, the claim of Christ as the one path to salvation. Mother and son argued the matter until Bar finally picked up the telephone.

"Get me Billy Graham," she told the secretary.

She waited a few minutes until the evangelist was on the phone. Graham agreed with W. but cautioned them both, "No one should try to play God."

One member of the family who increasingly shared W.'s evangelical fervor was his grandmother Dorothy Walker Bush. As her own church became increasingly liberal, Dottie found comfort by retreating to the works of evangelical writers such as John Stott and Francis Schaffer.

The change in W. took time, but old friends began to notice. Don Evans, his friend from Midland, invited W. to join a men's Bible study group at the First Presbyterian Church. Showing up was a sign of commitment in football-crazy Midland: It was held the same time as *Monday Night Football*.

The group studied the men of the faith, starting with the apostles. But they talked as much about themselves and their own struggles. At first, W. was nervous and characteristically used humor as a form of protection.

The teacher would ask, "What is a prophet?"

"That is when revenues exceed expenditures," W. would crack. "No one's seen that out here for years."

When one participant revealed the pressures he felt growing up as a "PK—preacher's kid," George W. chuckled. "You think that's tough? Try being a VPK."

But for W., these Bible studies were times of intimacy with other men that he had not really experienced before. What his grandfather had found at Brown Brothers and the Alibi Club and his father in Skull and Bones, W. found in a less formal and less regal setting.

As the presidential campaign began to heat up, W. and Laura moved to Washington, taking up residence in a Massachusetts Avenue apartment about a mile from the vice presidential mansion. W. took a permanent office next to Lee Atwater and Bob Mosbacher at campaign headquarters.

Mosbacher, George's old friend from Houston, was handling fund-raising, and he was getting plenty of help from the lifelong friends the family had collected over the years. Henry Kravis, partner in the LBO power firm Kohlberg Kravis Roberts (KKR), had made billions taking over firms with junk bonds and turning them around for resale at enormous profit.

George knew the Kravis family from way back. His father, Pres, had known Henry's father, Ray Kravis of Tulsa, and George had gone to see him in the late 1940s when he got into the oil business. He retained the friendship for more than forty years and maintained it with Ray's son Henry, who was at the time dominating the investment world. Kravis held a lavish fundraiser at the Vista Hotel in Lower Manhattan and invited his blue-chip friends and associates. He also joined George's Team 100 of the largest soft-money contributors.

Also playing an important role was Nick Brady. He, too, had known Pres Bush when he was with Dillon Reed Brady, the Wall Street investment banking firm. Brady would later go on to be George's treasury secretary.

It was a calculated decision to give W. responsibility for keeping in touch and working with these longtime family friends. It was a way for relationships to be extended to yet another generation of the family. But while his father had huddled with Brady at social clubs, W. chatted with him from his campaign office while sitting in a jogging suit with a dip of Red Man chewing tobacco in his lip. When needed, he would casually spit the chew into a nearby trash can.

Those who worked with both father and son saw immediately how different the two were. "George W. was absolutely fearless," recalls Doug Wead, who worked for W. during the campaign and served as a special assistant to President George H. W. Bush. "He had no interest in politics himself. Certainly he was not thinking about national politics. He didn't give a rip about publicity or attention. He wanted to help his dad get elected and then get out of town. He was very decisive, very energetic. The father never let you know what he was thinking. You had to present your case in points from one to ten. You didn't know if he agreed with number three or number ten. You had no idea; you had to present your whole case. The kid would say, yeah, yeah, one–three is okay, go ahead. And he gave you feedback."

Chairman Rich Bond remembers W. as almost consciously trying to be different from his father. "You might say it was almost exaggerated," Bond told us. "I don't know why because the father and son were very close. But George W. seemed to want to be defined differently from the beginning."

George seemed to carry himself with a complete lack of pretense that surprised many people. When W. and Doug Wead took a campaign trip through Chicago, Wead contacted United Airlines in advance.

"Hey, meet us at O'Hare," Wead told their service people. "I've got the vice president's son. We're flying through."

After the two landed, United Airlines sent a service agent to meet them at the gate.

"Mr. Bush!" he exclaimed, handing W. a little carnation before taking them to a private lounge and upgrading their tickets to first class.

As they sat in the lounge, Wead commented on the great service. W. grimaced.

"Wead, what's this?"

"You know, they do this for congressmen's kids and senators' kids, and you're the son of a vice president," he explained. "They do it so celebrities won't be bothered, and it doesn't cost anything. They've got empty seats, they upgrade you."

W. leaned forward.

"Wead, I want you to understand something right now. I am not a big shot, and I got news for you, pal, you are not a big shot, either."

W. could also be blunt and brusque. At campaign headquarters, two young campaign aides started flirting with W. He thought it was innocent enough at first and ignored it. But soon it became clear they were thinking about something more.

W. let them know in direct, blunt, and wide-open words that he "had absolutely no interest in them at all."

Indeed, his words were so biting that Doug Wead recalls sitting in W.'s office when an upset senior campaign worker came in. "G. W., you really made her feel bad, you really hurt her."

"Good," he snapped. "I'm married. No interest. Case closed. Good, I hope she feels bad. Glad she got the message."

———

W.'s MAIN ROLE AT CAMPAIGN HEADQUARTERS WAS TO SERVE AS THE FAMILY'S eyes and ears. But he relayed what he saw and conveyed messages to campaign aides not so much from his father as from Bar. If George was hardworking and largely affable when in campaign mode, it was Bar who was the enforcer, protecting her family and her husband's interests.

"There were times when people did some things that I think upset my mother," W. later recalled to a reporter. "Leaks, and staff siphoning off credit for ideas originating with the candidate especially infuriated her. I would then go talk to that person and inform them they needed to amend their ways—and explain to them that if they weren't careful, the wrath of the Silver Fox would fall upon them."

In December 1986 an article about Lee Atwater appeared in *Esquire* magazine. Bar wasn't so much irritated by what Atwater had said, but by the rather garish impression he made. The writer reported interviewing Atwater in his underwear, in the bathroom. It was roguish behavior that Bar believed reflected poorly on her husband. She spoke with W. about it and told him to pass along to Atwater her feelings about the matter.

"You're representing a great man," W. told Atwater. He advised him to issue a public apology, and fast. The campaign manager did, and interestingly enough apologized not to the vice president but to Bar. The episode was quickly forgotten, but Atwater was learning that it was Barbara Bush who was the heart and soul of the family.

Despite a few such clashes, W. and Atwater became fast friends. The two families would gather at the Atwater house and the men would order pizza and talk about the campaign.

"They both had these frantic minds," Sally Atwater recalled. "They were moving really fast and one almost always seemed to know what the other was thinking and would sometimes finish their sentences for them. They just fed off of each other."

---

W. DEVELOPED AS A QUICK-ACTION MAN, BECOMING LESS DELIBERATIVE AND more decisive than his father. "He made decisions that just took your breath away," recalls Doug Wead, "just bam bam bam bam, yes yes yes, no no yes no. Decisions that had been lying around, collecting dust for a long time that he could instantly get to the bottom line and decide."

Wead noticed that George W. wrestled with strategic, big-picture decisions. But once he made a commitment to a strategy, the tactical decisions were made quickly.

Bob Mosbacher noticed the same thing. "You could really see that George W. was a product of West Texas," he told us. "His edges had not been sanded down. His father, in contrast, had been raised in Connecticut and had been in politics for more than twenty years, through difficult periods like Watergate. It was more difficult for him to make those sorts of decisions."

W. was also fueled by the enormity of what was at stake in 1988. His father's political future was being decided, but his own future was being determined as well. "If his father lost, he would be the forgotten son of a vice president," said John Ellis. "If his father won, a whole world would open up. His fate would rise and fall with his father's."

---

LEE ATWATER WANTED TO TURN THE RACE FROM A CAMPAIGN ABOUT ISSUES into a campaign about values. It reflected the instincts of Reagan Democrats, who had gravitated to the GOP out of concern about declining moral values and an interest in social issues. George shared an interest in those areas as well, but he didn't seem to fit the part.

George had been a member of the moderate wing of the GOP and now found himself in the middle of the Reagan era. While he had been supportive of the president and even changed his position on some issues, he lacked identity as a conservative. He was by nature an instinctive conservative and not a movement conservative, as Buckley had so aptly put it.

A considerable portion of the GOP was now made up of religious conservatives, and George was well aware of the changing religious dynamics at work in the country. He had seen firsthand in 1980 what the evangelical churches were like and considered Billy Graham a good friend. But with his Episcopalian roots, George was decidedly out of place, even with his son's recent embrace of evangelism. His faith was private, not demonstrative. Worship for him was a somber experience in contrast to the emotionalism of the evangelicals. But to capture the GOP nomination, he would need to reach out to their votes.

In November 1985, on the advice of aides, he held a private meeting with evangelist Jim Bakker, head of Praise the Lord Ministries. Bakker certainly would have fit the definition of the temple-builders Bush had derided in 1981. But George put that aside and discussed the state of the country, his faith, and issues like school prayer with the evangelist. The two seemed to hit it off despite their differences.

More awkward was Bar's meeting two weeks later with Tammy Faye, whom she invited to join her at the vice presidential mansion and naval observatory. They had tea and struggled to find common ground.

"Can't you just see it?" says Nancy Bush Ellis. "Bar with her pearls and Tammy Faye with her overstated makeup. Two women could not have had less in common than those two."

But George's interest in evangelicals was more than a political gesture. He was genuinely interested in their expressions of faith, the demonstrative way in which they talked about God, and the personal relationship with Jesus that they placed such an importance on. His interest was no doubt sparked by his children's interest in spiritual matters.

———

THE MOVE FROM TEXAS TO WASHINGTON FOR THE 1988 CAMPAIGN WAS A DIF-ficult transition for Laura. She was leaving a new house in Texas and a passel of friends, many she had known most of her life, for a home in the nation's capital, where she knew few people. Also, her husband was going to be working long hours. The apartment on Massachusetts Avenue was nothing like their house in Texas, and the twins, Jenna and Barbara, had too little room to run around.

But Bar was nearby and took Laura under her wing. They had spent time together before, but this time Bar seemed instinctively to know that Laura was feeling very much alone.

"I think there was a kind of mentoring process going on," recalls Shellie Bush Jansing. "It wasn't planned that way, but Barbara was always looking for ways to share what she had learned. How to deal with people, what to watch out for, how to protect your kids, how to support your husband even if you question what he is doing. Bar believed in being a strong woman, and believed a good wife was by definition a strong woman."

With W. no longer drinking, his relationship with Laura seemed rejuvenated. The two spent more time together and became intimate once again. Family and friends noted the newfound synergy between W. and Laura and a level of supreme trust returning to their marriage.

"You could see that they were very much in love," recalls Sally Atwater. "And I began to notice that George was relying on Laura more and more. He was confident in so many ways, but uncertain at times. Laura steadied him when he was uncertain."

But in his relationship with his father, W. still seemed tentative. W. idolized his father, and that sense of awe remained. When a particularly important campaign decision needed to be made, W. would travel to a meeting with his father, full of ideas about what should be done. "But he was afraid a lot of times to bring [them] up," recalls Doug Wead. "He was afraid that the ideas might be foolish and other campaign aides would say so. So he simply didn't say everything that he wanted to."

While George would praise the work of his campaign team, he said little openly in support of what his son was doing. "For Big George, there is such an emphasis on the submersion of ego," Elsie Walker Kilbourne told us. "For W., that meant that his father would not praise him openly in front of others."

One time of uncertainty was when rumors circulated yet again about his father's alleged romantic involvement with Jennifer Fitzgerald. As ever, there was no real evidence of a physical relationship. Campaign aides were nonetheless in a panic as the press corps began running with the story, with articles appearing in both *Newsweek* and *U.S. News*, and Lee Atwater receiving fifty media calls in a single day.

The rumors angered George Sr. and hurt Bar, who was both furious with the media and upset with all the attention. W. then made a dramatic decision that would alter his relationship with his father completely.

As the media tempest continued to brew, W. approached his father to discuss the matter. For the first time in his life, he questioned his old man. "You've heard the rumors," the son asked the father. "What about it?"

"They're just not true," his father told him.

W. nodded, and that was all it took. He called up *Newsweek* magazine. "The answer to the Big A question is N-O."

The exchange represented a remarkable turn in their relationship. For the first time in their lives, the son had asked his father for an answer about a critical question. It represented more than a simple exchange about a family and campaign issue. It represented George W.'s rise to an adult equal with his father. "If there was any sort of leftover competition with being named George Bush and being the eldest, it really at that point was resolved," said Laura.

With the rumors of an affair squelched and his inquiry answered, W. fumed against the media. It was for the family only the latest in a series of offenses. W. had been raised on stories about how Walter Winchell had spiked his grandfather's first run for the Senate. His father had recorded how the news media had exaggerated battlefield reports in Vietnam when he had been there in 1967. And of course the family saw the story of Watergate not so much as a story about Nixon's abuses as about the media's efforts to get Nixon. Now it was continuing, and while candidate Bush would quietly respond to repeated probing questions, W. didn't feel so constrained.

When a particularly irksome question was fired at him by a reporter, W. would snap back, "No comment, asshole." Sometimes he wouldn't even acknowledge the question, but would simply give the reporter a look-over and walk away in disgust.

#### CHAPTER 28

# GOMEZ

O N THE FIFTH OF OCTOBER, 1986, A C-123K AIR TRANSPORT plane was cruising over the Nicaraguan countryside at twenty-five hundred feet when a surface-to-air missile pierced the morning air and found its mark, striking the plane and sending it reeling to the ground. A middle-aged man from Wisconsin named Eugene Hasenfus was behind the controls and bailed out, parachuting into the remote jungle. Hasenfus managed to hide out for the night and avoid detection. But the next morning he was taken prisoner by Sandinista soldiers and marched back to Managua.

Three days later he was headline news around the world. At a news conference in the Nicaraguan capital, Hasenfus explained that he was running supplies for the Contras, working out of Ilopango Air Base in El Salvador under the supervision of a man named Max Gomez. It was the first direct confirmation that, despite restrictions by Congress on federal aid for the Contras, money was somehow getting through to them.

After the news conference, reporters were scrambling to find out: Who exactly is this Max Gomez? Days later word leaked to the *Los Angeles Times* that someone named Max Gomez had been seen meeting with George Bush several times in the Old Executive Office Building. George was in Charleston, South Carolina, on a campaign stop when suddenly a reporter asked him about Gomez.

George responded that he knew Gomez and that he considered him a patriot. He also offered his complete support for the Contras because "to see the Contras prevail is clearly in the best interests of the United States." But then he misstepped.

"*Felix* Gomez is . . ."

Felix Gomez? Who was *Felix* Gomez? Reporters began scouring Washington and quickly figured out that Max Gomez was really the old CIA hand Felix Rodriguez.

Less than a month later, another shoe dropped. Shortly after the release of David Jacobsen, an American being held hostage in Lebanon, the Lebanese magazine *Al Shiraa* published a story about how the Reagan administration had secretly sold arms to Iran to get the hostages released. The Reagan administration was quick to confirm that arms sales had indeed been made, but claimed that it was part of an effort to encourage moderates inside the Iranian government.

Some weeks later Attorney General Ed Meese went to see President Reagan with something shocking. He told Reagan that they had discovered that the Iranians had paid some $30 million for military spare parts and equipment, but the U.S. government had received only $12 million from the middleman. What had happened to the rest? Meese explained that he went to see Oliver North, the National Security Council employee who was responsible for arranging the deal. North admitted that the missing funds had in fact been diverted to the Contras.

Reagan blanched at the news and literally turned ashen-faced.

Meese next broke the news to Bill Casey, the CIA director.

"Holy s———," was his response.

GEORGE WAS AT A CAMPAIGN FUND-RAISER IN PENNSYLVANIA PREPARING FOR a speech when he was handed a note by an aide. He sat there for several minutes in utter amazement, trying to gather himself. After giving his speech, George climbed into the back of his limousine and listened to a White House news conference about what would come to be known as the Iran-Contra affair.

In the early 1980s, much of Central America was aflame in revolution. Marxist guerrillas were waging war in El Salvador and Guatemala. In Nicaragua, the Sandinistas had just taken power and were imposing a Cuban-like government while talking about spreading the revolution to other countries. The Reagan administration had decided in 1981 to provide covert assistance to anti-Sandinista rebels, the so-called Contras, and military aid to the surrounding countries.

The Bushes had deep ties in Latin America going back more than forty years. Bert Walker had done business with Mexican railroads. Senator Pres Bush had spent time there, first because Brown Brothers Harriman invested there, and later as a senator on the Armed Services Committee. At one point he had traveled to Mexico City for a talk with the CIA station chief to discuss the Soviet threat to Latin America. Pres, Jr., had worked for Pan Am in

Recife and Rio. George, while running his oil company Zapata, had drilled for oil in Latin America, both near Cuba during the time of Castro's revolution and with a partner in Mexico. Later, as CIA director, he had taken a keen interest in the region.

Back in the 1960s, Sen. Pres Bush laid the turmoil in Latin America squarely at the feet of President John F. Kennedy for his failure to do what needed to be done at the Bay of Pigs. The plan to organize and train Cuban exiles for insertion into Cuba had been pieced together by his good friend Allen Dulles. Pres thought the scheme was "a well-planned, well-thought-out enterprise which had been developed over a period of six or eight months." The trouble was that Kennedy executed the plan without the air and naval support that Dulles had called for. Bush, a member of the Senate Armed Services Committee, was furious at what he saw as Kennedy's lack of nerve. "My feeling was then, and it hasn't been changed," he said in 1966, "that if the enterprise had been conducted the way it was intended to be conducted, and planned to be conducted—if the United States forces had co-operated to the extent that they were counted on to—that it might well have succeeded." But instead it was "a fiasco. It hurt Kennedy and it was really a reflection on his judgment, in my opinion. We should have gone through with that enterprise then."

When George and his brothers visited Pres at his home in Hobe Sound, they heard again and again about the mistake at the Bay of Pigs and the threat emerging in Latin America. Exposure to Cuban-Americans living in the area only heightened the family's sense of commitment to fighting communism throughout the hemisphere.

In the early 1980s, debate was raging in Washington over whether aid to El Salvador and the Nicaraguan Contras should continue. To George and his brother Pres, Jr., it must have seemed a cruel, slow-motion replay of the Bay of Pigs fiasco. Support was being provided to allies in the region, but was restricted in its use and under constant threat of being cut off by Congress.

On his vice presidential staff, George surrounded himself with men he had come to know from his time at the CIA. Donald Gregg, his chief of staff, had been CIA station chief in Vietnam. George knew him from his DCI days and was impressed with his abilities. Even more important, perhaps, he had that hallmark quality that mattered more than just about anything: Gregg was loyal. George was also in touch with old CIA hand Ted Shakley, aka "the Blond Ghost," who had headed up the CIA's Miami office during the 1960s.

With concerns about the on-again, off-again aid flow to Latin America, private efforts were being mounted in the United States to support the government of El Salvador and the Nicaraguan insurgents. Gregg was contacted by old friends and asked if he could recommend someone to organize operations in El Salvador. He had just the man.

Felix Rodriguez was a longtime CIA veteran who at the age of nineteen had participated in the ill-fated Bay of Pigs invasion. Rodriguez performed well in the midst of that debacle and the agency had kept him on the payroll. He went on to have an illustrious career, which included helping track down rebel leader Che Guevara. Indeed, Rodriguez wore Guevara's wristwatch as a memento.

Gregg hooked Rodriguez up with the right people, and then Rodriguez was on his way to Ilopango Airfield in El Salvador, working under the alias Max Gomez. He helped plan the counterinsurgency campaign and advised Salvadoran military officers on how to fight a guerrilla army.

Gregg introduced Rodriguez to George, who took a keen interest in what he was doing. They would occasionally meet in his office at the Old Executive Office Building, where Rodriguez would entertain the vice president with tales of adventure and spycraft. They also talked about the situation on the ground. George and Rodriguez shared a common belief: They would not let Central America turn into another Bay of Pigs.

A private effort to fight the battle in Central America was mounting. And the Bush family and their extensive network of friends were at the heart of it. One of George's old friends from Andover, Robert Macauley, contacted him about a humanitarian relief organization he was establishing called Americares. Macauley was an old hand at helping those who were resisting communists. During the Vietnam War he had helped organize rescue missions to assist Vietnamese children fleeing the advancing North Vietnamese Army. In 1975 he went into personal debt to secure the evacuation of pro-American Vietnamese following the collapse of Saigon.

Now Macauley wanted to help the people of Central America, and he needed the Bush family's assistance. George was enthusiastic and offered to lend his support. Pres Bush, Jr., agreed to join the advisory committee and help raise money. Pressy also joined the board of the National Strategy Information Center, a Washington think tank headed by former CIA employee Roy Godson.

Americares began soliciting contributions from pharmaceutical companies for medical supplies that could be shipped to the region. In the first two years of operation the group provided $14 million in aid to El Salvador,

Guatemala, and Honduras. When aid to the Contras was cut off by Congress in 1982, Americares sent $20 million to the region in one year. A portion of the aid went to Miskito Indians, who were waging a guerrilla war against the Sandinistas.

In Nicaragua the organization looked for opportunities to support Sandinista opponents, providing two hundred tons of newsprint to *La Prensa*, the opposition newspaper. As one critic put it, "Americares resembles a private foreign-policy operation of the U.S. government."

Other family members quickly became involved. Marvin Bush told friends and colleagues in the financial sector about the group and accompanied one shipment of supplies to Nicaragua. He was met by Roberto Alejos Arzu, a businessman who had allowed his plantation in Guatemala to be used by the CIA for training Cuban exiles for the Bay of Pigs invasion. Neil, who was living in Colorado, also told friends about the situation in the region, and one of his investors made a five-figure donation to a private Contra funding effort.

But the most active of the Bush sons was Jeb. Miami was ground zero as far as private efforts to support the anticommunists in Latin America were concerned. The sizable Cuban-American community there was being buttressed by tens of thousands from El Salvador and Nicaragua fleeing the Marxist forces in their countries. They all wanted to support the cause, and they saw Jeb as his father's eyes and ears in Miami.

Jeb would show up at anticommunist rallies dressed in a white guayabera and, in near-perfect Cuban-accented Spanish, talk about the need to defeat Castro and the Sandinistas. He was at a rally in front of the Orange Bowl put on by the Cuban Patriotic Association. When a shipment of $2 million in humanitarian aid for refugees "displaced by communist expansion" in Central America passed through the port of Miami, Jeb would be there to inspect the cargo. When Cuban political prisoners were released and brought to Miami, Jeb was there chanting *"Libre! Libre! Libre!"* along with the exiles. He was also an adviser to the Florida chapter of the National Defense Council, a private organization committed to fighting communism in Central America whose board members included Robert Brown, editor of *Soldier of Fortune* magazine, and retired general Jack Singlaub.

Jeb would raise money for the cause, and when people wanted help in official channels, he served as a willing intermediary. In 1984 a Guatemalan pediatrician named Dr. Mario Castejon approached Jeb for help. Concerned about what he saw as a threat from Nicaragua, Castejon wanted to establish an international medical brigade to help the Contras. He drafted a three-page letter to Vice President George Bush laying out his proposal in the name of helping "Nicaraguan patriots who are fighting for freedom against Sandinismo."

To make sure the letter was read, he gave it to a close friend in Miami who passed it on to Jeb, who in turn forwarded it to his father. Jeb added a cover note and wrote "Walker" on the envelope. It was the family's secret code, which ensured that his father would receive it from the mailroom right away. The vice president read the letter with interest but was advised not to meet with Castejon because he was head of the National Conservative Party in Guatemala, and it was important that he not appear to be meddling in the country's domestic politics. But George saw that the proposal was forwarded to a staff member on the National Security Council named Col. Oliver North, who was helping in the private Contra effort. North and Castejon did meet, and the Guatemalan doctor offered to create a Guatemalan-based supply line to the Contras.

BEFORE THE NEWS BROKE ABOUT IRAN-CONTRA, REAGAN'S APPROVAL RATING had stood at 70 percent. In the days after the revelations it plummeted to 46 percent. It was about as close as you could get to a meltdown in American politics; never since they had begun keeping such records in 1936 had poll numbers fallen so dramatically.

Over at campaign headquarters, Lee Atwater was worried. "Whatever lingering illusions we may have had about the invincibility of the Reagan mantle or the permanence of a broad-based GOP realignment must be put on the shelf," he wrote weeks later in a strategy memo to Bush. Riding the Reagan coattails until election day 1988 was no longer going to work.

The explosive revelations set off a firestorm in the Reagan administration. Secretary of State George Shultz went public: He knew nothing about the Contra diversion and had opposed secret arms sales to Iran. Privately he issued an ultimatum to Reagan, insisting that the president take certain steps or he would resign. Shultz was not alone. Recriminations and backstabbing rocked the White House, and the administration seemed to be fracturing as each agency tried to protect its own interests. George wrote with amazement in his diary as chaos loomed, "No President can have a cabinet [member] set the terms under which he will stay. It is impossible. The problem is . . . that Poindexter, Don Regan, and George [Shultz] are all out there with leaks and peddling their own line. Regan, for example, says 'I'm a team player.' Everybody at State rallies around George, and get him all upset. And, when Regan says, or uses the word 'negotiate' or allegedly makes some comment about Israel, everybody—State and NSC—gets upset with him."

George was aware that there were decision-making problems at the White House, which created a lot of confusion. "The truth of the matter is that the president makes his decisions in very oblique ways. I am not in the decision process . . . unless I am sitting in at the time the president makes a decision, then I can speak up."

But more than anything, George found himself impressed with Reagan in the midst of the maelstrom. The president "bears up beautifully" in the face of a difficult situation. "He smiles when the press fires these tough questions. That is something that I have got to learn better. I will keep trying."

Loyalty was the main issue for George. He wanted to be loyal to Reagan, but sticking with him was not going to be easy. By doing so, he was risking his own political future and the one chance he would have to fulfill his own presidential ambitions. He trusted Reagan and believed in the man's innate qualities. He was confident that Reagan's "basic integrity and honor will help him overcome his difficulties."

Nevertheless, as President Reagan's poll numbers sank, so did George's. Some people working for the campaign, particularly Lee Atwater, were concerned that George was too close to too many CIA types. Donald Gregg, his chief of staff, was a liability, Atwater told him. Meeting with Felix Rodriguez had not been a good idea. As George put it in his diary, they believed that Gregg "is hurting me very much in a political sense . . . They don't think I should have seen Felix Rodriguez. I disagree with that. There is a lot of pusillanimous worry here, but they are all trying to protect my interests."

Iran-Contra soon became the center of the political universe; everything seemed to revolve around it. At every press conference, every public appearance, the scandal was issue number one. With the release of classified material the paper trail began to emerge, and it became clear that George had been present at numerous key meetings where the sale of arms to Iran had been discussed or at least mentioned. The implication was that he had been involved in the arms transfers.

The idea of sending arms to Iran had been discussed at the National Security Council and then taken to Reagan by Bud McFarlane. When George finally heard about the initiative, Reagan was already on board. So his silence, or apparent lack of opposition to the deal, said more about his views on being a loyal vice president than about the merits of the proposal itself. But explaining that to the public would not be easy.

Only months earlier George had seemed the clear front-runner in the presidential sweepstakes, but now the ranks of potential Republican rivals for the nomination began to grow. Senator Bob Dole and Congressman Jack Kemp were joined by Al Haig, Pat Robertson, and others. And family enemies from the past reemerged.

Ever since George had turned down Ross Perot's offer to run his oil company, relations with the Texas billionaire had never been the same. Perot began looking for evidence of Bush conspiracies, hiring private investigators to scratch away at the family's veneer and reveal what he considered to be the true nature of the Bushes. He began by investigating Jeb and W., writing their father a letter in 1986 declaring that both were involved in nefarious activities. Perot gave no details, clearly hoping to pique George's interest. But the father didn't take the bait, instead writing back that he was proud of his sons and wasn't worried in the slightest about anything they were doing. Perot then paid Washington lawyer Berl Bern to research the tax deductions obtained by George's old business partner Hugh Liedtke while he was head of Pennzoil. Perot was convinced that this was a "mini–Teapot dome" scandal and that George was involved. He was also sure that one of George's other former business associates "maybe had a cocaine habit."

Perot was absolutely convinced that Americans were still being held in Southeast Asia and was clandestinely funding efforts to find proof. Many in the Reagan administration were open to being convinced, and George Bush was one of them. When Perot purported to have a videotape of Americans being held in Vietnam, he called George, who encouraged the Pentagon to look into the matter. The videotape proved to be a hoax, but Perot continued in his efforts. When George didn't share his passion, Perot became convinced that he had somehow been compromised, telling friends that George was being pressured by heroin traffickers and money launderers, some of whom, Perot claimed, where George's friends. It was a fantastic conspiracy theory that Perot wove into a spider's web of alleged deceit and deception. And Iran-Contra seemed confirmation enough for the Texas billionaire that conspirators were everywhere.

One morning in 1987 he called George and confronted him.

"Well, George, I am looking for prisoners [of war], but I spend all my time discovering the government has been moving drugs around the world and is involved in illegal arms deals . . . I can't get at the prisoners because of the corruption among our own covert people."

George responded by telling Perot that he didn't know what on earth he was talking about. Perot was furious.

"The world is full of lions and tigers and rabbits," Perot snapped. "And you're a rabbit." He promptly hung up the phone.

#### CHAPTER 29

# SILVERADO

I T WAS 1986 AND NEIL BUSH WAS RIDING HIGH. FOR THE FIRST TIME IN his life he was running in the circles that his older brothers seemed to thrive in. Neil and Sharon were attending all the lavish parties and society balls in Denver's gothic mansions, complete with Hollywood celebrities and corporate titans.

JNB Exploration, Neil's energy exploration company, might have been struggling just like all the others in the oil patch. But his entry into the highest orbit of Denver's social circuit came because of his name and his links to Silverado Savings and Loan.

Silverado was one of the biggest financial players in the area, loaning money to small homeowners but also to titans in the world of commercial real estate and development. As a board member, Neil attended monthly meetings for which he received a nice annual fee. He also received additional perks, such as a $289,000 mortgage with a $300,000 loan at a much lower rate. More important, he was moving in these circles as his own man, as a rising star in Denver. He was thinking of running for governor or senator soon, maybe even before his older brothers did.

But Neil seemed hopelessly naive about his business relationships. Family members saw him as ill-prepared to move in the business world, and he never revealed the true nature of his relationship with Silverado.

Bill Walters had sunk $150,000 into JNB and extended Neil a $2 million line of credit. Because business was bad, Neil owed him money. Kenneth Good, after his initial investment, was talking about pumping $5 million more into JNB and then merging it with his Florida-based real estate company, Gulfstream Land and Development. Neil was ecstatic about the idea but never questioned why they would want to merge JNB, which had nothing to offer, with a real estate company that had real holdings, like Gulfstream. Nor did he wonder what Good might want in return for his $100,000 contribution to the RNC for his dad's campaign. All he knew was that in his hypercompetitive family, Neil was finally becoming a name.

But Walters and Good were having problems of their own. They had made some bad land deals, speculated too much, bought too much, and paid too much for some of their properties. Both of their financial empires were teetering. They needed some help, and they needed it in the form of loans from Silverado. They expected Neil to be there for them.

Over the few years that Neil sat on the board, he voted to extend some $106 million in loans to Walters alone, all of which would go bad. Neil didn't actually act solo to do their bidding; all the loans were approved unanimously by the board. But it was a blatant conflict of interest, approving loans to people he was depending on to finance his own business interests.

In January 1986 federal regulators quietly sat down with Silverado's senior executives to discuss the thrift's financial picture. There were serious "concerns," they said. Fully two-thirds of the bank's loan portfolio was concentrated in high-risk loans backed by little collateral. The prospect of faulty loans was high. And the thrift's accounting procedures were creative, to say the least. Senior management was reporting a $12 million profit on paper in 1985, a number that had impressed Neil and other outside directors. But in reality the picture was bleak. Silverado had actually lost $10 million that year. It just wasn't reporting the bad loans on the forms that federal law required.

Every month Neil would sit with the other outside board members and approve loans. Like Neil, none of them had any background in banking. One member ran an auto dealership; another owned a real estate company in the resort town of Breckenridge. The one lawyer among them was Richard Vitkus, who worked for Beatrice Foods and knew next to nothing about banking laws and regulations. In a January 1986 memo, Silverado vice chairman Richard Vandapool wrote to S&L president Mike Wise and was stunningly frank in his assessment of the outside board. "Let's admit it. The board is a legal necessity, but you and Jim [majority shareholder W. James Metz] control the company and you control the directors. You know it and they know it. The [outside] directors simply ratify our actions and decisions. Why meet monthly? Why spend significant time and money to provide ten directors with information that the majority of them don't or won't comprehend?"

Neil's financial life became more complicated in October 1986 when Walters told him that he wanted to sell his $150,000 stake in the company and get out. It wasn't a matter of business per se; it was personal. Walters had discovered that Ken Good, Neil's other major investor, had been secretly sleeping with his wife, Mary Lou. Walters quickly filed for divorce, and Good began instructing her on how her husband might try to hide his assets.

In short, the last thing Walters wanted was to have anything to do with Ken Good.

Walters wanted his money, but JNB didn't have the cash to pay. He settled for $50,000 plus a promise to pay the other $100,000 later. Neil was never able to come up with the money.

With Walters gone, Neil became more dependent on the flamboyant Ken Good. The next month, Good's attorneys pressed Neil to get Silverado to extend a line of credit of more than $900,000 to keep one of his businesses going. Neil presumably had to deliver in order to keep JNB afloat, so he sent a letter to Mike Wise at Silverado and the deal was done.

By late 1986, Silverado had multiple big loans going sour and a credit rating so bad it couldn't even issue junk bonds on Wall Street. So the Silverado execs came up with an illegal plan to help the thrift raise cash. Those desperately needing loans would be given them, but they would be forced to invest in the company as a condition for getting their money. Real estate developers who wanted to buy land, for example, would be given a loan amount slightly higher than the property was worth, and the difference would be used to buy Silverado stock.

In December, Neil and the other board members attended a special meeting in the sky room to review thirteen deals. In each case, Silverado was offering loans to buy real estate for more money than the property was actually worth. Senior executives provided charts and graphs demonstrating that this was good business. All the loans were approved unanimously.

#### CHAPTER 30

# NEW HAMPSHIRE

I N MID-OCTOBER 1987, WITH THE IRAN-CONTRA AFFAIR SEEMINGLY sucking the lifeblood out of his campaign, George Bush made his announcement to run for president. As a high school band played "The Yellow Rose of Texas," the extended Bush clan looked on as he stepped to the podium of the Hyatt Regency Hotel in Houston. George picked his words carefully. "I am not a mystic, and I do not yearn to lead a crusade." He had no plans to go off in "radical new directions" but was offering the country "steady and experienced leadership." He promised in foreign policy to support "the freedom fighters of the world," something the family had been quietly doing for the Contras over the past half decade.

On domestic issues he announced his intentions to cut spending and not raise taxes. The Republican Party was "the party of Lincoln," so he was going to be "attentive to human needs and for racial justice." To those who said he couldn't do everything without raising more revenue: "They are wrong. I am not going to raise your taxes—period." The crowd erupted and red, white, and blue balloons dropped from the ceiling.

George hit the campaign trail with vigor, but there was the ever-present residue of the past in everything that he did. Reagan had understood the grand scale of being president, the need to convey the larger-than-life image of the man in the Oval Office. George H. W. Bush never seemed to understand it. Family members recall being with him on the campaign trail and seeing that he never quite seemed to "get it."

"I remember George Bush speaking at some place in Pennsylvania early in the fall campaign," recalls John Ellis. "And there were cheerleaders—and they were screaming—you'd think it was an Elvis concert. I remember seeing the expression on his face; he was looking around to see what they were screaming about. It didn't occur to him that they were screaming about him."

Those instructions hammered into him from childhood—no more than your fair share, avoid those *la-dee-dahs*—haunted him like specters in an election that required self-aggrandizement. George was uncomfortable talking about himself—Oh, let me talk about anything but that! His syntax was choppy as he avoided using the words "me" and "I," just like his mother had taught him as a young boy. He had also been told to avoid grandiosity. So when Margaret Warner of *Newsweek* asked him why he entered politics, he blathered: "It's hard to describe . . . I got intrigued with it, I felt fascinated, believe in the country, in its strength, in helping people. You know, all the reasons people go into politics. Challenges and rewards."

George seemed uncertain about his journey, convinced that talking about solid leadership based on principles was more important than the issues or talking about himself. If in 1980 he had campaigned on the theme "A President You Won't Have to Train," this time the slogan was "Ready on Day One to Be a Great President."

But president to do what? You could hear in his words that he was going through the motions. His priorities were "education, or *whatever*, and jobs, *whatever*." When talk turned to beliefs or abstract ideas, he retreated to the word "thing." Liberals were guided by the "post-Vietnam thing." He also mentioned the "limited government thing" and the "civil rights thing." And then of course there was "the vision thing." George's thinking did not naturally attach itself to ideas, but to people and certain principles such as loyalty and honesty. In 1985 someone had approached him and said, "How can you run for the presidency? You don't have a constituency." George had responded, "You know, I have a great big family and thousands of friends." That was his ideology, what Richard Ben Cramer called his "ideology of friendship."

George was faithful to friends, but some believed he lacked such fidelity to ideas. The indictment was that he lacked courage. Shortly after he announced his candidacy, *Newsweek* ran a cover story titled "Fighting the Wimp Factor." Conservative pundit George Will followed up with a piece that declared he was a "lap dog," incapable of making difficult decisions on his own. "The optimistic statement 'George Bush is not as silly as he frequently seems' now seems comparable to Mark Twain's statement that Wagner's music is better than it sounds."

George told his friend Lud Ashley that Will was a close friend of Nancy Reagan's, and he considered her the ultimate source for the story. As for *Newsweek*, he saw the article as a particularly nasty attack on his character. But as ever, he kept most of his fire to himself and avoided the larger question being raised. Not so George W., who called a *Newsweek* editor and announced that the campaign would no longer work with the magazine on any stories. Then, thinking about the speedboat the family kept in Kenne-bunkport, he told the editor, "I'd like to take the guy who wrote that head-line out on that boat . . ."

Polls showed that these criticisms and the growing furor over Iran-Contra were hurting him. In some key states he was behind his chief rival, Sen. Robert Dole, by twelve points. Republicans who liked Reagan were splitting their vote evenly between the two candidates, so there wasn't much of a Rea-gan coattail for George. And those in the GOP who were upset with Reagan were breaking by an almost two-to-one margin for Dole.

The first test came in Iowa, where George was in clear trouble. While the American economy overall was doing quite well, the Grain Belt was strug-gling with low prices and a high number of farm bankruptcies. In mid-October 1987 the state held a straw poll. Stunningly, George came in third, behind Dole and evangelist Pat Robertson. It was a surprising rebuff in a state where George had done quite well in 1980.

As the results came in, the way George tried to explain them added to the perception that he was out of touch. "A lot of people that support me, they were off at that air show, they were at their daughters' coming-out parties, or teeing up at the golf course for that all-important last round." Someone for-got to explain that Iowans weren't big on "coming-out" parties.

The challenge posed by Pat Robertson was particularly frustrating for George. He had been reaching out to evangelicals over the past several years. He tried to talk about his faith openly, behavior that came awkwardly to him because of the reticence of his Episcopalian faith. "If by 'born again' one is asking, 'Do you accept Jesus Christ as your savior?' Then I could answer a clear-cut yes. No hesitancy. No awkwardness."

Four months later, during the Iowa caucuses, the situation did not im-prove. Dole won with 37 percent of the vote and Robertson came in second with 25 percent. George could garner only 19 percent. Neil Bush was at George's campaign headquarters when the vote was finally tallied and was furious at his father's third-place finish. He blamed Robertson, declaring that his supporters had appeared out of nowhere like "cockroaches." W. on the other hand didn't offer any excuses. "What happened in Iowa is we got whipped," he declared.

But Doug Wead recalls seeing an eldest son overcome with emotion when he retreated to his hotel room. "Tears welled up in his eyes," Wead told us. "He was devastated." The two men read the Bible together and prepared for the next battle.

Atwater's strategy all along had been to play it safe, prevent mishaps, and coast into the general election. But George was now suddenly running behind and the campaign needed to take some risks. An opportunity presented itself when Dan Rather approached the campaign about doing a candidate profile for the *CBS Evening News*. CBS producers told the campaign they were going to do profiles on each of the candidates, and George was glad to do it. But soon word leaked that this was not going to be a general profile. Media adviser Roger Ailes advised George to go ahead with the interview, but prepped him on how to respond.

George had known Dan Rather from their days in Houston. The two had met through a mutual friend in the 1960s and even played tennis together. (George wupped him, family members say.) They were not exactly friends during those Texas days, but the relationship had always been cordial.

George sat for the interview at his desk in the Dirksen Senate Office Building, and Rather began with a less-than-flattering introduction. "Many feel, rightly or wrongly, that he is hiding things people want to know." Then he began listing the dates when George had been present at meetings where the arms deal with Iran had been discussed. "The record shows he never objected." Then Rather started talking about Felix Rodriguez and Donald Gregg's activities in Central America. Surely George had to know everything about this.

George was expecting questions on Iran-Contra and quickly began rebutting the charges. The Tower Commission had declared that George was not involved in the diversion, and Rodriguez, in sworn testimony, had "totally vindicated" him. George wasn't hiding *anything*, he told Rather.

But as Rather continued to press with laserlike focus on Iran-Contra, George's irritation became apparent. "If this is a political profile for an election, I have a very different opinion as to what one should be . . . I find this to be a rehash and a little bit, if you will excuse me, of misrepresentation on the part of CBS, which said you're doing a political profile on all the candidates, and then you come up with something that has been exhaustively looked into." Rather ignored George's protestations. "Let's talk about your record . . ." He probed the arms-for-hostages deals in the Middle East and asked about efforts to raise private money for the Contras. By now George's ire was rising and, with more than a hint of irritation in his voice, he asked: "How would you like it if I judged your whole career by those seven minutes when you walked off the set in New York?"

George was referring to an incident when the U.S. Open Tennis Championships had delayed the start of the *CBS Evening News*. Rather had been caught on the phone complaining when the program went on the air. Realizing what had happened, the broadcaster stormed off the set for more than seven minutes.

There was silence for a moment as Rather felt the blow right between the eyes. He ignored the comment and continued, but the damage was done. The broadcast ended with George coming off not as a wimp, but as the man who had vanquished Dan Rather.

George took particular relish in his performance. He had been able to strike back in a way that Pres never had. "The bastard didn't lay a glove on me," he later told a friend.

The exchange boosted George's ratings, particularly among conservatives who had a dislike of the media. But the exchange also seemed to fuel hostility between George and Rather. The family believed that Rather was consciously trying to push the network to a particular dislike of the Bushes, and there is some evidence to support the claim. A study by Robert Lichter determined that by 1992, fully 87 percent of all CBS stories were critical of the George Bush administration compared with 57 percent by NBC and 39 percent by ABC. Rather in particular seemed to go out of his way to target George. When riots erupted in Detroit during his administration, Rather began the broadcast: "In this Reagan/Bush era of budget cuts, riots erupted in Detroit tonight."

"No question Dan Rather and CBS gave us more trouble than anyone," Marlin Fitzwater said. "And it was personal. They purposely did things that were deceptive, the sorts of things no one else would do."

———

AFTER THE IOWA DEBACLE, THE NEXT TEST WAS NEW HAMPSHIRE. DOLE, coming off his big win, was determined to keep his momentum. While there were policy differences between him and George, Dole clearly believed that personal qualities were the key to winning. Again, as it had been in every other election, family, background, and privilege took center stage in the election. George was the spoon-fed rich kid while Dole was the hard worker who had risen on his own merits. "I'm a little disadvantaged," he would say on the campaign trail. "I have to work for a living . . . [I've] had some hard knocks in my lifetime. Nobody gave me anything."

It was the same sort of class politics that George had first heard in 1964, and it made him madder than ever. But it bothered him even more to talk about it; he didn't want to inflate himself or pat himself on the back. You'd have to "pour gasoline on Bush and light a match to him" to get him to fight back, recalled Victor Gold, a campaign aide. George figured that if he simply ignored the critics, they would go away.

Aides circled around him and insisted that he needed to run negative ads against Dole. Roger Ailes, Bob Teeter, and Lee Atwater were all of the opinion that only by going negative could he overtake Dole. George was uncertain; he disliked negative campaigning. But Bar, who also detested it, told her husband that he had no other choice. So he approved a slate of ads that painted Dole as a straddler who changed his position on issues such as taxes regularly.

The race remained tight and polls showed that George was still a couple of points behind. On the final weekend he reached into the family's deep reservoir of friendships and called on Sen. Barry Goldwater to make an appearance on his behalf. Mr. Conservative himself, Goldwater was an old friend of George's father and had served with him on the Senate Armed Services Committee. Goldwater flew to New Hampshire in Bob Mosbacher's jet and declared, "I believe in George Bush. He's the man to continue the conservative revolution we started twenty-four years ago." It was a stunning setback for Dole, who had served with Goldwater in the Senate for close to two decades. Three days later, George won New Hampshire by nine points.

After New Hampshire there were no more close calls. Two months later, on April 26, George won Pennsylvania and the nomination was finally locked up. He was one step closer to his lifetime goal.

With the Republican National Convention still several months away, George began thinking seriously about the all-important matter of a running mate. Other presidential aspirants such as Bob Dole and Jack Kemp had to be considered, and out of a host of governors, one might make an attractive candidate.

George began mulling over the question in great secrecy. However, he did solicit advice from his family and got varying opinions. Jeb, as ever with his pulse on the national political mood, suggested California governor George Deukmejian. Deukmejian was popular and carried more electoral votes with him than anyone. Brother Bucky Bush noted the qualities of Missouri senator John Danforth, who was known for both his sincerity and his earnestness.

George also sought the advice of several advisers, who forwarded the names of just about every prominent Republican in and out of Washington. But in the midst of it all, an unexpected twist shook up the entire process. Jimmy Baker, George's longtime friend and current treasury secretary in the Reagan administration, let it be known that he wanted the job.

Rumblings were heard starting in 1982 that Baker had presidential aspirations. Now he seemed to be confirming them. These two men, who had been through so much together, now faced one of the most awkward moments of their relationship.

Their partnership was one of two perfectly matched tennis players who each knew his role. George was always the front man, playing net, and Baker excelled with his line play. So it had been in politics. Now, for the first time, their ambitions were coalescing, and some in the family were wondering whether Baker could be the subservient vice president that George had been for eight years to Reagan.

But George wanted someone new and bold, a baby boomer who would add youth to the ticket. American politics was beginning to undergo a generational change, and Baker was, like George himself, a product of the Second World War.

Also lurking in the background was the mounting Iran-Contra probe, which Independent Counsel Lawrence Walsh would carry out with great gusto. The probe, which initially looked at the activities of the National Security Council, was quickly becoming a hunt for someone more senior. Walsh firmly believed that the buck did not stop with Oliver North, and with Reagan about to leave the scene, his number two was in the crosshairs.

George had seen the role that constant investigations had played in bringing Nixon down. He considered it to be a relentless partisan attack, a form of political warfare. What emboldened Nixon's enemies was the knowledge that Gerald Ford would be a competent replacement. All of this had a strong bearing on whom George would pick for vice president.

He quickly determined that Baker was not his man. In mid-July, George went on a Wyoming fishing trip with Baker and broke the news to him. Instead, he wanted his friend to run the campaign and then serve as secretary of state. Baker took the news in stride but was clearly disappointed, and in some respects their relationship would never be the same. A few years later, as the Bush presidency faced an internal crisis during the 1992 election, their relationship would be severely tested. "If you're so smart," George would snap to his friend, "*how come you're not president?*"

#### CHAPTER 31

# TRIUMPH

As the 1988 Republican National Convention began in New Orleans, the extended Bush-Walker clan gathered on an old-fashioned Mississippi riverboat to make their grand entrance into New Orleans. They were all wondering who George had selected as VP. "No one except George and Bar knew who his running mate would be," recalls Shellie Bush Jansing. "Not any of the boys or his brothers. We were all giddy about it." It was one of the few times that George had kept such a critically important decision from his family.

Nearby, walking among the crowds on Bourbon Street, were Indiana senator Dan Quayle and his wife, Marilyn. Suddenly Quayle's beeper went off; a call from Jim Baker. He hurried back to the hotel and returned the call.

In a muted tone, Baker informed Quayle that he was the choice. Minutes later, George called him and, with W. at his side, popped the question. Would he be willing to join the ticket? Back on the steamboat, word of his choice rippled through the family. The first words on everyone's lips were, "Dan who?"

Baker had told Quayle to go dockside to the Spanish Plaza to meet the riverboat, where he would join George for the public announcement.

"I'm looking at the Spanish Plaza on TV," Quayle responded, "and there are thousands of people there. There's no way you can get us there."

"Trust me," Baker told him. "Trust me . . . We'll find you in the crowd. We'll get you in there."

The Quayles made their way to the plaza and stood in a mass of people, looking for an advance man. They waited more than twenty minutes, but no one came. Jim Baker "didn't send a soul," Marilyn Quayle recalled. Instead, the couple had to push their way through the crowd to reach the stage.

Meanwhile, Baker was quickly making his unhappiness clear, telling reporters that Quayle was Bush's selection, "but not mine." Senior Republicans remember him denigrating the choice behind closed doors at the convention.

Quayle was virtually unknown on the national stage, and as reporters delved into his background, questions began to surface within hours of the announcement. How did he get a coveted slot in the Indiana National Guard during Vietnam? How did he get into law school with such low grades as an undergrad? What about the rumored golf outing in Florida that included Playboy Playmate Paula Parkinson? Campaign aides began scrutinizing his background to see if any of the allegations were true. A good scrubdown revealed that there was apparently nothing to them. But the questions came so fast and hard that Quayle seemed shaky when answering them.

Suddenly the candidate who George had hoped would boost his credibility with younger voters seemed too youthful and very inexperienced. As George later admitted in his diary, he came to view the choice as a mistake. "It was my decision, and I blew it, but I'm not about to say that I blew it."

That opinion was shared by George W., who was stunned at his father's decision. "When [W.] talked about Senator John Danforth it was John," recalled John Ellis. But when he talked about J. Danforth Quayle, "he always called him Q or 'the queely one.' " Jeb shared that opinion, telling family members that Quayle was "way out of his depth." W. mounted a brief attempt to get him replaced on the ticket, but his father stood firm, and W. had no other option but fall into line.

The selection was puzzling. Yes, George had been impressed with Quayle the first time he met him during the 1978 congressional elections. And he seemed to be everything he needed in a running mate: young, attractive, the first baby boomer on a major party ticket, and a senator with a good reputation on Capitol Hill. But he was also an attractive choice for another reason. With all the investigating going on over Iran-Contra, Quayle was "impeachment insurance," said nephew John Ellis. Members of Congress would think twice before going after George and trying to replace him with a greenhorn like Quayle.

———

THE 1988 CONVENTION WAS AS MUCH ABOUT GEORGE'S FUTURE AS IT WAS about the family's ambitions. He was on the cusp of being elected president, but other family members had ambitions, too. Jeb, for one, had been thinking about running for office for some time. His wife, Colu, not a great lover of politics, had just received her American citizenship. George, eager to encourage his son and daughter-in-law, asked Colu to give the seconding speech for his nomination in both Spanish and English.

Thirty-one members of the Bush-Walker clan were at the convention, many of them as delegates: from Missouri, Massachusetts, Connecticut, Texas, Florida, Colorado, and New York. Each had a role to play, and they all stayed in contact. It was the embryonic beginning of a new establishment within the GOP, one that by the mid-1990s some would consider to be the only real national network in the party.

That night the state delegations slowly made their vote counts known. As the eldest son and the head of the Texas delegation, it was left to George W. to put his father over the top. Fighting back tears, he declared that Texas was giving all of its votes to his father. "For a man we respect and a man we love, for her favorite son and the best father in America . . . the man who made me proud every single day of my life and a man who will make America proud, the next President of the United States."

George then walked out to the podium to deliver the most important speech of his life. He spoke about the country, but most important he spoke about himself. "I am a man who sees life in terms of missions—missions defined and missions completed. When I was a torpedo bomber pilot they defined the mission for us . . . But I am here tonight—and I am your candidate—because the most important work of my life is to complete the mission we started in 1980."

For the next twenty minutes George offered a look inside his vision for the future. What he talked about was continuity, the American Century, a phrase first coined by his father's friend and fellow Bonesman Henry Luce. And he laid out the grand design for the world that his father and his father's friends had developed after the Second World War.

"This has been called the American Century because in it we were the dominant force for good in the world. We saved Europe, cured polio, we went to the moon, and lit the world with our culture. Now we are on the verge of a new century, and what country's name will bear it? I say it will be another American Century."

A month earlier, Democrats had gathered for their nominating convention. Michael Dukakis, governor of Massachusetts, had won a bruising primary. The family gathered to watch the convention on television and listened as speaker after speaker took shots at George. Particularly irksome was the speech by Gov. Ann Richards of Texas, who let loose with "what a real Texas accent sounds like." She went on to declare famously, "Poor George, he can't help it . . . he was born with a silver foot in his mouth." Following the speech, W. perfected a wicked Ann Richards impersonation.

Dukakis was little known on the national stage, and there were early troubling signs for George. Thanks to Iran-Contra and the view that he was "wimpy," his negative rating was now 41 percent in many national polls. In contrast, Dukakis's negatives were only 15. It was clear that in order to win they would have to raise the negatives.

George Bush had always maintained a neat division in his mind. On the one hand there was the dirtiness of politics; on the other was the honor of governing. He had never much cared for negative campaigning. In all of his races for public office, only his first in 1964 had proved to be decidedly negative. But that would have to change in 1988.

It was apparent to everyone that he was uncomfortable with the idea. You could see it on his face and hear it in his voice. When on the attack, his voice would rise in pitch as his vocal cords tightened. "Should public school teachers be required to lead our children in the Pledge of Allegiance?" asked George. "My opponent says no—and I say yes."

Dukakis was soft on crime; witness the furlough of convicted felons like Willie Horton. "Clint Eastwood's answer to crime is 'Go ahead. Make my day.' My opponent's answer is slightly different. His answer is 'Go ahead. Have a nice weekend.' "

George was transforming the campaign from a race about issues into a race about values. For Bush, who was decidedly nonideological, his candidacy was ironically becoming defined by ideology. Dukakis was "a liberal," and George kept referring to it as the "L-word" and calling his opponent a "card-carrying member of the ACLU." Dukakis, said George, was someone who believed in "Harvard boutique liberalism."

At the same time, George tried to prove that he was indeed his own man, someone who respected Reagan but would also be different. At a flag factory in New Jersey, he told a group of workers that he wanted those who had succeeded in the economy to help "the little guys," and that he was "haunted" by children struggling in poverty, growing up "amidst the violence and horror" of the inner city. This was not the sort of imagery that Ronald Reagan had emphasized.

As George insisted to a reporter early in the campaign, issues mattered but character was more important, and if you could connect with people, they would remain loyal to you. That had been the idea behind all of the Christmas cards and handwritten notes he had sent out over the years. Now that he was running for the presidency, he took every opportunity to form that sort of individual connection.

George and Bar liked to call it the "limousine game." Riding around in the limousine with thousands of people lining the streets, they would take turns making eye contact with roadside spectators. The idea was that if you made direct eye contact, that voter would be a supporter for life. George and Bar reckoned they had collected several thousand additional votes simply by establishing eye contact.

Connecting in the debates was another matter. Early in his career in Texas, George had been quite good at verbal banter and forceful in defending his positions. But after more than a decade as a diplomat, head of the RNC, and vice president, it was as if the passion had been sucked out of him. Friends such as Bob Mosbacher knew that the old George was in there somewhere; he just didn't seem to want to come out.

Moreover, in Michael Dukakis he had an opponent who had mastered the art of the verbal duel. For years he had been on the television program *The Advocates*, debating a whole host of issues. No surprise then that Dukakis wanted to debate early and often. George was game for that, but Jimmy Baker said the earliest they would consider a debate was September 20.

When they did meet, it wasn't long before Dukakis began pounding away on Noriega, Iran-Contra, and the tax cuts. He also slammed George's criticisms of his liberalism, saying he was "questioning my patriotism . . . I resent it. I resent it."

George volleyed back but seemed uncomfortable. He left the meeting knowing he had not given a stellar performance. "I'm going to do a heck of a lot better the next time," he told Jim Baker later.

Bar watched the debate that night with her son-in-law Billy LeBlond and daughter-in-law Margaret Bush. She dealt with her tension about the campaign by eating and had put on some weight, which bothered her and added to her level of stress. After the debate was over she spoke with her husband. As always she was blunt and direct: Your attacks on Dukakis were too strong, she told him. George, as he almost always did, took her advice and overruled Lee Atwater's plans to stay on the offensive.

During the second presidential debate, George and Dukakis dueled on the issues. But the Massachusetts governor was weakened by a terrible flu and fever that had kept him in bed for most of the previous day. They seemed to battle to a standstill when CNN's Bernie Shaw asked Dukakis a question.

"Governor, if Kitty Dukakis were raped and murdered, would you favor an irrevocable death penalty for the killer?"

No one remembered the exact words Dukakis used to answer that question. It was his tone; unimpassioned, calm, as if he were giving a lecture in a college classroom on the mechanics of constitutional law. "I don't," Dukakis said, "and I think you know I've opposed the death penalty during all my life. I don't see any evidence that it's a deterrent..."

---

GEORGE AND BAR WATCHED EAGERLY AS DAN QUAYLE SQUARED OFF IN HIS vice presidential debate with Sen. Lloyd Bentsen. George had been looking for a candidate who was young and attractive, and he wasn't disappointed with the visuals. Quayle looked great next to the older and craggier Bentsen. As public relations veteran Joe Canzeri put it about Quayle, "The camera makes love to the guy." But he was also too handsome and too young for many voters to take seriously. "He looks twelve," complained Canzeri. "He got his hair cut one day and we all died. He looked ten."

During the debate, Quayle tried to turn his youth into an advantage. He appealed to voters for a generational change. He was like that other young politician of a generation earlier. "I have as much experience in the Congress as Jack Kennedy did when he sought the presidency..."

When Quayle was finished, Bentsen stepped up to the mike with a large grin. "Senator, I served with Jack Kennedy. I knew Jack Kennedy. Jack Kennedy was a friend of mine. Senator, you are no Jack Kennedy."

After that devastating blow, the attacks became relentless. Some argued that George should drop Quayle in favor of someone more experienced, like Senator Bob Dole. But George, ever the loyalist, stood by him.

Sometime after the debate, George sat down with Quayle. "What do you think of all those cartoons and editorials and attacks?"

Quayle just shook his head. "Wow!"

"Well, why don't you take the word 'Quayle' and insert the word 'Bush' wherever it appears, and that's the crap I took for eight years. Wimp. Sycophant. Lapdog. Poop. Lightweight. Boob. Squirrel. Asshole. George Bush."

---

ON ELECTION DAY, GEORGE AND BAR WERE AT THEIR APARTMENT IN HOUSton along with their children and grandchildren. They voted early that morning and then went over to campaign headquarters. George made a few calls to help get out the vote before going to lunch. The family then returned to the apartment.

At eleven o'clock George received a phone call from Dukakis, conceding the race. He had waited for the California polls to close before admitting defeat. When George hung up there was family jubilation. W. had worked at campaign headquarters and served as his father's enforcer. The other boys and Doro had each helped out in their own way. Dozens of other Bushes, Houses, Walkers, Ellises, and Jansings had made other contributions, large and small. That Christmas the Bushes sent out ninety thousand Christmas cards under Bar's direct supervision, thanking friends and family for their help.

The next morning the family gathered at St. Martin's Episcopal Church to give thanks. At a private 7:45 A.M. prayer service, it was George W. who rose to lead the family in prayer. "Many of us will begin a new challenge. Please give us strength to endure and the knowledge necessary to place our fellow man over self . . . please guide us and guard us on our journey, particularly watch over Dad and Mother." W. had not been much on prayer earlier in his life. But this time it was less perfunctory. Up until this time, the family had never experienced the full blast that celebrity would bring them. It was one thing to be the child of a vice president. It was quite another to be the First Family.

After the service, George went jogging in Houston with Lee Atwater. He made a brief announcement naming the members of his transition team and mentioned his appointment of Jimmy Baker as secretary of state. In the days ahead he would announce the appointment of longtime friends Bob Mosbacher to Commerce, Nick Brady to Treasury, and even Bruce Gelb, the former Andover classmate he had rescued from a bully, to be head of the United States Information Agency.

As George decided on the makeup of his new administration, Jimmy Baker began pushing the idea that a troika of presidential aides could run the place. He wanted Craig Fuller, Robert Teeter, and John Sununu each put in a slot. It was an arrangement that would serve Baker nicely. With three men running the White House, he was bound to find more influence in domestic policy even though he was at State. But George rejected the idea. He wanted John Sununu in the top spot. Sununu, a former governor of New Hampshire, was a mix of Lebanese, Greek, and Salvadoran heritage. He was born in Havana and grew up in Queens, New York, where he was weathered by the fights that took place after school and the tough training he undertook at a military academy on Long Island, where he was top of the class. He went on to MIT to study engineering.

By 1982, Sununu was running for governor and his campaign was short on cash. George flew to New Hampshire and raised a bundle of money for the campaign. Sununu didn't forget it, and when George made plans to run for president, he was one of the first to sign on.

―――――

DAYS AFTER THE VICTORY, THE FAMILY BOARDED A PLANE AND FLEW BACK TO Washington. Jeb, Marvin, and Neil all headed back to their homes and their jobs. George and Bar were joined on the plane by W., Laura, and the twins. The girls, now seven, released their nervous energy by stuffing big clods of paper down the airplane's toilet. When the toilet backed up, it was Bar who had to fish the paper out and stick it in the trash.

―――――

DESPITE THEIR EIGHT YEARS IN THE REAGAN ADMINISTRATION, GEORGE AND Bar had not been in the White House residence before. So shortly after the election, they got their first peek at the private living quarters. The Reagans had seen the residence as a retreat where they selectively entertained small groups of people. When the Bushes toured the place, George naturally had different ideas. When he saw the size of the living room, he instantly lit up. "I can have forty people in here!"

Bar picked the small room in the back that Reagan had used as a study to make a private sitting area. It was here that the family would conduct its private business, and it was also here that Bar would put the big needlepoint rug that she had patiently stitched over the past twenty years during the family's rise to power. She knew precisely which stitches she had made during the family's historic turning points. Now, as family, close friends, and distinguished guests met in the inner sanctum of the White House, they would literally be looking at the Bush family history as they conversed with the president.

Other changes were afoot, too, which reflected the family's informality. Shortly after the election, Bar took their dog Millie to Kentucky to be bred by a dog owned by their good friend Will Farrish. When the puppies came due, Bar replaced Nancy's row of hair dryers in the White House with a nest for Millie's new puppies. To make the place more comfortable, Bar put some of the White House antique furniture in storage and brought in their own bed and bedroom furniture. A chest of toys was added for visiting grandchildren.

The inauguration was a Bush family reunion as hundreds of family members crowded into the Capitol Building. With the Quayles preparing to move into the vice presidential home, Bar and George lived in Blair House and characteristically invited the whole Bush-Walker gang to join them. All ten grandchildren were there, rumbling all over the place as George worked on his inaugural address.

At the swearing-in ceremony, George and Ronald Reagan left the platform and walked to the Capitol to formally say good-bye to everyone on Capitol Hill. As Reagan left, the House sergeant at arms came forward to direct George.

"Mr. President," he said.

George didn't say anything.

Bar finally nudged him with her elbow: "He's talking to you." George was sworn in as Bar held two Bibles, one that had been used by George Washington, the other a gift from a Capitol Hill prayer group.

His first visitor that day in the Oval Office was his mother, Dottie, who was rolled in in a wheelchair. Even more than his father, his mother had shaped his very being. Now here she was, sitting in the Oval Office with her son. Someone asked her, "Isn't this the greatest experience in your life?" Dottie nodded, and in her characteristic spirit added, "The greatest thing in my life . . . *so far*." She was always quick to offer advice and remind her son that the Bushes were the unKennedys. "George, remember how President Reagan used to wait for Nancy as he got off the helicopter there on the White House lawn?"

"Mother, are you sending me a message?"

"Well, I think it would be nice if you didn't walk ahead like Jack Kennedy used to do."

After his mother and the other members of the family left, George looked in the president's desk and found a note from Ronald Reagan. Written across the top were the words "Don't let the turkeys get you down."

"Dear George," read the note, "You'll have moments when you want to use this particular stationery. Well, go to it. George, I treasure the memories we share and wish you all the very best. You'll be in my prayers. God bless you and Barbara. I'll miss our Thursday lunches. Ron."

George would remain supremely loyal to Reagan, never taking shots at him. Even when Jim Baker sent a note applauding him because the staff no longer had to sit through "those long gaps when President Reagan conducted those meetings," George would say nothing. After the Reagans left, twenty-eight of the Bushes spent the night at the White House.

———

THE INAUGURATION WAS A CHANCE FOR THE FAMILY TO ENJOY A TRIUMPH that had been more than two decades in the making. A Bush was now president; but there was plenty of talk about other contests.

George W. told family members that he was going to make a run for the governor's mansion in Texas, or maybe a Senate seat. The governor's office was going to be open in 1990 and he figured he had a great chance of winning it. The news surprised most in the family, who had never really thought of W.'s mounting a viable campaign. But they joked with him and teased him. By the end of the inaugural celebration, family members were calling him "Governor" in jest.

George W. had gone through a circuitous journey. He had turned his life around, and certain innate qualities were beginning to emerge. But after nearly four decades of being boisterous, of consciously downplaying expectations, of making clear that he was not competing with his father, family members had a difficult time taking the turnaround seriously. When campaign aide Doug Wead interviewed family members for a study of First Families, he asked Marvin Bush what sort of future he thought his oldest brother might have in politics. Marvin just laughed. "George?! Why he's the family clown."

In the days after the campaign, Doug Wead put his staff to work on making a report about presidential children. What did they end up doing? What were their lives like? "It was of interest to all the Bush children, but particularly W.," Wead said. "I think he had a greater sense of generational destiny than his siblings."

The report was blunt. "Being related to a president may bring more problems than opportunity. Almost any enterprise is criticized. If successful, it's assumed that it is because of the relationship. If not, the public assumes the son or daughter is lazy or incompetent . . . the presidential child in business faces the pressures of enormous scrutiny. Two things the media and the public won't allow? Success or failure. Keep the business mediocre, maintain a personal low profile and you will be left alone."

Contemporary examples were given. Steven Ford got a job as a journalist but was dismissed because it was assumed to be because of his father's influence. "Anything they do in life," Wead discovered, "they're discredited."

Wead went to work putting together the research. The result was a forty-four-page document that proved to be downright depressing. The fact was, most children of presidents had not fared well. Of particular interest was the life of Franklin Roosevelt, Jr., and some eerie parallels he had with W. He was born into a family of six kids, four sons and a daughter, and another daughter who had died at a young age. One of his brothers went on to serve in state government in Florida (where Jeb was now secretary of commerce). Roosevelt decided to run for governor in his home state, just like W. was considering. He lost. Wead said, "I remember W. looking at the document and rolling his eyes. 'Oh, great . . .' "

History weighed heavily on the Bush children. Fortunately, the Bushes are not a fatalistic lot, but the family did face tension when it came to defining precisely the role the children would play now that George had risen to the presidency.

#### CHAPTER 32

# FRIENDS

EORGE BUSH WAS A PRODUCT OF HIS PAST. AS PRESIDENT, HE seemed to carry forward those qualities he had been taught by his family over the generations. They were excellent attributes for a man, but for a president they were problematic.

Bush seemed determined to have the first presidency that didn't draw attention to itself. He told the Secret Service to stop the presidential motorcade at traffic lights and to drive through Washington without sirens. He also wanted the motorcade scaled back.

"He was always looking for ways to cut back on the size of the presidential motorcade," Marlin Fitzwater recalled. "He wanted to cut the communication people out, put all the staff in one van. I think in part it was an effort to escape some of his past, you know, riding the limousine to the country day school."

He seemed determined not to succumb to the la-dee-dahs and take himself too seriously. He joked about his linguistic abilities. ("Dirty Harry said, 'Make my day.' I say, 'Make my twenty-four-hour time period.'") Later, after he had broken his no-new-taxes pledge, he strapped on a George Bush mask and walked through a campaign plane full of reporters yelling, "Read my lips! Read my lips! Read my lips!"

This was more than an attempt at public relations. George Bush was determined not to take himself too seriously. In the bowels of the White House, he would wander around carrying a voice-activated stuffed monkey that would sock itself in the head whenever he began to speak. But in all the effort to make sure he didn't take himself too seriously, he risked having others not take him too seriously either.

He made a concerted effort to diminish his visibility, reducing the amount of time that he appeared on TV. In his first two years in office, George made the evening news only a third as many times as Ronald Reagan had. Reporters who covered the presidency created a new award called The Poppy, which went to the reporter who traveled the most miles with

Bush and generated the fewest column inches. "Demands no more than his fair share" was good protocol for a privileged young man, but not for a president.

As one of his first presidential acts, George revoked the White House mess privileges of the speechwriters, a clear indication that he considered their work less important than Reagan did. His speeches lacked the high-velocity rhetoric of Reagan, with its soaring peaks and valleys of emotion and language. George would instead include a large acknowledgments section that ran several paragraphs long, in which he said "thank you" to dozens of people. "The acknowledgments are the bane of our existence," one speech-writer declared. George would delete dramatic words from his speech and skip over emotional lines about patriotism. Fundamentally, he didn't believe that words and ideas could change peoples' minds. They had rarely done so in his life. Stimson had spoken with emotion about the need for the young men of Andover to stay in school before joining the fight. George had been visibly moved by the speech but it didn't change his mind. He had enlisted anyway. Instead, you changed people's thoughts by meeting with them one-on-one, making a personal and sincere appeal.

George also arrived in the White House with no clear vision of the direction he wanted to take. For George, campaigning and governing were two entirely separate matters. Campaigning was a test of stamina, strength, and character. Governing required different qualities. Several weeks after the election, he was asked about the campaign and what it meant in terms of how he would lead the country. "That's history," he told reporters, "that doesn't mean anything anymore."

Throughout their lives the Bush boys had been tested, whether on the athletic pitch or in the world of business. The presidency was no different. George hung a picture of President Lincoln on the wall of the White House Treaty Room. Entitled *The Peacemakers*, it showed the president talking with generals aboard a riverboat on the Mississippi. Lincoln was George's favorite president, not simply because of what he had done, but because he had passed the greatest test of any president. "He was tested by fire," George would tell family and friends, "and showed his greatness."

As it had always been for the Bushes, meeting a challenge was in large part a measure of stamina. In every previous campaign, George had been de-termined to outdo, outgo, outlast all of his opponents. George W. had done the same in his 1978 run for Congress. Now that George was president, he was determined not to sit still, not to be bested.

Physically, he was his same hyperkinetic self. When in Washington, Bush rose to go jogging at 5:30 A.M. and was in the Oval Office before 7. One time, after a state dinner for Lech Walesa of Poland, George slipped upstairs and jumped out of his tux and into his jogging clothes for a quick spin around the South Lawn. Some of the exiting guests got brief glimpses of him as he bestrode the White House grounds. And once, in Los Angeles after a church service, he was so eager to get to the tennis court for a few sets that he left behind the military aide who carried the briefcase containing codes for launching a nuclear strike.

When it came to relations with the media, always a thorny subject for the Bushes, he tried to simply befriend them and outlast them. Pool reporters on Air Force One got so much face time with the man that they eventually ran out of questions. When the interviews ended, he would engage in banter, talking about Millie's new puppies and the exercise machines he was using.

George was taking over a government more divided than any in recent memory. Reagan had enjoyed a Republican Senate for six years and a House that had included enough conservative Democrats to pass major portions of his agenda. George had none of that, meaning it was going to be difficult to push much of anything through.

It was as president that George emerged as a leader for the first time. He was a conservative, but not a movement conservative as Reagan had been. Bill Buckley called it a "conservative temperament." George was a conservative like Edmund Burke, nervous about change, progress, and changing institutions. Reagan had been a conservative revolutionary; George was a conservative pure and simple. As he made clear in his inaugural address: The mission of the Bush administration was "stewardship" of Reagan's legacy. He quoted former RNC chairman Ray Bliss, who had advised him years earlier to always wait a few days before making a decision or taking a position on a particular issue because "by then, you might not have to decide at all."

In the days following the election, administration advisers gathered at the vice presidential residence. Nick Brady, the new treasury secretary, and George's adviser Robert Teeter had come to discuss the looming budget deficit with the president and Vice President Quayle. Both Brady and Teeter mentioned the need to raise taxes to narrow the deficit, but George and Quayle said no.

Then George's old friend Congressman Dan Rostenkowski, a Democrat and chairman of the powerful House Ways and Means Committee, came to visit. Earlier in the year Rosty had endorsed Michael Dukakis for president. At the Democratic National Convention in Atlanta, he made a seconding speech for Lloyd Bentsen. But there was never really any question where his heart was. Rosty had forged a friendship with Congressman George Bush more than twenty years earlier, and the two had maintained it through all the political battles in Washington. Rosty had helped during Watergate to see that no indictments came from the House. And in early 1981, he had offered the Reagan White House advice, through George, on how best to proceed with the 1981 tax cut. In the summer of 1988, when friends visited Rosty at his office on Capitol Hill, he would take them to look at the portraits on the wall. "You know what those are? Those are all the [seven] members of the Ways and Means Committee that became president. Next year, one more's going up there." Of course, he meant George Bush.

So when Rosty came on December 6 to have lunch with his old friend, he came with an agenda in mind. Rostenkowski had just proposed a gas tax increase and was talking fiercely about the need to close the deficit by taxing people more. George had campaigned on the slogan, "Read my lips: no new taxes." The two friends talked about the old days, and Rosty offered to not raise the tax issue for one year if George would at least reconsider his views about raising taxes. George readily agreed to the compromise.

Rosty kept his end of the deal. Then in the fall of 1990, White House officials sat down with congressional leaders to discuss the mounting deficit. Budget Director Richard Darman in particular was convinced that tax increases were going to be necessary. Rosty was there, telling George that this needed to be done. In late September 1990, in the White House family dining room, George gathered with Sununu and Brady and Darman on one side of the large table and congressional leaders, including Rosty, on the other. They talked diligently, and in the end George did reconsider his stand and offered to back "tax revenue increases" in exchange for spending cuts. In George's mind this was not really breaking his pledge; it was about governing responsibly. And despite his political differences with Rosty and other Democrats, he trusted them because they were friends. "Rostenkowski, Joe Moakley, these were people that he liked and trusted," nephew John Ellis said. "And if they wanted to do something, it was probably a good thing."

When the deal was announced, Republicans were outraged and a flurry of angry phone calls came from voters across the country. George took it all in stride, convinced that his friendship with Rosty would preserve him. "Real friendships," he wrote Rosty in December, "survive these little bumps in the road." Indeed, when Rostenkowski was convicted a few years later of illegally using his postage funds on Capitol Hill and went to jail, Bush stood by his friend. As Rostenkowski told us, George Bush called him regularly at the prison, trying to cheer him up.

Friendship defined his vision of politics. As president he demonstrated the same discomfort in attacking Democratic leaders, organized labor, teachers' unions, or other institutions that opposed his agenda. Instead, he courted Congress, convinced that performing acts of kindness and thoughtfulness was not only the right thing to do, but would also yield results. When staying at Kennebunkport, George would call Maine senator George Mitchell to see if he wanted a ride back to Washington. During a signing ceremony for the Clear Air Act in 1989, he noticed that Tom Foley, the speaker of the House, was sitting in the second row. He immediately ordered staffers to move him to the front. George kept a locker at the House gym and played squash regularly with Democratic congressman Sonny Montgomery. His bonds of friendship were so deep that when he visited Mississippi, he declared, "I wish we had more like [Montgomery] in Congress." He could never understand why the Mississippi GOP was so upset with him.

When French president François Mitterrand made plans for his first trip to the United States, George insisted that he make a visit to Kennebunkport. He was hoping to take him for a spin in his speedboat *Fidelity* and ram into some of those eight-foot-high swells. Afterward, he wanted to have an informal lunch on the boat's deck.

Mitterrand was expecting the regalia of an official state visit: flags, a military band, and an honor guard. And if he was going to visit Walker Point, he would need a bidet and a special bed put into the family cottage to help with his back trouble. An allergy-free pillow would also be required. White House aides were shocked at the demands, but George told them to do what was necessary. When Mitterrand did arrive, there was no powerboat ride. But he did dress in a plaid shirt, corduroys, and hiking boots (undoubtedly his first and last time in such an outfit). They went for a quiet walk in the woods where George had played as a child six decades earlier.

In the Middle East he sought to create a friendship with Yitzhak Shamir. Relations were difficult, particularly later in the administration when Israeli settlements continued to go up on the West Bank over Washington's objections. But George was always looking for an angle. As he prepared for a meeting with Shamir, he asked his advisers: What were this guy's hobbies and interests? What could they do together and talk about? When security officials declared that Shamir had no interests outside of politics and his family, George was stumped. "How can I get through to this guy?"

If friendship failed him politically at times, other lessons from his youth served him well. George Bush came into office during revolutionary times. In Eastern Europe the Soviet Empire was falling apart, with hundreds of thousands of people in the streets of Prague, East Berlin, and Budapest. Historic events were revealing the triumph of democracy over totalitarianism, of capitalism over communism. It might have been a time for great celebration, of jubilation in the West, just as there was in the former Soviet bloc. But through it all George was cautious, more fearful of doing the wrong thing than doing nothing. "I don't want to do anything dumb," he told his cabinet. When pressed by the media, he quoted Yogi Berra: "I don't want to make the wrong mistake."

When the Berlin Wall fell in the fall of 1989, there were Germans dancing in the streets.

"Do you want to make a statement?" Marlin Fitzwater asked him.

"Why?"

"Why? This is an incredibly historic day. People will want to know what it means. They need some presidential assurance that the world is okay."

"Listen, Marlin, I'm not going to dance on the Berlin Wall. The last thing I want to do is brag about winning the Cold War, or bringing the Wall down. It won't help us in Eastern Europe to be bragging about this." It was the application to geopolitics of the principle of good sportsmanship that he had learned from his parents while young.

But for all of the grandeur of the presidency, George never seemed to lose touch with his sense of the past. Gerry Bemiss recalls the time he visited George and Bar at a private White House dinner party. Plenty of VIPs were in the room, but George and Gerry chatted about the old days in Kennebunkport. George then looked at his friend impulsively.

"Let's give 'em a call!" he blurted.

"Who?" asked Bemiss.

"Let's give the boys a call."

Right in the middle of dinner, the president popped up and grabbed a nearby phone and started dialing.

#### CHAPTER 33

# CREST

FOR THE ENTIRE FAMILY THE ELECTION OF GEORGE HERBERT Walker Bush represented a dramatic change. The family had always maintained a free flow of information. Everyone everywhere was accessible, and no one was more interested in preserving that than the new president. Family members were instructed to write "Walker" on the outside of the envelope. This would ensure that it would go directly to the president. He also made it clear that family members could call if they really needed something.

"You would call him with something," Elsie Walker Kilbourne said, "and he'd call you right back. In maybe fifteen minutes! And you'd say thank you very much, but you've got a job to do! He never made you feel that way at all. He wanted to be there for you, regardless of what was going on in his life."

He called his mother regularly, sometimes daily, and his uncle John Walker once a week. Fifteen members of the Bush-Walker clan participated in special ceremonies held around the world. Sister Nancy, with her love of history and literature, represented the United States at a special celebration of democracy in Greece. Brother Johnny went to the Ukraine for a ceremony and to a presidential inauguration in Argentina. Bucky went to Turkey and Malta for official ceremonies, Neil went to the African nation of Benin for an inauguration ceremony. Pres Bush, Jr., went to Bolivia, Doro to Paraguay and Morocco, and Jeb to Albania. Nephew Jamie Bush, Pres, Jr.'s, son, went to a swearing-in ceremony in Guatemala, and another cousin went to Poland on a goodwill mission. Craig Stapleton, who had married a Walker cousin, was given an appointment at the Treasury Department. And John Walker, Jr., an accomplished prosecutor in New York (he had cracked the famous French Connection heroin case), became a judge on the Federal Court of Appeals.

For George and Bar's children, this was a new and sometimes awkward experience. The president would sit and have a beer with Doro and Marvin, who lived nearby, and he talked to his sons W., Jeb, and Neil regularly. His sons would also make occasional appearances at official events. At one White House dinner, when the boys were all in town, the protocol office had dispersed them and put Marvin next to actress Melanie Griffith. The starlet was wearing a tight-fitting, low-cut black dress and it didn't take long for the notes to start to fly, carried back and forth by navy stewards.

W. fired a note off to Marvin. "Easy big fella."

Marvin fired a note back. "She can't keep her eyes off me."

W.: "You're irresistible!"

But these were also awkward times for those family members who didn't enjoy being in the spotlight. At a Washington charity fund-raiser, Marvin sat next to Princess Diana. She asked him several times for a dance, but Marvin refused.

The boys never really talked policy with their father or his advisers. "George W. almost never showed interest in politics or policy," recalls Marlin Fitzwater. "We would talk about baseball and then we'd chat about sports. But that was largely it."

Despite occasional forays by George and Bar's children into the White House, there was a strict division in the family. George was insistent that his children live their own lives. Doug Wead, who was serving as his special assistant and who was close to W., remembers how difficult it was. The media had an initial flurry of interest in the extended Bush family, and then it died off. After one appearance on the *Today* show, the president's children retreated into the background.

"The father's philosophy was raise the kids, give them a good education, and then they are on their own," Wead recalls. "And I found that personally almost heartless. 'The kids have their own lives, I have my life.' But by separating it, I wondered if he wasn't communicating to his own staff a lack of respect or fear of the kids."

At the same time, George W. seemed to emotionally distance himself from his parents. Wead recalls how President Bush and Bar would ask him, "How is George doing?" as if they really didn't know what was going on in his life.

Suddenly, too, there were security concerns that hadn't existed before. The president's brother Bucky and his family received a tip from law enforcement authorities that they might be the target of a deranged man who disliked the new president. In late 1989, hit men hired by Colombian drug cartels were said to be targeting George and family members. George W. received extra Secret Service protection when he attended Texas Rangers games just in case.

Even more difficult was keeping a clear line between public service and private interests. The extended Bush-Walker clan was involved in a host of business and commercial enterprises throughout the world. How to make legitimate use of the fact that George was now president, as opposed to exploiting it, was a difficult line to walk.

Nowhere was that more true than when it came to George's older brother, Pres. With his brother's rise in politics, Pres had ventured out from his work in the insurance business and Wall Street to seek lucrative international deals, particularly in Asia.

The president and Bar were returning to China in March 1989. It would be his first visit overseas as president and offer him the opportunity to return to a land where he had spent a year of his life fifteen years earlier. But just ten days before that trip, Pres made a visit to Beijing to drum up business. He was a partner in an $18 million venture to build a country club outside of Shanghai for foreign businessmen and was being paid $250,000 per year as a consultant by a New York firm. They wanted him to discuss with Chinese officials the possibility of setting up an international satellite communications network that would link Chinese businesses and universities. On the rare occasions when Pres talked about his dealings in Asia, he was insistent that "there's no conflict of interest." But he did admit, "It's doesn't hurt that my brother is the president of the United States."

Pres made other deals, some involving business entities that had apparent links to Asian organized crime. While there is no evidence that Pres did anything improper or illegal, it was troubling to the family. Pres's work in China "has always worried me," George wrote in his private diary. Other family members were likewise angry about his activities.

"I think everyone had a strong feeling of disapproval," recalls Caroline Bush Cole. "It was using the Bush name."

The situation became so troubling that George eventually had to discuss the matter with his brother. But Pres was immovable.

"Pres was just so damn stubborn about it," Gerry Bemiss said. "You couldn't even discuss it with him. It was very frustrating for George."

Family disagreements in the past had always been handled within the family. But this time George was forced to take other actions. He quietly told Jimmy Baker to send a cable to all U.S. embassies instructing them to avoid "any appearance of preferential treatment" to family members.

George's frustration with his brother caused a division from which their relationship would never quite recover. "They were never as close as they had once been," their sister Nancy Ellis said. "Sadly, they probably never will be."

For Bar, George's election had been a sort of confirmation that all the years of sacrifice, of sitting at home alone and caring for the children while George was off traveling somewhere, had paid off. To those who served in the Bush administration, Bar's central role was surprising. Lamar Alexander served as secretary of education and has known the family for more than a decade. "George and Barbara are as tight as a drum," he said. "They almost unconsciously work together in their political objectives. Barbara has a full share in the authority of it."

In a strange way, Bar was using the same tools of "soft power" in the family that Pres Bush had perfected at Brown Brothers. She influenced family decision-making because of her instincts and the trust that George and the rest of the family placed in her judgment. Above all, her authority comes from the fact that she seems most concerned about protecting the family. Her motives are above suspicion.

Her strong presence and maternal instincts led many American women to identify with her. The patented three-strand fake pearls that she wore so often to cover the wrinkles on her neck became a big seller across the country. The National Needlework Association saw interest in the craft blossom when women learned of her commitment to constructing the family rug. She also became an icon of sorts for women who were tired of the American obsession with being slender. "Having Barbara as First Lady means that women who weren't buying a new dress because they were a little overweight are buying new dresses now," reported designer Arnold Scaasi. "It means you don't have to try to look like your daughter anymore."

But Bar was still self-conscious about her weight and appearance. Once at an official dinner in Australia, Bar decided not to wear her eyeglasses. When her dinner plate came, Bar began cracking into a big thing in the middle of it. The prime minister quietly leaned over and said, "Barbara, that's the adornment."

She was always uncomfortable with the pull of celebrity. "If anything, Bar is always genuine," says Nancy Bush Ellis. And in the artificial world of celebrities, Bar could lose her patience quickly. In the weeks before every Mother's Day, the First Lady's office would be flooded with cards, letters, pictures, and notes from thousands of people. Some of the letters spoke as if they considered her part of their family. The letters were heartfelt but made her uncomfortable.

"Please don't write me," she finally wrote one of them. "I have children of my own. I'm not your mother."

IN THE FALL OF 1989, ONE OF THOSE CHILDREN WAS IN SERIOUS TROUBLE. The Denver office of the Federal Deposit Insurance Corporation was taking over management of more than a billion dollars' worth of assets from Silverado Savings and Loan, where Neil had been a board member. Neil had resigned from Silverado in the summer of 1988 after more than three years on the board and was now heading up a new oil and gas venture called Apex, which was looking for methane gas in Wyoming. But Silverado still lingered. The S&L's assets consisted of property and commercial real estate loans that were in serious trouble. The news caught the interest of the House Banking Committee, which announced on December 4 that it would begin hearings on Silverado. Committee members wanted the federal records unsealed.

Silverado was one of hundreds of S&Ls that failed during the 1980s—some 1,037 thrifts were facing closure, and losses for the federal government were going to be upward of $100 billion. None of those cases involved a member of the First Family. But to critics, Neil was the personification of what went wrong in the S&L industry. Regulators and members of Congress wanted him held personally responsible.

The Democrats hired a private investigator to look into the matter and began issuing press releases about "Bush sleaze." Wanted posters with Neil's face on it were soon going up around the nation's capital. "Jail Neil Bush" was next.

Federal regulators did not believe there was any criminal activity involving Neil. But he had made serious lapses in judgment concerning conflicts of interest. As a board member Neil had approved loans to men who were investing in his oil company. While not illegal, it certainly was a conflict of interest. The feds offered him a simple deal: agree never again to serve on the board of a financial institution and you're off the hook. But while he didn't want to be on another board, signing such an agreement would be an admission of guilt. It was a stain not only on Neil but on the family. Regulators backtracked and instead asked that he simply sign a consent for a cease and desist, which would amount to a wrist slap. But again he refused. So investigators pressed ahead.

The glare was devastating to Neil, and family members noticed the change. The normally happy-go-lucky optimist became brooding and angry. He started swearing in front of the camera, obsessively clipping newspaper articles about Silverado and piling them high on his desk.

"I didn't eat well," he recalls. "I didn't exercise. I became consumed with reading every newspaper and listening to every news account."

Family and friends immediately rose to his defense. A legal defense fund was established by Lud Ashley. The president told his son not to worry; he would be vindicated. But Neil, who had always been somewhat shy, disliked the attention and attacks. As George wrote to Ashley, "I saw him in Denver and I think he is worried about the publicity and the 'shame.' "

George defended his son's honor at a Houston conference. Bar sat in the front row and watched, trying not to cry. "I've got three other sons," he said, "and they all want to go to the barricades." He pledged that the family would fight and stand by Neil through everything.

But despite the strong defense, George was counseling patience. "You calm down now," he told his sons. "We're in a different role now. You can't react like you would if your brother was picked on in a street fight. That's not the way the system works."

While everyone in the family was pained, Bar was hit the hardest. She cried regularly and confided in family members that she and George had ruined their son's life. "She was devastated, just devastated," recalls Shellie Bush Jansing. "Neil was the most sensitive and the most kind of her boys. She had been with him through all the stuff with the dyslexia. Next to the loss of Robin and Marvin's near death, it was the most painful thing for her."

When reporters pressed Bar for comments on the matter, the normally combative First Lady simply looked at them with sad eyes. "You don't want to see a grown woman cry, do you?"

The issue for Bar was clear: "They are going after Neil because he is *our son*." George likewise blamed himself. They were going after his youngest son to get to him, and it was ruining Neil's life.

By the fall of 1990 the situation reached critical mass. The family was gathering in New York for the funeral of Dr. John Walker. For more than four decades he had been a pillar of the family. He had helped George and Bar in their desperate fight to keep Robin alive and had arranged for the sale of Walker Point from Herby's widow to George. Whenever there was heavy lifting to be done in the family, John Walker had been there.

After the service, the family milled around at the reception. Then George W. started dropping the bombshells: Dad may not run for reelection.

It was a shocking thing to say. After all, George was midway through his first term, and his standing in the polls was relatively high. But it was clear that the attacks on Neil were weighing heavily on both George and Bar. There was also the additional news that the president was having medical problems, that he was feeling tired and weak. Doctors had advised him that he had an overactive thyroid and the early onset of Graves' disease. Bar was diagnosed with the same disorder. It was a breakdown in her autoimmune system and was attacking her eyes, which were puffy and itching. They put her on Prednisone and then she started to undergo radiation treatments.

An additional concern was Dottie. George's strong and vibrant mother was now slowing down at eighty-eight years old. "She needed constant care," said Nancy Ellis. "George had all these things that he was doing, but he was always worrying about her." She was weak and her mind was slowly fading. "Mum was here," he noted in his diary of May 2, "she came yesterday and she looked very tired. Her cheeks were hollow and I was absolutely shocked as I walked across from the Oval Office to the Diplomatic entrance, and she said, 'Who's that? Who's that?' I said, 'Mum, it's George.' " His mind, he admitted, was not on the situation in Eastern Europe, but "on Mother and our family, and our love for her. She won the Mother's race when I was in the fourth grade, and she was the captain of the Mother's baseball team when I was in the 6th, 7th, or 8th grade—but it matters not. At Andover she was the most vivacious when she came, and I know my friends looked at her and said how wonderful she was. As the years went by, she was the leader for the Walkers, the Stapletons, the Bushes, the Jansings, and whoever—but now, she is a tired old lady. She stares a lot when she focuses, and it's that focus of love . . . Tomorrow she leaves, and maybe I'll never see her again, but I love her very much and that's what counts. All the criticism, all the fighting, all the ups-and-downs, all the right-wings, the left-wings, the press, and controversy—they all mean nothing. It's Mum's words: do your best; try your hardest; be kind; share; go to Church—and I think that's what really matters on this evening of May 2nd, 1990 . . ."

Here he was at the crest of his power, and George Bush was questioning whether to give it all up. The irony was that he was facing the choice at precisely the same age his father had been in 1961 when advised not to seek reelection. History was repeating itself. Many believed that he would step down and that his good friend Secretary of State Jim Baker would step in and run in his stead. And while George did eventually seek reelection, the issue was never really resolved in his mind until the final weeks of the 1992 campaign.

#### CHAPTER 34

# RANGERS

A FTER HIS FATHER WAS INAUGURATED IN JANUARY 1989, GEORGE W. decided that he didn't want to linger in Washington. He had been a paid campaign adviser to his father for eighteen months. Then in the weeks following the election, W. had remained the "loyalty" man for the campaign, serving as a member of the scrub team that would separate the friends from the opportunists seeking jobs in the new administration. He sat with a group including Lee Atwater, and they met six times to make sure that loyalists found positions in the administration.

But when this work was done, he, Laura, and the two girls returned to Texas. The excitement of the campaign, the focus for nearly two years on one single purpose, had been a thrilling time. But now he was again facing the reality of his own uncertain future. He had Harken Oil and Gas stock and a consulting gig with the firm, but things were very much up in the air.

A few days before the election, Bill DeWitt, who had brought him on board at Spectrum 7, called with the news that the Texas Rangers baseball team was up for sale. DeWitt's family had previously owned the Cincinnati Reds, and he knew that W. loved baseball and that the Walkers had owned the Mets. If you played your cards right and made some good decisions, he explained, a baseball team could be very profitable.

George quickly made a call to Eddie Chiles, the team's owner and a longtime family friend. Chiles had known his parents in Midland during the 1950s and had been on Bar's massive Christmas card list ever since. Chiles was desperate to sell and in financial trouble, just like everybody else with energy holdings in Texas. And the Rangers had been in the basement for quite some time. But Chiles could be a tough old bear. Raised planting cotton seeds in rural Virginia, he had amassed a fortune as owner of the Western Company, an offshore oil rig operation. Eddie had ridden the crest of the oil wave and bought the Rangers in 1980. But almost a decade later he was struggling, as his stock had plummeted from $32 a share to under $2.

"I walked into his house," George W. Bush later recalled, "and said, 'I would like to buy the team. I'm serious about it. I'll put together a group of people to buy it. I want you to give me serious consideration.' And therein began the courtship."

But Chiles was skeptical. "I'd like to sell to you, son, but you don't have any money."

Besides, there were plenty of other people courting Chiles to buy the team. Investors from Florida and New Jersey wanted to move the franchise to Tampa. Another investor in Oklahoma was eager to buy. W. had to convince Chiles that he should sell to him, and he used every ounce of his charm to do it.

It was the same sort of exercise he had engaged in a decade earlier in the oil business. He went to Craig Stapleton, who had married Lou Walker's daughter Debby and was with Marsh & McLennan. He went to Fred Malek, his father's friend from the Nixon White House. And he went to his old Yale friend Roland Betts.

"He saw it as a great opportunity all around," recalled George Bush. "A chance to do something for Texas and a chance to be involved in baseball. It was everything he wanted."

But W. was not only interested in baseball. The 1988 campaign had reignited his interest in politics. And while some in the family saw his interest in running for governor as a passing phase, W. was serious. Karl Rove told him that buying the Rangers would help move him in that direction, because it would establish "him clearly as a Texas businessman."

W. had always possessed an amazing amount of energy—like his father, he was a perpetual motion machine. Now that his drinking days were over, he was able to channel and direct his energy, like a raging river that had been tamed.

This time it was his Yale connections who proved most useful. Roland Betts, his fraternity brother, the man whose father had been like a surrogate father to him, offered to take a big stake in the team. But his offer came with a condition: "I don't want to make the investment if you plan to run in two years," Betts told his friend. W. would have to choose, baseball or politics. W. agreed, and announced that he would pass on the 1990 governor's race.

Baseball commissioner Peter Ueberroth was another longtime family friend, and when he was introduced to the plan he was concerned that not enough Texas money was involved. So in March 1989, Ueberroth approached billionaire financier Richard Rainwater.

Ueberroth stepped down as baseball commissioner on April 1, but his replacement was equally friendly. Bart Giamatti, former Yale president and longtime family friend, was the new commissioner and brought over longtime friend Fay Vincent to be second in command. It was a convergence of planets in the Bush universe. Vincent had grown up with the Bush kids in Connecticut.

W. and DeWitt assembled a team of investors who bought 86 percent of the team for about $75 million. Betts was the main investor. Also included in the group was a collection of Texans, including Richard Rainwater and Edward "Rusty" Rose. George W. himself put in only a little over $600,000. That might represent only about 1 percent of the team's value, but it was W. who had put the deal together and convinced Chiles to sell. He was appointed managing partner and would receive a 10 percent stake in the team after the other investors had recouped their money. His annual salary was $200,000.

The idea of George W. Bush, presidential first son, at the helm of a baseball team was greeted with derision in some quarters. Randy Galloway, a sports columnist for the *Fort Worth Star-Telegram*, considered him "a total smartass who didn't have a clue about baseball." Many of the players and manager Bobby Valentine wondered what to expect. They made a few phone calls and heard the stories about W.'s volcanic temper and his wild ways. Tom Grieve, the team's general manager, grimly looked forward to working with "a spoiled brat who thinks he runs the world because of his last name. Everyone felt that way."

W. was defensive, particularly when dealing with the media. "I've seen this before," he snapped when reporters pressed him on the team's investment group. "I'm a guy whose father was called a wimp on the cover of *Newsweek* the day he declared his race for the presidency. If it gets too bad, I'll let you know. I damn sure will let *Newsweek* know."

W. gathered the Rangers management to introduce himself and tell them about his history with baseball. He told them about his great-uncle Herby and his role in the Mets. But he also told them about his time on the Yale freshman baseball team as a pitcher. It was late in the game and Yale was down by ten runs. W. was warming up in the bull pen. The manager went onto the field and signaled that he wanted to make a pitching change. He glanced over at the bull pen and then signaled for the second baseman to take the mound and pitch. "And that was the end of my career."

W. relished the chance to be owner and was most directly involved in promoting the team. Only weeks after the deal was approved, W. convinced his mother to throw out the first pitch at a Rangers game. He asked his dad, the commander in chief, to sport a Texas Rangers baseball cap when he went fishing in Kennebunkport.

W. would sit in the stands at the home games in a box up front, chat with the fans, hand out baseball cards, and hold conversations with his players on the field. By sheer force of personality he was determined to make the team a success. The three-times-a-week team meetings were punctuated with jokes and nicknames. He organized a pickup game of baseball for the team's owners and took them all to a retreat in Mexico with cigars, cards, and fishing. He worked out in the weight room with the players and strutted around the office in casual clothes and a pair of ostrich boots. There were family picnics for team players.

He was not particularly concerned about getting credit for the team's success. But he did adhere to the family's strict code concerning loyalty. Shortly after he joined the Rangers, W. fired Mike Stone, the club president. W. believed that Stone had been trying to stir up differences with one of the partners. He ordered Stone to clear out his desk immediately. But he violated his own code when, instead of handling it quietly as Bushes had done in the past, he went public, standing before the cameras to explain and justify what he did. A whispering campaign followed, and anonymous sources derided him as "Scrooge Jr." and "head of complacency central." The next time he fired somebody, manager Bobby Valentine, he would do so quietly and with greater dignity.

When player Julio Franco got married, W. and Laura were there. He would speak Spanish with the Hispanic players and started explaining the team's financials to players at the end of the season. It was a recognition that players and management were all in this together. It was pure George W. — lock in on people, find commonalities, listen and remember.

Unlike the other owners, W. sat and ate peanuts in Section 109, Row 1, right behind the Rangers' dugout. Hot dog vendors and ticket-takers would walk by, and he soon knew them all by name. He made friendly banter with players as they stood in the on-deck circle. As one game went into extra innings, W. was sitting with family friend and commissioner Fay Vincent as Rafael Palmeiro waited on deck. "Hey, Rafa," W. shouted, "hit a home run so we can all go home." When Palmeiro went to the plate and with a mighty swing knocked one into the stands, W. yelled, "Way to go, Rafa man!"

W. had his own ideas about what made a team and a player great. For example, in scouting, too much emphasis was placed on statistics. Instead, he wanted scouts to look at players' character, "their makeup," as he called it. It was an essential virtue in the Bush family lexicon. At Brown Brothers the emphasis had not only been on production but also on character and trust. G. H. Walker and Company was concerned about the performance of the firm, not individual partners. It was the same formula his father had adopted in Washington: Wagon trains, not single cowboys, are what settled the West, as his grandfather used to say.

Not that all of W.'s deals went well. He traded for Harold Baines, a player at the end of his career, and gave up a young slugger named Sammy Sosa.

W. disliked prima donnas. He wanted to can players like Ruben Sierra, Jose Canseco, and Kevin Brown, who seemed to struggle to get along with their teammates. Instead, he brought in lesser-known players. "They want guys who want to be here," said Palmeiro. "They want everyone to fit in. I like that."

That attitude became central when in 1992 baseball would undergo a bitter debate over the tenure of commissioner Fay Vincent. Vincent was a baseball fan as well as an executive who was not in favor of plans to break the players' union. W. sided with Vincent, not only because he was a longtime family friend but because he agreed with him that fighting the union would ultimately be bad for baseball. "The idea was to break the union, bomb it into submission," Vincent told us. "George understood that wouldn't work and that it would be very bad for the game."

Vincent eventually lost his battle and Milwaukee Brewers owner Bud Selig was in charge. The suggestion was made that maybe George W. should be made commissioner as a gesture of conciliation with the forces that had supported Vincent. But when the offer came in early 1993, George W. was gearing up for his governor's race.

---

WHILE THE TEAM'S RECORD DID IMPROVE, MORE IMPORTANT FOR W. AND HIS investors was the fact that the value of the team skyrocketed. Through his efforts at marketing and creating a warm atmosphere, gross revenue more than doubled. The organization went from having 30 front-office employees to 170. He was clear that his family lineage helped. "Being the president's son puts you in the limelight," he told a reporter. "While in the limelight, you might as well sell tickets."

But to really make the team grow, it needed a new ballpark. The Rangers were playing at a stadium built in the 1960s for a minor league team. There were no skyboxes and seating was limited. Eddie Chiles had started discussions with the city of Arlington about making renovations or even building a new stadium. So George W. and the owners began dropping hints that the team might leave for another city.

The Rangers had always been a source of local pride for Arlington; a base-ball team was something that its bigger neighbors didn't have. So it didn't take long for the city to consider some sort of public funding. The two sides haggled, with W. leaving the intricacies of the negotiations to team lawyers. In the end a bargain was struck that proved to be a gold mine for the team. The city would cough up $135 million to fund the building of a stadium, and the Rangers would get $17 million to pay off a debt. They would also be exempt from paying some local taxes, have full control over the project, and be committed for only twelve years at a modest rent. The Ranger owners were supposed to come up with $90 million of their own for the project, but they raised that by dedicating future revenues from the luxury suites and concessions that would be available at the new ballpark.

#### CHAPTER 35

# VICTORY AND DEFEAT

O N THE EVENING OF AUGUST 1, 1990, GEORGE WAS SITTING
in the White House residence resting and relaxing with Bar.
Suddenly the phone rang. It was from the Situation Room in
the basement. The news was not good: Iraqi forces had pierced the Kuwaiti
border and were heading south. Thirty minutes later, National Security Adviser Brent Scowcroft and an aide were in the East Wing briefing him. Secretary of State Jimmy Baker was in Siberia meeting with Soviet officials, so
an aide, Robert Kimmett, consulted with George by phone.

Everyone was completely surprised. The consensus had been that Saddam was a "thug," but no one believed that he was capable of this. In the
1980s he had been seen by George and many others as a bulwark against
Iranian extremists. Still, Saddam's invasion should not have been a complete
surprise. In May the CIA had warned of a possible Iraqi invasion of Kuwait
in a short, top-secret report circulated to the cabinet. But hardly anyone paid
attention. Eyes were focused instead on events in the former Soviet empire.
A few months earlier Lithuania had declared its independence from
Moscow, a move denounced by the Kremlin as "illegitimate and invalid."
The Soviet Union was in chaos, and a summit with Gorbachev in Washington had led to complex discussions over arms control, human rights, and the
fate of the Baltic republics. Closer to home, the Bush administration only a
year earlier had invaded Panama to remove Manuel Noriega from power.
Iraq seemed a far-off concern.

But still the intelligence kept coming. In July, four KH-11 spy satellites focused on the Iraq-Kuwaiti border had detected some thirty thousand Iraqi
soldiers moving south. Infrared satellite photos showed Iraqi trucks carrying
ammunition and fuel. George did what he often did when confronting a
thorny question: He called on people he trusted and knew. He phoned his
friend King Hussein of Jordan, whom he had first met in 1964 while traveling to the Middle East for Zapata. Then he telephoned President Hosni
Mubarak of Egypt, whom he had met in 1981 during a vice presidential visit.

Both men told him Saddam was bluffing and would not invade Kuwait. George put more faith in these Middle East contacts than in his own intelligence analysts.

As they sat in the East Wing discussing the situation, George and his friend Brent Scowcroft remained convinced that Saddam would go only so far. He would probably stop at occupying the Kuwait oil fields along the Iraqi border; surely that was his primary interest. George had learned during his visits to the region in the 1960s that the oil fields were in dispute. But when Iraqi forces kept rolling south, to Kuwait City, it became clear that the Iraqi dictator had larger ambitions.

George issued a statement to the media. "We're not discussing intervention," he said.

The next morning George headed to Colorado to deliver a speech. By coincidence, British prime minister Margaret Thatcher was also there. When the two leaders finally had a chance to discuss Iraq, they had distinctly different views. George was uncertain whether military intervention was called for. By nature he was a cautious man, and with so much going on in the world, a war could be destabilizing. It could also undermine the cause of reform in the former Soviet Union. Thatcher, however, was insistent that the Iraqi invasion could not stand. "Don't go wobbly on me, George," she told him. George laughed, and the discussion seemed to move his opinion toward intervention for the first time. As one of her advisers later claimed, "The prime minister performed a successful backbone transplant."

The next day, August 3, George chaired an emergency meeting of the NSC. The CIA was convinced that Saddam was determined to turn Iraq into a Middle East superpower, with control over oil, a large collection of weapons of mass destruction, and a grip on strategic points in the Persian Gulf. Saudi Arabia was next on the invasion list, the CIA believed, and it concluded that the Iraqis would need only three days to overrun Riyadh, the Saudi capital. With this latest intelligence, his attitude continued to harden.

"This will not stand, this aggression against Kuwait," he said on August 5. It was his strongest statement yet. Some of his advisers were frankly surprised. To Gen. Colin Powell, chairman of the Joint Chiefs of Staff, it appeared as if a transformation had taken place. If before the president had seemed reluctant, now it was "almost as if the president had six-shooters in both hands and he was blazing way."

George Bush, like so many of the other men in his family, was obsessed with the notion of measuring up to a challenge. He was raised in a home where the biblical command "from those to whom much is given, much is expected" was as important as a profound sense of duty. George had become convinced in the early weeks of August 1990 that his great test would be the struggle against Saddam Hussein. For the first time in his life he made a geopolitical struggle intensely personal. Before, he had always spoken about war and geopolitics in terms of national interest and American security; now he was more direct and personal. "I've had it," he would say. "Consider me provoked." He stopped talking about Iraq and started talking about Saddam. In tennis, George would often taunt his opponents to gain a psychological edge. Now with Saddam he would do the same. He began purposely mispronouncing Saddam's name to emphasize the first rather than the second syllable of his name. By doing so, George was changing the Arab meaning of his name from "one who confronts" to "little boy who cleans the shoes of old men."

Competition helps the Bushes focus. In contrast to his uneven performance on domestic politics, George was focused and clear about his mission when it came to Iraq. The convoluted sentences were gone; instead, here was a leader who had military resolve and a steely nerve. And rather than relying on advisers for guidance, he was going to push this through himself.

On most issues George had been a consensus builder. But in this war he would make his own path. Few of his top advisers favored military action. General Colin Powell supported sanctions but no military invasion. Nick Brady, the treasury secretary and a good friend, talked about how the United States could "accommodate" and "adjust to" a Kuwait controlled by Iraq. His longtime friend Jimmy Baker, secretary of state, wanted a negotiated settlement. As George's subtle rival he asked George if he could go to Baghdad to bargain with the Iraqis; George refused.

One voice near the president who counseled a hard line was George W. Family members say that the father called his son less to talk strategy and more for support, and when it came to Iraq, W. took a hard line.

George quickly dispatched Secretary of Defense Dick Cheney to Saudi Arabia to meet with King Fahd, along with Gen. Norman Schwarzkopf, the head of Central Command, and Robert Gates of the CIA. They extended to the king greetings from his old friend George Bush and then showed him detailed satellite photos of what Saddam was up to.

GEORGE WAS VERY FAMILIAR WITH THE WAYS OF THE MIDDLE EAST. HE HAD done business in the region thirty years earlier, drilling for oil off the Kuwaiti coast. When his father was a member of the Senate Armed Services Committee, the old man filled him in on the complexities of the Middle East situation and the anguish he felt during the Suez Crisis in 1956. Later, as U.N. ambassador and CIA director, he had forged a close relationship with King Fahd. As VP, George had seen Fahd many times in the royal palace. The two men would have an official dinner with many guests present and then sit and chat for hours afterward, just the two of them and one or two aides. Given all this, George was well aware of the manner in which the Arab countries dealt with threats. If Western nations resisted their enemies, in the Arab world there was more often a dance of force and accommodation.

"My worry about the Saudis," George told advisers, "is that they're going to be the ones who bug out at the last minute and accept a puppet regime in Kuwait." To ensure that there were no unplesant surprises, he ordered the intelligence community to closely monitor the Saudis. NSA intercepts quickly revealed that some in the Saudi royal family were contemplating paying Saddam off with millions of dollars in oil money.

George began working the phones in a highly personal form of diplomacy that reflected how he had done business and played politics over the past forty years. He called King Fahd and Prince Bandar, the king's nephew and Saudi ambassador to Washington. Perhaps more than anyone, George understood the value that family contacts played in Saudi Arabia; the Bushes placed a similar primacy on family relationships. He also made dozens of calls to world leaders, from Mikhail Gorbachev to the emir of the United Arab Emirates. In the month of August alone he called sixty-two world leaders about the crisis. All the while he relied on NSA intercepts of foreign leaders' conversations as they talked among themselves.

Despite Saddam's naked aggression, many in the Middle East were shaky about how to respond. When Prince Bandar came to the White House for discussions, both men were frank. George said he worried about the Saudi commitment to expelling Saddam from Kuwait. Bandar for his part openly questioned American resolve. George took that comment personally. He had given his word, he told Bandar.

Questions were being raised by everyone, with the exception of Thatcher in Britain. Still, George remained confident. "I feel tension in the stomach and the neck," he wrote in his diary. "But I also feel a certain calmness when we talk about these matters. I know I am doing the right thing . . ."

Concern was being expressed in official Washington that what George Bush was asking for was wildly unrealistic. As diplomatic options went nowhere and war appeared inevitable, Pentagon briefers threw what they thought would be cold water on his plans. As he sat down for a Pentagon briefing in the early fall, the mood was sour. To expel Saddam, the military men told him, "We will require the Seventh Corps to move from Germany." This meant transferring two heavy divisions and an immense amount of logistical and support equipment. It would be an enormous undertaking, the biggest of its kind since the Second World War. Six carrier battle groups would also be needed, along with components from the National Guard and reserves. Bob Gates of the CIA came away with the clear impression that the briefing was meant to deter Bush from going ahead with his plans.

But after he absorbed it all, George pushed back his chair, smiled, and said, "Done! Come back if you need more." He then proceeded to walk out of the room. As Gates recalls, "These guys' jaws were absolutely on their chests."

IN EVERY AUGUST BUT ONE, GEORGE BUSH HAD GONE TO KENNEBUNKPORT for the summer. Even with the crisis looming in the Gulf, he was determined not to miss his time there in 1990. Changing his plans now would only encourage Saddam; he would not be captive in the White House, as Jimmy Carter had been during the hostage crisis. So to really tweak Saddam, the Bushes headed to Kennebunkport for a relaxing month of fishing, tennis, and cookouts. When George needed to talk to the media, he would show up in his K-port formals—a sport coat, starched white shirt, and club tie along with faded chinos and running shoes. All the while he continued his routine of golfing and fishing, taking Brent Scowcroft out on the water for bluefish while he was briefed on the situation in the Persian Gulf.

The family had gathered, as it always did, in August. Only this time they had a constant flow of visitors. When Prince Saud of Saudi Arabia came for a visit, the children were excited but Bar kept them at the beach while George discussed the crisis.

For George the prospect of war brought back events from his past. Family members remember his standing by himself among the rocks at Walker Point. When asked what was on his mind, he explained that he was replaying his experiences in the Pacific.

Family members tried to avoid discussions about Iraq, but Bar began reading up on the situation. Later she would sit down with a twenty-seven-page report from Amnesty International about human rights abuses in Saddam's Iraq: how they tortured handicapped children; how young children were shot in front of their parents; repeated rapes; tying people to ceiling fans by their arms so they would turn again and again. Bar was so horrified that she set the report down after two pages. Something needed to be done about that man, she said.

George W. came up from Texas. As he had been in 1988 during the campaign, the eldest son was a sounding board for his father. At times the president expressed doubts about what course to take. W., rock-hard as always, encouraged his father to do what he thought was right, regardless of the cost.

The two men would rise early and head over to the Cape Arundel golf course before 7 A.M. to catch a quick game. They would play eighteen holes in an hour and a half. It was an almost daily routine, and if the media pressed the president for answers to questions, W. would step forward and act as a shield. "Hey, hey!" he would shout. "Can't you wait until I finish hitting at least? My game is already bad, so when you are talking, my backswing is even worse."

The relationship between the two, which had been distant and strained at times, was changing. Confident and with direction for the first time in his life, W. was beginning to display an innate strength.

That summer was George W.'s first introduction to the world of geopolitics. As foreign leaders came and went, W. was often on hand for at least some of the socializing. Just as Sen. Pres Bush had given his children and grandchildren nice seats from which to watch history unfold, George made a conscious decision to allow future generations of the Bush clan to see as much of it as possible.

George's meetings in Kennebunkport were highly personal. When King Hussein of Jordan arrived, it meant seeing an old friend. When Prince Faisal of Saudi Arabia came, he was meeting with someone he had dealt with for more than two decades.

George's persistent diplomacy paid off. On November 27, the U.N. Security Council passed Resolution 678 authorizing the use of force to liberate Kuwait.

———

THAT WINTER THE FAMILY RETREATED TO CAMP DAVID, SNUGGLED IN THE cold, snow-capped Catoctin Mountains of western Maryland. As the deadline for war approached amid a flurry of diplomatic activity, George was under immense pressure. On Christmas Eve he went to bed and had a dream about his father. His dad was playing golf and George went to see him. "We embraced, and I told him I missed him very much," he recorded in his diary. "I could see him very clearly: big, strong, and highly respected . . ."

On Christmas Day all of the children were there—George W., Jeb, Neil, Marvin, and Doro. It was the first Christmas they had all been together in ages. They played games (the Bushes against the Marine guards) and reminisced. George tried hard not to seem moody, but he was concerned about what lay ahead. He wrote a letter to his children: "I guess what I want you to know as a father is this: Every human life is precious. When the question is asked 'How many lives are you willing to sacrifice'—it tears at my heart. The answer, of course, is none—none at all. We have waited to give sanctions a chance, we have moved a tremendous force so as to reduce the risk to every American soldier if force has to be used; but the question of loss of life still lingers and plagues the heart."

He worked hard to stay distracted. Much as he had done with Robin's death, he tried to immerse himself in activity. Sometimes he did it to a fault. Two days before the war started, Bar was sledding at Camp David with Arnold Schwarzenegger and his wife, Maria Shriver. As she sledded down the hill, out of control, George yelled, "Bail out, bail out!" But she held on tight and crashed into a tree. George laughed at the whole thing as Bar lay there with what turned out to be a broken leg. It didn't go over too well with Bar. When an ambulance came to take her to a hospital at the foot of the mountain, George elected to stay with the Schwarzeneggers. "I didn't handle it too well, I don't think," he recalled later.

The first phase of Desert Storm began with a massive aerial bombardment of Iraq on January 16, 1991. "I have never felt a day like this in my life," he wrote in his diary. "I am very tired. I didn't sleep well and this troubles me because I must go to the nation at 9 o'clock. My lower gut hurts, nothing like when I had the bleeding ulcer. But I am aware of it, and I take a couple of Mylantas."

Over the course of the next several weeks, Allied warplanes bombed Iraqi positions. George waited nervously to hear about any pilots who might be shot down. Barbara spent the time with her leg in a cast, watching CNN with her grandchildren. Old enough to be aware that it was grandpoppy who was involved in all of this, they were disturbed when they saw SCUD missiles striking Tel Aviv. Bar explained to them what was happening thousands of miles away. "We just talked about it, the things we were looking at," Bar later recalled. "I answered their questions."

The next morning George and Bar attended services at St. John's Episcopal Church. They sat and sang hymns with Dick Cheney and his wife, who sat in the pew behind them. Cheney passed him a note saying that things were going well. George and Bar said an extra prayer.

The American advance went quickly. In less than one hundred hours, General Schwarzkopf's forces had wreaked havoc on Iraqi units. Now a critical decision needed to be made. Hussein had been expelled from Kuwait, and his army was nearly broken. Should the Allies press ahead? Colin Powell and Dick Cheney called for an immediate cease-fire. General Schwarzkopf, in consultations with Powell, agreed. George accepted their advice and spoke to the nation. "Kuwait is liberated. Iraq's army is defeated. Our military objectives are met."

Then George and Bar retired to their White House residence with a small group of advisers. They sat and chatted with drinks in hand. Saddam Hussein was still in power, but probably not for long, they concluded. "I'm comfortable," George told Colin Powell. "No second thoughts."

In the days that followed, George expressed his belief that Saddam would not stay in power for long. Intelligence officials were convinced that his demise was imminent. That assessment had been an important factor in the decision to halt the Allied advance. For Bar, the end could not come soon enough. "I'd like to see him hung," she told reporters, and then quickly added: "If he were found guilty by a court, of course."

The stunning victory had come more quickly than anyone expected. George was confident that he had done what needed to be done. "Our pinpoint attacks have put Saddam out of the nuclear bomb–building business for a long time," he said. To make sure Saddam was gone for good, CIA covert operations designed to overthrow him quietly continued.

On March 6, George spoke before a joint session of Congress. It was the high point of his political career. His approval ratings put his popularity at 90 percent. One poll of white males in the South gave him an approval rating of 100 percent. George W. believed that things looked fine for 1992. "Do you think the American people are going to turn to a Democrat now?" he asked the media. But questions still loomed about whether his father really wanted the job.

Throughout the previous year it had become increasingly apparent that something was wrong with George. Patty Presock, his secretary, noticed that his handwriting was changing. No longer so clear, it was looping and slanted. Bar started to notice that his sleep patterns were erratic. Some nights he slept fine, but others he was wide-awake late at night or in the early morning hours. His clothes were loose; he was losing weight. His stamina was in decline and he had shortness of breath.

As the euphoria of the war faded, George continued to struggle through the battles that his son Neil was facing and his own difficult health condition. He was in a funk, almost depressed. It was something that the ever-sunny George had never really experienced before. Now at the pinnacle of his career, having achieved a stature that he had sought since 1964, George Bush was . . . ambivalent. Normally so outgoing and friendly, he would retreat and spend time alone. "Yesterday at Camp David I was a little down," he wrote his friend Alan Simpson. "I picked up two bright red leaves, and I did something I haven't done in the last 60 years. I put the leaves pressed into a heavy book in my little quiet office. I felt better—strange but I really did."

George was gearing up for an election that was destined to be difficult. Neil had become a poster-boy for the savings and loan scandal, and George believed that he was responsible for ruining his son's life. The war had gone well, but the economy was limping. The breaking of his read-my-lips pledge had angered many in his Republican base. As a result, he was facing challenges from three sides. Former presidential aide and commentator Pat Buchanan was entering the GOP primary, challenging him from the right, contending that he had failed to carry the conservative mantle inherited from Ronald Reagan. The Democrats had a crowded field of aspirants who were attacking him from the left, claiming that he had not done enough to help the economy. And then there was Ross Perot, who was challenging him from . . . well, somewhere.

It had begun for Perot shortly after George was elected president. In December 1988, noted the *Texas Monthly*, "Listening to Perot, one expects a declaration of candidacy at any minute—so evident is his scorn for the dummies in Washington and his sense that he could do better." Ever since the Texas days, Perot had been down on the Bushes. Perhaps it was George's rejection of his offer to head up an oil venture; but whatever the reason, Perot was angry and he had George in his sights. Over the course of the previous decade, Perot had slammed George's handling of prisoners of war, the drug war, and taxes. He had also criticized the administration's handling of the Gulf War. "We rescued the emir of Kuwait," he said. "Now, if I knock on your door and say I'd like to borrow your son to go to the Middle East so that this dude with several wives, who's got a minister for sex to find him a virgin every Thursday night, can have his throne back, you'd probably hit me in the mouth." Perot even went so far as to hire private detectives to dig up dirt on George W. and Jeb.

It was Bar who first fired a shot across Perot's bow, calling some of his comments "just nuts." Perot was furious, and, for a variety of reasons, threw his hat in the ring. As he later admitted, "I did this [run for the presidency] because I was upset at Bush."

Perot's entry into the race created a new dynamic. Given his record as a success in the business world, many were immediately attracted to Perot's no-nonsense style. He talked about reducing the deficit and attacked the NAFTA agreement, all the while spinning stories about Bush conspiracies. He claimed at one point that Bush minions were plotting to disrupt his daughter Carolyn's wedding as a way of getting back at him.

Often Perot's conspiracy theories were written off as fantasies. But when Perot told the FBI that the Bush campaign was trying to bug his offices, the bureau believed him. The FBI recorded Perot's voice on tape, and then an undercover agent arranged to meet with James Oberwetter, a friend of W.'s who was heading up the Bush campaign in Texas. Oberwetter met with the agent outside of his office and was offered a tape he said was from a secret Perot phone conversation in exchange for money. Oberwetter refused it and walked away. When President George Bush learned what the FBI had done, he was furious. Perot was "a bastard" and "very dangerous," he told one friend. And he vowed never to forgive the FBI. "I always defended the FBI," he said. "But not anymore."

Publicly George held his fire, but the family rallied. Pressy Bush proclaimed that Perot was "a psychopath," pure and simple.

George had always been a fighter. In every election he had been in, George was always determined to be the last man standing, out-hustling and out-working every other candidate in the field. But family members saw that the fire was not really in him. The family had faced difficult challenges over the past two years. Neil's troubles had haunted both George and Bar, their daughter Doro had gone through a difficult divorce, and George's health was weakening. He had an overactive thyroid, which was causing an irregular heart rhythm. He was taking five different medications, and friends and family could see how they were affecting him.

Gerry Bemiss recalls seeing George before the debate in Richmond. The president flew in on Air Force One, and Bemiss rode with him in the limo on the way to the debate.

"He was not himself," he told us. "Tired, his eyes seemed hollow. I knew something was wrong." The medication had taken effect and he was tired. It was during this debate that he infamously glanced at his wristwatch as if he had something better to do.

The medications also made him irritable. When a heckler yelled at him on the campaign trail, he uncharacteristically snapped, "Shut up and sit down."

Even with the Gulf War victory, the economy was in recession. And with attacks coming from three directions, it was no surprise that George's poll ratings were way down. The campaign tried everything. They even brought in Professor Robert Wellstein of the University of Michigan, an expert in setting up statistical models, to determine how people would respond to different messages. He had been doing it for years for the automobile industry, telling Detroit what kind of cars people might buy. If it worked for General Motors, why not try it on voters?

It was an amalgamation of personalities and people who seemed to fit George's style. But the campaign suffered from the problem personified by George Bush: the division between governing and campaigning. George had always believed that the two jobs were separate entities, distant cousins at best, and that campaigning should never dirty the world of governing. This created a tension that was never really resolved. As he had done during the 1988 election, George W. traveled to Washington to try to help the campaign focus. But his efforts failed. As the summer in Houston turned hot, George W. did something very strange: He stayed home.

Fifteen hundred miles away in Florida, younger brother Jeb was doing the same thing. Indeed, both sons seemed to make a conscious decision to stay at home during the 1992 election and prepare for their own campaigns in 1994. George W. was campaigning for his father in safe places like San Antonio and Houston. Jeb was spending lots of time speaking to Republicans in central Florida. These states were hardly up for grabs. They were, however, states that gave both sons the opportunity to forge relationships with party activists in the event of a run for electoral office.

As George continued to sink in the polls, there was a bid to recruit Jim Baker to leave the State Department and take over the campaign. It was not something that he needed to do. As far as Baker was concerned, the problems lay with George, who seemed lethargic and lacked focus. George took the criticism personally. "If you're so damn smart," he retorted, "How come you're not president?"

Conflicts also continued with the media, which George had made a concerted effort to win over during his presidency. Unlike Reagan, George held frequent and long press conferences during his tenure. He invited reporters to the White House residence and tried to forge relationships with them much as he had done through most of his career. But despite his best efforts, he largely failed. The coverage was decidedly negative and even slanted.

George's image as a rich man out of touch with American realities became fixed when he was visiting the National Grocers Association in Orlando, Florida. His hosts took him to a grocery scanner display set up by the National Cash Register company.

"This is the scanner, the new scanner?" George asked.

"Of course, it looks like the typical scanner you'd see in the grocery store," said NCR representative Bob Graham. "But there's one big difference."

Graham gave George a little card with a ripped up and jumbled universal product code number on it. The machine scanned it perfectly.

"Isn't that something," said George. He was simply "amazed."

The White House press corps used a pool reporter for these sorts of events, and the man on the hot seat was Andrew Rosenthal of the *New York Times*. Rosenthal, son of A. M. Rosenthal, the paper's onetime managing editor, put together a story that seemed to indicate that George had never seen a UPC scanner. The headline said it all: BUSH ENCOUNTERS THE SUPERMARKET, AMAZED.

George was furious. He wrote to Arthur Ochs Sulzberger, chairman of the paper's board, explaining how the report had been distorted. As Sulzberger later admitted in a letter, "There was no question that Andrew Rosenthal's article on the supermarket electronic checkout system was 'just a teeny-weeny bit naughty.' Little did any of us expect that the story would be picked up by others, including some not too subtle political cartoonists." But the *Times* never did run a clarification.

The family's ire rose further when they gathered at Kennebunkport in August. George was answering questions about the Middle East and his family was gathered around. Bar was there as were the grandchildren and Dottie. Suddenly CNN reporter Mary Tillotson of CNN fired off a question. Did he have an affair with Jennifer Fitzgerald?

George stood there stone-silent. His granddaughter Noelle started crying. Bar shielded her and led her away.

"No. It's a lie."

The Bushes were at war with the media as much as they were with the Democrats. Marlin Fitzwater called reporters "lazy bastards."

Bush tried to get himself fired up, to get those competitive juices flowing. In the final weeks of the campaign he started calling Al Gore "Ozone Man" because of his environmental views. Clinton and Gore were a couple of "bozos," he said. He would trust his dog Millie to handle foreign policy before he would trust the Democrats.

Despite his lack of focus, George managed to climb back into the race. Allegations about Bill Clinton's personal life seemed to trouble the American people. With the election only days away, a CNN poll put George only two points behind. It seemed as if he might actually pull it off.

But in Washington, Iran-Contra independent counsel Lawrence Walsh had been working feverishly. The grand jury had looked at Secretary of Defense Caspar Weinberger's diary and found an entry that seemed to indicate that George had known that the sale of arms to Iran was linked to the release of hostages. One of Walsh's assistants released the information to the media. The Friday before the election, front pages around the country blared the news: '86 WEINBERGER NOTES CONTRADICT BUSH ACCOUNT ON IRAN ARMS DEAL (New York Times); and BUSH STANCE, IRAN-CONTRA NOTE AT ODDS, WEINBERGER MEMO SAYS PRESIDENT "FAVORED" ARMS HOSTAGE PLAN (Washington Post).

What had been a neck-and-neck race changed immediately. Clinton was still at 39 percent, but George dropped 7 points to 32 percent. All of those voters had defected to Perot, who jumped to 19 percent in the polls.

The media pressed George for comments. Campaigning in Wisconsin, he bristled at the questions. "I thought you might bring all this up and dwell on it," he snapped after persistent questioning. "I think most people concede that the media has been very unfair." It was in his mind a replay of what had happened to his father thirty-eight years earlier: an eleventh-hour media story that could not be refuted.

The night of the election the family gathered in the family's suite at the Houstonian Hotel. If in 1988 they had been focused and intense, filled with anticipation, this time the mood was different. W. was walking around in gym shorts. Others were dressed in bathrobes. As the returns came in, everyone was quiet. Perot pulled in more than 20 percent of the vote in nine states. When the final numbers put Clinton over the top, George Bush sat there stunned. While family members had seen the writing on the wall months earlier, the president had never quite believed that he would lose. "He never thought that the American people would elect someone like Bill Clinton," says Nancy Bush Ellis.

Family members quietly got dressed for the concession speech. As they headed for the Houston Convention Center, George turned to his family and said, "Okay, let's go do this with style and dignity."

It was a stunning defeat, and the pain of the loss would not leave him quickly. "It hurts like hell," he would tell family and friends.

TWO WEEKS AFTER HIS LOSS, GEORGE SAT AND HELD HIS MOTHER'S HAND IN Greenwich. She was frail and old, seemingly fighting for every breath. Her whole adult life she had been the heart and soul of the family. "None of us," recalled Bucky Bush, "had ever seen our mother so weak and frail. She had been so strong, always." In the final years she had divided her time between Kennebunkport and the old pink bungalow that Pres Bush had bought in Hobe Sound, Florida, in 1960. Her youngest brother, Lou, lived next door, and daughter Nancy came down regularly to visit. She had round-the-clock nurses and a tiny black poodle named Petey, who would sit by her side. With the exception of a Thursday morning Bible class, she rarely got out.

When she breathed her last at 5:05 P.M. on November 19, everyone in the family cried. The loss of the presidency, which had hurt George so much, didn't seem to matter much anymore. "It's immaterial when you think of Mother, love, faith, life and death," he wrote in his diary.

More than ten years earlier Dottie had written out what she wanted at her funeral. Her instructions were explicit. She wanted a traditional Episcopal funeral with readings from the Book of Common Prayer. She had requested that the service be held in the 127-seat chapel at Christ Church in Greenwich, not the larger chapel. So, many were forced to gather outside to honor her memory.

The whole Bush-Walker clan seemed to be there, four generations in all, along with hundreds of friends from the community. The crowd was so large that it spilled out into the sidewalk. George and Bar sat in the front row but didn't speak. Instead, it was Pressy who had been asked to stand up and give the main eulogy. He spoke about his mother's indomitable spirit. Then a letter she had written for family and friends was read by her youngest son, Bucky.

"This is a service of gratitude to God for the easiest life ever given anyone to live on this earth and all because of LOVE. From my mother's knee I learned to know Jesus and that He would always be with me if at night in bed I would just tell Him any mean, selfish, even untrue things I had done during the day, He would lift them from my mind and I would awake refreshed, and later along the way if there was a steep incline, He would take my hand and help me up the hill. How right she was!

"In addition to Jesus' love I had the love of a saintly mother, loving father, sister and four brothers, all of whom stood fast through the years and brought wonderful in-laws into my life.

"Then, best of all, God sent into my life the most perfect human that ever lived and we had fifty-one glorious years together and he will be with me through eternity. When we first married I used to worry as I knew God's commandment 'Thou shalt love the Lord thy God with all thy heart and all thy soul and all thy mind' and I knew that was the way I was loving Pres, and then it came to me that God was showing me how great 'finite' love could be so that I would have a glimpse of what God's infinite love must be, and I could accept both in my heart."

Following the funeral, Dottie was cremated and the ashes were buried in the family's plot in a Greenwich cemetery. They were placed next to Pres and near her granddaughter Robin, who had died forty years earlier.

As the service ended, the members of the family slowly drifted back to their lives. "You really felt it was the passing of an era," Caroline Bush Cole told us. "For so long she had been the strength—the glue—of the family. And you couldn't help wondering what would hold it together now."

PART THREE

# CLIMB ANEW

#### CHAPTER 36

# OPERATION DESERT LOVE

W ITH THE DEVASTATING LOSS IN NOVEMBER, GEORGE FELL into a funk. Usually outgoing, he retreated from his relationships and the family. Walker Point, which had for so long been a retreat for the entire Bush-Walker clan, was now reserved for the immediate family; George and Bar wanted the place for themselves, their children, and grandchildren.

Longtime friends found that when they called him up, he was distant. Gerry Bemiss, who had known the man since childhood, found it impossible to get him to go fishing. Instead of his longtime friends, George became increasingly fond of celebrities. He would go fishing with Ted Williams and invite Kevin Costner to spend the weekend, then seemed to relish the opportunity to tell others whom he was spending time with. Nephew John Ellis recalled getting a telephone call from the former president.

"Guess who's coming over today to play golf?"

"I don't know."

"Roger."

Ellis thought it was Roger Ailes, George's former media adviser. "I didn't know Ailes played golf."

"Not Roger Ailes. Roger Clemens."

Gerry Bemiss and others were frustrated by all of this display. "I would tell him, George, you're a former president; you are the biggest celebrity there is. But he would just look at me and smile, and move on."

Ellis believes that these celebrity visits were less about celebrity worship than emotional self-protection. "They wanted to be around people who couldn't see the pain; and the celebrities couldn't see the pain," he told us. "They can bask in each other's celebrity."

Unwilling to believe that her husband had made mistakes or that the American people had simply made a bad choice, Bar blamed Jim Baker for failing to bring order to the campaign. Barbara, the arbiter of family relations, deemed that Baker was no longer a close family friend. After that he was no longer visible at many family functions, and the slights became obvious to everyone. At the opening of the George H. W. Bush Presidential Library in 1997, family members were shocked not to see Baker in one of the limousines that had been reserved for close friends and former cabinet officers. Instead, he rode to the event on a bus.

Baker believed that he had been singled out. He was being made a scapegoat for the failings of the entire administration and for George Bush himself. The feud would last until November 2000, when Jim Baker would go to Florida to lead the legal battle for George W.'s presidential race.

"The fact is that both Barbara and Jim Baker were right," said John Ellis. "Jimmy was right that George should have been slapped around and told to get with the program, sit up in his chair, watch his posture, and either do it or not do it. There is in the Bush-Walker clan a sort of—something happens that leads it on occasion to close ranks in this kind of mindless way, and it closed in this mindless way when Barbara was leading it against Jim Baker. That said, it is also true that Jimmy Baker worrying about what his title would be was totally unimportant. You either have the franchise or you don't. Jim Baker, stop whining about it and get your shoulder to the wheel and go. And if you don't want to, get out of the way for people who do. But don't go around telling people how screwed up they are at the White House. So both sides I think were right."

DESPITE ALL THE FINGER-POINTING AND THE SUBTLE DEPRESSION, SPIRITS were lifted in early April 1993 when George and Bar boarded a 747 outfitted with new carpets, couches, a royal bedroom suite, a formal dining room, and several posh guest rooms. They were heading to Kuwait at the invitation of the royal family. Along for the trip were Marvin and Neil and their daughters-in-law Laura and Sharon.

A few days before the Bushes arrived, seventeen men were apprehended at the Kuwait-Iraqi border. Their vehicles contained hundreds of pounds of plastic explosives and cloth belts designed to be worn by suicide bombers. They had grenades and detonator mechanisms.

The evidence indicated that the Iraqis had undertaken to kill George and members of his family. Twelve of the seventeen suspects were Iraqis, and the other five, while Kuwaiti citizens, were originally from Iraq. Ra'ad al-Assadi, the suspected ringleader, confessed to being a colonel in Iraqi secret intelligence, stationed in Basra.

Soon it became clear that they had support from the Iraqi government. Documents revealed that the men had trained at a military facility outside of Basra, which was tightly controlled by the military. The cars themselves had been stolen in 1990 during Iraq's occupation of Kuwait and still bore Kuwaiti license tags. FBI officials concluded that the group was "way too sophisticated, involving things too sophisticated, to be just some crazies with a complaint against the president."

With heavy Secret Service protection and Kuwaiti security personnel on high alert, the Bushes elected to go on with the visit despite the apparent conspiracy to kill them. At the Kuwait City airport, George and his family were greeted by whirling sword dancers, beating drums, and flower-bearing girls along with signs that read YOU ARE THE SUNSHINE IN OUR LIVES and WELCOME BOOSH. Thousands of children lined the airport access road, chanting, "Thank you, Bush." Others waved small U.S. flags or balloons.

For three days there was celebration and feasting. Sheikh Jaber al-Ahmad al-Sabah hosted a dinner for seven hundred men, and the emir presented George with Kuwait's highest honor, the Mubarak al Kabeer chain. (Bar was treated to a separate feast by Kuwaiti women.) He was also given a prized racing camel as a gift and an antique Arabian door inscribed with the names of U.S. soldiers killed during Desert Storm. As he left, his motorcade ran by thousands of signs that read SALAM ALAIKUM, YA AZEEM (PEACE BE ON YOU, OH GREAT ONE). One local merchant donated ninety-six bottles of perfume to be sprayed along Bush's route. But this was more than a simple celebration. For the Kuwaiti royal family, George and his family were now friends. "The visit has been a milestone in the history of Kuwait, about which we will keep telling our sons and our grandsons time after time," said one official announcement. "We await his next visit."

And other visits there would be, by both George and his sons. For Marvin Bush, the admiration of his father in the wake of the Gulf War proved to be particularly helpful. After graduating from the University of Virginia in 1979, Marvin had gone to work for Moseley, Hallgarten, Estabrook & Weeden, a Boston-based brokerage firm where he worked in investment management. Then he had gone on to Shearson Lehman Brothers and had taken a stake in a number of Blockbuster Video franchises. On the advice of family friend Mercer Reynolds, he invested in Mid-American Waste Systems, a Cincinnati waste management company. Three years later they had pocketed fifteen times the original investment. By 1993, he was getting ready to launch a money market investment firm called Winston Partners Group with a friend from college.

While in Kuwait, Marvin was introduced to the extended al-Sabah clan, which had ruled Kuwait since the nineteenth century. As a result, he became partners with Mishal al-Sabah, whose investment firm KuwAm invested in a variety of American companies. Within months of his return, Marvin was on the board of Securacom (later renamed Stratesec), a high-tech security firm where al-Sabah was a heavy investor. The company had security contracts with, among others, Dulles Airport in Washington, D.C.

Gratitude also came from the royal family in the nearby United Arab Emirates. The family had a large stake in the firm IAT, which in 1994 purchased Fresh Del Monte, a large producer of foodstuffs. Both Marvin and Jeb were placed on the company's board of directors in 1995. When the company bought real estate in south Florida, it used Jeb's Codina group to broker the deal.

Marvin would return regularly to the region, enjoying the goodwill that his father had developed there. In October 1998 he was in the United Arab Emirates meeting with the ruler, Sheikh Zayed bin Sultan al-Nahyan. He would also attend functions of the Saudi Arabian Chamber of Commerce in Riyadh.

Marvin's brother Neil was also active in seeking business relationships with the Gulf States. After the pain of Silverado Savings and Loan, he returned to live in Houston. During the family's visit in 1993, he raised the idea of several business ventures with the royal families of both Kuwait and Saudi Arabia. Over the course of the next decade, the Saudis would invest in both a high-tech company and an education software company that Neil had started.

#### CHAPTER 37

# TURNING POINT

W HEN HE MADE THE ANNOUNCEMENT, IT CAME AS LITTLE surprise to the family; everyone had been expecting it. Jeb had been methodically planning to run for office for years. With his father's advice that he needed to be financially secure first, he had worked hard to build up a number of businesses in Miami. Now, with a net worth over $2 million, he was finally ready to take the plunge.

In the days following his father's loss to Bill Clinton, Jeb had grown increasingly committed to the idea of taking on Gov. Lawton Chiles in Florida. Chiles was a long-serving politician who had been in the U.S. Senate before running for governor. "Walkin" Lawton was a Florida political legend; but he was also in political trouble. Poll numbers put his popularity in the high thirties.

By Christmastime in 1993, Jeb had mentioned his plans to several family members, who were all enthused about it. By January he was all but set and specifically asked family members to help him win. This was a turning point in his life that had long been expected. Jeb was the one who might be president one day, who had flirted with running for Congress, had served in the cabinet of Gov. Bob Martinez, who kept up on all of the issues. When word reached George and Bar that Jeb was going to take the plunge, both were enthusiastic. His father responded simply, "Go for it." Jeb had prepared for this; he had worked hard for this; he was ready to dive in.

But along the way there came a surprise. And it was the sort of surprise that Jebbie had come to expect from his big brother. If Jeb's bid to run for governor was expected and encouraged, news that George W. wanted to run for governor in Texas sent shock waves through the family.

Most in the family thought at first that it was another one of his jokes. When they found out he was serious, almost everyone declared it was a mistake. He went to his mother. "Mother, I've made up my mind. Laura and I are fixin' to announce for governor." "You can't win," snapped Bar. That was her simple answer, and Big George thought the same thing; so did W.'s levelheaded brother Marvin. Most Bush family friends shared former Bush aide Pete Tee-ley's assessment: "Jeb's got his feet on the ground. He doesn't suffer from the ego problems of George."

About the only one in the family who said give it a crack was his cousin John Ellis.

The concern was that Gov. Ann Richards was popular and effective in Texas, and that George would be taking on a legend in Texas politics. But they were also concerned about whether George W. had the savvy to run the race. As Bar put it, Jeb is "more like his father if the truth be known." He could think quickly, be politic, and be polite. George W. is more like his mother, she said. He spoke quick and asked questions later. He could show his temper and let people know exactly what he thought about them. "This is not a compliment to him," she added.

Truth be known, both Jeb and George W. had seen the handwriting on the wall early in their father's campaign. They saw the campaign's chaos and detected that their father wasn't completely into the race as he had been be-fore. They saw how fatigued he was and how he seemed to lack the neces-sary focus to win. So they thought ahead, beyond 1992.

Cousin John Ellis recalled, "I talked to George W. a lot during the 1992 campaign. He didn't come up to Washington like he did the last time [in 1988]. I was very alarmist about the campaign. I thought they would lose New Hampshire. W. never said, but his actions speak volumes. He didn't go to Washington; he used the entire campaign in 1992 to position himself in Texas. He had no illusions about the ultimate outcome after the convention. He was completely disconnected from the campaign after the convention, except what was going on in Texas."

George W. was able to effectively use the campaign as a springboard to develop contacts with Republican activists around the state of Texas. That and his good work as head of the Texas Rangers propelled him into a legiti-mate Republican standard-bearer in a matter of a year. For Jeb, his brother's announced plans were frustrating. As cousin John Ellis recalled, "I think Jeb felt, 'Well wait a minute, I've been the one doing the work here—I've been secretary of commerce of Florida, head of a local Republican committee, and now George is using the '92 campaign to run for governor.' He used it to shore up his base in Texas—and now all of a sudden they are running for governor together. That's where they started teasing each other back and forth."

Despite the awkwardness for both, the decision by the two eldest sons to seek elective office was a source of pride for their parents. After the painful

Above, Pres Bush with President Eisenhower. Bush was one of the earliest Republicans to encourage Ike to run for president. Once in the Oval Office, Eisenhower was a close friend and golfing partner of the senator from Connecticut. (*George Bush Presidential Library*) Below, Pres Bush (at left) with Governor John Lodge of Connecticut (center). In Washington, Bush forged alliances with liberals, conservatives, Democrats and Republicans—many alliances that he would pass on to his children. (*George Bush Presidential Library*)

Above, George Bush with his brother Bucky (left) and his sons in 1953. Ambitious and on the go, George didn't see much of his boys. "It was a matriarchal home," says Jeb Bush. *(Prescott S. Bush family scrapbook)* Below, the Bush boys, Little George, Jeb, and Neil, with little brother Marvin, in 1956. The boys were competitive and fought constantly. Jeb and Little George would eventually become rivals in adulthood. *(Prescott S. Bush family scrapbook)*

Above, George and Bar with their children George W., Doro, Neil, and Marvin. George W. struggled the most with living up to expectations and his name, but it was a problem for his brothers, too. *(Prescott S. Bush family scrapbook)*

Left, George and Bar await election results with the children during the 1970 Senate race. *(Prescott S. Bush family scrapbook)*

Right, George Bush as ambassador to the United Nations. With ambitions to be president, he attached himself to Nixon. In 1968 his father tried to help broker a deal to make his son the vice presidential candidate. *(George Bush Presidential Library)*

Below, the wedding of George W. and Laura Bush in 1977. Says one family member: "Laura and Bar have that same quality, in that the two Georges can get a little bit full of themselves. And those two women in a sentence or even with a wink or a look can get them right back down to where they belong." *(Prescott S. Bush family scrapbook)*

Above, Jeb and Neil working on their father's presidential campaign in 1980. If George W. was the prodigal, Jeb was the dutiful son. Always the first to arrive and the last to leave the campaign office, he had early political ambitions. *(Bettmann/Corbis)* Below, the Bush family at the inauguration ball in 1980. *(George Bush Presidential Library)*

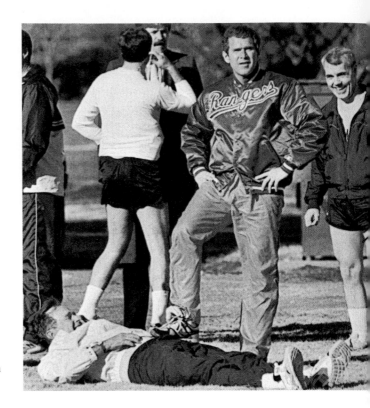

Right, George W. Bush joking around with his father in 1990. Long considered the family clown with little in the way of a political future, George W. was quietly plotting his own career in politics. *(Bettmann/Corbis)*

Below, the Bushes with the Reagans in the vice president's residence. While the men would move from rivals to close friends, relations between the women remained cold. *(George Bush Presidential Library)*

Above, the president's son Neil Bush testifying before Congress over the failure of Silverado Savings and Loan. Eager to prove himself to his brothers and parents, Neil dove in to a series of financial deals that ended him in legal trouble. He would blame his parents for his situation. *(Bettmann/Corbis)* Below, Jeb Bush on the campaign trail for governor, running the same year as his brother George. The year 1994 would prove to be the turning point in the dynasty. "Everyone thought George would lose and Jeb would win." *(Najlah Feanny/Corbis Saba)*

Above, Jeb and George embrace at a rally in Florida. Though they were longtime rivals within the family, often going long periods without speaking to each other, the crisis in Florida during the 2000 election would bring them back together. *(Brooks Kraft/Corbis)* Below, the former president relaxes on the golf course with his sons President George W. Bush and Governor Jeb Bush. Active involvement in both their careers has kept him at the center of America's most successful political dynasty. *(Brooks Kraft/Corbis)*

loss in 1992, it gave them a sense of affirmation. "They know it's ugly," Bar said in 1993, "and they're still willing to do it. In a way, that sort of vindicates our life."

---

JEB WAS OUT OF THE GATE FAST. HE HAD WORKED HARD OVER THE PAST decade to put together the sort of financial picture in his own life to make a run possible, so win or lose he knew that his family would be taken care of. He was now worth more than $2.25 million and his income in 1993 would be $1.65 million. In addition to his real estate work, he now had a stake in the new Jacksonville Jaguars football franchise, a portion of a shoe importing firm called Oriental Trading Corporation, a partnership that sold water pumps in the Third World called Bush-El Trading Corporation, and commissions coming from a small real estate company called U.S. Asia Realty. The company, headed by Richard Lawless, a veteran of the CIA, handled real estate transactions for Asian investors. Lawless had reportedly only a few years earlier worked as a private emissary for then vice president Bush to arrange the release of hostages in Lebanon.

In February 1993 Jeb announced his plans to run for governor. He hired Houston political consultant David Hill and Washington media consultant Alex Castellanos to work on the campaign.

But the path would not be easy. Also interested in the GOP nomination was State Sen. Ander Crenshaw, the president of the Florida Senate, and two members of the Florida cabinet: Insurance Commissioner Tom Gallagher and Secretary of State Jim Smith. All could count on having a steady fundraising machine in place, and none faced the challenge of being dismissed simply as "George Bush's son."

For all the friends that the family had, there were also plenty of enemies. One city council candidate in Bradenton had promised, "I'll shoot Jeb Bush if he's elected." To make the matter more troubling, the police actually confiscated a loaded .25-caliber pistol from the man's home.

The other candidates might have been better established and better able to count on plenty of special-interest money from companies doing business in Florida, but all of this was child's play in comparison to the Bush family money machine. All those family friends on Bar's Christmas card list and those who had been political donors to George H. W. Bush's campaigns were now getting letters asking them to give to Jeb's campaign. The results were, to say the least, impressive. In the first six months, Jeb raised more than $630,000. His leading contender could manage at most just half of that. Both his mom and dad chipped in $500 (George listed his occupation as "retiree" and Bar as "homemaker.") Checks also came from Marvin, Uncle Pres, Aunt Nancy, and brother Neil. Even more checks arrived from family friends like Bob Mosbacher, Marlin Fitzwater, and other members of George's father's cabinet.

For George Bush, life outside of the White House was a complete readjustment. The first few weeks of 1993 he would wake up and grope unsuccessfully for the button located beside his White House bed that would send a servant with coffee. He was also having trouble driving. Neither George nor Bar had been on the road without a driver in more than a decade. For twelve years they had had someone to chauffeur them around. But Bar for one seemed freed by it all. In the weeks after they left the White House, she was participating in, of all things, a lip-sync contest on a Caribbean cruise ship.

Jeb's announcement in Florida helped shake them from the blue period they were going through. It gave them a campaign, a race, a purpose, a goal; and the Bushes always work best with a fixed goal in mind.

To win in Florida, Jeb was going to need a lot of ingredients that his parents simply couldn't offer. But one that he did need and that they could provide was plenty of money. To get his name out to voters, to buy the necessary TV time, they needed to raise millions just to win the primary. So George and Bar started making frequent trips to Florida to host a flurry of fund-raisers for Jeb.

In November, George arrived in Boca Raton to participate in a celebrity tennis tournament. He was as competitive as ever when he played doubles with his partner, Chris Evert. He chose not to be miked during his doubles match, concerned that his competitive spirit might lead him to utter an expletive that he'd rather not share with the audience. But if there were any doubts whether he had forgotten his loss a year earlier to Bill Clinton, they were wiped away. As he smashed a winning shot against Regis Philbin and Billie Jean King, he was heard to exclaim, "Kill Bubba!"

After the tournament, George gave a series of speeches throughout south Florida to bring in the donors for Jeb. And bring them in he did. One luncheon in Naples yielded more than $230,000—any of his opponents would need weeks to raise that amount. In the first few months of 1994, George would hold more than nine fund-raisers for his son. Beyond Florida, the Bushes held fund-raisers for Jeb in their hometown of Houston. The family's efforts were critical to his fund-raising success. More than half of the $7 million he would raise for his campaign came from fund-raisers in Florida featuring his parents and fund-raisers out of the state sponsored by friends of the family.

But while the money was good, it also created a dilemma for the young candidate. By taking advantage of his father's limelight, he risked being in his father's shadow. When his father was speaking to the crowd, talking up Jeb, the son was taking second billing to the father. Jeb was a warm-up speaker and his father was the star. At some events Jeb even found himself stepping out of photos.

And yet the father was emotionally overcome by what his son was doing. He had watched as vice president and then later as president as his son worked methodically to erect his network in Florida. Now, seeing his second-eldest running for office was an overwhelming experience. At a campaign luncheon in early 1994, he went to the podium and made a few jokes about life after the White House. Then, in a cracked voice, he said, "I have concluded that what really counts in life is family . . . it's faith . . . and it's friends. We Bushes have been triply blessed in each single department. And the pride I have in my son, no . . ."

The words simply wouldn't come out; he dropped his head and started sobbing. Jeb started to tear up, too, and bounded up from the audience and embraced his father in a bear hug.

"Sorry," Jeb said over the applause of the audience.

This was a time of deep emotion for both. When father and son appeared the next day in Orlando, it was Jeb who struggled. He fought back tears when he described his father as "the man I love more than any other on the planet." When the father later campaigned for George W. in Texas, there would be no similar epiphany or overwhelming expression of emotion.

———

IN 1993, JEB WAS WORRIED ABOUT RAISING THE MONEY HE WOULD NEED TO challenge Lawton Chiles; George W. on the other hand was worried about Jose Canseco. The slugger for the Texas Rangers was being paid $4.1 million a year to hit balls out into the seats and he was good at it. But then someone in the dugout had the bright idea of actually letting the slugger *pitch* in a game against the Boston Red Sox. Canseco took to the mound, wound up, and let it rip. He came out of the game moments later with a torn ulnar ligament in the right elbow. He was lost for the season.

George W. was putting together his plans to run for governor in 1994, but before he did that he had baseball details to attend to. The Texas Rangers were, by any business measure, a successful venture. They were making money, and with the new ballpark in Arlington the value of the team had skyrocketed. Now if they could only get the team to actually win.

"George always loved his work with the Rangers for two reasons," his uncle Pres Bush said. "He loves business, but more than that he just loves the game of baseball."

Whether the team was winning or not, George W. was committed to the game. And when a meeting of baseball owners was held to discuss changes to the schedule, he was emphatic about it. Concerned about declining revenues and interested in expanding the playoffs, the owners were floating a proposal to include wild-card teams and add another round to the playoffs. It was a popular idea with both the owners and the commissioner. But when the owners' meeting was held in May, George W. was unconvinced. Knowing that he was alone in his opposition, he made a speech anyway. He explained how it would hurt the traditions of the game, about how the traditions needed to be respected. By the accounts of those in the room he was eloquent and impassioned. But when the vote came, it was tallied 1–27; George W. was alone in his views. He had known that before he went in, yet despite the overwhelming opposition he had gone ahead and stood his ground anyway.

Baseball was taking up a lot of his time, and since politics threatened to take even more, Laura was not enthusiastic over W.'s decision to run. She had a comfortable life, a North Dallas home with a pool, three fireplaces, and, most important for her, a library. Her two daughters Jenna and Barbara were enjoying a relatively anonymous life with their friends at school. Laura's instincts toward privacy were strong. She had seen how public attention had hurt the family. Neil was still reeling from the savings and loan scandal; you could see it in his eyes. And George and Bar were still hurt by the losses in November. For Laura, going into politics just didn't seem to make a whole lot of sense. But this was something that W. wanted to do.

W. contacted his father's former aide and his friend Karl Rove about putting together a campaign. Rove had drifted into the Bushes' lives in 1973 when he was with the College Republicans and George was chairman of the RNC. Like so many in the circle of Bush family friends, Rove stayed in orbit for the next two decades. Ever since his first encounter with George H. W. Bush, Rove had been part of the team, working on George's PAC and his political campaign in 1980 and offering W. advice for his 1978 campaign.

After the 1980 election, Karl Rove had stayed in Texas and developed a political consulting firm. He set up shop in Austin, Texas, when there were few Republicans around. But Rove had worked to change that, and by the early 1990s he had a string of political successes to trumpet.

Rove would be for W. what Jimmy Baker and later Lee Atwater had been for his father. Someone who could do the heavy lifting of politics—organize the events, coordinate the campaign, detect the land mines. As his father had done with Jim Baker, W. would confide completely in Rove and trust him with everything. In return he expected complete loyalty.

For Rove, this political marriage proposal was impossible to resist. He'd had a political crush on George W. Bush for almost twenty years. Rove and W. had met in 1973 when working for his father. When W. would come back to Washington to visit his parents while attending Harvard Business School in Boston, it was Rove who picked him up at the airport or train station and gave him the keys to the family car. Rove was immediately struck by the young man. He had "huge amounts of charisma, swagger, cowboy boots, flight jacket, wonderful smile, just charisma—you know, wow." It was a contrast to both Rove and the father, and a nice change from the uptight days of Watergate. Even then Rove had thought briefly about the possibility of turning the roguish son into a political candidate. And W. would confide in Rove his interest in politics on a grand scale long before he would confide in the family. Unlike the clan, which was familiar with the wisecracking, carousing, George W. the jokester, Rove never quite saw that side of him. As a result he didn't have that baggage of bad memories when he interacted with W.

W. also tapped Karen Hughes, executive director of the Republican Party of Texas, to be his press spokesperson. Like his grandfather and father, who had elevated women to senior positions of trust, W. saw in Hughes a person who exuded loyalty and savvy. Hughes was glad to join the campaign but quietly believed that W. didn't have much of a chance against Richards.

In early November 1993, George W. officially launched his gubernatorial race at a hotel about a mile from his parents' home. Jeb had already been running hard for more than half a year. George W. promised to return Texas to its former glory. "Texas is becoming like the rest of the nation," he said on the stump. "I don't want Texas to be like California. I worry Texas is changing."

He went off on a twenty-seven-city tour. To those who said he had not accomplished anything, George W. would point to the dark red brick and pink granite stadium that he had built for the Texas Rangers. The granite, he was quick to point out, came from the same field of Texas stone from which the State Capitol Building was cut.

As he announced his candidacy, his father was in Florida raising a quarter million dollars a pop at luncheons for Jeb. George W. was expecting his father to play a similar role in his campaign. "I don't think he'll be holding my hand campaigning everywhere for me," he said. "He knows I can handle my own self. But I hope he raises me a whole bunch of money."

---

BOTH W. AND JEB RAN SIMILAR CAMPAIGNS. THEY BOTH CALLED FOR THE ABO-lition or severe curtailing of the state departments of education. Both campaigned against "big government, big property taxes, and inefficient services." Both held proudly to the fact that they had never served in public office before.

But despite these common themes and even sentences, the two rarely spoke to each other. In part it was a reflection of Jeb's growing isolation in the family. While George W. was always talking to everyone on the phone, family members say you could go months or even a year before hearing from Jeb. Instead, it was their father who served as a sort of informal go-between, passing along campaign information, strategy, and gossip from one to the other.

Like Jeb in Florida, W. brought with him into the race a massive, nationwide network of Republican supporters and activists who had worked in his father's campaigns in both 1988 and 1992. Throughout the 1992 campaign, W. had been in touch with these people and made appearances around the state. More than inheriting his father's name, he was also inheriting his network, which was really the only national network of its type in the Republican Party.

As he watched Jeb preparing to slug it out in a tough GOP primary, W. saw that a unified Republican Party was critical if he was going to get a good crack at Richards. Lack of GOP unity had killed his father in 1992 and was forcing Jeb to raise a lot of money that he would have to burn even before he got to Lawton Chiles. So W. and Rove went around the state to visit other Republicans who were interested in running against Richards. Tom Craddick of Midland, Tom Luce, a former Perot man, and Bob Mosbacher, Jr., were all eyeing the race; fortunately, every one of them was a friend or longtime family acquaintance.

W. told them of his plans. He was committed to the 1994 race, and Rove was going to run his campaign. He told them about the network they had put together. "He had really laid the groundwork," says Robert Mosbacher, Sr. "He had everything in place." They all saw that he was serious, and each candidate agreed to pull out by August 30; the path was clear.

Many believed that W.'s campaign was a fool's quest. Ann Richards was riding high in the polls. Her approval numbers in the summer of 1993 were 63 percent, and it wasn't as if W. had much experience in being a candidate. His 1978 run had ended in failure, and when he got before the media during his father's run in 1988 he could have a quick lip. "George could have a short fuse, no question about it," his uncle Pres Bush said. "There was concern that he would say the wrong thing or explode in front of the cameras."

But W., as he had done so many times before, trusted his own instincts and went ahead. Contrary to what many people believed and what the polls seemed to indicate, W. believed that crime and education were big concerns in Texas. And he drew lessons from his father's stinging defeat and the high poll number he had enjoyed after the Persian Gulf War. "The big lesson I learned in 1992 is that you can't rest on your laurels and hope the voters will reelect you out of gratitude," he said as he was gearing up to run against Richards. "That doesn't work. Incumbents have to project into the future . . ." Ann Richards might be popular, just like his father had been, but that might not matter on election day.

George and Bar kept worrying that the run was a mistake, but W. stuck to his guns. "I don't have to erode [Richards's] likability," he would say. "I have to erode her electability."

W. understood in a way that his father and most in his family didn't that he wasn't running against just silver-haired Ann Richards. He was running against Democrats, and especially the head Democrat, President Bill Clinton. Ann Richards might be the queen of Texas, but Bill Clinton was as likable as dirt in a Texas sandstorm. While Ann Richards was rated "excellent or good" by 49 percent of the voters in Texas, only 18 percent felt the same way about Bill Clinton.

W. started by using the family's network of fund-raising friends. Bar's famed index cards were still up to date, although computerized by now. With W.'s extensive list of allies from Yale to Texas, raising money proved easy. The money came pouring in; he even raised $1 million in a single night at one point.

By the early fall, with George W.'s name circulating around, polls indicated that the race would be tight. Bush was only seven percentage points behind Richards, within striking distance.

"George understood that Ann Richards was likable but too liberal for Texas," cousin John Ellis said. "He had lots of polling done on the issues. Richards was out of step with Texas. He understood that in a way that his parents didn't appreciate."

As both members of the clan's new generation tossed their hats into the electoral ring, George H. W. Bush sat down at his home in Houston and wrote each of them a letter. They were letters from a father to his sons that spoke of his pride and also of a man at peace with himself. The sting of the loss to Clinton might still be felt, but that was for George a matter of the past. He was cognizant of and sensitive to the fact that, while he could benefit his sons in many respects, he might also be a hindrance. And he didn't want the sons to feel that they had to defend the reputation of their father at the expense of their own careers. He told them not to worry about political stories that "contrast you favorably to a father who had no vision and who was but a placeholder in the broader scheme of things." There was also no reason for them to fight his political battles. He also advised them not to be bothered by stories "that compare you to a Dad for whom English was a second language and for whom the word destiny meant nothing . . . So read my lips— no more worrying." He was making a point of passing the baton; the old man was no longer the bearer of the torch. That would be left to a new generation of Bushes. Family members revered their elders. George H. W. Bush often spoke proudly of his father. But when it came to charting his political course, he often stood for positions that were contrary to his father's. For the Bushes, this is an important ingredient in the recipe of their success: the past is an anchor but not a leash.

———

IN THE SPRING OF 1994, JEB WAS CHARGING HARD, RUNNING FOR GOVERNOR of Florida as a self-described "head-banging" conservative committed not simply to reinventing government, but to redefining it. And he was ever the policy wonk that family members knew him to be. He'd show up at a meeting with thirty parents to discuss the merits of school choice. He wanted to get rid of welfare and social services that "no longer work." He told a group in Bradenton about how food stamps, welfare payments, and housing subsidies provided a fifteen-thousand-dollar income for one woman. "I saw government up front, the inherent ineffiency," he told the audience, describing his tenure as Florida's secretary of commerce. "Success was measured on how much money you were willing to spend."

Jeb was also not shy about drawing a contrast with his father. "People from my dad's generation in the late sixties and seventies had a greater faith in government. My brand of conservatism is based on the fact that we have the benefit of hindsight and can see it doesn't work." He credited his stout antigovernment position as coming from "a gene that my Mom gave me. Barbara Bush always liked to challenge authority."

Jeb fought his way through the primary and won it decisively. As he prepared to take on Lawton Chiles in the general election, it quickly became very clear that Jeb's family would be an issue.

Jeb was on the campaign trail when a woman in the audience asked him, "You're familiar with the Skull and Crossbones Society? I mean Skull and Bones?"

Jeb rolled his eyes.

"Yeah, I've heard about it," he said.

"And you're familiar with the Trilateral Commission and the Council on Foreign Relations?"

"Yeah."

"Well, can you tell the people here what your family membership in that is? Isn't your aim to take control of the United States?"

Those sorts of exchanges were expected. But then Lt. Gov. Buddy McKay, a wily panhandle politician running with Chiles, said, "Jeb Bush's children are the children of privilege. He is a child of privilege."

Jeb bristled. "I am running for governor not because I am George and Barbara Bush's son; I am running because I am George P. and Noelle and Jeb's father." It was a nice line, and when W. heard it in Texas, he appropriated it. "I am not running for governor because I am George Bush's son. I am running because I am Jenna and Barbara's father."

Jeb was slightly amused. "He heard me say it in Dallas and he stole it," he said. "It was outright robbery. He said he was going to steal all my good lines."

Family members noted that Jeb seemed annoyed by the fact that his older brother was running for governor at the same time he was. Rather than focusing on the issues, the "two-brothers" angle was turning the campaigns into a "cover story for *People* magazine," he complained. His criticism was directed at the media, but the irritation went deeper.

Over the course of the previous several decades, family members had grown accustomed to W.'s bravado and sharp tongue. When his father or family was attacked, he could be counted on to angrily defend them. He had a short fuse and sometimes no fuse at all. "George really didn't take s———from anyone," said John Ellis.

For Gov. Ann Richards, who had built a career on a sassy tongue (recall her remark about George being "born with a silver foot in his mouth"), the strategy seemed simple. Needle, pester, and irritate W. until he blows up in front of the camera. If she kept it up, it was bound to happen.

Throughout the general election, she poked her finger in his eye. He was "little Bush," or "Junior," and sometimes she called him "Shrub."

"You just can't wake up one morning and decide you want to be governor," she told an audience. "You can't just be looking in the mirror shaving one morning and say, 'O Wheeee! You're looking good, you're looking real good—You're so good you ought to be governor.' " She called him a "jerk." Pretty soon it was the governor who was losing her cool.

"The last time I was called a jerk was at Sam Houston Elementary School in Midland, Texas," he responded evenly.

She attacked his daddy for being out of touch and called the family elitist. She kept it up on the stump and during the debates. Every chance she got, she took a shot at him. As family members watched the televised debates, they could see W. contorting his face and biting his lip. But when his turn came he did something no one expected—he remained under control. "It amazed me, just amazed me," recalls Elsie Walker Kilbourne. "You just kept waiting for it to come, like some sort of volcano. George W. is very protective of the family. But he just kept his cool. It was not the George we were all used to."

"He who guards his lips guards his life," he had read in Proverbs 13:3. "But he who speaks rashly will come to ruin." If there was any doubt that he was a changed man, this was further proof.

———

AS THE FATHER WATCHED HIS SONS CAMPAIGN, HE OFFERED HIS OWN ASSESSMENTS of their strengths. When it came to George W., it was all about his personality: "He is good, this boy of ours. He is uptight at times, feisty at other times—He includes people. He has no sharp edges on issues. He is no ideologue, no divider—All this talk about his wild youth days is pure nuts. His character will pass muster with flying colors." When he talked about Jeb, the focus was on his intellect and beliefs, and he declared that his second son had a great political future. "There is no question in my mind that he will become a major political figure in the country. He is passionate in his caring and in his beliefs. He speaks well and at six-foot-four is an impressive man."

In Texas, the father did little campaigning for his son. George W. made only one reference to his father, in a single campaign speech. Bar on the other hand was a common fixture on the campaign. W. spoke about what he had learned from her, and she made frequent appearances, perhaps in an effort to counteract Governor Richards's feisty silver-haired routine. Florida was another question. The old man was there all the time, raising money, shaking hands, and meeting with voters.

Family members supported both boys with vigor. But the subtext was clear. "Just about everyone in the family assumed that Jeb would win and George would lose," recalled John Ellis.

A WEEK BEFORE ELECTION DAY, POLLS INDICATED THAT BOTH RACES WERE close. In Florida, Jeb had first surged ahead but now was running neck-and-neck. Lawton Chiles countered Jeb's charges that he had failed the state on crime, welfare reform, and education by attacking Jeb's business record. He ran some ads claiming that he had profited from the savings and loan scandal. Jeb responded with attack ads of his own. A campaign that had been so well planned seemed to be losing focus.

Jeb's campaign mailed out half a million letters to older voters signed by his mother. But Chiles had learned that Jeb and his running mate, State Rep. Tom Feeney, were vulnerable on social security. Earlier in the campaign they had distributed a flyer claiming that Feeney had "co-sponsored" a resolution to "abolish the Social Security system." Feeny had done nothing of the sort, but it got a strong reaction from elderly voters. In the days before the election, the Chiles campaign began a massive phone bank effort to tell millions of seniors throughout Florida that if Jeb won, they might lose their social security.

In Texas, George W. was slugging it out with Ann Richards, who was now slightly behind in the polls. She tried to draw him off his core issues—crime, welfare reform, and education. But try as she might, he wouldn't take her bait. Instead, he began a dash across the state. In Houston he was joined by his parents at a rally. Unlike Florida, where both had made more than a dozen appearances, this would be their first and only appearance for George W.

On election night, members of the extended Bush-Walker clan huddled around their television sets to watch the returns. Jeb and Colu were in a hotel suite in Miami. George W. and Laura were in Austin at the Capitol Marriott. George and Bar stayed at their place in Houston, watching the news on different stations.

The early returns in both states looked promising. In Texas, George W. was leading in almost every region, even traditionally Democratic East Texas. He was also pulling in half the Hispanic vote. In Florida, Jeb was holding his own in some of the more traditional Democratic counties, aided no doubt by the Cuban-American vote. By seven o'clock it appeared clear that George W. was going to win. He was carrying almost every county in the state in what was turning out to be a stunning win. But as his vote count surged, the news in Florida was disappointing. Jeb was getting "hammered" in Broward County. In the condo communities of southeastern Florida, Lawton Chiles was carrying 80 percent of the vote. Chiles's gambit had worked; he would win with 52 percent.

As George W. prepared to make his victory speech at ten o'clock, he received a telephone call from his father. They chatted for perhaps ten minutes, and then George hung up the phone with more than a hint of disappointment on his face. "It's sounds like dad's only heard that Jeb lost," he told his aunt Nancy. "Not that I've won."

Texas had spoken, and George W. addressed the crowd that had gathered in the hotel. His three-hundred-thousand-vote victory was stunning and a symbol that "Texas is ready for a new generation of leaders." The crowd danced to country music while George and Laura toasted each other with ginger ale.

For the Bush family, however, it was a bittersweet night. Said the father, "The joy is in Texas; my heart is in Florida."

"Jeb would have been a great governor," George W. said. "But such is life in the political world. You cannot go into politics fearing failure."

Members of the clan saw the 1994 election as a turning point. George W. was now the one who would carry the torch in the new generation. It was a complete shock to most in the family. In a strange way, George W. was still the family rebel. Having gone against the advice of his family, he had done something his father had never succeeded in—winning statewide office in Texas.

"George is a diamond in the rough," says Elsie Walker Kilbourne. "Growing up he was always rougher-edged. He was very good at managing the Rangers. But politics didn't seem to be his chosen career. With Jebbie you always had this sense that methodical planning was going on and that he was going into politics. So it was a big surprise. It was just too bad in a way that they didn't both win because they are very competitive."

Open competitiveness and dissension was never tolerated in the family outside of games and sports. But between the sons, a subtle, emotive competitive spirit prevails. "Competitiveness matters because one is always measured against the other and they are both measured against their father, in their minds," said their cousin John Ellis.

#### CHAPTER 38

# HANDING OFF

I N AUSTIN ON THE MORNING OF JANUARY 21, 1995, THE BUSHES ROSE early and headed to the First United Methodist Church. The Reverend Leighton Farrell, the Bush family minister at Highland Park United Methodist Church in Dallas, was coming to deliver a special message before George W.'s inauguration. Standing at the podium, the reverend spoke about the importance of courageous leadership and the necessity of having humility in public office.

Afterward, President Bush was asked how his son would do as governor. "He'll be all right as long as he listens to the sermon," he said.

Right after the difficult loss in 1992, the whole family temporarily lost its sense of purpose. Some believed that perhaps a life on the national stage was behind them for good. When both sons had announced their plans for governor, most family members had pinned their hopes on Jeb. But instead, George W. wound up wearing the family mantle. For all their desire to be considered the "unKennedys," there was a nod to that dynasty on this historic day. "On this day," said Karl Rove, "George W. Bush clearly comes into his own, and no one can dispute that. We really do have a generational passage here. Sort of like Joe Kennedy handing off to young John."

As George W. approached the podium, there could be little doubt that the family's political aspirations now rested firmly on his shoulders. With the immediate clan gathered around him—Laura, his two daughters, his mother and father, Jeb, Marvin, Neil, and Doro—the Bushes were back in the game.

The elder George had seen his son transformed over the past decade. He had questioned W.'s judgment about running in the first place and had been proven wrong. He had underestimated his son, he told his own siblings Bucky and Nancy. Now he was overcome with emotion. When reporters shouted questions, he shook his head. "Don't ask me," he said with a lump in his throat. "I'll cry."

The Reverend Billy Graham rose to deliver the invocation. He prayed for W.'s protection and praised "the moral and spiritual example his mother and father set for us all." Then George W. put his hand on Sam Houston's Bible and was administered the oath.

The Democratic lieutenant governor, Bob Bullock (elected on a separate ballot), then rose and talked about the future. He too nodded to W.'s parents. "As a father I know the immense pride out there. As an American I thank you for your service to the state and to the country and for helping to bring world peace. And as a Texan, welcome home. We're glad you're here." George nodded gently and said nothing. But even in these first few moments of George W.'s life as governor, the shadow of his father would be difficult to escape.

George W. spoke from the podium about his family and his future plans for Texas. He glanced over at his brother Jeb, who was sitting quietly off to the side. "He's looking happy and proud, but also something else, maybe a little sad, too," he said. "It's a tough moment, tough for me to look at. I love my brother, you see."

Love there was, but also distance. Defeat had a bitter taste. Running for office was something Jeb had dreamed about since at least 1980 when he had worked on his father's first presidential campaign. But the price of his ambition had been high. Beginning in July 1993, a full fifteen months before the election, he had been campaigning full-time, he recalled. "Six days a week. Early morning until late night." He had pushed himself and stopped only when he was forced to slow down. "Twice I got dog sick. I couldn't stand up. I just had to rest for two or three days."

But all that time away from home had hurt the family. Little Noelle, his only daughter and now a seventeen-year-old at Gulliver Prep school in Miami, had been caught using drugs. And his older son, George P., had seen a relationship with a girlfriend end rather badly. Colu, who had never been excited by politics to begin with, was left to deal with much of it alone. Their marriage suffered with the distance, and she fretted about her children and the glare of public attention. Several family members recall hearing her tell him, in tears, "You've ruined my life."

After his father had lost in 1992, Jeb's future career had seemed to hold much promise. The run for governor was to be his first electoral step toward the White House. Now his family was in shambles.

While George W. reveled in the soft, white light of victory, Jeb was experiencing what he recalled as his most "humbling experience." The time for finger-pointing was ending. Determined to do what he could to pull his family together, Jeb called a series of family sessions of discussion and prayer. He took responsibility for his failure to be at home when he was needed, and recommitted himself to Colu and his kids. As a symbol of his commitment, he vowed to Colu that he would convert to Catholicism. Over the course of their marriage Colu had remained a committed Catholic, and all three children had been raised in the faith. Jeb, a nominal Episcopalian, had always gone along but never completely participated. Now that would change.

"They went through such a bad phase with Colu, with Noelle, the drug thing, and it was in that that they decided to commit to each other," says Shellie Bush Jansing, who lives in South Florida. "And he started it by saying, 'I'm going to commit to this, and then I'm expecting you all to fall in line,' including Noelle."

As painful as Jeb's loss was for the family, his parents would come to see it as a blessing. Had he been elected, it is doubtful whether his family would have stayed together. Barbara came to see it as a good thing. "She is very protective of Jeb," says Shellie Bush Jansing. "Don't say anything bad about Jeb or you'll get your neck squashed. But I know that she feels that way very strongly—that it was a wonderful thing that Jeb lost."

Two hours after W.'s inauguration, the Bush family rode in a parade as they headed through Austin for a barbecue lunch on the Capitol lawn. George and Bar rode in a limousine just ahead of their son. The enthusiastic crowd seemed just as excited—if not more so—to get a glimpse of the former First Couple as they were to see the new governor. Traditionally the outgoing governor was supposed to host a lunch for the incoming governor. But Ann Richards had left town; she was vacationing in California. That night there were three inauguration parties, and George W. and Laura made the rounds. "Dancing with Laura is the most nervous I've been all day," W. declared.

George and Laura moved into the governor's mansion with the twin girls, who had elected to pass on boarding school and instead attend a local school in Austin. Laura in particular fell in love with the two-story Greek Revival structure with its large twenty-nine-foot-tall Ionic columns. The slowly moving Colorado River was a short stop away. The place was at the center of power in Texas, and yet it seemed so serene.

Laura had always been a bit reluctant about W.'s run for governor. Her major concern had been that he was being pushed or talked into the race by family friends who were anxious to see another Bush in Texas politics. As Bar had done for the father, Laura constantly alerted George W. to hangers-on and would-be friends who tried to play off her husband's position in an effort to advance their own interests.

She was also shy in public. During the campaign she had made a few appearances at Republican women's clubs. But unlike Bar, who had quickly grown accustomed to the spotlight, Laura was shy and reluctant. She preferred to be active behind the scenes. She had also seen the pressures that public families could place, even indirectly, on their children. She told her husband that their daughters needed to be protected from that, and W. agreed. They also agreed that neither child should be forced to attend official functions; it would be their choice whether they came or not.

Laura did most of the heavy lifting with the girls, but George W. was also the doting father. Sometimes, if Laura was out of town, he would cut short a luncheon meeting by indicating that his daughters were home alone. "I better get home before I have to replaster some walls." When his daughters went to a sleepover, he would arrive at the house early and sit in his parked car out front, waiting for the appropriate time to pick them up.

It was also during his early years as governor that Laura began to assert herself as her husband's chief adviser and aide. As with Bar, it was less about the issues than matters of tone and people. And unlike anyone else around him, Laura could put her husband in his place.

"I've seen Laura do it to George any number of times," Shellie Bush Jansing recalled. "George will go on about something and she'll say quietly but strongly, 'Well, we've heard your side, now why don't we hear someone else's side.' "

"She is good at deflating his grandiosity," agreed John Ellis.

Laura's interest in politics was limited; her passion was culture. For the inauguration, she arranged for seven Texas writers to give readings at the Capitol. Few of them had actually voted for George W. But as far as she was concerned, this was a celebration of Texas as well as her husband's victory. Her interest in culture and his in politics created an inherent tension in their marriage that seemed to provide energy rather than heat. Laura had a massive collection of books, read frequently, and enjoyed thought-provoking literature such as Dostoevsky's *Brothers Karamazov*.

George W. might read a book about sports or a biography of Sam Houston, but his literary interests were limited. And as with his mother and father, the differences between George W. and Laura would at times turn into banter as a way of smoothing over their disparities. A public comment would lead to a private, humorous rebuke. On the stump, W. would sometimes joke about Laura's profession. "As a librarian, her idea of a conversation is 'Shhhhh!' "

Laura was not amused and told him to stop, which he did. But she would also strike back, explaining that her husband "thought that a bibliography was a biography—the life story—of the person who wrote the Bible."

Her commitment to literacy was passionate, and W. helped her advance the agenda. When the state legislature passed a $215 million program to encourage early reading, it was really Laura's triumph.

———

BAR HAD BEEN INTRODUCED TO HER HUSBAND'S FRANTIC SOCIAL ACTIVITIES back at Yale, when he would bring a half dozen friends by for dinner without notice. George and Bar relished having an active social life; they could seemingly never get enough of it. W. and Laura were decidedly less social. Through two terms in the governor's mansion, the Bushes never held one black-tie event. When they did have people over, they were usually smaller gatherings, maybe a barbecue on the lawn with ribs, hot dogs, and Laura's chili.

For Laura it was an idyllic life. Austin was a welcome and inviting place. Her childhood chum from Midland, Peggy Weiss, was owner of Jeffrey's, a casual, chic, dimly lit bistro that had an impressive wine list and art-lined walls. W. and Laura would slip into the restaurant for a quiet dinner alone, dining on crispy oysters with honey habanero aioli. It was the sort of life Laura wanted—making a difference but preserving some semblance of privacy.

The Texas legislature met for a few months every other year, so George would often be home for lunch. They would dine alone or with a few select friends. She could walk out the front gate of the mansion and down the street to the river. Or she could go with the girls over to Twin Lake for a nice four-mile walk.

"Laura absolutely loved Austin," said Bucky Bush. "This was the sort of place where she could thrive. The arts, friends, and she could maintain a certain level of anonymity that she really enjoys."

———

IN HIS OFFICE, GEORGE W. WOULD SIT BEHIND A LARGE, DARK MAHOGANY desk that was a bit scuffed up from use over the years. His grandfather had used it while in the U.S. Senate and his father had used it in Washington.

In the inner sanctum of his office, W. surrounded himself with artifacts that were visually appealing but also reminders. Unlike his father, for whom self-control seemed natural, W. found himself having to work at it. Some said it was that Walker blood. While Laura had placed oil paintings with sweeping images of the Old West in the governor's mansion, in his office he hung an oil painting of Sam Houston, his great hero, dressed in, of all things, a Roman toga. Houston had commissioned the portrait of himself posing as the Roman conqueror Gaius Marius when he had been particularly depressed in life.

George W. saw parallels between himself and Houston. "He wrestled with self-doubt, he wandered for years looking for direction," he recalled. "The turning point in his life came when he looked in the mirror and saw the reflection of a man he no longer respected. And that very day he vowed to turn his life around, and he did."

While others saw the painting as an odd choice of decor, George W. saw it as something more. "Evidently, he must have been in a drunken stupor to have done this, to go to Nashville and have himself painted as Marius," he explained.

W.'s addictive personality required him to fix in on something and maintain a hold on it. For George W., that meant a rigorous commitment to self-discipline. He kept to a strict schedule for meetings, and official dinners at the governor's mansion never went past 9 P.M. When all his work was done, even in the middle of an event, he would say, "Okay, you're outta here." He kept a vigorous exercise schedule and dutifully read his Bible every morning. In his youth his "addictive personality" had led him to drinking and other destructive behavior. Now in adulthood he was addicted to a sense of orderliness and rigor that he did not want to deviate from. It was as if he had turned a character weakness into a source of strength.

W. also placed photos in his office to remind him of the ancestral voices that he undoubtedly heard subconsciously from time to time: photos of his parents and Pres and Dottie in front of a prop plane at Midland airport; another of his grandfather Pres waving to an audience at a 1952 victory rally. They all reminded him of where he had come from and why he was here. They also in a certain way were pointing in the direction he needed to go.

As George W. looked at the lay of the political land in early 1995, it was a rocky horizon. He had won decisively, but the Democrats controlled both chambers of the state legislature. They also held the two most powerful legislative jobs, House speaker and lieutenant governor.

But instead of walking across the sharp terrain in bare feet, George W. decided to do what he had done so often before—make friends.

His father had done it as a young congressman and his grandfather as a senator. Both men had been popular even among members of the other party, his grandfather with Fulbright and other Democrats, and his father with congressmen like Dan Rostenkowski. They had done it by being sincere, shooting straight, and agreeing to disagree when necessary. Detaching the personal from the political was a key ingredient.

W. sought out a meeting with lieutenant governor Bob Bullock, a Democratic fixture in Texas politics for more than thirty years. George W. called him "Bully" because, like LBJ, he could be tough, direct, and shrewd. It was better to make him an ally than have him as an enemy.

W. approached politics the way he had everything else in his life, as an extension of his personality. He would casually drop by the offices of state legislators and kick up his feet for a nice chat. When he was grappling with the legislature on welfare reform, he spotted Elliott Naishtat, a Democrat, walking down the steps of the Capitol Building. Naishtat, a liberal, was opposed to much of what Bush was proposing. Suddenly he found himself in a headlock. "It's Bush, and he's very friendly," he later recalled.

Naishtat jokingly called for nearby police officers to help, but they ignored them. So W. guided him, still in a headlock, down the Capitol steps. "Elliott, I hear we're hung up on welfare. You know how important this is, I hope we can work it out."

Shortly after he became governor, W. learned that Sen. John Whitmire, a Houston Democrat, had lost a memento. After graduating from high school in Houston, he had received a congratulatory letter from a young congressman named George Bush. When George became president, Whitmire had given the framed letter to one of his aides to get the president to autograph it. The letter disappeared.

Whitmire casually mentioned the letter to W. shortly after he became governor. The two didn't know each other very well, but W. took note. Within hours the letter was suddenly found.

"What that goes to show you is George Bush is a people person," says Whitmire. "I've served under five governors, and he's probably the best people person in that respect of any. He understands that governing is about people, that politics is about relationships. And he pays a lot of attention to those relationships."

Suddenly Democrats found themselves wanting him to succeed.

And yet while he was like his father in recognizing the importance of personal relationships, he also relished keeping people off balance and keeping them guessing. He could also play the game that he had mastered as a young boy, of keeping expectations low. When he met with a group of university chancellors who wanted $1 billion added to the state budget, George W. said, "Would you accept five hundred million?" All the university heads agreed. He then told them that he was joking. But since they had settled for half, he wanted them to justify their full request.

But where the son seemed to differ from the father was that he put limits on friendship. His father had come of age during the war, when there was unity among all. At Yale, ideology had played a very small role in his formation. He had grown up in the shadow of his father who had been a moderate Republican. George W., on the other hand, had witnessed the limits to friendship in the world of politics. He had seen the schism over Vietnam and experienced the bitterness of the post-Watergate era. He had seen how his father's commitment to friendship had hurt him politically and made him a less effective leader. W. was not prepared to go so far. And while his father had downplayed what he called "the vision thing," that was the son's strength.

George W. was conscious of these differences, and he often made a point of drawing contrasts with his father. He had his dad's eyes but his momma's mouth; he was from West Texas and not Greenwich; his was a different generation with different experiences. This was more than a public relations strategy. Karl Rove, who had worked for both men, saw the differences up close. And while the men were similar in that they shared "a great sense of courtesy," it was becoming clear that the son was "a lot more philosophically driven" than the father.

Doug Wead, who served as a special assistant to the father and is friends with the son, saw how different the men were. The father had a thousand friends whom he wrote, phoned, spent time with, and connected with. Even many of his political opponents had nice things to say about the man. George H. W. Bush had few enemies and detractors who knew him on a personal basis. But W. was different. "You either got him or not," Wead told us. "Opinions about him ran hot or cold."

———

W. HAD CAMPAIGNED ON FOUR KEY POINTS—ROUNDING UP CRIMINALS, IN-creasing local control over education, reforming the tort system of lawsuits, and welfare reform. He stuck narrowly to those themes and was opportunistic in pursuing his agenda. He promoted opening hostels for welfare mothers and legislation to encourage religion-based drug treatment centers and prison ministries. He believed that he would be judged most on whether he delivered in those areas. But he was also not about to squander his political capital on causes that were nonstarters with a Democratic-controlled legislature. Observers concluded that he was much like his father—nonideological, a team player, noncontroversial. But W. was more than anything a realist. Ideas were important as a guide, but the real work in politics lay in getting them adopted.

They had started to notice it on the campaign trail, but now that he was governor it was apparent to everyone: George W. was and was not his father's son. He had that penchant for loyalty and that commitment to the verities of character, but the commonalities seemed to end there. And the father was understanding and not resistant to the fact that his son was very different in some respects.

As governor, George W. was a paragon of minimalist government. His first meeting was at 9 A.M., followed by two hours of "private time," which included lunch and a run. The last meeting would be finished by 5 P.M. He spent little time studying the issues and more time in meetings with groups and ceremonial occasions, and "photo opportunities." Impatient in long meetings, he was in short a governor the way Ronald Reagan would be, and not his father: He would dictate the principles of his administration and then delegate policy details to his subordinates.

His affairs in Austin were handled by what came to be known as the Iron Triangle: Karl Rove, Karen Hughes, and Joe Allbaugh. Big and burly at six foot four and 275 pounds, Allbaugh wore a flat-top haircut and shied away from the media. He was about keeping the system in line. And when Karl Rove and Karen Hughes competed for the governor's ear, it was Allbaugh who was the enforcer. In this respect, George W. was much different from his father. While his father had relied on a strong chief of staff and a cluster of friends who had direct access, George W. seemed to have a flat organizational chart that disciplined the way he operated. His MBA background had taught him how to handle decisions. You didn't need to be completely conversant on the state budget, but your advisers did, and they needed to give you the options.

He was also mindful that a powerful individual could come to dominate decision-making. Karen Hughes was smart, loyal, and had great instincts when it came to his image. In contrast to his father, who had held long and numerous interviews with the media, George W. and Hughes became focused on controlling the message. The difference here between father and son went to the root of their personalities. Lud Ashley recalls being amazed at how the father dealt with the media. After a particularly heinous article was written, "he would be so forgiving, more than I would be. He assumed it was just about them doing their job." The son didn't see it that way. Sometimes their dealings with the press had a unique irony. Maureen Dowd of the *New York Times* had written some hard pieces on the father when he was president. George W. would barely speak to her and referred to her with derogatory names in family discussions. But his father, who had been attacked, actually maintained an on-again, off-again e-mail exchange with her.

While Governor Bush had strong relations with all of his senior staff, his relationship with Rove was particularly complex. Rove was for W. what Lee Atwater had been for his father. He was a friend, but not particularly close. Rove called W. "sir" in telephone conversations. He was W.'s political confidant and adviser, but as so often with the Bushes, the relationship was strictly hierarchical. After a news conference one day on the lawn of the governor's mansion, W. noticed that the reporters were crowding around his aide and peppering him with questions. W. walked over. "Is the Rove news conference about over?" he snapped. Rove blanched and walked away from the reporters.

In other instances, when Rove seemed particularly pleased with something that had been accomplished, W. would deflate him. "Thank you, Mr. Big Shot."

For all their informal style, the Bushes don't like aides who draw attention to themselves. Leaders are the leaders, and everyone else is there to help them succeed. It's a rule that they themselves live by. When George H. W. Bush was vice president, he seemed to go out of his way not to draw attention to himself at the expense of Reagan. Deference is both a virtue and a necessity with the Bushes.

As he settled into the role of governor, it became clear early on that he was becoming a star of the Texas political scene. Skeptics who had dismissed him as a lightweight soon realized that he was a quick study who understood the art of political persuasion. He also had star power, a charisma that was particularly strong when he met with legislators in small groups or one-on-one. The family's longtime friends in Texas soon heard the buzz, and it wasn't long before someone uttered "the p-word."

A subsurface tug of war began to emerge. Family friends, seeing how natural George W. was as governor, also began seeing him in national office. "He had a very loyal band of followers in Texas," recalls Nancy Bush Ellis. "I think a lot of Big George's friends saw it early [that George W. could be president] and pushed him." It came first in the form of subtle hints and notes. He was a natural leader who could burst onto the national scene. "I don't really think it was an organized campaign per se," says his uncle Bucky. "But it probably seemed like it."

W. was rather enjoying the attention and interest, but Laura was protective and brought him back to earth. At one church service the pastor proclaimed that God was calling for moral leadership, and that people needed to step up and take charge. W. would later say that this sermon was central in his decision to seek the presidency. But Laura had her doubts. After the sermon, the family gathered at the governor's mansion. W. went around to his aunts and uncles saying, "I feel as if God were talking directly to me." He continued doing this until Laura slipped over and said to him gently, in front of the family, "I think that's a bit of a stretch, W."

W. tried to ignore the heady talk and his life slipped into a steady rhythm. Unlike his role at the Texas Rangers, he was very much his own boss in Austin. His weeks were filled with politics and his weekends revolved around family. His friend Don Evans had given him a *One Year Bible*, which included daily readings from the Old and New Testaments as well as Proverbs and Psalms. He read the Bible daily, and soon he was giving sermons, guest speeches really, at churches around Texas.

But George W. was determined to avoid being the conventional Christian. The residue of his West Texas past, the vein of rebellion that still ran through him, led him to take pains to demonstrate his independence from the typical evangelical Christian culture.

Doug Wead recalls a conversation he had with George W. after he had returned from a series of public events in California.

"Someone told me that at a receiving line in California, you took the Lord's name in vain."

There was a pause. "That's b——s——."

"It's important that evangelicals see you are sensitive to this issue."

"It's b——s——."

"Forty-nine percent of Americans describe themselves as evangelicals and if they—"

"It's b——s——."

"Words have important meaning and—"

"Doug, I'd never use the Lord's name in vain. I have, however, been known to use the word b——s——."

W. was also trying to come to a deeper understanding of broad cultural issues. He had an instinctive revulsion to the counterculture of the 1960s. Now with Bill Clinton in office, old wounds from that era seemed to reopen. George W. started reading books about the subject and the culture that the 1960s era had engendered. He read a book by Myron Magnet called *The Dream and the Nightmare: The Sixties' Legacy to the Underclass*. He also became intrigued with the exploits of those who had led the New Left in the 1960s and now had second thoughts. He read books like *Destructive Generation* by David Horowitz, who had once edited *Ramparts* and had become a Reagan Republican. And writings by Marvin Olasky, a one-time Marxist who was now a evangelical Christian. The sixties might be long over, but W. believed the sixties legacy was still being fought over.

#### CHAPTER 39

# WORLD TRAVELER

THE ELECTION OF GEORGE W. WAS AN ENORMOUS EMOTIONAL boost to his father. He took it as an affirmation of what he had done for the family name and for his chosen profession. But disappointment about 1992 was still lurking deep inside him. It wasn't so much that he was no longer president as the profound sense that he had somehow let people down.

"He must have said to me, I don't know, more than a dozen times," Bob Mosbacher said, " 'I'm so sorry I let you down.' He said that to a lot of people he's close to."

He was also still stunned that Jeb had lost in Florida. Jeb had gone the route he had taken in his youth, leaving home for a new state, working his way up in a new business, serving in the local Republican Party, serving in government, and becoming financially independent. But alas, that route had not worked this time. Instead, the rise of George W. mystified him in the same way that Ronald Reagan's did. Members of the family still believe that the father doesn't completely understand his son. John Ellis recalls how surprising it was—and still is—for the father. "[George W.] was a decisive winner in a way his father was not on a statewide ballot. They were now his constituents. And he was their governor. It took them a while—and I think that 41 [George H.W.] has still not wrapped his mind around it—he still doesn't get it."

George and Bar had their new, three-story brick house completed in Houston and moved in. The centerpiece of the home was Bar's large needlepoint rug, the family's most sentimental possession. After several decades' worth of work and travel—all the way from China, to Washington, back to Houston, then to Washington, and now back in Houston—it was completed and had found a resting place. Bar could still tell anyone which stitches she had put in place when W. got married and Jeb had his first child. As a final notation, she had placed her grandchildren's initials carefully in the corners.

Despite George and Bar's attempts to return to normalcy, it would not be so easy. The hope was to live a relaxed retirement in Houston. But when word of where they lived got out, hordes of people would drive by or stand on the corner and gawk at them. Eventually they had to put up a six-foot-high wall.

Still feeling that he had let his friends down and possessing that latent energy that never seemed to completely leave him, George threw himself into the business of making money. When George and Bar left the White House, their finances were not what one might think. With a net worth of $3.2 million and a pension of $150,000 per year, the Bushes were comfortable. But there were other considerations, most important, perhaps, Walker Point at Kennebunkport. It was the magnet George had been drawn to for more than five decades and was the closest thing he had to a permanent home. But his love for the Point was not particularly shared by his children. "George, Jeb, and all of them love the place because it's their dad's place," says Elsie Walker Kilbourne. "Beyond that they could all take it or leave it. It's not the sort of place they would keep and maintain."

For George H. W. Bush, however, Walker Point was the essence of the family, and so in the months after he left the White House, he made plans to preserve it through a perpetual private trust. Everything from painting to cutting the grass would be taken care of through a separate fund that would require large chunks of money.

So George took his energies and plied them in the commerical world. He would not act as a paid lobbyist, and he turned down opportunities to serve on corporate boards. But as so often happens with the Bushes, the commercial intersected with the political, in this case the geopolitical. And like several generations of the family, he was shrewd in the subtle use of connections and informal power to make things happen for himself, the family, or his clients.

The booming Asian economy was a subject of intense interest for both the family and numerous American corporations. After he left the White House, former President Bush would make regular, sometimes yearly, trips to Beijing, to meet with Chinese leaders, some of whom he had known more than twenty years. The trips would be paid for by companies that had commercial interests in China, and he would often deliver speeches for the companies while on the mainland. His visits almost always included private meetings with Chinese president Jiang Zemin. He would not lobby Chinese leaders directly, but he let them know who was paying for his trip and by doing so enhanced their prestige in Chinese eyes.

When the Chubb Group of Insurance Companies wanted a license to sell its products in China, it paid for George to travel to Beijing and gave him a fee to make a speech and an appearance at a reception. He never told the authorities to give Chubb the license, but he really didn't need to. It was just the sort of language that the mandarins in China spoke.

"If you're unknown in China and trying to get known and you're trying to get a license there, having a former president at a reception might get people to come who might not come otherwise," explained Mark Greenberg, senior vice president at the company.

George did much the same for the Carlyle Group, a Washington-based merchant bank. Chaired by Frank Carlucci, Reagan's last defense secretary, Carlyle also included his longtime friend Jim Baker as a senior counselor. Richard Darman, his former White House budget director, was also involved. Carlyle was a natural landing place for the former president, as it included many family friends and former aides who had been helpful to the Bushes in other ways. In 1990, when Carlyle acquired Caterair, a large airline-catering business, George W. was placed on its corporate board of directors.

George agreed to serve as a senior adviser on the company's Asia Advisory Board and became a regular fixture when Carlyle tried to acquire businesses overseas. Rather than take cash, he elected instead to put his compensation into investment accounts run by Carlyle.

When Carlyle was looking to purchase three South Korean firms, George went to South Korea and met with the country's president. As he chatted with Kim Dae Jung, they discussed both personal matters and world affairs. As in China, George didn't make a direct pitch for the bids; he didn't have to. His involvement spoke volumes to the Koreans he had befriended and worked with over the years.

Regular trips to Beijing, work for Carlyle, and a booming lecture business in the United States provided a small river of money for the recently retired first couple. But in those years, the father had no greater benefactors and friends than the royal families in Kuwait and Saudi Arabia.

One particularly long-lasting friend was Prince Bandar, son of Sultan, the Saudi defense minister and brother of King Fahd. Bandar was a former fighter pilot who had served as ambassador in Washington since 1983. The two had worked together on several important issues, including the sale of AWACS surveillance aircraft to the Saudis in the early 1980s and the war against the Sandinistas in Central America. But the relationship was sealed when Bandar came to visit George in Kennebunkport shortly before the Gulf War. The family was so taken by him that they quickly labeled him Bandar Bush. There was hardly a higher compliment the family could pay.

The relationship was based on mutual respect and trust. The Saudis had in the former president a supporter and friend who was sympathetic to their view of the threats from radical Islam. Also, while supportive of Israel, George also believed that the Jewish state was not doing enough for the Middle East peace process.

In the Saudis, George had financial benefactors and friends. He would hunt pheasant on Bandar's estate in England and visit with the Royals whenever he traveled to the region. For favorite family causes such as the construction of the Bush Presidential Library and Bar's literacy program, seven-figure checks were written.

On one occasion George traveled to Kuwait and Saudi Arabia and met with the Saudis' Crown Prince Abdullah at his compound outside of Riyadh. The Carlyle Group was hunting for investments there. In addition to seeing the crown prince, he took a yacht cruise on the Red Sea with Saudi business leaders.

Though out of office, George still had many friends who remained in power around the world. Argentine president Carlos Menem was a particularly close friend. First elected in 1989, Menem remained as Argentine president for ten years. George kept in close touch, visiting him in Argentina five times and then three times when Menem came to the United States. The relationship was not lost on companies interested in working the Argentine market. In 1994, George traveled to Buenos Aires twice and gave speeches to a pharmaceutical group and to bankers.

At one point Menem decreed that a casino could be built in Buenos Aires. Soon after, George received a call from another longtime friend, Steve Wynn, the gambling mogul who ran Mirage Resorts. Wynn had been a major donor, and George had visited his home and golf course. Wynn wanted to develop casinos in Argentina. George wrote Menem and indicated that he had no financial stake in the venture, but that Wynn was a good man. Menem agreed that Mirage was the right company for the job. But shortly thereafter, local officials became upset that such decisions were being made by federal authorities and Menem was forced to withdraw his approval.

The Bushes tend to thrive in foreign cultures where a primacy is placed on the family. It is no accident that the Bushes have found eager partners and investors in regions of the world such as Asia and the Middle East. The friendship with Menem was also of benefit to many in the family. Neil Bush tried to secure some oil and gas deals in Argentina and could count on support from Menem. When Menem was leaving office, he gave two hundred thousand dollars for a new Argentine Studies Center at the University of Texas. While visiting Austin, he had lunch with George W.

But there were instances when George went beyond simply making an appearance and exercising his "soft" power. He has on rare occasions specifically lobbied for individual companies. In 1995 his friend, former Canadian prime minister Brian Mulroney, became involved in the Barrick Gold Company, a Toronto-based mining firm. George came on as a consultant, offering advice about matters overseas. In 1996 he took the unusual step of writing to Indonesian president Suharto about a concession to a gold mine in the country. George had known Suharto since the 1960s, when he had done work in Indonesia with Zapata. Barrick wanted the exploration rights to an enormously promising patch of land on the Indonesian archipelago that was currently owned by another Canadian company, Bre-X. "I simply want to take the liberty of telling you how impressed I am with Barrick," George wrote the leader, "its visionary leadership, technological achievements and great financial strength." Soon after the letter arrived, Suharto issued a decree that Bre-X would be required to make Barrick a partner and give up three-quarters of its revenue rights. When Bre-X shareholders caught wind of what had happened, they mounted a media campaign in Indonesia that forced Suharto to back down.

On the speakers' circuit George made about fifty speeches a year. He went to trade associations, universities, and corporations. Sometimes he took company stock instead of cash and it proved to be a windfall. In 1998 he took stock in Global Crossing, Limited, which blossomed from $100,000 to $13.4 million.

He was traveling overseas, too, collecting six-figure speaking fees. Sometimes the opportunities were perhaps too inviting. He gave a series of speeches for the Reverend Sun Myung Moon. First he lectured throughout Japan for the Women's Federation for World Peace, which was led by Moon's wife. He talked about family values. Later he went to a black-tie dinner in Buenos Aires to launch *Tiempos del Mundo*, a Spanish-language daily newspaper owned by Moon.

The Moon-owned *Washington Times* had been a steady supporter of his presidency. But when George appeared in Buenos Aires, he was roundly criticized. His good friend President Carlos Menem would not attend the speech because, on the advice of aides, he believed it to be "blasphemous and anti-Christian." Then word leaked out from the Defense Intelligence Agency that Reverend Moon, who was born in North Korea, had a financial relationship with the North Korean government. According to DIA reports,

Moon had funneled money to both Kim Il Sung and his son and successor, Kim Jong Il. He was said to have hopes of building a shrine where he was born. After 1996, George stopped giving speeches for Moon-related organizations.

Only a few years out of office, and George was making about $4 million a year on the lecture circuit. But the real star of the family was Barbara. She, too, was giving speeches, but the public attraction to her seemed overwhelming. The two would make appearances together and while guests might come up and formally shake hands with George and chat for a few minutes, they seemed to gravitate toward Barbara. Five hundred letters a day poured into George's office and many of them were for Barbara. A Mother's Day poll revealed that Barbara was the woman most Americans would like to talk with on Mother's Day along with their own moms. To top it off, Bar was named "Biker Babe of the Year" by *Outlaw Biker* magazine.

While George seemed to have trouble adjusting to life after Washington, for Barbara it was easy. She kept abreast of family developments, talked with old friends, and kept a keen eye on national politics. At night she would lie in bed and watch A&E and the History Channel. ("There's too much Hitler," she would complain.)

There had been rumblings in the extended Bush clan as early as 1995 that George W. might make a run for the White House. Of course 1996 was out of the question: He had been governor only two years. If the family had a favorite, it was probably Dick Cheney, who had served as George's defense secretary. Cheney had expressed an interest in late 1994 in entering the race, and the former president encouraged it. Mel Sembler, a major fund-raiser for the Bush family (he had raised large sums for the father and both sons) who had served as ambassador to Australia during the administration, signed up to handle fund-raising for a Cheney campaign after consulting with the former president. Other members of the Bush family's network loved the idea and quickly jumped on board. But Cheney simply couldn't stomach the fund-raising that a presidential bid would require. Al Haig recalls, "I'd go with him to a fund-raiser and he'd lean up against the fireplace and hold conversations about policy. He just didn't want to work the room." By mid-January 1995, Cheney had made it clear that he didn't want to seek the nomination.

In the Republican presidential sweepstakes, George W. ended up supporting Sen. Phil Gramm while Jeb supported Lamar Alexander. When Sen. Bob Dole secured the nomination, no one in the family was particularly surprised. Like many in the GOP, there was a sense that the old boy deserved it after all his years of service to the party. Still, few in the family believed that Dole would win. The 1996 convention in San Diego was therefore less about the presidential election than about the year 2000.

Even with the family out of power in Washington, they remained active within the Republican Party. After George left the White House, he had remained engaged in party activities. He continued giving speeches to Republican groups and spoke regularly with party leaders from every corner of the country, talking about candidates, fund-raising, or just gossiping. Pres was involved in the Connecticut GOP and Buck was active in Missouri. In New York, Johnny Bush, the former fund-raising chairman of the state party, was still organizing fund-raisers for Republican aspirants. Then of course there were the dozens of close family friends who had served in the first Bush administration and were active in party functions. So as they planned the convention events in early summer, the word went out: George W. was a rising star and should address the convention in prime time. In short order, he was given a slot.

In August 1996 the Bush clan gathered in San Diego. For the first time in sixteen years, the family had no one on the national ticket, but they were nonetheless very active behind the scenes. The network of friends and supporters that had been built up over the previous three or four decades was still very much in place, and like any piece of machinery it needed tending.

Presidential candidate Lamar Alexander remembers noticing months before the convention that the family was positioning George W. for a possible future run. "I realized it the moment that I saw he was going to deliver a keynote at the national convention," he told us. "It was clear to me then that the family was making plans for something not too far down the road."

The move caught the interest of the national media, who asked former president Bush whether his son had presidential ambitions. In characteristic fashion, he disavowed any possible involvement in a presidential bid. After all, these were the unKennedys. "It'd be wonderful" if his son ran and won in 2000, he said. "But it's not—I'm not like Joe Kennedy sitting there: 'Here's a couple of hundred thousand—go out and win the West Virginia primary.' I, you know, it's not a scheme. It's not a dynasty. It's not a legacy." But according to family members he was actively making phone calls to party heavyweights around the country, asking them to keep their powder dry in 2000.

Of more immediate concern was Jeb's ambition to run for governor again in Florida. Much of the action in San Diego centered on the Florida delegation. When the delegates held a breakfast meeting, the family was there to boost Jeb's plans to run in 1998. George and Bar came to a luncheon to shake hands, visit old friends, and quietly pitch for Jeb. "I am blessed to be from the best state in the best country with the best parents," said Jeb with his parents standing nearby. "Ladies and gentlemen, *my* president, George Bush."

George W. also made an appearance. As the Texas governor entered the room, Florida GOP chairman Tom Slade turned to the younger Bush son and cracked, "Here is Jeb Bush to introduce his more successful brother."

George W. stood up and spoke a few words on his brother's behalf. As usual, he was more blunt and direct than the rest. "He's supposed to be coy and play like he's waiting to be recruited and everything," the Texas governor matter-of-factly said about his brother. "But I know better."

That fall the GOP went down to inglorious defeat. Bob Dole lost and did so solidly. To make matters worse, defeat had come at the hands of Bill Clinton, who many in the party and in the Bush family viewed with disdain. As GOP leaders licked their wounds in late 1996 and early '97, candidates were already lining up to run in 2000. Lamar Alexander was one of the first out of the gate. Soon there was news that everyone from Sen. Orrin Hatch to Sen. John McCain was going to enter the race.

George W. was saying no such thing, but behind the scenes the family was taking action. Shortly after the 1996 election debacle, major Republican donors began making plans for 2000 almost immediately. But the family wanted to make sure that none of them committed too early. Despite his public statements that he had no interest in "a dynasty" or a "legacy," the former president was actively working the phones. "George Herbert Walker Bush made several calls to key people in several states, telling them to keep their powder dry," says John Ellis. "The message was, don't commit just yet. We may have something for you in a year or so."

But before a possible run at the White House, there was the matter of running for reelection. George W. was enormously popular in Texas, but he needed to win and win big if a presidential bid were to be realistic. And he had thorny issues to tackle, one of the most difficult being capital punishment. Texas was sending more inmates to death row than any other state, but in the fall of 1997 the practice took an unusual turn when one Karla Faye Tucker became the next to die. The last time a woman had been executed in Texas was 1863. Tucker had been found guilty for the brutal slaying of two people in a drug-induced haze in 1983. She had used a pickax to commit her crime.

Since her conviction, however, Karla Faye Tucker had changed. After having a Christian experience similar to George W.'s, she became a model prisoner, was repentant for her crime, and asked for forgiveness. Her cause quickly received national attention from evangelicals such as Pat Robertson and even Pope John Paul II, who called for clemency. Bianca Jagger showed up in Texas representing Amnesty International. As the execution time approached, small crowds holding candles started appearing at the gate of the governor's mansion.

There had rarely been such controversy in Texas. Two days before the scheduled execution, George's daughter Jenna informed him over dinner, in a tense tone, that she too believed in commuting the sentence.

If he were to commute the Tucker sentence, it would certainly be a popular move with many religious conservatives who made up his core base of support. But despite the pleas, George W. was unyielding. While he obviously sympathized with her religious conviction and believed in the power of redemption, in his view the law was the law. And the laws of Texas were clear: Absent evidence of a mistake in the process, the law called for the death penalty. "May God bless Karla Faye Tucker," he said, "and may God bless her victims and their families."

The night of the execution he sat in his office waiting for news. Finally he received the word: "Prisoner is pronounced dead." The first thing he did was pick up the phone to call Laura.

Later, George W. would give an interview to Tucker Carlson of *George* magazine. During the course of that interview, he would mimic Karla Faye Tucker's pleading for her life; the cockiness emerged yet again. After the article was published, Laura had to only look at the magazine and give her husband a glance that demonstrated her disappointment. Family members say she didn't have to say a word about it; he got the message.

The whole notion of redemption is a powerful one in George W. Bush's life. Faith had changed his life, so the power of transforming faith was something he believed should be harnessed for the benefit of government.

The Texas prison system was bursting at the seams, and new prisons were being built regularly around the state. Through friends in the ministry he had heard about how faith-based prison programs could help lower the recidivism rate. He began visiting prisons to watch some of these programs in action. He would put his arm around a convicted murderer and sing "Amazing Grace" and pray with him. He visited a juvenile jail in Marlin, Texas. He talked with the young boys there for a few minutes and then asked if there were any more questions. One fifteen-year-old piped up: "Yeah. What do you think of me?"

The question stunned W., but he saw in that question the deep doubt of someone who "wondered whether there was any hope for him—any room for him—in society. He was basically asking, 'Am I worth anything?' "

On the campaign trail he would talk about issues and subjects. But when the subject turned to faith, he would light up. "We're all lowly sinners," he would tell students at a Christian college during the presidential campaign. "That's what redemption is all about, it seems like to me. And I'm doing the best I can do. And I don't know whether it's God's plan or not." W. proclaimed June 10 "Jesus Day" in Texas. He also backed the so-called Religious Freedom Restoration Act, which allowed the open expression of religious faith.

When twenty-one-year-old Steven Gonzales was one of three American soldiers captured in the Balkans by Serbian forces, W. not only called his parents in Palestine, Texas, but prayed with them on the telephone. When a gunman burst into a Fort Worth church in 1999 and killed seven people, W. was in Michigan fund-raising and returned to Fort Worth immediately and visited the home of the Reverend Al Meredith, pastor of Wedgwood Baptist Church. The meetings were private, without the presence of the media or television cameras. The two men prayed together. Then he went to visit Justin Laird, a sixteen-year-old high school football player who was paralyzed after being shot in the church. W. fought back tears. That Sunday, W. and Laura attended a community memorial service for the victims. Organizers asked him to make a few comments but he refused, declaring that it was a religious event, not a political one. He didn't even want to sit on the stage, but instead sat in the bleachers with the crowd of fifteen thousand quietly listening to the comments and the prayers.

On December 7, 1997, George W. returned to Sam Houston Elementary School in Midland to announce his reelection bid. "I proudly offer my record to the voters of Texas, because I have done in office what I promised to do."

In contrast to his father, who had struggled to find focus in his 1992 presidential campaign, George W. was completely focused on three or four narrow issues. He had promised to deliver on issues relating to crime, education, and tax reform, and during his first term he had focused on those very issues.

With a popularity rating in the seventies, George W. was seen as a formidable candidate by all. The Democrats found it hard to get any of their A-list candidates to run against him.

Endorsed by several leading Democrats, George W. sailed to victory in

November against Gary Mauro. He won nearly 70 percent of the vote and picked up a stunning 48 percent of the Hispanic vote. At his second inaugural address, W. again spoke about the need for renewal and redemption. "Government can't solve all our problems," he said. "Economic growth can't solve all our problems. In fact, we're now putting too much hope in economics, just as we once put too much hope in government. Reducing problems to economics is simply materialism." Only personal redemption could solve the nagging problems that had plagued our society for so long.

Days after the inauguration, the luncheons began. A group of Florida moneymen who had raised money for his father came to Austin to talk about a presidential bid. A few weeks later, his father's old friend Henry Kravis was in town to have the same discussion. The network of family friends and relationships going back two generations was there to help, but W. was still genuinely uncertain about whether he should take the plunge.

The biggest struggle was the question of his twin daughters. They were decidedly uninterested in politics and liked the level of anonymity that they had been able to find in Austin. Both were involved in activities at Austin High School and had a collection of friends who treated them just like everyone else. Their world would change radically if their father ran. George W. wrestled with the question for months. At one point he was on the phone with his friend Doug Wead, who recalled the conversation.

"I'm afraid if I run it is going to ruin their lives . . ." W. said with grim emotion.

"Did it ruin your life when your father ran?" Wead shot back.

"Ruin my life?! Heck, it *made my life*," he responded.

#### CHAPTER 40

# LIBERTY CITY

S HORTLY AFTER HIS DEFEAT IN 1994, JEB HAD CONCLUDED THAT HE was going to run again for governor. But Jeb, depressed about the loss and struggling with problems at home, was receding from the extended family. Relations with his brother in Texas were particularly strained. They would go half a year or more without speaking, and when they did, it was usually pro forma at a family function or meeting.

It was troubling to the gregarious George W. "From George W.'s point of view, it was Jeb who was the noncommunicative one," said cousin John Ellis. "Jeb was going through all this stuff with his daughter, complications with his marriage, and his conversion to Catholicism. And George was like, 'I'm here, why doesn't he talk? He doesn't talk to me. So if I'm going to call him up there is going to be big silence on the other end of the line. What am I supposed to do?' "

Despite the difficult time he was going through, Jeb was as determined as ever. After his loss, he was determined to stay in the political debate. He established the Foundation for Florida's Future, a think tank that raised hundreds of thousands of dollars each year from a stable of donors who had given to his gubernatorial campaign. With his former campaign manager in the post of executive director, the organization put together crime prevention seminars and published a book on character. He spent time on the board of the conservative Heritage Foundation in Washington, D.C. He also returned to the real estate business.

In some respects it was the same old Jeb, making plans and striving hard to reach them. But family and friends could see that he was different. The swagger he had always carried seemed to have mostly evaporated. He had clearly been humbled by his defeat, and the lesson was not lost on him.

In early 1996 he went to a dingy and crime-ridden suburb of Miami called Liberty City with a balding, bespectacled black man named T. Willard Fair. Head of the Greater Miami Area Urban League, Fair had been a fixture in the black community for a quarter century. Unlike some other black leaders who showed instant animosity toward people on the GOP side of the spectrum, Fair was willing to work with anyone who sincerely wanted to help his community.

A burgeoning movement was under way to create so-called charter schools, which would allow local communities to experiment with the curriculum and structure of schools that were failing. Liberty City, the center of Miami's black ghetto and the scene of intense race riots in the 1980s, was a good place to start. Two-thirds of households there were headed by single women, and the annual income was below eighteen thousand dollars, less than half of Dade County's average. More than half of Liberty City's students dropped out of high school before graduating, and its children scored well below the city's averages in reading comprehension and math.

Jeb wanted to develop and create a charter school in the community. The key was to keep it a small, neighborhood school. "Small schools are better than big schools," he said. "An elementary school with 1,200 students or 1,500 students is a factory." Jeb called on friends and patrons to get donations of chairs, desks, carpets, and school supplies. IBM even kicked in seventeen computers.

Willard Fair wanted academic success, but he also wanted to emphasize character, discipline, and a curriculum heavy on basics. Students would wear red, white, and blue uniforms. Parents would sign contracts pledging that their children would go to classes regularly, show up on time, and do their homework. Parents were also required to perform thirty hours of community service for the school.

In the summer of 1997, Jeb joined Fair and local parents in renovating an old two-story building on 87th Street and Fifth Avenue. The staff included many locals who had conquered adversity and gone on to college. To students who might complain about an irresponsible mother or drugs, principal Katrina Wilson was unapologetic. "I don't want to hear it. I don't want to hear about your mother on crack, your grandmother." She had herself grown up in a nearby one-bedroom house and shared a bed with three other members of her family. "How many people come from poverty, that's the American way. One girl here has one arm. She's expected to do her work. People go to the Olympics with less."

Academics was applauded but so was character. When a second-grader found a one-dollar bill in the hallway and turned it in to the principal's office, Fair was overwhelmed. "This is success."

Critics dismissed Jeb's efforts in Liberty City as a stunt. But it is easy to see how it fit in with the family's ethos. Jeb's great-grandfather in Columbus had pushed for better housing for black employees. His grandfather, while serving in the Senate, had been a champion of urban renewal programs in blighted neighborhoods like New Haven and Bridgeport. His father and Uncle Johnny had worked with the United Negro College Fund (Johnny was the finance chairman), and after college George W. had worked with PULL in the inner city of Houston.

When reporters accompanied Jeb during one of his regular visits, they were stunned to discover that he knew the students by name and that they were comfortable and affectionate with him. A six-year-old boy brought Jeb a picture with a bright yellow sun. "You're an excellent artist, Jarrell," he said, rubbing the boy's head.

"Look, Mr. Bush," one shouted from a distance, "I've got potato chips."

"Devon," he responded, walking over, "you aren't eating potato chips for breakfast, are you?"

The students came around and surrounded him, crawling onto his lap and telling him stories. He agreed to be the godfather of a small three-year-old black boy from Miami.

Jeb decided to announce early for the 1998 gubernatorial race to hold off potential challengers. He sent Cherry Perry, the mother of two children enrolled in his charter school, to file the papers. "I have seen, firsthand," she told reporters, "his commitment to children. He is compassionate, he is loving, and he is a doer—not just a talker."

Jeb then flew up to Tallahassee and stood at a podium as the rattle of drums and the clang of cymbals of the Florida A&M marching band warming up could be heard in the distance. "I can't work any harder than I did last time, but I know I will have to work at least as hard as I did in 1994," he said.

This time, however, he was determined to do things differently. Concerned about the strain on his family, he took shorter trips. He borrowed from his father's strategy in Texas three decades earlier, vowing to try to get home each night even if it was very late. But he worried about whether his running might create more family problems.

"Personally it was difficult," he said. "There was a huge strain on my family [in 1994]. I gave my heart and soul away and became so immersed in the campaign that I lost my balance in terms of my priorities. And I do better with that now. In '97, I did it with a little trepidation because I didn't want to relive the pain of '94 for the family."

Observers on the campaign trail saw a new Jeb in 1998. Gone was the "head-banging" conservative of 1994. Like both his grandfather and his father, he was adjusting his message in his second campaign. His grandfather had run a hard-line campaign and lost narrowly in 1950; his father was the consummate Goldwater conservative in 1964 and lost the Senate race in Texas. Both men had moved to the center the next time around. Jeb was determined to do the same.

In announcing his candidacy, he declared that his running mate as lieutenant governor would be Secretary of State Sandy Mortham, a pro-choice Republican. (She would later be replaced by Education Commissioner Frank Brogan after a series of allegations about financial matters.) And the rhetoric of rolling back government was changed to an inclusive message of a "fresh, energetic approach."

Back in 1994 he had been asked whether he would do "anything special" for black voters. "Probably nothing," he had replied. This time he spent countless hours visiting schools in poor inner-city neighborhoods where he had rarely campaigned four years earlier. He also went into Democratic strongholds in south Florida's retirement communities.

Black leaders saw the change. The political rough edges were being polished. Among those who jumped into his campaign was Rev. R. B. Holmes, Jr., pastor of the Bethel Missionary Baptist Church in Tallahassee. A registered Democrat, Holmes headed a church with more than five thousand members. To the surprise of his congregants, he joined the Bush campaign as a county chairman.

Jeb didn't run away from the fact that he was a different candidate now. "This is a part of the growth of any man or any woman and there is nothing cynical about it at all," he said. "It's quite natural for people who view life as a journey, not something that you just respond to and react to. I'm not that type of person. I'm a searcher."

The race was a reflection that he had changed, but also that the political climate was different. Like his father and grandfather, he learned to adjust to the times. "The campaign in '98 was totally different," he said. "Politics is a mirror image of life. It's a reflection more than an indicator of everything. The environment we were operating in in 1998 was different than in 1994. It didn't have the ideological edge. The whole style of campaigning was different. People didn't feel imperiled as much by the size of government as they did in 1994."

Raising money was not a problem. Mel Sembler, the Tampa developer who had served as finance chairman for his father's presidential campaign, held several early fund-raisers for Jeb. In addition to his existing base of donors from the Sunshine State, Jeb also made several fund-raising trips to Texas. Within six months he had raised eight hundred thousand dollars from his brother's supporters in Texas. It is not uncommon to find GOP donors who have given to all three Bushes—the father and the two sons.

The Democrats nominated Lieutenant Governor Buddy MacKay to be their standard-bearer. This was hardly a replay of the 1994 election when Jeb had faced the formidable Lawton Chiles. "In 1994 I ran against a legend," he said. "In 1998, against a mere mortal."

MacKay tried to pin on Jeb the label of a man with many "privileges." He also raised questions about Jeb's business career in Florida. But his campaign never gained any traction. By mid-1998, Jeb had raised three times more than Buddy MacKay. Public opinion polls never put them at closer than 10 percent.

In November, as his brother cruised to reelection in Texas, Jeb won big in Florida. George and Bar, who in 1994, when both sons were running, had carefully elected to stay at home in Houston, this time traveled to Florida to join Jeb and his family in Florida. And unlike 1994, when he had been hammered in south Florida, he picked up considerable support in traditional Democrat strongholds. Most surprisingly, he managed to double his portion of the black vote to 14 percent.

JEB'S ELECTION AS GOVERNOR REPRESENTED THE END OF HIS SIX-YEAR QUEST to enter the national political scene. It was easy to see the sense of satisfaction and relief on his face. A second defeat probably would have ended his political career. But there were still struggles on the home front. His daughter Noelle was continuing her battle with drug addiction. Over the course of the next several years she would have a number of relapses. For Colu, the victory was somewhat bittersweet. Glad that her husband had succeeded, she did not welcome a return to Florida's capital city. Jeb and Colu had lived in Tallahassee in 1987, when Jeb had served as commerce secretary. For Colu, who enjoyed the vibrancy of the Latin culture in south Florida, the sleepy capital was a downright depressing place. Also, her aversion to politics and being in the spotlight was strong. Family members saw those sentiments as a serious barrier to his future ambitions.

"Jeb carried a huge chip on his shoulder for a long time," says Shellie Bush Jansing. "Everybody in the family knew that, because of

Columba [not supporting his political ambitions]. Jeb was always the one who had the brains. Maybe in the real bosom of the family we never thought Jeb would go national because of Colu."

Shortly after they moved into the governor's mansion, Jeb sent Colu on a trip to Paris. When she returned days later, she arrived at the airport with more than nineteen thousand dollars worth of French fashions. But she failed to declare her purchases at customs. When the pile of clothes was uncovered, she was fined.

She had failed to declare the clothes because she was embarrassed by how much she had spent and didn't want her husband to know. Jeb forgave her, but to help Colu cope with the changes, both agreed that she could spend much of her time at the family's condo in south Florida to be near friends and familiar places while Jeb worked in Tallahassee.

LESS THAN TWO WEEKS AFTER BEING ELECTED GOVERNOR, JEB WAS IN NEW Orleans for a gathering of the Republican Governors Association. For the first time both he and George W. were on the public stage together as elected governors. For the first time since the Rockefellers sixty years earlier, two brothers were serving as governors of different states. To satisfy the media interest, the brothers gathered for an impromptu press conference.

Rumors about a possible presidential bid by George W. were already flying, and reporters started firing questions at him. George W. turned to his younger brother and tried to deflect the questions. "He's the tall one," W. said. Jeb laughed but resisted the temptation to call the Texas governor his "big little brother," in reference to his height.

One reporter asked W. whether he agreed with the description of Jeb as "the smart one" and himself as "the savvy one."

"I describe myself as the smart one," W. interrupted.

The two brothers were clearly on unfamiliar ground. As the media continued to ask questions, they would look at each other and try to figure out who would take the lead. But clearly George W. was more comfortable with it all. At one point he even pinched a male reporter from Texas on the cheek.

Though both brothers had won their elections, the Republicans had suffered setbacks in Congress. W. said it was not something to worry about, that the GOP would come back.

"Can I disagree on one thing?" Jeb asked.

"Just make sure it's a minor point," W. shot back with a smirk.

And so the banter continued.

"It's how the boys communicate," says Elsie Walker Kilbourne. "It's all in good fun. But it's kind of a hidden way of letting the other know what you want or what you think without saying it directly."

#### CHAPTER 41

# THE PHOTO

G EORGE W. BUSH HAD THOUGHT LONG AND HARD OVER THE course of 1997 and 1998 about a possible run for president. Public opinion polls that put him at the head of the pack appealed to his sense of service. The GOP wanted him, and who was he to turn them down?

But he also struggled with the question of his family. Laura was not particularly keen on the idea. And his daughters were borderline horrified at the thought that they would suddenly be under the national microscope as their dad sought the highest office in the land. But while his daughters expressed their opposition, his own experience indicated that being the child of a president could also be a blessing. "It made my life," he had told his friend Doug Wead. Would it not bring good things to his daughters as well?

Other issues also needed to be considered. He had been governor only four years and might need more seasoning. In the national political climate, the economy was booming and Bill Clinton had more than survived impeachment. Public opinion polls indicated that his popularity remained relatively high and that by a five-to-one margin, Americans believed they were better off than they had been four years before. Why would voters elect a Republican?

His brother Marvin had an immediate reaction. "Are you nuts?" The consumer confidence index was sky-high, the country was at peace. How on earth was he expecting to beat Al Gore? Cousin John Ellis came to the same conclusion. It was going to be a cold summer day in Texas before Gore would lose, given how well the economy was doing. George H. W., who had come to appreciate his son's political skills and gifts, was likewise worried about whether he could win.

On the other hand, W. was about to sell his stake in the Texas Rangers, which would bring in a cool $18 million. With that kind of cash on hand, the family could still live comfortably, could still buy the ranch in Crawford, and financing the girls' college education would not be a problem.

When the decision was finally made, the pressures and expectations that he had felt for much of his life seemed to evaporate. "I have a feeling of calm inside myself," he told a friend.

The contrast with his father was stunning. While the old man had determined in 1964 that he wanted to run for president someday and worked for the next decade and a half to make his presidential bid, George W. had in effect stumbled into it. Ten years earlier he had been worried about whether his past would preclude him from politics. When he did make a run, his career, unlike his father's, was haphazard and not well planned. The father, who so many in the family believed would be president one day, was being succeeded by the son whose own brother had considered him "the family joke" not too much earlier. If George W. had faith in the power of redemption, he need look no further than his own life.

Nor did George W. step into the presidential race for the same reason his father had twenty years earlier. For the father it had been about obligation, the belief that from those to whom much is given, much is expected. He was a member of the old school of civic idealism. George W. had no attachment to the idea of noblesse oblige. Was he running for president to fulfill his family's expectations?

Quietly, behind the scenes, some pieces of his campaign were slowly being moved into place. His father, despite his concerns, was discreetly contacting heavy hitters in the GOP and asking them to wait before committing to another candidate. By early 1999, eight other Republicans were already in the race, including former vice president Dan Quayle, Sen. John McCain, Lamar Alexander, and Elizabeth Dole. But all of them were finding it difficult to recruit big fund-raisers to their campaigns. Longtime Bush family friends and allies Mel Sembler, Robert Wood Johnson IV, John Hennessy, Wayne Berman, and Heinz Prechter were all asked to keep their powder dry and be patient.

For some of the other candidates who had longtime friendships with the family, it was a precarious situation. Dan Quayle, for whom George H. W. Bush had campaigned in 1978 and who had served loyally as his vice president, called the father shortly after W. announced his candidacy. They spoke for a few minutes in a tone that Quayle recalls as chilly. He had heard rumors that the son might be running, but he was hoping that because of his service the father might at least agree to some sort of nonaggression pact. The father wasn't interested. "We all have to do what we have to do," he said cryptically.

A few weeks later, when George W. announced his candidacy, the family fired a round right across Quayle's bow. One of the first Bush fund-raising events was scheduled for Phoenix, which both Quayle and Senator McCain considered their hometown. W. wasn't available for the event, so his father went instead.

The other candidates had local networks of supporters and some even had national followings. But the Bush clan had a nationwide network that included literally tens of thousands of family members, friends, and supporters. Their commitment was in a way to the Bush family itself, not simply to one particular candidate. George worked the telephones to line up supporters for his son. The support that the father had within the GOP was immediately transferable to the son and easily plugged into George W.'s own base of supporters. It all served to lock up the vast majority of the Republican establishment.

"The Bush family," said Tom Rath, a Republican fund-raiser, "has done everything they could to shut off the oxygen supply to everyone else—and it's worked." The endorsements quickly rolled in. By the spring of 1999, George W. had the total endorsement of ninety-four Republican congressmen, including the first-, second-, and third-ranking Republicans. Republican governors were also behind him.

In early August, father took son to a private gathering at the secretive and exclusive Bohemian Grove in California. George H. W. Bush had gone to a meeting there prior to his run, in 1979. He figured it would also benefit George W. to meet his circle of friends there, including corporate heads. The former president was a member of the Hillbillies Camp, which included William F. Buckley and Donald Rumsfeld as members.

But it would be a balancing act. Both the father and the mother were used to being in the limelight; they were now being asked to step back. In June 1999, George W. and his family traveled to Kennebunkport for their annual visit to Walker Point. This time, however, he arrived with 150 reporters in tow. On a sunny summer morning, father and son stood on the lawn with Bar as the wind blew in from the Atlantic.

"I had my chance," the father said, "and I got some things right. Maybe I messed some things up. But it's his turn now in the family."

As they stood there to answer questions it was clear that the baton had not been passed yet. The father dominated the joint appearance in front of twenty-eight camera crews, including those from Japan and Germany. After some Q&A, George W. headed back to the house for a nap. His father, however, stayed out on the lawn answering questions until a young aide tugged at his shirt and pulled him away.

While the Bushes have always maintained a strong loyalty and pride, they have felt relatively free to disagree on both policy and people. It is one of the strengths of the family, its ability to change and adapt to developing political circumstances. There is no strict adherence to a family ideology; family members can embrace their own ideas.

In the summer of 1999, George W. took his first public steps away from his father's legacy. Explaining that his father had clearly made a "mistake" when he broke his "read my lips" pledge as president, he was blunt in stating that he would be a different man. "I'll be a different candidate than the previous George Bush who ran for president . . . First of all, it shouldn't surprise you that there will be new names and new people involved. Second, people who will be working for me will be conservative-minded people."

Despite these early efforts to separate son from father, the family was having trouble finding the right tone. When George H. W. Bush chatted to a reporter or to an audience of supporters, he would go into a warm discussion about "my boy." "We're so proud of our boy," he would say. In New Hampshire he referred to the presidential candidate as "this boy, this son of ours." Clearly these words of affection were not helpful to the campaign. Calling a presidential aspirant "a boy" minimized George W. and made it hard for voters to envision him actually sitting in the Oval Office. As the habit continued, there was a flurry of e-mails fired between family members. In no uncertain terms the word went out to both George and Bar—stop it.

Bar was characteristically combative. When she was asked about it, she snapped back, "Don't you have a mother? Well, she feels the same way about you."

For George H. W. Bush, the criticism was stinging. Convinced that he was hurting his son, he made a conscious decision to step back. "He was just very nervous that he might make a mistake, say or do something wrong," explained his brother Pres, Jr., during the campaign. "He would rather do anything than that." He made few public appearances for his son, and given the hostility toward him among some in conservative Republican circles, George W. referred to him less frequently in his speeches.

But while the father retreated into the background, he remained a key player in the campaign. Karl Rove would travel to Houston regularly to brief the father privately. The old man would regularly trade e-mails with campaign advisers. (The Bush family has its own domain name and a private server.) He talked to friends and family around the country searching for gossip, new polling information, and more allies. During critical primaries he would call campaign headquarters sometimes every half hour to get the latest exit polling data. "It was even worse than when he ran for president," re-calls his brother Bucky.

He watched television compulsively to get glimpses of his son on camera. When he saw a shot on CNN of W. campaigning in New Hampshire, he contacted campaign aides. "Make sure he gets enough rest," he said.

The father also found the campaign difficult on another level. Asked to step back from a public role, he found himself unable to do anything when his son was attacked. "It's far more hurtful when your son is criticized than when you yourself are," he explained.

George W. Bush trusted his campaign aides, Karl Rove and Karen Hughes. But the experiences of the past had convinced him that familial loy-alty was the only kind you could depend on. Now it was the son who would talk to the father about the deepest matters of the campaign. "When he asks for advice," the father explained, "I give it. He knows I will never breach a confidence or tell anyone."

The Bushes have a protean nature; they are comfortable adapting and changing with the times. There is no rigid ideological tradition. If S. P. Bush was both a Taft man and a Democrat and Gampy Walker had railed against economic royalists, Pres Bush had been completely comfortable as a Re-publican liberal. His son felt equally at home as a moderate-conservative from Texas. Now, as a new generation arose, it reflected a new phase in the family's political development.

Outside of the family, a large orbit of advisers, aides, friends, and allies had labored with them for several decades. Many began to call the father for roles in the campaign. We want your help, they were told, and then they were all promptly told to contact the fund-raising operation. Virtually none were directed to policy or organizational channels.

To many it was a stunning response. Some even felt a certain embarrass-ment because "those with far weaker Bush connections," as one put it, were handling the most important tasks.

In mid-1999, an advisory board meeting of the George H. W. Bush Pres-idential Library took place in College Station, Texas. The former president was there along with a cluster of his closest advisers including Rich Bond, Marlin Fitzwater, Ron Kaufman, Andrew Card, and James Ciccone. While the meeting was ostensibly about the library, the discussion quickly turned to the upcoming campaign. Several pressed the former president to play a greater role in his son's campaign. The father listened quietly and told them to be patient; opportunities might still come up.

Worried about whether his son was getting the best advice, he made inquiries about bringing some of the old boys on board. He got back to several of his former aides a few weeks later.

"This is their turn," he said. "We had our turn."

The simple fact was that George W. was shunning many who had served in his father's administration. His exploratory committee, formed in March 1999, had included Reagan administration officials such as George Shultz and Haley Barbour. Conspicuously absent were members of his father's inner circle, including people such as James A. Baker.

Certainly this was good politics. He didn't want anyone to think that this would be a replay of his father's administration. But there was more to it than that. While his father had been familiar and comfortable in the culture of Washington, George W. couldn't stand the place. Part of it was the overtone of superiority that he had encountered at Yale. But more to the point, it was the absence of loyalty. When his father's electoral ship had been sinking in 1992, he saw those who were jumping off as "rats." He knew how the Washington game was played. Some people who wanted into the campaign were "feathering their own nests," he said. They were opportunists, and he wanted no part of them.

George W. Bush had come to resemble less his father, who had been a consummate establishment man, than Ronald Reagan the outsider. In part it reflected the fact that he had grown up in West Texas and still saw the world through that dusty lens. It also reflected his temperament. He was his father's son; but he was his mother's political protégé. "I learned more from her about politics and how to deal with people," he explains. "She's a natural. She has a lot of wisdom and she's not afraid to share it."

George W.'s embrace of Reagan's political legacy also reflected the changing tenor of the Republican Party. By 1999 the GOP was Reagan's party, and those who wanted to rise in its ranks needed to embrace the Reagan vision. W. had seen how the Reagan coalition of the 1980s had wedded economic and social conservatives. It was his experience in practical politics in 1988 and 1994 that gave him his political philosophy, not ideas forged together by reading or studying. Family members say that to understand George W., it is essential to understand how he learns.

"George W. has that sort of native intelligence, that non–merit scholar intelligence," says cousin John Ellis. "George is somebody who learns by doing. There is that great saying about golfers. Some learn by doing, some learn by watching, some learn by listening, some learn by feel. George W. is someone who learns by doing."

In the 1988 campaign he developed a habit of reading short memos but rarely long policy papers. Instead, he would want the policy people right there with him in the room. Instead of simply listening and receiving information, he would engage in an interchange.

"George W. doesn't learn something in a passive way," says Uncle Bucky Bush. "He's the sort who wants to be there and feed off of what he's hearing. He'll make up his own mind based on what he hears. Just as important as the ideas, however, is the person presenting them. If they're not behind it or can't answer tough questions, it tells him something about the underlying ideas."

That pattern became apparent when he began boning up on national issues for a possible presidential run. In April 1998, during a fund-raising swing through California, he linked up with several scholars at the Hoover Institution at Stanford University for an informal meeting at the campus home of George Shultz. For two to three hours Shultz and several economists and advisers discussed a variety of issues with W. The scholars found themselves impressed. Martin Anderson recalls, "We all kind of looked at each other and said, 'Hey, this guy's really good.' " Other meetings followed. Mayor Stephen Goldsmith of Indianapolis became a frequent interlocutor, as did UCLA professor James Q. Wilson and Princeton criminologist John DiIulio. In every single case, scholars found him to be much more animated by discussions than by looking at reading material.

As George W. scanned the political horizon in the 1990s, he came to the conclusion that the grand Reagan coalition had become unhinged. In part it was because of the political tremors that had shaken the 1990s. Bill Clinton had governed through "triangulation," which led him to incorporate ideas from both the left and right into his political philosophy. The old left-right dynamic, which had been evident especially since the Nixon-McGovern campaign of 1972, was changing. The second major event that influenced W.'s thinking was the public's general shrug over the Monica Lewinsky scandal. The cultural war seemed to be waning.

George W. was in the tradition of Reagan, but he also wanted to reform the Reagan coalition. Unlike most economic conservatives and libertarians, he believed that government could be a force for good. He believed, like his father, that government had a responsibility to help the weak, but he also believed that government's ability to do that was limited. He also blurred the old distinction between economics and other policy matters. Prosperity was not simply a resource question; it was a question of hope, faith, and character. That was the way it had been in his life. Only after he had turned his life around as a believer had he found the success he was looking for.

W.'s campaign theme became compassionate conservatism, a label that he affixed to a loose collection of policy ideas. Some were baffled. What precisely did it mean? Others ridiculed it as a marketing stunt, a reflection of some fine work done by pollsters.

Other candidates lashed out at the phrase. Lamar Alexander called them "weasel words." Former vice president Dan Quayle declared, "Conservatives ARE compassionate." Every one of the GOP hopefuls attacked his new political construct.

"Is compassion beneath us?" George W. shot back. "Should our party be led by someone who boasts of a hard heart?"

George W. was not the first one to use the phrase. Governor Thomas Dewey, an old family friend who had known his grandfather Pres Bush, had used the phrase. So had Bob Dole in 1988. But for George W., the phrase reflected how faith and politics fundamentally intersected.

At the center of his political philosophy was his vibrant Christian faith. When he stood at the podium and spoke about "the transforming power of faith, a belief no one is finally a failure or a victim, because everyone is the child of a loving and merciful God—a God who counts our tears and lifts our heads," he sounded like he was giving a sermon. In this case, however, he was speaking about filtering aid to the poor through churches.

But he also believed that charities should make demands of those who received the aid. Teen Challenge, a national drug treatment program, had a philosophy: "If you don't work, you don't eat." "This is demanding love," George W. would say, "a severe mercy. These institutions, at their best, treat people as moral individuals, with responsibilities and duties, not as wards or clients or dependents or numbers."

But he was also in a very direct way talking about himself and his own experience with redemption and transformation. In this way, for George W., the personal is the political. Christians did not only incorporate part of his political coalition; his faith is a center point of his political philosophy.

"I always laugh when people say George W. is saying this or that to appease the religious right," his cousin John Ellis said. "He *is* the religious right."

His quest for the presidency was about personal ambition as well as what he considered a spiritual calling. Elsie Walker Kilbourne remembers talking to him during the campaign and about what he was trying to do. She said that before the September 11 tragedy, he had a real sense of concern about the unity of the country and about a possible future calamity. "He talks about being a uniter not a divider, healing America's wounds together. His advisers have told him he needs to attack more, but he believes national unity is really important right now."

After the September 11 tragedy, Elsie Walker Kilbourne discussed with the president the fact that he had stressed national unity well before the tragedy.

"There are certain things—I don't want to get too spiritual—in the case of George it does seem that he was reluctant to get into the fray of the campaign because he knew [that a tragedy might take place]. If he had his druthers, he would have run for president later in life or maybe not at all. But I think he felt he was called for it, for a lot of reasons he understood, but for some he didn't. And I think that a lot of the things he said during the campaign have much deeper resonance now."

<hr/>

BUT GEORGE W.'S POLITICAL PHILOSOPHY IS A BREW THAT INCLUDES NOT only his belief in the centrality of redemption but also a keen sense of realism. Many had sought the presidency in the past two centuries and had incorporated faith as a central point of their campaigns. But most were like William Jennings Bryan, who, for all of his sermonizing, never came up with a realistic plan. George W. had a stronger sense of faith than his father, but he was also, oddly enough, more of a realist, too.

A cultural war of sorts had been raging during the previous thirty years. The flash points of the 1960s still hung heavy in American culture and were every bit as divisive as they had been during that turbulent decade. The presidency of Bill Clinton seemed to reopen some of those wounds. Conservatives had battled liberals on a host of social issues—abortion, the breakdown of the family, gay rights—with only limited success.

The culture war was real to George W., and it was a priority for his presidential campaign. Unlike his father, who grew up in the bosom of the Eastern establishment, George W. had an animosity toward it. "George W. really sees the world from West Texas," said his cousin John Ellis. "It's not that he's unaware of the establishment, it's just that by the time he was really exposed to it—those people were already attacking his father, those people were already attacking his friends in Texas. Those people were already culturally at odds with the people George feels the most comfortable with."

But he believed that you needed to fight the culture war on your own terms; conservatives had failed because they were not willing to adapt. George W. is, for example, decidedly pro-life. But rather than fight the straight-up political battle to ban abortion, which had produced few victories in the past twenty-five years, he wanted to overcome the issue by pushing alternatives, such as adoption programs, which would find even greater support among people.

This was a family campaign, and each member of the family played an important role. George H. W. Bush activated his network, assembling endorsements from dozens of members of Congress. In the U.S. Senate, the effort was directed by an enthusiastic senator, Paul Coverdell of Georgia, whose relationship with the family went back twenty-five years. When George H. W. Bush had served as ambassador to the U.N. he traveled to Atlanta to give a small talk on world affairs. In the audience that night was State Sen. Paul Coverdell. The two men hit it off, and weeks after they met, Bush invited the young politician to Kennebunkport to talk. When the father had run for president in 1980, Coverdell was the finance chairman in Georgia, and in 1988 he was the Southern steering committee chairman for the Bush campaign.

Coverdell had a critical role: get senators to endorse George W. instead of colleague John McCain. He was fabulous at his job; he managed to line up almost every Senate Republican.

George W. also inherited from his father a network of friends and supporters ranging from Staten Island borough president and former congressman Guy Molinari in New York to Sonny Montgomery, a Democratic congressman from Mississippi who had chaired the Armed Services Committee. Molinari had served as the father's chairman in New York during the 1988 presidential run, and Montgomery was a decades-old friend.

In Congress, W. picked up 117 congressmen and 10 senators by June 1999. They helped develop his agenda and raise money. It was a stunning gamble. At no time in modern American politics had a major party put its chips in the hands of a single candidate the way they were doing with George W.

***

BUT NOT ALL OF THE ENDORSEMENT CAMPAIGNS WERE SUCCESSFUL. THE FATHER had set his sights on Gen. Colin Powell even before the son had decided to run for the presidency. The efforts began in 1998, when Powell was asked by former President Bush whether he would consider a vice presidential slot. Powell said he wasn't interested. What's more, he was unwilling to commit to the Bush campaign so early. In part it was because he had reservations. He knew little about Bush and was fearful that he was not up to the job.

Others were concerned about whether George W.'s past might come back to haunt him during the campaign. In late March 1999 a delegation of GOP officials came from Massachusetts to check out the new apparent front-runner. They had a bite to eat at the trendy Shoreline Bar and Grill in Austin. As they chatted, Sandy Tennant started grilling W. about his past. Rumors about his young wild days had been circulating everywhere. At first W. responded with his pat "I was young and irresponsible" line. But when Tennant pressed him, W. got angry. "I have never been unfaithful to my wife, I haven't had a drink in ten years, and as far as I'm concerned, it is a nonissue." When the exchange was over, Tennant asked W. if he could control himself. W. stared at him. "You mean, can I smile when a bunch of jerks ask me questions? The answer is yes."

His uncle Pres helped organize a June 1999 fund-raiser in Greenwich, and Uncle Buck would do the same in St. Louis. Buck had managed to get three hundred new donors for George W.'s 1998 gubernatorial campaign and also helped line up the endorsement of a majority of the Republicans in the Missouri General Assembly. Uncle Johnny was raising money on Wall Street. As former finance chairman of the New York State Republican Committee, he would organize a splashy event for July in New York City, and another in Connecticut. Each brought in more than $1 million. Jeb held several fund-raisers in Florida. During one day he secured $800,000 at breakfast, $500,000 at lunch, $650,000 at a cocktail reception, and another $400,000 that evening. Jeb also assumed the role of attack dog, saying the things about Clinton and Gore that the family believed but W. couldn't say. Jeb's son, George P., struggled with his decision and finally wrote his father an e-mail to explain that he was planning to go to law school and would miss the campaign. Family members say he was nervous about how his uncle might take the news. George W. wrote him back and said that he was doing the right thing.

Meanwhile, Aunt Nancy left Boston and went to Columbus, Ohio, and checked into a fifty-dollar-a-night room. She worked on get-out-the-vote efforts. Why Ohio? She had heard that the race would be particularly close in that critical state.

In Denver, Bush cousin Joe Ellis, who was vice president of business operations for the Denver Broncos, helped organize a campaign rally featuring members of the team. Coach Mike Shanahan went so far as to offer an open endorsement. This was the amazing Bush family money machine, a self-lubricating operation that didn't even require the candidate's direct involvement. A quick $7.5 million was raised in the first few months of 1999 (more than even sitting vice president Al Gore could raise) without even leaving the state. George W. remained in Austin in order to keep a promise to Texas voters that he would remain focused on the state's business until the legislative session ended in late May. In the first six months the campaign raised $36 million.

Raising money is a barometer in politics, a sign of how large your support is. But in the case of the GOP primary, it also mattered because of the presence of Steve Forbes. The magazine publisher had spent millions in the 1996 GOP primary in an effort to beat Bob Dole. His massive media buys battered and bruised Dole, who limped into the general election without a unified party behind him. Forbes was running again, and Bush was going to have to spend a lot to match him.

A group of special friends called Pioneers was created to raise at least $100,000 each for the campaign. Of the four-hundred-plus people in this group, some came from the ranks of his mother's famed computerized card file. Longtime family friends or former aides to his father such as Wayne Berman, Zach Zachariah, and Ken Lay, chairman of Enron, were also among this group. The Houston-based law firm Vinson & Elkins kicked in $172,000. Efforts there were coordinated by Thomas Marinis, who had grown up with W. in Midland. From his Yale days he counted Roland Betts and Thomas Kuhn, who now headed the Edison Electric Institute.

Bill DeWitt and Mercer Reynolds, who had been his partners in the failed Spectrum 7, agreed to serve as his finance cochairmen in Ohio. They raised $1 million at a single reception in Cincinnati. "We're just a couple of guys with big families," they explained, "and we got a call from George asking us to help him out." Rusty Rose, his partner in the Rangers, was also a Pioneer.

Back in 1981 a successful Tucson auto dealer named James Click had sat between then–vice president George H. W. Bush and his mother, Dottie, at a White House event. They chatted and hit it off. "I immediately liked him," says Click. Click found his way onto the Bush family Christmas card list, and before he knew it he was raising money.

Other family friends raised enormous sums but didn't join the Pioneers. James Baker held a fund-raiser in Palm Springs, California, that netted several hundred thousand dollars. Sister Doro, Uncles Johnny in Connecticut and Bucky in Missouri, and cousin Dorothy Stapleton and her husband Craig were also Pioneers. At one point George W. mentioned that his brother Marvin was a Pioneer. When a reporter mentioned that he wasn't on a list that had been distributed, W. chuckled. "I think he's a Pioneer. If he's not, we need to expose that he's not."

This networking got the money machine primed, and it was soon churning along at a frightful pace. Bush could list an astonishing eighty thousand donors to his campaign who had made average contributions of $480. Clearly something more was afoot than simply the family network coming to life. Republicans around the country could sense that they might have a winner, and they desperately wanted one.

Once the decision to run had been made, the whole clan jumped aboard with enthusiasm. The father made appearances in Iowa, a state he had won from Reagan in 1980. Speaking on the lecture circuit, he would talk about his son and take an occasional swipe at Bill Clinton. In Orlando, Florida, car dealer Harold Wells got up and introduced the former president to fellow members of the National Automobile Dealers Association. As for the father, said Wells, "He's doing what you or I would do—he's helping his son get into the family business."

But while George made a few appearances in Iowa, Barbara was the star. A CBS News poll found that 63 percent of Americans had a favorable view of her and only 3 percent unfavorable. So Bar campaigned in Arizona, New Hampshire, Michigan, and Florida at a nonstop pace that tired her out. "She has been unleashed," her husband joked.

On the campaign trail, George W. spoke frequently about his mother and his wife. His references to his father were much more opaque. And yet, as the campaign progressed, it was clear that the torch was being passed. Bar, who for so long had been the feminine icon of the Bush family, was slowly giving way to Laura. It was Laura who got the featured speaking position and the last word at joint rallies. At the news conferences Bar would simply sit and watch.

But for all of the enthusiasm, the presidential race also complicated life for Jeb, who only months earlier had been elected governor in Florida. Still trying to establish himself in the minds of Florida voters, he was effectively forced to retreat from public view out of concern that he might hinder George W.'s campaign. On a few occasions he ventured out to campaign for his brother. He knocked on doors in New Hampshire and shook hands in South Carolina. But he turned down speaking opportunities around the country and even cut back on his own appearances in Florida. "Any bad things that might be said about me would be used negatively against George," he explained. "I don't see how I help George by having a high profile nationally. In fact, I see the opposite."

But as much as he might want to avoid complicating his brother's bid for the presidency, the mere fact that he was a Bush made it inevitable. Only weeks after he settled in to his job as governor, thunderclouds appeared on the horizon.

Ward Connerly, a determined opponent of affirmative action, had just won a victory in California with a ballot initiative to end the practice in state universities. Now he set his sights on Florida, launching a campaign to amend the Florida constitution to stop preference programs based on race, sex, or ethnicity. Florida was targeted specifically because of the Bush family connection. "I want this to be part of the presidential debate," Connerly said. "It scares the hell out of Jeb Bush, because he doesn't want it on the ballot when his brother runs for office."

Polls indicated that the move would be favored by a majority of voters. But Jeb and other Republican leaders in Florida worried that it might galvanize their political opponents and hurt them in the 2000 election. When Connerly arrived in Tallahassee, Jeb Bush, the Republican Senate president, and the House speaker all declined to meet with him.

In an attempt to defuse the issue, Jeb launched One Florida, an initiative strikingly similar to a program his brother had started in Texas. One Florida would end affirmative action and replace it with guaranteed placement in a public university to anyone who was in the top 20 percent of their class in high school. While it did halt Connerly in his tracks, it set off a firestorm that would have repercussions.

Jeb was convinced that One Florida would do in the Sunshine State what similar plans had accomplished in other states, namely boost minority enrollment without using race as the basis for admissions. While some black leaders welcomed the step, many others saw it as a direct assault. Students from nearby Florida A&M University, a predominantly black institution, began protesting the plan. Signs that read JEB CROW and WE NEED "ONE FLORIDA" LIKE WE NEED ANOTHER BUSH IN THE WHITE HOUSE sprouted up. Inside the State Capitol building itself, black lawmakers organized a sit-in at Jeb's office. Jeb was visibly angry. With a dozen reporters watching, he paced around the office and then turned to an aide. "Kick their asses out," he said. Later when asked to explain his comments, he said he wanted the reporters tossed, not the legislators.

One Florida did end up passing through the legislature, but the whole event set off a storm that would carry over into the 2000 election. Some might say the gambit to circumvent Ward Connerly would almost cost his brother the election.

George W. had been a witness to his father's loss in 1992 and he understood that, along with inheriting many of his father's friends, he would also inherit his enemies. Chief among them were Ross Perot and Pat Buchanan, who had a particular dislike for the old man. Now the two were joining forces. Buchanan would join the fold of the Reform Party and Ross would fund a presidential bid. No one really believed that Buchanan could win. But with Perot and his money behind him, Buchanan could do serious damage and peel off enough votes to hurt George W.'s chances.

W. wanted to fix this problem and do it soon. Knowing that Perot was hardened against his family, he went to his son, Ross, Jr. The two sons knew each other fairly well. Both were sports team owners, W. of the Rangers and Ross, Jr., of the Dallas Mavericks. "Despite the difference between the fathers," says Doug Wead, "the sons connected."

Back in 1988, Ross Perot had begun development of an air cargo airport outside of Fort Worth. By the mid-1990s the facility was in need of expansion, but the plans were being blocked by local authorities. "There was some airport that they blocked, but George got that all together again, through Tom Luce," says John Ellis. "There was very, very, very bad blood which had festered for some time. But W. got it back together again." George W. was able to help Ross, Jr., get his airport project back on track. Later, in the fall of 2000, Ross Perot would take the unusual step of endorsing George W. Bush for president.

The first big test was an Iowa straw poll. The event had no significance in terms of actual delegates, but it was an early barometer of strength. Throughout his life, growing up in an ambitious and competitive family, dramatically lowering expectations had been W.'s method of minimizing the impact of failure. Now, as his juggernaut of a campaign rumbled into Iowa, he faced the challenge of doing the same. George W. was so far out in front that many wondered if he was ready for a big fall. "The only thing we haven't done well," said Karl Rove, "is to lower expectations."

In Iowa, George W. would get his first real direct exposure to the extreme media scrutiny he had seen his father deal with a decade earlier. Unlike his father, however, who seemed to go out of his way to cater to the media, George W. seemed immune to its forces. TV reporter Mark Halperin asked him about the four national elections and how they had influenced his own political development. Halperin wanted a sort of soul-searching answer about W.'s own philosophy. What he got was: "Well, '88 was great and '92 stunk."

Running for president was about baring your soul. His father had found that out in 1988 when he had gone before the nation and spoken about the pain of losing his daughter Robin.

But George W. appeared determined not to get sucked into the media vortex. The impulse to avoid introspection at all costs extended to his own writing projects. The candidate's memoir had become a predictable part of any campaign arsenal, and W. agreed to write one with his friend Mickey Herskowitz of the *Houston Chronicle*. Herskowitz had written about sports and had known Bush for quite some time. He was expecting some inner-voice material about the real George W. What he got was a three-inch-high stack of old George W. speeches.

George W.'s relations with the media were cordial on the surface, but he had that deep, lurking suspicion inside. The media was constantly probing rumors concerning past drug use. George W. refused to play what he called the gotcha game of politics in Washington. But he was also concerned about how his past might influence his children. "I don't want to send a signal to children that whatever I may have done is okay." Rumors circulated about how he had danced naked on a bar in college, been arrested for using drugs. None of it was substantiated, but they continued to swirl.

W.'s suspicions were realized when the *New York Times* ran a story about some of the tutorials he was getting to bring him up to speed on the issues. The article concluded: "There may never have been a 'serious' candidate who needed it more." The editorializing was so outrageous that the *Times* later ran a correction. The offending sentence had been inserted by the editors. On NBC, reporter David Bloom suggested, "Many people don't believe the Texas governor is prepared to be commander in chief."

Frustrations with the media eventually would boil over late in the campaign when W. was caught on tape at a rally with Dick Cheney, pointing to Adam Clymer of the *New York Times*. "He's a major league asshole," Bush explained.

"Big time," Cheney concurred. (The response stuck with W., who started to call his running mate "Big Time.")

But larger than the candidate's suspicion for political reasons was the complete disconnect between the media and Bush. He was getting, in his mind, nonsensical questions that really didn't matter. When *New York Times* columnist Maureen Dowd asked about his reading list of books, he offered, "I've always liked John La Care, Le Carrier, or however you pronounce his name."

Dowd and George W. had, as they say, a history. When his father had been running for president in 1988, George W. had singled her out for particular scorn in family meetings. ("He would go off on riffs about her," recalls Shellie Bush Jansing.) Dowd returned the favor by predicting early in the campaign that the Bush ship was bound to sink and reach bottom quickly. "Yup," she wrote in June 1999, "the Republicans are bewitched. And that means soon they'll be bothered. And bewildered. Dreamboats always sink."

One bit of media scrutiny that the Bush clan enjoyed, however, was the imitations of George W. on *Saturday Night Live*. George W. as a clueless frat boy brought the family to tears from laughter. "I'd laugh so hard that I'd roll out of bed," recalls Nancy Ellis. "And we'd all talk on the phone to decide which skit was the best." The family consensus: the one in which George W. stumbles over the name of several visiting foreign dignitaries.

The attacks and parodies would continue throughout the campaign. And while presidential contenders like Sen. John McCain and Al Gore were intense and stern, George W. was just the opposite. "He's the most physically relaxed Republican in years," wrote columnist Mark Steyn. "The overwhelming impression is of a man at ease with himself."

That sense of ease led to speculation that he lacked curiosity about the world around him. His flubs started to mount. He called Greeks "Grecians" and Kosovars "Kosovians." Balkanize became "vulcanize" and ascribe became "subscribe." He explained that you "can't take the high horse and claim the low road." And he described millionaires "who have become rich beyond their means." There was also his sympathy: "I know how hard it is for you to put food on your family."

Often seen as a lack of intelligence, his butchery of the English language was seen as something all too familiar by family members. His speech pattern was similar to his father's. The old man had talked about "hyporhetorical questions" and "hypocthcate." He explained at one point in his presidency, "Please don't look at part of the glass, the part that is only less than half full." Another time he said: "I hope I stand for antibigotry, antiSemitism, antiracism."

But the father's intelligence had never been questioned. By the time he ran for president, he had a resume the length of his arm of proven accomplishments.

Elsie Walker Kilbourne grew up as one of the closest members of the clan to George W. She sees the mangled syntax not as a problem of intelligence but as a developmental problem that affects many others in the family. "I think he has some variety of ADD," she said. "I think that is where the speech thing becomes a problem. He doesn't have organizational issues. But he has reading issues and speaking issues. Some people with those sorts of circumstances self-medicate a bit. Also if they have addictive personalities—he also smoked a lot. But he exercised a lot, too. I had the same thing. We all [in the family] have vaguely some of these same issues."

GEORGE W. WOULD GO ON TO WIN THE IOWA STRAW POLL AND THE IOWA caucus: But his first big test would be New Hampshire, with its legendary independent voters. The Granite State had never been good to his father and viewed the family heritage as a matter of suspicion. George W. was determined to change that.

A vast network had been put together in the state, including campaign workers from the machine of longtime family friend, New Hampshire senator Judd Gregg. Julia Fifield, a Republican stalwart from Orford, New Hampshire, held a reception for George W. and Bar. Twenty years earlier she had hosted one of the first receptions for the father.

As the candidates gathered in New Hampshire for a presidential debate, family members were nervous. George H. W. was on a fishing trip in Argentina, trying to get his mind on something else. The day before the debate he had mistakenly called his wife.

"How was it?"

"How was what?" Bar responded.

"How was the debate?"

Bar simply shook her head before setting her husband straight.

George W. was nervous, too. He would call Laura in Austin to check on the girls, and called twice the same night to see who was responsible for feeding the dog.

Senator John McCain's independent campaign paid big dividends in New Hampshire, and he came out with a double-digit win. Many in the Bush family bitterly blamed the media for giving him so much favorable coverage. "That great sucking sound you hear is the sound of the media's lips coming off John McCain's . . ." said brother Marvin Bush before cutting off his comments to reporters.

McCain was ecstatic when the numbers came in.

"Someone yell 'Timber!' " he exclaimed in the presidential suite of the Nashua Crowne Plaza Hotel, as if a mighty tree had fallen. George W., feeling both anger at his loss and a sense of failing to measure up, instructed Karl Rove to call McCain and offer his congratulations. John Weaver, McCain's aide, took the call.

"Consultants don't concede to candidates," he snapped.

Moments later, George W. called back. With fierce competitive juices built up over a lifetime coursing through his veins, he offered his congratulations. But the conversation lasted a scarce ninety seconds.

John McCain set down the phone, convinced that he was going to take command of the election. But on the suite's wall was a reminder that it would not be so easy. After all, he was running against a legacy, a family, a dynasty. As he sat in the presidential suite celebrating with his wife and top aides, President George H. W. Bush looked down at them from a photo on the wall.

New Hampshire represented George W.'s first stumble in the race. That sense of invincibility, just recently so strong, had evaporated, and the other candidates were quick to pile on.

"Frankly," said Sen. Orrin Hatch to W. during one appearance, "I really believe that you need more experience before you become president of the United States. You'll make a heck of a president after eight years."

Even some supporters began hedging their bets. "I have endorsed Governor Bush," said Senator Al D'Amato, "[but] it doesn't keep me from marveling and enjoying and living vicariously through McCain." Precisely how deep was his support?

———

ATTENTION QUICKLY TURNED TO THE NEXT PRIMARY, IN SOUTH CAROLINA. Former governor Carroll Campbell, a close friend of his father's, had his machine behind George W. But a victory in South Carolina was going to require more than running as the most electable candidate and staying positive. Instead, W. would need to return to the politics of Lee Atwater and the sort of race that his father had run in 1988.

George W. had learned in 1988 that winning elections was about both driving up your own numbers and driving down your opponent's. By early 2000, John McCain had great momentum and his negatives were very low. In order to stop McCain, the Bush campaign would have to drive up his negative numbers. George W., in his 1978 campaign and both gubernatorial races, had never before resorted to such a strategy.

But he was fully prepared to do it. As he stood at a campaign stop, a local supporter, State Sen. Mike Fair, said, "Y'all haven't even hit his soft spots."

"We're going to," W. responded. They just were "not going to do it on TV."

Over the course of the next several days, an explosion of negative TV and radio ads was aimed at McCain. While George W. maintained his persona as an amiable and compassionate conservative, the ads ran and mailings were sent out questioning McCain's conservative credentials.

McCain was also attacked from outside of the Bush campaign. A professor at Bob Jones University sent out an e-mail charging McCain with fathering illegitimate children. Nasty rumors were spread about his wife. By the night of the South Carolina debate, tensions between the two camps were high. As the candidates stood next to each other, there was an awkward silence. McCain finally turned to Bush.

"George," he said shaking his head. He didn't need to tell him what he was thinking.

"John. It's politics."

"George, everything isn't politics."

The debate began and the testiness seemed to die down. Then when they broke for a commercial, George W. reached over to shake McCain's hand, in hopes that they could put their differences behind them.

"Don't give me that s——," retorted McCain. "And take your hands off me."

McCain and the Bushes had a history. McCain's grandfather, an admiral in the Pacific during World War II, had served with Admiral Kauffman, who was George W.'s great-uncle. Later, when W.'s father had been vice president, McCain had come to him concerning a controversy involving the Skull and Bones organization. Now, facing this barrage of attacks, McCain appealed to the legacy of the Bush family in an effort to get them to end. "I'm calling on my good friend George Bush to stop this now," he told the media. "Stop this now. He comes from a better family. He knows better than this."

George W. went on to win South Carolina by eleven points. South Carolina demonstrated that, for all the affability and even goofiness that people associated with George W., he also had the ability to rip someone's throat out. The flashes of steeliness that some had seen during his father's run in 1988 were back. It was the sort of bare-knuckled politics that his father and grandfather had never been comfortable with or good at. If it bothered George W., it didn't show.

---

GEORGE W.'S VICTORY IN SOUTH CAROLINA EFFECTIVELY STEMMED THE McCain tide, but on the heels of that victory came some very troubling campaign data. Polls indicated that a majority of Republican voters were expressing concern about whether George W. was ready to be president. It was a stunning number, particularly among those who would presumably make up his base of support in a general election. Given that reality, how could he expect to attract independents?

With that data in mind, the hunt for a running mate became all the more critical. The early favorite had been Gov. Tom Ridge of Pennsylvania. A Catholic governor of a vote-rich Northeastern state, Ridge made sense according to the political math. Ridge was also well known to the family. He had been friends since college with Craig Stapleton, who was married to a Walker cousin. That led to an introduction to the Bush clan in 1996.

But Ridge was virtually unknown to most Americans. Instead, W. needed a steady hand who would add experience to the ticket without taking the spotlight off of himself.

At the suggestion of his father, George W. appointed Dick Cheney to head up the effort. They had collected a short list of elder statesmen who might fit the bill. On several occasions W. called his father to talk about the choices. Most were longtime family friends such as Sen. John Danforth of Missouri. It soon became clear what the father thought: Dick Cheney was the ideal guy. He was smart, hardworking, loyal, and unconcerned about the limelight. Pretty soon George W. saw it that way, too.

Cheney's entrance into the race represented a full circle for both himself and the father. Twenty-five years earlier it had been Dick Cheney, chief of staff in the Ford White House, who had been favorably disposed to the idea of Ambassador George H. W. Bush as a running mate for Gerald Ford. Now it was the father pushing Cheney.

That spring, as his son was locking up the Republican nomination, the father continued with his visits overseas. He and Bar traveled to China to do some charity work. He also paid a visit to Chinese president Jiang Zemin, with whom he discussed the international situation and his son's campaign. The Chinese were watching the race closely, wondering if the election of George W. Bush would benefit them. They were also curious about the father's advocacy of closer relations while the son was campaigning on the theme that China was a "competitor" and not a partner.

The father also paid a social call on several longtime friends in the Middle East. He traveled first to Saudi Arabia and then to Kuwait, where he met with members of the al-Sabah royal family with whom he had been doing business for almost four decades. In 1991, after the Gulf War, both the Kuwaitis and the Saudis had made clear their preference for a second Bush term. They had even dramatically lowered oil prices on the eve of the 1992 election. But in the 2000 election, the al-Sabah family was not nearly so vocal in its preference. The Clinton administration was furious with the royal family, which it blamed for a boost in oil prices. Prices had tripled in the previous twelve months in light of lower production by Kuwait and other OPEC members, and the Clinton administration was pressing hard for prices to be lowered.

---

THAT SUMMER, WITH THE NOMINATION ALL BUT LOCKED UP, THE FAMILY gathered in Kennebunkport to celebrate Bar's seventy-fifth birthday. It was supposed to be a surprise—two hundred or so of their closest friends in town for a party. George almost pulled it off, but when Sen. Alan Simpson called to say he couldn't make it, he mistakenly left word with Bar.

Plenty of chatter went on about the campaign. "But the event was really a tribute to Bar," recalls Gerry Bemiss, who was in attendance. "It's interesting because nothing like it was ever done for George. Bar really is in so many respects the heart and soul of the family."

Toasts, short speeches, and skits by family members included a gentle ribbing. A couple of family members put on a spoof about how Bar married into the family, and no one heard of the Pierces again. The skit brought laughs but also hinted at a deeper truth. "The Walker energy and the Bush intensity," says Bemiss, "anyone who marries into it has a hard time matching it. Through the generations the other branches of the family seem to have just melted away in the face of it."

The Bush men played several rounds of golf, or the particular Bush brand of the game called "aerobic golf." Played in the same way the Bushes and Walkers move through life, fast and furious, they would play eighteen holes in seventy minutes. With the national convention looming, George W. also made time for seaside jogs and a quick spin in his father's new speedboat, *Fidelity II.*

On Sunday the family attended church together. When the two Georges tried to slip out a little early to meet with reporters, the ever-watchful Bar was close behind.

"Stay in church until the end," she told them.

---

ON JULY 31 THE BUSHES GATHERED IN PHILADELPHIA FOR THE REPUBLICAN National Convention. The convention represented the return of the Bushes to the center of the GOP. But they were mindful not to make themselves the center of attention. "We want to be careful it doesn't turn into a Bush family reunion," said convention cochairman Andrew Card.

Doro was a delegate from Maryland. Jeb was there with the Florida delegation. Neil and Marvin would go around to the various state delegations to give a small talk and rev up the crowds. Marvin had seen his fund management firm grow to over $300 million, investing in profitable but decidedly low-tech ventures. He had struck alliances with Christopher Brady, son of his father's treasury secretary Nicholas Brady, and with Sam Wyly, a longtime family friend. (Marvin also spent time on CBS News trying to handicap the finalists on the television show *Survivor*.) Cousin Elizabeth Walker Field was a member of the Delaware delegation.

Jeb's eldest son, George P., was another fixture at the convention. He had graduated from Rice University, where he stirred local controversy among liberal activists because of his failure to participate in "Hispanic organizations." Instead, he had spent his time on Saturdays helping kids through a Catholic Church mentoring program. After college, he had gone to work for a few years as a teacher in a poor south Florida neighborhood.

In all, four members of the clan would speak before a nationwide audience, including Laura, along with Jeb and George P., who was the convention's youth chairman. George and Bar were there, watching together as their eldest son accepted the nomination.

Eight years earlier the family had gathered as George H. W. Bush tried to keep the party unified. The conservatives had been down on him for breaking his tax pledge. In the end he had gone down to an inglorious defeat with only 38 percent of the popular vote. Now he and Bar were returning to see their son receive the nomination. And the law of familial politics seemed to be coming into play: As the son rose, the fortunes of the father rose with him.

Ron Kaufman, an adviser to the father, saw the change in the former president's standing among Republicans. "In '93, we'd get maybe two or three requests a month max [to speak] like, 'Can he do the Lincoln Day speech for the Harris County Republican Party in Texas?' I'd mostly get calls, 'Do you think the president would mind asking his son if he'd be the speaker?' But by 1999 he was getting twenty-five to thirty requests a week for him to be the headliner at events like the Republican National Committee's annual gala." The political tide was lifting all of the Bush boats.

At the convention, questions about the family's history and legacy were repeated. The father kept a low profile, refusing to answer most questions on the subject. When the dreaded d-word, "dynasty," came up, he rejected it out of hand. When Jeb was asked about it, he just shook his head. "Dynasty shmynasty," he retorted. It was the constant refrain.

"I don't think they ever had to have a meeting to say, don't mention dynasty," says Doug Wead.

For the Bushes, "dynasty" was a dreaded word not simply because it was politically dangerous but because it ran contrary to their ethos. It smacked of calculation and entitlement. For the Bushes, there had rarely been any detailed discussions about the political fortunes of the family. In the Bush home the young were taught about the nobility that could be found in public life, and then an unspoken code seemed to propel them into it. Public service was about something more than advancing the cause of the family; it is their identity. Dynasty-building would, in a sense, cheapen what they held to be a calling.

When the d-word didn't get a response from the family, more questions about family history and legacy arose. As one reporter noted to Bar, only one woman in American history knew what it felt like to be married to one president and mom to another, Abigail Adams: What would it feel like?

"I don't think she was living," Bar shot back. "I plan to be living."

One night the family gathered for a private dinner, with all of the laughing and crying that there usually was at these gatherings. Family members told stories about the past. But the high point came when Jeb stood up and said, with a lump in his throat, "I see my brother as presidential." Coming from a brother who had been a competitor in recent years and so distant to so many, it brought tears to the eyes of almost everyone in the room.

On a lighter note, Jeb and his son George P. put together a David Letterman "Top Ten List" of what a return to the White House might mean for the Bush clan.

#9 from George P.: "Great pickup line: 'You wanna take a stroll through my uncle's Rose Garden?'"

Jeb: "And the No. 1 reason George W. should be elected president: There definitely will be a controlling legal authority . . . Barbara Bush."

BUT FOR ALL THE EMOTION AND EXCITEMENT, THERE WAS ALSO A CURRENT of anger. In the run-up to the convention, President Bill Clinton had started with a series of potshots at the family. At a fund-raiser in Rhode Island, the commander in chief gave a wicked impersonation of George W. "My daddy was president. I own a baseball team. They like me down there."

The remarks sent the father into a tizzy. Always struggling to control his emotions in the face of the media, he snapped, "If he continues that, then I'm going to tell the nation what I think about him as a human being and a person."

It was a spectacle quite unseen—two American presidents on the verge of trash-talking each other. It was a sign of how deep the resentment and dislike really was between the Bushes and the Clintons. And yet it was also an emblem of the differences between the normally reticent Bushes and Clinton, the "let it all hang out" president.

The father had been fighting political battles for three decades now and it was difficult for him to stop. But the imagery was not helpful at all to his son. The father seemed to be fighting the son's battles. Bar saw the damage that could be done and advised her husband to put a stop to it quickly.

But while the father held his fire at the request of his wife, Bill Clinton kept blasting away. Over the course of the convention he would give no fewer than eight political speeches taking shots at both W. and his father. And that fall, George W. would square off against another son from a prominent political family.

#### CHAPTER 42

# CROSSING
# THE RIVER

G EORGE W. BUSH AND AL GORE—SEEMINGLY SO SIMILAR AND
yet worlds apart. Both grew up as the eldest sons in prominent
political families. Both were C students at Ivy League schools,
and both witnessed important events close up as their fathers made history.
Both families had also crossed paths in history.

When Prescott Bush had run for the Senate in Connecticut, a senator
from Tennessee named Albert Gore, Sr., had come to campaign vigorously
against him. When both served in the Senate, they often found themselves
on opposite sides of the most sensitive political issues, including civil rights.
In 1984, when Al Gore, Jr., ran for the U.S. Senate, George W. went to Tennessee to campaign for his opponent, Victor Ashe, a longtime family friend
and member of Skull and Bones.

In short, these were two very competitive political families. And yet they
functioned very differently. The Gores were a decidedly top-down dynasty;
the old man guided the son and imposed a future on him. Young Al's birth
was announced on page 1 of the *Nashville Tennessean*. By age six the
*Knoxville News Sentinel* was proclaiming him a rising political star. When he
reached high school, his father announced that he was setting aside a wall
in the home for his son's presidential years.

The Bushes operated very differently. Far from being top-down, the
Bushes were in a strange way bottom-up. For two generations, George W.
Bush had seen his forebears at the heart of national power. As he was growing up, it was never suggested that he would run for office. Instead, the unspoken question was—Would you fulfill your responsibility to serve? It was
more of a challenge than a command.

The two families' worldviews were also distinctly different. To the Bushes,
Al Gore seemed to walk around with a sixty-pound pack on his back, a knap-
sack of guilt and expectation that weighed on him. George W. and Jeb had
experienced that sense of suffocating guilt at Andover, and George W. later
at Yale and Harvard. When Al Gore saw the privileges he had grown accus-

tomed to in his youth, he felt guilty. When George W. Bush looked at his privilege, he was profoundly thankful for what his parents and ancestors had been able to pass along to him. He was also mindful of the burdens of privilege. Al Gore had grown up in Washington, D.C., and among the elite in Tennessee society, familiar places where the family was well established. The Bushes, by migrating to places such as Midland, Texas, had encountered the limits of privilege. Being the product of Yale was a negative in West Texas, as George W. found when he ran for Congress there in 1978.

The 2000 campaign was presumed to be a contest between an astute policy insider and a charismatic outsider. Al Gore understood the mechanics of power and was well versed on the issues. George W. understood the issues but in a far less detailed manner. He also had difficulty expressing himself extemporaneously when it came to explaining these complex issues.

The playbook for his campaign then became less the one that his father had adopted in 1980 and 1988. George W.'s campaign would be less Bush and more Reagan, demonstrating once again the family's ability and comfort in adapting to new realities without offending the sensibilities of earlier generations.

George W. understood Reagan politically in a way that his own father didn't. Reagan had always been a bit of a mystery to the old man. George H. W. Bush had grown up in the world of business, with its emphasis on practical knowledge. Reagan was not a businessman and his political identity was tied up in principles, not practical knowledge. George W. could identify with that, and through the course of the general election he often consciously and unconsciously wedded himself more to the Gipper than his father.

When critics labeled him a lightweight, he responded by saying, "I take great comfort in the fact that they said the same thing about President Ronald Reagan." When Gore took shots at him for lack of experience, he responded, "I remember what they did to Ronald Reagan. They belittled him and said, 'Oh, he can't possibly be smart enough to be president of the United States. He is simply an actor.' The man turned out to be a great president."

He also subconsciously mimicked Reagan. When asked about a comment Al Gore made about his tax plan, George W. responded, "There he went again." It was an echo of Reagan's reply to Jimmy Carter in 1980.

If for George W. the race was a replay of Reagan's in 1980 and 1984, Al Gore ironically looked to George H. W. Bush's 1988 campaign for inspiration. In that election, down by 17 points against Michael Dukakis, Bush was derided as a "lapdog" who lacked independence and vision. The same criticisms were now being leveled against Gore.

The Bushes were determined to see this through the lens of a young, ambitious man rising to the presidency on grit and determination. The Bushes are, after all, the unKennedys. "The family will take pride that he went as far as he did," George H. W. Bush said. "It is not that this is John F. Kennedy's father driving his sons to do something. We are not that way in this family. This is not about vindication or legacy or entitlement. It is about the love of a father for his son, the love of a mother for her son."

And yet there was no escaping the family's rich legacy. George W. traveled to Columbus, Ohio, and spoke to a high school only a few miles from where S. P. Bush used to work. There, he spoke about the need for tough compassion when dealing with the poor, the same sort of views that S. P. Bush had articulated almost a century earlier. And he did so standing on the podium with Sen. Bob Taft and Tony Roosevelt. Bob Taft's family had known the Bushes for ninety years. Roosevelt was the grandson of FDR, whom Bert Walker had met to talk about his political ambitions seventy years earlier.

By all objective measures the race should not have been particularly close. The American people were basking in what appeared to be a continued economic boom. And yet Bush was running neck-and-neck with Gore, sometimes even taking the lead. Gore made his appeal on the grounds of competence while George W. rallied on the theme of honesty and values. Neither seemed capable of knocking out the other.

On October 17 the Bushes gathered to watch the third and final debate between the two candidates. Jim Lehrer was the moderator. The two men came out and greeted each other before taking their respective places. When the questioning came, they alternated in their responses, one standing in front of the audience while the other took a seat on an assigned stool. Suddenly, as George W. started to answer a question, Al Gore walked toward him, clearly trying to intimidate him. Only inches away, he stared at George W. In 1996, Bill Clinton had done the same thing to Bob Dole, and the senator seemed to be unnerved by the tactic. This time, however, George W. glanced over at him, seemed to smirk, and then kept talking.

"My God!" yelled George H. W. Bush back in Houston, watching it on television.

"I thought he was literally going to hit him," Bar said later.

What had been a relatively civil campaign was now becoming nasty. Even George W.'s apolitical daughters, Barbara and Jenna, took a severe dislike to Gore that night. When Gore made an overt reference to his children being present at the debate, they took it as an insult, meaning why aren't your kids here? Afterward, both girls vowed to do more to help their dad. When George W. chatted with Jenna shortly after the debate, she was for the first time emphatic in her praise. George W. was so overcome, he cried.

In the waning days of the campaign, the father watched his son with a new sense of confidence. He had, in his words, "crossed a kind of river of doubt." His son had proven himself on the national stage in a way that the old man had not been able to.

Still, the race was neck-and-neck, and the former president saw even before election night that it would hinge on Florida. "A key state like Florida looked good a few days ago," he said days before the election. "Now I see a poll that shows us behind. How can that be? I wonder, are we lulling ourselves into a premature sense of false victory and complacency?"

Florida was indeed becoming ground zero in the waning days of the campaign. Jeb, who had won comfortably there two years earlier, was horrified that the race was as close as it was. His older brother had made clear on the campaign trail, "I'm going to rely on my little brother to carry Florida." And Jeb himself knew that his brother's rise to the White House would rest on Florida. "If we carry Florida," Jeb said in October, "my brother is going to be the president of the United States."

Jeb was feeling enormous pressure. "The stakes are very high now for Jeb," said Congressman Mark Foley. "You don't want your own brother calling and saying, 'What happened? I thought we were in pretty good shape.'" Along with constant inquiries from the family, there were also e-mails from his father who, in his frantic search for information about the race, was wondering how things looked in Florida. Before long, the Sunshine State was the family's most frequent destination. In the last week of September, George W. was campaigning in Orlando, Big George was in Miami, and Jeb was in Miami Beach talking about health care and his brother's campaign.

George W. had called his brother on numerous occasions to discuss the situation in Florida. In the waning days of the campaign across the Sunshine State, Jeb had looked his brother in the eye and assured him, "Florida is going to be Bush-Cheney country."

But Jeb was walking a tightrope. He could do a lot to help his brother, but he could also complicate matters by drawing attention to the dynasty question. The campaign wanted him to keep a low profile, which is what Jeb had been doing for the past eighteen months. When calls came to the governor's office for interviews with Jeb about the presidential race in Florida, callers were told to arrange them through his brother's campaign in Austin. Usually those requests were turned down. Jeb had also kept close to his knitting in Tallahassee, avoiding opportunities to speak to large audiences around the country. There was even the awkward balance to strike during campaign appearances in Florida. If Jeb was there, inevitably the media would draw comparisons between the two brothers, sometimes in a way that was not favorable to George W. On the other hand, if he didn't show up, people would wonder why. W. even found himself saying at some campaign appearances, "I'm a little disappointed the chairman of my campaign [in Florida, Jeb] is late."

Jeb was determined to see his brother succeed. "I don't want to live the rest of my life with the humiliation of not having it be that way," he said.

———

BAR HAD BEEN WARNING W. FOR QUITE SOME TIME. DESPITE HER DOWDY IMage and grandmotherly demeanor Bar had a real instinct for politics, and she had been warning for weeks that there would be "an October surprise." "I don't know what it will be," she said. "But something, something."

Family members from the former president on down were on the Internet daily, clicking on the Drudge Report, waiting for something to explode. Days before the election, news broke of George W.'s arrest in 1976 on a charge of drunk driving. The story had been leaked by a Democratic activist in Maine and soon it made headlines around the country. George W. had been out drinking with friends, including John Newcombe, the Australian tennis star. Pulled over by the police, W. had failed a sobriety test. It was a stunning bit of news that brought up images of his rowdy past. Critics claimed that by failing to reveal what had happened, George W. was being dishonest. Ironically, the news was not new to the organization Mothers Against Drunk Driving in Texas. George W. had told his staff about the arrest a long time ago, and they had shared it with MADD.

The Sunday before the election, George W. and Laura attended St. Andrews Church in Jacksonville, Florida, and had breakfast with Billy Graham. The two men had walked closely over the past fifteen years since their long discussions while strolling on the beach in Kennebunkport.

George W. had connected with Graham in a way that he never had with his father. Franklin Graham explained that the two men connected on a profound level. "The son and the father have a different faith," he told us. "The son studies the Bible, he reads it every day just like my father."

Shaking a bit as he stood before the media, one could see a sense of amazement in Graham's eyes about the man standing next to him. Graham had never come close to endorsing anyone for political office. But on this sunny morning, he said, "I've been praying that God's will shall be done. I don't endorse candidates. But I've come as close to it, I guess, now as any time in my life, because I think it's extremely important. I believe in the integrity of this man."

---

THE FINAL DAYS AMOUNTED TO A MASSIVE SPRINT THROUGH FOUR STATES— Tennessee, Wisconsin, Iowa, and Arkansas. Polls indicated that the race was a toss-up, but George W. seemed confident of victory. At his final rally in Bentonville, Arkansas, he jumped onto the stage as the speakers blared out "Don't Stop Thinking about Tomorrow." The song, by Fleetwood Mac, had been the Clinton campaign theme in 1992. But when the tune reached, "Don't stop thinking about tomorrow," the song was interrupted and replaced by the chorus of The Who's hit "Won't Get Fooled Again." George W., to the hoots of the crowd, danced to the beat in his cowboy boots. It was, at last, done. The campaign was over.

---

GEORGE W. SLEPT ONLY FIVE HOURS THE NIGHT BEFORE THE ELECTION. HE rose early, read his Bible, prayed, and then went to the gym at the University of Texas. That afternoon, exhausted from the heavy campaigning over the past months, he took a long nap.

At 5:30, W. called his cousin John Ellis, who was working the election desk at the Fox News Channel. Ellis, who had worked the NBC desk during two previous elections, was familiar with how the data came in and knew how to read the electoral tea leaves to see what it meant. Exit polls in Austin were indicating that the race was razor-close.

"Is it really this close?" W. asked him.

"Yeah, it's really close."

"Well, what do you think?"

"I have no idea."

"Well, keep in touch. Let me know if you hear anything good."

George W. and Laura gathered with his parents and Jeb at the governor's mansion in Austin. That evening they all went for a family dinner at a restaurant next to the Four Seasons Hotel. The extended family was in town, including Uncle Bucky, Aunt Nancy, and several cousins. It was a festive if nervous dinner until news suddenly leaked out that Al Gore was being declared the winner in both Michigan and Florida. It was dreadful news; both were considered states that George W. needed to win.

George W., losing his appetite, ended dinner and retreated to the governor's mansion. The plan had been for the family to watch the returns at a suite in the Four Seasons, but now the mansion would be the family fortress.

By 7:52, Fox News was calling Florida for Gore. Jeb was devastated. He called his cousin John Ellis.

"Are you *sure?*" he asked with emotion.

"Jeb, I'm sorry. I'm looking at a screen full of Gore."

"But the polls haven't closed in the Panhandle."

"It's not going to help. I'm sorry."

Jeb was simply devastated. He turned to his brother, apologizing for his failure to deliver Florida.

Frantic to do something—anything—he started making calls to radio stations on the West Coast—to Seattle and Medford, Oregon, among other places—in a desperate bid to help his brother. But the election seemed to be slipping away. "We've done all that we can do," George W. said. "It's up to the people of this country to make up their mind."

By 11 P.M. EST, John Ellis was back on the phone with W. He had looked over the numbers in Florida again and was no longer sure that Gore was going to win. Fox News was now retracting the call for Gore.

By 1:50 A.M., Ellis became confident that Gore could not win Florida. He called the mansion and asked for Jeb.

"I think you've got it," he told his anxious cousin. Fox News now had the state for Bush.

Minutes later the phone rang at Ellis's Fox News desk. "Gore called and conceded," W. told him. "He was good, very gracious." Ellis congratulated him.

By 2:16 A.M., Ellis believed that George W. had indeed won Florida and with it the presidency. He called W. to tell him the good news. John Moody, vice president of Fox News, made the official call moments later.

But the seesaw in Florida continued. Just as the tide seemed to swing for George W., it drifted toward Gore again. As quickly as he had called to concede, Gore was now on the phone to rescind his earlier concession.

George W. was confused. "Let me make sure I understand. You're calling me back to retract your concession?" W. went on to explain that Jeb had spoken with state election officials, who had assured him that the numbers were solid and that he would carry Florida by a narrow margin.

"Let me explain something," snapped Gore. "Your younger brother is not the ultimate authority on this."

Moments later the phone went dead.

The tension in the governor's mansion was palpable. Former president

Bush was "a nervous wreck," Jeb Bush told us. Bar, on the other hand, did her best to break the tension. "Gosh," she said with a chuckle, "it was great to be the mother of the president for thirty minutes."

As night turned to morning, Florida still hung in the balance, and it quickly became apparent that Jeb's gambit to deal with Ward Connerly through his One Florida plan had backfired. Rather than defusing the issue, it had made the Bushes the target of wrath for minority voters. While blacks had represented only 10 percent of voters in the 1996 presidential race, in 2000 they represented 15 percent, a surge directly attributable to the controversy surrounding One Florida.

That morning the outcome was still very much in doubt. George W. did what he had done every morning that year: He got up and read from his *One Year Bible*. His good friend Don Evans had introduced him to this edition, published by Tyndale, which allows the reader to consume the entire Bible (Old and New Testaments) in just one year. George W. had made it his practice to read through it every other year.

For George W. the words had the ability not only to inform but also to transform, and family and friends had noticed that one could literally track some of his thinking based on what he read.

On April 26 he had surprised many when, in an interview, he proclaimed that a "cycle of bitterness" was at work in Washington. The surprise came in that he said, "Some in our party have responded in kind . . . both parties bear some of the blame." It was a candid statement that took many, including those in his campaign, by surprise. His reading that morning had been from Proverbs and was about honesty: "A truthful witness does not deceive, but a false witness pours out lies."

In Akron, Ohio, he had become immersed in a verbal tussle with reporters about past drug use, a real concern for him throughout the campaign. George W. had said that he could pass a federal security clearance, which required one to be drug-free for twenty-five years. Instantly the media seized upon his comments and asked, Did that mean he had used drugs earlier than that? George W. tried to evade the question over the next twenty-four hours, answering selectively and parsing his comments. But eventually he stopped. The decision to stop came from campaign aides, but family and friends also point to the reading from his *One Year Bible* of August 21, which was Proverbs 21:23— "He who guards his mouth and his tongue keeps himself from calamity."

Now, the morning after the election, he had another reading from Proverbs (27:10): "Do not forsake your friend and the friend of your father, and do not go to your brother's house when disaster strikes you—better a neighbor nearby than a brother far away."

The reading proved to be prophetic. Minutes later he received a phone call from Dick Cheney. His running mate was suggesting that they send Jim Baker, the friend of his father, to oversee the recount in Florida.

The family's relationship with Baker had cooled after the 1992 election. Bar blamed him for not trying hard enough on her husband's behalf, but Baker was still close to the father. The two had been set to go hunting in the days after the election with Gen. Norman Schwarzkopf and basketball coach Bobby Knight in Spain. But Bar was still resentful.

"I think that George W. had shared some of his mother's resentments about Baker's conduct, particularly when he was perceived to be disloyal in the press," said cousin John Ellis. "But I think that George W. does not carry the parental grudges far along. He kind of wears them for a while and then he has his own interests. I don't think he was all bent out of shape about Jim Baker."

When Cheney mentioned sending Baker, George W. liked the idea. "Baker will do a fantastic job," he wrote to family and friends in an e-mail.

Baker agreed to cancel his trip and come to the aid of the family again, and he proved to be the perfect man for the job. Shrewd, bright, and loyal, he also had the stature and respect that would be essential in any bruising battle. He understood how to deliver a devastating blow with a smile, when to come on strong and when to gracefully back down. It would also bring him back fully in the family's graces. Bar would later pledge eternal gratitude for his work on behalf of her son.

AFTER CATCHING A CHARTER FLIGHT TO TALLAHASSEE, BAKER EMERGED from the Old Capitol Building with an announcement. As thirty TV cameras watched, he proclaimed, "The presidential election is on hold."

The battle lines were quickly drawn. Within twenty-four hours the Gore campaign had flown a planeload of seventy-two people into the state. Many of them were trial lawyers who were being asked to volunteer their services in Florida. The Republicans, a little slower on the move, were still trying to determine their strategy. The situation in Florida put Jeb in a quandary. Eager to help his brother, he also understood how his actions might be seen if he intervened unfairly in the process. So he recused himself from direct involvement but remained active. As he later explained it, "I recused myself as the chairman of the canvassing board. But I was not going to recuse myself as governor or from being my brother's brother."

Jeb knew the political landscape in Florida better than just about anyone, so he moved quickly to nail down the services of Barry Richard, the state's top election dispute lawyer. A registered Democrat, Richard had been Jeb's legal counsel on election issues.

Jeb also saw to it that the Gore team would be starved of local legal talent. Frank Jimenez, his acting counsel, began calling the state's leading law firms to make clear that working for the Gore recount effort would be a major political mistake.

"Jeb did whatever we asked of him," Jim Baker said. "He never looked at the political cost to himself." And, indeed, in a strange sort of way it was Jeb who faced the prospect of having the whole matter blow up in his face. He was up for reelection in two years, and how matters were handled would, fairly or unfairly, directly reflect on him. As Maureen Dowd warned in the *New York Times*, "Jeb's future is jeopardized."

Manual recounts began in Palm Beach and Dade Counties. It was an almost completely subjective process. Hanging chads or dimpled chads? What about pregnant chads or swinging chads? No clear guidelines emerged as to which ballots should actually be included. As the recount proceeded, the voter count began to seesaw, with Gore down by 1,700 votes and then less than 1,000.

Troublesome was the fact that Carol Roberts, who was overseeing the recount in Palm Beach, not only sported a Gore-Lieberman sticker on her car but had actually solicited funds for the Democratic campaign. Later, a statistical analysis by Matthew Spiegel of the Yale School of Management laid out the grounds for concern. Himself a Democrat, Spiegel concluded that the manual recount heavily favored Gore in a way that statistically didn't make sense. Gore was getting 15 percent more of the votes than the overall vote indicated. "Gore picked up 903 too many votes in the recount relative to what would have been expected by chance machine-read errors."

At the same time, the battle on the ground was heating up. Democrats brought in dozens of political operatives from Massachusetts, including Kennedy aides and the deputy mayor of Boston, to press the issue in Palm Beach. Republicans responded by bringing in staffers from Capitol Hill and Warren Tompkins, a protégé of Lee Atwater, who had run the campaign in South Carolina. Republican activists began organizing protests in south Florida to end the recount.

The Democrats countered by hiring a telemarketing firm to call voters in search of ballot problems. "If you have already voted and think you may have punched the wrong hole for the incorrect candidate," they told voters, "you should return to the polls and request that the election officials write down your name so that this problem can be fixed."

At the same time the recount was taking place in three south Florida counties, Democrats moved to stop the admission of military ballots from overseas because there was no independent record of requests or the date of the post-mark was challenged. It was clear that the standards in each county were different. In counties carried by Bush, 29 percent of overseas ballots were disallowed. But more than 60 percent were rejected in counties carried by Gore. The reason was simple: military ballots were breaking heavily for Bush.

The Bush family contacted Gen. H. Norman Schwarzkopf, who issued a public statement. "It is a very sad day in our country," he said.

In the early stages George W.'s aides in Austin tried to call the shots, but before long it was clear that managing from a distance would be unworkable. Jim Baker was put completely in charge in Florida. His gambit was simple: Calmly, he told the press that this was a question of law, not politics, and he called for an end to the recounts. "I thought we held the high moral ground," he later recalled. "Our position was: It's over. We won. Let's stop counting. Let's go home."

The Democrats filed in state court to order mandatory recounts. As Jeb Bush sat and watched, he knew where events were heading. The Florida Supreme Court was overwhelmingly liberal, and Jeb had poor relations with the justices. Many of them rejected the state's death penalty law, and Jeb had publicly taken them to task on the issue. Worried that the state court would seek its revenge on the family, Jim Baker called George W. and advised that they file a legal action in federal court. George W. accepted the advice.

---

AS DAYS BECAME WEEKS AND THE GROUND BATTLE CONTINUED IN FLORIDA, George and Bar watched the fiasco unfold from their home in Houston. Bar was advising everyone to calm down. George was simply too emotionally wrapped up in events to be of much help.

"In 2000, I wasn't getting advice from my dad, I was giving him the advice, and that was, 'Dad, chill out,' " Jeb Bush said. "My dad was a living wreck. It was horrible. He was so into this, and to have a son . . . I don't think there would be a way to describe the powerful emotions of pride, anger, love, and all the emotions to the max. And just stretch it out—ebbing and flowing."

Bar on the other hand was outwardly calm. "My mom is more stoic about things like this. She stopped watching, which was pretty wise and pretty smart. My parents had a deal in their home. My mother bought my father some earphones so he could listen to the cable television and she didn't have to hear all the stuff on Fox, CNN, and CBS. He was flipping around and watching all of this." Bar would sit there reading or doing some work and suddenly George would start mumbling or screaming because of what he was hearing. "That's how she followed the 2000 campaign, through these grunts and groans, expletive deleted. She handled it differently."

———————

IF THERE WAS ANY DOUBT THAT GEORGE W. WAS HIS MOTHER'S SON, THOSE doubts were dispelled as George W. withdrew to his ranch. Al Gore took an intense interest in every twist and turn of the electoral drama in Florida. But from Crawford, Texas, the court battles and ballot fights were far off. George W. didn't read many newspapers and instead spent his time on a Joe DiMaggio biography. He also kept up his routine of jogging and cleared cedar from a path he was creating.

It had become a pattern with George W. and one of his most puzzling attributes. When he learned that he had won the critical South Carolina primary, the staff had cheered. George W. went and lay down for a midafternoon nap. When he learned days later that he had lost in Michigan, he casually played "airbowl" on the campaign plane, rolling ripe grapefruits down the aisle.

While other candidates were determined to show that they had fire in the belly, George W. appeared to be a man at ease. Sometimes it was confusingly seen as a lack of concern. Now, with his political future on the line, he was unbelievably calm.

It wasn't that George W. didn't care. Rather, it was evidence of the enormous capacity for self-control he had developed since he'd quit drinking almost fifteen years earlier. As John Ellis explained, "There is that prayer from AA, 'Give me the courage to change the things I can, the serenity to accept the things I can't, and the wisdom to know the difference.' I think George is the living embodiment of that credo. And you see that in spades when he's dealing with something that he cannot control."

He would chat with Jim Baker and Dick Cheney by phone every morning at 8 A.M. At 8:45 there would be another call, this one including Baker, Cheney, and his aides Karl Rove and Karen Hughes and other staffers. He would talk with Baker maybe four or five times a day; his brother Jeb would sometimes sit in on these discussions. But it was generally Baker and Cheney who would make the logistical decisions.

———————

EVENTS MOVED TO A HEAD AS FLORIDA SECRETARY OF STATE KATHERINE Harris certified a Bush victory. Reporters encircled the State Capitol to watch the press conference. As it was unfolding, three of Jeb's aides arrived at the governor's mansion to give him the documents that would make it official. The Certificate of Ascertainment was a list of electors for the electoral college. Katherine Harris had already signed the document earlier. Now Jeb pulled out a pen and put his name on the dotted line. Jeb also made it clear that he would sign legislation naming his brother's electors even if the courts concluded otherwise. He was prepared to risk a confrontation with the judiciary.

"I can pull the trigger with the best of them," he said.

Over the previous several years the two brothers had experienced their differences. But now, in the heat of the Florida battle, the distance between them melted away. "Jeb was simply amazing," Jim Baker told us. "He did whatever we needed. And he was never once concerned with his own political future." After it was all over, the two brothers would find a new sense of unity.

"They are much closer now," said John Ellis, "after the battle in Florida."

As the battles continued and November stretched into December, the image of a President George W. Bush began to emerge. After a vote count, a recount, and another recount, in each instance Bush had come out the winner.

---

ON DECEMBER 12, GEORGE W. WAS ON THE PHONE WITH HIS FRIEND DON Evans. "I gotta call you back, buddy," said Evans, hanging up. The Supreme Court was coming in with its decision.

George W. dialed Tallahassee. He was looking for Jim Baker.

"Good evening, Mr. President-Elect," said Baker. Then Don Evans's cell phone rang. It was Dick Cheney wanting to speak to Baker.

"Jim," said Cheney. "Congratulations. Only under your leadership could we have gone from a lead of 1,800 votes to a lead of 150 votes."

---

A CROWD GATHERED OUTSIDE THE GOVERNOR'S MANSION IN AUSTIN. THE United States Supreme Court had decided in favor of George W. Bush. He would become the forty-third president.

The victory was a triumph for the family and also brought Jim Baker back into the family fold. "George and Bar went into great forgive and forget mode," recalled John Ellis. "And so all is happy in the family again. The Baker bashing has certainly stopped from Bar. I remember her saying, 'Jim

Baker did a fantastic job in Florida,' which really meant, 'We don't really hate you anymore.' "

The victory in Florida also served to enhance Dick Cheney's stature within the incoming new administration. The critical choice of whom to pick had paid off handsomely.

#### CHAPTER 43

# SETTLING IN

I N THE DAYS FOLLOWING THE SUPREME COURT DECISION THAT UPHELD
his election as president, George W. made a phone call to a powerful
figure on Capitol Hill. It was not to a Republican leader such as Den-
nis Hastert, Trent Lott, Dick Armey, or Mitch McConnell, with whom
he was in regular contact. Instead, it was a senator who was very much
his political opposite, but who for personal reasons might prove to be a
strange ally.

Over the decades the Bushes had prided themselves on being the un-
Kennedys. They considered the Kennedys as competitors. As Jeb Bush had
told one reporter in 1986, "I think we could probably beat the Kennedys in
touch football, we could beat them in basketball, baseball, any goddam sport
they want to play."

Not only were the two clans' politics different, they handled matters differently. Even when there were discussions during the 2000 election about
the site selection for a debate in Boston, George W. had been careful to
maintain the distinction. He told aides that he didn't want to have a debate
at the University of Massachusetts' Boston campus because it was close to the
John F. Kennedy Library.

Yet now that he was president, he was placing a call to Sen. Edward Kennedy. As he was the ranking Democrat on the powerful Education and Labor Committee, any major legislation in these critical areas would need his
agreement. But George W. was calling him for reasons that went deeper.

The two men were now the standard-bearers for the two largest political
dynasties in modern American history. They shared common purposes and
common burdens. And despite the talk of being the unKennedys, the Bushes
had ties going back forty years with the Kennedy clan.

For Ted Kennedy, that bond had been formed back in 1959 when he was
a law student at the University of Virginia. Needing to round up a speaker to
address the Student Legal Forum, he called his brother, then Senator John
Kennedy, for some suggestions. The first name that came out of his mouth

was that of his colleague, the affable senator from Connecticut, Sen. Prescott Bush. Young Ted extended an invitation and the senator kindly accepted. They spent an enjoyable evening together in Charlottesville and remained friends for years.

As so often with the Bushes, that friendship was passed down to George H. W. Bush, who as vice president and president maintained the quiet friendship and sometime alliance with now Senator Ted Kennedy. In 1990, Kennedy helped President Bush pass the Americans with Disabilities Act and also broad legislation reforming immigration laws. After they left the White House, George and Bar became close friends with Eunice Shriver, Ted Kennedy's sister, as they worked together on the Special Olympics.

In 2000 the relationship was extended to George W. when the Bushes and Senator Kennedy gathered for the funeral of Sen. Paul Coverdell of Georgia. After the service, George W. sought out the senator in the small crowd. "I've heard of you," W. said with a smile, extending his hand. "I understand that what you do, you do very well." Ted laughed, and the relationship was extended to a third generation of Bushes.

So when George W. Bush called Ted Kennedy in December 2000, they chatted first about the long relationship between the two families. Then George W. explained how he hoped to work with Kennedy. I hope we share "some mutual goals," he said. Kennedy concurred that they probably did. Later, after he moved into the White House, George W. invited the senator and other members of the Kennedy clan for a private screening of *Thirteen Days*, a new motion picture about JFK and the Cuban missile crisis. The tacit alliance between these two dynasties would prove helpful at times, but also difficult. Kennedy would help Bush pass some of his educational reforms in 2001, and two years later he would receive the George Bush Award for Excellence in Public Service. But he would also denounce the war in Iraq as "a failed, flawed, bankrupt policy . . . This was made up in Texas . . . This whole thing was a fraud."

But if relations with Kennedy warmed in the weeks before the inauguration, they were downright cool with the Clintons. The final straw for the Bushes came during the Florida recount, when Clinton couldn't resist the temptation to inject himself into a tense moment in American history. The only way Bush could win, the president told the media, "was to stop the vote count in Florida." George W. visited the White House in December for a two-hour meeting with President Bill Clinton to discuss world events. The meeting was cordial, but the mutual disdain was apparent to just about everyone. Clinton's personal attacks had angered the family, and they had been horrified at how he conducted himself in the Oval Office. George W. had campaigned against Clinton as much as against his actual opponent, Al Gore, and kept reminding family members of what he really felt about him. "He promised to have the most ethical administration in American history," he would say of Clinton. "He fell about forty-one presidents short."

A COLD RAIN FELL AS THE BUSH CLAN GATHERED ON THE SOUTH LAWN OF the Capitol for the inauguration. The family had again come to Washington, some 230 in all, to see another chapter in American political history inscribed with the family's name.

Despite the cold, which reduced attendance, the mood was genuinely upbeat. Former president Bush wore a dark overcoat and Bar covered herself with a clear plastic poncho. The only familiar face that did not appear was that of Billy Graham, who had been advised to skip the ceremony because of medical complications. Instead, his son Franklin delivered the invocation. As W. stood at the podium to be sworn in, he placed his hand first on a 1767 Bible that George Washington had used at his inauguration in 1789. Then he placed his palm on his family's Bible, the same one his father, his brother, and he had used (as governor).

His inaugural address was the shortest in recent history. He spoke for only twelve minutes and talked about the importance of national unity. Then he promptly exited the stage with family members watching and cheering.

As he left the podium, his Aunt Nancy leaned over and spoke to Jeb. "When can I come to Florida to campaign for your reelection?" she asked. Jeb smiled.

"I'm not sure I'm going to seek reelection," he told her.

Since his brother had won Florida narrowly in a disputed election, the long knives were out for Jeb. During the recount fiasco, the media had been fed rumors (all proven untrue) that Jeb had been involved in romantic liaisons first with Katherine Harris and then with an aide. The *New York Times* and *Washington Post*, among others, had committed several reporters to the story. Not a shred of evidence was found to back up any of the stories, but rumor had fed rumor in a destructive cycle.

Then came accusations that Jeb and his aides had undertaken a campaign to suppress minority voting. The U.S. Civil Rights Commission went so far as to organize a hearing in early January to determine whether Jeb had called out the state police in minority neighborhoods to discourage people from voting. Forget the fact that such a conspiracy could never have been kept secret, the attacks seemed more designed to wound Jeb than to get to any truth. The commission even subpoenaed Jeb for dramatic effect. A simple invitation was never extended.

———

THE NIGHT OF THE INAUGURATION, THE FAMILY CELEBRATED ITS TRIUMPH. George W. and Laura went to eight inaugural balls and danced for an average of forty-eight seconds at each one. They ended up back at the White House more than an hour ahead of schedule. Unlike his father, who enjoyed the socializing and the friendships in Washington, George W. made clear early on that in this respect, as in others, he was not his father's son. He was asleep before midnight.

As the Bushes toasted the family in the nation's capital, ancestral echoes were heard across the Atlantic. In Messing, England, residents of the small village gathered at a local "Bush Bar" for a Tex-Mex celebration. On the wall hung a signed photo from former president Bush, a thank-you letter, and a Bush family tree. The Bushes were direct descendants of Reynold Bush, a successful farmer who had left for America in 1631 to escape religious persecution.

Before the Bushes left England, Robert Bush, one of Reynold's forebears, was fined by the lord of the manor for killing a flock of doves. "Had he committed the same offense one hundred years earlier," said Roger Carter, chairman of the parish council, "he'd have been castrated for his foul deed—then where would the Americans be?"

———

FOLLOWING THE INAUGURATION, THE FAMILY WENT TO THE WHITE HOUSE, and George W. slowly walked into the Oval Office for the first time as president. He had been in it plenty of times before, when his father had governed from there. Now he walked to the center of the room and looked at the presidential seal on the ceiling and then at the same seal on the rug. Stepping behind the mahogany desk, he stood there silently for a moment.

Suddenly he heard footsteps in the hallway; it was his father. Chief of Staff Andrew Card watched as the former president stood at the door for a moment and looked at his son. "Mr. President," he said with a crack in his voice.

"Mr. President," responded W. Then both men began to cry.

It was the sort of raw emotion that punctuated the relationship between

the two men from time to time. In 1995, when George W. was being inaugurated as governor, a photographer had snapped a picture of his father
standing on the platform behind him, wiping away tears. When George W.
saw the shot a few days later, he had it enlarged and placed it prominently
behind his desk. Emotions between the two had been intense in both victory
and defeat over the decades, but the stakes had never been higher than
they were now. For the son, it represented the first time that he would finally
be out of his father's shadow, and he could dispel criticism that he could
accomplish only what his father helped him to. As if to remind himself
of the new reality, he had made a simple decision days before he moved
into the Oval Office. As governor, he had conducted business from behind
a desk his father had used. But now as president, he dispensed with his father's desk and instead had one pulled out that had been used by JFK.

As for the rest of the White House, he would have to give it "one hell
of a scrubbing" to make it livable, he said, and he made elaborate plans to rid
the Oval Office of artifacts of the Clinton presidency. The royal blue presidential rug, the golden drapes, and the plush red and cream silk-covered sofas that Clinton had put in were promptly removed. In came the beige terra
cotta rug and peach-colored sofas that Reagan had used as president.

George W. also pointedly declared that the old "Clinton dress code"
would be changing. Clinton's practice of allowing people in jeans, T-shirts,
or even running shorts to enter the Oval Office was now banned. Only men
wearing a coat and tie and women in suits would be allowed in. It was a rule
that he applies to himself. More than a dress code, for the Bushes it is about
reverence for the office.

Family friend Joe O'Neill recalled a recent visit to the White House.
"One evening we were watching a movie in the White House theater and
the president, who was wearing a sweater, went to fetch something from the
Oval Office. It's just sort of down the hall, and should have taken only a couple of minutes. But after about half an hour went by, I asked what had happened to the president. 'Oh,' his aide told me, 'he went upstairs to change
into a suit and tie.' He doesn't believe anyone, including the president,
should set foot in the Oval Office without correct attire. To him, it's hal-
lowed ground."

It is the sort of belief that echoes what his father had done thirty years earlier, when, as a young congressman, he insisted on going home before a
meeting with Richard Nixon so he could take off his loafers and put on wing
tips.

For the father, this was perhaps the most important element of what his son would do as president. "He's returning honor and dignity to the White House," he pointedly reflected.

The father was understandably proud of what his son had accomplished, but he was also going through a bit of an identity crisis. For more than three decades he had been the family patriarch, the one who carried the mantle in the corridors of power, the strong one whom everyone went to when they had trouble, the moneymaker who would save Walker Point. He had been the family's unofficial spokesman, using the expression "we Bushes" repeatedly. But now with his son as president, things seemed different.

At a private Houston dinner just before his son had been elected, he demonstrated some of that sentimentality and honesty that those in the family had seen through the decades. He noted that he was no longer "former president Bush," but had simply been given a number within the family: "41." "I used to be George Bush," he said wistfully. "Now I don't know who the hell I am. I'm going home Sunday and leave this to 'Mr. Quincy,' " the nickname he had given his son.

———

WITH THE BRUISING FLORIDA RECOUNT, LOYALTY HAD BEEN AT A PREMIUM. So W. made a point of rewarding those who had battled so hard for him— often at no compensation—in Florida.

In December 2000, John Bolton had entered a Tallahassee library. "I'm with the Bush-Cheney team, and I'm here to stop the count," he had said. Now he would be undersecretary of state for arms control. Matt Schlapp, who had organized protests at county government buildings in Miami, became assistant to the president. David Aufhauser, who helped fight the legal battle over military and overseas ballots, became general counsel at the Treasury Department. Alex Azar, who helped plot legal strategy in Tallahassee, became general counsel at HHS. Brad Blakeman, who organized rallies in south Florida, became director of White House scheduling. In all, fifty of the foot soldiers who had worked so hard in Florida joined the new administration in midlevel and senior positions.

Experience had also led W. to trust the family's dictum that, all things considered, blood runs thicker than politics. His father had relied on him to be his enforcer, and when making plans for his campaign he had sat the family on one side of the table and campaign aides on the other for a reason. So in this administration, family members and relatives of close aides and friends littered key positions. Craig Stapleton, married to George W.'s cousin, was appointed ambassador to the Czech Republic. Vice President Cheney's son-in-law, Philip Perry, was named deputy attorney general. Colin Powell's son, Michael Powell, was chairman of the FCC. Budget Director Mitch Daniel's sister was appointed assistant attorney general. Deputy White House press secretary Scott McClellan's brother was appointed to the Council of Economic Advisers. Ken Mehlman, the White House political director, could call his brother Bruce at the Commerce Department, where he was an assistant secretary. The children of Supreme Court justices Rehnquist and Scalia were also offered slots.

When it came to senior positions in his cabinet, George W.'s choices reflected his general attitudes toward Washington and the American establishment. His life was, in a sense, a devolution. He had been educated at Andover, Yale, and Harvard. His father and grandfather had worked their way through the veins and arteries of the American establishment. But George W. was uncomfortable in that world and indeed in rebellion against it.

When George H. W. Bush had put together his cabinet, it was filled with longtime friends who had Ivy League pedigrees. Jim Baker (Princeton) was secretary of state and Nicholas Brady (Yale) was secretary of the treasury in an administration that included numerous Ivy Leaguers. George W. Bush's cabinet, on the other hand, was largely devoid of Ivy League–educated members. With the exception of Energy Secretary Spencer Abraham and Secretary of Defense Donald Rumsfeld (neither of whom had a stereotypical Ivy League view of life), his cabinet was largely made up of people educated in state schools and private universities from the Midwest and West.

When his father had won in 1988, he had gathered with friends from Skull and Bones to talk about old times and unload thoughts and feelings about what lay ahead. Such a meeting never would have occurred to George W. Skull and Bones was a funny fraternity to him; he never took it seriously the way his father did.

In the early months of his administration, overtures were made by Yale University to repair the rupture between the Bushes and their alma mater. At the encouragement of friends, George W. did return to Yale in May to give a commencement address and receive an honorary degree. It was his first return to the campus in decades. Several hundred students protested his presence, and 171 faculty members signed a letter denouncing the decision by Yale trustees to invite him in the first place.

Using humor, he delivered a speech to disarm his critics. Making reference to his days of drinking he said, "If you're like me, you won't remember everything you did here." Lampooning his lack of academic achievement he said, "To the C students, I say, you, too, can become president of the United States." But behind the humor, he remained skeptical about Yale and what the campus had become.

Those early days were new to George W. but also familiar in a way that only the son of a former president could appreciate. He had seen up close what his father had done in the Oval Office, and in recent years he had become the foremost student of his father. For all the admiration and affection he felt, he also knew that his father was a flawed politician, and he seemed determined not to make the same mistakes.

His father had embraced the notion of bipartisanship in Washington and worked feverishly to court both Republicans and Democrats. This was in part out of necessity: The Democrats had controlled both the House and the Senate. But it also reflected the father's temperament. Like George's own father, Sen. Prescott Bush, President Bush had an ideology of friendship that made him less committed to an agenda than to those relationships. The son had witnessed how that approach had led to the tax increase in 1990 and doomed his father's reelection. He also had a very different temperament.

"George W. is tougher; his father is gentle," said Elsie Walker Kilbourne. "He can be strong, but he's always gentle. W. has thicker skin, and he gets that from Bar. He can take a punch and give a punch. Big George can take a punch, but he doesn't like to give a punch."

Instead of that old notion of bipartisanship, George W. spoke of civility. He wanted to be civil but also stay completely committed to his agenda. When asked about his agenda, he said he was "not backing off" of his conservative convictions. If Democrats chose not to work with his administration, "they're going to be left behind," he declared.

He had also seen how his father, who had perhaps the most extensive resume of any president in American history, had immersed himself in the details of government. He worked Capitol Hill because he had been in Congress; he closely watched global affairs and intelligence because he had been U.N. ambassador and CIA director. But somehow the details had taken over, and the "vision thing" had disappeared. George W. was determined to do the opposite.

Unlike his father, who had a vice president he didn't trust and never found a chief of staff with whom he was completely at ease, George W. felt comfortable handing over the administrative reins to Dick Cheney. In addition to knowing the family for more than a quarter of a century, Cheney was a sitting vice president who had no ambitions to run for president. He was in a sense the perfect prime minister. As one aide described it, "The president is the engineer, Cheney is the guy shoveling the coal."

But perhaps the most significant lesson he had learned from his father was how not to deal with the media. His father had made himself available to news people and tried to befriend them. He gave dozens of press conferences, lingering until every question was answered, and he maintained a private correspondence with many members of the press. (Even after his presidency, he kept up an on-again, off-again e-mail correspondence with Maureen Dowd of the *New York Times*.)

Yet George W. believed that the media had repaid his father by stabbing him in the back. Stung by a sense of betrayal, in the final year of his administration George H. W. Bush regularly lambasted the media and became obsessed with media bias.

George W. was determined to take an entirely different approach. Instead of befriending the media, his strategy was essentially to ignore them. "All the wagging tongues," he said in his first few days in office. "I personally am going to completely ignore them."

He remained detached from what the news media was reporting and saying. "It's not that he doesn't read the newspapers," said his cousin John Ellis. "It's just that he doesn't get mad or infuriated if they get it wrong."

Despite his public denials that he read the papers, it became part of his ritual. During his visits to the White House, Ellis recalled, he would join George and Laura in their bedroom at 5 A.M. George W. would be going through the papers in bed. "They got that wrong," he would say calmly and then move on to another. But he was determined not to let the media get under his skin in the way his father had. Moreover, George W. Bush combined an awe of the office with an unassuming and low-key manner. When he entered a room for an appearance, he often declined to have a band play "Hail to the Chief." This was a man completely comfortable with himself, not intoxicated with the power and pomp of the presidency. Five months after being inaugurated, as he and Laura sat in front of thousands of guests at the President's Dinner in the Washington Convention Center, he calmly told guests that he needed to leave early. "We've got to go home and feed Barney the dog."

The Washington social scene, which both his father and mother had mastered during their climb to the presidency, seemed to hold little attraction for him. The black-tie-and-sequin parties downtown or the small, intimate parties held by the powers that be in the nation's capital didn't interest George and Laura. *Washington Post* editor Ben Bradlee's wife, Sally Quinn, made comments about how the Bushes were wrecking the social scene in Washington. "Washington as we know it is over," she lamented. "Washington's social scene has come to a screeching halt."

Nancy Ellis recalled the time Laura told her husband about the story and suggested that perhaps they ought to do more entertaining.

"You're not going to ask me to sit next to Sally Quinn and Buffy Cafritz, are you?" he responded.

"No Bushie, I'm not. Maybe we can add their names to the Christmas party."

Rather than linger in Washington, George and Laura seemed eager to escape the city at the first opportunity. They would visit the ranch in Crawford regularly and, at times, for long visits. In the spring of 2001, Laura spent two straight weeks there, seeing to the decorating of the ranch. On weekends, they would head off to Camp David, a place that he had grown to love with his father. But unlike his father, who enjoyed a busy social time there with friends and celebrities, the son brought friends and members of the cabinet. These breaks, however, included precious little chum time. Often he wanted his guests to simply unwind, as he was doing. If he socialized at all, it was usually with his brother Marvin or sister Doro, both of whom lived in the D.C. suburbs. In all, during his first two years in office, the Bushes visited Crawford nearly two dozen times, more visits than Reagan had managed to make to his ranch in two terms. And they had been to Camp David sixty times, almost once every two weeks.

But as much as George and Laura tried to maintain a sense of normalcy, it was difficult for their daughters. When news of their underage drinking became the subject of international media attention, the girls were angry with their father. "If you weren't president, this wouldn't have happened," they told him. Increasingly it was their mother and not their father whom they communicated with.

———

TWELVE YEARS EARLIER, W.'S FATHER HAD WON BIG AGAINST MICHAEL Dukakis and come into the White House with a broad mandate. But in the months that followed, the administration had done little to boldly capitalize on its position. George W. had come into office with a minority of votes. Never one to squander an opportunity, he dived in with a bold agenda that surprised many in its ambition.

The centerpiece of that agenda was a large tax cut that he considered critical to helping an already sputtering economy. The economy had essentially fallen into recession a year earlier in the spring of 2000. W's prescription was one of the largest tax cuts in history, a $1.6 billion reduction in personal income taxes and a rebate for every taxpayer.

His greatest asset was that George W. Bush charm that had worked so well in Texas. His ability to befriend his political opposites carried over from Austin, and he was deft in his negotiations.

But George W. was constantly running into family members who were active in areas that presented a potential conflict. In late April, Interior Secretary Gale Norton announced plans to lease 6 million acres of the Gulf of Mexico for energy exploration. It was part of a broad national strategy to develop more offshore energy resources. But the move was highly unpopular, particularly in California and Florida. When the news broke, it took Jeb by surprise. Florida might be evenly divided between Republicans and Democrats, but offshore oil drilling was unpopular with almost everyone in the state. So Jeb wrote his brother an open letter declaring that he was strongly opposed to the move.

He pointed out that "few other issues so completely unite Floridians." He then phoned his brother to talk to him about it. A few weeks later the administration revised its plans, scaling the exploration area back to 1.5 million acres and moving it away from the Florida coast.

California governor Gray Davis was equally opposed to plans to drill in coastal waters in his state. However, when Gale Norton amended her plans, the leases near the coast of Florida had all but vanished while plans to drill off the California coast remained in effect.

———

IN THE EARLY MONTHS OF OFFICE, THE FOREIGN POLICY CHALLENGE THAT bothered W. most was not the continuing struggle with Iraq, but China. His father had been engaged with that country for close to three decades, and both his brother and uncle had extensive business dealings there with senior Chinese officials. But despite these familial links, George W. took a harder line toward Beijing than many expected.

Barely three months after taking office he announced plans to sell eight diesel-powered submarines to Taiwan. This was a reversal of over three decades of U.S. foreign policy in Asia, but George W. was convinced that China represented a long-term challenge to the United States. The move clearly irritated Beijing.

In April, George W. Bush was presented with the first international crisis of his presidency when a Chinese fighter jet collided with a U.S. Navy surveillance plane over the South China Sea. The American plane was forced to make an emergency landing on Hainan Island, and its twenty-four U.S. crew members were detained by the Chinese military. It was a case study in how the nexus of Bush family relationships both influences and fails to influence the conduct of his presidency.

Chinese president Jiang Zemin had a long history with the Bush family. George H. W. Bush had dined privately with him perhaps more than a dozen times, and they considered each other friends. So, too, did Neil Bush, the president's brother, who had traveled to Beijing to talk up a business venture called Ignite Software. He enjoyed a private dinner with the Chinese president, and Jiang's son agreed to have one of his businesses invest in Ignite.

W. was receiving contradictory advice. Some contended that he needed to show strength in the face of Chinese provocation. Others believed that he needed to allow the Chinese to save face; that they really didn't want a confrontation with the United States.

The former president's advice was clear: Keep a low profile and don't embarrass the Chinese. George W. did just that immediately after the incident, speaking about it only twice in two days to reporters. His main concern was whether the detainees were staying in officers' quarters at the Chinese base and whether they had access to Bibles. In the end, the decision to draft a carefully worded apology over the mishap was made, with the encouragement of the father.

As the U.S.-China standoff began, Uncle Prescott Bush, Jr., was by chance en route to Beijing on the inaugural flight of United Airlines' new Chicago-to-Beijing link. United was an active member in the U.S.-China Chamber of Commerce, and Pres Bush, as chairman of that organization, was also very well connected with the Chinese leadership. Among those he was close to was Rong Yiren, the former trade minister and vice president of China. Rong's family had made a fortune in textiles before the communist revolution in 1949. When Mao took power, he had elected to stay in the country. Though he never joined the Communist Party, he had risen to power with the backing of Deng Xiaoping, who in 1979 put him in place as head of the China International Trust and Investment Corporation (CITIC), which included thirty-eight subsidiary banks in Hong Kong, the U.S., Australia, and the Netherlands.

Back in 1993, when Pres, Jr., had made a visit to Beijing, Rong had introduced Bush as "an old friend." Rong was now the richest man in China. While other dignitaries on the ceremonial flight returned home after a few days, Pres Bush, Jr., stayed in China for two weeks and canceled plans he had in Hong Kong. While in China, he met privately with Rong and with the American ambassador, Joseph Prueher. It was Prueher who would deliver a carefully crafted letter to President Jiang Zemin to arrange the release of the servicemen. Pres Bush, Jr., left a day after the U.S. crew members were allowed to leave China.

As events in China indicated, family connections had the potential to both help and entangle W.'s foreign policy ventures. Since he had left Washington in 1993, the father and several of his sons had been very active around the world in their business ventures. When the Bush family did business in China or the United Arab Emirates, it involved having a strong relationship with those countries' leaders. How would George W. navigate in a world that had such countervailing interests?

Despite both his father's and his brother's dealings with Jiang, George W. was determined to strike an independent course. Jiang Zemin would be one of a handful of world leaders who would visit Bush at his Crawford, Texas, ranch. But W. would pull few punches in his relationships with the Chinese. When he visited Beijing in February 2002, he pressed Jiang on a number of issues, and he did so publicly. During their joint press conference, George W. made a point of bringing up the question of religious freedom, saying, "As a president of a great nation, Jiang would understand the important role of religion in an individual's life."

The next day, when he gave a speech at Tsinghua University that was broadcast live across the country, he spoke boldly about American values. "Ninety-five percent of Americans say they believe in God, and I'm one of them . . . My prayer is that all persecution will end, so that all in China are free to gather and worship as they wish."

During their private meetings, George W. told Jiang, a committed atheist, how faith had changed his life and how it was important to the life of the United States. When Jiang claimed that there was no religious persecution, Bush kept after him. When, at a joint press conference, reporters grilled the Chinese president over the recent imprisonment of fifty Catholic bishops and priests, George W. clearly enjoyed it, pressing his lips together and gazing away from his host.

———

IN EARLY JULY, GEORGE W. AND LAURA HEADED TO KENNEBUNKPORT FOR the long Independence Day weekend. Air Force One landed in nearby Sanford, and they were whisked to Walker Point. Once they got inside the house, it took only moments for the president to trade his suit for a T-shirt and shorts. Doro, Marvin, and Jeb also made the trip.

This was the first time the clan had been able to gather casually since the election. While the president kept in touch with advisers and even called world leaders on the phone, it was mostly a time to spend with his family. George W., Jeb, and their father would leave the house at 6:15 A.M. to play a quick eighteen holes, which took them just a tad over two hours. The competition between the two brothers had subsided in the professional realm, but on the greens it was as fierce as ever. When the president knocked a perfect wedge shot out of a sand trap, Jeb, convinced it was pure luck, grabbed another ball and tossed it into the trap. "George, do it again."

"Forget 181," replied George W., referring to the number for the proposed oil leases off the coast of Florida.

"All right," said Jeb, heading back to the sand trap. "I'll take the ball back."

It was while on the course that the two presidents donned their navy blue baseball caps, revealing to the world for the first time that they were now calling each other "41" and "43." Throughout most of George W.'s life, it had been "Big George" and "Little George." Now that he was president, that didn't seem quite right. A year later they would start calling Jeb's older son, George P., "44."

After golf and fishing, the president settled on Walker Point for a quiet birthday dinner. As George W. approached the table, his father signaled to him and offered him the seat at the head of the table. Proud of what his son had accomplished, he was still somewhat baffled about his son's rise to power. Asked what it felt like, he recalls: "You remember when your kid came home with two A's—and you thought she was going to fail? That's exactly what it's like."

Only once before had a president been the son of another president. But it was also rare in that George W. had a living father. The last American president who could claim that was JFK, and Joe Kennedy had suffered a debilitating stroke in the first year of his son's presidency.

So how exactly does the ex-president Bush interact with his son?

From the beginning he set strict limits on himself and tried to maintain a binary relationship with his son. There was the father-son relationship, and then there was the ex-president–president relationship. However artificial or difficult it would be to maintain this separation, the former president was determined to do so. Therefore, he offered advice only if asked. If a friend or adviser wanted to pass along advice to his son, he would relay it through official channels.

In the spring of 2001, George H. W. received a detailed memo from the former ambassador to South Korea, Donald Gregg. The two men had been friends for decades, and Gregg believed that the administration's hard line was counterproductive with regard to North Korea. The father read the memo and found it persuasive. He was loath to use the direct channel to his son, so he forwarded it to National Security Adviser Condoleezza Rice. It would then be her decision about how to forward it, with comment or without. The process made sense; if Condi Rice received anything from the former president, she would most likely pass it on.

In early November 2001, the former president traveled to South Korea for a three-day visit that included a luncheon meeting with President Kim Dae Jung. They discussed antiterrorism issues and the standoff with North Korea over nuclear weapons. After the meeting, the father wrote a memo and sent it to his son. It was the sort of thing he had done during the Clinton administration if something of particular concern had arisen during the discussions.

And yet the father was intimately involved in his son's decision-making process. Those familiar with the relationship say that the two men sometimes speak several times a day. They discuss family gossip because George W. sees Marvin and Doro more than the father does. If the conversation strays to policy matters, and it almost always does, it happens only at the behest of George W. Here he will ask his father a question such as "What do you think I should do about this?" or request him to make a call to a foreign leader on his behalf. The father does not sugarcoat his advice. "As long as the opportunity is offered up by W. to address an issue or concern, the former president is as candid as one would be with one's son," said cousin John Ellis. "He would move the world to help him in any way he could. There is this true deference to the son's position that prevents the former president from weighing in—or delays him from weighing in until the president asks him."

The father clearly relishes his role as his son's confidant. He religiously consumes his daily briefing from the CIA, which all ex-presidents are entitled to, and the secretiveness of their relationship serves him well. As a private citizen he is not required to disclose matters before Congress the way a public official might be. He insists publicly that he does not sway his son on policy matters, which generally seems to be the case.

"The great thing is that no one in the world—the West Europeans, the Asians, the Arabs—believes a word of it," said John Ellis. "They believe the father is intervening all the time. So they all pepper the old boy with everything. It's given him a new lease on life because he has that wonderful feeling of being at center stage, and he can pick and choose about what he thinks is relevant to pass on. After he was voted out, he felt pointless and stupid and then he just said, 'I'll just make a lot of money so the family can keep this place in Maine.' But now everybody calls him."

#### CHAPTER 44

# 9/11

GEORGE W. BUSH WAS SITTING IN FRONT OF A CLASSROOM FULL of children in Sarasota, Florida, when Chief of Staff Andrew Card approached him. "A second plane hit the second tower," he whispered in his ear. "America is under attack."

A look of horror came over George W.'s face like none ever seen before. Minutes before he had stepped into the classroom, he had been told that a single-engine plane had plowed into the World Trade Center in what everyone had dismissed as a tragic accident. Now everything had changed.

George W. tried to carry on for the next few moments as if nothing had happened. "Really good readers," he told the class. "These must be *sixth*-graders."

George W. stayed for the rest of the lesson, mindful that the press corps was with him and not wanting to create any added panic. Then he thanked the teacher and the students before exiting the room. He headed immediately to the holding room, where his aides were gathered to collect as much information as possible. He talked first with Dick Cheney at the White House. Cheney had been watching the news when he saw the second plane slam into the World Trade Center. They briefly discussed how they would organize the national security team and how terrorists were likely behind the attack. Then he spoke with his new FBI director, Robert Mueller. When he got off the phone, he turned to his top aides, Karl Rove, Andy Card, and Ari Fleischer. "We're at war," he said.

Laura Bush was in the Caucus Room in the Russell Senate Office Building in Washington, about to testify before a Senate committee, when word came of the attack. As she stood with Sen. Ted Kennedy, her face quickly turned ashen and tears welled up. Kennedy comforted her for a few moments until the Secret Service explained that it was necessary to take her to a safer place. George W. Bush would later express his thanks to Kennedy for comforting his wife.

Laura was taken in an armored SUV back to Secret Service headquarters while her daughters, Jenna and Barbara, were tracked down on their respective college campuses. Barbara (named "Turquoise" by the Secret Service) received added security at Yale and Jenna ("Twinkle") at the University of Texas.

The president quickly left Emma E. Booker Elementary School and headed for Air Force One. He wanted to return immediately to Washington, but the Secret Service insisted that there was an imminent threat of further attacks. Other hijacked planes could be out there, and the White House would be high on the target list. All airplanes were being grounded immediately by the Federal Aviation Administration (FAA), but that would be no guarantee of safety against determined terrorists. So Air Force One was diverted instead to Barksdale AFB in northwestern Louisiana. It was here that Bush made his first appearance to the American people on 9/11.

Standing in a conference room at the base, he stood and spoke with a halting voice, looking down at his notes and mispronouncing several words. It left some wondering whether he was up to the task.

After refueling, Air Force One headed north for Offutt Air Force Base outside of Omaha, Nebraska. En route, the president called his father on his cell phone.

"Where are you?" the president asked.

His father told him that both he and Bar were in Milwaukee.

"What are you doing in Milwaukee?"

"You grounded my plane."

They spoke for a few minutes about the attack. This time it was the son who steadied the father. "We're going to be fine," he told him.

———

THE NAME ON EVERYONE'S LIPS AS THE LIKELY CULPRIT WAS OSAMA BIN Laden, a name that the family had been familiar with for quite some time. And on this day in September, it could not help but release immense emotions in the Bush family.

Former president Bush had been in Washington a few days earlier attending a meeting of the Carlyle Group. Osama bin Laden's estranged half brother, Shafiq bin Ladin, was an investor with Carlyle and was present at the meeting. Also, literally dozens of extended bin Laden family members were in the United States at the time.

In the days immediately following 9/11 when commercial flights were grounded, the Bush administration allowed members of the extended bin

Laden family who were in the United States to leave, fearing that they might be subject to physical attack. Contrary to some published accounts, they were not allowed to leave the country and were subject to FBI screening. Bin Laden was also a familiar name to Neil Bush, who had corresponded with and stayed in a hotel owned by Mouldi Sayeh, who was a business partner with Mohammad bin Laden, one of Osama bin Laden's fifty-two siblings. Judge John M. Walker, Jr., who had been appointed to the bench by George H. W. Bush, was also familiar with the bin Laden name. Walker was now chief of the Second Circuit of the U.S. Court of Appeals, the court that only a year earlier had convicted bin Laden foot soldier Ramzi Yousef of trying to bring down the Towers in 1993.

For presidential sibling Marvin Bush, the attacks were also strangely personal. He was in New York on the morning of September 11, trapped in the subway. Only after a long delay was his car evacuated. He had to walk across Manhattan through the soot and smoke of the Towers in order to escape the catastrophe. The irony was that Marvin had served on the board of directors of Stratesec, a security company largely owned by a member of the Kuwaiti royal family. Until recently, Stratesec had handled security for both the World Trade Center and Dulles Airport, where some of the hijackers had taken off.

But for George W. the devastating nature of the attacks, the cruelty that they represented, led him to see this as something larger than a single man and his maniacal movement, and in the days that followed, his thinking moved quickly. "We have made the decision to punish whoever harbors terrorists, not just the perpetrators," he would tell his staff.

Such a broad goal represented an enormous challenge. Advisers cautioned him that CIA estimates put the number of terrorist sponsors at maybe sixty countries. George W. was undaunted.

"Let's pick them off one at a time," he said.

———

THE WEIGHT OF THE PRESIDENCY NOW SEEMED SO MUCH HEAVIER. HIS PRE-9/11 political life was suddenly in the past; fighting and winning this war was what mattered most. As he returned to the White House aboard Marine One, he looked down at the smoldering ruins of the Pentagon. "You're looking at the face of war in the twenty-first century," he said to the others in the helicopter.

But while the attacks fundamentally changed America, they also changed

George W. He now seemed different to the world; more decisive, more serious, and more focused. All of those qualities had been there all along, but in the minutiae of politics and complex domestic issues they had never come out. Says Elsie Walker Kilbourne, "People are saying that George is rising to the challenge; it isn't that he's rising to the challenge, it's just that it's given flower to what is already there in him."

But Franklin Graham did see a different president emerging. In the days following the attack, he visited with George W. "I have certainly seen a change in the man," he said. "There is a more somber seriousness in him. It's hard to describe. He knows what he has to do and he has the inner confidence to do it. He used to tell corny jokes a lot. He doesn't do that anymore."

Chief among the embedded qualities was his "addictive personality," which the Walkers had seen in their youth. "He's clear, he's strong, he doesn't waver from who he is," said Elsie Walker Kilbourne. "He's very consistent internally. So he could be a very strong force. I do think he has it in him. With terrorism, he's like a dog with a bone. He won't give up on it."

Family members said that they could see the Walker genes literally coming out in him. "We are going to find out who is responsible for this," he told Dick Cheney shortly after the attack, "and we're going to kick their asses."

He was suddenly tough and uncompromising in a way that his great-grandfather Bert Walker might have been, a bold risk-taker willing to face the odds for the sake of winning and winning big. Vice President Cheney saw the virtues of that approach during a time of crisis. "Oftentimes you can get too tangled up in the nuances and the fine points of diplomacy of dealing with these kinds of issues, engage in large debate. But the people who make things happen, the leaders who set the world, if you will, on a new course, who deal effectively with these kinds of threats that we've never been faced with before, will be somebody exactly like President Bush."

As he pondered the finer elements of diplomacy, you could almost see President Bush mouthing the words of Bert Walker, who had dismissed diplomats as "the striped-pants set."

But family members also saw in George W. a commitment to purpose that was tinged with his sense of a divine calling. During the 2000 campaign, recalls Elsie Walker Kilbourne, George W. had insisted on running as a "uniter, not a divider." Some advisers had dismissed the approach as too softheaded, but George W. had insisted on it. Now, in the shadow of the attacks, when the United States needed that sense of unity, it all seemed to make sense. Now, in the rubble of the World Trade Center, he had found his calling as president. "I think he thinks that," said Elsie Walker Kilbourne. "It's like, 'Ah, I get it now.'"

The battle against terrorism is not for him an abstract geopolitical struggle. "George sees this as a religious war," one family member told us. "He doesn't have a p.c. view of this war. His view of this is that they are trying to kill the Christians. And we the Christians will strike back with more force and more ferocity than they will ever know."

Franklin Graham, while stressing that he has not spoken specifically with Bush about the subject of terrorism and Islam, has had intimate conversations with him about the state of the world. He sees the same spiritual dimension in George W.'s views. "The president is not stupid," he told us. "The people who attacked this country did it in the name of their religion. He's made it clear that we are not at war with Islam. But he understands the implications of what is going on and the spiritual dimensions."

His daily practice of reading from the Bible in the morning influenced his actions and his words as much as they had done during the campaign. One morning shortly after 9/11, he woke up and read a passage from Proverbs 21:15. "When justice is done, it brings joy to the righteous but terror to evildoers." For several weeks after the attacks, he referred to the terrorists and their sponsors as "evildoers," with that passage firmly fixed in his mind.

George W. Bush had run for the presidency with the goal of trying to change the culture. He had spoken of the need for a faith-based approach on issues of poverty and crime. Now, in a single morning, his presidency was being changed to a war presidency. Before the attack, he had explained America's need to be "humble" on the world stage; now he was preparing to unleash a terrible and swift sword.

Ironically, his mannerisms became more relaxed after the attacks. He had always been a man of instinct, and the tenor of the times seemed to require the very sort of impulses that had ebbed and flowed throughout his life. He seemed more comfortable out in front of a crowd than he did in the Oval Office, and the bomber jacket seemed to suit him better than the tailored blue suit with the red tie.

His speeches seemed to improve, too. Because of his addictive personality, it was the sort of presidency that suited him well. Unencumbered by domestic issues, with their detail and ambiguity, he was now free to speak naturally in a way that reflected the way he viewed the world: black and white, good and evil. Life had been for him a struggle to conquer those things that had a bad hold on him; the struggle between good and evil was something that he had experienced in his own life.

George W.'s presidency had been transformed. So, too, was Laura's life. When the Bushes moved into the White House, Laura had been determined to maintain a low-profile in Washington. She moved her office to the East

Wing, where the First Lady's office had been before Hillary moved it to the West Wing. She was also able to have same privacy, leaving town early in the administration for two weeks to work on the ranch in Crawford. Now that all changed; the world was watching both her husband and her. She was before the cameras almost daily. He donated blood in front of television cameras and dropped in at Walter Reed Medical Center to visit Pentagon employees injured in the attack. She wrote two letters to children that would go to every school superintendent in the country. "I want to assure you that many people—including your family, your teachers, and your school counselor—love and care about you and are looking out for your safety . . . I want you to know how much I care about all of you. Be kind to each other, take care of each other, and show your love for each other."

Six days after the tragedy, she traveled to Pennsylvania to speak at a memorial service for the victims of United Flight 93. The next day she was on the *Oprah Winfrey Show* explaining about "How to Talk to Children about America under Attack." She also gave interviews to *60 Minutes* and *Good Morning America*. She produced two public service announcements that aired on television and she made an appearance at a concert at the John F. Kennedy Center. Throughout it all she was steady and calm. When staff members would cry, Laura would comfort them. The experience of Bar had been extremely helpful to her. "I have learned so much from watching her," Laura would say, "about what it is like to live in a public house like this one. Things that have to do with how to raise your children. And she does give me advice." Her role as the one who could trim her husband's sails without tearing the cloth became critically important. George W. revealed himself to be his mother's son—fiery, emotional, and impulsive. Laura on the other hand seemed to take on the role of his father—calm, prudent, and cautious.

On Friday, September 14, a little before noon, the presidential motorcade headed for the National Cathedral. President Bush had declared this a National Day of Prayer and Remembrance. It would be his first opportunity to address the nation at length.

The planned memorial service was an unprecedented event not seen in almost half a century. Gathering there would be former presidents Bill Clinton, Jimmy Carter, former vice president Al Gore, and former president George H. W. Bush. The cabinet was going to be there as well as most members of the Senate and congressional leaders.

Plenty of tears had been shed over the previous few days. Like his father, George W. was a sentimentalist, prone to tearing up for both good news and bad.

The president entered the cathedral as the children's choir sang "Father in Thy Gracious Keeping." He shook hands with former presidents Carter and Ford and also gestured to Bill Clinton and Al Gore. He then greeted his own father. Bar was sitting next to him.

The Very Reverend Nathan D. Baxter, dean of the cathedral, offered the prayer. "Guide our leaders, especially George our president. Let the deep faith that he and they share guide them in the momentous decisions that they must make for our national security."

Several other men of faith offered prayers, including Imam Muzammil Siddiqi, of the Islamic Society of North America. The final preacher was Billy Graham, who was silver-haired and needed help to reach the pulpit.

Then it was the president's turn to speak. He walked to the podium and looked out at the audience. He purposely avoided eye contact with his parents. "My biggest concern was looking at my parents," he told one reporter. "If I looked down at my mother and dad, and they'd be weeping, then I'd weep."

"We are here in the middle of our grief," Bush said. "So many have suffered so great a loss, and today we express our nation's sorrow. We come before God to pray for the missing and the dead, and for those who love them."

He spoke about the heroes of September 11, those who risked and lost their own lives in attempts to rescue strangers. "The commitment of our fathers is now the calling of our time," he said. The reference was to the Founding Fathers, but it also appeared as if he were speaking about his own forebears.

"As we have been assured, neither death nor life, nor angels nor principalities nor powers, nor things present nor things to come, nor height nor depth can separate us from God's love. May He bless the souls of the departed. May He comfort our own. And may He always guide our country. God Bless America."

When he stepped away from the pulpit and returned to his seat, no one clapped. As he sat in the pew next to Laura, his father reached across and patted him on the arm. Neither looked directly at the other for fear of crying.

For the father, September 11 brought back memories of the cold day at Andover in 1941 when he had heard about Pearl Harbor. As a young boy, it had inspired him to join the fight. Now, seventy-eight years old, he was nonetheless determined to do the same.

George W. enlisted him to be the official representative in London for a service commemorating British citizens killed in the attacks. The former president also made a point two weeks later of very publicly boarding a commercial flight to prove that the airlines were safe. But he was eager to do more than simply engage in symbolic acts. Much to his delight, his son was asking for his advice, and he had some clear and direct answers.

The Desert Storm president was convinced that military actions against Afghanistan should not be an attempted replay of that earlier battle. For all the talk of massive armored divisions winding their way through the valleys of Afghanistan, the father knew better. He advised that the CIA be unshackled. We have to "free up the intelligence system," he said. Instead of relying on noble motives, he wanted the agency to make greater use of "money or women" to ferret out secrets.

It was the sort of strategy that was eventually carried out by the son in Afghanistan, where the CIA played a key role in coordinating opposition to the Taliban. But there were also critical differences in their approaches. The father was a committed internationalist who had counted world leaders as close friends and relied on them heavily for advice and support during Desert Storm. The son was more of a unilateralist, closer to the Reagan tradition than his father.

"The world we live in today is very different than the world we lived in when this week began, very different indeed," George W. said.

———

JEB HAD FIRST HEARD ABOUT THE PLANES HITTING THE WORLD TRADE CENter during a cabinet meeting in Tallahassee. The day before, he had been with his brother in Jacksonville, meeting with teachers, parents, and students to talk about education. They had bantered in front of squirming first-graders and talked about reading.

When word of the attacks reached him on the morning of September 11, Jeb quickly ended the meeting and canceled official business before he headed to the state Emergency Operations Center. He declared a state of emergency and offered to do what he could to help officials in New York and Washington. After intensely watching the situation most of the day, he went to the Blessed Sacrament Catholic Church and attended mass.

He was deeply emotional about the whole situation. When a spontaneous prayer service of several hundred people grew outside the capital building, he joined them. His voice seemed deeper now, and it cracked as the emotion ran through him. "We are a loving and strong people," he said with tears in his eyes, "and we will respond to this challenge."

A policy wonk who is generally shy in public, he found it difficult to display his emotion outwardly. Two days after the attacks he spoke with his brother in Washington. "I love you," he said, in words that had scarcely been uttered between the two over the past several decades.

---

On September 15, while at Camp David, President George W. Bush spoke for the first time about what lay ahead.

"We're at war," he told the American people. We needed to "get ready" for a prolonged conflict. "This act will not stand," he said, using the precise words that his father had spoken a decade earlier. And in a certain way, 9/11 was not unlike what had happened when Iraq's invasion of Kuwait had transformed his father's administration. Domestic issues seemed to melt away as an international crisis drew all of his attention. But the similarities seemed to end there. If his father's methods were restrained, George W. revealed to the world how much he was his mother's son. In his highly personal radio address, he was blunt about the United States being interested in getting both justice and revenge. "Behind the sadness and the exhaustion, there is a desire by the American people to not seek only revenge, but to win a war against barbaric behavior, people that hate freedom and hate what we stand for."

Laura worked to temper this impulse in her husband. When he proclaimed that he wanted the culprits "dead or alive," Laura stepped up and told him it was a poor choice of words.

---

The challenge for 43 would be greater than it had been for 41. This war had started with the deaths of thousands of Americans and would be fought both overseas and within America's borders. Success in meeting the goal that his father had laid out in Desert Storm was easy to gauge: expel Saddam Hussein from Kuwait. Measuring success in a war on terrorism would be more difficult. Moreover, unlike his father, the son had little national security experience to fall back on.

Evidence quickly emerged that it was indeed Osama bin Laden, operating from a base in Afghanistan, who had masterminded the attack. George W. Bush made it clear that unless bin Laden were turned over by Afghanistan's Taliban rulers, America would begin military operations in the country.

The announcement sent shock waves through Europe. The French foreign minister feared that the attack had been part of "a diabolical trap" aimed at pulling the United States into a war it could not win. In Germany, Foreign Minister Joschka Fischer called for caution. "In the end, we should not create more instability than was the case previously by our reactions." But the two allies stepped forward and provided support that stood out in a hesitant Europe. In both instances, Bush family ties helped the American diplomatic effort enormously.

George W. Bush and Tony Blair are two distinctly different individuals. The social democrat from Scotland and the conservative Republican from West Texas had very little that would seem to bond them together. The bridge came in the form of a Scottish oilman named Bill Gammell. The Bushes had a long association with the Gammells. Bill Gammell's father, James Gammell, was a financier who back in the 1950s had invested in several American energy projects, one of which was a Texas offshore oil company called Zapata, where he sat on the board.

As with so many of the Bushes' business partners, the Gammells also became family friends. They became so close that during the summer of 1959, at the age of thirteen, young George was sent to Scotland to spend his vacation with the Gammells at their grand home in Perthshire.

The friendship remained strong, and when George W. established his own oil business, one of the first people he contacted was Bill Gammell. Over the next six years, Gammell would help finance several of George W.'s ventures. In 1983, George W. made a special trip to Scotland to attend Bill Gammell's wedding.

The relationship might have been one of hundreds that the family carried on over the years without much effect on world events, except for what Bill Gammell calls "a curious and extraordinary accident of fate." Gammell had attended the elite Fettes College in Edinburgh, where he became fast friends with an ambitious young man named Tony Blair. The two studied, socialized, and played soccer together, then lost touch in adulthood but became reacquainted in 1994. Gammell offered financial support for Blair's political ambitions, and when Gammell opened a new headquarters for his company, Cairn Energy, Prime Minister Blair was there to cut the ceremonial ribbon.

Tony Blair had never met George W. Bush. Like many in Europe, Blair tended to believe the European press stories about the new president's lack of seriousness, his gunslinging approach to global affairs, and his lack of intellect. For his part, George W. probably viewed Blair as being similar to most European leaders—socialists who were excessively cautious on the world stage. Bill Gammell helped both men see each other differently, and through their mutual friend Bush and Blair would forge a very special political relationship. Bush family ties going back nearly fifty years were paying enormous dividends at a critical juncture in American history.

"The two men are so comfortable with each other," said Nancy Bush Ellis, who, while staying at the White House, met Blair during one of his visits to Washington. "I saw them in the White House, smoking cigars just as candid and comfortable as can be."

The family's relationship with Spanish prime minister José María Aznar would also prove critical. Like Blair, Aznar would be one of the few Western European leaders to back the American strike against Iraq. Bush family ties with Aznar went back to the mid-1990s when Aznar, the conservative leader of his country, was first elected prime minister. George H. W. Bush's introduction to Aznar came through his longtime friend, hunting partner, and fellow golf fanatic, King Juan Carlos of Spain. George and King Juan Carlos had been friends since 41's days as vice president. It was a hunting trip with the king that drew Bush to Spain in November 2000 as the Florida recount began.

As with other leaders, the father had called Aznar shortly after the 2000 election to introduce him to his son. While Aznar no doubt joined the coalition of the willing because he believed it to be in the Spanish national interest, it is hard not to see the family bond as an important factor.

In the weeks following September 11, the Bush administration developed and executed a strategy to remove the Taliban from power in Afghanistan. CIA operatives working with anti-Taliban tribesmen (a strategy supported by former President Bush) and a precision air campaign succeeded in quickly removing the Taliban from power.

———

THE ATTACKS ON THE TWIN TOWERS HAD BEEN DEVASTATING. BUT WHILE THE national attention was focused on the smoke-filled skies of Manhattan, something emerged that the president found even more troubling. Envelopes filled with anthrax had been mailed to political leaders and members of the news media. Several had been sent on September 11; another on the first day of the war against Afghanistan. Unlike the airliner attacks, the authorities had been unable to find the culprits.

Biological weapons represented perhaps the gravest threat in the era of global terrorism. They could trump the American nuclear arsenal because if you couldn't figure out who the attacker was, you couldn't strike back. And if you couldn't strike back, the strategy of deterrence would go out the window.

Intelligence analyses were now crossing the president's desk that were literally hair-raising. Deterrence was at risk, and the reports were blunt and graphic in their depiction of what might happen. One report indicated that America could "lose a city" soon.

It was this sort of information that he was reading in the Oval Office every morning as part of the "threat Matrix" the CIA was providing. Family members say that the president was obsessed with preventing any sort of fresh attack on the United States.

He didn't verbalize his anxiety of burden. "These are enormous burdens for a president, but I've never, ever heard him whine," said the father.

Two months after the attack, Aunt Nancy Ellis came to the White House. That evening they walked the dogs around the White House grounds and admired the building's elegant designs. Through it all, recalled Ellis, "there was this profound sense that he needed to try to protect all of this beauty."

The stress manifested itself in other ways. For one thing, he began running more aggressively—at the White House, Camp David, even while on Air Force One. While en route to visit leaders in Beijing or Europe, he would jump aboard a treadmill for a brisk run. In the year after 9/11 he would shed fifteen pounds.

The summer after the attacks, cousin John Ellis saw him at Camp David. He was running on rugged courses with sharp inclines and making good time—twenty minutes for three miles. "He's in incredible physical condition—I've never seen him look better," he told us. "His hair has turned white, and your hair would turn white if you read those reports. But physically he's really strong."

Ellis commented to his cousin about his great physical condition.

"Well, I build this in," he told him. "This is part of my day. I'm so stressed out that I gotta do something."

#### CHAPTER 45

# SHI'ITE REPUBLICAN

D ESPITE SERIOUS MISGIVINGS IN EARLY 2001, JEB HAD DECIDED by the middle of the year to seek reelection. The decision had been based on a host of family and personal matters, but the bottom line was, he loved his job.

Jeb had run with the mind of a revolutionary. He had ideas about how he wanted government changed and streamlined. And during his first term he had thrown himself into that enterprise with abandon.

If his older brother was instinctive in his way of governing, Jeb was methodical. George W. had befriended Democratic leaders in Texas and courted Hispanic voters with great success. Jeb governed more like a bedrock conservative. Some Republican leaders in the state senate called Jeb and his top aides "Shi'ite Republicans."

Jeb had purposely picked outsiders for many top positions. His inner circle included a chief of staff from Mississippi, a budget director from Michigan, a policy director from Pennsylvania, and a communications chief from Alabama. Some had served in his father's administration in Washington, but none had extensive ties in Florida. The reason was simple: He didn't want people who had relationships with state agencies or lobbyists that might pull them away from his agenda.

He clearly relished his role as governor. He seemed to have his finger in every aspect of his broad agenda for Florida, with a voracious appetite for detail. During the legislative session, he would read bills personally. Often his staff would see him leaving the office at night with a foot-high stack of papers.

If a judicial slot needed to be filled, he reviewed the applications and interviewed the leading candidates himself. If the state was planning a land purchase, he would look over the wording of every deal, using his background in real estate to try to negotiate a better price. And for the governor of a large state, he was surprisingly accessible. He would respond sometimes to two hundred e-mails a day, many of them comments sent to him on his personal, nongovernmental server at jeb.org.

During his first term he had managed to make dramatic changes in Florida. He had slashed taxes by more than $1 billion, established rigorous statewide testing for schools, eliminated hundreds of state jobs by transferring their functions to the private sector, created the country's first statewide school voucher program, vetoed more pork barrel spending projects than the total for the entire history of the state of Florida, gained control over naming new members to the judicial branch, and extended his control over the public universities and colleges in Florida by abolishing the independent Board of Regents.

When he had the chance to appoint a member of the Florida Supreme Court, he did not hide his disdain for the court's behavior during the 2000 election or their activist approach. With the appointment of appellate lawyer Raoul Cantero, a pro-life Catholic, he declared, "As courts grow ever more powerful there is an even greater need for judges who are humble about the judicial role."

As his first term reached its end, it was clear to both friends and enemies that Jeb Bush was the most powerful governor of Florida in more than a generation.

With his bold moves and ambitious agenda, Jeb was generally popular with voters. But he had also amassed a large collection of enemies. Public employee and teacher unions were outraged at his reform of civil service. African-American groups opposed his One Florida plan to replace affirmative action. He had even made some enemies among developers, who didn't like his plan to get them to pay more for the cost of growth.

But the lurking giant that had not gone away was resentment among Democrats and liberals over the 2000 election fiasco. "All this crisis has taken place," Jesse Jackson had cried outside of the Florida Supreme Court building, "like in no other state, on John Ellis Bush's watch." Would their anger in 2000 translate into activism and energy in 2002?

Big-name Democrats from across the country believed it would, and they pledged to raise an unprecedented $10 million to help defeat him. High-profile candidates like Clinton attorney general Janet Reno were eager to take him on. Defeating Jeb was a way of getting to his brother, the president.

To counteract the challenge, Jeb and the family worked to crank up the money machine. It was now the most formidable campaign funding effort in American political history. George W. had set records with it. Now Jeb would do the same. During the first three months of 2002, an eye-popping $9.8 million was raised by the Florida GOP. It was seven times what the Democrats managed to raise during the same time period. Not surprisingly, half of it came from outside the state, with the two biggest sources being Texas and the nation's capital, where his father and brother had their political base. More than forty Texans suddenly took an interest in Florida politics and donated $10,000 to the state GOP. Several of them were Pioneers, who had raised more than $100,000 for his brother's presidential bid. The Republican National Committee also worked its stable of donors. It was an unusual move for the RNC, but party officials had been instructed by the president to do whatever they could to help his brother win reelection.

Bar arrived in Florida and became a key component in the effort to sway senior voters. Meeting with retirees along the southwest coast, she said, "He will not let you down—that's a mother's promise." In Sarasota she spoke about how Republicans could vote by absentee ballot. And she recorded a telephone message that was sent to hundreds of thousands, urging support for her son. "Your homes, your streets and your families are safer than before." Former president Bush spoke at a veterans rally in Jacksonville, and Laura made an appearance in Tampa.

George W. was deeply engaged in Florida. During eighteen months in office, he made close to a dozen trips to the state, often appearing with his brother. In May 2002 he arrived in Little Havana to bolster his brother's campaign. In front of a boisterous crowd the two brothers proclaimed their support for the cause of Cuban freedom. It was an echo of what their grandfather had said forty years earlier when he railed against Kennedy for failing to finish the job at the Bay of Pigs.

IN THE SUMMER OF 2002, JEB'S ELDER SON, GEORGE P. BUSH, RETURNED TO Florida to help in his father's campaign and further his own career interests. After graduating from Rice University and working for a year as a teacher at Homestead High School in troubled Miami, he had headed back to Rice to attend law school. (Younger brother Jebbie was at his father's alma mater, the University of Texas.)

Earlier generations of Bushes had spent their summers working at G. H. Walker and Company. But with the business sold off in 1977, a new generation looked outside for opportunities. A year earlier, George P. had interned in the Hong Kong office of Fulbright and Jaworski, a large Texas law firm run for years by his grandfather's old friend and Watergate prosecutor Leon Jaworski. That summer he would work at two firms, White & Case and Steel Hector & Davis, which had extensive dealings in Latin America. In his off time he would work on his father's campaign. He traveled to college campuses and delivered brief speeches about his father's candidacy. Like his father and grandfather, he didn't speak much about the issues during these campaigns. Instead, he focused on meeting and greeting.

Much as his grandfather had been, George P. was the star of the new generation of Bushes. If George H. W. Bush had become so with his wartime heroics, George P. was doing so in that thoroughly twenty-first-century manner—celebrity. *People* magazine named him one of the country's eligible bachelors; he had even done some modeling for Tommy Hilfiger. Attractive and articulate, he was the image of what a candidate should be in the era of television and the Internet. He would be the first in his generation to talk seriously about running for political office, but he would do so only after achieving financial independence, a necessity for members of the family who had the political bug. But clearly his father, grandfather, and uncle the president delighted in his bright political future. They began calling him by the nickname "44," the next in line after 41 and 43.

If George P. seemed to be flying high, his younger sister Noelle was still wrestling with her demons. First came news that she had tried to obtain prescription drugs in Tallahassee by forging a prescription. She had been sent to a drug-treatment center in Orlando, but by the fall counselors had found crack cocaine hidden in her shoe. Her nearly decade-old battle against drugs, which many in the family assumed had been won, suffered another setback.

Jeb, usually not emotional in public, was clearly struggling. "I pray every day that Noelle will see the path to a better life," he said at one point with tears in his eyes.

The news left him feeling defeated and depressed. Even in the midst of the campaign, he found it hard to get out of bed. At his bedside he kept a large photo of Noelle—five years old, smiling, and bright—taken at a happier, more innocent time. Jeb had it positioned so it was the first thing he would see when he woke up in the morning.

Barely a week before the election, Noelle would be released after a ten-day jail sentence in Orlando for violating the terms of her court-ordered drug treatment program. George P. and her Aunt Doro were there to provide moral support.

<hr />

ATTORNEY GENERAL JANET RENO HAD BEEN THE FRONT-RUNNER FOR MOST of the Democratic primary. Jeb relished the opportunity to run against her in what would certainly be a classic liberal/conservative contest. But when Reno was upset in the primary by political novice Bill McBride, the race suddenly took a different turn.

McBride was a trial lawyer and head of the state's largest law firm. An ex-Marine, he described himself as a moderate whose primary concern was education. Indeed, the centerpiece of his campaign was an initiative to improve schools by lowering class sizes. The race suddenly tightened.

In the two debates between the candidates, Jeb clearly stood out with his detailed knowledge of Florida government. In the waning days of the election, polls indicated that he had a steady eight-point lead. But Jeb was taking no chances, and the family rallied around him. George W. made another visit on his brother's behalf, his twelfth to Florida since being elected president. McBride, for his part, contacted former president Bill Clinton and asked him to make an appearance to rally voters in south Florida. The disdain between the Clintons and the Bushes was well known, and Clinton seemed to relish the opportunity to bring down a Bush. He canceled previous plans in order to appear with McBride days before the election.

On election night, Jeb became the first Republican governor in Florida's history to be reelected. He pulled in a record 2.8 million votes, 600,000 more than he had received in 1998. In the four years since he had first been elected, Jeb had worked hard and pushed his agenda through the legislature. But something else seemed different. In 1998 he had been just another candidate, albeit the son of a former president. Now, with a brother as president, an ambitious agenda accomplished, and flush with victory, he noticed something new when he ventured out in public.

Unlike before, when he might elicit a glance, a smile, or a handshake, now the crowds were flocking around. He had become a bona fide star.

In the final weeks of the campaign, while Jeb was working hard in Florida, George W. had been barnstorming through thirteen states in an effort to help GOP senatorial and congressional candidates. Unlike his father, who had neatly divided governing and campaigning into different spheres, George W. had grown to understand that he was president in the era of the permanent campaign. In order to govern, he needed allies on Capitol Hill. And to obtain those allies, he needed to work aggressively on their behalf. His efforts paid off handsomely. For the first time in more than a century, the party in power gained seats and captured the Senate in an off-year election.

#### CHAPTER 46

# IRAQ

O F ALL THE INTELLIGENCE REPORTS THAT CROSSED HIS DESK, those that seemed to trouble the president most concerned chemical and biological weapons. The anthrax attacks had indicated how dangerous the threat could be. Radiological bombs, contagious diseases, or hideous poisons could potentially kill hundreds of thousands of Americans. As he met with advisers to discuss the problem, one name kept coming up—Saddam Hussein. He had been in violation for more than a decade of United Nations resolutions to disarm, and most Western intelligence agencies identified Saddam as the world's leader in efforts to develop biological and chemical weapons.

The intelligence reports were alarming enough, but when the president consulted with his father on the subject, he learned something even more troubling. In 1990, when George H. W. Bush was president, he had been startled to discover the existence of a massive Soviet biological weapons program that employed forty thousand people. He didn't learn about it from American intelligence; the Soviets had managed to keep it hidden from the Americans. Only when Soviet defector Ken Alibek came forward did the world learn about the massive effort. That experience had to make the new president wonder: What horrible weapons could be under development in the dark corners of Iraq without our knowledge?

THE BUSHES TEND TO HAVE A HIGHLY PERSONALIZED VIEW OF FOREIGN AFfairs. If Henry Kissinger and other realists tend to focus on national interest and the role of power politics, the Bushes placed heavy emphasis on the personal responsibility of the leaders in power. That personalized approach grew out of the family's own experience in both business and politics. Pres Bush had learned at Brown Brothers and in the U.S. Senate about the importance of knowing whom you could trust and whom you couldn't. He developed close friendships with powerful leaders in the business world and political figures like Presidents Eisenhower and Johnson. His son George H. W. Bush had also learned that personal relationships and the character of individual leaders mattered greatly. His career in business and politics had allowed him to forge long-term friendships with foreign leaders such as the late King Hussein of Jordan, Hosni Mubarak of Egypt, and Jiang Zemin of China. And he had felt enormous betrayal when his friend Richard Nixon lied to him about Watergate.

But if they personalized their friendships and alliances, the Bushes also personalized their enemies. When President George H. W. Bush authorized the invasion of Panama in 1989, he did so with the sole purpose of bringing Mañuel Noriega to justice. He had dealt with Noriega fifteen years earlier as CIA director and discovered that he had protected Colombian cocaine shipments through Panama in the 1980s. Eventually convicted in a U.S. court, Noriega began serving a thirty-year sentence. When the ex-strongman came up for parole in 2000, former president Bush took the unusual step of writing a letter to the U.S. Parole Commission asking them to deny the request. He said that he feared for his life if Noriega were released early.

He had also personalized the war with Iraq in 1990. Although he carried it out for what he believed to be sound geopolitical reasons, he could often be found taking personal jabs at Saddam Hussein, even to the point of purposely mispronouncing his name as an insult. In his view, the problems in the Middle East arose less because of the lack of a balance of power and more because the leaders were evil.

George W. Bush would adopt a similar approach in his presidency. When in June 2001 he met with Russian president Vladimir Putin, the two men talked policy—aid, ballistic missile defense, and terrorism. But what touched Bush most was the fact that Putin wore a cross around his neck. "It amazes me that here you are a communist, KGB operative, and yet you were willing to wear a cross," he told the Russian president. Bush left the meeting saying he could do business with Putin because he had looked into his eyes and seen his soul.

Instead of looking at the Israeli-Palestinian crisis as a matter of two competing peoples fighting over land, Bush had proclaimed that the "path to peace goes through Chairman Arafat." Initially convinced that Arafat might be willing to talk peace, he changed his opinion when intelligence passed from the Israelis indicated that Arafat had personally authorized the transfer of twenty thousand dollars to the Al Aqsa Martyrs' Brigade. Suddenly George

W. was calling for his ouster. If the Palestinians would get rid of Arafat, George W. promised to support their bid for full statehood.

For three generations the Bushes had carefully worked to transfer friendships and relationships from one generation to another. If you befriend one generation, chances are that you will find yourself adopted by the next. In the world of international diplomacy the Bushes operated in the same manner. In the early months of his administration, George W. asked his father to place a call to Crown Prince Abdullah of Saudi Arabia. It was a courtesy call from an old friend, but the father also tried to convey that the Saudis should work cooperatively with his son. When it concerned the Middle East, his son's "heart is in the right place," he told Abdullah. He was in effect trying to transfer the close relations and goodwill that he had enjoyed with the Saudis to his son. The Saudis were concerned initially because they viewed George W. Bush, with his evangelical faith and supportive statements about Israel, as much less friendly to Arab interests than the father. The father would become an intermittent conversant with Crown Prince Abdullah as he tried to convey the message that the Saudis would get a fair shake from his son, and at critical times he would also speak with his friend "Bandar Bush," the Saudi ambassador in Washington.

This attempt at Bush family diplomacy did give the Saudis enough confidence to propose a peace plan that recognized Israel's right to exist in exchange for a withdrawal from the West Bank and Gaza Strip. No Arab state had ever accepted the Jewish state's right to exist.

But while such personalized diplomacy could help relations with other countries, it could also sour them, as an encounter between Bush and Jacques Chirac did in the spring of 2002. Tensions had already existed between the United States and France over how to deal with Iraqi noncompliance with U.N. resolutions. But the fissure widened substantially on May 29 when, during a Bush visit to France, as the two leaders exited a church service, Chirac surprised George W. by leading him to a stage where some media had gathered. Bush was ambushed by the mini press conference and fumed as he listened to Chirac deliver a sermon of his own, which included criticism of American policy. This was a violation of personal protocol and honor that ran contrary to the Bush approach. The Bushes are fine at handling disagreements behind closed doors, but they detest grandstanding and upstaging. (In 1991, when then–President Bush was greeting freshman senators, Minnesota's Paul Wellstone had upbraided him in front of the others for failing to deal with the country's economic problems. The president, shocked at Wellstone's lack of decorum, turned to the other newly elected senators and asked, "Who is this s——?")

Whatever chemistry, if any, existed between Bush and Chirac evaporated after the incident in May 2002. Thereafter, George W. would do "Jack Chirac" impersonations.

But in the pantheon of Bush enemies, none was greater than Saddam Hussein. The nature of the Hussein regime, his flaunting of international agreements, his continuing efforts to acquire and develop weapons of mass destruction, his gross violation of human rights, the continuing threat Iraq posed to its neighbors, were all related to the personal evil nature of this man and the system of governing he had created and controlled.

To President Bush, of course, Saddam Hussein was the "guy that tried to kill my dad." But even more important was the fact that Saddam had been identified by most international organizations and Western intelligence agencies as the leader who was most actively trying to develop chemical and biological weapons. Were he able to develop such an arsenal, the nightmare scenario of untraceable biological attacks could become a reality.

However, a regime change in Iraq had been a Bush family goal well before September 11. Both George W. and Jeb had become more hawkish over the previous decade. Always proud of their father, they were nonetheless free to move in their own direction, much as their father had moved to the right of their grandfather. Thus while George H. W. Bush had embraced the realist notion of seeking a balance of power to promote stability, the sons were increasingly in favor of a more "Reaganite" approach to the world.

In 1997, Jeb signed a letter produced by the Project for the New American Century organized by William Kristol, publisher of the *Weekly Standard* and a leading neoconservative thinker. Signed by hawks like Elliott Abrams, Dick Cheney, Eliot Cohen, Fred Ikle, Norman Podhoretz, Donald Rumsfeld, and Paul Wolfowitz, it called for robust "American global leadership." The document firmly embraced "a Reaganite policy of military strength and moral clarity." PNAC would go on to produce another letter (this one not signed by Jeb Bush), calling for the invasion of Iraq in 1998.

George W. had undergone a similar shift, propelled by his sense of duty. For his part, George H. W. Bush tried to contain himself when the subject came up. When asked about the assassination attempt, he would say stoically, "Nobody likes to be the target of assassination." The reason for Saddam's survival was in his mind clear-cut: "We underestimated the tyranny."

Saddam Hussein himself had seemed to personalize the war between himself and the Bushes. Saddam saw to it that murals poking fun at Bush were drawn around Baghdad. At one of his hotels, a picture of Bush was put on the floor so that guests could walk on his face, a supreme insult in the Islamic world. After the collapse of the Hussein regime, George W. was horrified to learn that Saddam's sons had even hung up pictures of his daughters on the walls of their palaces.

Former president Bush remained of the opinion that he had made the right decision to leave Saddam in power in 1991. Assured by his longtime friends Hosni Mubarak and King Hussein that the tyrant would not last, the father had stopped the advance on Baghdad in order to preserve the international coalition. Now those same voices were telling the son that containment would eventually lead to the demise of Hussein. Only this time the president wasn't listening.

Unlike his father, whose temperament and experience had taught him to be a consensus-builder, George W. was much more willing to go it alone if need be. He had seen the limitations of relying on friends in international affairs, and he was concerned about the prospects of a biological weapons attack.

In the weeks following September 11, he issued an intelligence order directing the CIA to be more aggressive in trying to oust Saddam Hussein. For the first time, a president authorized the CIA or U.S. Special Forces teams to kill Saddam if acting in self-defense. But it was clear that he was prepared to do more—very much more than his father or Bill Clinton had done—to deal with Saddam.

Beginning in January 2002, the U.S. military began quietly expanding Al Udeid Air Base in Qatar, making sure that the runway could handle heavy bombers. Hardened aircraft shelters and an upgraded command-and-control facility were completed by mid-2002. As work began in Qatar, Bush delivered his "axis of evil" speech before the nation. At this point, many in the family came to the conclusion that Saddam would be ousted one way or another. "George doesn't say he's going to do something and then not do it," says Elsie Walker Kilbourne. "When he says something so bold, he's committing himself. It's that simple."

The solution to dealing with rogue states seeking to develop and acquire weapons of mass destruction was a bold strategy of preemption. On June 2, George W. traveled to West Point to deliver a commencement address that would fundamentally change the course of American foreign policy. "New threats also require new thinking" he said. "If we wait for threats to fully materialize, we will have waited too long."

But preemption was a controversial strategy. The most likely target for its implementation was the long-festering problem in Iraq. But while the George W. Bush administration contemplated war against Saddam, the memory of the father still loomed large. George W. considered his father's victory in Desert Storm to be one of his greatest triumphs. Now, with a new war looming, questions arose about both the past war and the present. Sen. Joseph Biden, a member of the Senate Foreign Relations Committee, told the president that he was worried about how a new war might end.

"I told the president, there's a reason why your father stopped," recalled Biden. "He didn't go to Baghdad because he wasn't prepared to stay five years. We need a plan."

But many of those who were close to his father believed that an attack on Iraq and the policy of preemption was a dangerous course to follow. Foremost among them was Gen. Brent Scowcroft, his former national security adviser. Writing in the *Wall Street Journal*, he expressed concern that such a conflict could unleash a war between the Arabs and Israelis or, at the very least, destabilize the entire region.

George W. was frustrated when the article appeared, and when the subject came up he was quick to voice his frustration. "Scowcroft has become a pain in the ass in his old age," he said. But concerns about an attack on Iraq were coming from even closer to home. Although he never went public with them, the president's own father shared many of Scowcroft's concerns. As the prospects of war continued to grow throughout 2002, family members could see the former president's anguish. When his sister Nancy Ellis asked him about the war, he responded: "But do they have an exit strategy?"

On the first anniversary of the September 11 attack, George W. Bush rose early in the morning and read from his *One Year Bible*. It was appropriately a reading from Psalm 55:

My heart is in anguish within me;
The terrors of death assail me.

Destructive forces are at work in the city;
Threats and lies never leave its streets.

Let death take my enemies by surprise;
Let them go down alive to the grave,
For evil finds lodging among them.

Cast your cares on the Lord
And he will sustain you;
He will never let the righteous fall.
But you, O God, will bring down the wicked
Into the pit of corruption;
Bloodthirsty and deceitful men
Will not live out half their days.
But as for me, I trust in you.

#### CHAPTER 47

# SHOCK AND AWE

A s President Bush engaged in a vigorous diplomatic effort to fight the war on terrorism, members of his family continued and even expanded their business activities overseas. Neil was traveling the world, trying to raise money for a new education software company, Ignite, Inc. He had started the company in 1999 with $450,000 and established as his goal to make education fun, with pictures, sound, and video graphics. The idea for the company came out of his own difficult experiences in learning due to his troubles with dyslexia.

There were investors such as Michael Milken, the former junk bond leader and now head of Knowledge Universe. But of the sixty investors, many came from overseas, like Hamza El Khouli, an Egyptian business magnate.

Neil was in some instances doing business with national leaders (or their relatives) that his own brother was dealing with in the world of politics. In December 2001 he traveled to Beijing for a series of meetings with potential investors and retail distributors. Also on the itinerary was an intimate, private dinner with Chinese president Jiang Zemin in which the Chinese leader became overwhelmed with sentimentality and began singing military songs he had learned in his youth. Neil didn't discuss Ignite with Jiang. Instead, his dinner with the leader spoke volumes when he met with potential investors. One of those who did invest is Winston Wong, a Taiwan businessman who started Grace Semiconductor Manufacturing Corporation, established with Jiang Zemin's son and bankrolled by the Chinese government in Beijing. Neil receives a reported $400,000 in stock anually as a retainer.

Neil also made forays into the Middle East, another region where a great deal of emphasis is placed on familial relations. Neil clearly saw family contacts in the region as a lucrative field to develop. A month after September 11, Neil was in Dubai meeting with the crown prince. Crown Prince Sheikh Muhammad bin-Rashid al-Maktum, who was the defense minister and a critic of American sanctions against Iraq, hosted a gala dinner in his honor. Neil also met with Sheikh Abdallah bin Zayid al-Nuhayyan, the minister of information.

In January he traveled to Jiddah, Saudi Arabia, for a meeting of the Jiddah Economic Forum sponsored by Prince Alwaleed, a nephew of King Fahd. The family's links to Saudi Prince Alwaleed were indeed strong. The prince, who owned a large stake in Citibank and was active in numerous business ventures, was a big Bush fan. He even donated half a million dollars to Phillips Academy in Andover to establish a George Herbert Walker Bush Scholarship Fund.

In Jiddah, Neil spoke about the September 11 attack and the image of Muslims in the United States, and suggested that the Saudis and other Arab countries should work harder to improve their image there. The average American, said Neil, "sees Arab terrorists and has the desert-man image about them." He urged the Saudis to engage in a "sustained lobbying and P.R. effort" to counterbalance the stereotype. By doing so they might also overcome American public support for Israel, he told the audience, because "the U.S. media has been reporting Israelis defending themselves from rebels disrupting their stability." He gave a similar message at a speech for the Zayed International Centre, a Middle East organization backed by Sheikh Zayed bin Sultan al-Nahyan, president of the United Arab Emirates.

Neil Bush is no expert in Middle East politics. There can be little doubt that these opportunities arose more because the Arab sponsors saw them as a chance to curry favor with the Bush family than out of any sense that Neil could contribute to the discussion.

Family ties had the potential to cause problems in the execution of policy. But as with China, there is little evidence that George W. Bush was influenced by his brothers' foreign activities. Indeed, rather than be captive to the wishes of foreign powers, he seemed prepared to harness his family's ties overseas and use them to his advantage. In the ashes of 9/11, he had ambitions to revolutionize the Middle East and deal with the Israeli-Palestinian crisis. He began to speak about the possibility of establishing democracies in the Middle East and fundamentally transforming the region. And he came to believe that because of his family's unique links to the Arab world, he might be able to succeed where other presidents had failed. He had two brothers—Marvin and Neil—who had substantial business dealings with leading members of Arab royal families. (Jeb had briefly served as well on the board of Del Monte Fresh Produce, a company heavily financed by members of the royal family of the United Arab Emirates and headed by a Palestinian businessman.) His father had links to the royal families of Kuwait and Saudi Arabia going back in some instances forty years.

At the same time, George W. was deeply devoted to the Israeli cause. An emotional visit to the Holy Land in 1998 linked his Christian faith with the fate of the Israeli people in a deeply personal way. Israeli hard-liners such as Ariel Sharon viewed him as a staunch ally.

GEORGE W.'S FATHER HAD TASTED WAR IN THE PACIFIC AND STRUGGLED WITH the decision to strike during the first Gulf War. George W. had no personal experience of war, but when the responsibility of commander in chief was thrust upon him, he felt the demands almost instantly. In one of his first appearances before a military audience early in his administration, he had walked among the troops at Fort Stewart, Georgia, shaking hands and greeting them. But he also locked eyes with several servicemen and noticed how their eyes gravitated toward his.

"I think they were sending me a message," he later told friends. " 'If you're going to send us to war, you better be damned sure you know what you're doing."

And how could he be sure? For George W., making wise choices was about consulting with people he trusted. He was devoted to his regular Bible reading, and several of the passages he read seemed particularly apt. On the morning of September 27, George W. rose and read from Proverbs: "A wise man has great power, and a man of knowledge increases strength; for waging war you need guidance, and for victory many advisers."

Faith intersected with his daily decisions in a direct and profound way. While many Christian denominations were opposed to a war against Iraq on religious grounds, George W. Bush was confident that a war, if he believed it to be necessary, would be just. According to his good friend Doug Wead, that certainty grew out of his views of Christian responsibility. Wead recalled a lengthy and deep conversation he had with Bush a decade earlier, when the Catholic Church had issued a statement condemning nuclear weapons and the use of force except in self-defense. When Wead asked George W. his opinion, Bush reverted to a parable Jesus had told about the Good Samaritan. In that story, Jesus tells of several travelers walking along the road and encountering a man who had been robbed and was lying wounded at the side of the road. The purpose of the story was to speak about love and the need for people to help those who are injured and hurt, even if they are not our neighbors or friends.

But George W. also saw the story as a question of moral responsibility as it related to war. "What would be expected of us if we got to the wounded man fifteen minutes earlier?" In other words, what would Jesus expect one to do if we were present while the attack was taking place? To Bush the answer was clear, and the Iraqi people were under attack at that moment.

The security implications were important to his decision. So, too, was the suffering of the Iraqi people. As his mother and father had done on the eve of war in 1991, he thumbed through human rights reports to learn what sort of torture was being used by Saddam's regime to keep the Iraqi people in line. It gave him the sort of moral clarity that was necessary to make the decision.

But for all of his certainty, doubts arose. In addition to hearing his father's concerns about the lack of an exit strategy, there were profound spiritual challenges, too. With the turn of the calendar he began reading a new devotional book in 2003, *My Utmost for His Highest*, written earlier in the century by a Scottish preacher named Oswald Chambers. The devotional was largely about the relationship between man and God, but Chambers also had strong views about war. "War is the most damnably bad thing," he wrote later in his life. "Because God overrules a thing and brings good out of it does not mean that the thing itself is a good thing."

 On March 16, Bush offered Saddam Hussein one last opportunity to avoid war. Give up power and leave the country and war would be averted. Saddam refused the offer.

On the morning of March 19, George W. arose and read a warning from his Chambers devotional. "Living a life of faith means never knowing where you are being led," it read. "But it does mean loving and knowing the One who is leading . . . Faith is rooted in the knowledge of a Person, and one of the biggest traps we fall into is the belief that if we have faith, God will surely lead us to success in the world."

Later that evening he went to the Oval Office to deliver a four-minute televised speech to the nation. Moments earlier, three dozen Tomahawk cruise missiles, fired from navy ships and a submarine, had hit a section of Baghdad, followed by two F-117 Stealth attack planes carrying two-thousand-pound bombs. The hope was that the strike would kill Saddam Hussein.

"On my order," he said, "coalition forces have begun striking selected targets of military importance to undermine Saddam Hussein's ability to wage war. These are the opening stages of what will be a broad and concerted campaign."

Within hours of his speech, Iraqi television aired a predictable rant from Saddam. It was unknown whether it was a live shot or taped. But the message was clear. In Saddam's eyes this was a personal struggle. He fulminated against "Junior Bush," about how he had licked the dad and was now going to get the son. "The criminal little Bush has committed a crime against humanity."

George W. is the foremost student of his father's success and failure. The mistake of the first Gulf War had been not too much force, but too little. People had blamed his father for not going far enough. The same could be said for the American failure in Vietnam. It was not that LBJ had committed half a million troops that made him unpopular; it was that he was losing.

So for George W., the Iraq war needed to be bold with an overwhelming use of force. Very little should be held back; "shock and awe" would be the order of the day.

Through the two-week-long first phase of the war, the president watched very little on television. As was his habit, he kept a level of detachment that allowed him to be fully engaged but not emotionally sapped by the war. When Baghdad was captured he was relieved, but his father continued to worry about what lay ahead in Iraq. As the cessation of major combat operations passed and Iraqi attacks continued, he vowed to family members that he was prepared to risk everything—including the presidency—to win in Iraq.

In the summer of 2003, the clan gathered as it always did in Kennebunkport. There was talk about Neil's difficult divorce from Sharon. Neil had struck up a romantic relationship with Maria Andrews, whom he had met when she was working for the Barbara Bush Foundation. He also admitted to numerous other instances of infidelity with prostitutes while traveling overseas. Neil had filed for divorce earlier in the year and offered a small alimony payment to Sharon. She protested and went to George and Bar, who sided with their son. Claiming he was in debt and his business struggling, Neil said that he couldn't afford a higher payment. Only when George and Bar intervened and offered to purchase a home for Sharon was the divorce settled. But the children—Lauren, Ashley, and Pierce—were devastated. Marvin was doing well, and his business, Winston Partners, was booming. (Ironically he had recently handled investments for George Soros, who was now spending millions to defeat his brother.)

After everyone left, Bar sat in the swimming pool with Nancy Ellis, soaking up the sun. George W. was gearing up for reelection and Bar was looking ahead. "Jeb looks like he's doing so great," said Nancy. "Do you think he'll run for the presidency in '08?"

"Oh, we can't have that," responded Bar. "That's too much like the Kennedys. We can't do that." She paddled around the pool a bit and then amended her thoughts. "He's running out of money," she said, indicating that she and Jeb had talked about the subject. "He's not making any money as governor of Florida. And he needs to make some more money before he does something like that."

#### CHAPTER 48

# THE D-WORD

ASK BUSH FAMILY MEMBERS WHETHER THEY CONSIDER THEM-selves a dynasty and you are likely to get a strong reaction. Family members will grimace, roll their eyes, or simply shake their head.

"D and L—those two words, dynasty and legacy—irritate me," says former president Bush. "We don't feel entitled to anything."

"Dynasty schmynasty," says Jeb.

The Bush hostility to the very notion of dynasty runs deep because it runs contrary to the myth that they are self-made. While they are certainly more self-made than the Kennedys and have a strong drive to prove their worth, family members don't think twice about going to family and friends in their climb to the top.

Stephen Hess, in his fascinating work *America's Political Dynasties*, defines "dynasty" as "any family that has had at least four members of the same name, elected to office." The Bushes, despite their protestations, are thus by his definition a dynasty, but it is unlike just about any other in American history.

The Bushes do seem to lack a strong sense of entitlement when it comes to their aspirations for leadership. Their motive appears to be much more strongly linked to vindicating the family and perpetuating the strong sense of identity that they have developed over the decades, namely to serve through leadership. Aspirations also seem to be driven by a raison d'être that is as old as humankind itself: Do your brother one better.

The 2004 national election will not only shape the future of the country, it will likely determine the future course of the Bush dynasty as well. Since winning reelection for governor of Florida in 2002, Jeb Bush has been quietly talking to individuals around the country about a possible presidential bid in 2008, family members have reported. Should George W. win reelection, Jeb's chance to run in 2008 will be seriously open to question. Will Americans consider a third Bush for the White House?

America's other well-known dynasties—the Roosevelts, the Adamses, and the Kennedys—all have had their idiosyncrasies. Some have enjoyed seclusion, others theatrical recognition. Some have viewed public service as an opportunity, others more as a burden. But all to varying degrees have been top-down families.

It was Joe Kennedy who called the shots in his clan, determining for as long as he was alive which son would run for which office. He enforced a rigid hierarchy, giving special deference to older siblings. It was his eldest son Joe, Jr., whom he first saw as the politician in the family. When he died in World War II, the father moved on to the next eldest, John. When John was elected president, it was the father who pushed him to make his brother Bobby attorney general, then helped Ted become a senator. Even after Joe Kennedy passed away, this sense of hierarchy remained. In 1968 it was Bobby who ran for president, taking John's place, even though his younger brother, Ted, had seniority in the Senate.

The Bushes in contrast operate more like a high-tech start-up. Instead of creating a line of dynastic succession, they follow a process of natural political selection. The young charges in the Bush clan are never told or pushed to run for office. George W. Bush is fundamentally, at his core, a rebel. His life before politics was guided in part by a deep vein of rebellion against his father and the expectations that he believed were weighing on him. Even during his rise to power, he often made decisions that his parents disagreed with. It is not too much to say that had George W. Bush followed the guidance of his parents, he might never have appeared on the national political stage. Once in the White House, he has continued in a manner to buck the family tradition. In a top-down dynasty, this political success would have been doubtful.

The Bushes are also unique in that, for this family, success needs to happen far from home in order to be seen as success. Fiercely and loudly competitive in sports, the family is also quietly competitive in the realm of business and career. Striking out on your own in a new land garners greater respect than staying close to home and inheriting the old man's business. It is this impulse to establish themselves as self-made men that has led the last four generations of Bushes to stay clear of their father's home and actively seek out opportunities elsewhere. Pres Bush left Ohio for Connecticut; George H. W. Bush left Connecticut for Texas; George W. and Jeb Bush stayed clear of Washington, D.C., where their father effectively lived from 1970 on.

This sense of individual accomplishments is motivated in part by the simple fact that the Bushes lack the fabulous wealth of dynasties such as the Du Ponts and Kennedys. Were future generations of Bushes to stay at home and try to live off the family wealth, it would dissipate rather quickly. While the Bushes have over the course of the past century run in the social circles of the super-rich, their own wealth has been comparatively limited. Criticism that they are "out of touch" and living in an insular world simply does not ring true; their level of wealth doesn't make such insulation possible.

The Bush dynasty has been able to cultivate a mix of cooperation and competition among its members, which creates a strange dynamic in the father-son relationship. It is not simply coincidence that the last four generations of Bushes, while relying on their fathers' network of friendships, relied very little on the fathers themselves. Indeed, when George H. W. Bush and later his son George W. sought their fortunes in the oil patch, they turned to uncles rather than their fathers for financial advice, capital, and support.

At the same time, the Bush women are a critical factor in the rise and success of the dynasty. Dottie Bush, then Bar, and later Laura are all strong women in their own ways. Bush marriages are often marriages of opposites, which serve to temper troubling qualities in the Bush men and encourage positive ones. American history is replete with examples of what Stephen Hess calls "the coupling of political genes." But it is difficult to find an example of a member of the Bush-Walker clan marrying into another political family. It is equally rare to find a member marrying into big money.

Spurning luxurious living, which would have required a corporate career for their husbands rather than a political one, the women of the family play a vital role in keeping the men on an even keel. Each learned in her own way how to confront her husband about his shortcomings, limitations, or failures without compounding or deflating him. It is also the Bush women who have the most influence on the next generation. The men are often too consumed and preoccupied with all of their ambitions and ventures to spend considerable time with their children. They are admired from a distance and respected close up. But it is the women who give their children the sense of duty, moral values, and ambition that propels them when they get older. One can imagine them giving the sort of advice to their children that another mother gave to her sons. "Aim at the stars," Martha Washburn, a matriarch of the early-nineteenth-century Washburn political dynasty, wrote to them. "If you don't hit anything, you'll have the satisfaction of seeing your arrow go up and come back again."

Aiming for the stars is an apt metaphor for Bush ambitions. The Bushes are raised to be risk-takers. It comes from seeing their fathers trying to realize their ambitions. But it also comes from their mothers, who fuel them to extend their efforts beyond where they want to go.

Clearly the responsibilities of the women in the family are immense. Indeed, it is interesting to note that in most instances, the women in the family tend to move into the Bush-Walker clan rather than pulling their husbands into their own family orbit.

---

THE BUSHES ARE ALSO CURIOUSLY DIFFERENT FROM OTHER AMERICAN DYnasties in that they have consciously chosen to take a path of inverse social climbing over the past half century. While the other great American families rose to aristocratic stature and maintained their position as select and unique, the Bushes have in many respects moved in the opposite direction. George W. Bush is a prime example of this movement. Coming from a privileged family with a great Eastern establishment lineage, fine social standing, and access to elite schools, he has rejected this part of his past. The disdain that George W. Bush and his brother Jeb have for America's elite institutions is genuine and deeply felt. This is more than a public pose or an exercise in public relations. President George W. Bush draws his friendships and values from his youth in West Texas. The world of his grandfather and even at some level his father is not his.

Politically, this sort of devolution has allowed him to succeed where others might have failed. The Republican Party dominated by Eastern and Midwestern families like the Lodges and Tafts has long since passed. Since the Depression the party has found its zeal in Sunbelt America, in sons like Richard Nixon, Barry Goldwater, and Ronald Reagan. But it would be a mistake to dismiss George W.'s down-home persona as mere political posturing. Few if any of the new generation of Bushes, even those far from the public glare, are comfortable with the Eastern establishment, country club ways of their ancestors.

The Bushes have a strong sense of identity with the past. Jeb and George W. learned to respect what their grandfather did in the United States Senate. George P. Bush, Jeb's elder son, was able to witness events up close while his grandfather was president. But this is about more than having respect for the past. What the family has done tells younger members of the clan what is also expected of them. The Bushes have managed to strike a balance in which everyone is independent but still part of the whole.

---

SO HOW HAVE THE BUSHES SUCCEEDED IN ESTABLISHING THEMSELVES AS THE preeminent dynasty in American politics today? No doubt talent has something to do with it, as has their ability to make and keep alliances and friendships. They have also created an internal culture that helps perpetuate the family mission. But perhaps what separates them most from other political families is their sheer ability to adapt.

As the family has grown in influence and size, it has also become less close-knit. The days when Dottie Bush ran the clan, kept siblings close, and gently wove a sense of identity have faded. The divide between Jeb and George W., fueled by their mutual ambitions, would not have festered in previous generations. The current generation is not as close as previous ones, simply because they no longer have that sense of place their forebears did in Kennebunkport. For more than a century the Bushes have tethered their ambitions to the rise of America itself. As Americans migrated from the East to the Midwest, the Bush family was there. When the focus of opportunity shifted from Wall Street to Texas, Bushes were there. Even their politics have changed. Pres Bush was a Connecticut Republican—a moderate in the mold of President Eisenhower. His son was also a moderate conservative, to the right of Rockefeller but to the left of Reagan. George W. and Jeb are what could accurately be called Reagan Republicans. The family's political evolution reflects, not coincidentally, the political evolution of the Republican Party.

For all their sense of place at Kennebunkport, they are equally at home in Texas, Florida, or wherever their ambitions may take them.

Assuming that they maintain their adaptability, it is likely that the Bushes will continue to be the most powerful family in American politics for the next decade or more. If Jeb Bush does indeed run in 2008, it is safe to assume that he will be the man to beat. In a world where political fund-raising drives media coverage, which in turn drives national attention, even popular figures in the GOP cannot help but feel that they are a small merchant shop up against Wal-Mart.

In the early days of the Kennedy administration, a joke made its way around the White House. "We'll have Jack for eight years, Bobby for eight, and Teddy for eight. Then it'll be 1984." And yet for all the joking, all three sought the presidency and received public support. Americans may hate kings, but they love princes.

The bulk of the material for this book centers on more than sixty hours of interviews we conducted with members of the Bush family beginning in 1999 as well as more than forty hours with the family's close friends. Those we interviewed include George H. W. Bush, Jeb Bush, Pres Bush, Jr., William "Bucky" Bush, Nancy Ellis, John Ellis, Elsie Walker Kilbourne, Shellie Bush Jansing, Lou Walker, Teensie Bush Cole, Stu Clement, James Baker, Robert Mosbacher, Marlin Fitzwater, Lamar Alexander, Al Haig, Franklin Graham, Dan Rostenkowski, Fay Vincent, Rich Bond, Sally Atwater, Gerry Bemiss, Tim Ireland, William F. Buckley, Jr., Lud Ashley, Ed Meese, Victor Ashe, Bill Middendorf, William H. Draper, Jerry Finger, Harry Catto, Cap Weinberger, Pete Roussel, Rob McCallum, Robert Strauss, Doug Wead, Ron Kaufman, Jim Duffus, Vernon Walters, and a handful of others who asked not to be named. We also benefited enormously from the correspondence and family oral histories provided to the authors.

Other primary source material came from the Bush-Walker family, including transcripts from interviews with family members now deceased; the Thomas Ludlow Ashley Papers, Center for Archival Collections, Bowling Green State University; interviews with Prescott S. Bush by John T. Mason, Jr., for the Eisenhower Project, Oral History Research Office, Columbia University, conducted in 1967; the Prescott S. Bush Papers, University of Connecticut; the W. A. Harriman Papers at the Library of Congress; the Allen Dulles papers at Yale University; and the S. P. Bush and Buckeye Steel Papers at the Ohio Historical Society (OHS).

We also did rely on some excellent reporting in secondary sources. Those that proved most helpful include Herbert S. Parmet's *George Bush: The Life of a Lone Star Yankee* (New York: Scribner's, 1997), which includes exhaustive background material on George H. W. Bush's youth and rise to power. He is, thus far, the only writer to have been granted access to George H. W. Bush's diary. Richard Ben Cramer's *What It Takes* (New York: Vintage, 1993), which likewise charts George H. W. Bush's rise, is by all accounts the family favorite. Fitzhugh Green's *George Bush: An Intimate Portrait* (New York: Hippocrene Books, 1989), and Nicholas King's *George Bush: A Biography* (New York: Dodd Mead, 1980), both written by friends, were also useful.

For George W. Bush, Bill Minutaglio's *First Son: George W. Bush and the Bush Family Dynasty* (New York: Times Books, 1999) is thus far the most comprehensive of the biographies on his life and career. Elizabeth Mitchell's *W: Revenge of the Bush Dynasty* (New York: Hyperion, 2000) was particularly helpful when it came to George W.'s college career, his time in the Texas Air Guard, and his first congressional race. For Barbara Bush, we found Pamela Kilian's *Barbara Bush* (New York: St. Martin's, 1992) to be very helpful in reporting Barbara Bush's youth and early years of her marriage to George H. W. Bush.

For George H. W. Bush's World War II years, we relied on two superb and detailed accounts: Robert B. Stinnett, *George Bush: His World War II Years* (Washington, DC: Brassey's, 1992); and Joe Hyams, *Flight of the Avenger: George Bush at War* (New York: Berkley Books, 1992).

On the 2000 election, several books proved particularly helpful, including Frank Bruni, *Ambling into History* (New York: HarperCollins, 2002); Dana Milbank, *Smashmouth: Two Years in the Gutter with Al Gore and George W. Bush* (New York: Basic Books, 2001); and Robert Zelnick, *Winning Florida: How the Bush Team Fought the Battle* (Stanford: Hoover Institution, 2001). Two books on Karl Rove were also helpful, including James Moore and Wayne Slater, *Bush's Brain: How Karl Rove Made George W. Bush Presidential* (Hoboken, NJ: John Wiley and Sons, 2003); and Lou DuBose, Jan Reid, and Carl M. Cannon, *Boy Genius: Karl Rove, the Brains behind the Remarkable Political Triumph of George W. Bush* (Washington, DC: Public Affairs, 2003).

Of the published material by the family, George Bush's collection of letters, *All the Best, George Bush: My Life in Letters and Other Writings* (New York: Scribners, 1999), was the most helpful in providing background material, and we have quoted from some of those letters here. Barbara Bush's *Barbara Bush: A Memoir* (New York: Lisa Drew Books, 1994); and George W. Bush's *A Charge to Keep: My Journal to the White House* (New York: Perennial, 1999), helped provide context.

For George H. W. Bush's White House years, we were aided by outstanding reporting in Michael Duffy and Dan Goodgame, *Marching in Place: The Status Quo Presidency of George Bush* (New York: Simon & Schuster, 1992); and Christopher Andrew's *For the President's Eyes Only: Secret Intelligence and the American Presidency from Washington to Bush* (New York: Harper Perennial, 1995). The most useful memoirs of the Bush presidency came from Marlin Fitzwater's *Call the Briefing!* (New York: Times Books, 1995); and Robert M. Gates, *From the Shadows* (Touchstone, 1996).

To help put the notion of dynasty into a historical context, we found Stephen Hess's *America's Political Dynasties* (New Brunswick: Transaction, 1997) extremely helpful.

In addition to these primary sources and books, we also relied on the following material.

### INTRODUCTION

xiii   "The Kennedys flew too close . . ." Maureen Dowd, "Pappy and Poppy," *New York Times*, January 7, 2001; Michael Duffy and Nancy Gibbs, "The Quiet Dynasty," *Time*, July 30, 2000.

xvi   The Bush family genealogy is from Gary Boyd Roberts, *Ancestors of the American Presidents* (Carl Boyer, 1989), and Suzi Parker, "We Are Family," *Salon*, March 31, 2000.

### CHAPTER 1

Material on Columbus, Ohio, society and historical events is from *History of Columbus, Ohio: Events from 1900 to 1918* (Columbus, Ohio: Ohio Historical Society).

In addition to family interviews, information on Buckeye Steel is from Buckeye Steel

Castings Company Records, 1883–1977 (Ohio Historical Society), and Mansel G. Blackford, *A Portrait Cast in Steel: Buckeye International and Columbus, Ohio, 1881–1980* (Greenwood Press, 1982). The letters quoted in this chapter are from the S. P. Bush letters file at the Ohio Historical Society.

CHAPTER 2

In addition to interviews with family and friends, information on Skull and Bones and early Yale come from Walter Isaacson and Evan Thomas, *The Wise Men* (New York: Simon & Schuster, 1986), and G. White Edward, *The Eastern Establishment and the Western Experience* (Yale University Press, 1989). See also Ron Rosenbaum, "Inside George W.'s Secret Crypt," *New York Observer*, May 22, 2000; Alexandra Robbins, *Secrets of the Tomb: Skull and Bones, the Ivy League, and the Hidden Paths of Power* (New York: Random House, 2002); and Antony Sutton, *America's Secret Establishment: An Introduction to Skull and Bones* (Trine Day, 2003).

The alleged incident involving the skull of Geronimo is from *Continuation of the History of Our Order for the Century Celebration, June 17, 1933 by The Little Devil of D'121*. While the document has circulated publicly and through the ranks of Skull and Bones, it is impossible to determine whether it is truth or mythmaking.

Material on the War Industries Board is from Records of the War Industries Board (Record Group 61), National Archives, and drawn from Robert D. Cuff, *The War Industries Board* (Johns Hopkins University Press, 1973).

The poem about S. P. Bush is from the S. P. Bush Collection, OHS.

The account of Pres Bush's joking claims to military heroics and the later family retraction is from the *Ohio State Journal*, August 8, 1918; August 9, 1918; and September 6, 1918; available at the Ohio Historical Society.

CHAPTER 3

Background information on St. Louis and Ely and Walker is from James Neal Primm, *Lion of the Valley: St. Louis, Missouri, 1764–1980* (Saint Louis: Missouri Historical Society Press, 1998). Information on the Simmons Hardware Company is from "The Winchester-Simmons Merger," *Hardware Dealer's Magazine*, October 1922.

CHAPTER 4

Harriman's early activities in Russia are detailed in Joseph Finder, *Red Carpet* (New York: Holt, Rinehart & Winston, 1983). The first mention of Brown Brothers Harriman (BBH) investments in prewar Germany are to be found in Webster Tarpley and Anton Chaitkin, *George Bush: An Unauthorized Biography* (Washington, DC: Executive Intelligence Review, 1992). While the authors deserve credit for uncovering this story, their analysis descends into wild conspiracy theories. Documents they quote that we were able to verify for accuracy are mentioned here. Antony Sutton, *Wall Street and the Rise of Hitler* (Seal Beach, CA: '76 Press, 1976) also provides information concerning other investment activities in prewar Germany. The internal function and structure of BBH comes from Tim Ireland, a former BBH partner.

For more on Walker and golf, see John Gleason, "A Great Amateur," *Golf Journal*, July 1997.

CHAPTER 5

For information on the merger of Brown Brothers with W. A. Harriman and a useful history of the firm, see John A. Kouwenhouven, *Partners in Banking* (New York: Doubleday, 1969).

Additional background material and reporting on growing up in the Bush home comes from Walt Harrington, "Born to Run: On the Privilege of Being George Bush," *Washington Post Magazine*, September 28, 1986.

CHAPTER 6

Particularly helpful in this chapter were Parmet's *George Bush* and Kilian's *Barbara Bush*. Material on AUV and its practices is from Frederick S. Allis, *Youth from Every Quarter: A Bicentennial History of Phillips Academy, Andover* (Hanover, NH: University Press of New England, 1979). The Ted White story is from Hyams, *Flight of the Avenger*. The Pres Bush, Jr. letter to Fitzgerald Bemiss was given to the authors by Mr. Bemiss.

CHAPTER 7

Bush and baseball is from William B. Mead and Paul Dickson, *Baseball: The President's Game* (New York: Walker & Co., 1997). The old-timers game is from Aaron Epstein, "Bush's Low-Key Approach Wins Administration's Favor," *Philadelphia Inquirer*, August 23, 1984.

"like mentioning Skull and Bones . . ." Roger Hilsman, *From Nuclear Military Strategy to a World Without War* (Westport, CT.: Praeger, 1999). The Harvard Hasty Pudding Show story is from Cleveland Amory, *Who Killed Society?* (New York: Harper, 1960).

"We spent our time . . ." and information on time in the oil patch is from Barry Bearak, "His Great Gift, to Blend In: Team Player Bush, Yearning to Serve," *Los Angeles Times*, November 22, 1987.

CHAPTER 8

In addition to Pres Bush's exhaustive oral history, we relied on contemporary newspaper accounts, including "Connecticut GOP Chooses Bush; Mrs. Luce Is Third in Senate Race," *New York Times*, September 6, 1952.

CHAPTER 9

For an account of Pres Bush in the larger context of 1950s politics, see Leonard Schlup, "Prescott Bush and the Foundations of Modern Republicanism," *Research Journal of Philosophy and Social Sciences* 1 & 2 (1992). See also "Political Notes," *Time*, December 13, 1954. Background on the Alibi Club is from Sarah Booth Conroy, "A Peek at Privilege: Inside the Alibi Club," *Washington Post*, June 22, 1992. On Eisenhower viewing Pres Bush as a possible successor, see Steve Neal, *The Eisenhowers: Reluctant Dynasty* (New York: Doubleday, 1978). For the account of George Bush being pressured for his father's vote on natural gas deregulation, see the Prescott Bush oral history and Robert H. Ferrell, ed., *The Eisenhower Diaries* (New York: W. W. Norton, 1981).

On the GOP convention and civil rights, see "GOP Firmness on Rights Urged,"

*New York Times*, August 16, 1956. On the family and Pres Bush's career, see Pamela Colloff, "The Son Rises," *Texas Monthly*, June 1999.

139    "My mother fed . . ." Manuel Bravo and J. Quezada Gilberto, *Border Boss: Manuel B. Bravo and Zapata County* (College Station: Texas A&M University Press, 1999).

CHAPTER 13

Very helpful for this chapter was the reporting by Lois Romano and George Lardner, Jr., "Following His Father's Path—Step by Step by Step," *Washington Post*, July 27, 1999; Helen Thorpe, "Go East, Young Man," *Texas Monthly*, June 1999; Nicholas Kristof, "Ally of an Older Generation amid the Tumult of the 60s," *New York Times*, July 19, 2000; and Mitchell, W: *Revenge of the Bush Dynasty*. Information on Bradford Westerfield is from "Up Close CIA Keeps Presence on Yale's Campus," *Yale Daily News*, March 1, 1995.

167    On Calvin Hill, see Romano and Lardner, "Following His Father's Path." "Hey, it's not easy for him . . ." Lanny Davis, "The George Bush I Knew," *New York Times*, December 16, 2000.

171    For more on Garry Trudeau and his feud with Bushes, see Ron Hutcheson, "Cartoonist Lampoons Bush's Yale Fraternity Days," *Fort Worth Star Telegram*, September 22, 1999.

CHAPTER 15

Material on Neil Bush at St. Albans is from Steven K. Wilmsen, *Silverado: Neil Bush and the Savings and Loan Scandal* (Washington, DC: National Press Books, 1991).

182    Marvin Bush quote is from Fitzhugh Green, *George Bush: An Intimate Portrait* (New York: Hippocrene Books, 1989).

184    "I got a phone call . . ." Bearak, "His Great Gift to Blend In."

CHAPTER 16

George W. Bush and National Guard information are from George Lardner, Jr. and Lois Romano, "At Height of Vietnam, Bush Picks Guard," *Washington Post*, July 28, 1999. Mitchell, W. "Revenge of the Bush Dynasty." George W. Bush and Stratford Company is from Jo Thomas, "After Yale, Bush Ambled Amiably into His Future," *New York Times*, July 22, 2000.

CHAPTER 17

Additional information on the 1970 Senate race is from Rowland Evans and Robert Novak, *Nixon in the White House: The Frustration of Power* (New York: Vintage, 1972).

213    "Who picked up the check?" George H. W. Bush, Texas A&M University Distinguished Lecture, March 8, 1999.

CHAPTER 18

George W. Bush and PULL information is from Lardner and Romano, "At Height of Vietnam, Bush Picks Guard."

222    Cutbacks at the RNC is from Fitzhugh Green, *George Bush: An Intimate Portrait* (New York: Hippocrene Books, 1989).

223    Karl Rove's political antics and "dirty tricks" are in John Brady, *Bad Boy: The Life and Politics of Lee Atwater* (Perseus, 1996), and Wayne Slater, "Top Bush Aide Brings Aggressive Style to Effort," *Dallas Morning News*, March 21, 1999.


CHAPTER 19

Information on Bush as a vice presidential choice is from papers at the Gerald R. Ford Presidential Library. Additional information on the Bushes in China is from Fitzgerald Bemiss, "China Trip, April 17–May 9, 1975" (self-published paper), given to the authors by Mr. Bemiss. Also see Patrick Tyler, *A Great Wall: Six Presidents and China, an Investigative History* (Public Affairs, 1999).

237    "He thought he had it . . ." in Bearak, "His Great Gift, to Blend In."

239    "One of our best . . ." Henry Kissinger, memorandum of conversation with Qiao Guanhua, 10/2/74, United States State Department (TOP SECRET), Freedom of Information Act (FOIA), quoted in Tyler, *A Great Wall*.

244    "It's my impression . . ." Russell Rourke to Jack Marsh, March 20, 1975, John Marsh Files, Gerald R. Ford Presidential Library.

245    Dick Cheney's and Donald Rumsfeld's involvement in the selection of George H. W. Bush as CIA director are among the papers in The Richard B. Cheney Papers, Box 5. Of particular interest is Rumsfeld's memo to Ford on July 10, 1975.

249    CIA and Yale information is from Robin W. Winks, *Cloak and Gown: Scholars in the Secret War, 1939–1961* (New York: William Morrow, 1987).


CHAPTER 20

Reporting on George W.'s 1978 campaign and marriage to Laura is from Patricia Kilday Hart, "Not So Great in '78," *Texas Monthly*, June 1999; Lois Romano and George Lardner, Jr., "A Run for the White House," *Washington Post*, July 29, 1999; and Mitchell, *W: Revenge of the Bush Dynasty*.

260    Laura Bush and feminism story is from Frank Bruni, "For Laura Bush, a Direction that She Never Dreamed Of," *New York Times*, July 31, 2000.


CHAPTER 21

The 1977 trip to China details are from David S. Broder, "Out of Power in U.S., Republicans Still Popular in China," *Washington Post*, September 29, 1977; on the Chinese delegation in the U.S., see Bill Curry, "Tour By Chinese: Business Opportunity," *Washington Post*, January 17, 1978; and Hobart Rowen, "Peking in All-Out Hunt for Best Technology," *Washington Post*, August 11, 1978.

270    "Don, I've really gotta decide . . ." Cramer, *What It Takes*.

272    Sparks and Clark quotes from Benjamin Taylor, "Bush: An Image of Aristocracy," *Boston Globe*, July 17, 1980.

272    Bush 1980 announcement from Bill Curry, "Bush Declares Presidential Candidacy," *Washington Post*, May 2, 1979.

273    Early campaign account is from Paul Hendrickson, "Into the Marathon with Earnest George Bush," *Washington Post*, May 24, 1979.

276    Information on Bohemian Grove courtesy of Professor G. William Dumhoff.

279    Agents for Bush information is from Bill Peterson, "Coming in from the Cold, Going out to the Bush Campaign," *Washington Post*, March 1, 1980.

280    On Henry Cabot Lodge, see Myra MacPherson, "Patrician Politician," *Washington Post*, September 6, 1979.

280    Maine straw poll is from Martin Schram, "Maine Vote Gave All the GOP Strategists a Surprise," *Washington Post*, November 5, 1979.

CHAPTER 22

286    "Don't know what Greenspan . . ." Justin Martin, *Greenspan: The Man Behind the Money* (Cambridge, MA: Perseus Books, 2000).

287    The Leonard Garment story is from Leonard Garment, *Crazy Rhythm* (New York: Times Books, 1997).

288    Bush and conservatives are quoted from Martin Tolchin, "Conservatives First Recoil, Then Line Up behind Bush," *New York Times*, July 18, 1980.

CHAPTER 23

305    Investments in Arbusto information is from Richard A. Oppel, Jr., "Well Connected," *Dallas Morning News*, November 16, 1998.

CHAPTER 24

Background reporting on Jeb Bush in Miami is from Joel Achenback, "The Family's Business," *Miami Herald*, June 1, 1986. Neil Bush and Silverado background information are from Wilmsen, *Silverado*; Sharon LaFraniere, "Naivete and the Family Name," *Washington Post*, July 29, 1990; Brian Murphy, "Risk, Rise, Ruin," *Philadelphia Inquirer*, July 28, 1990; and Sharon LaFraniere, "Behind S&Ls, Lax Audits Losses Vanished after 'Opinion Shopping,'" *Washington Post*, October 24, 1990.

CHAPTER 25

Background on the Pres Bush, Jr. Senate race from David S. Broder, "Weicker Favored over Bush Clan in Preppy Grudge Match," *Washington Post*, July 24, 1982; and "Did Bush's Mother Know Best?" *Washington Post*, August 1, 1982.

CHAPTER 26

320    On Jeb Bush and Recarey, see Sydney Freedberg, "Paid to Treat Elderly, IMC Moved in Worlds of Spying and Politics," *Wall Street Journal*, August 9, 1988; Knut Royce, "The Jeb Bush Connection," *Newsday*, October 3, 1986; Lisa Getter, "Recarey Wired Cash, Then Fled," *Miami Herald*, August 15, 1988.

CHAPTER 27

330    On Harken Energy see, George Lardner Jr. and Lois Romano, "The Life of George W. Bush: The Turning Point," *Washington Post*, July 30, 1999.

341    W. approached his father . . . in Nicholas Kristof, "For Bush, Thrill Was in Father's Chase," *New York Times*, August 29, 2000.

CHAPTER 28

346    Information on Americares is from Joanne Omang, "$14 Million in Medical Aid Funneled to Central America," *Washington Post*, December 27, 1984.

350    For a detailed background of the Bush-Perot feud, see Gerald Posner, *Citizen Perot: His Life and Times* (New York: Random House, 1996), pp. 215–323.


CHAPTER 31

362    Baker-Quayle at Spanish Plaza is from David S. Broder and Bob Woodward, *Dan Quayle: The Man Who Would Be President* (New York: Simon & Schuster, 1992), pp. 56–57.

367    "He looks twelve . . ." from Germond and Whitcover, *Whose Broad Stripes? The Trivial Pursuit of the Presidency* (New York: Warner, 1989).

367    "What do you think . . ." from Broder and Woodward, *Dan Quayle*.

370    "Well, I think it would be nice . . ." Jim McGrath, ed., *Heartbeat: George Bush in His Own Words* (New York: Scribner's, 2001), p. 283.


CHAPTER 32

374    On the White House speechwriters, see John Podhoretz, *Hell of a Ride: Backstage at the White House Follies, 1989–1993* (New York: Simon & Schuster, 1993).

374    *The Peacemakers* information is from Michael Duffy and Dan Goodgame, *Marching in Place: The Status Quo Presidency of George Bush* (New York: Simon & Schuster, 1992).

376    "You know what those are . . ." James L. Merriner, *Mr. Chairman: Power in Dan Rostenkowski's America* (Carbondale: Southern Illinois University Press, 1999).


CHAPTER 33

384    "You don't want to see . . ." "President, Family Come to Defense of Neil," *Rocky Mountain News*, July 15, 1990.


CHAPTER 34

Background on the Texas Rangers and the stadium deal are from Dana Milbank, "Dispelling Doubts with the Rangers," *Washington Post*, July 25, 2000; Nicholas Kristof, "Road to Politics Ran through a Texas Ballpark," *New York Times*, September 24, 2000; Byron York, "George's Road to Riches," *American Spectator*, June 1999; and Lois Romano and George Lardner, Jr., "RBI: Revenue Brought In," *Washington Post*, July 31, 1999.


CHAPTER 35

393    "backbone transplant" and "consider me provoked" from Christopher Andrew, *For the President's Eyes Only: Secret Intelligence and the American Presidency*

*from Washington to Bush* (New York: HarperCollins, 1996); mispronunciation of name from Jean Edward Smith, *George Bush's War* (New York: Henry Holt, 1992).

395    "My worry about the Saudis . . ." Andrew, *For the President's Eyes Only*.

396    Bush's meetings at the Pentagon and with the CIA are from Fitzwater, *Call the Briefing!*

397    Bush on the Kuwait crisis and in Kennebunkport is from Duffy and Goodgame, *Marching in Place*.

398    On sledding at Camp David, interview with Peter Roussel, KUHT-TV, A Conversation with George Bush, November 18, 1994; tape provided by Mr. Roussel.

402    Scanner story from Fitzwater, *Call the Briefing!*

405    On Dottie Bush's funeral, see Christopher Keating, "Final Respects Paid to President's Mother," *Hartford Courant*, November 24, 1992.

#### CHAPTER 36

Info on Marvin Bush's business activities is from the Securities and Exchange Commission (SEC) EDGAR database (at secinfo.com). Also see "UAE President Receives a Message from Former U.S. President Bush," *Arabic News*, October 14, 1998; Bryan Curtis, "First Brother," *Washington Business Forward*, October 16, 2001; Rich Blake, "Make Room for Marvin," *Institutional Investor*, May 1, 2000; and "U.S. – Saudi Arabian Business Council Hosts H.R.H. Prince Sultan Bin Abdul Aziz Al-Saud," *U.S.-Saudi Business Brief* 5, no. 1 (2000).

#### CHAPTER 37

Information on Jeb Bush campaign from "Chiles Wins Squeaker," *Bradenton Herald*, November 9, 1994; Brian Crowley, "Mom, Dad Contribute to Son Jeb's Campaign," *Palm Beach Post*, October 13, 1993; Ellen Debenport, "Jeb Bush on Tightrope of Family Fame," *St. Petersburg Times*, March 24, 1994; Ellen Debenport, "Bush's Tears Are for Son Jeb," *St. Petersburg Times*, March 24, 1994; Mark Silva "Homespun Legend vs. Young Agent of Change," *Miami Herald*, October 30, 1994; and "Jeb Bush Sets Sights on Governor," *Palm Beach Post*, April 7, 1993.

423    "I am running for governor . . ." Curtis Wilkie, "Bush Sons Push Same Themes in Texas, Fla.," *Boston Globe*, July 4, 1994.

424    Comments on George W. and Jeb from George H. W. Bush are from Frank Davies, "Diaries Reveal the Intimate George Bush," *Miami Herald*, September 29, 1999.

#### CHAPTER 38

428    Bush inauguration is from Alan Bernstein, "The Bush Inaugural," *Houston Chronicle*, January 18, 1995.

434    Elliott Naishtat story is from Nicholas Kristof, "A Master of Bipartisanship with No Taste for Details," *New York Times*, October 16, 2000.

434    Whitmire story is from Ken Herman, "Personal: The Way Bush Likes to Work," *Austin American-Statesman*, May 16, 1999.

435    Karl Rove quote is from Ceci Connolly, "The Eyes of the Nation Are upon You, Gov. Bush," *St. Petersburg Times*, May 19, 1997.

CHAPTER 39

440    On the Bushes in retirement, see William March, "Bushes' Visit Fertilizes Son's Bid for Governor," *Tampa Tribune*, March 25, 1994.

442    For more on the Carlyle Group, see Dan Briody, *The Iron Triangle: Inside the Secret World of the Carlyle Group* (New York: John Wiley, 2003); Melanie Warner, "The Big Guys Work for the Carlyle Group," *Fortune*, March 18, 2002.

443    Background reporting on George H. W. Bush's speaking fees and business dealings is from Alan C. Miller and Judy Pasternak, "Problems with a Globe-Trotting Father," *Los Angeles Times*, May 7, 2000; and David Corn and Paul Lashmar, "Bush of Arabia," *The Nation*, March 27, 2000.

447    "Here is Jeb Bush . . ." Pamela Hasterok, "Jeb Bush Sowing Seeds for Race for Governor," *Daytona Beach News-Journal*, August 14, 1996.


CHAPTER 40

452    Visit to the charter school is from Bill Maxwell, "The Liberty School," *St. Petersburg Times*, May 25, 1997.


CHAPTER 41

460    Meeting at Presidential Library is from Lois Romano, "Bush Shuns Insiders, Father's Ex-Aides," *Washington Post*, September 26, 1999.

463    "I learned more from her . . ." Cokie and Steve Roberts, "Bush's Mother Is a Prime Political Asset in His Campaign for President," United Features Syndicate, November 13, 1999.

468    Sandy Tennant meeting with Bush is from "Tennant Turns Up Heat on Bush," *Boston Globe*, May 29, 1999.

468    On fund-raising for the Bush campaign, see Byron York, "Money for Nothing," *American Spectator*, September 1999.

471    On Ward Connerly, see Bill Duryea, "Mister Connerly," *American Spectator*, July 1999; on Jeb Bush and the One Florida plan, see Deborah Sharp, "Division Greets Jeb Bush's Plan for 'One Florida,'" *USA Today*, February 10, 2000; and "Jeb and the Black Vote," *Florida Trend*, January 25, 2001.

472    "The only thing . . ." Karl Rove, Mark Halperin story, and Herskowitz story are from Dana Milbank, *Smashmouth: Two Years in the Gutter with Al Gore and George W. Bush* (New York: Basic Books, 2001).

475    "Someone yell timber . . ." story appears in Milbank, *Smashmouth*.


CHAPTER 42

Background information on events and players related to the Florida recount are from Robert Zelnick, *Winning Florida: How the Bush Team Fought the Battle* (Stanford, CA: Hoover Press, 2001).


CHAPTER 43

497    On Kennedy and Bush, see Anne Kornblut, "Bush Tries to Build Ties with Kennedy," *Boston Globe*, January 11, 2001; "Kennedy Stands by Criticism of Bush on Iraq," CNN Washington Bureau, September 19, 2003.

497    Jeb Bush, "I think we could . . ." in Achenbach, "The Family's Business."

500    Messing, England, story is from Sue Leeman, Associated Press, January 19, 2001.

501    "One evening we were . . ." from Christopher Anderson, *George and Laura* (New York: Morrow, 2002).

502    Examples of George W. Bush rewarding those who worked for him in Florida are from "Recount Players Are Rewarded," *Tallahassee Democrat*, July 15, 2002.

508    Prescott Bush involvement in China and this incident are discussed in Debbie Howlett, "President's Uncle Shares Bush Family Ties to China," *USA Today*, February 19, 2002.


CHAPTER 44

The best-written accounts thus far of the early days after 9/11 are Bob Woodward, *Bush at War* (New York: Simon & Schuster, 2002); and Bill Sammon, *Fighting Back: The War on Terrorism—from Inside the Bush White House* (Washington: Regnery, 2002); and Dan Balz, "A Father-Son Bond Played Out in the View of History," *Washington Post*, September 16, 2001.

518    Laura Bush after September 11 background information from Antonio Felix, *Laura: America's First Lady, First Mother* (Avon, MA.: Adams Media, 2002).

522    Some background information on the Gammell-Bush-Blair relationship is from Auslan Cramb, "Mutual Friend Who Could Bring Together Two World Leaders," *Daily Telegraph*, December 18, 2000.


CHAPTER 45

525    Jeb as governor information is from Mary Ellen Klas, "Jeb's Lieutenants," *Florida Trend*, November 2000.

526    Details of Jeb's fund-raising are from Adam C. Smith, "Money Pours in to Benefit Gov. Bush," *St. Petersburg Times*, April 21, 2002.

527    Background on George P. Bush's work comes from Cindy Krischer Goodman, "Internship Lures Young Bush Back," *Miami Herald*, May 23, 2002.


CHAPTER 46

533    "Nobody likes to be the target . . ." GHWB interview, CNN's "After Desert Storm," February 27, 1996.

534    Background to Iraq buildup is from Anthony Shadid and Robert Schlesinger, "Strike Plans against Iraq Move Ahead," *Boston Globe*, August 18, 2002.


CHAPTER 47

537    Neil Bush's international travels, including his business dealings in Asia, are highlighted in "President's Brother Travels World Promoting Online Education Venture," *San Jose Mercury News*, April 8, 2002.

538    Neil Bush in Jiddah is from Khalil Hanware, "Win American Hearts through Sustained Lobbying: Neil Bush," *Arab News*, January 22, 2002; and Khalil Hanware, "Address Key Challenge Urgently: Alwaleed," *Arab News*, January 21, 2002.

541    Early stages of the war from John Burns, "In Baghdad, Sirens Wail as Missiles Strike," *New York Times*, March 20, 2003.

## ACKNOWLEDGMENTS

Many thanks to those in the Bush-Walker family who agreed to interviews, often multiple interviews, over the course of several years. We are particularly thankful to George H. W. Bush, Jeb Bush, Pres Bush, Jr., William "Bucky" Bush, Nancy Ellis, John Ellis, Elsie Walker Kilbourne, Shellie Bush Jansing, Lou Walker, Teensie Cole Bush, and Stu Clement.

Thanks also are due to friends of the family who spoke with us, including James Baker, Robert Mosbacher, Marlin Fitzwater, Lamar Alexander, Alexander Haig, Franklin Graham, Dan Rostenkowski, Fay Vincent, Rich Bond, Sally Atwater, Gerry Bemiss, Tim Ireland, William F. Buckley, Jr., Lud Ashley, Ed Meese, Victor Ashe, Bill Middendorf, William H. Draper, Jerry Finger, Harry Catto, Cap Weinberger, Pete Roussel, Rob McCallum, Robert Strauss, Doug Wead, Ron Wead, Ron Kaufman, Jim Duffus, the late Vernon Walters, and a handful of others who asked not to be named.

At the Hoover Institution at Stanford University, we are enormously grateful to John Raisian, who has not only supported Peter's work over the years but is also enthusiastic and encouraging. We also extend our thanks to Hoover colleagues Noel Kolak, Richard Sousa, Tom Henriksen, Charles Palm, and Peter Robinson.

At Doubleday we are blessed to have Adam Bellow as our editor, who along with his assistant, Jenny Choi, made sure that we got done what needed to get done on a reasonable time schedule. Thanks also are due to Bill Thomas for his support of this project and to Dean Curtis, who served as copy editor.

Finally, we want to thank our families and friends for their encouragement and love over the years. The authors alone are responsible for the content of this book.